CLASSICAL ECONOMICS, PUBLIC EXPENDITURE AND GROWTH

ECONOMISTS OF THE TWENTIETH CENTURY

General Editors: Mark Perlman, *University Professor of Economics, University of Pittsburgh* and Mark Blaug, *Professor Emeritus, University of London and Visiting Professor, University of Exeter*

This innovative series comprises specially invited collections of articles and papers by economists whose work has made an important contribution to economics in the late twentieth century.

The proliferation of new journals and the ever-increasing number of new articles make it difficult for even the most assiduous economist to keep track of all the important recent advances. By focusing on those economists whose work is generally recognized to be at the forefront of the discipline, the series will be an essential reference point for the different specialisms included.

A list of published and future titles in this series is printed at the end of this volume.

Classical Economics, Public Expenditure and Growth

Walter Eltis
Emeritus Fellow of Exeter College, Oxford

Edward Elgar

Published by
Edward Elgar Publishing Limited
Gower House
Croft Road
Aldershot
Hants GU11 3HR
England

Edward Elgar Publishing Company
Old Post Road
Brookfield
Vermont 05036
USA

A CIP catalogue record for this book is available from the British Library

ISBN 1 85278 741 4

Printed and Bound in Great Britain by
Hartnolls Limited, Bodmin, Cornwall.

Contents

Acknowledgements

The author and publisher wish to thank the following who have kindly given permission for the use of copyright material.

Basil Blackwell Ltd for the articles: 'Ricardo on Machinery and Technological Unemployment' in Giovanni A. Caravale (ed.), *The Legacy of Ricardo*, Basil Blackwell, 1985, 257–84; 'Some Implications of Deficit-financed Tax Cuts: These Will Always Increase Demand, but Will They Reduce Supply?' in Michael J. Boskin, John S. Flemming and Stefano Gorini (eds), *Private Saving and Public Debt*, Basil Blackwell, 1987, 318–46.

Economic Journal for the article: 'The Determination of the Rate of Technical Progress', *Economic Journal*, **81**, September 1971, 502–24.

Edward Elgar for the article: 'How Inflation Undermines Economic Performance' in Keith Shaw (ed.), *Economics, Culture and Education: Essays in Honour of Mark Blaug*, Edward Elgar, 1991, 81–94.

Encounter for the article: 'The Borrowing Fallacy: On the World Debt Crisis', *Encounter*, **67**, November 1986, [12]–[13], [16]–[20].

Lloyds Bank Review for the article: 'The Failure of the Keynesian Conventional Wisdom', *Lloyds Bank Review*, **121**, October 1976, 1–18.

Macmillan Press (London) for: 'Where Britain Went Wrong', Chapter 1 of Robert Bacon and Walter Eltis, *Britain's Economic Problem: Too Few Producers*, Macmillan, 1976, 1–34; and the article: 'Sir James Steuart's Corporate State' in R.D.C. Black (ed.), *Ideas in Economics*, Macmillan, 1986, 43–73.

National Westminster Bank Quarterly Review for the article (with Douglas Fraser and Martin Ricketts), 'The Lessons for Britain from the Superior Economic Performance of Germany and Japan', *National Westminster Bank Quarterly Review*, February 1992, 2–23.

Oxford Bulletin of Economics and Statistics for the article: (with Robert Bacon), 'The Implications for Inflation, Employment and Growth of a Fall in the Share of Output that is Marketed', *Oxford Bulletin of Economics and Statistics*, **37**, November 1975, 269–95.

Oxford Economic Papers for the articles: 'Investment, Technical Progress, and Economic Growth', *Oxford Economic Papers*, **15**, March 1963, 32–52; 'François Quesnay: A Reinterpretation 1. The *Tableau Économique*', *Oxford Economic Papers*, **27**, July 1975, 167–200; 'François Quesnay: A Reinterpretation 2. The Theory of Economic Growth', *Oxford Economic Papers*, **27**, November 1975, 327–51; 'Malthus's Theory of Effective Demand and Growth', *Oxford Economic Papers*, **32**, March 1980, 19–56; 'The Contrasting Theories of Industrialization of François Quesnay and Adam Smith', *Oxford Economic Papers*, **40**, June 1988, 269–88.

Oxford University Press for the articles: 'Adam Smith's Theory of Economic Growth' in Andrew Skinner and Thomas Wilson (eds), *Essays on Adam Smith*, Oxford University Press, 1975, 426–54; 'How Rapid Public Sector Growth can Undermine the Growth of the National Product' in Wilfred Beckerman (ed.), *Slow Growth in Britain: Causes and Consequences*, Oxford University Press, 1979, 118–39.

Introduction: How my economics evolved

My education as an economist

I was exceptionally fortunate to have had the opportunity to learn economics at Cambridge in the 1950s. John Maynard Keynes's closest colleagues, Richard Kahn and Joan Robinson, were at the height of their powers and taught extensively. Nicholas Kaldor had moved on to Cambridge from the London School of Economics, and Harry Johnson was there as a young lecturer. Dennis Robertson was still active as the Professor of Political Economy; he presided over Keynes's Political Economy Club and was very accessible to the young. Only 80 of us read Part II of the Economics Tripos and we knew each other well. I was lucky enough to be a contemporary of Jagdish Bhagwati, Sam Brittan, Amartya Sen and many others who have since established notable reputations. The confidence in Cambridge at that time was enormous. Keynes was universally regarded as the man who had turned economics upside down and got it right, and the new Keynesian policies on which official economics began to be based immediately after the war were proving very successful. Britain had less than 2 per cent unemployment; inflation was falling and it appeared that our recovery from the war, far more effective than that after the First World War, was also superior to France's and Germany's. We were firmly convinced that we were among the privileged 80 a year who were learning economics in the world's leading university, which offered both the highest theory and the key to policies that worked.

I did not get on top of the subject in my first year because I received the kind of tuition where, whatever I said, my tutors told me to add the six or seven further details I had omitted. In Oxbridge, quantity of knowledge produces only high Second Class marks. In my second year I was more fortunate, for which two major influences were responsible. One was a remark about my work by my Emmanuel College Director of Studies, Sandy Youngson, that 'an essay that reflects all the chaos of the real world will be as chaotic as the real world'. I took this as an encouragement to simplify and omit so that my economics could tell a clear story. I was overdoing this by the end of the year and when I told Youngson, after I was placed in the First Class in 1955, that in my final year I wished to go to Joan Robinson, he warned me, 'she doesn't care twopence what happens in any factory or office in this country, and there is a danger of your going the same way'. I went to her nonetheless.

A further major influence was David Ricardo. Everyone took an examination in the History of Economics at the end of their second year. We had lectures from Maurice Dobb who was actually booed at the end of his term because he had supported the wrong side (the North) in the Korean War: how students change! But Dobb introduced us to Ricardo whose *Principles of Political Economy and Taxation* was the first book I read which I found entirely logical and comprehensible. It was intellectually exhilarating to have it demonstrated in Chapter 1 with Ricardo's own assumptions (sufficiently remote from Britain in 1954 to make it an intellectual game) that if wages rose, most prices must fall. Adam Smith had made the error of supposing that wage increases would be passed on in higher prices. Ricardo showed by pure logic that the opposite must occur. As I went through the book I began to work out in advance what conclusions he would reach at the end of each chapter and generally I was right. Ricardo taught me to think as an economist.

When I went to Joan Robinson at the beginning of the following year, I thought I was one already. She removed every assumption I had made and asked me what then happened. I was not allowed to stick with a single one of my propositions. She then told me to come back the next week and to write the same essay again. I asked Sen who had been to her the year before what on earth she was expecting and he told me what she had regarded as the correct approach when he went to her. And so it went on, week after week. As I tried to say things she would find interesting, she removed every embellishment in my argument and left the bare bones. Finally, I received a letter which has stayed with me ever since:

> I have been hoarding over you and should like to offer a tentative suggestion. I think your trouble is lack of faith in your own ideas – you somehow feel that if they were set out clearly and simply step by step they would seem commonplace, whereas surrounding them with mystery makes them impressive. If so, this is quite mistaken. You have a very original and fertile mind. I know very well the sweat and tears involved in getting a new idea into shape, the painfulness of being criticised and the temptation to bluff.

That has remained with me as the case for saying everything in the simplest possible language and never to use technicalities unnecessarily. As she showed so magnificently in her own work, a great deal can be said in clear English, but some economic questions cannot be explained simply. As she said of *The Accumulation of Capital*, the book she was writing at this time which contained many difficult passages reflecting capital theory as she understood it, 'I was the messenger who brought the bad news'.

I also had the pleasure of being taught by Harry Johnson who would talk for half an hour at a time and then say, 'but you don't need all that for a First'. There were Statistics papers in the Cambridge Tripos (nobody there spoke of Econometrics), but they were taken by those whom the future economic theorists regarded as the dimmer people. We were astounded when someone in our year got a First on the basis of high marks in Statistics. This may well have reflected the way in which the greatest in Cambridge had never presented detailed statistical support for any of the principal Keynesian theories. This hardly seemed necessary, given Colin Clark's demonstration (about which Keynes had expressed scepticism) that the multiplier was always two and Kaldor's statement that the major economies (by which he meant the UK and US) had always had a capital output ratio of three, a share of profits in the national income of 30 per cent and a rate of profit of 10 per cent. There was no attempt to verify such observations; they were referred to instead as 'stylized facts' which were so clear that they required no demonstration. Similarly I recall Kaldor standing in front of the fireplace in the Political Economy Club and telling us that 'in the last two centuries money wages have never fallen'.

Instead of acquiring some statistical theory I supplemented economic principles and the economics of Money, Industry and Labour (taught mainly as theory) with

Political Theory where I was taught by a young King's Apostle, Christopher Foster, who subsequently achieved the double distinction of being (the Labour) Barbara Castle's Head of Transport Planning and 30 years later (the Conservative) John MacGregor's Privatization Adviser. Together with a Knighthood, he has also emerged as Chairman of one of the industrial Sector Groups I ran when I became Director General of the National Economic Development Office (NEDO) in 1988.

We theorists, mainly Joan Robinson's pupils, together with the one statistician, duly got our Firsts in Part II of the Economics Tripos in 1956 and I went on to become a graduate student in Oxford. Nuffield College, which consisted entirely of graduate students and faculty in the social sciences, was an especial attraction. In Oxford too at that time very few graduate students studied econometrics or statistics in any systematic way. Those of us who were following the Oxbridge mainstream were very puzzled when two young Fellows of Nuffield College, Martin Feldstein and John Flemming, presented a paper on the econometrics of the investment function. One Fellow jokingly remarked that he would begin to take econometrics seriously when the equations started to have pluses and minuses in the right places. But Feldstein and Flemming were right; serious economics was becoming empirical. Theories were being tested, not merely illustrated with a few stylized facts. In the great American Departments this was understood, with the result that a generation of Oxford and Cambridge graduates was inadequately trained to reach the peak of the profession, a matter about which Harry Johnson has written extensively.

Coming to Oxford from Cambridge, I was fortunate to be looked after by Roy Harrod who was very different from Joan Robinson. He would pretend an enormous ignorance of the subject and ask very elementary questions, and we had to explain the basic grammar to him. He spoke as if he were coming upon this for the first time. But he was also editor of the *Economic Journal* so the most important economic research in British universities came to him. He expressed deep scepticism when Kaldor perpetrated the heresy of wishing to measure capital in tons of steel; Kahn and Joan Robinson actually wrote to beg him not to publish his article because it would confuse the young. Cambridge was dividing. I, as a graduate student, asked Harrod hopefully if one of my 50-page chapters on capital theory contained an article and Harrod, with marvellous courtesy, responded, 'Certainly, there are several articles in this chapter'. He went on to explain that a publishable article developed just one line of argument and that there was a knack to it which was quite easily learned.

Harrod actually rescued my academic economics by inviting me to write a textbook on economic growth. My attempts at high theory were either long and expositional, or else they consisted of sharp undeveloped insights, neither of which were publishable. In those days graduate students at Oxford rarely produced theses because most were elected to Fellowships and University Lectureships rather quickly (I became a Research Fellow of Exeter College two years after I left Cambridge), so there seemed no need to produce anything as tedious as a doctoral dissertation. But young Fellows had to publish something and Harrod's suggestion of a textbook proved absolutely right. I published the first chapter as the article, 'Investment, Technical Progress, and Economic Growth' in 1963, managing to include in this almost everything I then understood about growth theory. I reproduce it here as Chapter 1 in this volume. The language was non-technical and it said a good deal. Joan Robinson described it as a vulgarization but she was kind enough to add, 'a vulgarization of the best kind'. Harrod helped me greatly at this stage. Later it became my responsibility to be one of the editors of the Festschrift presented to him when he retired, and five years after his death I wrote the article about him in *The New Palgrave Dictionary of Economics*.

Working for government in the 1960s

The publication of my first article in 1963 had one important consequence. The distinguished Norwegian economist Odd Aukrust drew it to the attention of Sir Robert Shone, the first Director General of the newly-established NEDO, and Shone asked Sir Donald MacDougall, the first Economic Director, to get me to join his team. Harold Macmillan's Conservative government had established NEDO to attempt to achieve in Britain what indicative planning had contributed in France. Enjoying great prestige when first established, it proposed a growth target of 4 per cent per annum in the belief that, with the government's support (which it had in full measure), the private sector would achieve 4 per cent. The way of thinking that lies behind this is summarized in my account of the 'full natural rate of growth' in pages 37–41 of my 1963 article (pages 8–12 in this volume). Working for Shone was an enormous stimulus as he established unending economic seminars in NEDO and brought a wealth of practical experience from the steel industry (he had been chairman of the Iron and Steel Board, a British body established to fix the price of steel in the private sector) and from other industries in which he had held high positions. It was a period from which much was expected.

NEDO suffered a setback in 1964 when Labour won an election and Harold Wilson became Prime Minister. On the day after the election MacDougall's desk and carpet left the building. MacDougall had become Director General of a newly-established Ministry, the Department of Economic Affairs (DEA), which was taking NEDO's indicative planning to the heart of Whitehall. He and his team produced *The National Plan* in 1965 which reduced Britain's growth target from NEDO's 4 per cent to 3.8 per cent. Left behind in NEDO with Sir Robert Shone (I actually became Chief Economist of the rump that remained), I noticed one miscalculation in *The Plan* which was to foreshadow a good deal of my later work on the significance of public expenditure. I wrote a note to Shone in September 1965:

> The departments responsible for estimating Public Expenditure in 1970 have failed to take account of the rise in personal incomes which is envisaged in the Plan. It is planned that income per employee will rise 20% (in terms of constant prices) in the six years 1964–70. Presumably this means that the incomes of nurses, doctors, dentists and teachers will rise by something like 20% in the period 1964–70, but no account appears to have been taken of this in the Plan, with the result that Public Expenditure in 1970 is substantially underestimated. A consequence of this is that government expenditure is likely to rise at a rate exceeding 4¼% per annum if the full extension of public services envisaged is carried through.
>
> According to the Minister of Health, the estimates in the Plan are 'in terms of constant pay and prices'. This must lead to underestimation. If prices are constant, the living standard of Public Sector employees can only rise if pay rises. If their living standard is increased by 1970, their pay (in constant price terms) will rise, and Public Expenditure will then exceed that planned for. Several consequences are possible:

(i)   Public expenditure may rise by more than 4¼ % per annum.
(ii)   The extension of social services, etc. may need to be less than that envisaged in the Plan.
(iii) Public sector wages and salaries may rise less than the national average, but in this case it is hard to see how the public sector will be able to recruit enough people (in conditions of full employment) to carry through the programmes envisaged in the Plan.

One of my Oxford colleagues who was working in the DEA told me on the Oxford train where many of us met that my note had been unwelcome.

I left NEDO at the end of 1966. In 1965 Shone had been replaced by Fred Catherwood, the Managing Director of British Aluminium (now Sir Fred and a Euro MP) and this ended the lengthy economic seminars conducted by the Director General which had made Millbank so interesting to an Oxford economist.

I returned to the theme of the adverse impact of growing public expenditure in a paper to a Business Economists' Group Conference in April 1968, 16 months after leaving NEDO. Here I foreshadowed a good deal of the theory I was to present with Robert Bacon seven years later:

Since productivity rises little, if at all, in the public sector, a 4 per cent per annum increase in public spending in terms of constant wages amounts to an increase in employment by the public sector of almost 4 per cent per annum. Hence, if we actually achieved 4 per cent per annum growth between now and the year 2000, and government spending increased 4 per cent per annum in terms of constant wages and prices, employment in the public sector might increase almost 4 per cent per annum between now and year 2000 and the share of public spending in total spending would not be constant: with a 4 per cent per annum growth in employment in health, education and central and local government administration, these would absorb about 40 per cent of the labour force by the year 2000, as against about 12 per cent today. The economic system would probably break down long before then, but the pressures in the interval would be overwhelming. In the past three years we have experienced a small measure of these pressures.

	real GNP (1964 = 100)	Public expenditure	GNP *minus* public expenditure
1951	69	28	41
1964	100	38.5	61.5
1967	106	47.5	58.5

Source: National Income and Expenditure, HMSO, 1961 and 1968.

The table shows that from 1951 to 1964, the United Kingdom's *real* GNP, net of all central and local government spending, increased 3.2 per cent per annum. From 1964 to 1967, it *declined* 5 per cent. In previous recessions it did not decline. This is the inevitable consequence of rapidly growing public spending in a period when real output increased only 2 per cent per annum. It is disturbing that since 1964, there has been a 5 per cent fall in real GNP net of public spending, for it is widely agreed that living standards will fall further in the next two years because of devaluation. It would be surprising, given this situation of declining real resources available to the private productive sector of the economy, if every business and every group of workers and salary earners which could obtain more money through higher prices or higher wages and salaries failed to exploit its full market power. Before 1964, some businesses and some workers may have refrained from maximising their incomes. With declining real profits and declining real incomes net of all taxes, there has been little restraint and there will be little restraint in the next few years. That is part of the price which is now being paid for growing public spending.

My 1965 note to Shone was seen by only a handful of NEDO staff and civil servants in the DEA, and this 1968 Conference paper (published in a low-key Conference booklet) will have been seen by few who were not actually there. Those present hardly reacted, but a North American told me that there was a Congressman, Wilbur Mills, who had views similar to mine: this was a put down because Mills had the reputation of an eccentric outside the mainstream at this time. My remarks were also well outside the British mainstream in 1968 but I mention them here to show how early my disillusionment with Cambridge Keynesian orthodoxy began.

My contributions to Growth Theory

A consequence of my Conference paper was that Thomas Wilson, a fellow speaker, invited me to come to Glasgow as an external examiner. When I was there, he asked me to contribute to the bicentenary *Essays on Adam Smith* which he and Andrew Skinner were editing as part of the Glasgow edition of *The Works and Correspondence of Adam Smith*. He knew that my conference statements about public expenditure were close to several in Smith, but at that time I had no idea of this. I started to work on my Smith essay, 'Adam Smith's Theory of Economic Growth', which is reproduced as Chapter 3 in this volume, in the early 1970s after a thorough study of *The Nature and Causes of the Wealth of Nations*, but in 1968 that was in the future. My main preoccupation was still capital theory and the modern theory of economic growth, my three years in NEDO having been something of a diversion from what I regarded as my main research.

In 1966 when my textbook *Economic Growth: Analysis and Policy* appeared, my Oxford colleague George Richardson courteously challenged my underlying belief that Britain's underperformance must be associated with something in the nature of machinery and technology, and remarked that he had just read in a newspaper that what it took seven men to produce in Britain required only three women working with identical machinery in the US. Our weaknesses might therefore have relatively little to do with the nature of machinery and its cost, and a good deal to do with management, skills, education and restrictive practices. I am not aware that Joan Robinson or Kaldor ever saw labour as anything other than an homogenous commodity; indeed, in 1934 she had published an article in which she described the appropriate rewards to entrepreneurship in a well-run competitive economy as zero. I had therefore been educated, like most contemporary British economists, to ignore these considerations, including the possibility that three American women might be better trained or motivated and more productive than seven British men.

I believed that the best hope of further elucidation of the technological gap between Britain and the US lay in the development of an economist's technical progress function which would penetrate further into the relationship between research and development, learning by doing and technical advance. Between 1968 and 1971 I managed to evolve a function which built on the work of Kenneth Arrow and Kaldor but produced the result, unlike theirs, that more investment will lead to faster technical progress and a higher equilibrium rate of growth. I believed this must be right because economies that invest more will also have larger knowledge-creation sectors which in turn can be expected to produce a faster stream of results. The consequent article, 'The Determination of the Rate of Technical Progress', published in the *Economic Journal* in 1971 and included as Chapter 2 in this volume, had this characteristic. It had another quality that pleased me. Since my Cambridge student days, I had hoped to discover an explanation of the supposed constancy of the capital output ratio, the share of profits and the rate of profit. If, as my 1971 article suggested, higher investment would be associated with faster technical progress and a higher equilibrium rate of growth, then the capital output ratio would be more stable than in Arrow's or Kaldor's model. I therefore had a partial answer to the question Kaldor had posed.

This article became one of the principal chapters in *Growth and Distribution* which I published in 1973. This book provided a coherent framework for all my contributions to growth theory. I was pleased by the reviews, but it had relatively little impact on the work of others: there were rather few citations in the principal journals which is a particular test of influence. The book failed to arouse the attention I had hoped for from my 17 years of intermittent but fairly persistent work on growth theory. Like others in the subject, I ignored a good deal of what we now regard as significant in the explanation of differences in growth between economies. Like Kaldor and Joan Robinson I focused especially on the nature of plant and machinery and rather little on how it was used. I succeeded in following Kaldor, however, by working through the consequences of increasing returns and Verdoorn's law. Like many contemporaries with an interest in capital theory, I ignored anything associated with the role of people in economies as against the role of steel and concrete and all that enters into the multi-faceted nature of physical capital.

One year later, in 1974, a new colleague, the econometrician Robert Bacon, and I published a piece of research for NEDO entitled *The Age of US and UK Machinery*. NEDO had asked us to examine the available statistics on the age of the actual machine tools in Britain and Germany. It rapidly emerged that there were no comparable German data, so we earned our consultancy fee by comparing Britain with the US instead. Detecting no significant differences in the quality or age structure of the machinery in use, we concluded along Richardson's lines. The Americans used the same machinery, got far more output from it and used fewer people to man it. We therefore diagnosed British industrial weaknesses as underproduction – getting too little output from capital – and overmanning – using too many people to get that output. This study attracted a good deal more attention, including that of Bruce Page, the Managing Editor of *The Sunday Times* responsible for commissioning features, than the 17 years of theoretical research which had led to *Growth and Distribution*.

The modern significance of Classical Economics

When Bruce Page came to see Bacon and myself in Oxford in 1974 to offer us space in his paper because he believed the readers of *The Sunday Times* were so worried about their personal finances that they would wish to read about economics on Sundays, we did not ask for space to write about overmanning and underproduction.

I believed I had acquired a considerable understanding of what was happening in Britain as a result of my research on Adam Smith which Wilson had set off. This represented a return to my concerns about the significance of public expenditure which I had expressed in 1965 and 1968, but which I now realized were a central element in *The Wealth of Nations* and in other great classical economic writings. The insights of the great classical economists into the potentially destabilizing impact of excessive growth in public expenditure had been lost sight of after the Keynesian revolution, and Bacon and I felt it necessary to bring them back to the forefront of attention because we believed it was precisely excessive public expenditure growth that was destabilizing the British economy. I had sensed that something was wrong in the 1960s, but I did not have a model to demonstrate the full potential destabilizing impact of growing public spending; moreover, I had only had the opportunity to put my *ad hoc* concerns to a handful of people. Now Bacon and I were to be offered nine pages of *The Sunday Times* spread over three successive Sundays ('Bacon and Eltis for Sunday Breakfast' was how *The Economist* described it), together with an invited response from leading economists, politicians and trade unionists, and an eventual reply by Denis Healey, the Chancellor of the Exchequer. (A fortnight after this appeared, I met Sir Douglas Wass, the Permanent Secretary to HM Treasury, who told me, 'I have just written a reply to your articles. I signed it Denis Healey'.)

The economic model which lay behind the Bacon and Eltis articles in *The Sunday Times* is entirely classical and owes much to what I had learned from Adam Smith and François Quesnay. I approached the challenge of writing about Smith after Wilson's invitation by attempting to set out the structure of the argument of *The Wealth of Nations* in the manner in which modern economics is presented: the assumptions are stated clearly and conclusions are derived from them. I was convinced that Smith's book must have an underlying logical structure as well as much fascinating and important detail; the problem was to find it. I therefore read *The Wealth of Nations* with care, derived the central strands of the argument and decided how this might be set out today, the challenge being to arrive at Smith's principal conclusions, including in particular those that were surprising. The late Klaus Hennings had emphasized to me that there must be no significant passages in Smith which contradicted my attempted restatement. To my great pleasure I managed to restate his argument with increasing industrial returns playing a central role – I had learned how to model these in my work on Kaldor in *Growth and Distribution*. In addition, despite continual advances in manufacturing productivity, in my restatement wages and profits eventually diminish and growth in the end falls towards zero as the economy approaches the stationary state. Previous commentators on Smith had succeeded in describing him either optimistically, with the economy all the time growing, or else pessimistically, with an emphasis on the eventual stationary state. The challenge I met was to find a statement where these were both integral to the argument. As with my later restatements, I allowed Smith's own words to present most of the argument.

During my 17 years at Oxford prior to 1973, I had sent my work on growth theory to Sir John Hicks and he had responded courteously that there was much he would wish to talk about when he had the time. I was therefore delighted when he wrote on this occasion that my article on Smith was, 'certainly the best case for Smith that has ever been made'. I had never before had so warm a reaction from him and it came to me that this might be the area of economics where I could make my best contribution.

I greatly enjoyed the year it took me to write the Smith article and I decided to produce similar restatements of Quesnay, Malthus, Ricardo and Marx. The articles which resulted became *The Classical Theory of Economic Growth* which I published in 1984; the two articles on Quesnay and the one on Malthus, which appeared first in *Oxford Economic Papers*, are reproduced in this volume (Chapters 4, 5 and 7 respectively).

It was the two years I spent on Quesnay that led especially to my understanding of the developing crisis in the British economy. The challenge Quesnay presents to an economist is to understand the *Tableau Economique* – the first technically-stated economic model set out by a distinguished economist. His many accounts of the Tableau are replete with illustrative numbers which do not appear to fit the argument. Every early effort to replicate the argument made me aware that there was more to understand. Quesnay was unquestionably a genius, a farmer's son who became a member of the French Academy of Sciences, a Fellow of the Royal Society of London, Madame de Pompadour's personal physician and one of Louis XV's principal doctors. He established his scientific reputation with books with titles such as *A Treatise on Gangrene*. Then at the age of 61 he became an economist, wrote on the subject in Diderot's *Encyclopédie* and invented the Tableau. The king is even said to have played a part in the correction of the proofs as printing was one of his hobbies. Gradually, by reading everything Quesnay wrote, including his books in collaboration with Victor Riqueti, Marquis de Mirabeau, I found a modern way of restating the argument that replicated all of Quesnay's significant numerical illustrations. I had managed to pin down his model. After completing this task, I felt that I had decoded the work of an economist vastly cleverer than myself and that for the rest of my life I could live off his ideas. That in a way is what then happened.

His account of the collapse of the French economy in the decades that led towards the revolution (he died in 1774) was based on the proposition that the agricultural sector produced the surplus which financed the rest of the economy including especially the Court, the Army and the Church. Despite this the government was taxing agriculture to destruction. Money was being taken from agriculture in a Colbertian policy to finance both industries which could not pay their way and vast and ostentatious public spending. Taxes on agriculture had the particular effect of reducing capital intensity on the land which greatly reduced the rate of surplus on which the rest of the economy depended. Quesnay had sequences of Tableaux which set out the decline of the economy year by year as a consequence of these self-destructive policies, and I believed I had found the key to decoding these series.

There were close parallels with what was happening in Britain in 1974. The surplus-producing sector was manufacturing industry and commerce. Bacon and I called this the market sector, but industry's workers and companies were being taxed at rising rates so that the surpluses it could make available to the remainder of the economy were declining. The other areas which were not surplus-creating were mainly in the public sector and they included certain nationalized industries which were increasingly absorbing the surpluses that successful companies created. British industrial policy (like France's before the revolution) was Colbertian. As private sector companies were squeezed, their ability to finance capital-intensive investments was all the time diminishing. Unemployment was rising and I greatly feared the Keynesian reaction of a further expansion of public spending to create jobs for those whom industry could no longer employ, leading in due course to still higher taxes on companies and those who worked in industry and commerce. With the growing structural weaknesses in the economy, I expected inflation all the time to rise. The rate of growth of the money supply would be accommodated to the growth of public spending judged to be necessary to maintain full employment, as it always had been up to 1974.

It required a considerable intellectual adjustment to appreciate that 18th-century economics could illuminate the 20th century. In 1973 I had been impressed by Adam Smith's proposition that excessive increases in the employment of those who produce no investable outputs (such as soldiers, bishops and civil servants) would undermine an economy's ability to grow, and in my essay for the Wilson and Skinner volume, I wrote: 'The labour of all these professions is included in modern National Income statistics, but few could doubt that if two developing countries had equal National Incomes, and one employed one-third of its labour in the above ways and the other one-tenth, the latter would find growth easier to achieve'.

By November 1974 when Bruce Page called on Bacon and myself in Oxford, we believed that it was not just in *developing countries* that a rapid increase in the employment of those who produced no investable outputs (whom Smith called unproductive) was slowing growth. By then we realized that this was also true of Britain. But we did not believe that others would be impressed if we told them that we were basing our analysis of the British economy on Adam Smith. Nor indeed did we think that this would appeal to the editors of *The Sunday Times*. In November 1974 when we published our first article, 'A Budget Message for Mr Healey: Get More People into Factories', we judged that we would get most credibility from the newspaper and its readers by stating, in acknowledgement of the origins of our theory, that the Russians use the illuminating division of the economy into productive and unproductive sectors, and that 'they got it from Marx who got it from Adam Smith'. During the 1970s and the 1980s the intellectual climate has been transformed so that an acknowledgement of the good sense in *The Wealth of Nations* now has credibility, while any suggestion that Marx or the Russians have had any positive insight would appear bizarre. But we had to influence opinion in 1974 and 1975, not 1992.

Economic theories that have died can come back. Hicks, one of Britain's three Nobel Prizewinners in economics, has reminded us that economics is not the kind of scientific subject where good theories are continually being superseded by better ones which fit more of the experimental data. Instead, in economics there is a continuous switching of ideas in which attention shifts from one theory to another equally good one which is more appropriate to a particular society. There may indeed be a reswitching of ideas, so that the most appropriate theory in the 18th century becomes inappropriate in the late 19th, but again becomes relevant in the 20th.

The reason why excessive public expenditure could appear damaging to growth in both the 18th and the 20th centuries but not the 19th was primarily that defence and administration absorbed a high fraction of the economic surpluses potentially available from investment in much of Europe in the 18th century, and again in the late 20th (when public expenditure reached or exceeded 50 per cent of the national income in many countries). In the 19th century, public expenditure was only about 10 per cent of the national income in the richest countries. Economists who attributed significance to the extent of public expenditure could thus appear relevant to policy-makers in the 18th and again in the late 20th century when Bacon and I began to command attention by placing this 18th-century theory in the public domain in *The Sunday Times* articles. Those who were aware of what had been happening in Whitehall and in Britain's Town Halls regarded what we were saying as highly credible. The Prime Minister, Harold Wilson, remarked in the House of Commons immediately after our 1975 articles were published that Whitehall had 'too many chiefs and too few Indians'.

The Bacon and Eltis articles and book
Our three substantial articles appeared in *The Sunday Times* in November 1975. They were published then to coincide with significant Cabinet discussions on public expenditure. Harold Evans, the Editor, described them as the 'Declining Britain' articles and invited 20 senior politicians, bankers and economists to respond in the next four issues. These included Lord George Brown, who had presided over *The National Plan* in the DEA. He wrote: 'One of the many valuable contributions by Bacon and Eltis to any useful debate on "The Way Ahead" is to enable us to make a fresh evaluation ... I agree pretty wholeheartedly with the authors' own choices of what we should do now ... One thing there can be no disputing: we must have really massive cuts in Government expenditure on non-productive items.' Denis Healey, the Chancellor of the Exchequer, almost echoed this when he said, 'The "Declining Britain" articles have provided the most stimulating and comprehensive analysis of our economic predicament which I have yet seen in a newspaper ... I strongly support their basic proposition that ... a faster growth in our manufacturing output will require more investment in industry; this will not be possible unless we limit the increase in the claims on the nation's resources which are made by public and private consumption.' David Basnett, the distinguished trade unionist General Secretary of the General and Municipal Workers' Union, wrote, 'Many points made in Eltis and Bacon's valuable analysis echo what the TUC and the unions have been saying with increasing force but as yet with little serious attention from the economic establishment. We agree, for example, on the total failure of the present system to direct anything like sufficient investment towards the productive industries.'

Support for our analysis came equally from the right. Sir Geoffrey Howe wrote: 'I have no doubt that we need to proceed broadly in the direction of the "Right" solution, foreshadowed by Bacon and Eltis'. In their book on *The British General Election of 1979*, David Butler and Dennis Kavanagh were kind enough to say that we had strongly influenced both parties. 'Conservatives seized on these findings as their explanation of de-industrialisation and inflationary pressure in the economy; Bacon and Eltis seemed to confirm the wisdom of their policies for holding back the public sector, reviving private enterprise and cutting direct taxation. The gradual change in direction of the Labour government's economic policy also appeared to heed this analysis.'

The newly elected leader of the Opposition had herself spoken very much in this vein in September 1975 when she said:

> The private sector creates the goods and services we need both to export to pay for our imports and to provide the revenue to finance public services. So one must not overload it. Every man switched away from industry and into government will reduce the productive sector and increase the burden on it at the same time.

When I met Mrs Thatcher later she singled out three statements in particular. She was struck by the opening sentence of the first article: 'Those who seek to manage economies or advise on their management are either tinkerers or structuralists'. She felt that many of her predecessors had been 'tinkerers'. We owe this opening sentence to Bruce Page who advised us to regard the first sentence of Machiavelli's *Prince* as the ideal opening to get a reader's attention, our model thus being: 'All states and dominions which hold or have held sway over mankind are either republics or monarchies'. A good article, we were being advised, should open with a striking half truth. Secondly, Mrs Thatcher referred to our statement that 'Oxfordshire County Council employs more workers in Oxfordshire than British Leyland' (which my wife drew to my attention from the *Oxford Mail*) and, thirdly, to our observation that 'workers and salary earners with just average earnings now suffer deductions of nearly 30 per cent from their paypackets, which is more than bank managers and university professors had to pay in tax and National Insurance contributions in 1963'. Proposals to reverse this increased taxation on those with ordinary paypackets had a significant impact on the outcome of the next four general elections, three of which she won.

We rapidly followed the publication of the 'Declining Britain' articles with the book *Britain's Economic Problem: Too Few Producers*, which included the full versions of the three articles, a statement of the economic theory that lay behind our analysis, and a complete explanation by Bacon of the derivation of the data we presented. In the present volume I reproduce the first chapter based on the first article, 'Where Britain Went Wrong', which was by far the most striking and influential, and also the theoretical chapter, 'The Implications for Inflation, Employment and Growth of a Fall in the Share of Output that is Marketed' (from the version we published in *The Oxford Bulletin of Economics and Statistics*). Thirdly, I reproduce an article published three years later in a volume edited by Wilfred Beckerman which extends our argument from Britain to New York, Canada and Chile which have also suffered destabilization from rapid public expenditure growth. (These are Chapters 10, 11 and 12 respectively.)

The reviews included one from my Cambridge undergraduate supervisor, Harry Johnson, who said that our book was 'interesting, both for its explanation of "the British disease" and for the economic theoretical foundations on which its analysis is based'. I was especially pleased when Sir Fred Catherwood, the second Director General of NEDO whom I served, said that ours was 'one of the very few books which gave a convincing diagnosis of our economic problems'.

Britain's real public expenditure was cut by more than 8 per cent from 1975–76 to 1977–78, I believe the largest cut ever achieved over a two-year period. The IMF's famous visit in 1976 was the main explanation of the extent of these cuts, but the reception of the 'Declining Britain' articles and subsequent book, as well as the absence of an effective answer at a level policy-makers would be aware of, may have contributed to the creation of an intellectual and political climate where government could more easily depart from the previous Keynesian orthodoxy. The effectiveness of our analysis owed much to its presentation in clear English without embellishment – as Joan Robinson had recommended so strongly when I was an undergraduate in Cambridge. When I later became Economic Director and Director General of NEDO and had to write papers to be read and discussed by Ministers and senior industrialists and trade unionists, I became very much aware that those who actually take the decisions that influence our lives are mainly in their 40s, 50s and 60s; if they have economics degrees, which few do, these will mainly date from the period before economics was taught mathematically. They therefore only read English prose and because of the pressures on their diaries, which are intense, they will rarely have the opportunity to read papers of more than about ten pages. Economists who wish to influence the decisions that are actually taken therefore have to present their arguments non-technically and concisely. That is why articles published in newspapers, or else official papers of equivalent length, are an important means to get through to the generation that takes decisions. I realized none of this in 1974 and 1975, and it was accidental that Bacon and I had the opportunity to write in the one medium of communication that actually stood a chance of having some effect.

My disillusionment with the Keynesian conventional wisdom

In 1976, a few months after the publication of our book, I produced a statement of my other principal doubts concerning the Keynesian approach which had dominated British economic policy since the war. This was the *Lloyds Bank Review* article, 'The Failure of the Keynesian Conventional Wisdom' which I reproduce as Chapter 13 in this volume. It too aroused a good deal of attention and elicited a response in a subsequent issue from Lord Kahn, who had invented the Keynesian multiplier in 1929. From the mid-1960s onwards, I had become increasingly uncomfortable with the economics we were teaching in Oxford. I recall that in 1966, I was examining in the Final Honours School of Politics, Philosophy and Economics with two distinguished colleagues who wished to write in our report that 'several undergraduates were so muddled, they believed that faster inflation would raise the rate of interest'. I protested to my colleagues that the undergraduates must be right – though that is not the answer that emerged from Keynesian textbooks. These had a monetary theory where the wealthy could only hold cash or government bonds in their portfolios. If they thought cash would lose its value because of inflation, they could not protect themselves because their only alternative was to switch to government fixed-interest bonds. In the real world the far-sighted can of course protect themselves from inflation by holding equity shares, commodities and houses; as portfolio holders seek to escape from cash into assets which will hold their value, the rising prices of commodities and houses is one of the principal inflationary transmission mechanisms.

Milton Friedman made the world aware of this, but we knew nothing of his work in Oxford in 1966.

Another discontent I had was with the Keynesian theory of the determination of the rate of interest by liquidity preference and the quantity of money. We were expected to teach that you receive interest because you are prepared to take the risk of not holding cash. But by 1966 you could get 4 or 5 per cent interest from a cash deposit in a bank or building society, so where was the risk? My colleagues explained that you had to give a week's notice to take your money out, so that was what you were being rewarded for with interest. I noted in my 1976 article that in 1936 Joan Robinson had wished to publish an essay which suggested that interest rates would be influenced by matters other than British liquidity preference, but Keynes had written begging her not to publish saying, 'you do not seem to realise that if you are right the whole theory of liquidity preference has to be thrown overboard'. Joan Robinson cooperated four days later by cutting the 'controversial matter' out of her 1936 essay. In October 1976 she wrote to me after the publication of my article, stating that 'in that correspondence with me, Keynes was completely off the rails ... he was having an aberration'. In 'The Failure of the Keynesian Conventional Wisdom' I expressed all my doubts about the main elements of the Keynesian approach to policy, the incorrect analysis of the impact of money and interest, the potentially disastrous impact on the balance of payments of using deficit financing policies to expand demand, the bias in Keynesian policies towards low saving which is bound to influence growth adversely, and the general indifference to government borrowing and its impact. I used a quotation from Kahn's evidence to the Radcliffe Committee: 'To my mind the [government's] "overall" deficit is of no significance'.

I was pleased that in his response in the April 1977 issue of *Lloyds Bank Review*, Kahn actually conceded that faster inflation would be associated with a higher rate of interest. My article was quoted extensively in *The Wall Street Journal* and attracted the attention of Tony Boeckh, the Editor of *The Bank Credit Analyst*. He invited me to his next annual conference in Bermuda where I met Art Laffer, the inventor of the Laffer Curve which was actually drawn for me on a napkin by his principal colleague, Jude Wanniski. Bacon and I were probably the first economists to carry this curve – which shows that cutting taxes can raise government revenues (and will inevitably do so at especially high tax rates) – to this side of the Atlantic. We included it in our article for the *Second Report* of the House of Commons Expenditure Committee which was published in 1978. I drew Sir Geoffrey Howe's attention to the argument in February 1978 after he had said that cutting the highest rates of tax would cost revenue. He replied, 'I am sorry that I have been guilty of back-sliding into the orthodox Treasury position on the subject of higher rate tax cuts. I am sure you are right; but I sometimes find that my puritan instinct gets the better of my reason!'

In his first budget when he became Chancellor of the Exchequer 15 months later, Sir Geoffrey cut the top rate of tax on the highest unearned incomes from 98 to 75 per cent and the top rate on earned incomes from 83 to 60 per cent. He also cut the standard rate of tax on most incomes from 33 to 30 per cent. Research has since suggested that the reductions in the top rates increased eventual revenue from those who paid the highest rates, the Laffer effect, but the reductions in the standard rate cost substantial sums, as HM Treasury and Sir Geoffrey fully understood and expected. The Laffer argument applied only to reductions in the very highest rates. I had an opportunity to publish a mathematical derivation of the Laffer Curve (which is sometimes despised because it can be drawn on a napkin) in a conference on Private Saving and Public Debt which Stefano Gorini organized in Sardinia in 1985. I reproduce the consequent article, 'Some Implications of Deficit-financed Tax Cuts: These Will Always Increase Demand, but Will They Reduce Supply?', as Chapter 14 in this volume.

The Bacon and Eltis book was published in Italy in 1977 with an introduction by Guido Carli, the Governor of the Bank of Italy, and many invitations to give seminars in Italy followed. I therefore became very much aware of the problems raised by Italy's budget deficit of over 10 per cent of GNP and its continually growing ratio of public debt. I went back to the early Keynesians and in particular to Evsy Domar to discover how they had managed to ignore the adverse long-term impact of growing government borrowing. It emerged that they were convinced that the growth rates from successfully implemented Keynesian policies would universally exceed the real interest rates at which governments had to borrow. With that assumption, government debt and its financing become a continually falling burden, and governments can safely be advised to borrow whatever a country needs to achieve full employment and its growth potential. That message was well heeded in Italy and in many developing countries which became financially crippled in the 1980s when the world's real interest rates rose to a level far above the rates of growth that most of them managed to achieve. In the 1980s real interest rates became 5 or 6 per cent throughout the world, so that countries growing at only 2 per cent found that the cost of servicing their debt rose very sharply as a share of national income. The previous encourage-ment to achieve high employment and economic development by borrowing thus proved to be a trap after the huge rise in real interest rates. I presented my critique of the Keynesian approach to public borrowing at a conference in Poland in 1985 which then, as now, was massively in debt to the West. Melvin Lasky, the Editor of *Encounter*, was at the conference and asked if he could publish my paper. I reproduce it here as Chapter 15.

With increasing involvement in financial seminars and conferences, and consequent invitations to write regular quarterly articles for Rowe and Pitman, the London stockbrokers (now part of Warburg), and for *The International Bank Credit Analyst*, as well as continuing opportunities to write in *The Sunday Times*, a good deal of my economic attention shifted to the financial sector. However, I continued to work on the History of Economics. My article on 'Ricardo on Machinery and Technological Unemployment', which I reproduce as Chapter 8 in this volume, gave me particular pleasure because many in the 1980s were beginning to believe that there had been a twist in technology so that technical advance was destroying jobs instead of creating them. Ricardo had developed an example where this occurred. He had told the House of Commons that 'the use of machinery was prejudicial ... to the working classes generally', and in a letter he wrote, 'If machinery could do all the work that labour now does, there would be no demand for labour. Nobody would be entitled to consume any thing who was not a capitalist and who could not buy or hire a machine.' Marx took Ricardo's argument further, the tendency of machinery to destroy jobs being a central element in *Das Kapital*. In my 1985 article I go through Ricardo's and Marx's arguments carefully to isolate the circumstances where investment in new machinery will reduce the demand for labour: fortunately they are remote. Ricardo's argument, for instance, requires that the introduction of machinery should reduce the level of production: if it increases aggregate output, jobs will not be destroyed. Even in this case, Ricardo insists that if foreigners introduce cost-cutting machinery, there is no alternative but to introduce it in Britain.

In 1986 the Eighth World Congress of the International Economic Association was held in Delhi, its theme being the balance between industry and agriculture. I was invited to present the paper, 'The Contrasting Theories of Industrialization of François Quesnay and Adam Smith', and I reproduce it as Chapter 6 in this volume. I argued that Quesnay was speaking directly to countries such as Argentina, India and Pakistan today. In Argentina agriculture yields a rate of surplus of 80 per cent, but it is heavily taxed and farmers are obliged to sell food below world prices, as in 18th-century France. These measures were introduced after the Second World War to help industry, which still requires vast subsidies and has few exportable products. Agriculture, which has had to pay for these policies, has not unexpectedly grown less than population. In Pakistan, where similar policies were pursued, industry's value added has been negative measured at world prices. In effect Pakistan has been subsidizing manufacturers to turn perfectly good raw materials into finished products that are worth less. Once again, I argued, the world should learn from Quesnay.

The final contribution to the history of economics that I include as Chapter 9 in this volume is my essay on 'Sir James Steuart's Corporate State' which I was invited to write shortly before I returned to NEDO in 1986 as Economic Director. Steuart wrote a 1300-page book in 1767 in which he recommended every inflationist and interventionist nostrum that any country has introduced in the 20th century. He advocated export subsidies, import controls and even the European Community's agricultural policy (the State should buy food at a price adequate for the farmer, sell it at a price suitable for the consumer and store the difference in State granaries). He proposed that paper money should be printed until interest rates fell to 2 per cent, that the State should place directors in major companies, that it should spend massively on the infrastructure, that it should borrow more than the total capital of the nation, renege on its debt and then borrow all over again because no one would remember. Taxes should be raised sharply to oblige people to work harder, while the expenditure of tax revenues would allow government to reward its supporters. Smith said in a letter that he would destroy Steuart's arguments without once mentioning his name; and indeed, the latter's work was soon forgotten after the publication of *The Wealth of Nations*. Steuart was even distressed enough to say that a 1300-page book about his dog would have aroused more attention, but he was rediscovered and much praised in the period of Keynesian ascendancy and everything he recommended was tried in many countries. I show in my essay how Steuart's underlying assumption that governments have total knowledge of everything and can therefore take far better decisions than the business community contrasts with Smith's assumption that statesmen are ignorant and prejudiced and should be kept as far as possible from business decisions. Reading Steuart and seeing all the fallacies in his corporatism was a marvellous education before my return to NEDO in 1986.

Leading the National Economic Development Office and practical economics
When Mrs Thatcher's government was elected in 1979, I greatly welcomed its declared policies to strengthen the supply side of the economy by creating room for tax cuts through reductions in the relative size of the public sector. But because of the sharp recession in the early years, the market sector declined in the short term and the relative size of the public sector actually grew. Like most British economists, I was extremely concerned about the rise in sterling in 1979 and 1980, because this was making it difficult for industry to compete. I organized a conference in Oxford in 1981, chaired by Robin Matthews, to which Adam Ridley (now Sir Adam), Sir Geoffrey Howe's Special Adviser, came and to which some of the most distinguished macroeconomists contributed. Their papers became the book, *The Money Supply and the Exchange Rate* which I edited together with Peter Sinclair in 1982. It emerged at the conference that no one had expected or wished for the extent of the rise in sterling that occurred. Because I was quite closely identified with the cutting of public expenditure part of the policy mix of the new government, friends did not hesitate to hold me responsible for what was going wrong. One senior Bank of England economist came up to me at a party and said 'You have written a book which has wrecked the British economy, could you write another that would save it?' My only official contacts until 1986 were occasional invitations from the Chancellor to join seminars with nine invited economists which were held in HM Treasury about once a year. Geoffrey Howe used to ask the changing membership of this group, which the Treasury labelled the 'gooies' (from the acronym GOOIE for Group Of Outside Independent Economists), whether money was loose or tight according to whichever measure we most recommended to his attention. Nigel Lawson's focus shifted from control of the money supply and in 1985 he asked us to advise him on the question, 'What should the public sector borrowing requirement be if inflation were zero?' It was reassuring that we were being invited to consider what should be done after the inflation problem had been solved. After such peripheral involvements with government in Mrs Thatcher's first seven years, I was delighted when my name was mentioned to Sir John Cassels, the Director General, as a possible Economic Director of NEDO, and I emerged as the successful candidate.

Cassels was a marvellous Director General to work for as he left economics entirely to me, confining his attentions to the improvement of my English and the removal of the hectoring statements to government that Oxbridge economists are apt to adopt. The discipline on my economics came from quite other quarters. Since NEDO was set up to serve government, the CBI and the TUC, everything we wrote had to be de-politicized. Our terms of reference were 'to give independent advice on ways of improving the economic performance, competitive power and efficiency of the nation' and 'to increase the rate of sound growth'. This we had to do in a manner which would retain the confidence of government, unions and industry. I never found that the need for impartiality prevented me from saying what needed to be said, but it was a useful discipline. The problem I became most aware of was an entirely different one. We had to put the essence of our papers to the very distinguished industrialists, trade unionists and bankers who chair our industrial Sector Groups and Working Parties. They would continually question what the purpose of a piece of economic analysis could possibly be, whether any useful practical actions could result, and whether the facts put forward (all drawn from official publications) reflected what was actually happening in their industries.

My difficulties resembled those that the distinguished American economist Fritz Machlup foreshadowed. He once told us that nuclear physicists had achieved great progress using the assumption that electrons follow random walks. He spoke of the consternation there would be in any of the great nuclear laboratories if voices started to emerge from electrons telling scientists of the reasons for their movements. Physics would be entirely held up while the voices of the electrons were recorded, analysed and modelled. But in NEDO we actually heard what industrialists were saying and had to take it seriously, which could make life extremely difficult for those of us who had been trained to see the world in academic terms.

It was not long before I began to learn. When businessmen and bankers said that a piece of economic analysis did actually describe what concerned them, we could arrive at a higher truth by combining logical economic analysis with what mattered in British industry. This first happened to me with a paper on the cost of borrowing which I presented to the Committee on Industry and Finance (which I later chaired as Director General). The members of the Committee had said that high nominal interest rates mattered just as much as, if not more than, high real rates. If real interest rates are 5 per cent, nominal rates will be 5 per cent if inflation is zero but 15 per cent if inflation is 10 per cent. Why should businessmen mind paying 15 per cent interest if inflation is removing 10 per cent of their debt each year?

In fact it matters a great deal because companies have to pay out far more actual money as interest when the nominal rate is 15 per cent. If anything goes wrong in the first two or three years of an investment (such as strikes, technical breakdowns or recessions creating hiatuses in sales), companies will still have to pay out interest and will fail if their banks let them down. With 5 per cent nominal interest and nil inflation, the negative cash flows required to pay interest in the early years of an investment are only one-third as great. The businessmen on our Committee were talking sense when they said that these considerations mattered, whereas those who assume that investment is riskless and that unlimited sums can be borrowed at the market rate of interest have failed to notice this vital consideration in the world of business. It is also central to the concerns of workers when they buy houses. With 15 instead of 5 per cent nominal interest rates, they have to pay their banks or building societies three times as much each week when they first buy their homes and are thus far more likely to lose possession if they are temporarily unemployed.

The bankers and industrialists on our Committee on Industry and Finance convinced me that these considerations were of key importance. The implications are very powerful because, with the free capital movements of the 1980s and the 1990s, real long-term interest rates are nearly the same in all the major economies. This means that the only sustainable way of bringing nominal interest rates down is to reduce inflation. If Britain has 5 per cent more inflation than Germany, nominal interest rates will be roughly 5 per cent higher in London than in Frankfurt. They have come down sharply in 1992 now that British inflation is close to the German rate.

Until I learned the details and implications of this line of argument from the members of our Committee, I had been lukewarm about the priority the government was attaching to getting inflation down towards zero. I had believed in 1986 that

5 per cent was low enough and I had welcomed the devaluation in 1987 which had greatly improved the competitiveness of British exports without apparently raising inflation. When I remarked that 5 per cent is low enough, Sir Peter Middleton countered that the danger in acquiescing in 5 per cent inflation is that, with all the difficulties of controlling it, you might accidentally get 7 per cent which is too high. Aiming for 3 per cent and getting 5 (if there were a miscalculation) would be far safer. We actually reached 10 per cent inflation in 1990 and so paid a very high price for our apparent acquiescence in 5 per cent inflation in the 1980s.

The argument that inflation damages company liquidity because it raises nominal interest rates inevitably points to an inflation target of zero, because that is what will minimize the vulnerability of companies and home owners to adverse cash flows in the early years of their investments. I developed the argument I had presented to the Committee on Industry and Finance in the Bateman Memorial Lecture which I delivered in Perth (Australia) in May 1990; I first published it in *The National Westminster Bank Quarterly Review* in February 1991 where it aroused a good deal of attention. The version of the article 'How Inflation Undermines Economic Performance', which I include as Chapter 16 in this volume, has benefited from further suggestions from Robin Matthews and Milton Friedman. Margaret Thatcher, Geoffrey Howe, Nigel Lawson, Norman Lamont and John Major had appreciated the case for nil inflation long before I did, but I was pleased to find strong economic arguments that underlined the economic rationality of the objective to which they attached such significance.

When I became Director General of NEDO in November 1988, it fell to me to obtain the fullest contribution that the Chairmen of our industrial committees were able to make. Instead of continuing to try to convince them how important our insights were, we decided to discover what they considered vital to the improved performance of the British economy. We therefore held a series of meetings from which a paper by all the Chairmen evolved. I include a version of this, 'The Lessons for Britain from the Superior Economic Performance of Germany and Japan', as the final article in this volume (Chapter 17). The Chairmen are listed and include distinguished heads of companies, Sir Ivor Cohen, Sir John Cuckney, Ian Gibson, Sir Ronald Halstead and Sir Brian Wolfson; distinguished trade unionists, Bill Jordan and Eric Hammond; John Ashworth, the Director of the LSE, and George Bain, the Principal of the London Business School. By listening to them, we learned that in their judgement a key difference between producing in Britain and producing in Germany and Japan was that those who run our companies have to spend much of their time dealing with financial questions. In contrast their opposite numbers in the world's most successful economies have been free to concentrate on the development of products and markets. British businesses above all need a stable and predictable financial environment within which those concerned with production and product development and marketing can take long-term decisions. They endorsed the objective of a near-nil inflation rate especially because it would minimize nominal interest rates. There is much else of importance in this Chairmen's article which was drafted jointly with Douglas Fraser and Martin Ricketts, NEDO's Industrial and Economic Directors.

Readers will see how far this article, which is entirely concerned with what is now needed to increase the growth of the British economy, differs from the one which opens this volume and which impressed Shone, our first Director General, in 1963. There are now no formulae concerning investment ratios and capital output ratios. The emphasis is instead on the conditions which will allow companies to operate effectively. There is much on training and Industry/City cooperation which was entirely absent from my 1963 article. I believe my economics has developed greatly in the 29 years that separate the first article from the last. To quote Keynes, the development of my economics in this book has been 'a long struggle of escape'. The ideas I have moved towards – with their emphasis on the case for supply-side reforms leading to economies in public expenditure and consequently low taxation, on the case for nil inflation, for low government borrowing and for predictable economic management – represent a very significant departure from the economics I was introduced to in Cambridge in the 1950s.

I only came to understand the full range of arguments I present in the later articles after I saw a great deal of senior industrialists and trade unionists in NEDO. I was obliged to listen. We had to take on board and learn from a wide range of opinion. We benefited from this and I greatly hope that, after the decision to close NEDO in June 1992 (which, ironically, by marginally diminishing the non-market sector, I have every reason to understand), it will not merely be the Department of Trade and Industry (where I have moved to become Chief Economic Adviser to the President of the Board of Trade) that listens to Britain's industrialists. It is equally important that HM Treasury, which takes the principal economic decisions, should have strong, close and institutionalized links with the business community.

A particular lesson I began to learn in the 1970s is the overwhelming need for collaboration between economists. Working together, most of us can achieve far more penetrating and valuable insights than we are capable of individually. In my own case, the work I produced with Bacon had far more impact and commanded more respect among professional economists and in the outside world than anything which either of us had previously published. My work on classical economics is cooperative in the sense that the originality is theirs. I have merely attempted to bring their work to life and make its continuing relevance evident in another century.

In NEDO, I discovered that papers for the NEDC and other research had considerably more value when those with different perceptions and areas of expertise cooperated in their preparation. I found it a particular privilege to have the opportunity to work with Martin Ricketts, a distinguished microeconomist Economic Director (an area of economics to which I have scarcely contributed) and Douglas Fraser, an Industrial Director with a rich and extensive knowledge of what happens in companies here and overseas. Few of us are expert in macroeconomics, microeconomics, econometrics and the worlds of industry and finance, so most of us must work with others if we are to produce economics that illuminates and commands attention.

Bibliography: Publications by Walter Eltis 1963–92

(1963), 'Investment, Technical Progress and Economic Growth', *Oxford Economic Papers*, **15**, March.
(1965a), *Economic Growth: Analysis and Policy*, Hutchinson. Italian translation (Il Mulino).
(1965b), 'A Theory of Investment, Distribution and Employment', *Oxford Economic Papers*, **17**, July.
(1965c), 'Underestimation of Public Expenditure in the Plan', Internal NEDO Memorandum, 25 September.
(1967), 'Economic Growth and the British Balance of Payments', *District Bank Review*, December.

(1968a), 'Inflation: Some Problems', paper read at the Business Economists' Group Conference, Business Economists' Group, April.

(1968b) 'Technical Progress, Profits and Growth', *Oxford Economic Papers*, **20**, November.

(1969), 'Is Stop-Go Inevitable?', *National Westminster Quarterly Bank Review*, November.

(1970a), Joint Editor (with M.FG. Scott and J.N. Wolfe), *Induction, Growth and Trade: Essays in Honour of Sir Roy Harrod*, Oxford University Press.

(1970b), 'Capital Accumulation and the Rate of Industrialization of Developing Countries', *Economic Record*, **46**, June.

(1971a), 'The Determination of the Rate of Technical Progress', *Economic Journal*, **81**, September.

(1971b), 'The Australian Economy Today', *Lloyds Bank Review*, April.

(1971c), 'Taxation and Investment' in Sir Robert Shone (ed.), *Problems of Investment*, Basil Blackwell.

(1973), *Growth and Distribution*, Macmillan (London) and John Wiley (New York).

(1974a) (with R.W. Bacon), *The Age of US and UK Machinery*, NEDO Research Monograph, HMSO.

(1974b) (with R.W. Bacon), 'A Budget Message for Mr Healey: Get More People into Factories', *The Sunday Times*, 10 November.

(1975a), 'Adam Smith's Theory of Economic Growth' in Andrew Skinner and Thomas Wilson (eds), *Essays on Adam Smith*, Oxford University Press.

(1975b), 'François Quesnay: A Reinterpretation 1. The *Tableau Économique*', *Oxford Economic Papers*, **27**, July.

(1975c), 'François Quesnay: A Reinterpretation 2. The Theory of Economic Growth', *Oxford Economic Papers*, **27**, November.

(1975d) (with R.W. Bacon), 'The Implications for Inflation, Employment and Growth of a Fall in the Share of Output that is Marketed', *Oxford Bulletin of Economics and Statistics*, **37**, November.

(1975e), 'How Public Sector Growth Causes Balance of Payments Deficits', *International Currency Review*, January–February.

(1975f) (with R.W. Bacon), 'Stop-Go and De-Industrialization', *National Westminster Quarterly Bank Review*, November.

(1975g) (with R.W. Bacon), 'The Declining Britain Articles': (i) 'Where We Went Wrong', (ii) 'The Chances We Missed', (iii) 'What We Would Do', *The Sunday Times*, 2, 9 and 16 November.

(1976a) (with Robert Bacon), *Britain's Economic Problem: Too Few Producers*, Macmillan (London) and St Martin's Press (New York), 1st ed. 1976, 2nd ed. 1978. Italian translation (Etas Libri), 1977; Japanese translation.

(1976b), 'The Failure of the Keynesian Conventional Wisdom', *Lloyds Bank Review*, October.

(1977), 'The Keynesian Conventional Wisdom' (a reply to Lord Kahn's 'Mr Eltis and the Keynesians' April 1977), *Lloyds Bank Review*, July.

(1978) (with Robert Bacon), 'Memorandum', Annex 1 in *Second Report from the Expenditure Committee*, House of Commons (Paper 257), 10 March.

(1979a) (with R.W. Bacon), 'The Measurement of the Growth of the Non-Market Sector and its Influence: A Reply to Hadjimatheou and Skouras', *Economic Journal*, **89**, June.

(1979b), 'How Rapid Public Sector Growth can Undermine the Growth of the National Product' in Wilfred Beckerman (ed.), *Slow Growth in Britain: Causes and Consequences*, Oxford University Press.

(1979c), 'The True Deficits of the Public Corporations', *Lloyds Bank Review*, January.

(1980), 'Malthus's Theory of Effective Demand and Growth', *Oxford Economic Papers*, **32**, March.

(1981a), Joint Editor (with P.J.N. Sinclair), *The Money Supply and the Exchange Rate*, Oxford University Press.

(1981b), 'I Nuovi Esperimenti dei Conservatori in Gran Bretagna e Negli Stati Uniti: Avranno Successo?', *Micros*, Giugno.

(1982), 'Do Government Manpower Cuts Correct Deficits when the Economy is in Deep Recession?', *Political Quarterly*, January–March.

(1983a), 'Policy for the Nationalised Industries: The British Problem' in Herbert Giersch (ed.), *Reassessing the Role of Government in the Mixed Economy*, Mohr: Tübingen.

(1983b), 'The Interconnection between Public Expenditure and Inflation in Britain', *American Economic Review*, **73**, March.

(1983c), 'A Neoclassical Analysis of Macroeconomic Policy', *Journal of Money, Credit and Banking*, **15**, November.

(1984), *The Classical Theory of Economic Growth*, Macmillan (London) and St Martin's Press (New York); Japanese translation, 1991.

(1985), 'Ricardo on Machinery and Technological Unemployment' in Giovanni A. Caravale (ed.), *The Legacy of Ricardo*, Basil Blackwell.

(1986a), 'Sir James Steuart's Corporate State' in R.D.C. Black (ed.), *Ideas in Economics*, Macmillan.

(1986b), 'The Borrowing Fallacy: On The World Debt Crisis', *Encounter*, **67**, November.
(1987a), 'Some Implications of Deficit Financed Tax Cuts: These Will Always Increase Demand, But Will They Reduce Supply?' in Michael J. Boskin, John S. Flemming and Stefano Gorini (eds), *Private Saving and Public Debt*, Basil Blackwell.
(1987b), Articles on 'Falling Rate of Profit', 'Harrod–Domar Growth Model', 'Roy Forbes Harrod', 'Sir James Steuart' and 'Thomas Mun' in *The New Palgrave Dictionary of Economics*, Macmillan.
(1988a), Joint Editor (with Peter Sinclair), *Keynes and Economic Policy: The Relevance of the General Theory after Fifty Years*, Macmillan.
(1988b), 'The Contrasting Theories of Industrialization of François Quesnay and Adam Smith', *Oxford Economic Papers*, **40**, June.
(1989), 'The Obstacles to Monetary Union', *International Currency Review*, August–September.
(1990a) (with Andrew Murfin), 'The Contribution of the Service Sector to the Growth of the United Kingdom Economy' in Christopher Moir and John Dawson (eds), *Competition and Markets*, Macmillan
(1990b), 'Marx on the Unproductiveness of the Financial Sector and its Tendency to Grow' in Giovanni Caravale (ed.), *Marx and Modern Economic Analysis*, Edward Elgar.
(1990c), 'British Industrial Policy for the 1990s' in Graham Mather (ed.), *The State of the Economy*, Institute of Economic Affairs.
(1991a), 'How Inflation Undermines Industrial Success', *National Westminster Bank Quarterly Review*, February.
(1991b), 'How Inflation Undermines Industrial Performance' in G.K. Shaw (ed.), *Economics, Culture and Education: Essays in Honour of Mark Blaug*, Edward Elgar.
(1991c), 'United Kingdom Investment and Finance' in Geoffrey Wood (ed.), *The State of the Economy*, Institute of Economic Affairs.
(1992a) (with Douglas Fraser and Martin Ricketts), 'The Lessons for Britain from the Superior Economic Performance of Germany and Japan', *National Westminster Bank Quarterly Review*, February.
(1992b), 'Financial Crises and Credit Cycles', *The New Palgrave Dictionary of Money and Finance*, Macmillan.
(1992c) (with Douglas Fraser), 'The Contribution of Japanese Industrial Success to Britain and to Europe' *The National Westminster Bank Quarterly Review*, November.

Other references

Arrow, Kenneth (1962), 'The Economic Implications of Learning by Doing', *Review of Economic Studies* **29**, June.
Basnett, David (1975), 'A Critical Engine of Change', *The Sunday Times*, 23 November.
Brown, George (1975), 'How Near We Came to the Right Answers 10 Years Ago', *The Sunday Times*, 30 November.
Butler, David and Dennis Kavanagh (1980), *The British General Election of 1979*, Macmillan.
Catherwood, Fred (1978), 'Bosses Must Take Control', *The Sunday Times*, 7 May.
Clark, Colin (1938), 'Determination of the Multiplier from National Income Statistics', *Economic Journal* **48**, September.
Department of Economic Affairs (1965), *The National Plan* (Cmnd 2764), HMSO, London.
Domar, Evsy (1944), 'The Burden of Debt and the National Income', *American Economic Review*, **34** December.
Economist (1975), 'Economics: New Oxford', 29 November.
Healey, Denis (1975), 'The Government Alone Cannot Put Britain Back On Its Feet', *The Sunday Times* 14 December.
Hicks, John, Letter to the author dated 13 May 1973.
Hicks, John (1975), 'The Scope and Status of Welfare Economics', *Oxford Economic Papers*, **27**, November
Howe, Geoffrey (1975), 'Industrial Growth with a Diminishing Work Force', *The Sunday Times*, 30 November.
Howe, Geoffrey, Letter to the author dated 23 February 1978.
Johnson, Harry G. (1976), 'How Good Was Keynes's Cambridge', *Encounter*, **47**, August.
Johnson, Harry G. (1977), Review of *Britain's Economic Problem: Too Few Producers*, *Canadian Public Policy*, **3**, Winter.
Kahn, Richard (1977), 'Mr Eltis and the Keynesians', *Lloyds Bank Review*, April.
Kaldor, Nicholas (1957), 'A Model of Economic Growth', *Economic Journal*, **67**, December.
Kaldor, Nicholas (1966), *Causes of the Slow Rate of Growth of the United Kingdom*, Inaugural Lecture Cambridge University Press.
Keynes, John Maynard (1936), *The General Theory of Employment, Interest and Money*, 1st edition, London Reprinted as Vol. 7 of *The Works and Correspondence of John Maynard Keynes*, Macmillan, 1973

Marx, Karl (1867–91), *Capital*, 3 vols. Republished in 1974 by Progress Publishers for Lawrence & Wishart.

Mirabeau, Victor de Riqueti, Marquis de, and François Quesnay (1756–60), *L'Ami des Hommes*, 1st edition, Avignon. Reprinted in 1972 by Scientia Verlag Aalen.

Mirabeau, Victor de Riqueti, Marquis de, and François Quesnay (1763), *Philosophie Rurale*, 1st edition, Amsterdam. Reprinted in 1972 by Scientia Verlag Aalen.

Quesnay, François (1749), *Traité de la Gangrène*, Paris.

Quesnay, François (1758–60), *Tableau Économique*, 1st edition (Paris); 2nd edition, 1759; 3rd edition, 1759. Republished and translated in Marguerite Kuczynski and Ronald L. Meek (eds), *Quesnay's Tableau Économique*, Macmillan, 1972.

Ricardo, David (1817), *Principles of Political Economy and Taxation*, First edition, London, Reprinted as Vol. 1 of P. Sraffa (ed.), *The Works and Correspondence of David Ricardo*, Cambridge University Press, 1951.

Robinson, Joan (1934), 'Euler's Theorem and the Problem of Distribution', *Economic Journal*, **44**, September.

Robinson, Joan (1956), *The Accumulation of Capital*, Macmillan.

Robinson, Joan, Letters to the author dated 31 January 1956 and 14 October 1976.

Smith, Adam (1776), *An Inquiry into the Nature and Causes of the Wealth of Nations*, 1st edition, London. Reprinted as II in *The Glasgow Edition of The Works and Correspondence of Adam Smith*, Oxford University Press, 1976.

PART I

GROWTH THEORY

[1]

INVESTMENT, TECHNICAL PROGRESS, AND ECONOMIC GROWTH

By W. A. ELTIS

Introduction

GROWTH in the productive capacity of a developed economy with full employment is inevitable because there are additions to its technical knowledge and to its capital every year, and these additions either increase or permit increases in its productive capacity. Its output can grow from year to year (as well as its productive capacity) providing its government allows demand to rise.

Two elementary approaches to the determination of the rate of growth focus simply on the increase in capital or the increase in knowledge. The approach which attributed growth solely to investment and the quantity of capital will be explained first.

Investment and Economic Growth—the S/C Formulation

It is argued in this approach that the rate of growth of net output is S/C per cent. a year, where S is the percentage of the Net National Product (subsequently written as NNP) which consists of net investment, and C is the capital output ratio of new capital. With a capital output ratio of C, net investment of £C would add £1 to the following year's NNP,[1] net investment of £1 would add £$1/C$, and the total net investment made in a year, S per cent. of the NNP altogether, would add (S per cent. of the NNP)$/C$ to net output in the following year. Since output in the following year would then be higher by NNP times S/C per cent., the rate of growth of the NNP would be S/C per cent. in the year concerned.[2] An increase in S would increase the rate of growth, while an increase in C would reduce it.

If C is defined as the increase in capital which is actually made in a particular period divided by the increase in output which actually occurs in that period, the S/C formulation is a tautology, and it was as a tautology that Sir Roy Harrod originated it in 1939.[3] Sometimes, however, C is not

---

[1] It is assumed that 'depreciation' is the amount of investment that is needed to keep net output constant, and then all *net* investment must add to net output.

[2] If S equalled 12 per cent. of the NNP and the capital output ratio of new capital was 4, the rate of growth of the NNP would be 12/4 per cent., or 3 per cent. a year. If the NNP was originally 100, 12 of the 100 units produced in the first year are net investment, and can be added to the capital stock. Every 4 of these extra units of capital can produce a unit of net output a year, so the following years output will be the original 100 units, plus a quarter of 12 units, or 103 units altogether—a growth rate of 3 per cent. from the previous year's 100 units.

[3] See R. F. Harrod's 'An essay in dynamic theory', *Economic Journal*, 1939. Reprinted in *Economic Essays*, Macmillan, 1952, essay 13. If C is defined as the $\dfrac{\text{net increase in capital}}{\text{net increase in output}}$

defined as the actual capital output ratio, but a value of C derived from
past experience is used to estimate the effect on the *future* rate of growth
of a particular rate of investment. For instance, Professor W. Fellner
wrote in 1956 of the U.S.A.: 'It is quite conceivable that by doubling net
capital formation, our growth rate could be fully doubled.'[1] Here the
argument that a doubling of S would quite conceivably double the rate
of growth implies that doubling S would leave C unaltered.

Capital per worker rises continuously in an economy with full employment, and an increased share of investment in the NNP would increase
the rate at which it rose. It is well known that 'When, in a given state of
knowledge, factors of production which are in variable supply are added
to another factor of production which is in fixed supply, the marginal
products of the variable factors eventually diminish'. According to this
principle, if there was a *given state of knowledge*, increases in capital per
worker would *eventually* lead to a lower marginal product of capital, i.e.
to a higher marginal capital output ratio, a higher C, and therefore to a
slower rate of growth from a given share of investment. Because there
is not a *given state of knowledge* in any actual economy, since knowledge
about methods of production is added to continuously, certain additions
to capital per worker can be made each year without bringing the point
of diminishing returns nearer. There is the further possibility that the
point where diminishing returns to capital would begin might be distant
in some economies because of a large backlog of unexploited investment
opportunities, and capital per worker could then be increased rapidly for
many years without a rise in C.[2] When a past value of C is extrapolated
into the future it is implicitly assumed that either technical progress, or
a large backlog of unexploited investment opportunities would prevent C
from rising in the period of the prediction.

If there is not full employment in an economy there is no reason why
there should be diminishing returns to capital, and there is then no reason
why C should rise when S is increased. In such an economy, doubling S

over a given period of time, S as the $\dfrac{\text{net increase in capital}}{\text{net output}}$ in the same period of time, and
the rate of growth in this period of time as $\dfrac{\text{net increase in output}}{\text{net output}}$,

$$\frac{S}{C} \text{ equals } \frac{\text{net increase in capital}}{\text{net output}}$$

divided by $\dfrac{\text{net increase in capital}}{\text{net increase in output}}$ which equals $\dfrac{\text{net increase in output}}{\text{net output}}$ which is identically
equal to the rate of growth.

[1] *Trends and Cycles in Economic Activity*, by Professor W. Fellner, Holt, New York,
1956, p. 74.
[2] The circumstances in which this would occur are considered in detail later in the
argument.

would be much more likely to double the rate of growth. It is also evident that with unemployment, a given amount of *gross* investment would add more to *gross* output than it would with full employment. Suppose a machine costs £3,000, requires one worker to work it, and adds £1,500 a year to gross output. In an economy with unemployed workers, one of these could work the machine and there would be an addition to gross output of £1,500. In an economy with full employment, a worker would have to be taken from other work where he was producing output worth say £800 (with an older machine) a year to work the new machine. In this economy gross output per year would be increased by £1,500 less £800, or by £700.[1] Thus identical investments would add £1,500 to gross output in one economy and £700 in the other.

The S/C formulation would be affected in the following way by these investments. The capital output ratios of the machines themselves would be much the same in both economies, so the C's due to the investments would be similar. On the other hand, since the depreciation of capital is 'whatever amount of investment is needed to keep net output constant', the fall of £800 in the output of old capital in the economy with full employment would raise depreciation in that economy (by an amount approximately equal to the cost of the capital needed to produce £800 worth of output) and consequently reduce its S, while the S of the economy with unemployment would not be reduced. Thus the growth resulting from investment in this type of machine would be less in an economy with full employment because the latter would have more depreciation, a lower S, and therefore a lower S/C. If the types of capital installed in the two economies differed, capital with a higher capital output ratio would probably be installed in the economy with full employment (because of labour scarcity, and its effect in raising capital intensity), and this too would reduce its S/C.

It would consequently be particularly inaccurate to try to predict the rate of growth which would follow from a greater share of gross investment in the GNP of an economy with full employment by looking at the effect on the rate of growth of a similar share of gross investment in an economy with unemployment. An argument, for instance, that Britain's rate of growth in the 1960's would be the same as West Germany's in the 1950's, if Britain invested the same proportion of her GNP as West Germany invested in the 1950's, would be particularly inaccurate for this reason.

[1] If the economy with full employment installed a great deal of capital of this type, it would after a time run out of workers who were only adding £800 to gross output, and it would need to use workers adding perhaps £900 each to gross output to work the new machinery. The addition to gross output from investment of £3,000 in this kind of machine would then fall from £700 to £600, which illustrates part of the process through which a faster rate of investment does not raise the rate of growth in the same proportion when there is full employment.

The S/C formulation is a truism if it refers to the past, and it can only be used safely to help to predict the future growth rates which would follow from particular investment policies if there is either sufficient unemployment, or sufficient technical progress, or a sufficient backlog of unexploited investment opportunities to prevent diminishing returns to capital in the period of the prediction.

Technical Progress and the 'Natural' Rate of Growth

An alternative formulation of the problem[1] attributes growth almost entirely to technical progress and population increase. It is assumed throughout this section and the next that demand is always maintained at a level just sufficient to permit the full employment of labour, that the supply of finance is infinitely elastic at the ruling rate of interest, and that individual entrepreneurs always push investment to the limit of profitable opportunity.

The importance of technical progress and population increase is best seen if a situation is envisaged where both are absent. It is supposed that there is a labour force of constant size and that there are no additions to technical knowledge. There would then be certain known ways in which capital could be used to raise output. If the rate of interest was initially 5 per cent., for instance, only those uses of capital which raised the value of net output by more than 5 per cent. of the cost of the capital required could possibly be profitable, and when all the investment projects which could yield more than 5 per cent. had been carried out, net investment would fall to zero. If the rate of interest then fell to 4 per cent. there would be some further investment opportunities which would be profitable at the lower rate of interest but in time these too would be exhausted. If the rate of interest then fell to the lowest level which was possible, net investment would fall permanently to zero after all the investment projects which were profitable at that rate of interest had been carried out.

It is now supposed that the rate of interest is constant, that there is given technical knowledge as before, but that the labour force increases by 1 per cent. each year. If labour and capital were the only factors of production, it would be profitable to extend every kind of capital installation by 1 per cent. each year (if capital was infinitely divisible), and with the extra 1 per cent. of labour, raise output by 1 per cent. each year; and if capital was not infinitely divisible, to extend capital and raise output by an average of 1 per cent. a year over a period of years. If there were possible economies of scale it would be profitable to expand output by more than 1 per cent. a year, while if factors of production other than labour and capital were needed and some of these were in scarce supply,

[1] See R. F. Harrod, *Towards a Dynamic Economics*, Macmillan, 1948, pp. 20–24.

36   INVESTMENT, TECHNICAL PROGRESS, AND ECONOMIC GROWTH

it might be unprofitable to expand output by as much as 1 per cent. a year because of diminishing returns. One per cent. would be the order of magnitude of the annual increase in output which would be profitable, and a limited amount of investment would be needed each year to produce the extra output.

It is now supposed that the size of the labour force is constant, that the rate of interest is constant, but that there are additions to technical knowledge each year. An advance in technical knowledge could be defined as 'new knowledge which would either permit existing products to be produced at lower cost,[1] or which would permit the production of new products'. By taking advantage of an advance in knowledge, entrepreneurs would make a greater profit than their competitors until all entrepreneurs manufacturing the good in question used the new method of production. Some new methods of production require investment, and this would of course be the case if the new method was made possible by the development of superior machinery. As soon as the new machinery began to be used, the price of the product would begin to fall relatively to the costs of production of entrepreneurs not using it (through competition), and their profits would consequently fall. In time, a point would be reached where it would pay them to scrap their old machinery and replace it with machinery incorporating the new knowledge.[2] Because of such staggering of investment, an advance in knowledge requiring the use of new capital would normally permit profitable investment stretching over many years. Other advances in knowledge might simply require a rearrangement of existing factors of production, and these would permit reductions in cost without investment. It would pay entrepreneurs to adopt an improvement of this kind immediately. All reductions in cost would lead to increases in total output because the factors of production released could be used elsewhere in the economy. For instance, any cost reductions which permitted economy in the use of labour would release workers, and it would then be profitable to extend capital throughout the economy with consequences which were analysed above. Through the replacement of capital and the redeployment of labour, advances in knowledge of all kinds would permit a certain increase in output each year. A certain amount of investment would be needed to obtain the full increase in output

---

[1] New knowledge might permit lower costs and therefore constitute an advance with one rate of interest, while with a different rate of interest it would not permit production at lower cost, and it would not therefore constitute an advance at that rate of interest. This problem is avoided here because it is assumed that the rate of interest is constant.

[2] The traditional view is that this point is reached when cost per unit of output with the new method of production is less than cost per unit *excluding capital cost* with existing machinery. The discovery of this point requires entrepreneurial judgement and not merely accountancy, because the economic life of the new capital has to be estimated before the cost of production with the new method can be calculated.

made possible by advances in knowledge each year, but only this amount of investment could be made profitably.

Either a fall in the rate of interest, or an increase in the size of the labour force, or an advance in technical knowledge permits an increase in output, and when investment is always pushed to the limit of profitable opportunity these together determine the rate of growth of output. If the effect of changes in the rate of interest is disregarded, the rate of growth would depend on the increase in the labour force and on advances in technical knowledge alone. If, for instance, the growth of the labour force made possible an increase in output of p per cent. a year, and technical progress made possible an increase in output of t per cent. each year, criteria of profitability would permit an increase in output of approximately $(t+p)$ per cent. each year. Sir Roy Harrod has called 'the rate of advance which the increase in population and technological improvements allow', the 'natural' rate of growth,[1] and this rate of $(t+p)$ per cent. is the 'natural' rate of growth.

If the 'natural' rate of growth was, for instance, 3 per cent. a year, and the capital output ratio of the new capital required averaged 4, it would be profitable to add four times 3 or 12 per cent. of the NNP to the capital stock. In this case S would equal 12 per cent., C would be 4, and S/C per cent. would equal 3 per cent., the 'natural' rate of growth. The growth in output of 3 per cent. a year would be made possible by technical progress and population increase, and the net investment of 12 per cent. of the NNP would simply be needed to realize this potential increase in output. If investment was 13 per cent. of the NNP, the thirteenth per cent. would be unprofitable,[2] while if less than 12 per cent. of the NNP was invested, output would rise by less than the possible 3 per cent.

The 'Full Natural' Rate of Growth

So far it has been assumed that the rate of technical progress which (with the rate of increase of the labour force) determines the 'natural' rate of growth does not depend at all on the rate of investment, and the rate of expansion of output. Investment was simply needed to take advantage

---

[1] R. F. Harrod, *Towards a Dynamic Economics*, Macmillan, 1948, p. 87.

[2] It might appear at first sight that if the rate of interest was r per cent., and investment was pushed to the limit of profitable opportunity, marginal investment of £100 would add just £r to net output, so the marginal capital output ratio would be $100:r$. Unprofitable investment, i.e. investment in excess of that needed to realize the 'natural' rate of growth, would then have a capital output ratio of more than $100:r$ and the contribution to the rate of growth of an extra 1 per cent. of the NNP (extra to that needed for the 'natural' rate) would be less than $r/100$ per cent. This would follow exactly if there was perfect competition in all markets, constant returns to scale, and no change in the rate of interest. With increasing returns to scale, or imperfect competition, the increase in output would be greater. If the extra investment was accompanied with a lower interest rate, the cost of capital would alter relatively to the price of its product which would also affect the calculation.

of such technical progress as occurred, but it did not itself influence the rate of technical progress. Because the development of superior methods of production is both more profitable and more practicable when the rate of investment is high,[1] it could be argued that there might be some connexion between the share of investment in the National Product and the rate of technical progress.[2] If technical progress depended on investment, it would be more likely to depend on gross investment than on net investment, because all investment would be likely to contribute to it. There would be some technical progress even if gross investment (in capital goods) was zero (due to the forces influencing technical progress which are independent of investment such as research in the universities, in government research institutions, and in business research departments which are not closed down in depressions, and improvements spontaneously discovered by workers and managements), and the technical progress in addition to this would depend on the amount of gross investment, or, it could be supposed, on the share of gross investment in the National Product.

Then if net investment was zero (and the NNP was consequently constant) there would be technical progress due to the research which continued whether there was investment or not, and additional technical progress due to the gross investment which would be needed to cover depreciation. If, for instance, the technical progress from these two sources amounted to 2 per cent. a year altogether, the 'natural' rate of growth would be 2 per cent. per annum when net investment was zero (and the labour force was constant). If the additional technical progress which was due to investment was, for instance, 1 per cent. per annum for every 6 per cent. of S (the share of net investment in the NNP),[3] the rate of technical progress and consequently the 'natural' rate of growth would be 2 per cent. plus 1 per cent. for every 6 per cent. of S. The rate of technical progress would then be 2 per cent. a year when S was zero, 4 per cent.

---

[1] If the rate of investment is high, a greater quantity of a new kind of machine can be sold which permits the use of more economies of scale in its manufacture, which reduces its cost and so encourages users of machinery to purchase machinery which had a higher capital output ratio formerly. The development of technically superior machinery would also be more profitable to manufacturers of machinery. A high output of machinery might also accelerate the eradication of weaknesses in the design and performance of new machinery. These points have all been made by Mr. N. Kaldor.

[2] See N. Kaldor, 'A Model of Economic Growth', *Economic Journal*, 1957; 'Capital Accumulation and Economic Growth', in *The Theory of Capital*, edited by F. A. Lutz, Macmillan, 1961; and 'A New Model of Economic Growth' (with Mirrlees) in *Review of Economic Studies*, June 1962.

[3] When S is higher, the amount of investment which is needed to cover depreciation is also higher (because more workers have to be transferred from old capital to work new capital, and the annual fall in the output of old capital is consequently greater), and the extra technical progress of 1 per cent. for each 6 per cent. of S is due, both to the net investment of 6 per cent., and to the extra investment which is needed in consequence to cover higher depreciation, because it depends on the share of gross investment in the National Product.

a year when S was 12 per cent., and 6 per cent. a year when S was 24 per cent. Doubling S from 12 to 24 per cent. would then increase the 'natural' rate of growth from 4 to 6 per cent. (i.e. it would be less than doubled), and the S/C formulation would not predict future growth rates accurately, because doubling S would not induce enough extra technical progress to overcome diminishing returns.

If the rate of interest was given, and there was a capital output ratio which was most profitable at that rate of interest, the rate of growth would tend towards one particular 'natural' rate of growth if entrepreneurs pushed investment to the limit of profitable opportunity. If, for instance, the most profitable capital output ratio was 3, S would tend towards 12 per cent. where both the actual and the 'natural' rates of growth would be 4 per cent. If S was less than 12 per cent., the actual rate of growth would be less than the 'natural' rate, so entrepreneurs would find it profitable to increase S, while if S was more than 12 per cent., the 'natural' rate of growth would be insufficient to allow the investment in excess of 12 per cent. to be profitable, and S would fall to 12 per cent. If there was a lower rate of interest, and the most profitable capital output ratio was consequently 4 instead of 3,[1] S would tend towards 24 per cent. where both the actual and the 'natural' rates of growth would be 6 per cent. With each interest rate, there would be a most profitable capital output ratio (which would only be constant if technical progress was 'neutral'), and a most profitable 'natural' rate of growth which the economy would tend towards.[2]

It is profitable for entrepreneurs to take full advantage of the growth made possible by technical progress, even in imperfect competition, because in general technical progress permits cost reduction with existing levels of output,[3] but it might not always be profitable for them to take

---

[1] With the assumption (which is made here) that entrepreneurs push investment to the limit of profitable opportunity, a fall in the interest rate must raise the most profitable capital output ratio (in the absence of 'perverse' cases). The effect on the argument of inelasticity in the supply of finance, risk, and entrepreneurial inefficiency is considered later.

[2] If t_1 per cent. is the technical progress which is due to research and the replacement investment which is made when S is zero, $t_2 S$ per cent. is further technical progress which is due to investment, and p per cent. is the growth made possible by population increase, the 'natural' rate of growth is $(t_1 + t_2 S + p)$ per cent. When investment is pushed to the limit of profitability, the actual rate of growth, S/C, equals the 'natural' rate, and C the actual capital output ratio is also C' the most profitable one. Then $S/C' = t_1 + t_2 S + p$, $S = \dfrac{C'(t_1 + p)}{1 - t_2 C'}$, and the 'natural' rate of growth is $\dfrac{t_1 + p}{1 - t_2 C'}$. (N.B. An increase in p of 1 per cent. raises the 'natural' rate of growth by $\dfrac{1}{1 - t_2 C'}$ per cent. (i.e. by more than 1 per cent.), so it raises the rate of technical progress. Thus with these assumptions, faster growth of the labour force leads to faster technical progress, and faster growth of output per worker.)

[3] Some technical progress might only reduce costs with higher outputs than those currently being produced, but this possibility is neglected here.

full advantage of the growth made possible by potential economies of scale because this would require increases in output. There might then be important unexploited economies of scale in many industries producing in conditions of imperfect competition. The firms in these industries might find it impossible to lower their costs at existing levels of output, but because of potential economies of scale they might be able to produce larger outputs at lower costs per unit and without extra workers. They would then have profitable investment opportunities whenever the demand for their products expanded. Many firms and industries might then be able to expand their outputs rapidly if they expanded simultaneously, because they would then help to create markets for each other's products by their own expansion and the consequent expansion in incomes,[1] and unexploited economies of scale would prevent the interference of diminishing returns to capital. No one firm could do this without the simultaneous expansion of other firms, because while one firm could produce a larger output at a lower cost per unit, its market would be insufficient without the expansion of other firms to allow the extra output to be sold profitably.[2]

It is possible that those commentators who believe that the mere statement of a 'target' rate of growth for the economy would allow that 'target' to be realized if the expansion of output by each industry needed to realize the 'target' was worked out and publicized, might have this kind of situation in mind. The situation is one where full employment and simultaneous profit maximization by all entrepreneurs would not be sufficient to realize the fastest rate of growth which was possible and compatible with profitability, and where some kind of stimulus to persuade entrepreneurs to expand more quickly than they would otherwise choose to would be needed to realize the 'full natural' rate of growth of the economy.

The 'natural' rate of growth could be thought of as 'the rate of advance which the increase in population and technological improvements allow when entrepreneurs maximise their profits independently', and then 'the greatest rate of advance compatible with profitability which the increase in population and technological improvements could allow' would be the 'full natural' rate of growth.

The 'full natural' rate of growth would be higher than the 'natural' rate if there were unexploited economies of scale which could only be exploited if industries expanded simultaneously. If these economies of scale were exploited, there would be an increase in the rate of growth due to this, and an additional increase because there would be a rise (which would

---

[1] See Allyn Young's 'Increasing Returns and Economic Progress', *Economic Journal*, 1928.
[2] The firm would only be precluded from selling a larger output at lower prices if there were lapses from perfect competition. But this is precisely the situation likely to prevail where economies of scale are important.

otherwise have been unprofitable) in S, and this would raise the rate of technical progress and the highest 'natural' rate of growth which could be profitable. In these circumstances, government intervention to raise the rate of investment, or to institute planned rates of expansion by different industries, might well result in a faster rate of growth than the rate which would be achieved without intervention.

Difficulty in obtaining Finance, Entrepreneurial Inefficiency, and Economic Growth

It has been assumed so far in the argument that the supply of finance is infinitely elastic at the ruling rate of interest, and that investment is always pushed (by individual entrepreneurs) to the limit of profitable opportunity. In fact, it has been assumed that all investments capable of earning any profit in excess of the interest cost of obtaining finance are always carried out. In an actual economy there are many reasons why this might not happen, and the ways in which the rate of growth would be affected by inelasticity in the supply of finance, and entrepreneurial inefficiency will now be worked out.

If the supply of finance was not infinitely elastic, some firms would be unable to take advantage of profitable investment opportunities because of difficulty in obtaining finance. The difficulty could be due to the decisions of banks and other financial institutions, or to the consequences of government policy to restrict credit. Firms might also be unable to invest as much as they wished because of difficulty in obtaining machinery without delivery delays, or because of builders' delays before factory extensions could be completed. All these factors would either have the effect of lengthening the actual life of capital because of occasional delays to new investment, or of raising the notional rate of interest an investment had to be expected to earn before a firm would be prepared to carry it out. The effect of a higher notional rate of interest would be both that new capital with a lower capital output ratio might be preferred to new capital with a higher capital output ratio, and that the replacement of capital might be postponed because the cost of production with new capital would be raised (by the effect of the higher notional interest rate on capital cost), while the cost of production with existing capital would be almost unchanged.[1] The effect of these factors is then to lower the capital output ratio of new capital, and to increase the actual length of life of capital.[2]

---

[1] It would be raised very slightly because the interest cost of work in progress (including the interest cost of the wages paid in the period between the start of production and the sale of the product) would be increased.

[2] A higher notional interest rate would also give incentives to entrepreneurs to design or install new capital of a less durable kind, because the higher interest rate would increase the cost of durability. It is assumed in the argument that follows that the immediate effect

42   INVESTMENT, TECHNICAL PROGRESS, AND ECONOMIC GROWTH

There is the further possibility that while entrepreneurs might be able to afford to carry out potentially profitable investments, they might not do so because of inefficiency, or the risk involved. Because of risk, entrepreneurs are said to require a much higher yield from new investment than the actual cost of finance. If they required, for instance, 12 per cent. from a marginal investment, 12 per cent. would be the relevant rate of interest in the above argument.

Because of inefficiency, firms able to obtain finance might not invest as soon as was profitable (when investment yielding more than the notional 12 per cent. was regarded as profitable) for reasons of ignorance, conservatism, or lack of the expertise needed to supervise the working of more complex machinery. In particular their managements might continue to use old machinery long after it had become profitable to replace it. There might also be restrictive practices in an industry which held up profitable investment. In all these cases, entrepreneurs and managements with better judgement and skill would eventually take over the markets concerned, but at any one time there would be many entrepreneurs who (for some reason or other) did not take full advantage of the profitable investment opportunities open to them.

The effect of risk through its effect on the notional interest rate required from new investment would again be to lower the capital output ratio of new capital, and to lengthen the actual life of capital by postponing replacement. The effect of the various kinds of entrepreneurial inefficiency outlined would also be to lengthen the actual life of capital; and because inefficient or conservative entrepreneurs are likely to be biased against more complex methods of production which are also likely to be the most capitally intensive, the capital output ratio of new capital would sometimes be lower than the most profitable capital output ratio.

In all the cases considered the likely effects of inelasticity in the supply of finance, risk, and entrepreneurial inefficiency are a longer life of capital than the most profitable length of life, and a lower capital output ratio of new capital than the most profitable capital output ratio, and these affect the rate of growth. Their effect on the rate of growth will now be shown.

The effect on the rate of growth of a longer life of capital (than the most profitable length of life) will be worked out first. If the life of capital lengthens in an economy, the proportion of workers who are equipped with old capital must grow, and since 'output per worker' (referred to subsequently as 'labour productivity') is lower with old than with new

of a higher interest rate of making new capital more expensive relatively to existing capital, and so of lengthening the actual life of capital, would outweigh any effect it might have in shortening the life of capital through reductions in the durability of new capital. Thus it is assumed that on balance, difficulty in obtaining finance lengthens the actual life of capital. It would be very strange if it shortened it.

capital, its average labour productivity must fall. Thus where two economies are similar in every respect except that their lives of capital are
different, the one with the longer life of capital will have lower average
labour productivity, and therefore lower total output. It might be thought
that it would also have a slower rate of growth, but this is not so. If the
life of capital is fifty years in one economy and ten years in another, they
would both have the same rate of growth if the rate of technical progress
and the rate of population increase was the same in both, and the capital
output ratio of new capital was constant.[1]

The effect of a shortening of the life of capital on the rate of growth is
illustrated in Fig. 1. It is assumed that the capital output ratio of new
capital is constant, so changes in labour productivity with new capital
depend only on technical progress. $G_1 G_1$ is the growth path an economy
would follow if the length of life of its capital was forty years, while $G_2 G_2$
is the growth path an economy would follow with a life of capital of twenty
years. The slopes of these GG lines show what the rate of growth would be
if these lives of capital were maintained, and they depend simply on

---

[1] Mrs. Joan Robinson pointed this out in lectures she gave in Cambridge in 1956. It is
proved in the Mathematical Appendix to this article, but non-mathematical readers might
find the following argument convincing. It refers to a situation where the labour force is
constant, but it could easily be extended to apply to a situation where the labour force is
growing. It is assumed that labour productivity with any capital is higher than with capital
a year older by d per cent. because it has been used a year less, and by t' per cent. because
it has benefited from an extra year's technical progress, so altogether it is $(d+t')$ per cent.
higher. If labour productivity with new capital is 1, and the number of workers equipped
with it is p, its total output is $1.p$. If p workers also work with one-year-old capital, labour
productivity with it is $(d+t')$ per cent. less, so its total output is $1.p\left(1-\dfrac{d+t'}{100}\right)$, and if p
workers work with two-year-old capital, its total output is $1.p\left(1-\dfrac{d+t'}{100}\right)^2$, and total output
with r-year-old capital is $1.p\left(1-\dfrac{d+t'}{100}\right)^r$. If the life of capital is L years, total output is:
$1\left\{p+p\left(1-\dfrac{d+t'}{100}\right)+p\left(1-\dfrac{d+t'}{100}\right)^2+ \ldots +p\left(1-\dfrac{d+t'}{100}\right)^{L-1}\right\}$. In the following year, with
technical progress of t per cent., where t equals t' plus t'' (where t'' is technical progress of the
kind which applies to both old and new capital), labour productivity with new capital is t per
cent. greater than in the year before, so labour productivity with it is $\left(1+\dfrac{t}{100}\right)$ instead of 1,
but labour productivity with one-year-old capital is $(d+t')$ per cent. less than this as before,
and labour productivity with r-year-old capital is $\left(1-\dfrac{d+t'}{100}\right)^r$ times labour productivity with
new capital, as before. Total output in the following year is then:
$$\left(1+\dfrac{t}{100}\right)\left\{p+p\left(1-\dfrac{d+t'}{100}\right)+p\left(1-\dfrac{d+t'}{100}\right)^2+ \ldots +p\left(1-\dfrac{d+t'}{100}\right)^{L-1}\right\},$$
which is just t per cent. higher than the total output of the year before, since the term inside
the large bracket is unchanged, and the term outside it has increased from 1 to $\left(1+\dfrac{t}{100}\right)$,
i.e. by t per cent. The rate of growth of output is then $(t'+t'')$ per cent. or t per cent., when L
the life of capital is constant.

Classical Economics, Public Expenditure and Growth 15

44   INVESTMENT, TECHNICAL PROGRESS, AND ECONOMIC GROWTH

technical progress and population increase, i.e. on the 'natural' rate of growth, and an economy which is moving along a GG line simply grows at its 'natural' rate.

If the economy with growth path $G_1 G_1$ started to invest in new capital more quickly at time T_1, the life of its capital would begin to get shorter (because it would be replaced sooner) and it would rise above $G_1 G_1$. If at time T_2 its life of capital was twenty years, it would reach $G_2 G_2$, and it would move along $G_2 G_2$ instead of $G_1 G_1$ for as long as the life of its capital

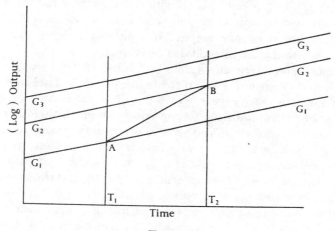

FIG. 1.

remained twenty years. Between times T_1 and T_2 it would move from A to B, and its rate of growth would be faster than the 'natural' rate because the slope of AB is necessarily steeper than the slopes of $G_1 G_1$ and $G_2 G_2$. Once it reached B its rate of growth would revert to the 'natural' rate unless its life of capital continued to shorten, in which case it would move towards a still higher growth path $G_3 G_3$ (where the life of capital is ten years). Its rate of growth would only be higher than the 'natural' rate while it was being augmented by an actual *shortening* of the life of capital, i.e. while it was moving from one GG line to a higher one. If there is an upper limit to the share of gross investment in the National Product which is practicable (for political reasons, for instance), there would also be a limit to the extent to which the life of capital could be shortened, and when that limit was reached the economy would reach a high GG line and move along it, and then its rate of growth would simply depend on the slope of that GG line, i.e. on the 'natural' rate of growth.

In Table 1 in the mathematical appendix the effect of various lengths of life of capital on average labour productivity are worked out, and it is possible to work out the effect of a move from $G_1 G_1$ to $G_2 G_2$ on output and the rate of growth with its help. For instance, supposing labour productivity with any capital is always 5 per cent. higher than with capital which is a year older (because ageing of capital causes a fall in labour productivity of d per cent. a year, and capital which is a year less old has benefited from technical progress of t' per cent. a year, and $(d+t')$ per cent. $= 5$ per cent.), average labour productivity when capital has a forty-year life is 43·2 per cent. of the labour productivity with new capital, and it is 63·2 per cent. when capital has a twenty-year life, and so average labour productivity is 46·8 per cent. higher with a twenty-year life (since 63·2 is 46·8 per cent. higher than 43·2), and therefore output along $G_2 G_2$ where the life of capital is twenty years is 46·8 per cent. higher than output along $G_1 G_1$ where the life of capital is forty years.

Thus when an economy moves along AB, it has 46·8 per cent. of growth in addition to the 'natural' rate. If the 'natural' rate is 3 per cent. a year, and T_1 and T_2 are twenty years apart (i.e. if it takes twenty years to shorten the life of capital from forty years to twenty), there is an extra 46·8 per cent. of growth spread over these twenty years, or an extra 2·0 per cent. a year, and the overall growth rate in this twenty year period is $(3+2\cdot0)$ per cent. or 5 per cent. If $(d+t')$ per cent. is 2 per cent. instead of 5 per cent., $G_2 G_2$ is only 19·8 per cent. above $G_1 G_1$, and the extra growth along AB is only 19·8 per cent. spread over the twenty years, or 0·9 per cent. a year, and the overall growth rate in the twenty-year period is 3·9 per cent. instead of 5 per cent. Other examples can be worked out with the help of Table I in the mathematical appendix. Naturally enough, a smaller $(d+t')$ always reduces the extra growth due to a shortening of the life of capital.

When the life of capital is reduced, the share of gross investment in output has to be increased,[1] and so the share of consumption is reduced. The growth in consumption is consequently less than the growth in output referred to in the last paragraph. For instance, when the life of capital is reduced from forty years to twenty (and output is consequently increased 46·8 per cent.), it can be seen in Table I that the share of gross investment in output is increased from $5\cdot8C$ per cent. (where C is the gross capital output ratio of new capital) to $7\cdot9C$ per cent., so an extra $2\cdot1C$ per cent. of output has to consist of investment, and as a result of this the growth in consumption is less than 46·8 per cent. If C equalled 2 the growth in

---

[1] It would be wrong to suppose that halving the life of capital (when the size of the labour force is constant) would double the *share* of gross investment in the National Product. Twice as many workers would need to be equipped with new capital each year if the life of capital was halved, and if the new capital workers were equipped with was unchanged, twice the total *amount* of gross investment would be needed, but because the National Product would be higher owing to the shorter life of capital, twice as great a *share* of the National Product would not need to be invested. This was pointed out to me by Professor Peter Wiles.

46 INVESTMENT, TECHNICAL PROGRESS, AND ECONOMIC GROWTH

consumption would be 39·3 per cent., if C equalled 3 it would be 35·0 per cent., and if C equalled 4 it would be 30·1 per cent. If the life of capital was reduced further from twenty years to ten years in a move from $G_2 G_2$ to $G_3 G_3$, output would rise a further 24·5 per cent., but the further rise in consumption would only be 10·3 per cent. if C was 2, 1 per cent. if C equalled 3, and consumption would actually fall by 9·4 per cent. if C equalled 4. There would be a particular life of capital which maximized consumption ($10\frac{1}{2}$ years if C equalled 2, 14 years if C equalled 3, and 17 years if C equalled 4), and once this life was reached, further shortening of the life of capital would cause a reduction in consumption.

It was suggested earlier that the rate of technical progress might be higher when the share of investment was higher, and if this was the case higher GG lines would have a steeper slope than lower GG lines, and when an economy moved to a higher GG line its rate of growth would be higher permanently, because its rate of technical progress would be higher when capital was replaced more frequently. A move to a higher GG line than the line where consumption is maximized might be justifiable then, because the rate of technical progress would be higher on the higher GG line, and consumption would become higher eventually on this line because of the faster rate of technical progress associated with it.

The argument can be reversed. If there was a lengthening of the life of capital because of increased risk, entrepreneurial inefficiency, or difficulty in obtaining finance, the economy would move to a lower GG line. There would then be an abnormally low rate of growth while the *lengthening* of the life of capital occurred, but once the economy was adjusted to the longer life of capital it would move along the GG line appropriate to that length of life, and output would once again grow at the 'natural' rate. There would, of course, be a permanent reduction in the rate of growth if the longer life of capital caused a reduction in the rate of technical progress.

The same analysis can be used to illustrate how the rate of growth changes when the capital output ratio of new capital is raised.[1] Labour productivity must also be higher with capital with a higher capital output ratio. An economy where new capital had a higher capital output ratio (and a constant length of life of capital) would therefore be moving along a higher GG line than an economy with a lower capital output ratio of new capital (and the same length of life of capital). An economy would therefore be able to move to a higher GG line if the capital output ratio of its new capital was raised, and its rate of growth would be higher while the

---

[1] It might be raised, either because of increased availability of finance, or reduced risk (or because a reduction in the rate of interest made it profitable for entrepreneurs to purchase new capital with a higher capital output ratio).

move to the higher *GG* line occurred. As with the life of capital, an increase in the capital output ratio of new capital would raise the share of investment which would be needed, and the growth in consumption would consequently be less than the growth in gross output. As with the life of capital, if there was a connexion between the share of investment and the rate of technical progress, the higher *GG* lines would have a steeper slope, and a higher capital output ratio would then permanently raise the rate of growth. A reduction in the capital output ratio would take the economy to a lower *GG* line, and result in a lower rate of growth while the reduction occurred, and also subsequently if technical progress was less.

Economies move along lower *GG* lines than they could move along because of inelasticity in the supply of finance, risk, and entrepreneurial inefficiency, which lengthen the actual life of capital, and lower the capital output ratio of new capital. Their levels of output are consequently always some way below the levels which could be achieved if the supply of finance was elastic, risk was absent, and entrepreneurs always invested when it was profitable for them to do so. Their rates of growth, on the other hand, depend on the slope of the *GG* lines they move along, and these depend on their 'natural' rates of growth, which depend on their technical progress and population increase.[1] When risk, or entrepreneurial inefficiency, or inelasticities in the supply of finance are reduced, an economy can move to a higher *GG* line, and while this move is made (and the move will require an increase in the share of gross investment) the economy's rate of growth will be higher than the 'natural' rate.

Conclusion

It is now possible to summarize the various ways in which the rate of growth of an economy with full employment could be raised. Fundamentally its rate of growth depends on technical progress and population increase, and any policy which resulted in a higher rate of technical progress would raise the rate of growth. An increase in the rate of technical progress would steepen the *GG* line the economy was moving along, and its rate of growth would consequently rise.[1] If faster technical progress took the form of a more rapid annual increase in the productivity of new capital relatively to older capital (i.e. an increase in t'), it would also become profitable to replace capital more frequently (because the cost of production with new capital would fall more rapidly relatively to the cost of

[1] Cf. Professor Peter Wiles's distinction between 'brakes' and 'handicaps', in his *The Political Economy of Communism*, Blackwell, 1962, pp. 385–8.

[2] It would do this however inefficient entrepreneurs were, because the degree of entrepreneurial inefficiency in the economy is already allowed for by the fact that the economy is moving along a lower *GG* line than the highest one it could move along.

production with old capital), and the economy would also move to a higher *GG* line. Thus the effect of a higher rate of technical progress could be, both steeper *GG* lines, and a move to a higher *GG* line, so there might be a particularly rapid rate of growth in the years immediately following an increase in the rate of technical progress.

A second and further increase in the rate of growth would be possible if there was a 'full natural' rate of growth higher than the 'natural' rate because of unexploited economies of scale in imperfectly competitive industries. Government stimulation of expansion (through stimulation of investment, and possibly through planned 'target' rates of growth for each industry) might then cause an economy to grow at its 'full natural' rate, when otherwise it would simply grow at its 'natural' rate.

The third way in which the rate of growth could be raised would be through the elimination of some of the factors causing inelasticity in the supply of finance, risk, and entrepreneurial inefficiency. The elimination of restrictive practices, the maintenance of steady growth of demand (reducing risks), and changes in the tax system designed to lessen or counteract entrepreneurial inefficiency would all help here.[1] Any reduction in entrepreneurial inefficiency or risk, or an increase in the availability of finance would allow an economy to move to a higher *GG* line through consequent shortening of the life of capital, and increases in the capital output ratio of new capital, and this would temporarily increase the rate of growth, and it would increase it permanently if a larger share of investment raised the rate of technical progress. A reduction in the rate of interest would also allow an economy to move to a higher *GG* line.

There is a fourth possibility which has not been discussed yet. If, in an economy, there was a shortage of certain kinds of skilled labour such as scientists of certain kinds, engineers, or managerial staff with the ability to plan and supervise complicated processes of production, industries with substantial opportunities for growth might not be able to expand,

---

[1] The following would be a particularly helpful change. At present firms pay a certain proportion of their profits in taxation. The result is that a firm with lower costs of production than competing firms pays about 50 per cent. of the extra profit due to this to the government, while a firm with high enough costs to prevent it from making any profit pays almost no tax. If there was no taxation of profits, and instead all the firms in the economy paid the same amount of tax altogether, but paid it in proportion to their use of labour (through a pay-roll tax), and capital (they could be taxed in proportion to their present depreciation allowances—the purchase of a Rolls Royce would then increase their tax liability instead of reducing it), the entire profit due to lower costs of production than competitors would go to the firm concerned, and there would be a great increase in the tax liability of firms with high costs of production. The rates of tax on the use of labour and capital could be varied according to the relative scarcity of labour and capital in the economy. A change of this kind would place high-cost firms in a much weaker competitive position, and it would consequently speed up the rate at which efficient entrepreneurs could take over the markets of less efficient entrepreneurs. (Mr. N. Kaldor and Lord Franks have made suggestions of this kind.)

and the products concerned would often need to be imported. If the rate of technical progress was higher in these industries than in others, an economy in this position would have a lower overall rate of technical progress, and therefore a lower rate of growth. Its rate of technical progress, and so its rate of growth, would be raised if more workers of these kinds were trained, and there would probably also be a beneficial effect on the balance of payments.

An increased share of gross investment in the National Product is not needed to take advantage of opportunities for growth created by a steepening of the slope of the GG line the economy is moving along, but an increased share of gross investment is needed to take advantage of opportunities to move to higher GG lines. Thus an increased share of gross investment would not be needed to take advantage of faster technical progress, but it would be needed to take advantage of opportunities to move to higher GG lines created by increased availability of finance, or increased entrepreneurial efficiency, and it would also be needed to take advantage of a 'full natural' rate of growth higher than the 'natural' rate.

If an opportunity for growth was created by the elimination of some of the conditions which kept the economy on a low GG line, and there was no subsequent fall in the share of consumption in the National Product, so that the share of investment could not be increased, there would be demand-induced inflationary pressure, and factors such as increased difficulty in obtaining finance (due possibly to government measures to restrict credit) and increasing delays in the time needed to obtain machinery would prevent the economy from moving to a higher GG line.

Thus an increased share of investment in the National Product is often needed to take advantage of opportunities for faster growth, but investment only creates opportunities for growth in so far as the rate of technical progress is related to the share of investment, and investment is unlikely to create enough technical progress to overcome diminishing returns. There is then likely to be a limit to the share of an economy's National Product which can be invested profitably when the rate of interest is given. To obtain the highest possible rate of growth when there is full employment as much technical opportunity for growth as possible must be created, and it must then be ensured that there will be sufficient investment to allow this to be exploited.

In an economy with substantial unemployment, or underemployment of labour, the technical opportunity for growth is almost unlimited, and there is no reason to suppose that an increase in the share of investment would not raise the rate of growth in the same proportion. The problem of obtaining the fastest possible rate of growth is then mainly one of obtaining the largest possible share of investment.

MATHEMATICAL APPENDIX[1]

1. It is shown here that the total labour force grows at rate p when the number of workers equipped with new capital at each point in time grows at rate p, and the life of capital is constant. The number of workers available to work new capital grows at an exponential rate p, and at time n it is ke^{pn}. Then the number of workers available to work new capital at time $(n-r)$ was $ke^{p(n-r)}$. If all the workers available to work new capital are always equipped with it, and capital is worked until it is L years old, the total labour force at time n is $\int_0^L ke^{p(n-r)}\,dr$ which equals $ke^{pn}\left(\dfrac{1-e^{-pL}}{p}\right)$. This grows at exponential rate p when k, L, and p are constant.

2. It is shown here that output grows at rate $(t+p)$ when labour productivity with new capital equipment produced at successive points in time grows at exponential rate t, and where p, t, L, and d (the rate at which labour productivity falls as capital becomes older) are all constant. Labour productivity with capital equipment produced at time n is at an annual rate of je^{tn} when the equipment is new. Labour productivity with all equipment falls at rate d as the equipment becomes older, so at time $(n+r)$ labour productivity with equipment produced at time n will be je^{tn-rd}. Labour productivity with capital equipment produced at time $(n-r)$ was $je^{t(n-r)}$ when it was new, and is $je^{t(n-r)-rd}$ at time n. $ke^{p(n-r)}$ workers were equipped with capital which is r years old in year n, so that the total output of r-year-old capital equipment at time n is at an annual rate of $ke^{p(n-r)}je^{t(n-r)-rd} = jke^{n(p+t)}e^{-(p+t+d)r}$. Total output at time n is then at an annual rate of $\int_0^L jke^{n(p+t)}e^{-r(p+t+d)}\,dr$, if capital is scrapped when it is L years old, which equals $jke^{(p+t)n}\left(\dfrac{1-e^{-(p+t+d)L}}{p+d+t}\right)$. This grows at an exponential rate of $(p+t)$ when j, k, p, d, t, and L are constant, and the result follows *a fortiori* if p or d is zero, i.e. if the labour force is constant or if capital does not deteriorate.

3. Average labour productivity in the economy at time n is now worked out. Since the labour force at time n is $ke^{pn}\left(\dfrac{1-e^{-pL}}{p}\right)$ and total output at time n is at an annual rate of $jke^{(p+t)n}\left(\dfrac{1-e^{-(p+d+t)L}}{p+d+t}\right)$, average labour productivity at time n must be at an annual rate of $je^{tn}\dfrac{p}{p+d+t}\dfrac{1-e^{-(p+d+t)L}}{1-e^{-pL}}$. This grows at an exponential rate of t when j, p, d, t, and L are constant. If $p=0$, i.e. if the labour force is constant, average labour productivity is

$$je^{tn}\frac{1-e^{-(p+d+t)L}}{(p+t+d)L} \quad \left(\text{since } \frac{p}{1-e^{-pL}} = \frac{p}{pL-(p^2L^2)/2!\ \dots}\right.$$

which tends towards $1/L$ as p tends towards zero.

4. The share of investment in output is now worked out. If the cost of the capital needed to equip a worker is C times the annual output per worker of that capital when new (so that C is the gross capital output ratio of new capital), then since the annual rate of output of new capital at time n is $jke^{(p+t)n}$, gross investment at time n is $Cjke^{(p+t)n}$. Since gross output at time n is at an annual rate of

$$jke^{(p+t)n}\left(\frac{1-e^{-(p+d+t)L}}{p+d+t}\right),$$

---

[1] The mathematics in this mathematical appendix has been much influenced by the work of J. Black. See 'Technical Progress and Optimum Savings', by J. Black, in the *Review of Economic Studies*, June 1962.

the share of gross investment in gross output at time n is $\dfrac{C(p+d+t)}{1-e^{-(p+d+t)L}}$, which is constant when C, p, d, t, and L are constant.

5. The complications due to different kinds of technical progress are now incorporated in the argument. If technical progress consists partly of improvements which result in increases in labour productivity with all capital (so that this increases at rate t''), and partly of improvements which result in increases in labour productivity which are confined to new capital (labour productivity with new capital rises at

TABLE I

L		Constant population ($p = 0$) $d+t'$						$(d+t') = 4\%$ p			
		1%	2%	3%	4%	5%	10%	0%	1%	2%	3%
5	Average labour productivity	97·6	95·2	92·9	90·6	88·5	78·7	90·6	90·7	90·8	90·8
	Investment/worker	20C	20C	20C	20C	20C	20C	20C	20¼C	21C	21½C
	Share of investment	20·5C	21·0C	21·5C	22·1C	22·6C	25·4C	22·1C	22·6C	23·1C	23·7C
10	Average labour productivity	95·2	90·6	86·4	82·4	78·7	63·2	82·4	82·7	83·0	83·2
	Investment/worker	10C	10C	10C	10C	10C	10C	10C	10¼C	11C	11¼C
	Share of investment	10·5C	11·0C	11·6C	12·1C	12·7C	15·8C	12·1C	12·7C	13·3 C	13·9C
20	Average labour productivity	90·6	82·4	75·2	68·8	63·2	43·2	68·8	69·7	70·7	71·6
	Investment/worker	5C	5C	5C	5C	5C	5C	5C	5·5C	6·1C	6·7C
	Share of investment	5·5C	6·1C	6·7C	7·3C	7·9C	11·6C	7·3C	7·9C	8·6C	9·3C
30	Average labour productivity	86·4	75·2	65·9	58·2	51·8	31·7	58·2	59·9	61·7	63·4
	Investment/worker	3·3C	3·3C	3·3C	3·3C	3·3C	3·3C	3·3C	3·9C	4·4C	5·1C
	Share of investment	3·9C	4·4C	5·1C	5·7C	6·4C	10·5C	5·7C	6·4C	7·2C	8·0C
40	Average labour productivity	82·4	68·8	58·2	49·9	43·2	24·5	49·9	52·5	55·0	57·6
	Investment/worker	2·5C	2·5C	2·5C	2·5C	2·5C	2·5C	2·5C	3·0C	3·6C	4·3C
	Share of investment	3·0C	3·6C	4·3C	5·0C	5·8C	10·2C	5·0C	5·8C	6·6C	7·4C

$$\text{Average labour productivity is } \frac{p}{p+d+t'} \; \frac{1-e^{-(p+d+t')L}}{1-e^{-pL}} \; 100.$$

$$\text{Investment/worker is } \frac{Cp}{1-e^{-pL}} \; 100.$$

rate t, but since labour productivity with old capital rises at rate t'', the increase in labour productivity due to technical progress involving new capital alone is at rate $(t-t'')$ which equals t'), the argument is affected in the following ways. First $(t'+t'')$ can be substituted for t, and secondly $(d-t'')$ can be substituted for d, since labour productivity with old capital falls at rate d because of deterioration with use, and rises at rate t'' because of technical progress which affects all capital. Substituting these it can be seen that total output at time n is $jke^{(p+t'+t'')n}\left(\dfrac{1-e^{-(p+d+t')L}}{p+d+t'}\right)$, average labour productivity at time n is $je^{(t'+t'')n} \dfrac{p}{p+d+t'} \dfrac{1-e^{-(p+d+t')L}}{1-e^{-pL}}$, and the share of gross investment at time n is $\dfrac{C(p+d+t')}{1-e^{-(p+d+t')L}}$, which is less than the share of gross investment in paragraph 4 since t' is less than t. The effect of the change is to leave the rate of growth unaltered, but to raise average labour productivity, and to reduce the share of investment.

52   INVESTMENT, TECHNICAL PROGRESS, AND ECONOMIC GROWTH

6. Table 1 is worked out to show the effect of the rate of technical progress, the rate of deterioration of capital, and the life of capital on average labour productivity (which is given in this table as the percentage of average labour productivity to labour productivity with new capital), and the share of investment.

Exeter College, Oxford

[2]

THE DETERMINATION OF THE RATE OF TECHNICAL PROGRESS [1]

IT is clear from almost all approaches to what determines an economy's equilibrium rate of growth that the rate of technical progress has a dominant influence upon it. The rate of technical progress is also a major factor in the determination of an economy's capital–output ratio, its rate of profit and its distribution of income. The rate and bias of technical progress and how these are determined are therefore matters of the utmost importance.

In the real world an economy's rate of technical progress will clearly depend upon a large number of factors, many of which will fall outside the usual boundaries of economics. A view which is widely taken is that the influence of these " non-economic " factors is all important, and that the influence of the factors normally analysed by economists in the context of growth models is relatively slight. With this view of the matter, it can be assumed for purposes of growth theory that there is an exogenously given rate of technical progress—for this is given exogenously so far as a model which ignores scientific activity, educational structure, trades union activity, managerial skills, attitudes to change, the rapidity with which foreign technical advances are adopted and so on, is concerned. This approach to the problem is the simplest, but it may ignore important aspects of the real world, for factors which are customarily included as variables in economic models may influence the rate of technical progress in important ways.

In particular, it can be argued that the rate of technical progress will be influenced by some aspect of an economy's investment activity. It may be influenced by the rate of growth of the capital stock,[2] or the share of the National Product invested, or the period of time over which the capital stock is replaced, or the accumulated sum of past investment.[3] Technical progress will be endogenous to the processes analysed by growth models rather than something which is exogenous to those processes in so far as the rate of technical progress depends upon investment.

In this paper the reasons for expecting a positive relationship between the rate of investment and the rate of technical progress will be analysed. The central arguments will rest upon two propositions: that the incentive to develop superior capital goods will vary with the quantity of a new capital good that can be sold; and that weaknesses in the design of plant and

[1] I am grateful to Professor I. I. Bowen, Professor G. C. Harcourt, and Mr. R. W. Peters for very helpful comment on an earlier draft of this paper which I completed in a sabbatical year in the University of West Australia. The responsibility for the errors that remain is entirely mine.

[2] See, for instance, N. Kaldor, " A Model of Economic Growth," ECONOMIC JOURNAL, December 1957.

[3] See, for instance, K. J. Arrow, " The Economic Implications of Learning by Doing," *Review of Economic Studies*, Vol. XXIX, June 1962.

502

machinery will be eradicated as more of a particular type of capital good is used or produced. These propositions will be analysed in turn. An object of the analysis will be to derive a plausible " technical progress function," *i.e.*, a plausible functional relationship between investment and the rate of technical progress. It will be argued that there may well be a strong relationship between the rate of investment and the rate of technical progress, and that this will differ, with important consequences for growth theory, from the relationships suggested by Kaldor and Arrow.

INVESTMENT, RESEARCH AND DEVELOPMENT, AND TECHNICAL PROGRESS

The first reason for expecting an association between the rate of investment and the rate of technical progress is that it will be more profitable to invent and develop superior methods of production where the rate of investment is high. The reasoning behind this argument can be seen with the help of Figs. 1 and 2. Here, the schedule *RR* shows the amount entrepreneurs expect to have to spend on research and development *per annum* in order to discover how to produce capital equipment which will permit

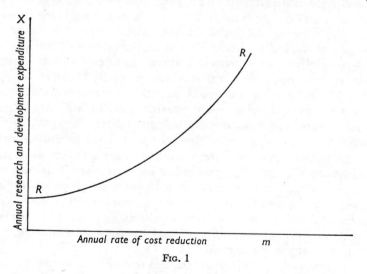

FIG. 1

reductions in unit costs of production with new equipment at various proportional annual rates. *RR* will cut the vertical axis because it is reasonable to suppose that some minimum sum must be spent on research and development before results begin to be achieved. Once results are achieved, it is reasonable to suppose that a high annual rate of cost reduction will be more expensive than a low rate, and that beyond a certain point it will become increasingly expensive to reduce cost at a higher proportional rate. With these assumptions, *RR* will slope upwards at an increasing rate, as in Fig. 1.

More formally, if X is the annual cost of research and development, and the annual rate of cost reduction is m, it is being assumed that $\dfrac{dX}{dm} > 0$, and that $\dfrac{dX}{dm}$ varies with m so that $\dfrac{d^2X}{dm^2} > 0$.

A number of crucial assumptions are implicit in this formulation, and these must be discussed before the RR function can be used in the subsequent analysis.

The expression of the results of research and development expenditures as an annual rate of cost reduction is what is necessary if this is to influence an economy's equilibrium rate of growth, but it is not obvious that the results of research and development can be properly expressed in these terms. It could be argued that successful research will produce a given once-for-all reduction in costs, and that further reductions will be progressively more difficult to obtain, with the result that RR should be drawn as a *static* curve with cost of research and development instead of *annual* cost of research and development on the vertical axis, and reduction in cost instead of *annual* reduction in cost on the horizontal. Then the diagram would suggest that it is progressively more difficult and expensive to reduce costs of production, with the result that no *steady* rate of technical change could emerge from the analysis. There are objections to this view and arguments in favour of the view which is taken in Fig. 1 that RR can be drawn as a dynamic schedule. If there were diminishing returns to research and development in the sense that discoveries by one research department typically became more expensive through time, companies would maintain research and development departments during the period when research could be fruitful, and contract them when the cost of further discoveries passed a certain point; but that is not what is typically observed. Research and development departments generally grow, and many produce a continuous stream of results. There is no evidence that their growth is generally associated with falling profitability. This suggests that discoveries may often be jumping-off points for further discoveries, with the result that the concept embodied in Fig. 1 of a research department of a given size producing results at a certain annual rate may approximate more closely to reality than the concept of diminishing research opportunities in any one direction.[1]

If this is accepted, it may be questioned whether the slope of RR should become steeper as the annual rate of cost reduction is increased. If discoveries are often starting points for further discoveries, there is apparently no reason why doubling research expenditure should not double or treble the annual results achieved. The fundamental basis for an increasing upward slope to RR rests on an obvious principle which has been documented

[1] Cf. J. Conlisk, " A Neoclassical Growth Model with Endogenously Positioned Technical Change Frontier," ECONOMIC JOURNAL, June 1969, where it is argued that research and development expenditure in an economy's " productivity sector " produces technical progress as an " output."

as a result of work done in the Rand corporation.[1] The cost of a new development will increase if the time span within which it must be completed is contracted beyond a certain point. Thus, writing in 1971, the aggregate cost of reaching Mars by 1976 must be greater than the cost of reaching Mars by 1981, which means that *annual* research and development expenditure would need to be more than doubled in the period 1971–76 to double the annual rate of technical progress, *i.e.*, to achieve ten years' progress in five. That is the basis for the increasing upward slope of *RR*.

A further difficulty is associated with uncertainty. To draw *RR* is implicitly to assume that entrepreneurs expect particular rates of research and development expenditure to produce particular rates of cost reduction, but this ignores uncertainty, which is likely to be particularly great where research and development is concerned. A question which then arises is how far a function like *RR* can allow for uncertainty. The rates of cost reduction that entrepreneurs expect from particular rates of research and development expenditure can be represented by a single schedule in an uncertain world only if this shows something as simple as, for instance, the weighted average of the various possible rates of cost reduction multiplied by their (subjective) probabilities. Otherwise the results of research and development will need to be represented in more than one dimension, for instance by expected yield and variance. If the initial argument is to be kept simple it will be desirable to represent expected results by a single rate of cost reduction, and the argument could always be extended to deal with uncertainty in a more sophisticated way by making use of some of the results of portfolio theory—with firms undertaking a portfolio of risky research projects. It will be assumed that the fundamental problems can be analysed without this.

A final problem is due to the fact that *RR* shows the expected rate of cost reduction of *existing products* when, in the real world, a very high proportion of research and development activity is associated with new products and improvements to products. The problems associated with this necessarily have to be tackled wherever the growth of a country's National Product is measured, for qualitative changes then have to be expressed as an increase in quantity. It can, perhaps, be assumed in the present argument that a quality change which raises the value of a product of unchanged real cost at a rate of *m* (in the estimation of the statisticians who compute the real National Product) can be represented as a rate of cost reduction (of an unchanging product) of *m*. Then cost reduction and product improvements will have the same analytical effect, and they can equally be regarded as technical progress. In both cases, firms will find that technical progress adds to their potential profits, and it will now turn out that this plays a significant part in the determination of the amounts which they will find it profitable to spend on research and development.

[1] See Edwin Mansfield, *The Economics of Technological Change* (Longmans, 1969, pp. 72–5).

In Fig. 2 a further curve, DD, has been added to RR, and this shows the amount that firms expect to earn from successful research and development activity. It can be supposed that the development of capital equipment which permits production with unit costs which are lower than they otherwise would be by a proportion of m (or the production of an equivalently superior product) will allow the firm responsible for these developments to charge a price for the equipment it markets (or to obtain a royalty from other firms licensed to market it) which is higher than it otherwise would be by a

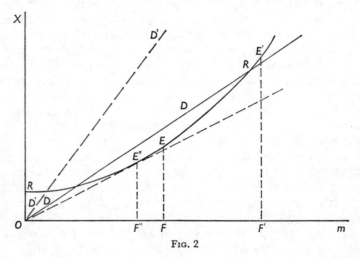

FIG. 2

proportion of $u \cdot m$ (where u is a constant). Thus it is assumed for simplicity that a firm can expect to earn twice as much extra profit from marketing equipment which permits the exploitation of 10% technical progress as it can earn as a result of 5% technical progress. If a firm expects to sell equipment which is worth I per annum, and it makes a discovery which cuts costs by m, it can expect to obtain extra profits of I times $u \cdot m$ per annum. This extra profit is shown as the schedule DD, and it will be a straight line, passing through the origin, with a slope of $u \cdot I$. With these assumptions, the extra profits from successful research and development will be proportional to the percentage cost reductions which are made possible by the development, and proportional to total expected sales of equipment. Thus it is assumed that twice as much extra profit will be earned from a particular cost reduction in an economy where there is twice as much investment in equipment to which the cost reduction is relevant.

The costs of research and development, and returns from this, must clearly be measured in the same units. Initially it will be assumed that the relative prices of capital goods (which influence I and therefore DD) and research and development activity (which influences RR) are given and constant. This assumption will be relaxed in a later stage of the argument, where it will be found that a continuous increase in the cost of research and development activity relatively to capital investment may have an important role to play in the growth process.

A profit maximising firm will push research and development expenditure to the point where the extra profits obtained from the development of superior capital equipment exceed the cost of developing such equipment by the greatest possible amount, and this is found where the gap between DD and RR is maximum, *i.e.*, at E, where DD and RR are parallel.

There will naturally be cases where expected sales of equipment are so low that DD is entirely below RR, and then the point where DD and RR are parallel will show a loss, with the result that research and development will not be viable and the firm will not have a research department. However, where DD is above RR as in Fig. 2, the firm will earn maximum profits by pushing research and development to the point where DD and RR are parallel, and in Fig. 2 the firm will find it optimal to spend EF on research and development *per annum*, and reduce costs in consequence at a rate of OF *per annum*. A firm which expects to market capital goods worth $2I$ instead of I will have the DD curve $D'D'$, where each point on $D'D'$ has twice the height on the vertical axis of the corresponding point on DD, but it will have exactly the same RR curve as the other firm. $D'D'$ is parallel to RR at E', and this shows the annual amount that the firm with twice the original firm's market for capital goods will choose to spend on research and development, while OF' shows the annual rate of cost reduction that it will achieve. The second firm will spend more, and it will achieve more, for OF' is bound to exceed OF.

A question which immediately arises is whether a firm which expects to sell twice as much equipment as another firm will achieve twice, more than twice or less than twice the annual rate of cost reduction of the other firm. It can be shown that these are all possible. Doubling expected sales of equipment doubles the slope of DD, and the new equilibrium will be where the slope of RR is also doubled, *i.e.*, where its $\frac{dX}{dm}$ is doubled. Doubling investment will more than double m, *i.e.*, it will more than double the rate of technical progress if, on RR, m more than doubles where $\frac{dX}{dm}$ doubles; it will double technical progress if m varies proportionately with $\frac{dX}{dm}$, and it will less than double technical progress if m varies less than proportionately with $\frac{dX}{dm}$. The critical point where doubling investment doubles technical progress occurs where m is proportional to $\frac{dX}{dm}$, *i.e.*, where $\frac{d^2X}{dm^2}$ is a constant. If $\frac{d^2X}{dm^2}$ varies positively with m, doubling investment would more than double technical progress, while it would less than double if $\frac{d^2X}{dm^2}$ varied inversely with m.   Each of these is inherently possible, for all that is clear from the proposition that getting results quickly increases their expense is that $\frac{d^2X}{dm^2}$ must be positive, but this says nothing about how it will vary with m.   A functional relationship between X and m which would produce the result that doubling investment doubled technical progress, *i.e.*, that $\frac{d^2X}{dm^2}$ is a constant, would be $X = A + B \cdot m^2$ (where A and B are constants, A being the intercept of RR on the vertical axis in Figs. 1 and 2) so that $m = \sqrt{\frac{X - A}{B}}$ This allows fully for diminishing returns to research and development by suggesting that the rate of technical progress will vary approximately with the square root of research and development expenditure, but this apparently produces the result that doubling the expected sales of equipment will double the rate of technical progress.

A faster rate of technical progress must, of course, require a more than proportional increase in research and development expenditure—*i.e.*, in annual investment in research and development as opposed to investment in new equipment.   The average cost of technical progress in terms of expenditure on research and development will be $\frac{X}{m}$, or the slope of a line from the origin to RR in Fig. 2, and this will be minimum at E''.   Any move up RR beyond E'' must raise the slope of a straight line from the origin, so it must raise the cost (in terms of research and development activity) of an extra 1 % *per annum* on the rate of technical progress.   Hence, if doubling the expected demand for equipment doubles the rate of technical progress, it will more than double required research and development expenditure.

The results obtained so far have depended upon the assumptions that firms undertaking research and development seek to maximise their profits, and that there is no entry into research and development.   However, the abnormal profits made by firms undertaking research and development shown by a gap between DD and RR might well attract other firms into this activity.   Suppose initially that there is free entry.   In this case firms will always enter where DD is above RR.   With the entry of each extra firm seeking to develop better equipment, the expected sales of equipment per firm will fall, with the result that the slope of DD will fall for each firm.   So long as DD is above RR at any point, abnormal profits can be earned through research and development, so the limit set by free entry is that entry will continue until DD has fallen to dd, which is tangential to RR at E'' in Fig. 3.   The position of E'' is independent of an economy's rate of investment, etc., for it can be found by simply drawing a tangent from the origin to RR, so it will simply be a function of the schedule RR.   This means that any connection between aggregate investment and the distance along *RR* which it pays firms to choose will completely disappear where free entry into research and development is assumed. Where expected sales of equipment are high, more firms will engage in research and development, but individual firms will not push expenditure further along their research and development functions. This would be beneficial to technical progress in that a larger number of research and development departments should increase the range of what is discovered, but this is not a benefit which will show in the analysis represented by Figs. 1, 2 and 3. Here, there will simply be more firms, each offering new equipment which permits an annual rate of cost reduction of *OF''*.

It then appears that where there is free entry into research and development, the rate of cost reduction achieved will vary with expected sales of equipment only in the rather imprecise sense that the number of firms engaged in research and development will vary with this, with the result that something extra should be achieved where more equipment is marketed, though how much extra can hardly be clear.

However, it will not be rational for the firms originally engaged in research and development to allow themselves to be pushed back to *E''*. If they could anticipate that this would be the consequence of earning abnormal profits at *E*, they would realise that they would do much better (in terms of market share, size and aggregate profits—though there would be no abnormal profits) by pushing research and development to *E** where *DD* and *RR* intersect. This would represent the maximum research and development activity which was compatible with normal profits, and it would represent the maximum financially sound rate of technical advance that a firm could achieve. It would also preclude loss of markets through entry. *E** is clearly a position of *long-run* profit maximisation in an industry where entry is thought to be the likely consequence of abnormal profits.[1]

The dominance of research and development in computers, chemicals, aircraft and so on, by a few firms with giant research departments, suggests that it may be more realistic to argue that firms carry out as much research and development as they can afford than to assume that they limit it so as to maximise short-run profits and invite consequent entry. Naturally it may be that *E** is chosen because the motivation of managements in these cases is biased towards technical progress and the achievement of technical excellence,[2] with the result that the principal objective of those responsible for the management of a firm is movement as far as possible along *RR*. Financial constraints will limit such movement to the point *E**. Whether this is the reason why *E** might be preferred to *E*, or whether it is long-run profit maximisation, it appears that the argument that the final equilibrium position will be at *E''* is not a strong one. If there is profit maximisation and

[1] Cf. R. F. Harrod, " Imperfect competition revisited," *Economic Essays* (Macmillan, 1956).
[2] Cf. J. K. Galbraith, *The New Industrial State* (Hamish Hamilton, 1968).

no fear of entry, equilibrium will be at E.   With either the anticipation o
entry, *or* a preference for sales, growth or technical progress maximisatior
over profit maximisation, the firm will choose $E*$. E'' will be reached onl>
if the firm pursues profit maximisation in the short run, and completely fail:
to take the possibility of entry into account where this is indeed a possibility

It has already been shown that where equilibrium is found at E, a highe:
expected rate of investment might increase the rate of technical progres:
in the same, a higher or a lower proportion.   Where firms reach equili
brium at $E*$, the same result will follow.   Doubling expected investmen
will double the slope of DD, so it will double $\frac{X}{m}$ at $E*$.   Technical progres:
will also double at $E*$ provided that, on RR, m doubles where $\frac{X}{m}$ doubles
i.e., provided that X varies with m^2 or that m varies with $\sqrt{X}$. It is clearl>
compatible with the general principle of diminishing returns to research an<
development (and the assumptions on which RR is drawn that both $\frac{dX}{dm}$ an<
$\frac{d^2X}{dm^2} > 0$) that m should vary more or less than proportionately with th<
square root of research and development expenditure, so the rate of technica
progress may vary more or less than proportionately with the expectec
market for equipment.

As with the equilibrium at E, there will be a need to increase investmen
in research and development more than proportionately with the rate o
technical progress, but a doubled market for equipment is as likely to lead t<
a more than doubled rate of technical progress as to a less than doubled rate

Figs. 1, 2 and 3 show the incentive to the individual firm to undertak<
research and development, but if there are barriers to entry into researc}
and development, or if firms choose points such as $E*$ (in Fig. 3) on thei:
research and development functions which preclude entry, the number o
firms undertaking research and development in each industry will not chang<
significantly, and RR in Figs. 1, 2 and 3 will then represent the position o
an industry.   An increase in an industry's expected demand for capita
equipment (and in equilibrium, this means an increase in actual investmen
as well) will then shift the point of equilibrium to the right, with the resul
that there will be a higher rate of technical progress, though whether thi
will be higher in a greater or a smaller proportion than the rate of investmen
is not clear.   Similarly, the rate of technical progress in the whole econom
will vary (less or more than proportionately) with the rate of investment.

The case for expecting an endogenous relationship between investmen
and the rate of technical progress is therefore strong, and this follows directl
from the assumption that there is a schedule such as RR which allows a1
annual rate of expenditure on research and development to be transforme<
into an annual rate of cost reduction.   The case for the existence of a schedul

of this kind is therefore crucial to the argument, but once this is accepted, the rest follows fairly straightforwardly.

It is now necessary to see how the argument will work out in the very long run. This is necessary, because a technical progress function which can be of use in a growth model must show the long-term equilibrium relationship between investment and technical progress. No attempt will be made in

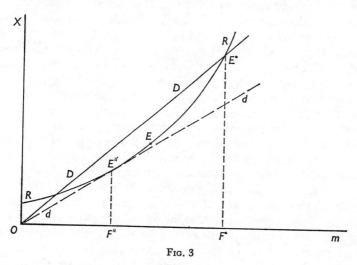

FIG. 3

this paper to prove that there will be steady growth with particular technical progress functions. Instead, the object will be to show the form that technical progress functions must take if steady growth is to be a possibility. The procedure will therefore be to assume some of the conditions necessary for steady growth (such as a constant share of saving and investment, a constant capital–output ratio, a constant share of wages), and to find forms for technical progress functions which will permit steady growth where these conditions hold. Whether there will, in fact, be steady growth where the technical progress function takes these forms is a problem which extends beyond the limits of this paper, but there will be no possibility at all of steady growth if the technical progress function does not permit it in the conditions postulated.

Suppose an economy saves and invests a constant share of a growing National Product. Then investment will grow at the same rate as the National Product, and in Figs. 2 and 3 the slope of the *DD* curve will rise through time. If the *RR* curve does not also rise, *i.e.*, if the " real " expenditures needed to produce various rates of cost reduction do not grow with the National Product, *E* (where *DD* is parallel to *RR*) and *E** (where *DD* and *RR* intersect) will move continuously to the right, with the result that there will be a continuous increase in the rate of technical progress until *RR*

becomes vertical.   There will then be no possibility of steady growth until
RR becomes vertical.   This is a perfectly plausible result, for there ha
arguably been a fairly continuous increase in the rate of technical progres
in the past 150 years, especially in the United States, and this has been
accompanied by growth in research and development in relation to the
National Product.[1]   More attention will be devoted to the possibility that
there may be an increasing rate of technical progress in a growing economy
below, but this is not the only result that is possible.   There is also the possi
bility of steady growth.

Suppose that a given rate of *employment* in research and development (with
a given ratio of labour costs to total costs) will produce given annual rates o
cost reduction.   It may be more plausible to assume this than to assume tha
given resources in terms of final physical outputs will produce constant re
search and development results.   With economic growth, a university
department with given staffing will become steadily more expensive in term
of an economy's final physical outputs as the real wages and salaries o
professors and their secretaries increase with other incomes.   If the cost of
department had to be kept constant in terms of the economy's physica
outputs, its staffing would steadily decline, and it could hardly be expected
to achieve a constant stream of results.   For this, constant employmen
would surely be necessary, and in so far as industrial research and develop
ment corresponds to university research, it will be right to assume that con
stant employment in research and development will be required if a constan
rate of cost reduction is to be achieved.   With this assumption, *RR* wil
be constant as a schedule on a diagram where the vertical axis is denominate
in " wage units."   If an economy with a constant labour force and a con
stant share of wages invests a constant fraction of its output, investment wil
also be constant in wage units.   Investment will grow in physical units with
the growth of final outputs, but any rise in output will be associated with an
equal rise in output per worker (because of the assumption of a constan
labour force) and in wages per worker (because the share of wages is con
stant), so any rise in physical investment will be associated with an equal ris
in the wage.   With investment constant in wage units, there will be n
tendency for *DD* to alter if the vertical axes of Figs. 2 and 3 are denominate
in wage units.   With no tendency for *DD* to shift in relation to *RR* as eco
nomic growth takes place, steady growth will be a possibility, and there wil
be particular possible equilibrium points—where *DD* and *RR* are parallel
and where they intersect.   The rate of technical progress will be constant a
each of these points.

---

[1] Statistics on technical progress in the nineteenth century are not generally thought to be ver
meaningful.   For the twentieth century, it has been estimated that the growth in total factor pro
ductivity in the United States was 1·8% *per annum* from 1900 to 1929, 2·3% from 1929 to 194
and 2·8% from 1948 to 1966.   The ratio of research expenditure to G.N.P. approximately treble
from 1930 to 1944, and doubled between 1953 and 1966.   W. Fellner, " Trends in the activitie
generating technical progress," *American Economic Review*, Vol. LX, March 1970.

Suppose two economies with different shares of investment are compared, where both have *the same* constant labour force. Then both will have the same RR schedule (measured in wage units), but the one with a higher share of investment will have higher investment measured in wage units, and therefore a higher DD curve. This will be parallel to (or intersect) the RR curve further to the right, so the economy with a higher share of investment will have faster technical progress, and a faster equilibrium rate of growth. The rate of technical progress may vary more or less than proportionately with the share of investment for reasons which were outlined earlier.

Suppose now that both economies have the same share of investment and that both have constant employment, but that one has a larger labour force than the other. Both will have the same RR line (measured in wage units), but the one with higher employment will have higher investment (measured in wage units) so it will have a higher DD curve, and therefore a faster (though constant) rate of technical progress. Hence, on this analysis, the rate of technical progress should vary with the size of the labour force, as well as with the share of investment.

The evidence is perfectly compatible with this rather startling result. The argument points to a strong connection between the rate of technical progress and *aggregate* sales of capital goods, which will depend on factors such as the share of investment and the *level* of employment. This suggests that economies with large potential markets for capital equipment, the United States and the European Common Market economies, for instance, should enjoy more technical progress than economies with smaller domestic markets which are precluded by tariffs from selling in large international markets. This may be one of the most fundamental, if not the most fundamental, argument in favour of large common markets for manufactured goods.

The argument suggests that a technical progress function which takes account of the effect of research and development expenditures on the rate of technical progress is likely to take the following form. The rate of technical progress will be proportional, less than proportional, or more than proportional to S, the share of investment in the National Product, and L, the level of employment, provided that this is constant. Where comparisons between economies with different levels of employment are avoided, the rate of technical progress will depend simply on S, and the following function will produce the desired result:

$$m_r = A_r + B_r . S \qquad . \quad . \quad . \quad . \quad . \quad (1)$$

where m_r is the rate of technical progress attributable to research and development, while A_r and B_r are constants, with A_r either positive or negative. If A_r is positive, m_r will vary less than proportionately with S, while it will vary more than proportionately if A_r is negative.

This technical progress function can be expected to apply to economies with a constant share of investment and constant employment.   Suppose, however, that an economy has a constant share of investment and *growing* employment.   Then, measuring in wage units, *RR* will not shift through time, but *DD* will rise continuously with the growth of the labour force. Then the points where *DD* and *RR* are parallel, and where they intersect, will shift continuously to the right, and this must mean a rising rate of technical progress through time.   Hence, there is apparently no possibility of a steady rate of technical progress, and of steady growth, where the labour force is growing.   The only possibility of steady technical progress with a growing labour force would arise if the research and development expenditure that was required to achieve a given annual rate of cost reduction was a constant fraction of the National Product.   This would mean that if there were two economies which were similar in every respect except that one had labour growth while the other did not, the one with labour growth would need to spend *increasingly* more than the other to achieve the same research and development results.   There is no plausible reason why this should be, and it would indeed be peculiar if the cost of research and development needed to increase with the rate of growth of employment.

This means that in so far as the rate of technical progress depends upon research and development, there is likely to be an increasing rate of technical progress where the labour force is growing—and the labour force grows in most developed economies.[1]   Steady growth will be possible only if it is assumed that the sectors of the economy where the rate of technical progress is influenced by research and development expenditure are so unimportant in relation to the economy as a whole that they can safely be neglected.   This will be a justifiable assumption in some cases, especially if attention is focused on growth in the nineteenth and the earlier part of the twentieth century. In such cases the rate of technical progress will depend principally on other factors, and a steady rate of technical progress will be possible.   In all other cases, there is likely to be an increasing rate of technical progress where there is growth in the labour force.

Before the argument can be taken further, the second principal endogenous relationship between investment and technical progress, the relationship based on " learning-by-doing " effects, must be analysed.

" LEARNING-BY-DOING " TECHNICAL PROGRESS FUNCTIONS

The best known form of the argument that a high rate of investment will be associated with rapid technical progress, because weaknesses in the design and development of capital equipment will be eradicated more quickly,

---

[1] Cf. William D. Nordhaus, *Invention, Growth and Welfare* (M.I.T. Press 1969), p. 106.   " The assumption that technical change is a function of the relative amount (of either the labour force or production) devoted to research is not satisfactory.   Empirical studies . . . indicate that the absolute amount of resources devoted to research should be the determining variable.   The correct formulation does not allow a steady state equilibrium."

is due to Arrow.[1] His model owes much to evidence obtained from the United States aircraft industry,[2] where it was found that if successively produced airframes were given serial numbers rising from 1 upwards, the cost of airframes varied with $N^{-\frac{1}{3}}$, where N was the serial number of an airframe. This is a plausible relationship, for it is fully to be expected that "learning," an element in total technical progress, will depend upon cumulative output.

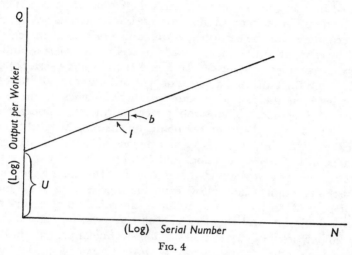

Fig. 4

If proportionality between unit costs, and N^{-b}, where b is a constant, applies universally, the basic equation for unit costs, H, will be as follows:

$$H = J \cdot N^{-b} \qquad \qquad (2)$$

where J is a constant.

If the share of wages is constant, labour costs will be a constant proportion of unit costs, so labour costs will be a constant proportion of H, *i.e.*, a constant proportion of $J \cdot N^{-b}$. Labour productivity is the inverse of labour inputs per unit of output, so labour productivity (Q) will vary in inverse proportion with $J \cdot N^{-b}$. Hence:

$$Q = U \cdot N^{b} \qquad \qquad (3)$$

where U is a constant. Taking the log of (3):

$$\text{Log } Q = \text{Log } U + b \cdot \text{Log } N \qquad \qquad (4)$$

(4) is plotted in Fig. 4. This shows labour productivity rising along a straight log line on a double log scale, where the axes are independent of the passage

[1] Kenneth J. Arrow (*op. cit.*).

[2] T. P. Wright, "Factors affecting the cost of airplanes," *Journal of the Aeronautical Sciences* (1936), pp. 122–8; and H. Asher, *Cost–Quantity Relationships in the Airframe Industry*, R-291, The Rand Corporation, 1956.

of time.   It is as if there is a succession of possible techniques of production, *1, 2, 3, 4, 5*, etc., with successive labour productivities which ascend along a straight log line on a double log scale.   Investment in *1* will automatically make investment in *2*, with a consequent rise in productivity, a possibility, and this will make possible investment in *3*, which will lead to a further increase in labour productivity, and so on.   At the same time, an economy which stagnates for generations, using *2*, cannot start to use *5* until it has first invested in *3* and learnt to use it, and then gone on to *4*.   Whether *3* and *4* are used only briefly, or for generations, is immaterial.   What matters is that an economy must be equipped with *3* and *4* before it can begin to use *5*.   Thus, investment automatically leads to technical progress, and it is a *sine qua non* for technical progress.[1]   In Fig. 4 there is not a series of distinct techniques of production, but a succession of techniques with infinitesimal differences between them, and labour productivity rises as the economy moves up the schedule.   The same general principle applies that the economy must pass along all the low points on the schedule if it is to reach any particular high point.   This is a general principle involved in a learning-by-doing technical progress function, and it is plausible that it describes an important feature of the real world.   It is now time to examine the particular features of the function which follow from the precise form of (2) and (3).

The effect of (3) is that each doubling of the serial number raises labour productivity 2^b times; and each increase in the serial number in the ratio $q:1$ raises labour productivity q^b times.   This technical progress in the ratio $q^b:1$ will be achieved over any period, however short or long, in which the serial number is raised q times.   Labour productivity will rise q^b times in ten years if it takes ten years to raise the serial number q times, and it will rise q^b times in a year if the serial number is raised q times in a year.   Halving the period over which the serial number is raised q times would involve doing the same amount of investment in half the time, which would double the amount of investment which was done in a given period.   Then technical progress in the ratio $q^b:1$ would be achieved in half the former time, which would mean that the annual rate of technical progress was doubled.   Hence, doubling the rate of investment (in the sense that the same investment is done in half the time) will double the rate of technical progress, and it follows from this that the annual rate of technical progress will be proportional to the rate of investment.

More simply, if something (investing: raising the serial number: anything) is done in half the former time, the rate at which it is done per unit of time will be doubled, and (as the technical progress which follows from a particular amount of investment is independent of the time taken to complete it) the consequences of this (whatever it is) will come through twice as fast per time unit.   Then doubling investment, per time unit, must double

[1] Cf. M. FG. Scott, " Supply and demand refurbished," *Oxford Economic Papers*, N.S. Vol. 19, July 1967, p. 163.

technical progress, per time unit; so the annual rate of technical progress will be proportional to annual investment.

For growth equilibrium, a technical progress function must be capable of producing a steady rate of technical progress where a constant share of the National Product is saved and invested, and the circumstances where a learning-by-doing technical progress function is compatible with this will now be analysed. The eventual function must be one where doubling investment doubles the rate of technical progress, but it does not follow that a function will necessarily be found where doubling *any constant* share of investment will produce a constant doubled rate of technical progress. A constant share of investment may produce an increasing or a declining rate of technical progress, and in this case doubling this constant share would double the increasing or declining rate of technical progress.

Technical progress will occur at a constant rate through time if the serial number is raised at *any* constant proportional rate, for successive increases in the serial number in the ratio $q:1$ will advance labour productivity in constant successive steps of $q^b:1$. Then what is needed for a steady rate of technical progress is *any* steady proportional rate of increase in the serial number.

Up to now, exactly what the serial number is applied to has not been specified. It could apply to successively produced machines, each worked by one worker, or to successively produced machines where each produces the same quantity of output; or to cumulative gross investment, or to cumulative net investment, each measured in terms of consumer goods.

Arrow in fact applies the serial number to cumulative gross investment since the beginnings of industrialisation. In steady growth, with any particular depreciation assumption, net investment will be a constant fraction of gross investment, so it will be equivalent to Arrow's assumption to assume that the serial number is applied to c times cumulative net investment, i.e. to c times the net capital stock, where $\frac{dc}{dt}$ is zero in steady growth. Then, substituting $c \cdot K$ for N in (3):

$$Q = U \cdot (c \cdot K)^b \quad . \quad . \quad . \quad . \quad . \quad (5)$$

Total output at time t, Y_t, will be output per worker (Q) times the total labour force, which will be $L_0 \cdot e^{nt}$, where L_0 is the labour force at time 0, and n is the rate of growth of the labour force, *i.e.*

$$Y_t = Q \cdot L_0 \cdot e^{nt} \quad . \quad . \quad . \quad . \quad (6)$$

substituting for Q from (5):

$$Y_t = U \cdot (c \cdot K)^b \cdot L_0 \cdot e^{nt} \quad . \quad . \quad . \quad (7)$$

differentiating (7) with respect to t:

$$\frac{1}{Y} \cdot \frac{dY}{dt} = n + b \cdot \frac{1}{K} \cdot \frac{dK}{dt} + b \cdot \frac{1}{c} \cdot \frac{dc}{dt} \quad . \quad . \quad . \quad (8)$$

In steady growth, the rate of growth of output $\left(\dfrac{1}{Y} \cdot \dfrac{dY}{dt}\right)$ will equal the rate

of growth of capital $\left(\dfrac{1}{K} \cdot \dfrac{dK}{dt}\right)$, and g and k can be written for these. Also,

in steady growth $\dfrac{dc}{dt} = 0$. Then where $g = k$, and $\dfrac{dc}{dt} = 0$:

$$g = \frac{n}{1 - b} \qquad \cdot \quad \cdot \quad \cdot \quad \cdot \quad \cdot \quad (9)$$

This is Arrow's equation for the only possible rate of steady growth which can follow from his assumptions.[1] The rate of growth of labour productivity (p) will be ($g - n$), so (from (9)):

$$p = n\left(\frac{b}{1 - b}\right) \quad \cdot \quad \cdot \quad \cdot \quad \cdot \quad \cdot \quad (10)$$

It is evident from (9) and (10) that except where $b = 1$, the equilibrium rate of growth is very narrowly restricted. Even though doubling investment doubles technical progress, the only possible rate of *steady* growth will be solely a function of the rate of growth of the labour force, and the technical coefficient, b. Investment will not influence it at all. The reason for the independence of steady growth rates of investment, and their dependence on the rate of growth of the labour force, even though " learning by doing " *should* make investment the dominant influence, can be explained quite simply.

It was explained earlier that a q-times increase in the serial number will raise output per worker q^b times. With proportionality between the serial number and the capital stock, this means that a q-times increase in the capital stock will raise output per worker q^b times, and if b is less than *one*, this means that a q-times increase in the capital stock will raise output per worker less than q times. With steady growth, output must increase at the same rate as capital. If labour productivity rises less than q times when the capital stock and output rise q times, labour requirements will increase, but if the labour force is constant, more labour cannot be made available. This means that a q-times increase in output cannot be arranged. Then no growth at all is possible if the labour force is constant (and b is less than one), a result that is shown by (9) and (10). It will still be true that raising the capital stock twice as fast will raise labour productivity twice as fast—the proposition arrived at earlier—but in steady growth it will also raise labour requirements twice as fast, and this will vitiate the whole process for an economy with a constant labour force. Then the freedom to enjoy a wide range of growth rates which should result from freeing the rate of technical progress from any time constraint apparently fails to result. Instead, the steady growth rate is dominated by the discipline of the annual rate of labour

[1] Kenneth J. Arrow (*op. cit.*), p. 165.

growth, and there can be no technical progress if there is no quantitative or qualitative growth in the labour force.

It is, however, possible to define a " learning by doing " technical progress function which is very similar to Arrow's, but where any steady growth rate is possible, and where the rate of growth will depend substantially upon the share of investment.

With Arrow, a q-times increase in the capital stock will increase labour productivity q^b times, and each successive increase in the capital stock by a fixed proportion will produce the same increase in labour productivity. Suppose that the unit for an increase in the capital stock is stated differently. Suppose the unit is the complete replacement of the capital stock by another with the same capital–output ratio, and that this always raises labour productivity in the ratio $e^M : 1$, where M is a constant. e^M can be $1\cdot02$ or $2\cdot50$: this will not affect the argument. With this assumption, the main essentials of a learning-by-doing technical progress function are retained. It is the act of investment that produces technical progress. An economy moves up a straight log-line as it replaces successive capital stocks, as with Arrow's function, and a succession of techniques, *1, 2, 3* and *4*, must be passed through before *5* can be used. Technical progress is defined independently of time, for given investment—replacing the capital stock with another with the same capital–output ratio—will produce the same e^M-times advance in labour productivity, whether it takes one year or a hundred. The results are, however, very different from those arrived at with Arrow's technical progress function.

If it takes T years to replace the capital stock with another with the same capital–output ratio, labour productivity will rise e^M times in T years, which means that it will rise at an annual exponential rate of $\dfrac{M}{T}$. The period needed to replace the capital stock, T, will vary in inverse proportion with S, for if there is twice as much investment each year, the capital stock will be replaced in half the time. If $T = \dfrac{D}{S}$, where D is a constant, the annual rate of technical progress due to learning-by-doing effects, m_z, will be $\dfrac{M}{D} \cdot S$ where M and D are constants. If the constant, B_z is substituted for $\dfrac{M}{D}$, a learning-by-doing technical progress function which is very different from Arrow's is arrived at, *i.e.*

$$m_z = B_z \cdot S \qquad \cdot \quad \cdot \quad \cdot \quad \cdot \quad \cdot \quad (11)$$

The economy's rate of steady growth will be this plus n. With the slight modification to Arrow's formulation made here, *any* rate of technical progress will be compatible with steady growth, and any rate of steady growth will be possible. There will be an infinite range of possible rates of technical progress, and the rate an economy actually achieves from learning-by-doing effects will depend entirely on investment, and it will be proportional to the share of investment.[1]

There is no reason why bringing learning-by-doing effects into the argument should produce results which are more restrictive than those in a Cobb–Douglas world. Learning-by-doing assumptions should increase the influence which an economy's saving and investment decisions can have upon its equilibrium growth rate. The formulation of learning-by-doing effects which is made here has that consequence, and as a result it is clear that the element of overall technical progress which is due to such effects will be proportional to the share of investment.

A Comprehensive Technical Progress Function

It can be argued that total technical progress will be due to a wide range of factors. There will be factors which are entirely exogenous to economic models as these are usually defined. These may be assumed to produce technical progress at an annual rate of A_e. Then there is the technical progress which is endogenous to the investment process, which can be divided into technical progress which is due to the investment process's stimulus to research and development activity, and to the learning effects which will go along with continuous investment. It has been argued that in steady growth, with a constant labour force, these will produce annual technical progress of $A_r + B_r \cdot S$ (where A_r can be positive or negative) and $B_z \cdot S$ respectively. Adding these effects together, it is to be expected that total technical progress, m, will depend on the following equation:

$$m = (A_e + A_r) + (B_r + B_z) \cdot S \qquad . \quad . \quad . \quad (12)$$

The constants $(A_e + A_r)$ can be replaced by the constant A, which will be positive provided that the technical progress which is due to factors which are exogenous to the investment process (A_e) amounts to more than the constant (and possibly) negative term (A_r) which is needed to allow for the possibility that higher investment may stimulate a more than proportionately higher rate of technical progress from research and development. The constants $(B_r + B_z)$ can be replaced by the constant B. Then:

$$m = A + B \cdot S \qquad . \quad . \quad . \quad . \quad . \quad (13)$$

(13) easily simplifies into the limiting cases where technical progress is entirely exogenous (and B is zero so that $m = A$), or entirely due to investment (where A is zero so that $m = B \cdot S$). A technical progress function

---

[1] This technical progress function, and the results which follow from it, were first outlined in W. A. Eltis, " Technical Progress Profits and Growth," *Oxford Economic Papers*, Volume 20, No. 2 July 1968.

for the real world should lie in between the limits where $m = A$ and $m = B \cdot S$, which points to the function shown by (13).[1]

The relationship between A and B will vary quite considerably between economies. The world's technological leaders will obtain much of their technical advance from their own research and development, which will give them a relatively high B_r, while backward economies which rely mainly on foreign technology will have negligible B_r's. There is no reason why B_z, the learning function, should be stronger for the technical leaders, but their higher B_r's should ensure that they have relatively higher B's and therefore a higher proportion of endogenously determined technical progress.

Where the labour force grows, steady growth is only possible where research and development produces negligible technical progress in relation to other sources. This will not be the case with most advanced economies, and this means that research and development is likely to produce a growing rate of technical progress in such economies, with important implications for growth theory.[2]

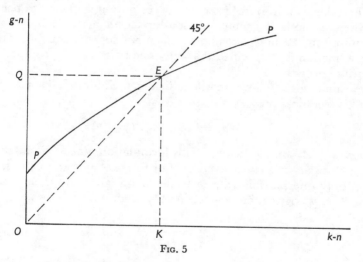

FIG. 5

The technical progress function arrived at in this paper is very different from Kaldor's pioneering technical progress function which is illustrated in Fig. 5.[3] There, the vertical axis shows the rate of growth of labour pro-

---

[1] I first used a technical progress function which took this form in W. A. Eltis, "Investment, Technical Progress, and Economic Growth," *Oxford Economic Papers*, Vol. 15, March 1963, but I did not then fully appreciate the arguments in its favour.

[2] There are also important implications for the future. If the growth rate doubles as a result of accelerating technical progress, the growth achieved over any given period will be *squared*—since an exponential is doubled—which means that science fiction results may be achieved with frightening rapidity. It must be remembered that in the real world technical progress usually takes the form of new products rather than a cheapening of existing products, and in the twentieth century these have created as many social problems as they have solved.

[3] N. Kaldor (*op. cit.*).

ductivity, while the horizontal axis shows the rate of growth of capital per worker. The technical progress function, PP, cuts the vertical axis to show that there will be some growth in labour productivity, even where capital per worker is constant, because of factors contributing to technical progress which are independent of capital accumulation. After this, the rate of growth of labour productivity is assumed to vary with the rate of growth of capital per worker. The 45° line shows all points where capital per worker and output per worker grow at the same rate, and as capital and output will grow at the same rate in steady growth, an economy in steady growth must be somewhere on the 45° line. It must, at the same time, be somewhere on its technical progress function, and if it is to be on this as well as the 45° line, it must be at E where the two lines intersect. This will be the only point where equilibrium growth is possible. Then OQ and OK will be the only growth rates of output and capital per worker which are compatible with steady growth. Therefore if two economies have the same technical progress function, PP, but different saving and investment propensities, both will have the same equilibrium growth rates of output and capital per worker. Thus there is no endogenous relationship at all between investment and the equilibrium rate of technical progress in Kaldor's model, for his technical progress function is so specified that only one point on it is compatible with equilibrium growth.

The same result follows mathematically. Kaldor's algebraic formulation of his technical progress function is:

$$(g - n) = A_1 + A_2 \cdot (k - n) \quad . \quad . \quad . \quad . \quad (14)$$

where A_1 and A_2 are constants. This formulation makes PP a straight line while he draws it as a concave curve, but this does not affect the result that there is only one possible rate of technical progress in equilibrium where $g = k$. If m is written for $(g - n)$ in (14), and $g = k$:

$$m = \frac{A_1}{1 - A_2} \quad . \quad . \quad . \quad . \quad . \quad (15)$$

Hence m is a constant, and if the constant, A, is substituted for $\frac{A_1}{1 - A_2}$, Kaldor's technical progress function becomes (13) with $B = 0$, *i.e.*, he would have arrived at the same result if he had assumed that the rate of technical progress was exogenously given. Indeed, with (14), he has assumed a function which implies a Cobb–Douglas relationship between output, capital and labour, for (14) can be rewritten as:

$$g = A_1 + A_2 \cdot k + (1 - A_2) \cdot n \quad . \quad . \quad . \quad (16)$$

Integrate (16) with respect to time:

$$Y = D_1 \cdot e^{A_1 \cdot t} \cdot K^{A_2} \cdot L^{(1-A_2)} \quad . \quad . \quad . \quad . \quad (17)$$

where D_1 is a constant.[1] It is naturally also the case that Kaldor's technical progress function will be arrived at if a Cobb–Douglas production function is differentiated with respect to time.

Superficially, Kaldor's (14) is almost identical to (13), but whether the rate of growth of productivity partly depends upon S (as in (13)) or on k (as in (14)) is a matter of crucial importance. If it depends upon k, this is simply another way of making Cobb–Douglas assumptions. If, on the other hand, it depends on S, economies with different saving and investment propensities will have different rates of technical progress, and different steady growth rates. If the argument of this paper is accepted, it will be right to assume that m will partly depend upon S, and that saving and investment propensities will therefore influence an economy's growth rate, even in the long run.

In formal terms, an economy's equilibrium rate of growth is $(m + n)$, where m is the rate of Harrod neutral technical progress, and if $m = A + B \cdot S$:

$$g = A + n + B \cdot S \quad \cdots \quad (18)$$

Hence, two otherwise similar economies with different shares of investment will have different equilibrium growth rates where technical progress is partly endogenous.[2]

The equilibrium capital–output ratio, V, must equal $\frac{S}{g}$, so from (18):

$$V = \frac{S}{A + n + B \cdot S} \quad \cdots \quad (19)$$

Then, where technical progress is partly endogenous, doubling the share of investment will less than double the capital–output ratio, and, indeed V will always equal $\frac{1}{B}$ if there is no labour growth and technical progress is entirely endogenous so that A and n are zero. It is clear from (19) that if steady state results say something about the development of actual economies, the capital–output ratio will differ less between economies, and it will be less variable in a single economy through time, the larger is B in relation to A and n. Thus there will be less variation in the capital–output ratio the greater the proportion of growth that is due to endogenous technical progress, and this is a result that Kaldor sought from his technical progress function.

[1] See H. A. J. Green, "Growth Models, Capital and Stability," ECONOMIC JOURNAL, March 1960; and J. Black, "The Technical Progress Function and the Production Function," *Economica*, Vol. XXIX, May 1962.

[2] The result that an economy's equilibrium rate of growth varies with S is also arrived at in J. Conlisk (*op. cit.*), and W. Vogt, "Kapitalakkumulation und Technischer Fortschritt", *Weltwirschaftliches Archiv*, 100 (1968).

Both Kaldor and Arrow wrote long and forceful passages to argue that there is likely to be a strong endogenous relationship between investment and technical progress in the real world. Unfortunately their subsequent mathematical specification of the relationship precluded any endogenous connection in equilibrium, in their growth models. With the specification of the technical progress function adopted here, that $m = A + B \cdot S$, it is possible to obtain results which are in line with the view of the technical process which Kaldor and Arrow initiated.

W. A. ELTIS

Exeter College,
Oxford.

PART II

CLASSICAL ECONOMICS

[3]

IX

Adam Smith's Theory of Economic Growth

W. A. ELTIS*

ADAM Smith's theory of growth has provided better predictions of the course that economic development was to follow in the nineteenth and twentieth centuries than the theories of his great successors, Malthus, Ricardo, and Marx, who predicted at best constant living standards for the great mass of the population. In Smith's account, increasing returns and 'learning by doing' (as growth theorists now call it) in industry play a central role, and in an economical and well-governed society these can be expected to continually increase the *manufactured* goods that workers can afford to buy. Right at the start of *The Wealth of Nations* he pointed out that as a result of the division of labour, an 'industrious and frugal peasant' enjoyed, as well as enough food for subsistence, a woollen coat, a coarse linen shirt, shoes, a kitchen grate, knives and forks and kitchen utensils, earthenware or pewter plates, and glass windows with the result that his 'accommodation' greatly exceeded that of an African King.[1] Workers, like peasants, gained from the division of labour which produced these benefits, and Smith certainly did not believe that the maximum possible advantages from this had been obtained by 1776.

The compatibility of Smith's theory of growth with what has happened since is not, however, its principal claim to modern attention. It is possible that this rests on a most persuasive line of argument it contains which modern theory has almost wholly lost sight of. In twentieth-century growth theory, the rate of investment generally has no effect at all on an economy's long-term rate of growth of output and living standards. This is true of almost all neoclassical growth theory, and of some Keynesian growth theory in addition.[2] In Smith's theory, however, capital accumulation leads to increased population and employment, and provided that the market for manufactured goods is widened by this, an increased division of labour will follow which will have favourable effects on labour productivity. If competition is sufficient, and an increase in capital will generally increase

* Fellow of Exeter College, Oxford.

I am grateful to Professor B. J. Gordon and Dr. K. Hennings for very helpful comments on an earlier draft of this paper.

[1] Adam Smith, *An Inquiry into the Nature and Causes of the Wealth of Nations*, ed. Cannan (1930), I.i.11. All subsequent references are to this edition.

[2] See F. H. Hahn and R. C. O. Matthews, 'The Theory of Economic Growth: A Survey', *Economic Journal*, lxxiv (Dec. 1964).

competition, the prices of manufactured goods will then fall with unit labour costs with the result that the quantity and range of manufactured goods that workers can afford to purchase will increase. It follows therefore that in Smith's account of growth, faster capital accumulation is associated with a faster rate of growth of employment and output, and faster growth in living standards. In modern growth theory, Arrow comes nearest to Smith's results with his 'learning by doing' model where the rate of growth of labour productivity and wages per head depend on the rate of growth of employment opportunities provided by new machines.[3] Very few other modern theorists have arrived at Smith's results. Thus, if a strong interconnection between investment and growth is central to the development process, Smith's theory of growth must stand high, for it is one of the very few where investment has highly favourable long-term effects.

A number of problems are naturally involved in any attempt to present Smith's theory of growth in modern terms. *The Wealth of Nations* was not written with the rigour of modern growth theory, or indeed that of Ricardo's *Principles of Political Economy and Taxation*. It is most unlikely that Smith's book would have had the vast influence it achieved if the argument had been presented in the form of a logical derivation of conclusions from carefully stated premises, with each term precisely defined. Because the book was written to persuade and to carry any literate reader along, definitions and assumptions often need to be inferred from the general argument, and as this deals with much more than growth and development, some of the propositions that relate to growth must be obtained from other parts of the argument.

In the present paper, an attempt will be made to present an account of Smith's theory of growth and development in modern terms, but before this is done, something must be said about Smith's basic assumptions, for these involve a number of problems of interpretation which must be resolved before a theory that can genuinely pretend to be his can be outlined. Part I of this paper, 'Adam Smith's Assumptions', will be concerned with these problems, and the various propositions that are to be found in *The Wealth of Nations* about returns to scale in industry and agriculture, the distinction between productive and unproductive employment and its relevance to the rate of capital accumulation, the effect of accumulation on wages, and so on, are discussed there with the object of arriving at the appropriate assumptions for a modern restatement of Smith's theory of growth. In Part II, 'A *Wealth of Nations* Growth Model', the theory that follows from the assumptions arrived at in Part I will be set out and discussed, and finally, in Part III, 'The Results of the Model and some of Adam Smith's Conclusions', the results arrived at in Part II will be

[3] See Kenneth J. Arrow, 'The Economic Implications of Learning by Doing', *Review of Economic Studies*, xxix (June 1962).

compared with various propositions and predictions about growth and development that are to be found in *The Wealth of Nations*. Smith does not merely predict continuing progress based on industry, for he clearly believed that growth would eventually cease when a country's potential for development was fully realized, the development then achieved depending in part on a society's laws and institutions. He expected the rate of profit to fall as full development was approached, and this means that a model that predicted an indefinite continuation of growth would not be Smith's.[4] In addition, it is clear that Smith thought that agriculture provided a more useful foundation for growth than industry, even though industry offered greater potential benefits from the division of labour. This apparent paradox must be explained by any model that claims to be Smith's. The model outlined in this paper passes these tests (and others) and it will be argued that the results it produces correspond to those in *The Wealth of Nations*.

I ADAM SMITH'S ASSUMPTIONS

In this part of the paper, Smith's basic assumptions about four of the factors that influence the development of economies will be discussed, namely his assumptions about returns to scale in the different sectors of the economy; about the relationship between the ratio of productive to unproductive employment and the rate of capital accumulation; about how requirements for fixed and circulating capital vary with growth; and about how growth and income distribution interact. His assumptions about returns to scale in industry and agriculture will be considered first.

Chapter 1 of Book 1 of *The Wealth of Nations* opens with an account of the advantages to be derived from the division of labour, and after illustrations including the famous pin factory, Smith writes:

This great increase of the quantity of work which, in consequence of the division of labour, the same number of men are capable of performing, is owing to three different circumstances; first to the increase of dexterity in every particular workman; secondly, to the saving of the time which is commonly lost in passing from one species of work to another; and lastly, to the invention of a great number of machines which facilitate and abridge labour, and enable one man to do the work of many.

(WN I.i.5)

The first two of these are now very familiar, but the third is less so, and it will be seen that it is important. It is obviously relevant to the correspondence between Smith's argument and Arrow's 'learning by doing' growth model that has been remarked upon.

[4] The dichotomy between Smith's arguments that point to indefinite progress as a result of increasing returns, and those that point to an eventual stationary state, is very clearly brought out in an unpublished paper by Dr. R. N. Ghosh.

The extent to which it is possible to take advantage of the division of labour depends on the number of workers who can be concentrated to manufacture a good at a single place, and this will depend on the market for the good. Smith points out that it takes 50 to 100 families to buy the product of a shoemaker working on his own, or an artisan in a single trade (WN IV.ix.45), and many more where the division of labour is pushed far, so a workshop with 100 workers will produce for far more than 5,000–10,000 families. Such a workshop can only exist if transport facilities are available to distribute products widely, and as water transport was by far the cheapest form of transport until the nineteenth century, there is much in *The Wealth of Nations* about the influence of the Mediterranean and navigable rivers on the location of the areas of the world able to exploit the potential advantages inherent in the division of labour.[5] Provided that the extent of the market is sufficient (and that the division of labour depends on the extent of the market is one of the best-known propositions in *The Wealth of Nations*) industrial output can be expanded more than proportionately with the labour employed in industry. Each increase in employment will lead to a further subdivision of tasks, which will lead to higher labour productivity:

What takes place among the labourers in a particular workhouse, takes place, for the same reason, among those of a great society. The greater their number, the more they naturally divide themselves into different classes and subdivisions of employment. More heads are occupied in inventing the most proper machinery for executing the work of each, and it is, therefore, more likely to be invented.

(WN I.viii.57; see also II.3–4)

Thus with tasks further subdivided, new machines will be invented, and once they are, labour productivity will rise to the level appropriate to that degree of division of labour. A further increase in labour productivity will be achieved when tasks can be still more subdivided, and this will be possible when there is a further increase in employment.[6]

Thus, if employment per firm rises with total industrial employment, the economy will move up a line like AB in Fig. 1 on p. 430 which shows the productivity level that is reached in the long run with each successively higher level of employment. The same diagram follows from Arrow's model, but there the horizontal axis would show successively produced machines, each worked by one worker, instead of aggregate industrial employment. However, the effect of these is the same, and in each case productivity advances at a rate depending on the rate at which the economy

---

[5] Joseph J. Spengler has emphasized the importance of this in 'Adam Smith's Theory of Economic Growth', *Southern Economic Journal*, xxv–xxvi (Apr. and July 1959), an article which gives a comprehensive account of the many different factors that influence growth in Smith's argument.

[6] See Samuel Hollander, *The Economics of Adam Smith* (1973), 208–12, for a similar account of the relationship between employment and technical progress in *The Wealth of Nations*.

expands its industrial labour force and capital stock. An account of Smith's lectures delivered in the early 1760s in Glasgow suggests that he may have thought that AB rose very steeply, for the following statement has been attributed to him: 'For twenty millions in a society, in the same manner as a company of manufacturers, will produce 100 times more goods to be exchanged than a poorer and less numerous one of 2 mill.'[7] This implies that each 1 per cent rise in employment might be associated with an increase in labour productivity of 1 per cent,[8] which suggests exceedingly favourable production conditions wherever the division of labour can be usefully extended, and it was certainly Smith's view that it could be much further extended in industry.

Agriculture was, however, of considerably greater importance than

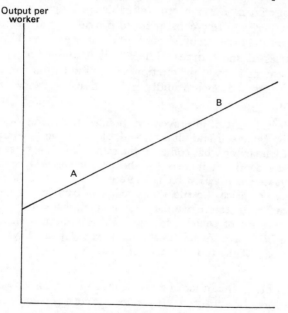

FIG. 1   *Employment in Industry*

[7] LJ (A), vi.166. A student who took lecture notes in a different year attributed a still more favourable statement to him, 'Twenty millions of people perhaps in a great society, working as it were to one anothers hands, from the nature of the division of labour before explained, would produce a thousand times more goods than another society consisting only of two or three millions' (LJ (B), 265; Cannan, 206). This student may well have added a nought to make a 'hundred' a 'thousand'.

[8] This also implies that a 1 per cent increase in output might be associated with an increase in labour productivity of $\frac{1}{2}$ per cent, implying what would now be called a Verdoorn coefficient of 0·50 in the long run. It is interesting to note that this is very close to the Verdoorn coefficient N. Kaldor found for the industry of developed economies in the period 1954–64 (*Causes of the Slow Rate of Growth of the United Kingdom* (1966)).

industry in an eighteenth-century economy, and here two to four families can consume the output of a farm worker (WN IV.ix.45), and:

> The nature of agriculture, indeed, does not admit of so many subdivisions of labour, nor of so complete a separation of one business from another, as manufactures. It is impossible to separate so entirely, the business of the grazier from that of the corn-farmer, as the trade of the carpenter is commonly separated from that of the smith. The spinner is almost always a distinct person from the weaver; but the ploughman, the harrower, the sower of the seed, and the reaper of the corn, are often the same. The occasions for those different sorts of labour returning with the different seasons of the year, it is impossible that one man should be constantly employed in any one of them.
> (WN I.i.4)

The fact that a farm of maximum attainable efficiency requires few workers to work together, and few consumers to provide a market, means that the potential from the division of labour will be fully exploited in agriculture in most countries at most times. There will then be no reason to expect increasing returns in food production. Some foodstuffs will have the same real labour costs, however rapidly productivity advances elsewhere, for instance, corn:

> In every different stage of improvement, besides, the raising of equal quantities of corn in the same soil and climate, will, at an average, require nearly equal quantities of labour; or what comes to the same thing, the price of nearly equal quantities; the continual increase of the productive powers of labour in an improving state of cultivation being more or less counterbalanced by the continually increasing price of cattle, the principal instruments of agriculture. Upon all these accounts, therefore, we may rest assured, that equal quantities of corn will, in every state of society, in every stage of improvement, more nearly represent, or be equivalent to, equal quantities of labour, than equal quantities of any other part of the rude produce of land.
> (WN I.xi.e.28)

Over much of the remainder of agriculture and mining, however, diminishing returns are to be expected: 'If you except corn and such other vegetables as are raised altogether by human industry, that all other sorts of rude produce, cattle, poultry, game of all kinds, the useful fossils and minerals of the earth, &c. naturally grow dearer as the society advances in wealth and improvement, I have endeavoured to show already' (WN I.xi.i.3). These all grow dearer in terms of both labour and corn. The exceptions in raw produce are vegetable foods, which fall in price relatively to corn because they are a cheap by-product of improved methods of cultivation; and other by-products, for instance hides, which may fall in price because their supply is increased relative to demand because of a faster increase in the number of cattle than in the demand for leather.

It then turns out that Smith assumes increasing returns throughout industry, and with the exception of vegetable foods and hides, etc., that unit costs will be constant, or that they will rise as employment increases in agriculture and mining where there is much less scope for the division of labour. It follows that whether the demand for manufactured goods grows as capital and employment rises will have a very great effect on the course that development follows. This is indeed the case, and it will turn out that the taste of the rich for manufactured goods, and potential export markets for these have a very great effect on the growth of economies.

If there is increased employment, and increased demand for manufactured goods, productivity in industry will rise, and the next step in the argument is to discover what, according to Smith, determines the rate of growth of employment. This depends on the rate of growth of capital, for an increase in aggregate employment will only be possible if there is an increase in the capital stock, since more wage goods and raw materials will be needed in advance of production if more workers are to be employed, and more fixed capital will be needed as well: 'As the accumulation of stock must, in the nature of things, be previous to the division of labour, so labour can be more and more subdivided in proportion only as stock is previously more and more accumulated' (WN II.3). Clearly the rate of growth of capital is crucial, and here one comes to the line of argument in *The Wealth of Nations* which is furthest from modern economics. The best starting-point to an understanding of Smith's approach to the determination of the rate of capital accumulation is perhaps the following passage:

In all countries where there is tolerable security, every man of common understanding will endeavour to employ whatever stock he can command, in procuring either present enjoyment or future profit. If it is employed in procuring present enjoyment, it is a stock reserved for immediate consumption. If it is employed in procuring future profit, it must procure this profit either by staying with him, or by going from him. In the one case it is a fixed, in the other it is a circulating capital. A man must be perfectly crazy who, where there is tolerable security, does not employ all the stock which he commands, whether it be his own or borrowed of other people, in some one or other of those three ways.

(WN II.i.30)

This immediately disposes of the possibility that part of a country's capital stock will not be fully utilized (provided that the institutions of a country maintain 'tolerable security' for creditors), and this proposition is a vital component of Say's law. Whatever goods are available that are not immediately consumed by their owners must either be used to make a profit, or sold (or lent) to those who expect to be able to make a profit. No one (if the above proposition is accepted) will allow goods to stand idly in warehouses, for this would be 'crazy'.[9]

[9] It may not be possible to use *fixed* capital at a profit at any reasonable set of factor prices if demand is insufficient, but this difficulty which is one of those that make Keynesian

Now, so far as circulating capital is concerned, and attention will be focused on this for the moment, a profit is made by getting more goods back at the end of a period than went out at the beginning, for instance, by feeding corn or its equivalent to farm workers who will then grow more corn than the cost of their wages and the necessary seed corn. Thus, that part of *circulating* capital that is not consumed by its owners must increase from period to period wherever profits are earned. However, circulating capital as a whole need not grow, because part of it is consumed (directly, or indirectly through the employment of unproductive workers, for instance servants) by its owners each year. If the owners consume $\frac{1}{4}$ of circulating capital each year, and then receive back $\frac{4}{3}$ times the $\frac{3}{4}$ they employ productively, the capital stock will neither rise nor fall from period to period. If they consume $\frac{1}{3}$, and receive back $\frac{4}{3}$ times the remaining $\frac{2}{3}$, the capital stock will fall by $\frac{1}{9}$ in each period; while it will grow by $\frac{1}{9}$ if they consume only $\frac{1}{6}$ and receive back $\frac{4}{3}$ times the remaining $\frac{5}{6}$. Thus, whether the capital stock grows or declines depends on the proportion that is used productively, and on how productive this is.

Both productive and unproductive labourers, and those who do not labour at all, are all equally maintained by the annual produce of the land and labour of the country. This produce, how great soever, can never be infinite, but must have certain limits. According, therefore, as a smaller or greater proportion of it is in any one year employed in maintaining unproductive hands, the more in the one case and the less in the other will remain for the productive, and the next year's produce will be greater or smaller accordingly; the whole annual produce, if we except the spontaneous productions of the earth, being the effect of productive labour.

(WN II.iii.3)

Something must obviously be said about Smith's distinction between productive and unproductive labour, which has disappeared from modern economics. This distinction is clearly crucial to Smith's argument, and he says the following about it:

There is one sort of labour which adds to the value of the subject upon which it is bestowed: there is another which has no such effect. The former, as it produces a value, may be called productive; the latter, unproductive labour. Thus the labour of a manufacturer adds, generally, to the value of the materials which he works upon, that of his own maintenance, and of his master's profit. The labour of a menial servant, on the contrary, adds to the value of nothing . . . A man grows rich by employing a multitude of manufacturers: he grows poor, by maintaining a multitude of menial servants . . . the labour of the manufacturer fixes and realizes itself in some particular subject or vendible commodity, which lasts for

unemployment possible was not noticed by Smith, and it may well have had little importance in the eighteenth century.

some time at least after that labour is past ... [the menial servant's] services generally perish in the very instant of their performance, and seldom leave any trace or value behind them, for which an equal quantity of service could afterwards be procured.

(WN II.iii.1)

Here, there are three criteria for the distinction between productive and unproductive labour: (i) whether employment produces a profit, (ii) whether employment produces something storable, and (iii) whether a particular kind of employment can be continued indefinitely without new infusions of capital. Some activities, for instance agriculture and manufacturing, are productive according to all three criteria, while others, for instance, domestic service are unproductive according to all three, while there are activities, for instance teaching or building an extension to a palace, which satisfy some and not others. There are obviously difficult borderline cases (as there are in the modern distinction between investment and consumption) and the distinction has lapsed, but it may have force in distinguishing activities which contribute to growth from those that do not. As Smith continues:

The labour of some of the most respectable orders in the society is, like that of menial servants, unproductive of any value, and does not fix or realize itself in any permanent subject, or vendible commodity, which endures after that labour is past, and for which an equal quantity of labour could afterwards be procured. The sovereign, for example, with all the officers both of justice and war who serve under him, the whole army and navy, are unproductive labourers. They are the servants of the public, and are maintained by a part of the annual produce of the industry of other people. Their service, how honourable, how useful, or how necessary soever, produces nothing for which an equal quantity of service can afterwards be procured. The protection, security, and defence of the commonwealth, the effect of their labour this year, will not purchase its protection, security, and defence for the year to come. In the same class must be ranked, some both of the gravest and most important, and some of the most frivolous professions: churchmen, lawyers, physicians, men of letters of all kinds; players, buffoons, musicians, opera-singers, opera-dancers, &c.

(WN II.iii.2)

The labour of all these professions is included in modern National Income statistics, but few could doubt that if two developing countries had equal National Incomes, and one employed one-third of its labour in the above ways and the other one-tenth, the latter would find growth easier to achieve.

In Smith's growth argument, the real distinction is between labour that produces and makes available goods *that can be used as capital* and labour that does not. Thus, as Smith points out, 'artificers, manufacturers and merchants' (WN IV.ix.29) and for the same reason those concerned with transport, etc. are productive. The above distinction will suffice for the argument that follows, so long as workers do not consume services.[10]

The distinction between productive and unproductive labour is one feature of Smith's account of growth that has become obsolete. Another that is equally unfamiliar is the proposition that, so long as investment in fixed capital (which was a small fraction of the National Product in 1776) is ignored, the entire National Income is consumed in each period:

> What is annually saved is as regularly consumed as what is annually spent, and nearly in the same time too; but it is consumed by a different set of people. That portion of his revenue which a rich man annually spends, is in most cases consumed by idle guests, and menial servants, who leave nothing behind them in return for their consumption. That portion which he annually saves, as for the sake of the profit it is immediately employed as a capital, is consumed in the same manner, and nearly in the same time too, but by a different set of people, by labourers, manufacturers, and artificers, who reproduce with a profit the value of their annual consumption.
>
> (WN II.iii.18)

Thus, while part of the income of the rich is saved, the entire National Income is also consumed—saving by the rich amounting to the employment of productive rather than unproductive workers. This terminology confused Malthus, but not Ricardo as the following note on a passage in Malthus's *Principles of Political Economy* shows:[11]

Malthus. Parsimony, or the conversion of revenue into capital, may take place without any diminution of consumption, if the revenue increases first.

Ricardo. I say it always take place without any diminution of consumption. Mr. Malthus clogs the proposition with a condition 'if the revenue increases first'. I do not understand what Mr. M. means:—if the revenue increases first. Before what?

Malthus clearly saw saving as 'that part of income which is not consumed', while Ricardo appreciated that all the goods (with the exception of fixed capital) that are produced in one period are consumed in the next, either productively or unproductively.[12] If those who own the capital stock are

---

[10] The sole echo of Smith's distinction in modern theory is in Piero Sraffa's classically based *Production of Commodities by Means of Commodities* (1960) where goods (and presumably services) that are used as factors of production and those that are bought by workers influence the prices of other goods, the wage, the rate of profit, etc., while goods (and presumably services) that are solely consumed by non-workers do not.

[11] *The Works and Correspondence of David Ricardo*, ed. P. Sraffa (1951), ii.326.

[12] It is clear from the 6th chapter of *Commerce Defended* (1808) that James Mill also thoroughly understood Smith's argument (before he met Ricardo). Thus, 'We perceive, therefore, that there are two species of consumption; which are so far from being the same, that the one is more properly the very reverse of the other. The one is an absolute destruction of property, and is consumption properly so called; the other is a consumption for the sake of reproduction . . .' (69).

rugal, and governments are modest in their expenditure, most of the
capital stock is consumed by productive workers with the result that it
grows from period to period. If those who own capital, and, most important
of all, governments, are extravagant, unproductive employment will
predominate with the result that the capital stock will decline:[13] and in
both cases the nation's circulating capital (apart from money) will be
consumed each year.

That is Smith's theory of accumulation, and it has lapsed, presumably
because of the difficulties in drawing a sharp borderline between productive
and unproductive employment, and because of the growth in the ratio of
fixed to circulating capital that has occurred since 1776.[14]

There is, of course, fixed capital in *The Wealth of Nations*, and it will be
seen that this plays an important role in the argument, but it plays no part
in the passages that deal with consumption and thrift that have just been
discussed.[15] Fixed capital is part of the gross product of productive labour,
and once this is allowed for, the entire product of productive labour in one
period is not used up in the next, and with growth, fixed capital per worker
must evidently rise:

The quantity of materials which the same number of people can work up,
increases in a great proportion as labour comes to be more and more subdivided;
and as the operations of each workman are gradually reduced to a greater degree
of simplicity, a variety of new machines come to be invented for facilitating and
abridging those operations. As the division of labour advances, therefore, in
order to give constant employment to an equal number of workmen, an equal
stock of provisions, and a greater stock of materials and tools than what would have
been necessary in a ruder state of things, must be accumulated beforehand.

(WN II.3)

Thus growth in industrial production will be accompanied by growth in
both raw materials (in volume, and relative price also in the case of some
minerals) and in fixed capital per worker.[16] The same is true in agriculture
where there is an increase in cattle and sheep per worker as development
continues, and in addition, as was noted earlier, the price of cattle will rise
relative to the cost of labour.

[13] 'Great nations are never impoverished by private, though they sometimes are by
public prodigality and misconduct. The whole, or almost the whole public revenue, is in
most countries employed in maintaining unproductive hands.' (WN II.iii.30).
[14] How difficult it is to return to Smith's assumptions is illustrated by Haim Barkai
whose stimulating modern restatement of Smith's theory of growth ('A Formal Outline of
Smithian Growth Model', *Quarterly Journal of Economics*, lxxxiii (Aug. 1969)) has
distinct saving and investment functions, where planned investment depends on the rate
of profit and planned saving on thriftiness conditions. In consequence he believes that
Smith needs an 'extreme' version of Say's law to achieve $I = S$.
[15] See Hollander, op. cit. 188–204, for a possible explanation of this.
[16] Spengler (op. cit. 7) has noted the importance of this line of argument in *The Wealth of
Nations*.

Now because raw materials and fixed capital requirements per head grow as capital accumulates, employment will not increase as quickly as the capital stock. Smith has Malthus-type arguments, though it will turn out that there are important differences, to show that population will expand with the demand for labour: '. . . the demand for men, like that for any other commodity, necessarily regulates the production of men; quickens it when it goes on too slowly, and stops it when it advances too fast' (WN I.viii.40). However, increased raw material and fixed capital costs per worker will act as a leakage which prevents population and employment from growing *pari passu* with the capital stock. Moreover, if wages also rise as capital accumulates, there will be a further 'leakage' of circulating capital—to the payment of higher wages per worker—which would reduce the rate of growth of employment still further in relation to the rate of growth of capital. Whether wages rise with the rate of growth of the capital stock is therefore a matter of some importance.

At first sight, it appears in contradiction to what was said at the start of the paper that wages will not rise continuously as capital accumulates, for as Hollander points out, it is apparently the *level* and not the rate of growth of wages that depends on the rate of capital accumulation.[17] Thus:

It is not the actual greatness of national wealth, but its continual increase, which occasions a rise in the wages of labour. It is not, accordingly, in the richest countries, but in the most thriving, or in those which are growing rich the fastest, that the wages of labour are highest. England is certainly, in the present times, a much richer country than any part of North America. The wages of labour, however, are much higher in North America than in any part of England.

(WN I.viii.22)

. . . it is in the progressive state, while the society is advancing to the further acquisition, rather than when it has acquired its full complement of riches, that the condition of the labouring poor, of the great body of the people, seems to be the happiest and the most comfortable. It is hard in the stationary, and miserable in the declining state.

(WN I.viii.43)

These passages, and others like them, suggest that Smith's theory of wages corresponds to that illustrated in Fig. 2 where the wage at different rates of growth of circulating capital is shown by the schedule WW. Where there is no growth of capital, the wage is oW_s, Malthus's 'natural' or 'subsistence' wage, and it will exceed this if capital is growing as in England, or better still, North America, and fall short of it if capital is declining as in Bengal.

If this were Smith's theory, a country with a faster rate of accumulation than another would need to pay higher wages, but once the wage in each country reached that shown in Fig. 2, no further increase in wages would

[17] See Hollander, op. cit. 157–8.

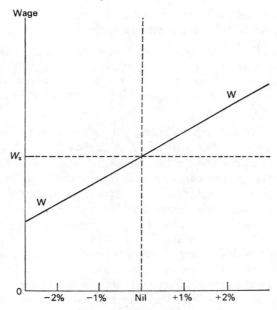

Fig. 2   *Rate of Growth of Capital*

be needed to produce the appropriate rate of population growth. Thus, if the rate of accumulation increased in any country, there would be a leakage into higher wages at first as part of the extra capital stock had to be diverted to the payment of higher wages per head, but this would cease once wages had risen sufficiently to produce the new rate of population growth. After this only extra fixed capital and raw materials per head would prevent employment from rising as fast as the capital stock.

However, the view that wages will reach the *level* appropriate to the rate of accumulation and then rise no further is only correct if two important qualifications are made. First, it must be possible for employment and population to grow fast enough to prevent a continuous rise in wages. This is evidently not always possible: 'Notwithstanding the great increase [in population] occasioned by such early marriages, there is a continual complaint of the scarcity of hands in North America. The demand for labourers, the funds destined for maintaining them, increase, it seems, still faster than they can find labourers to employ' (WN I.viii.23). Wages must obviously go on rising so long as this situation persists—and similar conditions have applied to many countries since 1776.[18] The second

[18] M. Blaug points out that wages may rise continuously in Smith's argument where the demand for labour grows faster than the supply in *Economic Theory in Retrospect* (1962), 46–7.

qualification is that, as Smith points out, the argument represented in Fig.
applies precisely to the wage measured in corn:

> . . . the money price of labour, which must always be such as to enable the labour
> to purchase a quantity of corn sufficient to maintain him and his family either
> the liberal, moderate, or scanty manner in which the advancing, stationary
> declining circumstances of the society oblige his employers to maintain him.
>
> (WN IV.v.a.1?

Hence, Fig. 2 corresponds to Smith's theory of wages if the vertical ax
shows wages measured in corn. Now, as capital accumulates and emplo⁻
ment grows, the prices of most manufactured goods will fall continuous
in relation to the price of corn as labour is more and more subdivided in th
manufacture of each good.[19] This means that the wage will rise when it
measured in manufactured goods, and this is precisely the line of argume⌐
that was presented at the start of the paper as the great feature th
distinguishes *The Wealth of Nations* from later classical writing.

To sum up Smith's theory of wages: measured in corn, only the level ⌐
wages will vary with the rate of growth of capital, but measured in man⌐
factured goods, the rate of change of wages will also vary with this so th
manufactured goods a worker can buy will rise continuously with capit
accumulation—as goods become cheaper relative to corn and labou⌐
Measured in cattle or poultry, wages fall as capital accumulates becau⌐
these become continuously dearer in relation to corn, but measured ⌐
vegetables, wages rise, and in Smith's opinion cheaper vegetables w⌐
matter more than dearer meat to most poorer workers (WN I.xi.m.10
Thus as the wealth and population of a country grow, workers may come ⌐
eat a little better or worse (depending on their relative expenditure ⌐
vegetables and meat), but they will enjoy a continuous growth in purchasir
power in terms of manufactured goods, and as only a small fraction of th
labour force is so poorly paid that most of its income must go on food, th
great majority of workers will gain substantially. Thus, as capital accum⌐
lates, most workers will become better off, and they will continue ⌐
become better off for so long as accumulation is able to continue. Th
means that as a society advances, employment will grow less quick⌐
than the capital stock, both because of the need to increase fixe
capital and raw materials per worker, and because wages per worker w⌐
rise—if these are thought of as a weighted average of corn, meat, an
manufactures.

The above argument suggests that Smith's theory of wages differs ⌐
several important respects from the 'iron law of wages' to which it is ofte

---

[19] It might be thought that the increased subdivision of labour would reduce the relati⌐
prices of all manufactured goods, but in a 'few' cases the unfavourable effects of rising ra⌐
material costs outweigh the favourable effects of increasing returns in the manufacturi⌐
process (see WN I.xi.o.2).

supposed that the classical economists all subscribed. This should not appear surprising. Malthus certainly thought that he had discovered something new in 1798, and he would have rejected the view that his theory of population and wages was all in Smith. There are, moreover, optimistic passages about the effect of economic development on living standards in *The Wealth of Nations* which have no parallel in the work of Malthus and Ricardo. It should not therefore be taken for granted as it often is that Smith's theory of wages was the same as that of his successors.

To turn now to profits, these are determined by two main considerations in *The Wealth of Nations*. On the one hand, capital accumulation reduces profits:

> The increase of stock, which raises wages, tends to lower profit. When the stocks of many rich merchants are turned into the same trade, their mutual competition naturally tends to lower its profit; and when there is a like increase of stock in all the different trades carried on in the same society, the same competition must produce the same effect in them all.
>
> (WN I.ix.2)

However, new investment opportunities raise the rate of return:

> The acquisition of new territory, or of new branches of trade, may sometimes raise the profits of stock, and with them the interest of money, even in a country which is fast advancing in the acquisition of riches . . . Part of what had before been employed in other trades, is necessarily withdrawn from them, and turned into some of the new and more profitable ones. In all those old trades, therefore, the competition comes to be less than before.
>
> (WN I.ix.12)

Perhaps the crucial factor is stock in relation to the business that is transacted, or in modern terms, the ratio of capital to output:

> In a country fully stocked in proportion to all the business it had to transact, as great a quantity of stock would be employed in every particular branch as the nature and extent of the trade would admit. The competition, therefore, would every-where be as great, and consequently the ordinary profit as low as possible.
>
> (WN I.ix.14)

This suggests that the rate of profit may rise or fall in the course of development, and that it should certainly tend to fall where the rate of capital accumulation much exceeds the rate of growth of output.

This completes the consideration of *The Wealth of Nations* that enables us to state the assumptions about returns to scale, capital accumulation, fixed capital requirements, and wages that are appropriate to a modern restatement of Smith's theory of growth. The essential assumptions that must be carried forward to Part II are that there will be increasing returns to scale in industry until a country's full potential for development is

realized, and constant or diminishing returns in agriculture and mining
that the ability to exploit the inherent potential for growth that follow
from increasing returns depends on capital accumulation which is a
function of the ratio of productive to unproductive employment and the
profitability of productive employment; and that fixed capital, raw
materials, and wages per head (as a weighted average of manufactures and
food) will all rise as the economy grows, while whether there is upward or
downward pressure on profits should depend largely on the relative growth
rates of capital and output. There is no production function where the
substitution of capital for labour depends on relative factor prices in *The
Wealth of Nations*.

II A WEALTH OF NATIONS GROWTH MODEL

In this section of the paper, the growth model that follows from the
assumptions arrived at in Part I will be presented in two stages. A very
simple version of the model will be presented first, and in this the com-
plicating effects of fixed capital will be ignored. It will emerge that it is
possible to arrive at most of Smith's results with a very simple circulating
capital model. However, fixed capital plays an important role in *The
Wealth of Nations*, and it will be brought into the second stage of the argument to produce a richer and more general model, though one that is a
little more complex than the circulating capital model that is presented
first.

It emerged in Part I that returns to scale play a crucial role in *The
Wealth of Nations*, and that they depend on the extent to which the tasks
performed by labour can be subdivided. A function which shows the effect
of this is:

$$Y = \lambda . L_p{}^Z \tag{1}$$

where Y is the output achieved in the very long run at each level of
productive employment, L_p, while λ is a constant, and Z shows whether
returns to scale are increasing, constant, or diminishing. If there are constant
returns, Z will equal 1 and doubling L_p will then double Y. If there are
increasing returns, Z will exceed 1, causing Y to vary more than proportionately with L_p, while it will vary less than proportionately if Z is less
than 1.[20] In the example from Smith's lectures that was quoted in Part I, a
ten-times increase in L_p raised Y a hundred times in industry, and this
result would be produced by a Z of 2.

It follows from (1) that:

$$g = Z . n_p \tag{2}$$

[20] Equation (1) can be written as $(Y/L_p) = \lambda . L_p{}^{Z-1}$, and this produces the schedule, AB
of Fig. 1, i.e. a rising straight line (on a double log scale) with a slope of $(Z-1)$.

where g is the long-term rate of growth of output ($1/Y . \mathrm{d}Y/\mathrm{d}t$), while n_p is the rate of growth of productive employment ($1/L_p . \mathrm{d}L_p/\mathrm{d}t$), so the long-term rate of growth of output is Z times the rate of growth of productive employment.

Of course, employment cannot be increased without capital accumulation, and two equations are relevant to the relationship between the rate of growth of employment and the rate of capital accumulation. First, there is the population supply equation, where the rate of growth of population and the labour force (and these will be assumed to grow at the same rate) depend on the rate of capital accumulation. This equation can be written as:

$$n = A . k_c \tag{3}$$

where n is the rate of growth of the total labour force ($1/L . \mathrm{d}L/\mathrm{d}t$), k_c is the rate of growth of circulating capital ($1/K_c . \mathrm{d}K_c/\mathrm{d}t$), and A is a constant. In a purely Malthusian model, A would be 1, but it will be less than 1 in a *Wealth of Nations* growth model because raw material[21] and possibly also wage costs per head[22] rise with capital accumulation. It is to be noted that the proposition that A is less than 1 (which will prove to be of crucial importance) does not rest solely on the argument that wages rise with capital accumulation. An increase in raw material costs per worker as capital accumulates is quite sufficient to make A less than 1, even if wages are entirely unaffected by the rate of capital accumulation.

The second equation that relates the rate of growth of employment to the rate of capital accumulation is the 'wages fund' equation that follows from the proposition that circulating capital is used to provide wages and raw materials prior to production. If the proportion of the labour force that is employed productively is q, it can be assumed, following Smith, that a fraction, q, of circulating capital, i.e. $q . K_c$ is used to provide wages and raw materials for L_p productive workers, and if the cost of providing wages and raw materials for each productive worker is W:

$$q . K_c = L_p . W. \tag{4}$$

Then, if q, the proportion of the labour force that is employed productively, is constant, the rate of growth of circulating capital will equal the rate of growth of productive employment *plus* the rate of increase in the cost of employing a worker, i.e.

$$k_c = n_p + w \tag{5}$$

where k_c and n_p are the rates of growth of circulating capital and productive

---

[21] See p. 436 above.   [22] See p. 439 above.

employment as before, while w is the rate of increase in the wage and raw material costs of employing a worker $(1/W . dW/dt)$.

If q is constant, $n_p = n$, and (2), (3), and (5) will then allow the long-term rates of growth of output, employment, and the wage and raw material costs of employing a worker to be expressed as multiples of the rate of growth of circulating capital. Thus:

$$g = A . Z . k_c \qquad (6)$$

$$n = n_p = A . k_c \qquad (7)$$

$$w = (1 - A) . k_c. \qquad (8)$$

Then the rate of growth of circulating capital determines the rates of growth of output, population, and wage and raw material costs per head, and a faster rate of capital accumulation will produce faster long-term rates of growth of each of these. Output may grow faster or more slowly than the capital stock, but population and wage and raw material costs per head must both grow more slowly than capital, since A must be less than 1.

To complete the model, what determines k_c, the rate of growth of circulating capital, must be set out. This has been worked out for a circulating capital model of the kind outlined here by Sir John Hicks, and his equation can be arrived at as follows.[23] Y_t, the output of productive workers in period t, can be regarded as the economy's circulating capital in period $(t + 1)$, so $K_{c,t+1} = Y_t$. An expression for $K_{c,t}$ can be obtained from (4), i.e.

$$K_{c,t} = \frac{1}{q}(L_{p,t} . W_t),$$

with the result that

$$\frac{K_{c,t+1}}{K_{c,t}} = q\left(\frac{Y_t/L_{p,t}}{W_t}\right).$$

Then:

$$\frac{K_{c,t+1} - K_{c,t}}{K_{c,t}} = q . \left(\frac{Y_t/L_{p,t}}{W_t}\right) - 1. \qquad (9)$$

Now $(K_{c,t+1} - K_{c,t})/K_{c,t}$ is the rate of growth of circulating capital per period. Up to now, k_c has been written for this, and these are equivalent but the correct form of the accumulation equation is necessarily a period one since one year's output is the next year's capital. (9) shows that the rate of growth of circulating capital depends on q, the proportion of the labour force employed productively, and on the ratio of output per productive worker, Y/L_p, to W, the cost of employing a worker, and this clearly corresponds to Smith's own argument. Thus, if for instance two economies

[23] See J. R. Hicks, *Capital and Growth* (1965), Ch. 4.

have equal technical opportunities for growth, and one has less un-productive employment than the other, i.e. a higher q, that economy will also have a faster rate of capital accumulation (from (9)), and therefore faster growth rates of output, population and wages per head (from (6), (7), and (8)).

The next step in the argument is to consider the question of whether the rate of capital accumulation will rise or fall through time. If q is given for various economies as is being assumed, the rate of capital accumulation will grow if $(Y/L_p)/W$ grows, i.e. if Y grows at a faster rate than $L_p . W$, and vice versa. The rate of growth of Y is g which equals $A . Z . k_c$ (from (6)), while the rate of growth of $L_p . W$ is $(n_p + w)$ which equals k_c (from (7) and (8)), so the rate of capital accumulation will rise through time if $A . Z . k_c$ exceeds k_c, and fall if $A . Z . k_c$ is less than k_c. This leads to the very simple condition:

$$\text{Rate of change of } k_c \gtrless 0 \quad \text{where } Z \gtrless 1/A. \tag{10}$$

Then, whether an economy will enjoy a rising or a falling rate of capital accumulation will depend simply on whether Z, the returns-to-scale variable, is greater or less than $1/A$, and $1/A$ must exceed 1 since A must be less than 1. Then accumulation can only continue at an increasing or constant rate in conditions where increasing returns predominate, and these must be sufficient to hold Z at or above $1/A$. Thus, it is to be noted that the mere existence of increasing returns will not be sufficient to produce indefinite progress.

It turns out that the relationship between Z and $1/A$ does not merely determine whether the rate of capital accumulation will rise or fall through time. It is evident from (6) that g will exceed k_c, i.e. that an economy will enjoy a rising output-capital ratio, if Z exceeds $1/A$, and vice versa.[24] More-over, as 'profits and rent' are the excess of output over wage and raw material costs, the share of 'profits and rent' in output will grow where $(Y/L_p)/W$ grows, and decline where this declines, so this too will depend on the relationship between Z and $1/A$. Where Z exceeds $1/A$, the share of 'profits and rent' in output will grow, and it will decline where Z is less than $1/A$. Furthermore, as (output/capital) rises where Z exceeds $1/A$, and (profits and rent)/output also rises,

$$\left(\frac{\text{output}}{\text{capital}}\right) \times \left(\frac{\text{profits and rent}}{\text{output}}\right) \text{ which equals } \left(\frac{\text{profits and rent}}{\text{capital}}\right)$$

must rise, and as profits are likely to gain in relation to rent where output

[24] In Irma Adelman's interesting restatement of Smith's theory of growth (*Theories of Economic Growth and Development* (1962)), Ch. 3, increasing returns together with capital accumulation always produce a falling marginal capital–output ratio. She arrives at this result because she does not allow for the need for increasing raw materials per worker. etc., as capital accumulates.

grows faster than capital, it is particularly clear that (profits/capital) or th
rate of return on capital will rise through time where Z exceeds $1/A$.

Three possible development paths for growing economies can then b
distinguished:

1. Where Z exceeds $1/A$, the rate of capital accumulation will increas
from period to period, while the capital–output ratio will fall and the rat
of profit on capital and the share of 'profits and rent' in output will rise
2. Where Z equals $1/A$, the rate of capital accumulation, the capital
output ratio, the rate of profit, and the share of 'profits and rent' will b
constant.
3. Where Z is less than $1/A$, the rate of capital accumulation, the rate c
profit, and the 'share of profits and rent' will fall continuously, while th
capital–output ratio will rise continuously, until capital accumulatio
ceases, and once capital accumulation ceases, there will be no furthe
change in the capital–output ratio, the rate of profit, etc.

Thus, whether Z is greater or less than $1/A$ is a matter of the utmos
importance. It is no wonder that there are numerous passages in *Th
Wealth of Nations* (which will be mentioned in Part III of this paper) wher
attention is drawn to the favourable effects on the long-term growtl
opportunities of the economy of growing demand for industrial goods a
home and abroad (as a result of the full exploitation of trading opportunities)
for these will increase the over-all Z of the economy since industry has ;
high Z.

The economy's Z will be high where the proportion of the labour forc
employed in industry is high, and the opportunities to benefit from a furthe
subdivision of labour are still considerable. If a point is reached wher
further subdivision produces diminishing benefits, Z will fall from perio
to period, and it must then eventually become less than $1/A$, however higl
its original starting point. The rate of capital accumulation will slow dow
as soon as Z becomes less than $1/A$, and the capital–output ratio will star
to rise, while the rate of profit on capital and the share of 'profits and rent
in output will both start to fall—until a point is reached eventually wher
accumulation ceases altogether, and a society will then have realized its ful
potential for development, given its ratio of unproductive employment, etc

These are the principal results that follow from the circulating capita
model that has been considered so far. It is now time to introduce fixe(
capital into the argument, and this can be done in the following way. U|
to now, it has been supposed that the employment of L workers will merel
require a circulating capital of $W.L$, and it can be assumed from this poin
onwards that a fixed capital of $\Phi.L^B$ will also be needed, where Φ is ;
constant, and B exceeds 1. With $B > 1$, fixed capital requirements will grov
more than proportionately with population and employment as Smitl

assumed. Writing K for total capital, K_c for circulating capital, and K_f for fixed capital, it is being assumed that:

$$K = K_f + K_c = \Phi.L^B + W.L. \tag{11}$$

The introduction of fixed capital will not alter the basic returns-to-scale equation which led to (2): more capital is now needed to provide employment for a given labour force, but its output can still be written as $\lambda.L^Z$.[25] Moreover, fixed capital will not affect the population supply equation or the wages fund equation ((3) and (5)), so (6), (7), and (8) will be unaltered. It is only (9), the capital accumulation equation, that will be altered, and this will be affected in the following way. It was assumed earlier that the entire output of period t became the circulating capital of period $(t+1)$ so that $Y_t = K_{c,t+1}$, but part of the output of period t will now need to consist of additions to fixed capital. Provided that Y_t is the output of period t *net* of the depreciation of fixed capital, Y_t will become the circulating capital of period $(t+1)$ *plus* the addition to fixed capital between periods t and $t+1$. Thus:

$$Y_t = K_{c,t+1} + (K_{f,t+1} - K_{f,t}).$$

Now $K_{c,t}$ will equal $1/q.L_{p,t}.W_t$ as before so that:

$$\frac{K_{c,t+1} - K_{c,t}}{K_{c,t}} = q\left(\frac{Y_t/L_{p,t}}{W_t}\right) - 1 - \frac{K_{f,t+1} - K_{f,t}}{K_{c,t}}.$$

As

$$A.B.K_{f,t}\left(\frac{K_{c,t+1} - K_{c,t}}{K_{c,t}}\right)$$

can be written for $(K_{f,t+1} - K_{f,t})$:[26]

$$\frac{K_{c,t+1} - K_{c,t}}{K_{c,t}} = \frac{q\left(\dfrac{Y_t/L_{p,t}}{W_t}\right) - 1}{1 + A.B.(K_{f,t}/K_{c,t})}. \tag{12}$$

Now a comparison between (9), the capital accumulation equation in the earlier circulating capital model, and the present capital accumulation equation shows that the rate of growth of capital in the earlier equation now has to be divided by $[1 + A.B.(K_f/K_c)]$. Thus the rate of growth of capital will always be lower (*cet. par.*) in the present fixed capital model.

---

[25] It is to be noted that Z will exceed 1 to a greater extent than before if increasing returns are stronger in a fixed capital model (and fixed capital certainly plays a substantial part in Smith's account of increasing returns in industry), but a higher Z would have no effect on the basic form of (2).

[26] $K_{f,t+1} - K_{f,t} = \phi.L^B_{t+1} - \phi.L^B_t = \phi.L^B_t((1+n)^B - 1) = n.B.\phi.L^B_t$ since n will be small in a single period. Now $K_{f,t}$ can be written for $\phi.L^B_t$, and $A.(K_{c,t+1} - K_{c,t})/K_{c,t}$ for n (from (7)) using the period form of this equation which is legitimate where n is small).

This is because the provision of fixed capital for extra workers is an additional factor in the capital cost of growth, so more resources will be needed, for instance a higher ratio of productive employment, to produce any given growth rate.

It was shown above that the critical condition for a constant rate of growth in the circulating capital model was that Z should equal $1/A$. Clearly, if Z equalled $1/A$ in (12), $(Y/L_\mathrm{p})/W$ would be constant, but the growth rate would still fall continuously if $K_\mathrm{f}/K_\mathrm{c}$ was rising, and rise if this was falling. Thus, if the ratio of fixed to circulating capital rose through time, the need to invest in fixed capital as employment grew would act as an increasing brake on accumulation, while it would act as a brake of diminishing intensity if the ratio of fixed to circulating capital was falling. Whether this ratio rises or falls through time is therefore important.

The ratio of fixed to circulating capital will rise if k_f, the rate of growth of fixed capital, exceeds k_c, the rate of growth of circulating capital, and vice versa. k_f is the rate of growth of K_f, i.e. the rate of growth of $\Phi.L^B$, and this is $B.n$, or $A.B.k_\mathrm{c}$ (from (7)) so that:

$$k_\mathrm{f}/k_\mathrm{c} = A.B. \tag{13}$$

Then the ratio of fixed to circulating capital will be constant if $A.B = 1$, i.e. if $B = 1/A$: and it will rise through time if B exceeds $1/A$, and fall if B is less than $1/A$. Hence, the need to provide fixed capital for a growing labour force will act as an increasing brake on growth if $B > 1/A$, and a diminishing brake if $B < 1/A$.

In the earlier circulating capital model, the rate of capital accumulation and the economy's other major variables were constant through time when Z equalled $1/A$, and this proposition will not be disturbed if the ratio of fixed to circulating capital is also constant, i.e. if B also equals $1/A$. Then the condition for a constant rate of growth, a constant rate of profit, a constant capital–output ratio, and constant distribution is that $B = Z = 1/A$.

Clearly the development of the economy through time will depend on how high B and Z are in relation to $1/A$. The simplest way of analysing the effect of values of B or Z that are inappropriate for a constant rate of growth is to assume in each case that the value of the other is appropriate, i.e. that $Z = 1/A$ where the value of B is inappropriate, and that $B = 1/A$ where Z is inappropriate. These possibilities will be considered in turn.

1. The effect of an inappropriate B

If B exceeds $1/A$ (and Z), the ratio of fixed to circulating capital will rise continuously, and this will reduce the rate of capital accumulation from period to period. Moreover, the capital–output ratio will rise continuously. Equality between Z and $1/A$ will ensure that the ratio of circulating capital to output is constant (from (6)), but as fixed capital rises continuously in relation to circulating capital, the over-all capital–output ratio must rise from period to period. Equality between Z and $1/A$ keeps the share of 'profits and rent' in output constant, but if a rising capital–output ratio acts against profits relative to rent, then the share of profits will fall and the share of rents rise. A rising capital–output ratio will reduce the rate of profit on capital, even if the share of profits is constant, and if this falls, the rate of profit will be doubly reduced. Hence a higher B than Z and $1/A$ will produce a declining rate of growth, a declining rate of profit, a rising capital–output ratio, and possibly a declining share of profits also. A lower B will produce the opposite effects.

2. *The effect of an inappropriate* Z

If Z exceeds B and $1/A$ where these are equal, the ratio of fixed to circulating capital will be constant, so the model will behave exactly as the circulating capital model that was analysed earlier, i.e. a higher Z will produce accelerating growth, a rising rate of profit, a rising share of profits, a falling capital–output ratio, etc. A lower Z will produce the opposite effects.

It appears then that the effects on the economy of a high B and a low Z are rather similar. The analysis has, of course, been simplified by focusing attention on one variable at a time. Smith may well have envisaged a growing ratio of fixed to circulating capital, especially in view of what he said about cattle, i.e. a B that exceeded $1/A$, and strong increasing returns for a time if a country could so arrange its affairs (through trading opportunities and so on) that it could take advantage of the potential gains from increasing returns in industry over a considerable range of its output: this being followed by a period where increasing returns became less important as the advantages from further subdivisions of labour diminished. Here Z would start high and then fall. If this was his view, then the present model would produce the result of either accelerating or declining growth while B and Z both exceeded $1/A$: the high Z would act as a stimulus and the high B as a brake, and either could exercise the dominant influence, though obviously a high enough Z would be bound to do so. Once Z fell, however, the high B and low Z (in relation to $1/A$ which must always exceed 1) would both act as an increasing brake on growth. Moreover, the high B and low Z would both reduce the rate of profit from period to period, etc. More will be said about the relationship between Smith's predictions in *The Wealth of Nations* and the predictions of the model in Part III, the concluding section of this paper.

However, before the present account of the model is completed, it may be worthwhile to relax one further assumption. Up to now, in the account that has been given, the various sectors of the economy have been considered together, so that Z has been a kind of weighted average of returns to scale in industry and agriculture, etc. Suppose instead that the various sectors are considered separately, starting with corn where it is clear Smith thought that Z was 1 (since he assumed constant costs), and that $1/A$ and B exceeded 1 because of the need to increase fixed capital (i.e. cattle) and raw materials per worker. With these assumptions, the rate of growth, the rate of profit, and the share of 'profits and rent' would all decline (at a rate depending on the extent to which B and $1/A$ exceeded Z), and the capital–output ratio would rise continuously, when these were all measured in corn. Then a declining rate of profit in agriculture would be the only possible result of the model, and assuming that profit rates are equalized between sectors, manufactured goods would have to be so priced that a declining rate of profit was also earned on the manufacture of these, with the result that the entire benefits from increasing returns would be more than reflected in lower prices. Real wages (measured in manufactured goods) would then benefit substantially. The agricultural part of this argument has perhaps a little too much of Ricardo in it, and it may well be more sensible to think of Smith's as a 'weighted average' model with each sector playing a part, rather than one where production conditions in the corn sector determine the rate of profit in the other sectors of the economy. However, Smith's chapter on corn bounties has a lot of Ricardo in it (though there may be some special pleading in this chapter), and the possibility that he had an underlying corn model of the kind considered in this paragraph in mind cannot be excluded. Both this model and the 'weighted average of sectors' model can be set out with the help of the basic relationships that have been outlined.

III THE RESULTS OF THE MODEL AND SOME OF ADAM SMITH'S CONCLUSIONS

The model, like *The Wealth of Nations*, attributes overwhelming importance to the rate of capital accumulation. Without this, population and the labour force would not grow, industry would not expand so the potential gains in productivity that could follow from increased subdivisions of labour could not be exploited, and the manufactured goods that workers could buy would not increase. The rate of capital accumulation itself depends on the proportion of the labour force that is employed productively, and on the efficiency of productive workers. The first three paragraphs of *The Wealth of Nations* bring out that these are, in Smith's view, the key factors, so the central features of the model certainly correspond to Smith's own view of what is crucial.

   This preliminary correspondence is not surprising, because an account of *The Wealth of Nations* could hardly be produced which failed to attribute overwhelming importance to accumulation and what causes it, and the virtues of thrift, '. . . every prodigal appears to be a public enemy, and every frugal man a public benefactor' (WN II.iii.25), and of economies in public expenditure. These were among Smith's main legacies to the nineteenth century.

A second central feature of the argument of the model is the role of increasing returns, and Smith devoted the first three chapters of *The Wealth of Nations* to the division of labour, so a modern account of his argument must allow these to play an equally crucial role. In the model that has just been outlined, the relationships between Z, the returns-to-scale variable, and A and B are crucial, and Z is perhaps best thought of as a weighted average of returns to scale in industry and agriculture. Hence, if Smith's view was similar, there should be a number of passages in *The Wealth of Nations* which speak of the crucial effect on the rate of development of an economy of the size of the industrial sector of the economy in relation to the agricultural. Perhaps two quotations will suffice to demonstrate the importance of building up a manufacturing sector:

A small quantity of manufactured produce purchases a great quantity of rude produce. A trading and manufacturing country, therefore, naturally purchases with a small part of its manufactured produce a great part of the rude produce of other countries; while, on the contrary, a country without trade and manufactures is generally obliged to purchase, at the expence of a great part of its rude produce, a very small part of the manufactured produce of other countries. The one exports what can subsist and accommodate but a very few, and imports the subsistence and accommodation of a great number. The other exports the subsistence and accommodation of a great number, and imports that of a very few only. The inhabitants of the one must always enjoy a much greater quantity of subsistence than what their own lands, in the actual state of their cultivation, could afford.

(WN IV.ix.37)

And two pages later:

Without an extensive foreign market, [manufactures] could not well flourish, either in countries so moderately extensive as to afford but a narrow home market; or in countries where the communication between one province and another was so difficult, as to render it impossible for the goods of any particular place to enjoy the whole of that home market which the country could afford. The perfection of manufacturing industry, it must be remembered, depends altogether upon the division of labour; and the degree to which the division of labour can be introduced into any manufacture, is necessarily regulated, it has already been shown, by the extent of the market.

(WN IV.ix.41)

There are also passages which speak of the benefits derived by European industry from the colonization of America (WN IV.vii.c.7), and of the advantages that are derived where the rich buy manufactures instead of employing servants, and these refer to other advantages of a demand for manufactures (WN II.iii.38–42).

Clearly capital accumulation and increasing returns play a central role in *The Wealth of Nations*, but there are other propositions in the book which do not at first sight fit the view that a thrifty society will enjoy indefinite progress as a result of increasing returns, provided that the market for manufactures grows. There are two types of proposition in *The Wealth of Nations* that do not correspond with this first approximation to Smith's argument, and these must be explained in any attempt to provide a modern reconstruction.

First, Smith argued that a given employment of capital in agriculture would provide a larger surplus for reinvestment (and therefore more growth of employment) than an equivalent investment of capital in industry —which apparently contradicts the view that growth is a function of the ratio of industrial to agricultural output. Thus:

When the capital of any country is not sufficient for all . . . purposes, in proportion as a greater share of it is employed in agriculture, the greater will be the quantity of productive labour which it puts into motion within the country; as will likewise be the value which its employment adds to the annual produce of the land and labour of the society. After agriculture, the capital employed in manufactures puts into motion the greatest quantity of productive labour, and adds the greatest value to the annual produce.

(WN II.v.19)

For

The labourers and labouring cattle, therefore, employed in agriculture, not only occasion, like the workmen in manufactures, the reproduction of a value equal to their own consumption, or to the capital which employs them, together with its owners' profits; but of a much greater value. Over and above the capital of the farmer and all its profits, they regularly occasion the reproduction of the rent of the landlord.

(WN II.v.12)

And, Smith adds:

It has been the principal cause of the rapid progress of our American colonies towards wealth and greatness, that almost their whole capitals have hitherto been employed in agriculture . . . Were the Americans, either by combination or by any other sort of violence, to stop the importation of European manufactures, and by thus giving a monopoly to such of their own countrymen as could manufacture the like goods, divert any considerable part of their capital into this employment, they would retard instead of accelerating the further increase in the value of their annual produce, and would obstruct instead of promoting the progress of their country towards real wealth and greatness.

(WN II.v.21)

Now these statements, which superficially contradict what has been said so far, follow directly from the model that was outlined in Part II. There, the rate of capital accumulation which determines the growth of employment depends very substantially on q, the ratio of productive employment, and on $(Y/L_p)/W$, the ratio of output per worker to the cost of employing a worker, and any increase in $(Y/L_p)/W$ will more than proportionately raise the rate of capital accumulation. Now, $(Y/L_p)/W$ is clearly highest in agriculture for the reasons that Smith gives, and it is even proper to include rent in Y/L_p for the purposes of this accumulation equation if there are constant costs in agriculture. However, the argument appeared incorrect to Smith's successors, for instance Ricardo,[27] but it follows directly from the re-statement of Smith's theory in this paper. The unimpeded use of resources in agriculture is central to the achievement of an adequate rate of capital accumulation, because the ratio of output per worker to the cost of employing a worker is highest in agriculture. However, the *effects* of accumulation as distinct from what causes this depend upon Z, and the effect of a Z greater than 1 will be more favourable, the higher the ratio of industrial output in total output. There is thus a trade-off between agriculture which favours the *rate* of accumulation, and industry which favours the *effects* of accumulation. Smith was fully aware of both propositions, but in the context of a world where some countries achieved no accumulation at all, while Great Britain and most other European countries had taken five hundred years to double the population they could support, (WN I.viii.23) the first priority could reasonably be the achievement of accumulation: and to obstruct this through *artificial* policies to raise Z by helping industry *at the expense* of agriculture was misguided, and these policies are criticized throughout Book III of *The Wealth of Nations*. In the case of North America, accumulation was so rapid that it was continuously raising wages even in terms of corn, and there was nothing to be gained by slowing down the rate of accumulation.

A second set of passages in *The Wealth of Nations* which stand in the way of the simple interpretation that accumulation and increasing returns will lead to unlimited progress are the passages which speak of the eventual completion of the accumulation process, after which wages and profits would both become low, for instance:

In a country which had acquired that full complement of riches which the nature of its soil and climate, and its situation with respect to other countries, allowed

[27] See Ricardo, *Principles (Works and Correspondence*, i), Ch. 26. Hollander, op. cit. 195, 280–7, has also suggested that this part of Smith's argument is 'unsound'. He has, however, seen the argument as the purely static one that the employment of capital in agriculture produces an *immediately* higher *level* of employment, and this only follows if capital costs per worker are lower in agriculture, which is not clear. He does not mention Smith's dynamic argument that agriculture produces a faster *rate of growth* of employment, as in North America, and therefore a level of employment that rapidly becomes higher.

it to acquire; which could, therefore, advance no further, and which was no·
going backwards, both the wages of labour and the profits of stock would probabl·
be very low.

(WN I.ix.14·

Here, there are low wages, low profits, and zero growth, even thougŀ
thriftiness conditions, etc., may be very favourable. The implication of 'fuľ
complement of riches' is, however, that gains from the division of labou·
are no longer possible. Once increasing returns cease in the model outlinec
in this paper, Z falls to 1 or below, and this leads to a declining rate o·
growth, a declining rate and share of profits, and a rising capital–output ratio
etc. Now, as the rate of capital accumulation falls, the wage (measured i·
corn) will fall which will restore profitability for a time, but the low Z wiŀ
always set profits on a downward path again until, as Smith says, the wag·
(in corn) has become appropriate to a stationary state, and profits will alsc
have fallen very low when this is reached. Thus, passages of the kind jus·
quoted are fully in line with the predictions of the model if it is assumec
that the benefits from the division of labour have upper limits.[28]

In the stationary state that has just been described, the wage is, of course
high in terms of manufactured goods, since the division of labour ha·
reached an upper limit, and Smith did not mention this, though it follow·
from his argument where there are many passages which explain that th·
relative prices of most manufactured goods must fall as a society progresses
and there is no suggestion that this trend is ever reversed. He spelt out th·
details of the stationary state no more than Keynes bothered to provide ·
detailed description of the ultimate destination of a Keynesian econom·
with the rentier 'euthanised', and the rate of profit reduced to negligibl·
proportions. Such propositions were not relevant to the main work o·
Smith and Keynes, which was to provide an account of the working of th·
economies that they lived in.

Smith was arguably as successful as Keynes in this great task. His wa·
recognized as an accurate and plausible account of the way in whicŀ
eighteenth-century economies worked by most of his contemporaries, anc
his influence on public policy was as great as that of Keynes, and, it ma·
turn out, longer lasting, for the central policy propositions of *The Wealth o,*
Nations dominated British economic policy and legislation for over ·
century.

[28] William O. Thweatt in 'A Diagrammatic Representation of Adam Smith's Growtŀ
Model', *Social Research*, xxiv, no. 2 (1957), shows a continuous increase in the rate o·
profit as capital accumulates, and following Schumpeter, he describes Smith's growtŀ
model as a 'hitchless' one. His diagrammatic representation clearly fails to take the factor·
which produce a declining rate of profit in *The Wealth of Nations* into account. A. Low·
mentions one of these in 'The Classical Theory of Growth', *Social Research*, xxi, no. ·
(1954), the article on which Thweatt's lucid diagram is based, but he says that a Smithiar
economy will move forward in 'dynamic equilibrium' in the absence of 'disturbances fron·
without'. See also the article by Lowe in this volume.

Smith did not, however, write out an account of his theory of growth and development that had the impact that it should have had on the thought of professional economists. Something like the model in this paper is needed to integrate increasing returns and the accumulation equation with his propositions about increasing raw material costs, etc., and while Smith may well have understood the full complexities of his argument—a great thinker will hardly arrive at consistent results by chance—he only published (and he may only have put on paper) what could be understood by all. Because of this, increasing returns in industry played virtually no part in the thought of his successors; their books omitted anything equivalent to Smith's first three chapters, and without this, a crucial element in classical economics was lost.[29]

[29] Cf. N. Kaldor, 'The Irrelevance of Equilibrium Economics', *Economic Journal*, lxxxii (Dec. 1972).

4

FRANÇOIS QUESNAY: A REINTERPRETATION
1. THE *TABLEAU ÉCONOMIQUE*

By W. A. ELTIS[1]

The class shall learn : 1° To know and understand the Tableau as it is . . . 2° After this, the assumptions will be changed . . . and they should be left to do the addition and work out the result themselves ; this to be continued until they can work out each case easily, be it of growth or decline. 3° When they are at this stage, we should come to the problems, that is to say of arbitrary disturbances to distribution . . .

This completes that part of education of this type which is absolutely necessary and indispensable for all those who have received enough education to learn the four first rules of arithmetic ; . . .—Victor de Riqueti, Marquis de Mirabeau, 1767.[2]

FRANÇOIS QUESNAY'S achievement is one of the most remarkable in the history of economics. He published his first article on an economic problem in 1756 when he was 62 years old, and in the following twelve years he produced a series of influential articles and successive versions of his famous *Tableau Économique*. He also became the centre of the first school of economists, the Physiocrats or Économistes of pre-revolutionary France. The Tableau has two multipliers, one of them almost Keynesian, and Leontief has said that he was following Quesnay when he constructed his input-output table of the United States economy in 1941.[3] Marx, who according to Schumpeter derived his fundamental conception of the economic process as a whole from Quesnay,[4] called it '. . . an extremely brilliant conception, incontestably the most brilliant for which political economy had up to then been responsible',[5] and in 1935 Schumpeter himself described Quesnay as one of the four greatest economists of all time.[6]

Born the son of a farmer, Quesnay first achieved distinction as a surgeon, becoming Secretary of the French Association of Surgeons, a member of the French Academy of Sciences, and a Fellow of the Royal Society of London. In addition he became one of four consultant doctors

[1] The author is grateful to J. W. Y. Higgs, E. F. Jackson, M.FG. Scott, and J. F. Wright for very helpful comments on an earlier draft of this paper.

[2] Georges Weulersse, *Les Manuscrits économiques de François Quesnay et du Marquis de Mirabeau aux Archives Nationales*, Paris, 1910, p. 96 (E). (E) after a page reference signifies that the responsibility for the translation is the present author's.

[3] Wassily W. Leontief, *The Structure of American Economy 1919–39*, Oxford University Press, New York, 1941, p. 9.

[4] Joseph A. Schumpeter, *Capitalism, Socialism and Democracy*, Allen and Unwin, London, 1943, p. 22.

[5] Karl Marx, *Theories of Surplus Value (Volume IV of Capital)*, Lawrence and Wishart, London, 1961, vol. i, p. 344.

[6] See Paul A. Samuelson, 'Economists and the history of ideas', *American Economic Review*, vol. lii, Mar. 1962, pp. 3–4.

to King Louis XV, with an entresol at Versailles where he was also Madame de Pompadour's private physician.[1] His first economic publications were two articles, *Fermiers* (1756) and *Grains* (1757), which Diderot and D'Alembert published in the Encyclopedia, and these provide a more detailed account of the agriculture of the time than the work of any other great classical economist, and they set out the foundations of Quesnay's theory of the working of economies, and the policies needed to ensure France's recovery from expensive wars and rural depopulation. The first edition of the Tableau followed a year later, and this was gradually modified and refined until, in 1764, Quesnay's principal collaborator, Victor de Riqueti, Marquis de Mirabeau, was able to write in a Preface to *Philosophie rurale*, the book (written with Quesnay) which 'provides the most complete and authentic account of the Physiocratic system considered as a whole',[2] that he was providing all the propositions needed to form an exact and complete theory of the working of economies, and:

> The *Tableau Économique* is the first rule of arithmetic which has been invented to reduce elementary economic science to precise and exact calculations . . .
> Calculations are to economic science what bones are to the human body . . . economic science is deepened and extended by examination and reasoning, but without calculations it will always be an inexact science, confused and everywhere open to error and prejudice.[3]

By 1764 Quesnay had indeed evolved a complete model of the working of economies as Mirabeau claims, and this allowed the full *dynamic* effects of changes in, for instance, the productivity of the soil, taxation, and the propensities to consume food and manufactures to be estimated. However, subsequent writers who have attempted to reconstruct the model have faced considerable difficulties, for each version of the argument, read in isolation, contains assertions that have no clear logical basis, and apparent gaps in the argument, inconsistencies, and puzzling calculations. Almost all the problems are solved, however, and the apparent inconsistencies removed when Quesnay's published works are read as a whole (and most have still been published only in French), and in addition, the important books he wrote in collaboration with Mirabeau, in particular Part VI of *L'Ami des hommes*[4] entitled 'Tableau Économique avec ses Explications', and *Philosophie rurale*. Clearly only scholars with a particular interest in his work will go to this much trouble to understand

[1] See Jacqueline Hecht, 'La Vie de François Quesnay', which is published in *François Quesnay et la Physiocratie*, Institut National d'Études Demographiques, Paris, 1958. This two-volume publication contains the most recent and complete edition of Quesnay's works, and it will be referred to subsequently as *Quesnay*.

[2] This is the view of Louis Saleron, the editor of *Quesnay* (see p. 687).

[3] *Philosophie rurale*, Amsterdam, 1764 (reprinted in 1972 by Scientia, Verlag Aalen), vol. i, pp. xl–xli (E). It is to be noted that there are two 1764 Amsterdam editions with different pagination. The first edition was published in 1763.

[4] *L'Ami des hommes*, Avignon, 1756–60 (reprinted by Scientia, Verlag Aalen in 1970).

him, but those like Schumpeter who persevered until they understood the model developed a great admiration for its originator.

In this and a following paper on François Quesnay's theory of economic growth, an attempt will be made to present a modern reconstruction of Quesnay's account of the working of economies. In the present paper an account will be given of the basic assumptions on which his analysis is based, and how these lead directly to the famous *Tableau Économique*. The successive versions of the Tableau will then be explained. In the paper that will follow on Quesnay's theory of economic growth, the effects of departures from the Tableau's equilibrium proportions will be shown. As in Marx's analysis, the scheme of simple reproduction depicted in the Tableau is merely the starting-point for the analysis of real problems, and any departure from the Tableau's exact equilibrium proportions must produce clearly analysable effects, including growth or decline in the economy's level of output and employment. The conditions which produce growth and decline will be systematically set out, and it will be shown that they are precisely those that Quesnay emphasized when he discussed real economies.

Quesnay's assumptions

In this part of the paper, Quesnay's basic assumptions about the factors which influence the development of economies will be outlined in turn. The first stage of the exposition is an account of his assumptions about techniques of production in agriculture and industry and their effectiveness, for this leads to the fundamental Physiocratic proposition that only agriculture produces a surplus or 'net product' over costs (where these arguably include a 'normal profit'), the size of the surplus depending on the capital intensity of agriculture. The second stage of the exposition which follows directly from this is an account of Quesnay's remarkable assumption that the economy's effective demand for marketable output depends on the expenditure of the agricultural surplus by landlords which has a multiplier effect on demand, and the further assumption that the relative size of the agricultural and industrial sectors of the economy depends upon how demand is distributed between them. The best known Physiocratic propositions all follow from these assumptions, i.e. that agriculture which alone produces a 'net product' must be the ultimate source of all tax revenue: that the economy cannot grow without agricultural growth: and that the industrial sector is wholly dependent on the agricultural, since the demand for manufactures depends on the size of the 'net product' which is wholly derived from agriculture.

The foundation of the whole system of thought is Quesnay's analysis of agricultural techniques of production which he first outlined in his

170   FRANÇOIS QUESNAY: A REINTERPRETATION

Encyclopedia articles of 1756 and 1757. There he distinguished three techniques of production: the cultivation of land with labour alone, cultivation with ox-drawn ploughs, and cultivation with horse-drawn ploughs.

Where labourers cannot find employment with a *métayer* using oxen or a farmer using horses:

. . . they leave the countryside, or else they are reduced to feeding themselves on oatmeal, barley, buckwheat, potatoes, and other cheap products which they grow themselves, and which they don't need to wait long to harvest. The cultivation of corn takes too much time and effort; they cannot wait two years for a crop.[1] Its cultivation is reserved for the farmer who can meet the expense, or the *métayer* who is helped by the landlord . . . [1756][2]

and:

When the peasant works the soil himself, it is evidence of his wretchedness and uselessness. Four horses cultivate more than a hundred *arpents* [125 acres]; four men cultivate less than eight. [1756][3]

and finally:

A poor man who only draws from the land by his labour produce of little value such as potatoes, buckwheat, chestnuts, etc., who feeds himself on them, who buys nothing and sells nothing, works only for himself: he lives in wretchedness, and he and the land he tills bring nothing to the state. [1757][4]

Thus, where farming must be undertaken without the capital of either a landlord or a rich farmer who employs others, there is no marketable agricultural surplus. The standard of living is so low that anything which reduces it further causes actual deaths through starvation,[5] and the peasant can pay no rent to the owner of the land. He thus makes no contribution to his landlord, the Church, or the State.

However, a surplus can be earned with the two alternative techniques, the cultivation of the land with ploughs drawn by either oxen or horses, and Quesnay makes a series of detailed comparisons between these techniques.[6] Before the economic differences are examined, there is an important institutional difference:

It is only wealthy farmers who can use horses to work the soil. A farmer who sets himself up with a four-horse plough must incur considerable expenditure before he obtains his first crop: for a year he works the land which he must sow with corn, and after he has sown he only reaps in the August of the following year: thus he waits almost two years for the fruits of his work and his outlay. He has incurred the expense of the horses and the other animals that he needs; he provides the seed

---

[1] Quesnay assumes a system of crop rotation where the land is ploughed but left fallow in the year before it is sown with corn. This was widely used in the eighteenth century (see B. H. Slicher van Bath, *Agrarian History of Western Europe 500–1850*, Edward Arnold, 1963, pp. 59, 244–5).   [2] *Quesnay*, pp. 446–7 (E).   [3] *Quesnay*, p. 453 (E).
[4] *Quesnay*, p. 498 (E).   [5] See *Quesnay* [1757], p. 553.
[6] Cf. the much less detailed comparisons in Fitzherbert, *Booke of Husbandrye*, 1534, Folio 6, 'Whither is better a plow of horses, or a plow of oxen'.

corn for the ground, he feeds the horses, he pays for the wages and the food of the servants; and all these expenses he is obliged to advance for the first two years' cultivation of a four-horse-plough demesne are estimated to be 10 or 12 thousand livres: and 20 or 30 thousand livres in a farm large enough for two or three plough teams.[1]

In the provinces where there are no farmers able to obtain such establishments, the only way in which the landlords can get some produce from their land is to have it cultivated with oxen by peasants who give them half the crop. This type of cultivation calls for very little outlay on the part of the *métayer*; the landlord provides him with oxen and seed corn, and after their work the oxen feed on the pasture land; the total expenditure of the *métayer* comes down to the ploughing equipment and his outlay for food up to the first harvest, and the landlord is often obliged to advance even these expenses. [1756][2]

Thus farming with horse-drawn ploughs which Quesnay calls '*la grande culture*' is undertaken by entrepreneurial *farmers*, while ox-drawn ploughs are used by *métayers* and Quesnay calls this kind of farming '*la petite culture*'. Where entrepreneur farmers are not available, landlords cannot have their land cultivated with horse-drawn ploughs, for:

. . . they would not find *métayers* or ploughmen [*charretiers*] able to handle and supervise horses in these provinces. They would have to arrange for them to come from far away, which could involve considerable inconvenience, for if a qualified ploughman falls ill or retires, work ceases. Such events are highly damaging, especially in busy seasons: and besides the master is too dependent on his servants, whom he cannot easily replace when they wish to leave, or when they work badly. [1756][3]

This means that the availability of rich farmers is the crucial factor that determines which technique is used. As soon as *la grande culture* and *la petite culture* are compared in detail, it emerges that the use of ox-drawn ploughs has great disadvantages. First, many more oxen are needed:

The work of oxen is much slower than that of horses: besides the oxen spend a lot of time grazing on the pastures for their own food; that is why normally twelve oxen, and sometimes as many as eighteen are needed in a farm which can be worked by four horses. [1756][4]

These large numbers of oxen need to be fed:

These oxen eat up the hay from his meadows, and a large part of the land of his demesnes remains fallow for their pasture; thus his property is badly cultivated and almost worthless. [1756][5]

Moreover, the oxen will be used part of the time for the peasants' own profit:

. . . the *métayers* who share the crop with the owner keep the oxen entrusted to them busy as often as they can by pulling carts for their own profit, which is more in their interests than ploughing the land; thus they so neglect its cultivation that most of the land stands fallow if the landlord fails to pay attention . . . [1756][6]

[1] See *Quesnay*, p. 428 (E)   [2] *Quesnay*, p. 428 (E).   [3] *Quesnay*, p. 429 (E).
[4] *Quesnay*, p. 429 (E).   [5] *Quesnay*, p. 445 (E).   [6] *Quesnay*, p. 431 (E).

172   FRANÇOIS QUESNAY: A REINTERPRETATION

The land which the oxen need for pasture, and the land that is otherwise uncultivated can be very profitably stocked with other animals. Quesnay specifies herds of sheep, beef cattle, calves, pigs, and poultry, but he points out that these cannot be entrusted to *métayers*. A particularly important point here is the manure that is obtained from the herds that can be stocked when the horse-drawn plough technique is used by rich farmers: Quesnay suggests that this may almost double grain yields.[1] Moreover, with the assumptions of *la grande culture* a wide variety of products can be grown by the rich farmers on land that is not quite good enough for wheat farming, and these are outlined in *Grains*.[2]

Quesnay makes detailed comparisons between the profitability of *la petite culture* and *la grand culture* in the context of the France of the 1750s, costing horses, oxen, animal feeding stuffs, farm workers, etc., and making assumptions about soil yields with the various techniques, and the prices at which grains will be sold over an average of good and bad harvests. He summarizes his results as follows:

It has been seen from the previous details that the cost of farming 30 million *arpents* of land with *la petite culture* is only 285 million [livres]; and that one would have to lay out 710 million to farm 30 million *arpents* with *la grande culture*; but in the first case the product is only 390 million [livres], and it would be 1,378 million in the second. Even greater outlays would produce still greater profits; the costs and men needed in addition with the best methods of cultivation for the purchase and management of farm animals bring in on their side a product which is scarcely less than that of the crops.[3] [1757]

With *la petite culture* the *net product* or the excess of output over the annual costs of agriculture is 390 *minus* 285 million livres, or 105 million livres, and the ratio of this to annual expenditure, one of the crucial ratios of the Physiocrats, is $\frac{105}{285}$ or 36 per cent. With *la grande culture* the *net product* is 1,378 *minus* 710 million livres, or 668 million livres, and 710 million livres of annual advances then yield a rate of return of $\frac{668}{710}$ or 93 per cent, which Quesnay later rounds up to 100 per cent, legitimately in view of the fact that not all the products of agriculture have been included in the actual calculations.

These are rates of return on what Quesnay calls the 'annual advances' or circulating capital—the equivalence is nearly exact—of agriculture, i.e. the investment in raw materials, wages, etc., that must be made each year to produce a harvest. Farmers must also provide 'original advances' or fixed capital, i.e. animals including horses in particular, ploughs, farm buildings, etc., which do not need to be paid for each year, but these depreciate, or need regular replacement and it is assumed that 'interest' at a rate of 10 per cent must be earned on the total capital of farmers to

---

[1] *Quesnay*, pp. 430–1.   [2] *Quesnay*, p. 477.   [3] *Quesnay*, pp. 504–5 (E).

cover this.[1] In his later writings Quesnay assumes that the original advances of farmers are four or five times their annual advances with the methods of *la grande culture*[2] (no figure for *la petite culture* is given) and a rate of return on annual advances of 100 per cent will be 20 per cent on total farm capital if original advances or fixed capital are four times annual advances, so that total capital is five times annual advances. Similarly, the rate of return with *la petite culture* will be less than 36 per cent, and if original advances or fixed capital with this technique are twice annual advances, the rate of return on total capital will be about 12 per cent.

It will be evident that Quesnay attributes overwhelming importance to the agricultural technique of production. With no agricultural capital, grain farming is impossible, and the commercial yield of agriculture is zero, while the standard of living is barely sufficient to support life. With the low capital per acre ox-drawn-plough technique, agriculture yields a return over annual advances of between 30 and 40 per cent and a return on total capital of perhaps 12 per cent, while with the capital intensive horse-drawn-plough technique, agriculture can yield 100 per cent on annual advances and perhaps 20 per cent on total capital. With the assumptions of modern economics, the horse-drawn-plough technique which is superior at virtually all factor prices would rapidly drive *la petite culture* out of existence, but it must be remembered that the institutional factors which Quesnay enumerated prevent this. Thus, only rich farmers can use the techniques of *la grande culture*, so landlords must have recourse to *métayers* who will farm with the techniques of *la petite culture* if there are too few rich farmers. Moreover, in the absence of banks able to lend at moderate rates of interest, farmers cannot add significantly to their own capital by borrowing, so the supply of capital of the rich farmers is inelastic.

It is interesting to contrast Quesnay's very detailed assumptions about agricultural techniques with the propositions of his great successors. Thus Ricardo who believed that farm workers must generally produce high outputs on good land apparently thought that '. . . the adoption of

---

[1] In addition to the annual and original advances of the farmers, landlords' advances (*avances foncières*) to make the land fit for farming are also needed. These are hardly ever mentioned by Quesnay himself, but they play a considerable part in the work of later Physiocratic writers; L'Abbé Baudeau in particular saw rent as partly a return on the *avances foncières* of the landlords (*Explication du Tableau Économique à Madame de ****, 1770, included in E. Daire's *Physiocrates* of 1846 which Otto Zeller, Osnabrück, reprinted in 1966, pp. 822–67).

[2] In the 'Explication du Tableau Économique' of 1759, annual advances are said to be 1,050 million livres and original advances 4,333 million livres (*Quesnay's Tableau Économique*, edited M. Kuczynski and R. L. Meek, Macmillan, 1972, 3rd edition (1759) pp. v and viii), while in the 'Analyse de la formule arithmétique du Tableau Économique' of 1766 original advances are said to be five times annual advances. (*Quesnay*, p. 795.)

spade husbandry, and the dismissal of the horses and oxen from the work of the farm' might reduce agricultural output by about one-tenth.[1] According to Quesnay this would entirely destroy any agricultural surplus, and reduce the farmers to penury. In his account of agriculture, it is capital and not labour or land that is of crucial importance:

Inefficient cultivation however requires much work; but as the cultivator cannot meet the necessary expenses his work is unfruitful; he succumbs: and the stupid bourgeois attribute his bad results to idleness. They probably believe that all that is needed to make the land bear good crops is to work it and agitate it; there is general approval when a poor man who is unemployed is told 'go and work the land'. It is horses, oxen, and not men who should work the land. It is herds which should fertilize it; without these aids it scarcely repays the work of the cultivators. Don't people know besides that the land gives no payment in advance, that on the contrary it makes one wait a long time for the harvest? What then might be the fate of that poor man to whom they say 'go and work the land'? Can he till for his own account? Will he find work with the farmers if they are poor? The latter, powerless to meet the costs of good cultivation, in no state to pay the wages of servants and workers, cannot employ the peasants. The unfertilized and largely uncultivated land can only let them all languish in wretchedness. [1757][2]

And finally, even the farmer must not be regarded as one who obtains his income from work. This is not what is needed:

We do not see the rich farmer here as a worker who tills the soil himself; he is an entrepreneur who manages his undertaking and makes it prosper through his intelligence and his wealth. Agriculture carried on by rich cultivators is an honest and lucrative profession, reserved for free men who are in a position to advance the considerable sums the cultivation of the land requires, and it employs the peasants and gives them a suitable and assured return for their work. [1757][3]

Thus capital in the hands of rich entrepreneurs who are willing to farm is the mainspring of an efficient agriculture, which will provide employment at good wages on the land. It is interesting in this context that Quesnay suggests that a rate of return of 100 per cent or more really is earned on annual agricultural advances in England where *la grande culture* predominates and there are sufficient rich entrepreneurs who are willing to farm. The contrast between England which has an efficient agriculture, and France which does not, is brought out several times.[4]

Quesnay assumes quite clearly that capital and entrepreneurs are the only factors of production that are needed to expand agricultural production, for he states quite specifically that the availability of land and labour is not a problem. So far as land is concerned, he writes:

The cultivation of corn is very expensive; we have far more land than we need for it ... [1757][5]

[1] David Ricardo, *Works and Correspondence*, edited P. Sraffa, Cambridge, 1951, vol. ii, pp. 237–8.   [2] *Quesnay*, p. 505 (E).   [3] *Quesnay*, p. 483 (E).
[4] See, for instance, *Quesnay* [1757], p. 479, *Quesnay's Tableau Économique*, 3rd edition (1759), p. 20 and *Quesnay* [1763], pp. 713–19 where it is argued that a rate of return of 150 per cent on annual agricultural advances is earned in England.
[5] *Quesnay*, p. 473 (E).

In the Kingdom there are 30 million *arpents* of cultivable land which are fallow, and the rest is poorly cultivated; because the production of grains does not repay the outlay. [1757][1]

and he quotes approvingly from De Plumart de Danguel:

If one travels through some of the provinces of France, one finds that not only does much of the land that could produce corn or nourish animals lie fallow, but that the cultivated lands do not produce anything approaching what they could, given their fertility; because the farmer lacks the means to bring them to their true value. [1757][2]

There are also numerous passages where Quesnay speaks of the rural devastation of whole provinces, and the depopulation that followed taxes that were unfavourable to agriculture. Clearly scarcity of land will not act as an obstacle to development, nor will the availability of labour. Quesnay follows Cantillon who wrote 'Men multiply like mice in a barn if they have unlimited means of subsistence . . .',[3] and it was very much his view that the growth of capital determined the growth of population. Thus:

It is however only with the help of wealth that an agricultural state can enrich itself more and more; *for an abundance of wealth contributes more than an abundance of men to the growth of wealth; but on the other hand the growth of wealth increases the number of men in all remunerative occupations.*[4] [1757]

It is therefore through the increase of wealth that a nation can achieve the greatest advances in wealth, population and power. It would then be in vain for it to try to increase the number of men without first setting out to increase wealth.[5] [1757]

Moreover

If the government diverts wealth from the source which reproduces it perpetually, it destroys wealth and men. [1757][6]

and more fully:

Men bereft of edible wealth could not live in a desert, they would perish there if they found no animals or other natural products to feed themselves on up to the time when by their labours they had forced the land to supply them with the products necessary to satisfy their needs continuously. Hence wealth is needed in advance to obtain in succession other wealth to live on, and to come to live in comfort which favours propagation. A Kingdom where revenues are growing attracts new inhabitants through the earnings it can procure for them; therefore the growth of wealth increases the population. [1757][7]

Hence lack of population would not be an obstacle to growth. With land also available, it is abundantly clear that Quesnay believed that the accumulation of agricultural capital was what was primarily necessary to produce growth of output and population.

[1] *Quesnay*, pp. 549–50 (E).   [2] *Quesnay*, p. 493 (E).
[3] R. Cantillon, *Essai sur la nature du commerce en général*, 1755 ed. and translated H. Higgs, London, 1931.   [4] *Quesnay*, p. 570 (E). The italics are Quesnay's.
[5] *Quesnay*, p. 571 (E).   [6] *Quesnay*, p. 542 (E).   [7] *Quesnay*, pp. 537–8 (E).

Quesnay gave a detailed account of his assumptions about how labour and capital had to be combined to produce food with the various techniques of production he described, but he was at no point so explicit about the sectors of the economy responsible for manufacturing, personal services, transport, commerce, and trade—which he called 'sterile'. The choice of the word 'sterile' to describe the sectors of the economy responsible for these activities proved unfortunate and many nineteenth- and twentieth-century economists concluded that Quesnay's and the Physiocrats' analyses of the working of economies need not be taken seriously because of the absurdity that they regarded manufacturing as sterile. However, if Quesnay's assumptions about manufacturing and commerce are followed carefully, and the word 'sterile' is put on one side until what he is saying becomes clear, it emerges that Quesnay's propositions are not very far from the analysis of the relationship between industrial costs and prices that subsequently became conventional. Thus in 1757 Quesnay gave the following account of the connection between industrial costs and prices:

> The works of manufacture demand from those who make them expenditures and costs which are equal to the value of the manufactured goods; . . .
> . . . the workman who makes a cloth buys the raw material and lays out the expenditure for his own needs while he is making it; the payment he receives when he sells it reimburses him what he has bought and his expenses; what he receives from his work is only the restitution of the expenses he has incurred, and it is by this restitution that he is able to continue to live by his work. The competition of workers who seek a similar return to live on limits the price of the work of manufacturing to this same return. [1757][1]

Thus competition ensures that the prices of manufactures are no more than the raw material and labour costs required to produce them. There is thus apparently no allowance for profits in the prices of manufactures. However, it is evident from Quesnay's work taken as a whole that the wages that manufacturers receive include something that is very close to the modern concept of a 'normal profit'. In 1763 he set out the incomes of all the workers of the economy in very great detail in Chapter 7 of *Philosophie rurale* which he contributed, and in manufacturing, commerce, etc., he assumed that there were 300,000 '*Gagistes supérieurs*' who earned an average of 2,000 livres each, and 1,800,000 '*Gagistes inférieurs*' or artisans who earned an average of 500 livres each.[2] The entrepreneurs in agriculture who farmed two four-horse-plough demesnes had an average income of just 1,200 livres, while servants and agricultural workers had incomes ranging from 125 to 500 livres a year.[3] Of the 1,200 livres that the farmer or agricultural entrepreneur received, 600 livres were for 'their subsistence and that of their family', while the whole 1,200 livres were

[1] *Quesnay*, p. 583 (E).   [2] *Quesnay*, p. 712.   [3] *Quesnay*, pp. 702–3.

for 'the enterprise of working two demesnes', which included a return for 'the work and risks of his enterprise'.[1] Clearly the *'Gagiste supérieur'* in industry who received 2,000 livres also received a return for enterprise and risk, i.e. a return which is not so far from the concept of a 'normal profit'.[2] There is no specific reference to a return to an entrepreneur's own capital, i.e. to profits on capital, as part of this 'normal profit', but it is most reasonable to think of the excess of the entrepreneur's income over subsistence as a return to the entrepreneurial capital he has to supply, and a return to enterprise and risk taking, and several of the passages that have been quoted make it very clear that entrepreneurs had to provide a great deal of capital to earn the kind of incomes that have been set out. Unfortunately the position is not quite as clear as this because agricultural entrepreneurs also receive 'interest' to provide for the depreciation and replacement of their capital, and to provide a margin against contingencies. There is no reference at any point to similar provisions in industry (although in the detailed account of the income and capital of the economy in the 'Explication du Tableau Économique' of 1759, industry was assumed to require the same fixed and working capital in relation to output as agriculture[3]). Quesnay's failure to refer to 'interest' in industry is usually regarded as a simplifying assumption, and it is most natural to assume that the return to industrial entrepreneurs which is set so high in relation to subsistence includes a return to risk and enterprise, and sufficient income to make it worth while for industrial entrepreneurs to continue their activities, i.e. that it includes what is now regarded as a 'normal profit'—the return that must be earned if they are to maintain constant output.

A point that should be noted here is that industry resembles agriculture in that 'advances' are needed for production, and in the subsequent *Tableau Économique* these advances (principally raw materials which must be bought in advance) form half of industrial costs, so output is twice annual advances in both the 'productive' and the 'sterile' sectors. However, in agriculture this doubling of advances produces a surplus as

---

[1] *Quesnay*, pp. 702–3 (E).

[2] It is interesting that Professor R. L. Meek has suggested that 'In particular, a number of the problems of interpretation which have subsequently arisen are cleared up in the seventh chapter [of *Philosophie rurale*] which seems to have been written largely by Quesnay himself and which has been unduly neglected by most modern interpreters' (*The Economics of Physiocracy*, Allen and Unwin, 1962, p. 278. This book is referred to subsequently as Meek).

[3] *Quesnay's Tableau Économique*, 3rd edition, pp. viii–ix. The annual advances of the 'sterile' sector are said to be 525 million livres, and the original advances for 'tools, machines, mills, forges, and other works, etc.' 2,000 million livres. This has led R. V. Eagly to reconstruct Quesnay's argument with a sterile sector that produces the fixed capital for *both* sectors ('A physiocratic model of dynamic equilibrium', *Journal of Political Economy*, vol. 77, Jan./Feb. 1969. See also his *The Structure of Classical Economic Theory*, Oxford University Press, 1974, Chapter 2).

substantial further costs are not incurred, while in industry further costs, mainly the wage costs of working up raw materials into manufactures, are incurred as production proceeds, so the fact that output is twice advances does not mean that a surplus is produced, and in formal terms a rate of return of zero is earned on the advances of the 'sterile' sector. With the present interpretation of Quesnay's argument, the 'normal profits' on these are included in the exceptional income of the *'Gagistes supérieurs'*, which is part of total wage and salary costs.

The fundamental assumptions which underlie the basic Physiocratic propositions that industry produces no surplus over costs while agriculture can produce a surplus if it is sufficiently capital intensive have now been outlined. The argument is basically that agriculture can earn something over and above costs (where these include a 'normal profit') while industry and commerce cannot. The extra earning power of agriculture is called its 'net product', and this is paid as rent or 'revenue' to the landlords. It is, however, basically a return on capital and not land, and it varies with the capital intensity of agriculture. The fundamental question arises of why 'labour and capital' can produce a surplus over wages and normal profits in agriculture and not in industry. Competition between entrepreneurs prevents the emergence of a surplus over costs in industry,[1] so an increase in industrial efficiency will eventually cheapen products and not produce a surplus for the producers. In contrast, an increase in agricultural efficiency supposedly increases the size of the agricultural net product or surplus. The fundamental assumption that allows Quesnay to arrive at this result, and it is also made by the great English classical economists, is that agricultural costs are largely fixed in terms of food. Thus the subsistence needs of farm labourers which determine what they are paid in the long run with an elastic supply of population are largely food,[2] and the farmer-entrepreneur gets a multiple of what labourers get. As the product of a farm is also food, an increase in agricultural efficiency, i.e. in food production per farm, must raise output relatively to agricultural costs (which can both be measured in food) and so increase profits which must go to someone. In stationary state conditions, Quesnay allows no more to the farmers than the multiple of the

---

[1] Quesnay was naturally asked to explain the existence of large commercial fortunes, and specific cases where industrial output was sold at a high multiple of costs. For instance, in 1766 he discussed the problem of how ten manufacturers at Nîmes were able to make a profit of 150 per cent on costs by buying silk in Spain or Italy, and selling it as cloth in Germany (*Quesnay*, p. 759). His explanation is basically that if there were perfect competition [*concurrence libre*] this could not happen, and that the abnormal profit that arose as a result of its absence was earned at someone else's expense (*Quesnay*, pp. 771–80).

[2] See *Quesnay's Tableau Économique*, 3rd edition (1759), p. 10 (M). 'The daily wage of a labourer is fixed on the basis of the price of corn, and amounts to a twentieth of the price of one *setier*.' (The letter (M) after a page reference signifies that the translation is Professor R. L. Meek's.)

labourers' long-term subsistence needs that ensures constant output, and with growth farmers only receive more than this for a few years until leases come up for renewal, so what they receive is limited. There is no reference to the possibility that landlords might sometimes allow farmers to earn more, to attract tenants. Hence the bulk of any agricultural surplus must go to the owners of the land in the form of rents or 'revenue'— or indeed to the Church or the King. At a more fundamental level, it is the institutions of society—limitation of land ownership to the nobility, and property rights, which give the surplus to the landlords, even though land is not scarce. Voltaire's reaction to the role of the Sovereign in 1767 (and the hereditary landlords are similarly placed) goes to the root of the matter:

> It is quite certain that the land pays everything; what man is not convinced of this truth? But that one man should be the proprietor of all the land, that is a monstrous idea . . .[1]

This account of how agriculture can produce a 'net product' which is paid to the landlords, the Church and the State, while industry cannot, concludes the present account of what would now be called Quesnay's microeconomic assumptions. His macroeconomic analysis of how effective demand for agricultural and industrial output is determined, and how this influences the growth of the two sectors of the economy makes use of the propositions that have been arrived at.

The macroeconomic analysis of demand determination developed gradually. In his Encyclopedia articles of 1756–7 Quesnay makes it clear that the demand for manufactures and personal services, i.e. the demand for the products of the 'sterile' sector, and therefore for labour in manufactures and services, depends on the expenditure of the revenue or surplus of agriculture by the landlords who receive it. Thus:

> Industry procures subsistence for a multitude of men by paying for their workmanship; but it produces no revenue whatsoever and it can only be sustained by the revenue of the citizens who buy the works of the artisans. [1757][2]

> The works of agriculture make good their expenses, repay the costs of work, procure incomes for the workers; and in addition produce the revenues of the estates. Those who buy industrial goods pay for the costs, and the workmanship, and the merchant's return; but these goods produce no income beyond this.

> Thus all the expenditure on the works of industry only draws revenue from landed income; for works which do not generate revenue can only exist through the wealth of those who pay for them. [1757][3]

---

[1] From a letter to Damilaville on 16 Oct. 1767 (see G. Weulersse, *Le Mouvement Physiocratique en France (de 1756 à 1770)*, Paris, 1910, vol. i, p. 147 (E)). Voltaire's common ground with the Physiocrats was limited as is evident from *L'Homme aux quarante écus*, which he published in the same year.

[2] *Quesnay*, p. 480 (E).   [3] *Quesnay*, p. 496 (E).

and moreover:

> The expenditure of these revenues constitutes the returns of the citizens who follow well paid professions. [1757][1]

As well as emphasizing the importance of the expenditure of the revenue, these passages make clear the full reasons for the total dependence of all other economic activities on agriculture, and therefore why Quesnay used the word 'sterile' to describe them. Not only does the production of industrial goods and services produce no surplus over 'normal profits', but in addition because demand depends on the expenditure of the surplus, the markets for the output of the remainder of the economy depend on expenditure flows which originate in agriculture. Moreover, the 'sterile' sector is dependent on the 'productive' sector for its raw materials. Agriculture in contrast is in no way dependent on the other sector.[2]

Quesnay's Encyclopedia articles show that as well as creating demand for manufactures and labour, the revenue is spent several times. Thus:

> The wealthy must be left free to spend. If affluence brings them to feed and pay for useless people, one must not place these domestic servants, it is true, in the ranks of men who play a part in the production of wealth; but one must at least see them as consumers who ensure the distribution of the money of the rich to all the well-paid professions; for the servants do not pile up wealth taken away from the circulation of the money that is destined to return continually to the source of annual wealth . . . It is with these servants as it is with the workmen engaged in making luxury articles for the nation's use: as these workmen are useful only in so far as they cause the rich to spend and as they spend themselves what they draw from their work. [1757][3]

The expenditure of rents or revenues is not merely necessary to produce demand for manufactures, services, and the lucrative professions, for it is clear from the above quotation that it is essential that there is sufficient expenditure that returns to 'the source of annual wealth', i.e. to agriculture. Thus again:

> A farmer has sold 100 *setiers* of corn for 1,600 livres. The landowner has received 1,600 livres for the rent of the land; he uses this sum to build; the workers to whom he has distributed it spend it on corn to feed themselves; thus the 1,600 livres returns to the farmer who sold them the corn. This farmer spends this sum on cultivation, to make more corn grow; thus the expenditure of the landlord becomes the returns of the workers, who restore to the farmer the sum that he has paid to the landlord. If this sum is taken away from the landlord, or from the workers, or from the farmer, its return in sequence is destroyed; the source will provide it no longer neither to the landlord, nor to the workers, nor to the farmer. Its perpetual reproduction, the expenditure of the landlord, of the workers, of the farmer, are all suppressed; the corn which was the real wealth, which came into being again, and

---

[1] *Quesnay*, p. 548 (E).
[2] H. Woog sets out Quesnay's reasons why industry is dependent on agriculture very clearly in *The Tableau Économique of François Quesnay*, A. Francke, A.G. Verlag, Bern, 1950, pp. 20–1.
[3] *Quesnay*, p. 568 (E).

W. A. ELTIS   181

which was consumed each year to feed the men is destroyed, and men must look elsewhere for their subsistence, and the State is impoverished and depopulated . . . [1757][1]

The maintenance of a continuing expenditure flow is crucial:

It is necessary that the owners of landed property who receive these revenues spend them each year so that this kind of wealth is distributed to the whole nation. Without this distribution the State could not subsist; if the landlords held back the revenues, it would be essential to despoil them of these; thus this type of wealth belongs as much to the state as to the landowners themselves; the latter only have the enjoyment of it so that they can spend it. [1757][2]

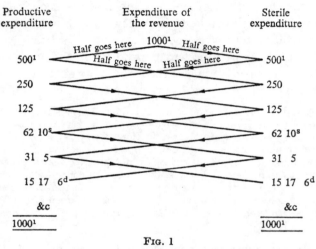

FIG. 1

(l. s. d. stands for livres, sous, and deniers; one livre = 20 sous, 1 sou = 12 deniers.)

These passages outline the position Quesnay had reached in 1757, namely that the expenditure of rents or revenues has an important influence on demand for the products of both industry and agriculture, and he may have owed much to Cantillon's account of the role that rents play in the circulation of demand.[3] A year later Quesnay set out the effect of the expenditure of rents formally for the first time in his first draft of the *Tableau Économique*, and this is illustrated in Fig. 1 which shows the circulation of the revenue as it is set out in the early editions of the Tableau of 1758–9, with the revenue changed to 1,000 livres. He assumed here that landlords, farmers, and artisans each spend half the money they receive on the outputs of the 'productive' sector, i.e. on the products provided by 'agriculture, grasslands, pastures, forests, mines, fishing, etc.', and the remaining half on the products of the 'sterile'

---

[1] *Quesnay*, pp. 541–2 (E).   [2] *Quesnay*, p. 582 (E).
[3] See R. Cantillon (op. cit.), (1755) Chapters XII–XVI. Quesnay knew the book, and quotes from it in *Grains* (*Quesnay* [1757] pp. 482–3).

sector, i.e. on 'manufactured commodities, house-room, clothing, interest on money, servants, commercial costs, foreign produce, etc.'[1] It is also assumed that the expenditure flows between the classes which are initiated by the expenditure of the 1,000 livres of revenue that the landlords receive continue until the productive and sterile sectors have each received 1,000 livres, as in Fig. 1. The expenditure of rents gives the productive and sterile sectors 500 livres each. Both sectors retain half of this until the end of the circulation process, supplying themselves with half their consumption needs from their own sector, and spend the remaining half of the 500 livres on the products of the other sector.[2] Both sectors therefore receive a further 250 livres from the other, and when this is spent, half on each side, they receive a further 125 livres each, and so on as in the diagram, until total expenditure is twice the original expenditure of the landlords. Quesnay underlined precisely this aspect of the expenditure flows of the Tableau in 1763 in Chapter 7 of *Philosophie rurale*:

> With the assumptions of the present Tableau in which the advances of the productive class give rise to 100 per cent of revenue, this revenue which is spent in the year passes in its entirety to the productive class, and in entirety to the sterile class through the reciprocal transfers between one class and the other . . .' [1763][3]

Thus a multiplier of *two* can be applied to the expenditure of rents, and the aggregate domestic *market* demand for the products of the two sectors will be exactly twice the initial expenditure of rents—where the three classes (landlords, productive workers, sterile workers) always spend half the money they receive on the products of each sector. They may divide their expenditure differently, and a progression is illustrated in Part VI of *L'Ami des hommes* which was published in 1760 where five-twelfths of all expenditures go to the productive and seven-twelfths to the sterile class. The revenue in the Tableau in question is 1,050 livres, and the zigzags then bring 915 livres in all to the productive and 1,146 livres to the sterile class, with the result that the expenditure multiplier is slightly less than two.[4] The money receipts of the two sectors can always be inferred precisely from (i) total rents or revenues, and (ii) the proportion of money receipts that each class spends on the output of the productive sector of the economy. The precise formulae are set out in Fig. 2, where total rents are R, and the proportion of all incomes that is spent on the productive side is q. The formulae set out in Fig. 2 produce the exact totals outlined in the 'Tableau Économique avec ses Explications' of 1760.[5]

[1] *Quesnay's Tableau Économique*, 3rd edition, Explanation, p. i (M).
[2] What happens to the money that is retained until the end of the circulation process will become evident when the full Tableau is explained below.
[3] *Quesnay*, p. 699 (E).   [4] *L'Ami des hommes*, Part VI, p. 192.
[5] Fig. 2 is derived from Diagram (1.1) in Izum Hishiyama, 'The Tableau Économique of Quesnay—its analysis, construction, and application', *Kyoto University Economic Review*,

The exact results arrived at by Quesnay and Mirabeau clearly depenc
on the assumptions that all receipts will be spent at every stage of the
circulation process, and that none of the revenue is lost overseas, anc
these are Quesnay's first assumptions in each edition of the Tableau o

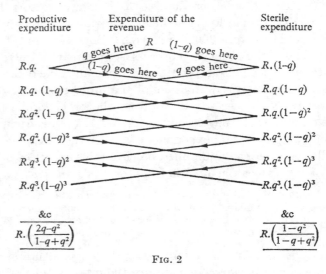

Fig. 2

1758–9. Thus, from the first printed edition where the total revenue i
600 million livres :

But in this distribution it is assumed :

1. That the whole of the 600 millions of revenue enters into the annual circulation, and runs through it to the full extent of its course ; and that it is never formed
into monetary fortunes, or at least that those which are formed are counterbalanced
by those which come back into circulation ; for otherwise these monetary fortunes
would check the flow of a part of this annual revenue of the nation, and hold back
the money stock or finance of the kingdom, to the detriment of the reproduction
of the revenue and the well-being of the people.

2. That no part of the sum of revenue passes into the hands of foreign countries
without return in money or commodities. [1758][1]

The assumption that the net product or rents of agriculture determine
the effective demand for the marketed output of agriculture and industry
is a most remarkable one, and it is unique to the Physiocrats. It has been
suggested that Quesnay's previous published work on the circulation of
the blood may have led him to believe that the circulation of money played

vol. xxx, Apr. 1960. The totals are derived in each case by summing two geometric progressions. The left-hand column, for instance, can be written as :

$$[(R.q+R.q^2(1-q)+R.q^3(1-q)^2...)+(R.q.(1-q)+R.q^2(1-q)^2+Rq^3(1-q)^3...)]$$

The formulae can be checked against the totals in *L'Ami des hommes*, Part VI, Tableau on
p. 192. R. V. Eagly has also set out the multiplier effects of the circulation of the revenue
very clearly (op. cit.).

[1] *Quesnay's Tableau Économique*, the Second Edition (1758), p. 3 (M).

a similar role in the working of economies, and that this led him towards the Tableau.[1] The circulation of the blood is referred to in a passage in *Philosophie rurale*, but this is in a part of the book that Quesnay commented on extensively rather than one that he wrote himself:

> Here it is necessary to observe that it is with this circulation of the money of the revenue as it is with the blood. It is necessary that all circulates without slackening, the least stoppage will produce a clot.[2]

The parallel between the circulation of money and of the blood is not, however, brought out in any passage clearly drafted by Quesnay himself.

The crucial assumptions on which Quesnay's analysis rests have now been outlined. It will be evident that his assumptions about the relationship between inputs and outputs in industry and agriculture, and about income distribution and the determination of effective demand for food and manufactures produce an account of the working of economies that is far from simple. Quesnay could doubtless have set out his argument in algebra (for his last book was concerned with mathematical problems) but he chose instead to use diagrammatic methods of exposition based on the *Tableau Économique* which he invented in 1758, and he later showed dynamic processes with a series of Tableaux which represented the economy in different years. Quesnay may well have believed that an argument based on the Tableau would be more widely accessible,[3] but the loss of clarity in not also providing an algebraic account made it immensely difficult for later generations (and indeed his own contemporaries) to grasp the argument fully.

In this paper, an attempt will be made to supplement Quesnay's diagrammatic exposition with an account of the basic interrelationships that underlie it.

Quesnay's *Tableau Économique*, and its explanation

Quesnay's basic Tableau of the early editions of 1758–9 is set out in Fig. 3, with Annual Agricultural Advances, the base of the Tableau, set at 1,000 livres. This Tableau incorporates the expenditure flows that were discussed in the earlier part of the paper, and in addition some of Quesnay's other important propositions. Perhaps the most important of these is the principle that agriculture (or the productive sector) can produce a surplus

---

[1] See V. Foley, 'An origin of the Tableau Économique', *History of Political Economy*, Vol. 5, No. 1, Spring 1973.   [2] *Philosophie rurale*, vol. i, p. 66 (E).
[3] The following passage from 'Tableau Économique avec ses Explications' is interesting in this context: '. . . we have not claimed to make of it a work of Algebra, considered with all the relationships to which it is susceptible; that would be the amusement of a Geometer, useless to the aim of the Author, who has only presented in the Tableau the points of view that are indispensably necessary, and as it is, one will still find it only too complicated'. *L'Ami des hommes*, Part VI, p. 129 (E).

W. A. ELTIS   18

or 'net product' of 100 per cent, while industry produces no surplus. Thi
is firmly incorporated in the Tableau, for it will be noted that agains
each receipt of the productive sector in the left-hand column are the word
'reproduce net' followed by an identical sum of money printed in th

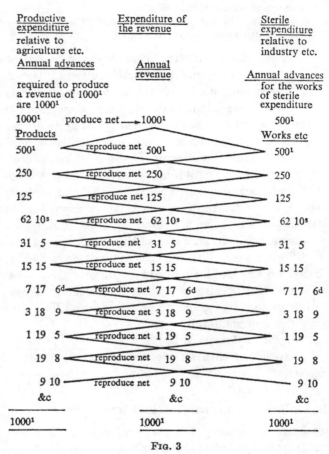

Productive expenditure	Expenditure of the revenue	Sterile expenditure
relative to agriculture etc.		relative to industry etc.
Annual advances	Annual revenue	
required to produce a revenue of 1000^1 are 1000^1		Annual advances for the works of sterile expenditure
1000^1	produce net ⟶ 1000^1	500^1
Products		Works etc
500^1	reproduce net 500^1	500^1
250	reproduce net 250	250
125	reproduce net 125	125
62 10^s	reproduce net 62 10^s	62 10^s
31 5	reproduce net 31 5	31 5
15 15	reproduce net 15 15	15 15
7 17 6^d	reproduce net 7 17 6^d	7 17 6^d
3 18 9	reproduce net 3 18 9	3 18 9
1 19 5	reproduce net 1 19 5	1 19 5
19 8	reproduce net 19 8	19 8
9 10	reproduce net 9 10	9 10
&c	&c	&c
1000^1	1000^1	1000^1

FIG. 3

column headed 'Annual revenue', so each 100 livres that the agriculturist
receive from the year's expenditure flow reproduce and become 200 livre
that can be disposed of in the following year. There is no extra colum
to the right of the 'Sterile expenditure' column, so 100 livres spent o
manufactures produce only 100 livres at the foot of the table. As a resul
of this asymmetry between the 'Productive' and 'Sterile expenditure
columns the 1,000 livres of revenue that comes to the 'Productive
column generates a further 1,000 livre total in the central 'Revenue
column; while the 1,000 livres that goes to the right-hand 'Sterile expendi
ture' column produces a total of just 1,000 livres. The fact that the 1,00

livres that is spent on the products of agriculture becomes 2,000 livres shows that the land can produce enough to pay 1,000 livres to the landlords at the end of the year, and still retain 1,000 livres for the 'Annual advances' of the farmers, so that both the demand for food (which requires 1,000 livres of revenue) and its supply (which requires 1,000 livres of annual advances) can be maintained at the same level from year to year.

One point that is not clear from the Tableau alone is what happens to the economy's stock of money during the course of the year. This is 1,000 livres and the landlords hold it at the beginning of the year.[1] They then distribute it equally to each class, and the Tableau's zigzags continue its distribution, but it would be wrong to think that the sterile class will be left with half the stock of money at the end of the year. The sterile class consumes half of the 1,000 livres that it receives, and it uses the other 500 livres as advances for the following year (shown at the top of the 'Sterile expenditure' column), and these consist principally of raw materials which are bought from the agricultural sector for the next year's production.[2] The sterile sector will therefore exchange such money as reaches it in the course of the year for produce with the result that the economy's whole stock of money will reach the productive sector by the end of the year. Thus, at the end of the year, the productive sector is left, not with 2,000 livres of 'food', but with 1,000 livres worth of 'food', and 1,000 livres of money. The 1,000 livres of 'food' passes to the top of the 'Productive' column to become the productive sector's advances of the following year. The 1,000 livres of money passes to the top of the 'Revenue' column, i.e. the money is paid to the landlords, and this generates the following year's circulation or effective demand, while only 500 livres passes to the top of the 'Sterile expenditure' column to act as the advances of the sterile sector—for only the raw materials of the sterile sector actually remain in being from year to year.

The process can continue indefinitely if it is not disturbed. Each year 1,000 livres of annual advances in the productive sector in the form of food and raw materials, 1,000 livres of money in the hands of the landlords, and 500 livres of food and raw materials in the hands of artisans and merchants, become outputs of 2,000 livres of 'food' and 1,000 of manufactures; which are then marketed and leave precisely 1,000 livres of food

---

[1] 'Thus the total money stock of an agricultural nation is only about equal to the net product or annual revenue of its landed property, for when it stands in this proportion it is more than sufficient for the nation's use', *Quesnay's Tableau Économique*, 3rd edition (1759), Maxims, p. 17 (M). See also Explanation, p. ix, and *L'Ami des hommes*, vi (1760), pp. 165 and 226.

[2] See p. 198 n. 1 below. Dr. Henri Woog (op. cit., pp. 72–83) has suggested that the sterile class holds its advances in the form of money, but this would make the money supply exceed total revenue, which would contradict Quesnay's several statements that it equals this.

and raw materials in the hands of the farmers, 1,000 livres of money in the hands of the landlords, and 500 livres of food and raw materials in the hands of the artisans and merchants at the end of the year. Quesnay's construction has been widely agreed to be a beautiful one, involving elegance, economy, and the several levels of meaning that characterize some of the eighteenth century's greatest works of art. The factors that may disturb the Tableau's equilibrium and so produce growth or decline will be discussed in the paper that follows this one, but it may be noted here that both of Quesnay's multipliers have the same value. Thus the equilibrium of the Tableau depends partly on the fact that a multiplier of *two* can be applied to the Revenue to ascertain its effect on aggregate market demand, and the same multiplier of *two* is applied to what agriculture receives because of the proposition that agricultural outputs are twice agricultural inputs. Thus the multiplier involved in the expenditure of the revenue is the same as the multiplier of the soil, for it is only in these conditions that each class will get back at the end of a year what it had at the beginning.

Successive generations have found the Tableau exceedingly difficult to understand, and some of the reasons for this will already be evident. Quesnay's achievement in showing monetary flows with his zigzags, and the production of goods on a single diagram is a remarkable one, but the fact that these are both shown makes the Tableau that much more difficult to comprehend. A second difficulty is that the Tableau shows only part of Quesnay's model. Thus the 'interest' costs of farmers and the receipts they need to meet these are not shown, and international trade is also left out—which matters, for consistency between the demand and supply of food and manufactures cannot be achieved in a closed economy. Only half the economy's consumer demand is for agricultural produce, but according to the Tableau, two-thirds of its output is agricultural. 'Food' must therefore be exported and manufactured goods imported, and Quesnay makes this clear in the 'Explication du Tableau Économique' that he published with the Tableau in 1759.[1] Finally the Tableau leaves a number of questions unanswered. Thus, it is not clear from the Tableau alone just what goes where in the process of consumption, for exactly how the agricultural output of 2,000 livres and the industrial output of 1,000 livres is divided between the classes is not shown on the diagram. Quesnay had to supply his 'Explanation' to show that the food and manufactures produced were exactly what was needed by the various classes and for international trade. Clearly the Tableau cannot give a full account of the economy's activities without some further information and interpretation.

[1] *Quesnay's Tableau Économique*, 3rd edition (1759), Explanation, p. iii.

The complete interactions of the Tableau depend on a number of fundamental equations that must hold when it is in equilibrium. First, the productive class and the sterile class must each receive just enough money from the Tableau's zigzags, etc., to meet their financial requirements. If they receive more money than they need, or less, their level of activity will rise or fall, so in the stationary state conditions that the Tableau describes, it is necessary that they receive exactly the right amount. In addition, there must be equality between the demand and supply of both

TABLE I

The solutions to the original version of the Tableau Économique

	Solution
Annual agricultural advances	A
Rate of return on agricultural advances	100%
Total rents or revenues	A
Wages and entrepreneurial incomes in agriculture	A
Interest of agricultural entrepreneurs	any value
Raw materials used in agriculture	any value
Exports of agricultural produce	$\frac{1}{4}A$
Raw materials used by industry	$\frac{1}{2}A$
Wages and entrepreneurial incomes in industry	$\frac{1}{2}A$
Gross industrial output	A

agricultural and industrial production if the Tableau is to be in equilibrium. The system of equations that determines the crucial values in the Tableau is completed with Quesnay's assumption that the costs of the industrial sector are half labour and half raw material costs,[1] and the further assumption that each class spends half its income on the agricultural and half on the industrial side of the Tableau. The equations that are produced by these conditions are outlined in the first section of the Appendix to this paper, 'A Mathematical Explanation of Quesnay's Tableau'. The equations are in fact very simple and straightforward, and the solutions that result with Quesnay's specific assumptions about propensities to consume, etc., are outlined in Table I above.

It will be seen that the solutions underline Quesnay's crucial argument that almost all the economy's quantities are multiples of annual agricultural advances, which are A in Table I. Thus total rents or revenues equal annual agricultural advances, wages in agriculture equal agricultural advances, wages in industry are one-half agricultural advances, and therefore half wages in agriculture, total industrial production equals agricultural advances, exports are one-quarter agricultural advances, and

---

[1] See p. 198 n. 1 below.

W. A. ELTIS   189

so on. The capital of the entrepreneurial farmer therefore determines everything else as Quesnay argued in everything he wrote from 1756 onwards, and if this can be doubled, then so can all the other quantities in the economy, once this reaches equilibrium. As for the details of the solution, the first crucial one is that the rate of return on annual agricultural advances is 100 per cent, and this is what he was at such pains to show to be practicable, both because it was achieved in part of the French economy, and more to the point, because it was achieved in the whole English economy. With a rate of return on annual agricultural advances of 100 per cent, total rents or the economy's aggregate revenues equal agricultural advances, and this is the case in every edition of the Tableau.

The result that the raw material and interest costs of the agricultural entrepreneurs can take any value without disturbing the equilibrium of the Tableau is an interesting one. It is arrived at because the raw materials that are used in agriculture, and the horses, etc., that are bought to replace others with the 'interest' received are wholly supplied and used up within the same sector, so they must affect the costs and receipts of the agricultural class equally. This is not true of wages, rents, exports, and the agricultural raw materials that are used up in the industrial sector, and these must all be the precise proportions indicated in Table I.

The result that industrial wages are half agricultural advances and half agricultural wages is exactly what Quesnay states, for with agricultural advances and therefore wages of 600 livres in the printed editions of both 1758 and 1759, the wages of the sterile expenditure class are said to be 300 livres,[1] and in the economy as a whole it is said that there are 3 million workers' families (all quantities in the Tableau should be multiplied by a million to arrive at figures for the whole economy) which receive an average of 300 livres each, of whom 2 million are in the productive and one million in the sterile sector.[2] Finally, it is specifically said that exports of agricultural products are 150 livres (where agricultural advances are 600 livres), so exports are one-quarter of agricultural advances as in Table I.[3]

The fact that the results arrived at are precisely Quesnay's is a check that his fundamental argument has been followed. It also shows that it can be arrived at rigorously, and that his conclusions follow from his assumptions. He may either have followed the model through to the conclusions arrived at in Table I without publishing his actual reasoning or he may have perceived intuitively that it all added up.

However he proceeded, he must also have appreciated that the Tableau as it is outlined in his diagram and in Table I can only take the argument

---

[1] *Quesnay's Tableau Économique*, 3rd edition (1759), Explanation, p. iii.
[2] Ibid., pp. iv–v.   [3] Ibid., p. iii.

so far. It presents a coherent account of an economy with one particular relationship between its various outputs and incomes: it is of course an economy in stationary state equilibrium, but the Tableau cannot be used to compare economies with different export ratios, or different rates of return on agricultural advances. This is because exports have to be one-quarter of annual agricultural advances and the rate of return 100 per cent in all economies that conform to the basic assumptions. Quesnay could not therefore use the Tableau to compare the French economy where advances yielded much less than 100 per cent with the English, so the Tableau was unsuitable for the kind of comparison that interested him most.

Quesnay and Mirabeau decided to deal with the problem by modifying some of the assumptions of the original Tableau so that an extra degree of freedom could be obtained. The crucial assumption they modified was the one that effective demand originates in the expenditure of the revenue, which is what limits the applicability of the Tableau because a very high revenue and therefore a very high rate of return on advances (i.e. one of 100 per cent) is needed to produce sufficient effective demand. The opportunity that Quesnay and Mirabeau took to give the argument extra freedom was the publication in 1763 of *Philosophie rurale* (its original title was to have been *Grand Tableau Économique*[1]) in which they planned to give a complete account of Quesnay's theory of the working of economies, and for this they needed a more flexible Tableau.[2]

They obtained this by inventing a Tableau which allowed the rate of return on annual agricultural advances to take any value whatsoever. The device they used to achieve this was the assumption that some agricultural incomes could be spent by rich farmers *as if they were rent.* Rich farmers could hold back some money after the harvest, and spend this for their consumption in the following year on the products of others, and this money would have the same effect on the circulation process as

---

[1] G. Weulersse, *Le Mouvement Physiocratique en France*, vol. i, p. 86.

[2] It is highly probable that Quesnay was author and not just part-author of the passages in *Philosophie rurale* where the new Tableau is set up, and where sequences of Tableaux are used to show growth or decline when its equilibrium is disturbed. This can be inferred (i) because the passages in question are stylistically Quesnay and not Mirabeau, (ii) Quesnay wrote to Mirabeau of a passage he had drafted for *Philosophie rurale*, 'This spiritual chemistry demands more from the readers than arithmetical hieroglyphs, which displease you more than them' (Weulersse, *Les Manuscrits économiques de François Quesnay et du Marquis de Mirabeau*, p. 81 (E)), which clearly indicates that Quesnay may have taken more interest in the calculations than Mirabeau, and these are almost all based on the manipulation of Tableaux. Professor R. L. Meek has also drawn attention to Mirabeau's self-confessed dislike of calculation to attribute authorship of an important section of *Philosophie rurale* to Quesnay (Meek, p. 38). (iii) The author of '(Premier) problème économique' of 1766, and this is undoubtedly Quesnay, at several points describes increases in an unorthodox way: an increase of 20 per cent is described as an increase of one-sixth throughout the article. The identical unorthodoxy is to be found in an important passage containing sequences of Tableaux in *Philosophie rurale*. See vol. ii, pp. 184–5 and 188.

equivalent sums circulated by landlords. This is illustrated in Fig. 4 which is based on a similar diagram in the section of Chapter 9 of *Philosophie rurale* headed:

RULES

To form an abridgement of the Tableau in all the different cases where the advances of the productive class yield more or less than 100 per cent of net product, and where it is supposed in addition that there are no causes of decline or growth in the annual reproduction.[1]

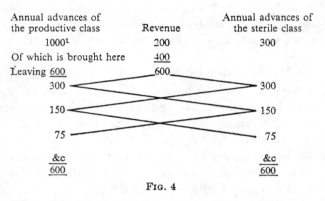

Annual advances of the productive class	Revenue	Annual advances of the sterile class
1000[1]	200	300
Of which is brought here	400	
Leaving 600	600	
300		300
150		150
75		75
&c		&c
600		600

Fɪɢ. 4

In Fig. 4 the rate of return on the annual agricultural advances of 1,000 livres is only 20 per cent, and a revenue of 200 livres will provide a total market demand of only 400 livres which is much less than total production. However, if 400 livres of the agricultural advances of 1,000 livres are spent as if they are revenue, leaving 600 livres to be spent as wages, the total expenditure of 'revenue' (including 400 livres of agricultural advances) is 600 livres, while the agricultural advances that are spent as 'wages' are also 600 livres, and with industrial advances at 300 livres, the precise ratios of the original Tableau are obtained. This will be confirmed if Fig. 4 is compared with Fig. 3. The rule which must be followed to achieve this result is that equal total sums should be *spent* as agricultural advances and rent, and if poor landlords spend some of their income as if they are workers, and rich farmers some of theirs as if they are landlords, this can always be achieved. Quesnay and Mirabeau give several examples in the ninth chapter of *Philosophie rurale*.[2]

With the assumption that the expenditure of some advances as revenue (and vice versa) always maintains the correct rate of effective demand,

---

[1] *Philosophie rurale*, vol. ii, p. 162 (E). Fig. 4 is based on the diagram on p. 175 of vol. ii.

[2] The theory clearly requires that where rates of return are substantially less than 100 per cent, there are sufficient 'rich' farmers who hold and spend money during the 'winter'. Otherwise the economy will contain regions where money hardly circulates, and monetization will be confined to the areas where landlords congregate and spend their revenues—these being insufficient to circulate money universally. This would limit the applicability of the Tableau in obvious ways.

FRANÇOIS QUESNAY: A REINTERPRETATION

Quesnay and Mirabeau were able to drop the Tableau's zigzags and set out a much simpler diagram, while they explained that the economy's money stock was circulating as before, and producing precisely the same results. They called the result a précis of the original Tableau, and the one equivalent to the Tableau set out above is shown in Fig. 5.

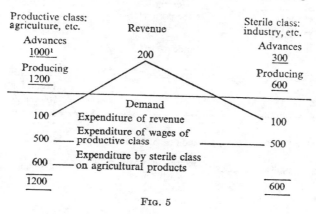

FIG. 5

All that needs to be said here is that half the revenue of 200 livres goes to each side: half the wages of the productive class go to each side: and the entire 600 livres the sterile class receives from the other two then comes back to agriculture, half being spent on agricultural products for consumption, and half on raw materials for the next year's advances. The assumption that the sterile class spends all it receives on the agricultural side of the Tableau is an apparent departure from the propositions of the original Tableau of which more will be said below. A similar précis Tableau can be drawn at all rates of return on advances, and in each case demand from these sources will equal precisely what is produced on each side, as in Fig. 5.[1]

The précis of the Tableau in *Philosophie rurale* was modified further in Quesnay's final version of the Tableau which he published in 1766 as 'Analyse de la formule arithmétique du Tableau Économique'.[2] This is the version of the Tableau that Marx admired and discussed in 30 pages of his *Theories of Surplus Value*,[3] and it is the version that has been turned into an input-output Table.[4] The Tableau of 1766 is the Précis Tableau

---

[1] The rule that must be followed to produce this result is to make the advances of the sterile sector one-quarter of the sum of annual agricultural advances and rents, as in the original Tableau. Only this makes the reproduction of the original Tableau possible. The rule is stated in *Philosophie rurale*, vol. i, p. 124, and again in vol. i, p. 328.

[2] *Quesnay*, pp. 793–812. It is translated in Meek, pp. 150–67 with one omission.

[3] Marx (op. cit.), vol. 1, pp. 308–44.

[4] A. Phillips, 'The Tableau Économique as a simplified Leontief model', *Quarterly Journal of Economics*, vol. lxix, Feb. 1955.

W. A. ELTIS   193

of *Philosophie rurale* with the single modification that the 'interest' costs of the agriculturists (which are assumed to equal 50 per cent of annual agricultural advances[1]) are directly included in the Tableau for the first time. The final version of the Tableau is outlined in Fig. 6, largely as

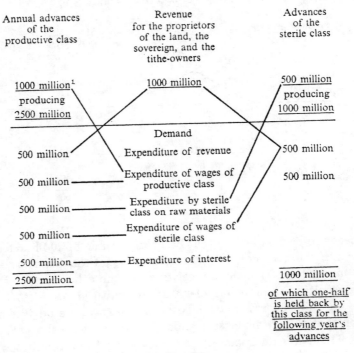

FIG. 6

Quesnay set it out with a rate of return on agricultural advances of 100 per cent but with some extra explanatory detail to help readers (and Quesnay's own text is printed underlined). Because of the inclusion of 'interest' at 50 per cent of advances, the annual agricultural advances of 1,000 livres produce a total agricultural product of 2,500 livres in place of the 2,000 livres of the original Tableau of 1758–9, and the extra 500 livres is used up because farmers spend their 'interest' on the agricultural side to replace horses, etc. The final version of the Tableau is set out in Fig. 6 on the assumption of a rate of return on advances of 100 per cent, but it can be set out similarly with any rate of return, and there are examples of this version of the Tableau with rates of return of less than 50 and of 150 per cent in subsequent published articles of Quesnay's.[2] It

---

[1] It is presumably assumed that interest is earned to replace original advances which are five times annual advances in the 1766 version at a rate of 10 per cent per annum.
[2] See *Quesnay* (1766) p. 863 and (1767), p. 980.

is to be noted, however, that it is only where the rate of return is 100 per cent that there is the correct amount of revenue to carry through the financial transactions indicated by the lines of the diagram.[1] At all other rates of return, some farmers must spend like landlords, or vice versa as in *Philosophie rurale*.

The final version of the Tableau, and the précis of the Tableau in *Philosophie rurale*, both suffer from one serious weakness or omission: there is no reference in them to the consumption of industrial products by the sterile class, who are assumed to spend their wages exclusively on agricultural products. There is thus an apparent asymmetry of a highly implausible kind between the expenditure pattern of agricultural workers who spend half their income on agricultural and half on industrial products, and industrial workers who spend their whole income on food. Quesnay was far too subtle a thinker to have an asymmetry of this kind in his *real* or underlying model, and what he published always contained certain abstractions in the hope that this would make for easier comprehension.

One way of dealing with the difficulty is to examine the equations which lie behind the final version of the Tableau. These are outlined in the second section of the Appendix where the mathematical basis of the Tableau is discussed, and they produce the solutions that are presented in Table II.

TABLE II

The solutions to the final version of the Tableau Économique

	Solution
Annual agricultural advances	A
Rate of return on agricultural advances	r
Total rents or revenues	$A.r$
Wages and entrepreneurial incomes in agriculture	A
Interest of agricultural entrepreneurs	$\frac{1}{2}.A$
Raw materials used in agriculture	any value
Exports of agricultural produce	$\frac{1}{8}.A(1+r)$
Raw materials used by industry	$\frac{1}{4}.A(1+r)$
Wages and entrepreneurial incomes in industry	$\frac{1}{4}.A(1+r)$
Gross industrial output	$\frac{1}{2}.A(1+r)$

It will be evident that as in the original Tableau, all quantities are multiples of annual agricultural advances, and moreover, here the rate of return on

---

[1] There is a very extensive literature on the expenditure flows indicated on the diagram, and the major controversies are very comprehensively outlined and discussed in Henri Woog (op. cit.), pp. 38–72. However, the only explanation that will work where the rate of return on annual agricultural advances differs from 100 per cent (and none of the ones Dr. Woog refers to will) is the one set out in *Philosophie rurale*, so it must be assumed that this also applies to the final version of the Tableau.

annual agricultural advances (r) can take the value that is appropriate to the economy in question. One of the most interesting conclusions that emerges from Table II is that Gross Industrial Output varies with both agricultural advances and the rate of return in agriculture—it is $\frac{1}{2}.A(1+r)$. Then an economy with a highly profitable agriculture will have a larger industrial sector than another with an equal agricultural wage bill but less efficiency on the land. These are among Quesnay's most basic propositions, and they are arrived at here as the result of a highly technical argument.[1]

Turning to the problem of the apparent asymmetry between the consumption patterns of agricultural and industrial workers which was remarked on above, Table II indicates that there is a solution to the problem. In this table, which is derived on the assumption that all classes have the same propensities to consume food and manufactures in Quesnay's underlying model, the discrepancy is removed because industrial workers export half the agricultural products they buy with their wages, and trade these for manufactures overseas. Their wages are $\frac{1}{4}.A(1+r)$, and if they export $\frac{1}{8}.A(1+r)$ of food and exchange this for manufactures, they will have the same proportion of food and manufactures in their own consumption as everyone else, and as Professor Meek who first discovered this solution points out, the precise manufactures they import could be consumed by anyone including the richest landlords. Exports of food of half of industrial wages and corresponding imports of manufactures will ensure that sufficient total manufactures will be available to allow each class to spend half of its income on food and half on industrial products.[2]

It can only be conjectured that this solution to the problem is part of Quesnay's underlying theory which he never published completely, but the ratio of trade to agricultural advances in Table II is the same as that

---

[1] Smith might have carried the argument an interesting stage further and said that the *larger* industrial sector associated with a more efficient agriculture would also produce more efficiently because the division of labour could be further extended in industry; and this leads directly to the proposition that England should be more efficient in industry than France (given the greater profitability of its agriculture) in the conditions of 1766–76.

[2] See Meek, pp. 282–3. J. J. Spengler (in 'The Physiocrats and Say's Law of Markets', *Journal of Political Economy*, vol. liii, Sept.–Dec. 1945) following Baudeau's *Explication du Tableau Économique à Madame de* *** of 1770 (op. cit.) suggests that the final Tableau understates the total output of the sterile class because it does not include the products that the sterile class produces for itself. Thus the total wages of the industrial class should equal $\frac{1}{2}.A.(1+r)$ and not the $\frac{1}{4}.A.(1+r)$ indicated in Table II. They can then spend $\frac{1}{4}.A.(1+r)$ on food for their own consumption as Quesnay says, and supply themselves with equivalent manufactures without needing to trade. However, the Baudeau–Spengler argument makes industrial wages twice the industrial sector's raw material costs, and it is clearly stated in each of Quesnay's accounts of the Tableau that wages are one-half and not two-thirds of the industrial sector's costs, so it is unlikely that their solution is the one he had in mind. Moreover, their solution makes industrial wages as great as agricultural wages where r is 100 per cent, and the industrial wage bill is substantially smaller than the agricultural wherever Quesnay refers to this relationship.

196   FRANÇOIS QUESNAY: A REINTERPRETATION

in the original Tableau if $r = 100$ per cent, i.e. one-quarter of these, and there are two indications that Quesnay may have intended the precise solution of Tables I and II to apply to his final Tableau. In Chapter 7 of *Philosophie rurale* (which contributes so much to the interpretation of his thought) he set out a fully itemized Tableau showing each branch of agriculture and the sterile sector separately, itemizing types of income in each branch, and arriving at equal totals for the output of agricultural products and purchases of these. In this Tableau which resembles modern National Income accounts, he includes the following item among the purchases of agricultural products:

| The Sterile Class buys of these | For the advances of its works and the business of exporting: 1,437,066,667[1](1) |

Now, if the formulae of Table II are applied to the itemized Tableau, exports plus the advances of the sterile class come to 1,470,750,000 livres,[2] which is exceedingly close to the 1,437,066,667 livres that Quesnay allows for these items. There are a number of small arithmetical errors in this detailed Tableau, and it contains some more complex relationships than the simplified Tableaux that have been outlined in this paper, which must produce substantial differences in some results. However, the fact that Quesnay's complete Tableau shows almost precisely the answer for exports plus industrial raw materials that is arrived at in Table II indicates that the solution suggested there may very well be the one he had in mind. This is supported by the further evidence of a statement in the '(Premier) Problème Économique' of 1766 (which is based on the final version of the Tableau) where Quesnay says: 'Foreign trade can be estimated at about one tenth of the total product [of agriculture] . . .'[3] in a situation where the rate of return on annual agricultural advances is 30 per cent. According to the solutions of Table II, the ratio of trade to agricultural output should be 9·03 per cent in these conditions.[4]

This completes the present account of Quesnay's *Tableau Économique*. The importance of the Tableau is that it sets out with great precision the conditions in which an economy will achieve continuous reproduction with a constant level of output in each sector. The conditions for stationary state equilibrium are, as Quesnay and later Marx appreciated, the

---

[1] *Quesnay* (1763), p. 712 (E). Professor Meek drew attention to this item in Meek, p. 283.

[2] According to Table II, exports plus the advances of the sterile class, which equal exports plus its raw material purchases, total $\frac{3}{4}A.(1+r)$ or $\frac{3}{4}\times$(Agricultural advances + Revenues.) In Chapter 7, annual agricultural advances total 1,921,000,000 livres, and Revenues total 2,001,000,000 livres (*Quesnay*, p. 710), so $\frac{3}{4}\times$(Agricultural advances + Revenues) equals 1,470,750,000 livres.

[3] *Quesnay*, p. 866 (M).

[4] In Table II, the ratio of trade to agricultural output is $(1+r)/(12+8r)$, agricultural output totalling wages *plus* rents *plus* interest where the cost of agricultural raw materials used in agriculture is disregarded as in the case in question. This comes to 13/144 where r, the rate of return on advances, is 30 per cent.

starting-point for an analysis of the conditions where growth will be achieved. Clearly there will be growth or decline in aggregate output if the equilibrium of the Tableau is disturbed. That is why the precise conditions in which the Tableau is in equilibrium are of such importance, and why such care has been taken to ascertain exactly what those conditions are. They form the starting-point of Quesnay's theory of economic growth, which is the subject of the paper that will follow.

APPENDIX

A Mathematical Explanation of Quesnay's Tableau Économique

1. *The Original Tableau of 1758-9*

The best starting-point for an understanding of the equations that underlie the original Tableau is to work out the implications of the condition that in equilibrium the total output or supply of the productive or agricultural sector, Y_a, must equal D_a, the demand for food and raw materials. Similarly, the total output of the sterile or industrial sector, Y_i, must equal D_i, the demand for manufactures and services.

Y_a, the gross output of the agricultural sector, must be equivalent to the sum of the incomes earned in this sector plus raw materials used up in production. Thus if the raw materials, etc., used up in agriculture are M_a, the 'interest' costs of the agricultural entrepreneurs I, the wages and entrepreneurial incomes earned in agriculture W_a, and the net product, i.e. the total rents or revenues of the landlords are R:

$$Y_a \equiv M_a + I + W_a + R. \tag{1}$$

Similarly, Y_i, the gross output of the industrial sector will be equivalent to the sum of wages and entrepreneurial incomes in that sector, W_i, and the raw materials used up, M_i, so that:

$$Y_i \equiv M_i + W_i. \tag{2}$$

D_a, the demand for agricultural output, is made up of the demand for the raw materials for both sectors, $M_a + M_i$, the expenditure of 'interest', I (for the replacement of farm animals that die, etc., is always made good from the agricultural sector), that part of wages and rents that is spent on agricultural produce, $q.(W_a + W_i + R)$ where q is the propensity to consume the products of agriculture of all classes,[1] and T_a, the net export demand for food and raw materials—and it is assumed by Quesnay that agriculture is always a net exporter. Then:

$$D_a = M_a + M_i + I + q.(W_a + W_i + R) + T_a. \tag{3}$$

Similarly, D_i, the demand for manufactures and services is made up of the demand of workers and landlords who all spend a proportion, $(1-q)$, of their incomes on the products of the 'sterile' sector, so they will spend $(1-q).(W_a + W_i + R)$ on these. However, some manufactures come from abroad, and T_i, net imports of manufactures, must be subtracted from home demand to produce the demand for the output of the home country's industrial sector. Hence:

$$D_i = (1-q).(W_a + W_i + R) - T_i. \tag{4}$$

In equilibrium, Y_a will equal D_a so that:

$$M_i + T_a + q.W_i = (1-q).(W_a + R)$$

---

[1] It is to be noted that Quesnay always assumes that workers and landlords have the same propensity to consume 'food'.

and Y_i will equal D_i so that:

$$M_i + T_i + q \cdot W_i = (1-q) \cdot (W_a + R)$$

It will be seen that these equations are identical provided that T_a, net agricultural exports, equals T_i, net imports of manufactures. They are thus the same equation provided that trade is balanced as Quesnay always assumes. If T is written for both exports and imports, the equation becomes:

$$M_i + T + q \cdot W_i = (1-q) \cdot (W_a + R). \tag{5}$$

This is one of the fundamental equations on which the *Tableau Économique* is based. It will be noted that M_a and I, the raw material and 'interest' costs of the agricultural entrepreneurs, play no part in the equation, so any level of these is compatible with equality of supply and demand for food and manufactures.

The principal further condition that must be satisfied in the Tableau is that the money receipts of the farmers and artisans, which depend on the circulation of the revenue, must be just sufficient to meet their financial needs. This produces two further equations, one for each class.

The agricultural sector receives the expenditure flows that originate from the revenue, and the calculation in Fig. 2 on page 183 above shows that these amount to $R \cdot [(2q-q^2)/(1-q+q^2)]$. In addition, the agricultural sector receives M_i from the sale of raw materials to the industrial sector for its advances.[1] It spends $(1-q) \cdot W_a$ on wage goods from the industrial sector in the course of the year, and at the end of the year it pays rent of R to the landlords. In equilibrium, what it receives must equal what it spends, so that:

$$R \cdot \left(\frac{2q-q^2}{1-q+q^2} \right) + M_i = (1-q) \cdot W_a + R.$$

i.e.
$$R \cdot \left(\frac{3q-2q^2-1}{1-q+q^2} \right) = (1-q) \cdot W_a - M_i. \tag{6}$$

Turning to the industrial sector, this receives $R \cdot [(1-q^2)/(1-q+q^2)]$ from the Tableau's zigzags in Fig. 2, and it uses this to spend M_i on raw materials from the productive sector, T, on agricultural products for export,[2] and $q \cdot W_i$ on agricultural products for the consumption of its workers. Hence, in equilibrium:

$$R \cdot \left(\frac{1-q^2}{1-q+q^2} \right) = M_i + T + q \cdot W_i. \tag{7}$$

(6) and (7) provide two equations that must be satisfied, given the circular flows of the original version of the Tableau, and (5) is an equation that a Physiocratic economy must always satisfy. These three equations can be supplemented by a

---

[1] Quesnay's precise assumption in his *Explication* to the 3rd edition of 1759 is: 'Circulation brings 600 livres to the sterile expenditure class, from which 300 livres have to be kept back for the *annual advances*, which leaves 300 livres for wages' (*Quesnay's Tableau Économique*, 3rd edition, p. iii (M)). It is evident from this that the sterile sector buys the next period's advances after the circulation of the revenue is completed. Moreover, in the above quotation, wage goods are distinguished from the advances of the sterile sector, so these must, strictly speaking, be raw materials—and this is Quesnay's precise assumption in the later versions of the Tableau (see *Quesnay* (1763), p. 712, and (1766) p. 795). He is not, however, consistent on this point in his explanation of the Tableau of 1759 where the advances of the sterile class are sometimes said to include subsistence goods and there is no specific statement about the amount it spends on raw materials, which can only be inferred from the above quotation.

[2] International trade is one of the activities of the sterile sector, so it buys the goods that are exported as one of its own inputs, and the economy's imports are sold together with its own products via the Tableau's zigzags.

fourth, because Quesnay states frequently through the various versions of the Tableau that the costs of the sterile sector are half wages and entrepreneurial incomes, and half raw materials, i.e.

$$M_i = W_i \tag{8}$$

With this fourth equation, there are sufficient equations to express R, T, W_i, and M_i in terms of W_a and q; i.e.

$$R = W_a \cdot \left(\frac{1-q+q^2}{2q-q^2}\right) \tag{9}$$

$$M_i = W_i = W_a \cdot \left(\frac{1-q-q^2+q^3}{2q-q^2}\right) \tag{10}$$

$$T = W_a \cdot \left(\frac{q-q^3}{2-q}\right). \tag{11}$$

These are the general relationships that must hold in a Tableau of Quesnay's type. He at no point set them out in general terms, but he simply outlined the particular solutions arrived at where $q = \frac{1}{2}$, which he assumes wherever the Tableau is in equilibrium. Before the very simple results arrived at in the particular case where $q = \frac{1}{2}$ are presented, something must be said about a further assumption of Quesnay's which does not influence the results, but only the way in which these are presented.

In his various expositions of the Tableau, Quesnay assumes that annual agricultural advances, A, equal or nearly equal W_a, total wages and entrepreneurial incomes in the productive sector of the economy. Where the Tableau is set out in very great detail in Chapter 7 of *Philosophie rurale*, annual agricultural advances at 1,921 million livres are close to the incomes of agricultural workers and entrepreneurs which total 2,180 million livres,[1] and everywhere else these totals are identical. Presumably the non-wage components of advances, and Quesnay mentions animal feeding stuffs in the *Explication* to the Tableau of 1759,[2] are just balanced by wages and entrepreneurial incomes which are not included in advances, and this allows Quesnay to assume that $W_a = A$.[3] With the simplifying assumption that annual agricultural advances equal labour costs, A can be substituted for W_a in (9), (10), and (11), and this allows the results to be presented as Quesnay actually presented them, so that where $q = \frac{1}{2}$, $R = A$, $M_i = W_i = \frac{1}{2}.A$ and $T = \frac{1}{4}.A$. The results are set out in this way in Table I on page 188. In addition, as rents are explained as a rate of return (of r) on annual agricultural advances in Quesnay's argument, $R = A.r$, and r must then be 100 per cent where $R = A$.

2. The Final Version of the Tableau of 1766

There must be equality between the demand and supply of both food and manufactures when the final Tableau is in equilibrium, and if all classes have the same propensity to consume agricultural products (and it can be supposed that they do in Quesnay's underlying model), equation (5) must be satisfied as in the original Tableau. Moreover, equation (8) which states that the industrial wage bill equals the cost of industrial raw materials also definitely applies to the final Tableau.

However, because of the change in the circular flow assumption, the financial receipts of the two sectors are no longer derived directly from the zigzags originating

---

[1] *Quesnay* (1763), pp. 710–11.

[2] *Quesnay's Tableau Économique*, 3rd edition, p. iii.

[3] The actual level of expenditure on animal feeding stuffs and other agricultural raw materials, M_a, is of course irrelevant to the Tableau's interrelationships because these are wholly produced and consumed in the same sector. For this reason they do not enter the basic equations that determine the model and this can be in equilibrium with M_a at any level.

from the Revenue. This means that equations (6) and (7) do not apply to this version. There is, however, an equation peculiar to the final version that replaces them. This is the proposition that the advances of the sterile sector must be one-quarter of the sum of annual agricultural advances and rents; and it was seen on pp. 191–2 above that this guarantees that the financial requirements of both sectors are always met. The equation that produces this result is written as:

$$M_i = \tfrac{1}{4}.A + \tfrac{1}{4}.R \tag{12}$$

and it replaces (6) and (7). Equations (5), (8), and (12) are sufficient to produce the results outlined in Table II on p. 194 where $q = \tfrac{1}{2}$, and these are written down on the presumption that $W_a = A$ and $R = A.r$.

Exeter College, Oxford

5

FRANÇOIS QUESNAY: A REINTERPRETATION
2. THE THEORY OF ECONOMIC GROWTH

By W. A. ELTIS

QUESNAY believed that population and output had been falling in France for a century. He thought that the population was 16 million in 1758, and that it had been 24 million a hundred years earlier, and about 19·5 million in 1701.[1] His detailed Tableau in Chapter 7 of *Philosophie rurale* was intended to show that France could support a population of 29·9 million, while the population in his final Tableau of 1766 was said to be 30 million.[2] These figures, and what growing and declining population and output meant in both human and national terms explain Quesnay's great concern with the causes of economic growth—and its opposite. He wished to explain the decline in France's output, population, and wealth that he believed had occurred, and to discover how this trend could be reversed. The invention of the *Tableau Économique*, the subject of a previous paper,[3] provided the tool with which both these objectives could be realized.

It will be evident that Quesnay had to use the Tableau to show two kinds of progression: to explain decline when the France of Louis XIV and Louis XV was under discussion, and to show growth when proposals to correct the weaknesses in the French economy were being put forward. The starting-point for the sequences of Tableaux which showed decline was a Tableau in equilibrium with a rate of return on annual agricultural advances of 100 per cent, and in one case of even 150 per cent. The economy then fell from this state of 'bliss' for one of several reasons. Quesnay used so favourable a starting-point because he believed that agricultural advances really had yielded rates like this in the past[4]—when Sully had applied the correct policies to agriculture and the finances of France which the Physiocrats were rediscovering. The downward progressions could then show realistically how Sully's successors had

---

[1] See *François Quesnay et la Physiocratie*, Institut National d'Études Démographiques, Paris, 1958, pp. 513–14. (This two-volume publication will be referred to subsequently as *Quesnay.*) Recent research suggests that the population may have fallen until 1720, but by much less than Quesnay believed. It is widely agreed that it increased slowly after this (with interruptions in years of famine) at an average rate of perhaps 0·2 or 0·3 per cent per annum, and reached about 22 million by 1760 and 27 million by the end of the century. It is believed that agricultural output increased at a similar rate. See J-C. Tutain, *La Population de la France de 1700 à 1959*, Cahiers de l'Institut de Science Économique Appliquée, Supplément no. 133, Janvier 1963; and J. Dupâquier, 'Sur la population Française au 17ᵉ et au 18ᵉ siècle', *Revue historique*, vol. xcii, Jan.–Mar 1968.

[2] See *Quesnay* (1756), p. 712, and (1766), p. 795.

[3] W. A. Eltis, 'François Quesnay: a Reinterpretation. 1. The Tableau Économique', *Oxford Economic Papers*, vol. 27 (2), July 1975, pp. 167–200.

[4] See *Quesnay* (1767), p. 978.

impoverished France, and Colbert was blamed in particular for the industrial and commercial bias of his policies. The upward progressions used the France of the 1750s and 1760s as their starting-point, and these assumed an initial rate of return on annual agricultural advances of about 30 per cent, which was rapidly raised as 'correct' policies were applied to the economy.

The equilibrium of the Tableau can be disturbed in a number of ways to produce growth or decline, and it can be assumed that the sequences of Tableaux that Quesnay actually published were intended to demonstrate the causes of decline and the methods of achieving growth that he considered most important. He certainly believed that the Tableau was a powerful tool of analysis and exposition, and it is reasonable to suppose that he used it to explain what mattered most. He published two sequences of Tableaux in 1766 and 1767 to illustrate the applicability of the final version to practical problems,[1] and it was suggested in the previous paper on Quesnay's *Tableau Économique* that he was probably responsible for the many sequences of Tableaux that demonstrate the causes of growth and decline in *Philosophie rurale*, the book he wrote in collaboration with Victor de Riqueti, Marquis de Mirabeau, in 1763.[2] He was certainly at least part author of these. The accounts of the Tableau in disequilibrium in Part VI of *L'Ami des hommes* which Quesnay and Mirabeau published in 1760 add further information about Quesnay's theory of economic growth.[3]

An examination of this evidence suggests that there are three causes of disequilibrium which Quesnay and Mirabeau considered particularly important. First, the proportion of incomes that is spent on the products of agriculture may be less or more than the one-half that produces stationary state equilibrium. Second, a change in methods of taxation may affect the rate of return that farmers actually receive on their advances with consequent decline or growth in these, and third, the rate of return may be raised in agriculture by increasing the price of food as a result of better marketing policies at home and overseas. Quesnay and Mirabeau used the Tableau to outline the dynamic effects of these three causes of disturbance, and they did this because they believed that the causes of French impoverishment were too much consumption of manufactures and services,

---

[1] These are '(Premier) Problème Économique', 1766 (*Quesnay*, pp. 859–77); and 'Second Problème Économique', 1767 (*Quesnay*, pp. 977–92). These are translated into English with the omission of one passage in R. L. Meek, *The Economics of Physiocracy*, Allen and Unwin, 1962, pp. 168–202. This book will be referred to subsequently as Meek.

[2] See Eltis (op. cit.), p. 190, n. 2. Sequences of Tableaux are to be found in *Philosophie rurale*, Amsterdam, 1764 (reprinted in 1972 by Scientia Verlag Aalen), vol. i, pp. 405–11, vol. ii, pp. 179–98, 298–325, and 354–75, and vol. iii, pp. 33–53.

[3] Tableaux in disequilibrium are to be found in *L'Ami des hommes*, Avignon, 1756–60 (reprinted in 1970 by Scientia Verlag Aalen), Part VI, pp. 192, 204, 214, and 254.

and they attributed particular importance to excessive *luxe de décoration*, and methods of taxation which caused agricultural advances to diminish. In their opinion, the best way to restore the situation was to substitute taxes which did not fall on the capital of farmers for those that did, and to adopt commercial policies which restored the profitability of agriculture.

The effect of these on the growth of the economy can be shown quite straightforwardly with the assistance of the Tableau, and they will be outlined in turn below. Quesnay and Mirabeau usually gave an account of growth or decline by publishing two Tableaux, one for the beginning and one for the end of a period where the equilibrium of the economy was disturbed. Each Tableau described an economy in stationary state equilibrium, and their method of analysis was therefore generally that of comparative statics. The one exception to this is the analysis of the effects of a propensity to consume the products of agriculture which differs from one-half, and it will be shown below that this must continue to produce growth or decline for so long as the discrepancy persists. The other causes of growth and decline can all produce once-for-all effects which can be analysed with the methods of comparative statics, but they can also produce indefinite growth or decline. Both possibilities will be outlined in the present account of Quesnay's argument.

Quesnay and Mirabeau used the final version of the Tableau, or the précis of the final version in their accounts of growth and decline in *Philosophie rurale* and the later articles, and these versions are obviously superior to the original Tableau for the analysis of dynamic processes because they can show rates of return which differ from 100 per cent, and because they are more flexible and less cumbersome. The original version of the Tableau should, however, be used for the first of the problems which will be considered, the effect on the rate of growth of a propensity to consume the products of agriculture of more or less than one-half, for the final Tableau will only give an accurate account of the expenditure flows that go to each sector where the propensity to consume is exactly one-half.

The effect of the propensity to consume agricultural products on the rate of growth[1]

This is best analysed by focusing attention on the financial receipts of the agricultural producers. These receive money from the landlords and the artisans of the sterile class via the Tableau's zigzags, and in addition to this they receive money from the industrial sector for the sale of raw materials for its advances. The agriculturists use the money they receive

---

[1] Accounts of the effect of this on growth are to be found in *Philosophie rurale*, vol. iii, pp. 33–53, and *L'Ami des hommes*, Part VI, pp. 192–202.

to buy manufactured goods for their own consumption and to pay rent. This relationship is set out in detail in Table I, where it is assumed that the rate of return on annual agricultural advances is 100 per cent, as in the original Tableau. In Table I, it is assumed that the Tableau is in equilibrium initially with a propensity to consume the products of agriculture, q, of one-half. Annual agricultural advances are 1,000 million livres in the initial year, and with a rate of return of 100 per cent rents are also 1,000 million livres. The agriculturists then receive 1,000 million livres in the

TABLE I

Declining production where the propensity to consume agricultural products (q) is less than 0·5

Annual agricultural advances	Rents	Farmers' receipts from circulation of revenue	Industry's receipts from circulation of revenue	Farmers' purchases from industry	Industry's purchases for advances	Farmers' financial surplus (+) or deficit (−)
A	$R = A$	Z_a	Z_i	$(1-q).Z_a$	$\frac{1}{2}.Z_i$	
						millions of livres
		Initial equilibrium relationships where $q = 0\cdot5$				
1,000	1,000	1,000	1,000	500	500	0
		q becomes 0·4: successive years				
1,000	1,000	842	1,105	505	552·5	−110·5
945	945	796	1,044·5	477·5	522	−104·5
893	893	752	987	451	493·5	− 98·5
844	844	711	933	426·5	466·5	− 93
797·5	797·5	671·5	881·5	403	441	− 88

$$Z_a = R.\left(\frac{2q-q^2}{1-q+q^2}\right), \quad Z_i = R\left(\frac{1-q^2}{1-q+q^2}\right).$$ See Eltis (op. cit.), Fig. 2, p. 183.

course of the year from the circulation of the revenue, i.e. from the Tableau's zigzags as in all of Quesnay's accounts of the original Tableau, and 500 million livres from the sale of raw materials to the industrial sector (i.e. half of what this sector receives from the circulation of the revenue). The agriculturists use this 1,500 million livres for two purposes —to buy industrial products for their own consumption via the Tableau's zigzags which costs them 500 million livres, and to pay rent to the landlords which costs a further 1,000 million livres. Then the 1,500 million livres the agricultural class receives is just sufficient for its full financial needs when the Tableau is in equilibrium as it is in the top line of Table I where farmers have no financial surplus or deficit.[1]

[1] The expenditure flows of the original Tableau on which Table I is based are explained in general terms in Eltis (op. cit.), pp. 184–8, while the precise equations are set out on pp. 197–9.

Suppose now that q, the propensity to consume agricultural products, becomes 0·4 so that the propensity to consume manufactures is 0·6. The effects of this are oulined in the second line of Table I. Here the Tableau's zigzags bring 842 million livres instead of 1,000 million to the agricultural sector, and 1,105 million instead of 1,000 million to the industrial—all sums of money being quoted to the nearest half million livres. The agricultural class receives a further 552·5 million livres from the industrialists for sales of raw materials, i.e. half of the 1,105 million livres the industrial class receives which is what Quesnay says this class puts aside for its advances. However, the agricultural class spends six-tenths of the 842 million livres it receives from the zigzags or 505 million livres on manufactures for the consumption of its workers and entrepreneurs. When its full transactions are taken into account as in Table I, it receives $842 + 552·5 = 1,394·5$ million livres, and it spends 505 million livres on consumer goods and owes rents of 1,000 million livres so it requires 1,505 million livres. The agricultural class therefore has a financial deficit of 110·5 million livres which is shown in the final column of Table I. If it pays the 1,000 million livres agreed to the landlords, the farmers must sell 110·5 million livres of their advances for the next year to get enough money to pay their rents. In the sequence of Tableaux that deals with this case in *Philosophie rurale* Quesnay and Mirabeau actually assume that half the deficiency is met by the landlords who accept lower rents than those previously agreed.[1] Then half the farmers' deficit of 110·5 million livres is met by a fall in annual advances from 1,000 to 945 million livres, and half by a reduction in rents so these will also become 945 instead of 1,000 million livres in the following year. It will be noted that the assumption that Quesnay and Mirabeau make in this case is the only one which keeps annual agricultural advances and rents in line with each other, which is necessary if the basic relationships of the Tableau are to hold from year to year.

While annual agricultural advances and rents both fall from 1,000 million livres in the first year of a lower propensity to consume to 945 million livres in the second, Table I shows that the advances of the industrial sector increase from 500 million to 552·5 million livres. What has happened in general terms is that the circulation of demand has brought more money than before to the industrial sector, and less to the agricultural with the result that a higher proportion of the harvest has been allocated to the industrialists and a smaller proportion to the farmers themselves. This has produced the present situation where industrial advances are larger than usual, 552·5 instead of 500 million livres, and agricultural advances and rents are both 5·5 per cent lower. Looking further ahead, the 5·5 per cent fall in annual agricultural advances reduces

[1] *Philosophie rurale*, vol. iii, pp. 33–53.

agricultural output by 5·5 per cent in the following year, while the reduction in rents reduces demand for both food and manufactures by 5·5 per cent. The increase in the advances of the industrial sector will raise the following year's physical output of manufactures, but this has no effect on the Tableau's circular flows, and the amount of money the manufacturers receive for their increased production depends solely on the expenditure of rents and the subsequent zigzags, and these must bring 5·5 per cent less to the industrial class than in the previous year because rents are 5·5 per cent lower. In fact, an examination of Table I shows that each quantity is 5·5 per cent lower than in the previous year. Both sectors receive 5·5 per cent less from the circulation of the revenue, the industrial sector's purchases of raw materials (for advances) are reduced 5·5 per cent from 552·5 to 522 million livres, and the financial deficit of the farmers also falls 5·5 per cent from 110·5 to 104·5 million livres. However, the correction of this deficit requires a further 52 million livres reduction in both annual agricultural advances and rents in the third year, and this is again a fall of 5·5 per cent. Indeed it will be clear from Table I that with the present assumptions, all quantities in the Tableau must fall at an annual rate of 5·5 per cent after the first year because annual agricultural advances fall at this rate, and because of this the advances of the sterile sector which rose from 500 to 552·5 million livres in the first year fall back below 500 million livres after only two further years. Hence an increased propensity to buy manufactures increases the wealth of the industrialists for only two years, and after this, all classes become poorer at a rate of 5·5 per cent per annum because this is the rate at which annual agricultural advances are falling.

The converse situation where the propensity to consume agricultural products rises from 0·5 to 0·6 is outlined in Table II. Here with the same assumptions as in the previous case, annual agricultural advances increase at a rate of 4·2 per cent per annum, and all other quantities grow with them. In the first year of the higher propensity to consume their products, farmers receive 1,105 instead of 1,000 million livres from the Tableau's zigzags, and when their other transactions are taken into account, they have a financial surplus of 84 million livres. If Quesnay's and Mirabeau's assumption that this is divided equally with the landlords is followed, their annual advances will then increase 4·2 per cent from 1,000 to 1,042 million livres in the second year, and this initiates growth at this rate which will continue for so long as the propensity to consume agricultural products remains 0·6. The advances of the sterile class are initially reduced from 500 to 421 million livres by the lower propensity to consume its products, but growth at 4·2 per cent will restore these to 500 million livres after five years and raise them above this initial level from that point onwards.

The industrialists will therefore become better off than they were originally after the sixth year as a result of a fall in the propensity to consume their products.

It will be evident that a propensity to consume agricultural products of more than 0·5 must produce growth, and that there must be declining output followed soon afterwards by declining population where this propensity is less than 0·5. There is naturally a formula which relates g_a, the

TABLE II

Growth where the propensity to consume agricultural products (q) exceeds 0·5

Annual agricultural advances	Rents	Farmers' receipts from circulation of revenue	Industry's receipts from circulation of revenue	Farmers' purchases from industry	Industry's purchases for advances	Farmers' financial surplus (+) or deficit (−)
						millions of livres
Initial equilibrium relationships where q = 0·5						
1,000	1,000	1,000	1,000	500	500	0
q becomes 0·6: successive years						
1,000	1,000	1,105	842	442	421	+84
1,042	1,042	1,151·5	877·5	460·5	439	+88
1,086	1,086	1,200	914·5	480	457·5	+91·5
1,132	1,132	1,251	953	500·5	476·5	+95
1,179·5	1,179·5	1,303·5	993	521·5	496·5	+99
1,229	1,229	1,358·5	1,035	543·5	517·5	+103·5
1,281	1,281	1,416	1,078·5	566·5	539·5	+108

rate of growth of annual agricultural advances, to q, the proportion of income spent on agricultural products, and if x is written for $(q-0·5)$, i.e. x is the excess of the propensity to consume agricultural products over one-half:

$$g_a = \tfrac{1}{2}.x.\left(\frac{1-1\tfrac{1}{3}x-1\tfrac{1}{3}x^2}{1+1\tfrac{1}{3}x^2}\right) \qquad (1)[1]$$

and where x is small so that terms in x^3, x^4, etc., can be disregarded:

$$g_a = \tfrac{1}{2}.x-\tfrac{2}{3}.x^2 \qquad (2)$$

[1] If annual agricultural advances are initially A, so that rents (R) are also initially A, the financial surplus of the agricultural sector in Table I will be the $A\left(\frac{2q-q^2}{1-q+q^2}\right)$ it receives from the circulation of the revenue, *plus* half the receipts of the sterile sector, i.e. $\tfrac{1}{2}.A.\left(\frac{1-q^2}{1-q+q^2}\right)$ for sales of raw materials, *minus* $(1-q)$ times $A.\left(\frac{2q-q^2}{1-q+q^2}\right)$ for purchases of manufactures *minus* R (which equals A) for the payment of rent, and this comes to $A.\left(\frac{2q+q^2-2q^3-1}{2-2q+2q^2}\right)$. If half of this is added to the next period's advances, these grow from A at a rate of $\frac{2q+q^3-2q^3-1}{4-4q+4q^2}$. (1) is arrived at by substituting $0·5+x$ for q in this expression.

Thus the rate of growth varies with x, the excess of the propensity to consume agricultural products over one-half, provided that this excess is not very great, and quite small deviations from one-half produce very significant rates of growth or decline.[1] The maximum growth rate that the above formula (the completely accurate (1)) permits is 6·73 per cent per annum, which is reached where $x = 0.249$, i.e. where the propensity to consume the products of the agricultural sector is approximately three-quarters. There is virtually no limit to the rate of decline of output that the formula can produce, and a propensity to consume agricultural products of only one-quarter (i.e. an x of -0.25) will produce an annual reduction in agricultural advances and rents of 14·42 per cent if the landlords bear half the losses. Even a very modest departure of the propensity to consume agricultural products from one-half will suffice to produce massive growth or decline in output in eighteenth-century terms, in one or two generations.

Quesnay did not actually believe that the rates of growth or decline that can be inferred from his Tableau would be achieved in the economies he wrote about, because of a number of further factors the Tableau does not take fully into account which will be discussed later in this paper. It is, however, best to start by confining the argument to the actual working of the Tableau, and this produces the formula for the rate of growth that is set out above.

There is no doubt that Quesnay fully recognized that the Tableau produced the result that there would be *continuing* decline in production where the propensity to consume the products of agriculture was less than one-half, and vice versa, and the following passage (among many) which is taken from the Maxims that were published with the 1759 or 3rd edition of the Tableau brings this out very clearly:

It can be seen from the distribution delineated in the *Tableau* that if the nation's expenditure went more to the sterile expenditure side than to the productive expenditure side, the revenue would fall proportionately, and that this fall would increase in the same progression from year to year successively. It follows that a high level of expenditure on luxury in the way of ornamentation and conspicuous consumption is ruinous. If on the other hand the nation's expenditure goes to the productive expenditure side the revenue will rise, and this rise will in the

---

[1] The rates of growth and decline that are arrived at in *Philosophie rurale* (vol. iii, pp. 33–53) as a result of a q of 0·6 and 0·4 are rather different from those produced by the above formula, but the précis Tableau is used there, in spite of the fact that this gives answers which differ from those of the original Tableau's zigzags where q does not equal one-half. I. Hishiyama ('The Tableau Économique of Quesnay—its analysis, construction and application', *Kyoto University Economic Review*, vol. xxx, Apr. 1960) arrives at a different result by simply assuming that the total at the foot of the advances column in the original Tableau will always be precisely the following year's advances, which fails to take the full financial transactions of the agricultural class into account.

same way increase successively from year to year. Thus it is not true that the type of expenditure is a matter of indifference. (1759)[1]

Those who are only familiar with modern theories of growth will find it remarkable that the rate of growth can be a function of *what* is consumed rather than the ratio of investment to consumption. Just how different Quesnay's argument is can be seen from the following passage from one of the early Encyclopedia articles:

> [A nation which is reduced to subsisting on industrial activity] can only extend and sustain its trade, its industry and its shipping through saving; while those which have landed property increase their revenues through their consumption. (1758)[2]

This follows quite naturally if each livre spent on food produces an addition to rents, while no other form of expenditure has similar favourable 'external' effects. Quesnay was far from alone in believing that consumption of the 'correct' goods produced growth, for it was a central argument in the *Wealth of Nations* that the rate of growth depended partly on the ratio of 'productive' to 'unproductive' consumption. Ricardo followed Smith here, though they both had a borderline between the productive and unproductive sectors of the economy that differed substantially from Quesnay's, and their argument did not lead to specific calculations like those that follow from his very precise model.

Taxation and the rate of growth

The propensity to consume the products of agriculture is not, of course, the only factor that can produce growth or decline in Quesnay's argument, and according to the Physiocrats a major factor responsible for the supposed decline in France's population and wealth, in addition to excessive *luxe de décoration*, was the use of methods of taxation which fell on the capital of farmers, i.e. on agricultural advances. One of the two articles which Quesnay published to illustrate the application of the final version of his Tableau to practical problems was concerned with the effects of indirect taxation, and there are two sequences of Tableaux in *Philosophie rurale*, of which one is wholly Quesnay's, and two Tableaux in *L'Ami des hommes* which demonstrate these.[3] There is no doubt that Quesnay thought that taxation which fell on agricultural advances was immensely harmful to production in the actual conditions of eighteenth-century France, and that the Tableau could be used to illustrate this.

---

[1] *Quesnay's Tableau Économique*, edited by M. Kuczynski and R. L. Meek, Macmillan 1972, 3rd edition, p. 12 (M). (M) after a page reference signifies that the translation is Professor Meek's.

[2] *Quesnay*, p. 499 (E). (E) after a page reference signifies that the responsibility for the translation is the present author's.

[3] See Quesnay's 'Second Problème Économique', of 1767; *Philosophie rurale*, vol. i, pp 393–411, and vol. ii, pp. 298–325. (The first passage is from Chapter 7 which Quesnay drafted); and *L'Ami des hommes*, Part VI, pp. 204–11, and 254–70.

With Quesnay's model the taxation of the revenue of the landlords has wholly neutral effect on the economy, because it has no effect at all on ıe Tableau. It is clearly a matter of complete indifference to the workers ıd entrepreneurs of agriculture and industry whether the revenue is ıent by the landlords themselves, or the Church, or the King and his .inisters. Their sole interest is that it be spent. If the King needs 30 per ınt of the revenue for the government of the country and for military ırposes (and Quesnay generally assumed that the government should

TABLE III

How taxation of rents at 30 per cent affects growth

| *Annual agricultural advances* | *Rents* | *Marketed farm output* | *Taxation of* | | *Tax revenue* | *Farmers' financial surplus (+) or deficit (−)* |
			Farm output	*Rents*		
initial year						millions of livres
1,000	1,000	2,000	0	300	300	0
second year						
1,000	1,000	2,000	0	300	300	0

ave two-sevenths of the revenue, the Church one-seventh, and the land-ırds themselves four-sevenths), the arrangement that suits agriculture est is that illustrated in Table III where the landlords pay 30 per cent f their revenues directly to the government which can then spend this ıstead of the landlords themselves. In Table III the Tableau in its final ırm is assumed with a rate of return on annual agricultural advances of 00 per cent. Then if annual agricultural advances are 1,000 million livres ı the initial year, rents will also be 1,000 million livres, and agricultural utput is worth 2,500 million livres, of which, in stationary state equi-brium, 1,000 million livres go to the farmers to allow them to maintain heir advances, another 500 million livres go to them for their 'interest' osts, and the remaining 1,000 million livres go to the landlords. How-ver, of the 2,500 million livres that agriculture produces, half the agri-ultural wages or advances of 1,000 million livres are obtained by farmers :om their own crops, so this 500 million livres of agricultural output does ot need to be sold, leaving 2,000 million livres to be marketed.[1] It will e evident from Table III that if rents are taxed at 30 per cent while sales f farm produce are untaxed, farmers' incomes will be unaltered, for it

---

[1] The expenditure flows of the final version of the Tableau on which Table III is based re explained in detail in Eltis (op. cit.), pp. 192–4.

is immaterial to them whether the revenue is spent by the landlords or th
state. There is therefore no effect on the following year's annual agricu
tural advances (unless these are changing for some other reason) so th
Tableau is in no way disturbed by the tax on rents, and constant outpu
can be maintained from year to year as in Table III. It is obviousl
assumed that the government spends the same proportion of its income o
agricultural products as the landlords.

TABLE IV

*How the taxation of rents and marketed farm output at 10 per cent
affects growth*

Annual agricultural advances	Rents	Marketed farm output	Taxation of Farm output	Taxation of Rents	Tax revenue	Farmers' financial surplus (+) or deficit (−)
Initial year						millions of livrε
1,000	1,000	2,000	200	100	300	−200
Second year						
900	900	1,800	180	90	270	−180
Third year						
810	810	1,620	162	81	243	−162

Suppose now that the landlords oppose a situation where they bear th
entire costs of taxation, and that an alternative system is therefore adopte
where an equal rate of tax is applied universally. The simplest case t
take to obtain the essence of Quesnay's analysis is the one illustrated i
Table IV where the rate of return on advances and the other initial con
ditions are the same as in Table III. The government seeks to obtai
300 million livres a year by taxing the landlords at 10 per cent which i
expected to raise 100 million livres, and in addition by taxing all marketed
agricultural output at 10 per cent which is expected to yield another 20
million livres. The landlords apparently have their taxes reduced fror
300 million to 100 million livres, but as Quesnay says of them in his simila
but more complex example of 1767:

> Poor calculators that they are, they do not have an inkling that by entering int
> this plausible arrangement they are providing the spade which will be used to di
> their own graves. (1767)[1]

The difficulty becomes rapidly apparent. When 2,000 million livres o
agricultural products are marketed (and the cash flows of the Tableau wi

---

[1] *Quesnay*, p. 987 (M).

.ot allow the harvest to be sold for more than this—so the tax cannot be
·assed on), 200 million livres must be paid to the government so the
armers will receive 200 million livres less than in the previous year when
he Tableau was in equilibrium. They therefore have a financial deficit of
00 million livres in Table IV. If they split this loss equally with the
andlords as is assumed in Table IV, their advances for the next year
·ill be reduced from 1,000 to 900 million livres, while rents will also be
educed from 1,000 to 900 million livres. With agricultural advances
own 10 per cent to 900 million livres, the following year's taxable agricul-
ural output will be 1,800 million instead of 2,000 million livres, and a
0 per cent tax on this will now yield only 180 million livres which,
ogether with the 90 million livres the government now obtains from the
andlords through the 10 per cent direct tax on rents, produces a total tax
evenue of 270 million livres in place of the previous year's 300 million
vres. Thus agricultural advances, rents and total tax revenues will all
e 10 per cent lower than in the previous year. Moreover, Table IV
hows that annual agricultural advances will continue to fall at an
nnual rate of 10 per cent for so long as sales of agricultural produce
re taxed at 10 per cent and landlords expect farmers to bear half the
ost of this, and rents and total tax revenue will both fall with agricul-
ural advances. There will thus be a continuing decline of all incomes
t an annual rate of 10 per cent, and this is half the rate at which annual
gricultural advances are taxed, for the 10 per cent tax on sales of food
, in effect, a 20 per cent tax on agricultural advances. The economy's
nnual rate of decline is thus half the rate at which agricultural advances
re taxed, and it is half this rate because of the assumption that land-
rds accept a reduction in rents each year equal to half the farmers'
nancial deficit.

The argument can be put in the following way, which incidentally makes
; quite clear why the farmers cannot pass a tax on sales of food on to
nother class. In the conditions assumed, the state uses its full powers to
btain 10 per cent of that part of each harvest which is marketed, and the
andlords then take what is, in effect, one-half of the remainder, whatever
his may be, or 45 per cent. This leaves the farmers just 45 per cent of
ach marketed harvest in place of the 50 per cent that they need to main-
ain constant output where annual agricultural advances yield 100 per
ent. (They would need two-thirds of each harvest to maintain constant
utput if agricultural advances yielded 50 per cent.) With Quesnay's
ssumptions, if the farmers receive 45 per cent of the marketed harvest in
lace of the 50 per cent that they need to maintain constant output, pro-
luction will fall in proportion, i.e. at an annual rate of one-tenth. As
gricultural output falls 10 per cent per annum, government revenue

(which is one-tenth of output) and rents (which are half the remainder
will fall at the same rate.

The decline in the National Product will continue until the landlords hav
sufficient appreciation of what is going on to accept a reduction in rents tha
corresponds to the full tax burden. When this happens, the landlords wil
agree to accept just 40 per cent of the harvest after the state has taken l
per cent, and this will leave the farmers the 50 per cent of each markete
harvest that they need to maintain constant output. In Quesnay's view
the landlords are likely to appreciate this quite quickly, but the Nationa
Product, rents and government revenues will all fall during the year o
years before they realize that the tax must not be allowed to fall on th
farmers who work their land, and they will fall at a rate corresponding t
half the effective rate of taxation that agricultural advances have to bea

There are a number of points to note about this simplified account o
Quesnay's argument. First there has been no reference to the industria
sector of the economy which is also taxed in Quesnay's examples. Thi
can safely be omitted because the taxation of industrial output shoul
have an approximately neutral effect on growth with Quesnay's assump
tions. Industrial products are in no way *inputs* necessary for agricultur
so their price has no effect on the proportion of agricultural output whicl
can be reinvested by farmers, which is what determines the growth rate
Moreover, the government can be expected to spend any money it take
from industry so the aggregate demand for food will be unaffected. Th
essentials of Quesnay's argument can therefore be set out without referenc
to the 'sterile' sector of the economy, which obviously much simplifies th
exposition.

A second point to note is that the above account greatly exaggerate
the revenue the government will receive by assuming that it will actuall
obtain 10 per cent of the value of the food that is marketed. In his articl
of 1767 Quesnay estimated that the cost of collecting this kind of tax wa
generally about half the money paid to the tax collectors,[1] so the govern
ment might only receive about 100 million instead of 200 million livres i
the first year from the tax on sales of food, the tax collectors, etc., receivin
the other 100 million. This would not affect what is spent in the followin
year if the tax collectors spend what the government does not, but Quesna
in fact argues that they are likely to form monetary fortunes, and thes
are '... a clandestine form of wealth which knows neither king nor country'.
and their formation will certainly slow down the flows of the Tableau. Th
costs of collecting direct taxes on the rents of the landlords are alway
assumed to be very slight.

[1] *Quesnay*, p. 983.
[2] *Quesnay's Tableau Économique*, 3rd edition (1759), Maxims, p. 13 (M).

340   FRANÇOIS QUESNAY: A REINTERPRETATION

A third point to note is that the above account has understated the adverse effects of falling agricultural incomes on growth because it has been assumed throughout that annual agricultural advances yield 100 per cent. This is only possible with *la grande culture* which depends on the existence of rich farmers. As agricultural advances are taxed away, farms will increasingly revert to *la petite culture* which yields only about 30 per cent on annual advances,[1] and this will accelerate the decline in production, rents, and tax revenues.

Finally, as tax revenues fall as a result of the continuing decline in agricultural advances, the reversion to less capital intensive methods of farming, and the higher cost of collecting indirect taxation, the state will be under continuous pressure to raise rates of taxation, and this will especially be the case in times of war when revenue cannot easily be dispensed with. Clearly any increase in rates of taxation as government revenues fall will cause the fall in the National Product to accelerate.

It follows very strongly from the above argument that given Quesnay's assumptions, there is an overwhelming case for taking tax revenue from the 'net product' of agriculture rather than its produce, since this is where it must come from in any case in the end. Any departure from this rule will have highly adverse effects on growth. As Quesnay wrote in 1767:

The nobility and the clergy have demanded limitless exemptions and immunities, which they have claimed are bound up with their property and their estate. Sovereigns have also thought it appropriate to grant complete exemptions to their officers, and to all those who are invested with posts or employments in all the different branches of government administration. As a result of this state of affairs the revenue of the Exchequer has been reduced to such a low level, and the proprietors have put forward so much opposition to its direct increase, that sovereigns have had recourse to indirect taxes of various kinds, which have extended further and further in the proportion that the nation's revenue has diminished as a result of the deterioration which is the inevitable consequence of these taxes themselves. The landed proprietors, who did not foresee these consequences, and who during the time that they were destroying their revenue did not understand, did not even perceive the cause of the reduction in their wealth, gave their approval to these indirect taxes, by means of which they believed they could evade taxation, which ought to have been laid directly and immediately on the revenue of their property, where it would have caused no decline in the annual reproduction and would not have required to be successively increased; whereas in fact, as a result of the progressive increase and disastrous effects of the indirect taxes, successive increases in both indirect and direct taxes alike become necessary in order to meet the state's needs. In addition, the landed proprietors have not only got out of the payment of the *two-sevenths* of the revenue which belongs to the sovereign, but have also brought upon themselves indirect taxes, causing a progressive and inevitable deterioration which destroys their own revenue, that of the sovereign, and the wealth of the nation. (1767)[2]

---

[1] See Eltis (op. cit.), pp. 170–3, for an account of Quesnay's propositions about the relative profitability of *la grande culture* and *la petite culture*, and the capital intensities needed with these alternative methods of farming.   [2] *Quesnay*, p. 982 (M).

Quesnay's final comment on what this meant in human terms looks forward to what was to happen twenty years later:

> The increase of beggars, which is a consequence of the indirect taxes which destroy wages or subsistence by obliterating part of the reproduction of the nation's annual wealth. This increase of beggars is a large added burden on the cultivators, because they dare not refuse to give alms, being too exposed to the dangers which the discontent of vindictive beggars may draw down upon them. (1767)[1]

It is obviously an exaggeration to suppose that any taxation of sales of food must lead to the day of the vindictive beggar. The argument has superimposed taxation of the advances of farmers on a Tableau which was otherwise in equilibrium, i.e. on a stationary state. Taxation of farm incomes need not produce actual falls in production if another factor, for instance, a propensity to consume food which exceeds one-half, is simultaneously producing growth in farm incomes. Quesnay's analysis of the factors which produce growth and decline always takes a Tableau in equilibrium as the starting-point, and this is disturbed for one reason only, so he invariably shows the effect on a stationary state of one kind of departure from equilibrium proportions. The total effect on growth will be the sum of *all* departures from equilibrium proportions, so the taxation of farmers' receipts will be perfectly compatible with growth if its adverse effects, and these are undoubtedly very strong with his assumptions, can be outweighed by favourable effects from other directions. In Quesnay's view, there was a most important possible favourable effect (in addition to a high propensity to consume the products of agriculture) which could produce growth, namely an increase in the profitability of agriculture, and the effect of this on growth will now be outlined.

The profitability of agriculture and the rate of growth

The most obvious way to increase the profitability of agriculture is to increase its technical efficiency, and this requires either the application of new knowledge, which played no part in Quesnay's argument, or an increase in the capital of farmers, which he discussed at great length. However, with his analysis, farm capital can be increased only if growth is in any case occurring, and up to now this has been producible only by a propensity to consume the products of agriculture which exceeds one-half. If the technical efficiency of agriculture cannot readily be increased until growth is actually proceeding, then the profitability of agriculture must be increased in some other way, and Quesnay suggested that this could be achieved by improving the conditions in which its products were marketed, which was the only policy lever for raising farm incomes that made practical sense to him.

---

[1] *Quesnay*, p. 992 (M).

42   FRANÇOIS QUESNAY: A REINTERPRETATION

The first of Quesnay's two articles which illustrate the application of the final version of the Tableau to practical problems was concerned with the favourable effects that a higher price of food and better marketing policies should have on agricultural advances and rents, and there is a similar sequence of Tableaux in *Philosophie rurale* which follows through in a most detailed way the effects over a nine-year period of the cumulative reinvestment of such extra advances as are obtained from an initial improvement in farmers' incomes.[1] In the mid-eighteenth century the free movement of food within France itself was only allowed intermittently, and sales abroad were generally only allowed in years of plenty. The object of these policies for which Colbert was blamed was to provide cheap food for the cities to help manufacturers. In his article of 1766 Quesnay argued that full internal and external free trade in the products of agriculture could be expected to increase the rate of return on annual agricultural advances from about 30 to about 50 per cent, for this should substantially *increase* the prices French farmers obtained for their products, turn the terms of trade in France's favour, and greatly reduce fluctuations in prices which affected farm incomes adversely. This was the easy way, because it only required 'correct' decisions at Versailles to set in motion a favourable sequence of Tableaux. Louis XV had in fact issued an edict permitting grain exports, subject to certain restrictions, in July 1764, largely as a result of the arguments and influence of the Physiocrats, and freer internal movements of food were also permitted for a time. Unfortunately, by 1767 the price of bread had risen 30 per cent and wages had not kept pace, whatever their long-run behaviour might have been, with the result that opposition to the edict became strong, especially in the cities, and it was suspended in 1770.[2] Turgot, however, managed to establish complete internal free movements of agricultural products in his brief tenure of the Finance Ministry from 1774 to 1776.

There is no need to go into the precise details of Quesnay's analysis of the effects of free trade in agricultural products because what is really important is the effect of an increase in farm incomes on growth. More favourable marketing conditions are just one way of bringing this about. Suppose that for some reason the rate of return on annual agricultural advances is raised from 30 to 50 per cent, and that as has been assumed hitherto in this paper, only half the increase in agricultural incomes goes to the landlords, while half is retained by the farmers. Then half the 20 per

---

[1] See Quesnay's '(Premier) Problème Économique' (*Quesnay*, pp. 859–77); and 'Progression de la réparation de l'agriculture par l'abolissement des causes de son dépérissement', *Philosophie rurale*, vol. ii, pp. 354–78.

[2] See Georges Weulersse, *Le Mouvement Physiocratique en France (de 1756 à 1770)*, Paris, 1910, vol. i, pp. 111–19, 154–5, 180–5, 199–212 and 223–6, and in addition Livre Quatre, 'La Réalisation du programme Physiocratique'.

cent increase in the rate of return will go to the farmers with the resu
that annual agricultural advances will increase 10 per cent, and this wi
raise agricultural output 10 per cent in the following year and raise agr
cultural advances again if farmers are allowed to retain half the frui
of growth.

The argument corresponds to the one which showed that the taxation
agricultural receipts at a rate of 10 per cent should reduce output by 1
per cent per annum. In the present case advances yield 50 per cent, s
farmers must reinvest 1,000 out of each 1,500 livres of agricultural sal
to maintain constant output. However, the landlords were content to tal
300 out of each 1,300 livres when agricultural advances yielded 30 p
cent, and if they are content to take 400 out of 1,500 livres when the ra
of return rises to 50 per cent, then the farmers will be left with 1,100 o
of 1,500 livres which is 10 per cent more than the 1,000 out of 1,500 livr
that they need to maintain constant output. With Quesnay's assumptio
this will produce an initial 10 per cent rate of growth in agricultur
advances and therefore in rents, government revenues and industri
production also, and growth will continue for so long as landlords are co
tent to leave farmers with half the increase in the returns to agriculture.

Where Quesnay discusses the effects on growth of an increase in far
incomes he does not actually make the mechanical assumption that ha
the benefits go to the farmers, but he assumes instead that farmers hav
fixed period leases, and obtain the whole benefit from an increase in th
rate of return during the remainder of their leases, after which this go
in its entirety to the landlords.[1] In the passage cited from *Philosoph
rurale* of which Professor Meek says 'All the evidence, stylistic and othe
wise, points to Quesnay as its author',[2] the period of leases is assumed
be nine years, and farmers reinvest all the extra income they receive unt
their leases expire. The effect of an increase in the rate of return on annu
agricultural advances from 30 to 50 per cent in these conditions is outlin
in Table V. This Table is drawn up with the same assumptions as Tabl
III and IV. However as the rate of return on advances is only 50 per ce
instead of 100 per cent, marketed farm output is advances *plus* 50 per ce
instead of advances *plus* 100 per cent. The farmers need to retain a
amount equivalent to their advances to maintain constant output. ar
any excess they produce over this together with the previous level of ren
is their potential surplus.[3] Thus in year 1, the first year when a 50 per ce
rate of return is earned, their output is 1,500 million livres which excee
advances which are 1,000 million livres and rents of 300 million livres b

---

[1] See *Quesnay* (1766), pp. 870–1.   [2] Meek, p.

[3] It is assumed for simplicity that farmers' transactions with the industrial sector ju
balance, to bring out the principal effects of the higher rate of return in agriculture as sharp
as possible.

200 million livres, and this is the farmers' financial surplus. With the assumption of nine-year leases, one-ninth of the farms are in the final year of their leases, and in these cases the rent agreed for the next nine years will be based on the new 50 per cent rate of return, so one-ninth of the 200 million livre financial surplus will be absorbed in higher rents. The other eight-ninths, 178 million livres, will be reinvested as in Table V, with the result that the second year's advances are raised by eight-ninths of the

TABLE V

Effect on growth of an increase in r *the rate of return on annnal agricultural advances from 30 per cent to 50 per cent in Year 1*

Year	Advances	Rents	Marketed farm output	Farmers' financial surplus	Unexpired leases	Addition to	
						Advances	Rents
	A	R	A(1+r)	S	h	h.S	(1−h).S
							millions of livres
0	1,000	300	1,300	0	..	..	..
1	1,000	300	1,500	200	8/9	178	22
2	1,178	322	1,767	267	7/8	234	33
3	1,412	355	2,118	351	6/7	301	50
4	1,713	405	2,569	451	5/6	376	75
5	2,089	480	3,133	564	4/5	451	113
6	2,540	593	3,810	677	3/4	508	169
7	3,048	762	4,572	762	2/3	508	254
8	3,556	1,016	5,334	762	1/2	381	381
9	3,937	1,397	5,905	571	0	0	571
10	3,937	1,968	5,905	0	..	..	..

farmers' financial surplus of the first year. In the second year, a financial surplus will only be earned by the farmers whose leases have not yet come up for renewal, and one-eighth of these come up for renewal at the end of the year, so only seven-eighths of the surplus will be reinvested. Similarly, six-sevenths will be reinvested in the third year, five-sixths in the fourth year until finally, in the ninth year the last leases expire, and the entire remaining farm surpluses are absorbed into rents. After this, in the tenth year of a 50 per cent rate of return in agriculture, rents will be 50 per cent of advances, so there will no longer be a financial surplus for farmers. There will therefore be no further growth in farm incomes and output, but Table V shows that in the nine years where there is growth, annual agricultural advances increase incredibly at an annual rate of 16·4 per cent from 1,000 million livres to 3,937 million livres, while rents increase at an annual rate of 23 per cent from 300 million to 1,968 million livres. The alternative assumption of an equal division of gains between rents and advances produced indefinite growth at an initial rate of 10 per cent per annum. Whichever assumption is used therefore produces growth that is quite capable of counteracting adverse effects from other causes, and thus achieving *la réparation de l'agriculture*. The actual growth rates produced by the argument are obviously implausibly high, as were the rates of decline that indirect taxation caused, but it is best to set out exactly what rates of growth and decline result from the direct application of the assumptions of the Tableau before the appropriate correction factors are applied.

A Quesnay growth formula

Combining what has been said about growth so far, g_a the rate of growth of annual agricultural advances will depend on three sets of factors. First, if the propensity to consume the products of agriculture exceeds one-half by x, annual agricultural advances will grow at a rate of approximately $\frac{1}{2}x - \frac{2}{3}.x^2$ (from (2)), if the dynamic assumption that all gains and losses in farm incomes are shared equally between farmers and landlords is made. Second, if annual agricultural advances are taxed at an effective rate of T_a, they will decline at a rate of $\frac{1}{2}.T_a$ if gains and losses are shared equally by farmers and landlords; it was argued above that a 10 per cent tax on sales of food, which was in effect a 20 per cent tax on agricultural advances, would produce a 10 per cent rate of decline in incomes and advances in these conditions. Finally, if the actual rate of return on annual agricultural advances is r and rents are based on a rate of return of r^*, then agricultural advances should grow at an annual rate of $\frac{1}{2}(r-r^*)$ if farmers are allowed to reinvest half the excess, as in the example that has been outlined, and growth from this source will continue until r^* becomes as high as the new and higher r. Combining the three effects:

$$g_a = \tfrac{1}{2}x - \tfrac{2}{3}x^2 + \tfrac{1}{2}.(r - r^* - T_a) \tag{3}$$

Quesnay believed that the French National Product had declined because x was negative, and because of T_a, while there was no compensation from an r in excess of r^*, i.e. a more favourable rate of return in agriculture than the one on which rents were based. He believed, however, that the situation could be rapidly restored because it was open to the government to make T_a zero, and to make r exceed r^* for nine years at any rate, which would produce considerable growth. It is now thought that there was, in fact, slow growth during much of his lifetime,[1] so there may have been favourable underlying factors that play no part in the formula, or x may have been positive and not negative. Growth was slow, however, there was great agricultural distress, and French governments went through a

See p. 327, n. 1.

series of financial crises which contributed to the events of 1789, so Quesnay's proposals were very much to the point.

The formula can very easily produce extraordinarily rapid rates of growth or decline, and Quesnay was fully aware of this, and a number of correction factors are applied in *Philosophie rurale* to produce more plausible rates of growth. These involve departures from the strict calculations of the Tableau in equilibrium, but this was not designed to deal with dynamic progressions in detail so some adjustment is appropriate. The principal adjustment, which is really all that is needed, is to bring the *original* advances of agriculture, i.e. its fixed capital, fully into the argument. It has been assumed so far that agricultural output is proportional to A, the *annual* advances or circulating capital of farmers, and that in addition to this, farmers earn enough to cover 'interest' which can be regarded as the replacement of such fixed capital as wears out. It has therefore been assumed, in effect, that agricultural output can be doubled in the short period by doubling employment and seed corn without also doubling expenditure on horses, ploughs, etc., which are part of the farmers' fixed capital. The assumption that 'interest' is earned allows these to be replaced at a higher rate, but it does not allow for actual investment in more horses and ploughs as output expands. It is clear that more fixed capital is needed as output expands, as this is central to Quesnay's argument about the productivity of *la grande culture*, and the financing of any long-term growth process must require that fixed capital be increased at the same rate as circulating capital. Quesnay does not introduce this complication in the relatively small progressions and regressions that are shown in most of his published sequences of Tableaux, but the growth in farm incomes in the nine-year period where farmers continually reinvest what they gain until their leases expire is so great that the calculation in *Philosophie rurale* concerned with this problem does allow for the need to expand fixed capital in line with circulating capital. It is assumed in this calculation that the fixed capital of farmers is four times their circulating capital, i.e. that it is four times *annual* advances, so total farm capital is five times *annual* advances.[1] Elsewhere in his writings, Quesnay sometimes assumes that fixed capital is five times annual advances so that total capital is six times annual advances.[2] With the assumption of *Philosophie rurale* that total farm capital is five times annual agricultural

---

[1] *Philosophie rurale*, vol. ii, Table opposite page 366 (translated in Meek, p. 145), which shows the 'PROGRESSION of the Cultivators' Profit' from 1761 to 1770 on the assumption that four-fifths of the 'increase in the net product' is added to 'original advances' and one-fifth to annual advances.

[2] See *Quesnay* (1766), p. 795. See Eltis (op. cit.), pp. 172–3, for a more detailed account of the relative requirements for *annual* advances and *original* advances in Quesnay's argument.

advances, only one-fifth of any increase in the incomes that farmers receive can go to increase annual agricultural advances, and the remaining four-fifths has to be invested in new fixed capital which must grow at an equal rate in the long run. Applying the same principle, any shortfall in farm incomes can be partly made good at the expense of fixed capital in the long run, and this means that in periods of decline, annual agricultural advances need fall by only one-fifth of any fall in farm incomes, and Quesnay points out that fixed capital is run down where advances decline.[1] The long-term rise or fall of rents will depend on the rate at which circulating capital or annual agricultural advances rise or fall, and all the other important trends in the economy depend on this, and once the need for fixed capital is fully allowed for it becomes evident that annual agricultural advances will not grow or decline as rapidly as has so far been supposed.

The actual formula for the rate of growth of annual agricultural advances can be adjusted very simply to the need to expand the fixed capital of farmers in line with their circulating capital. If the ratio of total capital to circulating capital is V, and this is five or six in Quesnay's work, all growth rates will simply be reduced by a factor of V. Thus in the calculation in *Philosophie rurale* where fixed capital is four times circulating capital, V is five, and the rate of growth of annual agricultural advances is one-fifth that so far supposed. More generally, with the need to invest in fixed capital allowed for, (3) will become:

$$g_a = \frac{1}{2V}(x - 1\tfrac{1}{3}.x^2) + \frac{1}{2V}(r - r^* - T_a) \qquad (4)$$

In terms of modern growth theory, it would be said that (3), the earlier formula which neglected the need to expand fixed capital in line with annual advances, understated the capital–output ratio by a factor of V. (4) recognizes the existence of fixed capital, and that this raises the capital–output ratio V times, and a V-times increase in the capital–output ratio reduces the growth produced by given investment by a factor of V.

(4) recognizes the need to increase the fixed capital of farmers at the same rate as annual agricultural advances, but there has been no reference yet to the need to increase the money supply and landlords' own capital (*avances foncières*) at this rate. Quesnay assumes that countries will automatically obtain sufficient money for their needs through international trade (and it will not be farmers who pay for it) and there is no reference to the possibility that insufficient *avances foncières* might restrict progress. The growth of farmers' advances will therefore be the growth rate that matters.

Much more plausible growth rates are obtained with (4) than with th

[1] *Quesnay* (1767), p. 987.

earlier formula, which neglected the need to expand fixed capital. Thus if V is five, a propensity to consume the products of agriculture of 0·6 will produce a growth rate of about 0·8 per cent per annum instead of over 4 per cent, while a propensity of 0·4 will produce an annual rate of decline of only about 1·1 per cent. Similarly, the taxation of farm income at 20 per cent will produce an annual rate of decline of 2 per cent and not 10 per cent, while an increase in the rate of return on advances from 30 to 50 per cent will produce growth at just 2 per cent per annum. In the alternative calculation of the effect of the reinvestment of farm profits until all leases come up for renewal, the annual rate of growth in the nine-year period is 3·3 per cent, and not the incredible 16·4 per cent calculated previously. These slower and more plausible rates of growth and decline would be more than sufficient to account for any supposed decline or increase in population, incomes, and wealth in France in the seventeenth and eighteenth centuries. They would moreover, as Quesnay says, allow a Kingdom to reach '. . . a high degree of strength and prosperity in a short period of time',[1] where correct policies are pursued.

It is pointed out in *Philosophie rurale* that an 'essential condition' that must be fulfilled if the calculated growth is to be achieved is that it must be possible to increase population and farm animals in step with the progression, which will be realized only if this 'indispensable condition' can be met.[2] Hence it is recognized that the maximum achievable rate of population growth, etc., sets an ultimate constraint to growth, and this could even affect the slower rates of growth produced by the modified formula. This could be particularly important in North America, for Quesnay's account of the effects of the reinvestment of the extra profits of agriculture over a nine-year period concludes with a few words about what could be achieved in a new colony:

> Nevertheless, if the rapid advance of the simple arithmetical progression shown above is applied to vigorous colonies with a large territory, which can be cultivated with the labour of animals, assisted by large advances supplied by a wealthy metropolis, it can be seen that such colonies may be able to make very great progress in a short time. 1. Because new land when it has been cleared yields a large product. 2. Because in such places little or no taxes are paid. 3. Because the cultivators are themselves proprietors, so that all the profits from cultivation are all the time continually used to increase the wealth employed in cultivation . . . (1763)[3]

With no taxation of the products of agriculture, and no diversion of growing farm incomes to landlords, r^* and T_a will be zero, and the basic growth formula will become:

$$g_a = \frac{1}{V} \cdot (x - 1\tfrac{1}{3} \cdot x^2) + \frac{r}{V} \qquad (5)[4]$$

[1] *Quesnay* (1757), p. 504 (E).
[2] *Philosophie rurale*, vol. ii, p. 368.   [3] Ibid., p. 369 (M).
[4] Translating this formula into the concepts of modern economics, r/V is the rate of return

which will evidently produce more rapid growth than the earlier formula appropriate to the institutions of eighteenth-century France. Quesnay estimated that these, together with the other factors that held back the growth of agriculture in France reduced the growth that could follow from a given increase in the profitability of agriculture by nine-tenths.[1] Clearly in North American conditions, the maximum rate at which population and farm animals can be expanded is likely to act as the effective constraint on growth, for the rate of capital accumulation produced by the above formula is likely to exceed any physically sustainable rate of growth.

This insight into what is achievable with the institutions of a new economy concludes the present account of Quesnay's theory of economic growth. It is an interesting, powerful, and highly original theory, and it focuses attention on causes of growth and decline which are arguably of real importance. Moreover, no economist since has set out a growth model with plausible assumptions (once these are understood) where agriculture plays such a crucial role.

Quesnay and his successors

Quesnay's successors developed concepts which would have allowed him to express his argument more clearly. In particular, the adoption of Smith's division of the categories of income into wages the return to labour, profits the return to capital, and rent the return to land, would have allowed Quesnay to say what he had to say much more comprehensibly. In his theory wages and the normal profits of both farmers and artisans are always expressed as a single total. They are already separated by Turgot in his *Réflexions sur la formation et la distribution des richesses* of 1770, but Turgot followed Quesnay in supposing that the normal profits of industry are a cost and not a taxable surplus.[2] It is perfectly plausible that this was largely the case in France in 1770—though industrial profits certainly began to provide a surplus, i.e. a *net product*, in some countries in the course of the nineteenth century, and they may well have provided one in England in the late eighteenth century. Quesnay's theories would have been taken more seriously if it had been appreciated that he was simply assuming that industry provided no taxable surplus, and not that

on *total* farm capital, so the rate of growth of agricultural capital is assumed to equal the rate of profit that results from agricultural investment, plus a further term in x which depends on whether demand trends favour agriculture relative to other sectors. Leaving aside the term that depends on x, the formula simply states that the rate of growth equals the rate of profit, which is what modern theory would say if all profits are reinvested once the subsistence needs of farmers have been met as Quesnay assumes, and provided that the constraint which Quesnay explicitly recognizes does not limit growth to some lower rate.

[1] *Philosophie rurale*, vol. ii, p. 370.

[2] See sections XCIX and XCVI in R. L. Meek's translation of the 1788 edition (*Turgot on Progress, Sociology and Economics*, translated and edited by Ronald L. Meek, Cambridge University Press, 1973, pp. 180 and 178).

it made no economic contribution to production which is another meaning of the word 'sterile'. It would also have been helpful if Quesnay had been able to answer the criticisms of his theory which followed from Ricardo's theory of rent. According to this, no rent accrues at the margin of cultivation, and given sufficient competition, an addition to agricultural and industrial investment must then produce the same total return, for agricultural capital will produce no return in addition to the normal profits that farmers receive.[1] Quesnay's response to this might well have been that agricultural output is principally a return to capital, and landlords must in all practical cases be able to obtain part of the return on this *once leases expire*. Then marginal industrial investments will yield wages and entrepreneurial returns, while marginal agricultural investments will yield wages, entrepreneurial returns, and an addition to rents on the expiry of leases, so agricultural investment must generally yield more. He would only have conceded the relevance of Ricardo's theory to a country where there was no need for farmers to invest at the margin of cultivation in any way that improved their farms in the course of their leases. These were not the conditions of eighteenth-century France where agricultural expansion meant taking the capital-intensive methods of *la grande culture* to land which was not being efficiently farmed. Thus Ricardo's assumptions are appropriate to a country where all the land that can be farmed by efficient capital-intensive methods is already being so farmed, while Quesnay assumes a country where there is still scope for the extension of these methods. This is often a more appropriate assumption than that of a fully stocked agriculture, and a particular case can be made for Quesnay's assumptions along these lines.

It is therefore arguable that Quesnay's theory of economic growth deserves serious attention. It is obviously of considerable historical interest for the light it throws on the underlying causes of the French Revolution, and for its undoubted influence on Smith (who met Quesnay in 1766, and would have 'inscribed' *The Wealth of Nations* to him if he had not died two years before its publication[2]), and through him, on Malthus, Ricardo, and their successors. Quesnay's influence on Marx is also important, for only Quesnay before him formulated a precise scheme of reproduction where attention was focused above all on the production of a surplus and its expenditure. That is not, however, all that can be learnt from his theory of economic growth. Quesnay analysed the problems involved in achieving growth in an economy where land was not

---

[1] David Ricardo, *Principles of Political Economy and Taxation, Works and Correspondence*, edited P. Sraffa, Cambridge, 1951, vol. i, chapters 2 and 24.
[2] Dugald Stewart, 'Account of the life and writings of Adam Smith, LLD', *The Works of Adam Smith*, London, 1812, vol. v, p. 470.

W. A. ELTIS   351

scarce in the sense that there was much land in use that was producing negligible rates of return because of the low capital intensity of the methods of production in use. These are precisely the conditions today in many developing countries, which have mostly adopted policies similar to Colbert's of favouring industries that can hardly produce a surplus at the expense of agriculture which can. The failures of these policies in the twentieth century would have surprised Quesnay no more than their failure in his own time.

Exeter College, Oxford

[6]

Oxford Economic Papers 40 (1988), 269–288

THE CONTRASTING THEORIES OF INDUSTRIALIZATION OF FRANÇOIS QUESNAY AND ADAM SMITH

By WALTER ELTIS[1]

THE BENEFITS from industrialization as seen by the great French Physiocrats and Adam Smith were immensely different. François Quesnay argued from 1759 onwards that the industrial sector of the economy was 'sterile', and that state support for industrialization in France in the seventeenth century had reduced population, cut living standards and undermined government finances. Adam Smith insisted just seventeen years later in *The Wealth of Nations* that the benefits from the division of labour which could only be enjoyed in industry had already raised the standard of living of a British labourer above that of an African King. (pp. 23–4)

Quesnay and Smith both used rigorously formulated economic argument to arrive at these radically different results. What led Quesnay to his conclusion which astonished his contemporaries no less than subsequent generations of economists was a belief that industry as constituted in France in the seventeenth and eighteenth centuries could make no kind of net contribution to the nation's tax revenues. Its 'net product' [*produit net*], or taxable capacity or economic surplus was zero, which meant that at best, if its support cost the rest of society nothing, it could made no contribution to the military and welfare needs of the State. In less favourable circumstances where industry actually needed to be subsidized or protected, such diversions of real resources would impoverish the primary producing sector which provided the surpluses on which French governments relied. Smith too believed that agriculture had the potential to provide a vastly greater economic surplus than industry, but in his judgement the surplus industry offered was not zero. In addition, industry could be expected to provide external benefits of great importance to the whole economy through the productivity advances associated with the division of labour, though according to Smith, these would be maximized if industrial development was left to market forces.

Virtually all subsequent economists have preferred Smith's analysis to Quesnay's, but there is an important line of argument in Quesnay which several developing countries have overlooked to their cost. This is the proposition that industry fails to provide a taxable surplus comparable to that offered by agriculture. In twentieth century Argentina the agricultural surplus is equivalent to 80% of output, and the state has prevented significant agricultural growth by diverting a high fraction of this suplus to

[1] A preliminary version of this paper was presented to the 8th World Congress of the International Economic Association in New Delhi in 1986, and this will be published with the Conference Proceedings. The present developed version has benefited from comments by Peter Sinclair, Andrew Skinner, and Gianni Vaggi.

the support of industries which cannot compete internationally.[2] In Pakistan the value-added of various industires, measured at world prices, has recently been shown to be negative.[3] Such industries cannot be net contributors to the nation's tax revenues. Instead as in seventeenth and eighteenth century France, they are net absorbers of revenues, and via protection, net inflators of agricultural costs. So such government support for industry may well damage the supluses primary producers generate and therefore reduce the size of the sectors of the economy which have a true net capacity to support government expenditure and to finance economic growth. If the extraction of real resources from a primary surplus-generating sector and their dissipation in an industrial surplus-absorbing sector can occur as readily in twentieth century Argentina and Pakistan as in seventeenth century France, it is unfortunate for such countries that Quesnay's detailed theoretical and practical accounts of this line of argument are so largely neglected today.

The twentieth century development of Argentina, Pakistan and other economies that protect industry at the expense of agriculture will also be damaged through two further effects which are well known in the twentieth century international trade literature. In so far as industrial protection reduces the national income in the short-term it will lessen saving and so have a tendency to reduce the rate of capital accumulation. Moreover, in so far as the costs of imported capital equipment are raised through the protection of domestic capital goods industries (which is an endemic policy in the Indian sub-continent), such saving as actually results in accumulation will be deployed less effectively so that growth will be still further reduced.[4]

In this paper the essence of Quesnay's and Smith's arguments will be set out at the start, and it will be suggested that there are important elements of truth in both. Twentieth century economies may therefore find that they are applying industry-boosting policies which derive from propositions Smith established in conditions where Quesnay's reasoning is more appropriate.

François Quesnay on the relationship between agriculture and industry in economic development

In Quesnay's analysis primary production offers an economic surplus [*produit net*] over wage and raw material costs which ranges up to 100% of these.[5] He contrasts three agricultural techniques of production of which the most capital intensive, *la grande culture,* yields a surplus to landowners and

---

[2] See Cavallo and Mundlak (1982) for estimates of the surpluses generated in Argentinian agriculture in the 1960s and the 1970s, the rates at which they were absorbed by the State, and the consequently low levels of agricultural investment and growth.

[3] Little, Skitovsky and Scott (1970), pp. 58, 64 and 113.

[4] These lines of argument are admirably set out in Corden (1985).

[5] Quesnay's account of the techniques of production available to agriculture is set out in detail in the articles 'Fermiers' and 'Grains' which he contributed to Diderot's and d'Alembert's *Encyclopedia.* These are summarised in Eltis (1984), pp. 4–11.

the state equal to approximately 50% of output. With the more modestly capital intensive intermediate technology, *la petite culture*, the *produit net* is between 30% and 40% of annual agricultural advances and perhaps 25% of agricultural production, and in the most labour intensive conditions where peasants use only spades and hoes, the land yeilds no surplus over their own meagre subsistence. Competition between farmers ensures that the physical rates of surplus appropriate to these techniques of production are translated into the money rates of return Quesnay set out. His detailed calculations to demonstrate this always assume an average seven year run of good and bad harvests.[6]

La grande culture which offers a surplus of 50% of output to landlords or the state involves heavy investments by farmers themselves, while with *la petite culture* which yields around 25% of output, farmers invest modestly or else use landlords' capital and divide the harvest equally with them. The establishment of the high-surplus-yielding *la grande culture* requires a wealthy entrepreneurial class willing to invest in a capital intensive and highly efficient agriculture, with firm expectations that landlords and the state will allow them to enjoy the high profits that efficient farming can be expected to yield. These high farmers' profits are part of the 50% of agricultural costs and not the 50% of pure surplus or *produit net* that accrues to landlords and the state.

In industry in contrast there is no taxable surplus, and in conditions of perfect competition [*concurrence libre*], prices cover no more than wage and raw material costs. But the assumed wages of master craftsmen and the owners of manufacturing businesses are set very high in relation to average living standard to enable their incomes to include an element of normal profit to cover risk, trouble and a reasonable return on their capital.[7] Quesnay and Turgot after him took it for granted that the element of extra income of industrial proprietors was not a taxable surplus, for they would gradually cease to manufacture if this element in their rewards was removed.

It is an inevitable consquence of these assumptions of Quesnay's that the financial needs of the state can only be met from the economy's primary producing sector, because only this yeilds taxable surpluses. But it was nonetheless a notable fact which all including Quesnay recognised that French industrialsists and the merchant class that traded their goods often made vast fortunes. His insistence that industry and commerce could not support the needs of the state, or finance economic growth and that their

[6] There is a careful analysis of the link between physical and value rates of return with the different agricultural techniques of production in Quesnay's article 'Grains' (1757).
[7] The evidence of the higher incomes of industrial entrepreneurs is set out in Chapter 7 of *Philosophie Rurale*, and summarised in Eltis (1984), pp. 12–13. Meek (1962) did not accept that their higher incomes contains an element of normal profit. but Adam Smith who had had the benefit of extensive contacts with the leading Physiocrats in Paris believed it did in his summary of their system in *The Wealth of Nations*, pp. 666–7.

production was *sterile* therefore bewildered his contemporaries. These also noticed that manufacturing and commerical states like Venice and Holland had accumulated wealth and power, so how could it possibly be argued that agriculture provided the ultimate source of all wealth and of all net government revenues?

It has always been a mark of the greatest economic thinkers that they can dispute the underlying explanation of facts that are self-evident to the untutored, and Quesnay insisted that taxable industrial and commercial profits could only arise where businesses had managed to achieve elements of monopoly power.[8] This had arisen in Quesnay's Europe in a variety of ways. States frequently granted monopoly privileges to political supporters, or else they sold future monopoly rights for current cash, or they allowed corporations with monopoly power to emerge by protecting their own countries' industries. Such policies were prevalent throughout Europe and they had allowed extremely profitable corporations to emerge. And it was also true that industrial innovators could sell at monopoly prices, but these would disappear as soon as others learned to make the same new products. In addition France's great jewellers and furniture makers of the *ancien régime* had temporary monopoly-rights over their distinguished products which allowed them to sell at home and overseas at very high prices which yielded financial surpluses.

Quesnay insisted that any taxable industrial and commercial profits which arose in these ways could only result from such elements of monopoly power, which had the unfortunate effect of diverting a fraction of the true surpluses generated in the primary sector to wealthy industrial and commercial proprietors.

The agricultural surplus is the excess of agricultural output over the costs farmers must meet, and anything which reduces their expenses will increase the suplus as Quesnay explains in the 'Dialogue on the Work of Artisans':

> we have to divide the reproduction generated by the cultivator into two portions, namely, the portion which provides for his own subsistence, and the portion which is in excess of this subsistence. Whence it follows that if it is possible, without detrimentally affecting the total reproduction, to cut down on the first portion, the second will be correspondingly increased. For example, if we assume that the reproduction is 20, the cultivator's expenses 10, and the surplus 10, then if the expenses can be cut down to 8 the surplus will be 12. (p. 227[M])

The purchase of industrial goods required for the subsistence of labourers

---

[8] Quesnay discusses the relationship between industrial and commerical profits, the degree of competition and the national interest in three important articles which he published in 1766 in the *Journal d'Agriculture* of which the Physiocrat, Du Pont de Nemours was then editor. These are, 'Répétition de la Question Proposée dans la "Gazette du Commerce" au Sujet du Bénéfice que la Fabrique des Bas de Soie Établie à Nîmes Produit à la France', and the two dialogues between Monsieur H. (Quesnay pretending to be an intelligent critic of Physiocracy) and Monsieur N. (Quesnay the Physiocrat), 'Du Commerce', and 'Sur les Travaux des Artisans'. In the passages from these articles quoted below, [M] after a page reference signifies that a translation is by Ronald Meek, and [E] that the responsibility for a translation is mine.

are a cost to agriculture. Quesnay explains in the same article how tailors make clothing so that 'the husbandman is not obliged to leave his plough in order to work at making his clothing' and this saving of the husbandman's time increases 'his productive labour' and therefore the rate of surplus in agriculture (226[M]). Increasing the cost of manufactures as a result of protection or monopoly privileges, which permit the generation of industrial profits, will therefore reduce the rate of surplus in agriculture. Part of the agricultural surplus is in effect diverted to monoplist merchants or industrial producers.

The restrictions on competition which make this state of affairs possible divert part of the agricultural surplus to industry or commerce, but the state cannot tax these *de facto* monopoly profits in the same way as the revenue from the agricultural surplus, for according to Quesnay in the 'Dialogue on Commerce', commercial traders:

> know how to keep their profits and protect them from taxation; thus their wealth like the traders themselves has no country; it is unknown, mobile, and dispersed throughout all the countries in which they have dealings, and their true wealth is so confused with debts, active and passive, that it is impossible to evaluate it or assess it for proportional taxation. If their merchandise is taxed, the taxes will fall equally on domestic and foreign merchants and both will ensure through their sales and their purchases that the taxes fall on the nation ... (p. 851 [E])

Thus commercial capital is controlled by multinationals (to use a twentieth century label) which are in effect untaxable,[9] and it makes no difference whether these enterprises are nominally domestic or foreign.

Profits of French companies are sometimes made at the expense of foreign countires, but foreign companies will equally gain at the expense of France, as Quesnay explains in the 'Dialogue on Commerce':

> Merchants transport and re-transport, and profit turn by turn in every country ...
> Commerical costs are always paid at the expense of producers, who would benefit from the full price that purchasers pay if it were not for the expenses of intermediaries ... These costs, it is true, may increase the wealth of the traders who profit from them. but not at all those of the nations which mutually contribute them. Since, once again, the traders do not allow nations to share in their wealth, but they themselves share in the wealth of nations. (pp. 835–6[E])

If governments cannot obtain tax revenues from industrial and commercial producers, how are the great City states financed? Quesnay argued in the 'Dialogue on Commerce' that, 'the nations involved in maritime commerce may have a large number of wealthy merchants, but the State is always poor'. (p. 829[E]) Holland is an apparent exception, but Quesnay insists that the Dutch Republic is not merely commercial, 'It is also necessary to envisage it as proprietor of a territory which produces much: of colonies

---

[9] Cf. also Quesnay's statement in the *Maximes* that he published with the third edition of his original *Tableau* in 1759 that monetary fortunes are 'a clandestine form of wealth which knows neither king nor country' (p. 13 [M]).

whose produce is extremely profitable to it, and of seas where it obtains a large product through fishing'. (p. 852 [E])

If the state cannot tax industrial and commercial profits, it can at any rate borrow from wealthy producers and traders, but this has obvious disadvantages as Quesnay makes clear in the 'Dialogue on Commerce':

> to lend is not to give, and it does not even contribute to the needs of the State, and to borrow is no proof of wealth and power in a State . . . If you say that it is at least a resource for a nation to have the power to borrow, you should also perceive that this ruinous resource is hardly to the advantage of the nation which provokes the usury of the lender. (p. 826 [E])

Since the industrial and commercial fortunes which arise from monopoly power and accrue at the expense of the agricultural surplus are difficult to tax and dangerous to borrow, there is an overwhelming case for removing the privileges, and import and export restrictions, which allowed them to emerge.[10] It is argued powerfully in the 'Diaglogue on Artisans' that a nation's overwhelming interest is always:

> to extend commercial competition as far as possible . . .
> It is only by means of absolute liberty of commerce that the number of domestic and foreign merchants can be multipled, monopoly be made to disappear, and burdensome costs reduced, nations be assured the highest possible prices in their sales, and the lowest possible prices in their purchases, and thus procure for themselves the most extensive and advantageous commerce they can hope for. (p. 858 [E])

This will have the added advantage of encouraging the growth of agriculture, for:

> the highest possible price in the sale of your products, and the lowest possible price in the purchase of foreign produce will procure the greatest possible growth for your agriculture, which will then furnish you with the only true and solid means to increase your commerce, your wealth and the enjoyment you derive from it. (p. 842 [E])

Once the ideal state of perfect competition in industry and commerce is actually attained, the calculations set out in the *Tableau Économique* show the precise relationship between the output and the rate of return achieved in the surplus-generating and state-financing primary producing sector, and the consequent demand for the products of the industrial and commercial sector that this idealised economy will actually be able to sustain.

The question of the size of the economy's industrial and commercial sector in relation to the agricultural can be examined in two stages. The first and simplest is to examine the relative size of the two sectors in static

---

[10] Vaggi (1985) emphasises the significance Quesnay attached to the merchant class as an intermediary between agriculturalists and final consumers, which exploits the opportunities open to intermediaries with local monopoly power to deprive producers of some of the real incomes that would otherwise accrue to them.

conditions, and this is found by examining their relative size when the *Tableau Économique* is in stationary state equilibrium. Using the results of the static *Tableau* as a starting point, the dynamic conditions which will produce industrial growth or decline can then be derived.

Industry and commerce will provide employment for a considerable fraction of the population. The effective demand for their produce derives from landlords and the government who are assumed to spend half their incomes on the products of industry and commerce, and farmers who are also assumed to spend half their incomes in the industrial and commercial sector. Quesnay shows that when the full inter-relationships of the *Tableau Économique* are set out and analysed, the aggregate demand for domesically produced industrial and commercial production will total $\frac{1}{2}(A + R)$, where A is farmers' total incomes (which also equals total agricultural costs or advances) and R is the agricultural surplus or *produit net*.[11]

If agricultural advances, A, yield a return of 100% as in *la grande culture*, R the *produit net* will actually equal A, so that $\frac{1}{2}(A + R)$, the aggregate demand for the output of domestic industry and commerce will actually equal A. If the level of agricultural technology is merely that of *la petite culture* where agricultural advances yield no more than 30% to 40% the total *produit net* or aggregate rents will be perhaps one-third of agricultural advances, so R will equal no more than $\frac{1}{3}A$ and the aggregate demand for home produced manufactures, $\frac{1}{2}(A + R)$ will total $\frac{2}{3}A$. Hence the demand for manufactures will approximately equal annual agricultural advances with *la grande culture* but be only two-thirds with *la petite culture*.

The level of industrial and commercial employment will therefore depend upon both the level of agricultural investment, and the capital intensity of agricultural technology which determine the rate of surplus in agriculture. That is a summary of Quesnay's static analysis, which explains the size of the industrial and commercial sector in a stationary state. In the formula where industrial production is $\frac{1}{2}(A + R)$, anything which raises A, the level of agricultural advances, and R the agricultural surplus or *produit net*, must raise demand for the ouput of the industrial and commercial sector.

The stationary state equilibrium set out in the static *Tableau* may be disturbed in a number of ways to produce economic growth or decline.

A possibility which concerned Quesnay was that the effective demand of landlords and workers might shift away from agriculture towards industrial products. An extraordinary result he arrived at which has no parallel in modern economics is that if a population wishes to purchase more industrial production, in his words if it acquires a greater taste for *luxe de la décoration*, then the level of industrial production and employment will not

---

[11] The annual advances of the industrial and commercial sector will be half its output and it is stated twice in *Philosophie Rurale* that these advances will indeed total half of $\frac{1}{2}(A + R)$, that is $\frac{1}{4}(A + R)$. (Vol. 1, pp. 124 and 328: the formula is explained in Eltis (1984), pp. 27–9 and 37–8).

increase: *it will actually decline.* This astonishing result follows directly from his assumptions.

Starting from an initial stationary state, if demand shifts away from agriculture and towards industry and commerce, these will receive extra cash flows (as calculated in two series of disequilibrium *Tableaux* which he published[12]) while agricultural producers will receive smaller cash flows than in the previous year. Because the agriculturalists suffer a financial shortfall, the advances or investment for the following year's production that they can afford will be reduced. The industrialists in contrast will receive an initial financial boost because demand shifts in their favour, and they will invest more in order to produce more in the following year. In consequence, in the second year, agricultural output (which is twice advances) will be lower while industrial production will be higher than before. But only agriculture yields a *produit net*, so if the land yields 100% as with *la grande culture*, each 100 livre fall in agricultural advances will also produce a 100 livre fall in the following year's agricultural surplus. If the landlords accept an immediate and parallel reduction in rents, farmers will achieve a new static equilibrium in which they invest less and produce less (to match the now reduced demand for food) and landlords will receive less rent. But the new situation is not a potential equilibrium redistribution of resources because Quesnay assumes that where the agricultural surplus falls, landlords are at first unwilling to reduce rents by the fall in the agricultural surplus which no one predicted when rent contracts were initially arrived at. Tenant farmers themselves therefore initially have to meet the whole or most of the financial loss consequent upon a lower *produit net* until leases come up for renegotiation, perhaps nine years later. This financial loss to tenant farmers will cause them to invest still less in the following year which will reduce the agricultural surplus yet again, but the rents they will have to pay will again be reduced by less than the fall in the *produit net*, so they will be forced to cut their advances still further, and each time they reduce their advances, production will fall in parallel and squeeze rents and farm profits still further. So agriculture will slide downwards, falling production levels continually reducing the *produit net*, and contractural rents falling more slowly than the *produit net* with the result that farmers are perpetually short of cash and are therefore obliged to sell off more and more of their advances instead of being able to invest them in the land to generate future harvests.

The domestic demand for industrial production derives quite largely from landlords spending a fraction of their rents on the products of industry, and farmers spending a fraction of their wages on the industrial side of the *Tableau*. If both these classes are becoming poorer each year, their demand for industrial production will all the time fall. The industrial producers gain

---

[12] These are to be found in *Philosophie Rurale*, Vol. III, pp. 33–53, and in *l'Ami des Hommes*, Vol. VI, pp. 192–202. A modern restatement is presented in Eltis (1984), pp. 42–9.

in the initial year in which the nation's tastes first move in their favour, and the extra cash flows they then receive enable them to invest and produce more in the second year, but after this, falling demand from agricultural producers and landlords will gradually reduce the domestic market for industrial production. This will be higher than it was originally for perhaps four years, but after that it will gradually decline in parallel with the falling trend in agricultural incomes.

Quesnay explains, correspondingly, that if the nation's tastes switch towards agriculture, industry and commerce will lose out for a few years but the growing agricultural sector will generate extra demand for industrial products which will steadily raise the demand for manufactures from then on. Within a few years the extra markets for manufactures from A and R which are both growing will more than make good the initial loss.

The formula for the growth (or decline) of agricultural production (δg_a) consequent upon a deviation in the propensity to consume the products of agriculture of δC_a from the steady state propensity (normally 0.5) can be shown to be:[13]

$$\delta g_a \approx \tfrac{1}{2}\delta C_a - \tfrac{2}{3}\delta C_a^2$$

Then if C_a rises from 0.5 to 0.6 (so that $\delta C_a = 0.1$), agricultural output (and therefore the effective demand generated from agricultural incomes) will grow at approximately 4.3% per annum. If the propensity to consume food falls from 0.5 to 0.4, agricultural production will decline at an annual rate of approximately 5.67%. When the propensity to consume food first declines from 0.5 to 0.4, the demand for manufactures rises by one-fifth (i.e by 20%) because the propensity to consume manufactured goods increases from 0.5 to 0.6. If agricultural output and hence the effective demand for manufactures then declines at a rate of 5.67%, it will fall below its initial level after four further years, despite the 20% increase at the start.

The logic behind this process is that agriculture generates a *produit net* while industry does not. Every 100 livres of demand that shifts the pattern of production away from industry and towards agriculture therefore generates *an external benefit* of 100 livres to the landlords (or the State where rents are taxed). Similarly, an increase in the demand and supply of manufactures and a corresponding reduction in the output of food has a negative external impact on rents. The lower level of rents then adversely influences the effective demand for manufactures so that industrial producers lose on balance as soon as this unfavourable *external* effect on the demand for their produce outweighs the initial favourable effect.

The *dynamic* effect in the above processes is due to a lag between the generation of a higher or lower *produit net* and the market fixing of the rents farmers are actually obliged to pay. Where the *produit net* falls, farmers are squeezed because their contractural rents are still based on the

---

[13] See, Eltis (1984), p. 47.

formerly higher *produit net,* so output slides downwards. Where the *produit net* rises so that farmers benefit, output will rise from year to year until market determined rents in the end catch up with the rising agricultural surplus. Then, as the agricultural surplus and agricultural advances rise or fall, so will the demand for the products of industry and commerce which is always $\frac{1}{2}(A + R)$. Anything at all which produces an unpredicted rise or fall in the agricultural surplus will have these dynamic effects which strongly influence the long-term growth of both agriculture and industry.

Quesnay's own examples focus on the benefits from the establishment of free trade which raises the agricultural surplus and sets off a dynamic expansion of the economy,[14] and the damaging effects on both agriculture and industry of a reduction in the agricultural surplus as a result of the adoption of protectionist policies misguidedly intended to foster industrial expansion. Quesnay's criticisms are especially levelled at the pro-industrial policies of Louis XIV's great Finance Minister, Colbert, and in his '*Maximes Générales du Gouvernement Économique d'un Royaume Agricole*', a vital summary of Physiocratic economics which appears three times in his published work,[15] he outlines the disastrous effects of Colbert's efforts to foster industrialisation, which actually resemble those that many countries have adopted in the twentieth century:

> It will never be forgotten that a minister of the last century, dazzled by the trade of the Dutch and the glitter of luxury manufactures, brought his coutry to such a state of frenzy that no one talked about anything but trade and money, without reflecting on the true employment of money or on a country's true trade.
>
> This minister, whose good intentions were so worthy of esteem but who was too much a prisoner of his ideas, tried to bring about the generation of wealth from the work of men's hands, to the detriment of the very source of wealth, and put the whole economic constitution of an agricultural nation out of gear. External trade in corn was stopped in order to bring about a low cost of living for the manufacturer; and the sale of corn inside the kindom was subjected to an arbitrary system of regulation which cut off trade between provinces. The protectors of industry, the justices in the towns, in order to procure corn at a low price, ruined their towns and provinces through poor calculation by causing a gradual decline in the cultivation of their land. Everything tended to bring about the destruction of the revenue of landed property, manufactures, trade, and industry, which, in an agricultural nation, can be maintained only through the produce of the soil. For it is this produce which provides trade with a surplus for export, and which pays revenue to the proprietors and wages to the men engaged in remunerative activities . . .

[14] Examples are set out in Quesnay's '(Premier) problème économique', and in *Philosphie Rurale*, Vol. II, pp. 354–78, and restated in modern terms in Eltis (1984), pp. 57–61. The principal factors that influence the rate of economic growth in Quesnay's work are explained quite similarly in Barna (1976).

[15] These maxims first appeared in 1757 in the article, 'Grains': a longer version followed in 1759 in the third edition of the *Tableau Économique*, and the full thirty maxims were published in 1767 in the volume of Quesnay's writings, *Physiocratie*, that Du Pont prepared, which reached Adam Smith's library.

Luxury in the way of ornamentation [*luxe de la décoration*] was encouraged, and made very rapid progress. The administration of the provinces, harassed by the needs of the state, no longer offered any security in the countryside for the steady employment of the wealth necessary for the annual reproduction of wealth, which caused a large part of the land to be reduced to small scale cultivation [*la petite culture*], to be left fallow, and to become valueless. The revenue of the proprietors of landed property was uselessly sacrificed to a mercantile trade which could make no contribution to taxes. It became virtually impossible for agriculture to provide for them, depressed and overburdened as it was; their coverage was extended more and more to include men, food, and trade in raw produce; they were increased through the expenses of collection and through the destructive plundering of the reproduction; and a system of finance grew up around them which enriched the capital with the spoils of the provinces. Traffic in money lent out at interest created a very important kind of revenue based on money and drawn from money, which from the point of view of the nation was only an imaginary product, eluding taxation and undermining the state. This revenue based on money, and the appearance of opulence, maintained by the splendour of ruinous luxury, imposed upon the vulgar, and reduced further and further the reproduction of real wealth and the money stock of the nation. Unhappily, alas, the causes of this general disorder remained unknown for too long a time (pp. 245–6 [M]).

That passage underlines France's various seventeenth errors in the manner priority was given to industrial development. The attempt to achieve a low cost of living for industrial producers by forcing agriculturalists to sell in the home market reduced agriculture's *produit net*, and therefore its output and the economy's rate of growth. The towns themselves were ruined by the destruction of agriculture in the surrounding countryside. The encouragement of luxury consumption added to the deterioration of agricultural markets. The impoverishment of the agricultural producers reduced the level of agricultural technique from *la grande culture* which yielded a *produit net* equivalent to half of output to *la petite culture* which yielded no more than 25%. The tax-contributing agricultural sector was allowed to decline in relation to the industrial and mercantile sector which yielded no tax revenues, and tax collectors became increasingly desperate to obtain revenues so that methods of collection became increasingly supply-destructive. In the same 'General Maxims', Quesnay quotes Boisguilbert's calculations to suggest:

the revenue from landed property, which was formerly 700 millions (1400 millions in terms of our money today) diminished by one-half between 1660 and 1699. He notes that it is not to the level of taxes but to the injurious form of assessment and the disorder which it brought about that this huge decline must be attributed. ... The assessment became so irregular that under Louis XIV it rose to more than 750 millions but yielded to the royal treasury only 250 millions ... (p. 262[M])

The increasing disorder in the nation's finances led to the creation of yet larger untaxable financial fortunes, and raised interest rates, and these higher interest rates then added to the adverse effect on the surplus-producing agricultural sector.

Quesnay's analysis led him towards very simple policy principles which he summarised in the 'Dialogue on Commerce':

> Consumers multiply wherever subsistence expands; but it is only free competition with foreign buyers which can ensure the best possible price, and it is only a high price that can procure and sustain the opulence and the population of a kingdom through success in agriculture. That is the alpha and omega of economic science. (p. 824[E])

How Adam Smith's analysis of the relationship between agriculture and industry in economic development differed from Quesnay's

Smith's account of the potential benefits from industrialization departs sharply from Quesnay's. He believed that in its progress towards opulence an economy's investment will initially be mainly agricultural, and after that industrial and finally commercial, so the latter must in due course offer very large economic benefits. Before attention is focused on Smith's differences with Quesnay, it is important to emphasise the extent to which he learned from him. Smith spent ten months in Paris in 1765–66 where he discussed economic issues extensively with several of the leading Physiocrats, and in particular with Quesnay himself. The lectures he gave in Glasgow before 1765 include no hint of the close interconnection between capital accumulation and growth which was to play so fundamental a rôle in *The Wealth of Nations*. It has been inferred that he owed his grasp of this to the thorough grounding in Quesnaysian economics he acquired in 1765–66.[16] The editors of the Glasgow edition of *The Wealth of Nations* have commented that 'the model [of Physiocracy] which Smith expounds [in Book IV Chapter 9] is rather more elaborate than that offered by Quesnay' (pp. 672–3), which underlines how much he learned during this Paris visit. It may be added that in Paris Smith also saw a good deal of Turgot whose *Réflexions sur la Formation et la Distribution des Richesses* of 1770 reached his library, and in this book Turgot who is sometimes regarded as a near-Physiocrat recognised that industry generates a surplus in the form of investable profits, so Physiocratic thought on industrialization quickly moved on from Quesnay's stark insistence that industry's potential contribution to growth is at best zero.

It is to be noted that while Smith (and Turgot) progressed from Quesnay's negative analysis of the potential benefits from industrialization, there are still vital issues where they follow him. Smith wholly agreed that agriculture offers a far larger taxable and investable surplus than industry which is one main reason why he believed that in a society's natural

[16] That view has been expressed by Skinner (1979), Chapter 5.

progress towards opulence, agricultural investment must come first:

> The labourers and labouring cattle, therefore, employed in agriculture, not only occasion like the workmen in manufactures, the reproduction of a value equal to their own consumption, or to the capital which employs them, together with its owner's profits; but of a much greater value. Over and above the capital of the farmer and all its profits, they regularly occasion the reproduction of the rent of the landlord. (pp. 363–4)

Smith thus comes to the same view as Quesnay and the Physiocrats that extra agricultural demand and production provide the *external benefit* that unlike industrial production they raise aggregate rents. Because agricultural production adds to rents while industrial production does not, increments to agricultural production will have more potential to finance the needs of the State than equal increments to industrial production. The Ricardian theory of rent, originated by Malthus, West and Ricardo in 1815, insisted that this line of argument of Quesnay's and Smith's was incorrect. If, as the Ricardian theory insisted, marginal land yields no rent, a *marginal increment* to agricultural production will add no more aggregate ouput than the increase in wages and profits that it generates, and precisely the same is true of manufacturing. Ricardo therefore insisted that there is not reason to suppose that expanding agriculture will generate more 'revenue' [profits plus rents in his analysis] than an equal expansion of industry.[17] On this issue, Smith's position was identical to Quesnay's, and the Ricardians found them equally in error.

There is a further vital issue on which Smith and Quesnay were in complete agreement. Both wholly supported free trade and the maximization of international competition, and they saw the benefits from these in very similar terms. Smith's position is better known than Quesnay's, and a very well-known passage from *The Wealth of Nations* in juxtapositon to a similar passage from Quesnay's 'Dialogue on the Work of Artisans' will underline the similarity of their reasoning. First Smith:

> every system which endeavours, either, by extraordinary encouragements, to draw towards a particular species of industry a greater share of the capital of the society than would naturally go to it; or, by extraordinary restraints, to force from a particular species of industry some share of the capital which would otherwise be employed in it, is in reality subversive of the great purpose which it means to promote. It retards, instead of accelerating, the progress of the society towards real wealth and greatness; and diminishes, instead of increasing, the real value of the annual produce of its land and labour.
>
> All systems either of preference or of restraint, therefore, being thus completely taken away, the obvious and simple system of natural liberty establishes itself of its own accord. Every man, as long as he does not violate the laws of justice, is left

---

[17] His objections to Smith's argument are developed in Ricardo (1817), Chapter 26. Hollander (1973) pp. 195 and 280–7, has also strongly criticised Smith here.

perfectly free to pursue his own interest his own way, and to bring both his industry and capital into competition with those of any other man, or order of men. (p. 687)

and now Quesnay:

> You will come round again to the necessity of accepting the greatest possible freedom of competition in all branches of trade, in order to cut down as far as possible on the burdensome costs involved in them. As soon as you have calculated the effects of this general freedom prescribed by natural right, by virtue of which *each person should have the legal power to render his situation as good as he possibly can, without infringing upon the rights of others*, it will become self-evident to you that it is an essential condition of the growth of public and private wealth. (p. 229[M])

Despite this identity of argument on the desirabiliy of a system of natural liberty in industry and commerce, where all should be equally free to buy in the cheapest market and sell in the dearest (though Quesnay's support for this system is tempered by the qualification that it should be administered through benevolent despotism[18]); and also their agreement that agricultural expansion offers the largest potential economic surplus, Smith believed that there were significant errors in Quesnay's analysis. But the extent of their agreement should not be underrated. Smith said that Quesnay's system, 'with all its imperfections is, perhaps, the nearest approximation to the truth that has yet been published upon the subject of political economy. (p. 678)

The first important difference between Smith and Quesnay is that Smith (like Turgot a few years earlier) believed that industrial profits include an element of economic surplus in the sense that industrial capitalists can save and invest from their profits, with the result that they have the potential to add to the growth of the economy:

> The increase in the quantity of useful labour actually employed within any society, must depend altogether upon the increase of the capital which employs it; and the increase of that capital again must be exactly equal to the amount of the savings from the revenue, either of the particular persons who manage and direct the employment of that capital, or of some other persons who lend it to them. If merchants, artificers and manufacturers are, as this system [Quesnay's] seems to suppose, natually more inclined to parismony and saving than proprietors and cultivators, they are, so far, more likely to augment the quantity of useful labour employed within their society, and consequently to increase its real revenue, the annual produce of its land and labour. (p. 677)

It was extremely prescient of Smith to appreciate that merchants and manufacturers have the power (and the inclination) to save some of the ordinary or 'normal' profits which accrue to them in conditions of perfect

---

[18] See Fox-Genevese (1976) and Vaggi (1987) for accounts of these aspects of Quesnay's thought. It is to be noted that Vaggi doubts that Quesnay would have advised his Monarch to permit the free importation of manufactures that constitute a mere *luxe de la décoration*.

competition. That merchants and manufacturers have the power to raise the rate of growth through their saving does not necessarily signify that they will generate a taxable surplus. A sufficient profit to leave something over for potential saving may be a necessary condition for the investment of private capital in industry and commerce, so profits sufficient to enable individuals to save may be part of the supply price of manufactures. But it does not follow that any part of these profits will necessarily be available to the State, for a lower net of tax return could discourage the supply of industrial capital. Smith does not actually discuss Quesnay's propostion that industry and commerce fail to generate a taxable surplus, but the history of the next century underlines that the industrial surplus soon became large enough to generate substantial tax revenues in addition to private saving. By the time the first volume of Karl Marx's *Capital* was published in 1867, industrial and commercial profits amounted to 30% of Britain's gross domestic product and agricultural rents plus the profits generated in agriculture amounted to no more than 13%.[19] So within a century, Britain's industrial and commercial surpluses were to become vastly larger than the agricultural. Smith's analysis (and Turgot's) was compatible with this development, but not Quesnay's.

Smith's main objection to Quesnay's argument is of course its neglect of the enormous advantages a society can obtain from the division of labour which can be taken far further in industry than in agriculture, for the 'labour of artificers and manufacturers . . . is capable of being more subdivided, and the labour of each workman reduced to a greater simplicity of operation, than that of farmers and country labourers'. (p. 676) Because of these potential advantages:

A small quantity of manufactured produce purchases a great quantity of rude produce. A trading and manufacturing country, therefore, naturally purchases with a small part of its manufactured produce a great part of the rude produce of other countries; while, on the contrary, a country without trade and manufactures is generally obliged to purchase, at the expence of a great part of its rude produce, a very small part of the manufactured produce of other countries. (p. 677)

So Smith argues that a country which successfully develops its industry can attain far more favourable terms of trade between agricultural produce and manufactures than one that is still without a substantial industrial sector. Smith formulated the benefits from the division of labour in industry so that each expansion in industrial employment leads to more extensive subdivisions of employment, and hence to the achievement of higher productivity through the invention of superior machinery to exploit the opportunities this offers:

What takes place among the labourers in a particular workhouse, takes place, for the same reason, among those of a great society. The greater their number, the

[19] Matthews, Feinstein and Odling-Smee (1982), p. 164.

more they naturally divide themselves into different classes and subdivisions of employment. More heads are occupied in inventing the most proper machinery for executing the work of each, and it is, therefore, more likely to be invented. (p. 104)

The proposition that industrial productivity will be higher the more extensive the division of labour was present in lectures Smith gave in Glasgow just before and immediately after his Paris visit, where different students have recorded his words as, 'Twenty millions of people perhaps in a great society, working as it were to one anothers hands, from the nature of the division of labour before explained would produce a thousand times more goods than another society consisting only of two or three millions' and 'For twenty millions in a society, in the same manner as a company of manufacturers, will produce a hundred times more goods to be exchanged than a poorer and less numerous one of 2 mill',[20] As industrial employment grows and the division of labour is extended, industrial productivity will continually increase, so the quanity of production of each industrial worker will all the time rise. If the relative prices of manufactures do not fall entirely in line with continuing increases in industrial productivity, the amount of corn the product of a manufacturing worker can be traded for will all the time rise. Thus if manufacturing productivity grows at a rate of 2% a year, and the relative prices of manufactures fall only 1% per annum, while agricultural productivity and the price of corn are constant, the output of a manufacturing worker will be tradable for 1% more corn in each successive year. Hence the basis for Smith's statement that '[A trading and manufacturing country] exports what can subsist and accommodate but a very few, and imports the subsistence and accommodation of a great number'. (p. 677)

The country that succeeds in expanding its manufacturing employment sufficiently to achieve the highest productivity levels and the greatest terms of trade benefits implicitly faces only modest competition from other manufacturing countries, so it will be able to reduce the relative prices of its manufactures less than the annual advance in its relative productivity. In Smith's argument, other countries will only achieve matching industrial productivity if they can attain comparable employment and production levels, so those who first attain high industrial production and efficiency will enjoy advantages which will not be readily competed away in the manner Quesnay assumed throughout his analysis of the tendency of competition to eliminate industrial profits.

The logic of Smith's argument indicates that a country with inferior industrial output and productivity might be able to compete with its more efficient competitors if it could pass through an initial loss making phase as

---

[20] These are reprinted in *Lectures on Jurisprudence*, pp. 392 and 512.

it expands its industrial production to their levels. Its companies could only survive these losses if, during the interval in which they were still inefficient owing to an inadequate scale of production, they were protected from the competition of overseas industries which had already attained high output and productivity. Smith discussed this case for infant industry protection which followed so directly from the logic of his argument:

> By means of such regulations, indeed, a particular manufacture may sometimes be acquired sooner than it could have been otherwise, and after a certain time may be made at home as cheap or cheaper than in the foreign country. But though the industry of the society may be thus carried with advantage into a particular channel sooner than it could have been otherwise, it will by no means follow that the sum total, either of its industry, or of its revenue, can ever by augmented by any such regulation. The industry of the society can augment only in proportion as its capital augments, and its capital can augment only in proportion to what can be gradually saved out of its revenue. But the immediate effect of every such regulation is to diminish its revenue, and what diminishes its revenue, is certainly not very likely to augment its capital faster than it would have augmented of its own accord, had both capital and industry been left to find out their natural employments.
>
> Though for want of such regulations the society should never acquire the proposed manufacture, it would not, upon that account, necessarily be the poorer in any one period of its duration. In every period of its duration its whole capital and industry might still have been employed, though upon different objects, in the manner that was most advantageous at the time. In every period its revenue might have been the greatest which its capital could afford, and both capital and revenue might have been augmented with the greatest possible rapidity. (p. 458)

In Smith's argument an extensive scale of production and large capital stock are both necessary if high levels of industrial efficiency and employment are to be attained. Infant industry protection can create a large captive home market, but by reducing the economy's overall net revenue, or *produit net* as Quesnay described it, protection actually reduces the economy's capacity to expand the capital stock and therefore to take advantage of its newfound opportunities for industrial growth.

So while Smith saw far greater benefits from the growth of manufacturing industry than Quesnay, he entirely agreed that the State should not interfere with market forces to further industrial growth. The very different analyses of Smith and Quesnay therefore indicate an identical policy stance.

Conclusion

Since the Second World War, Hong Kong, Taiwan, South Korea and Singapore have followed policies which have much in common with those that Smith and Quesnay advocated,[21] while the countries of the Indian

[21] The policies these countries have pursued are set out and discussed in detail in Chen (1979).

sub-Continent have preferred to pursue Colbertian policies involving massive tariff protection, industrial subsidies, agricultural price controls, and the diversion of agricultural surpluses in order to seek to build up industry.

The theory of infant industry protection and of the potential external benefits from industrial development have advanced greatly since 1776, but the eighteenth century propositions of Smith and Quesnay that these policies will not actually assist long-term industrial development pose question which twentieth century economists cannot safely lose sight of.

The first questions are raised by the line of argument which is most powerfully present in Quesnay's work. This focuses attention on the taxable surplus or *produit net* that industry and agriculture generate. Quesnay was of course wrong to suppose that only agriculture generates a *produit net,* but the question still needs to be asked of countries which have devoted vast real resources to industrial growth: Is industry a net generator of funds capable of supporting government defence and welfare spending, or is it actually a net absorber of such funds? Is industry capable of supporting social welfare, or is it a part of the welfare system that the sectors which are truly surplus-generating are required to finance?[22]

A second vital question is raised most sharply by Smith's analysis: Have pro-industrial policies actually raised or alterntively have they perhaps reduced the long-term rate of capital accumulation? If they transitorily reduce the gross national product because they force the substitution of low (or even negative) value-added production (when measured at world market prices) for production which offers a higher value-added, then the probability is that there will be less saving and capital accumulation from this lower real national income (as the twentieth century neoclassical trade literature also suggests). If saving and capital accumulation are diminished in the short-term, does the evidence indicate that long-term capital accumulation is truly raised as the advocates of twentieth century Colbertian policies invariably suppose?

It certainly appears that the questions raised by the eighteenth century analyses of François Quesnay and Adam Smith may still be pertinent to the development policies of several countries in the Third World.

Exeter College, Oxford.

REFERENCES

BARNA, TIBOR (1976), 'Quesnay's Model of Economic Development', *European Economic Review*, Vol. 8.

---

[22] It is shown in Eltis (1979) that even in a country with industries as advanced as Britain's, the nationalized industries were for many years part of the welfare state which the rest of the economy had to finance from its surpluses, instead of generating real resources to provide the wherewithal to finance social welfare.

BOISGUILBERT, PIERRE DE (1707), *Le Détail de la France* (Paris). Reprinted in *Pierre de Boisguilbert ou la Naissance de l'Économie Politique*, 2 Vols, (Paris: Institute National d'Études Démographiques.

CAVALLO, DOMINGO and MUDLANK, YAIR (1982), *Agriculture and Economic Growth in an Open Economy: The Case of Argentina* (Washington: International Food Policy Research Institute).

CHEN, EDWARD K. Y. (1979), *Hyper-Growth in Asian Economies: A Comparative Study of Hong Kong, Japan, Korea, Singapore and Taiwan* (London: Macmillan).

CORDEN, W. M. (1985), 'The Effects of Trade on the Rate of Growth', in *Protection, Growth and Trade* (Oxford: Blackwell).

ELTIS, WALTER (1979), 'The True Deficits of the Public Corporations', *Lloyds Bank Review*, January.

ELTIS, WALTER (1984), *The Classical Theory of Economic Growth* (London: Macmillan).

FOX-GENOVESE, ELIZABETH (1976), *The Origins of Physiocracy* (Ithaca: Cornell University Press).

HOLLANDER, SAMUEL (1973), *The Economics of Adam Smith* (Toronto: University Press).

LITTLE, IAN, SKITOVSKY, TIBOR and MAURICE SCOTT (1970), *Industry and Trade in Some Developing Countries* (Oxford: University Press for OECD).

MALTHUS, T. R. (1815), *An Inquiry into the Nature and Progress of Rent* (London).

MARX, KARL (1867–83), *Capital*, 3 Vols. Reprinted (Moscow: Progress Publishers for Lawrence and Wishart).

MATTHEWS, R. C. O., FEINSTEIN, C. H. and ODLING-SMEE, J. C. (1982) *British Economic Growth, 1856–1973* (Oxford: University Press).

MEEK, RONALD L. (1962), *The Economics of Physiocracy* (London: Allen & Unwin).

QUESNAY, FRANÇOIS (1756), 'Fermiers'. Reprinted in L. Salleron (ed.), *François Quesnay et la Physiocratie* (1958), 2 Vols, (Paris: Institute National d'Études Démographiques) [Abbreviated below as INED].

QUESNAY, FRANÇOIS (1757), 'Grains'. Reprinted in INED.

QUESNAY, FRANÇOIS (1758–9), *Tableau Économique*, Three Editions in 1758–9. Republished and translated in Marguerite Kuczynski and Ronald L. Meek (eds) (1972) *Quesnay's Tableau Économique* (London: Macmillan).

QUESNAY, FRANÇOIS (1756–60), with RIQUETI, VICTOR DE, MARQUIS DE MIRABEAU, *L'Ami des Hommes*, 6 Vols. Reprinted (1972) (Scientia Verlag Aalen).

QUESNAY, FRANÇOIS with RIQUETI, VICTOR DE, MARQUIS DE MIRABEAU, (1973), *Philosphie Rurale*, 3 Vols. Reprinted (1972) (Scientia Verlag Aalen).

QUESNAY, FRANÇOIS (1766), 'Répétition de la Question Proposée dans la "Gazette du Commerce" au Sujet du Bénéfice que la Fabrique des Bas de Soie Établie à Nîmes Produit à la France'. Reprinted in INED.

QUESNAY, FRANÇOIS (1766), 'Dialogue entre M. H. et M. N. 'Du Commerce''. Reprinted in INED.

QUESNAY, FRANÇOIS (1766), '(Premier) Problème Économique'. Reprinted in INED.

QUESNAY, FRANÇOIS (1766), 'Second Dialogue sur les Travaux des Artisans'. Reprinted and translated in Meek (1962).

QUESNAY, FRANÇOIS (1767), *Physiocratie, ou Constitution Naturelle du Gouvernement le Plus Advnatageux au Genre Humain*.

QUESNAY, FRANÇOIS (1767), 'Maximes Générales du Gouvernement d'un Royaume Agricole'. Reprinted and translated in Meek (1962).

RICARDO, DAVID (1815), *On the Influence of a Low Price of Corn on the Profits of Stock* (London).

RICARDO, DAVID (1817), *On The Principles of Political Economy and Taxation* (London).

SKINNER, A. S. (1979), *A System of Social Science: Papers Relating to Adam Smith* (Oxford: University Press).

SMITH, ADAM (1776) *An Inquiry into the Nature and Causes of the Wealth of Nations*, 2 Vols (London). Republished, R. H. Campbell, A. S. Skinner and W. B. Todd (eds) (1976) 2

Vols, as II of *The Glasgow Edition of the Works and Correspondence of Adam Smith* (Oxford: University Press).

SMITH, ADAM *Lectures on Jurisprudence*, delivered in 1762–3 and 1766. R. L. Meek, D. D. Raphael and P. G. Stein (eds) (1978), V of *The Glasgow Edition of the Works and Correspondence of Adam Smith* (Oxford: University Press).

TURGOT, A. R. J. (1770) *Réflexions sur la Formation et la Distribution des Richesses* (Paris).

VAGGI, G. (1985) 'A Physiocratic Model of Relative Prices and Income Distribution', *Economic Journal*, Vol. 95, December.

VAGGI, G. (1987) *The Economics of François Quesnay* (London: Macmillan).

WEST, EDWARD (1815) *Essay on the Application of Capital to Land* (London).

[7]

MALTHUS'S THEORY OF EFFECTIVE DEMAND AND GROWTH

By W. A. ELTIS[1]

THE challenge posed by Malthus's theory of effective demand is underlined by the multiplicity of modern interpretations and reinterpretations to which it has given rise.[2] From Keynes onwards, a very large number of twentieth century economists have considered that there may be important truths or errors in Malthus's analysis, but as Professor Denis O'Brien has pointed out, "... there are as many secondary interpretations as authors."[3] There is scarce agreement between any two modern commentators on the fundamental nature of his contribution.

One way of reinterpreting Malthus in the twentieth century is to endeavour to reconstruct his argument, using the tools of modern economic analysis. If a modern economist makes his assumptions and constructs an economic model from them, the results should ideally be those that Malthus himself arrived at. This will be the case if Malthus's own argument followed consistently from similar premises.

A model can in fact be constructed which is derived from his assumptions that arrives at some of his most important results. In particular, it can be shown rigorously, following his premises, that growth will be an *impossibility*, if saving by landlords is high, while spending by capitalists and the government fails to make an equivalent extra contribution to annual expenditure flows.

Malthus's argument will be presented in three stages. First, and uncontroversially, in Part I, Malthus's theory of fluctuations will be set out. In so far as "general gluts" are merely the slump in the cycle, they will be fully covered in this section. In Part II the argument will be extended to show how the economy's maximum potential rate of growth is determined. Finally, in Part III, the link between the saving of the various classes, unproductive expenditure by the government and aggregate profits will be set out. It will be shown there that the crucial variables can all too easily get locked into values where growth is a sheer impossibility. As Malthus himself

[1] The author is grateful to Dr. R. Dixon, Professor S. Hollander, and Mr. J. F. Wright for very helpful comments on a previous draft of this paper. He also benefited greatly from the discussion which followed his presentation of an earlier version at the History of Economic Thought Conference in Loughborough in September 1978.
[2] See, for instance, R. D. C. Black (1967), Mark Blaug (1958), B. A. Corry (1959), Robert V Eagly (1974), B. J. Gordon and T. S. Jilek (1965), Samuel Hollander (1962 and 1969), Paul Lambert (1956 and 1966), R. G. Link (1959), J. J. O'Leary (1942 and 1943), A. S. Skinner 1969), Thomas Sowell (1963 and 1972), J. J. Spengler (1945), Harold G. Vatter (1959) and of course J. M. Keynes (1933).
[3] See D. P. O'Brien (1975), p. 238.

20   MALTHUS'S THEORY OF EFFECTIVE DEMAND AND GROWTH

put it:

> "Production and distribution are the two grand elements of wealth, which, combined in their due proportions, are capable of carrying the riches and population of the earth in no great length of time to the utmost limits of its possible resources; but which taken separately, or combined in undue proportions, produce only, after the lapse of many thousand years, the scanty riches and scanty population, which are at present scattered over the face of the globe."[4]

It is evident from this passage that something far more profound than the slump of a trade cycle can go wrong with an economy, and Part III of this paper will be concerned with the problem of how a lack of effective demand can produce near-permanent underdevelopment.

I. Malthus's theory of cyclical fluctuations

Malthus's theory of fluctuations is best seen in terms of two cobweb style diagrams which are illustrated in Figs. 1 and 2.[5] Fig. 1 shows the relationship

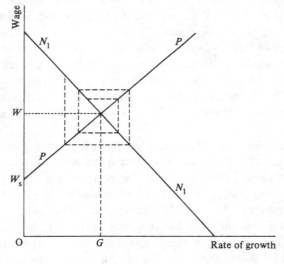

FIG. 1

[4] Malthus, *Principles of Political Economy*, (subsequently *Principles*), First Edition, p. 426 Second Edition, p. 371. Most of the passages cited from the First Edition are to be found in the partial reprint in David Ricardo, *Works and Correspondence*, Vol. II, which also provides the pagination of the original 1820 edition. This 1820 edition will be referred to specifically wherever the modern edition is insufficient.
[5] Mr. J. F. Wright used diagrams similar to these in a most interesting unpublished paper on Malthus's theory of effective demand which he presented in 1962. Two of the insights of this paper are published in J. F. Wright (1965). There are similar diagrams in Sowell (1963), Lev (1976) and Eltis (1973), Figs. 9.1 and 9.2. In the present article the schedules are drawn arbitrarily as straight lines. There is, of course, no reason why the relationships they represent should be linear, and whether they are or not has no effect on the argument.

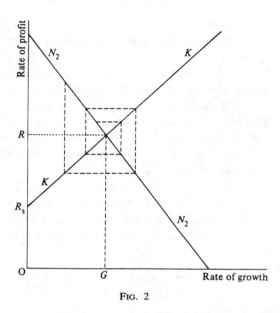

FIG. 2

between the *ex-ante* rate of growth of the labour force and the wage, while Fig. 2 shows the relationship between the *ex-ante* rate of growth of capital and the rate of profit. *PP* in Fig. 1 is based on the classical population supply function which states that the *ex-ante* rate of population growth will vary with the real wage. Malthus gives a succinct account of this relationship in the *Principles of Political Economy* (and a similar assumption is clearly to be found in the work of Smith and Ricardo):

"And whatever may be the state of the effectual demand for labour, it is obvious that the money price of labour must, on an average, be so proportioned to the price of the funds for its maintenance, as to effectuate the desired supply. It is as the condition of the supply, that the prices of the necessaries of life have so important an influence on the price of labour. A certain portion of these necessaries is required to enable the labourer to maintain a stationary population, a greater portion to maintain an increasing one; and consequently, whatever may be the prices of the necessaries of life, the money wages of the labourer must be such as to enable him to purchase these portions, or the supply cannot take place in the quantity required."[6]

It is reasonable to draw the inference from this, and indeed from the whole body of Malthus's work on population that the rate of growth of *supply* of

[6] *Principles*, Second Edition, p. 218; there is a briefer parallel passage in the First Edition, p. 41.

22   MALTHUS'S THEORY OF EFFECTIVE DEMAND AND GROWTH

population will vary with the real wage measured in the "necessaries of life," and it will not distort his argument to identify "necessaries of life" with "circulating capital".

KK in Fig. 2 is an identical function which relates the rate of growth of the *supply* of capital to the rate of profit. Capital breeds like labour if the rate of return is sufficiently high in relation to OR_s, the "subsistence minimum" return where the capital stock is constant. OR_s is precisely equivalent to OW_s in Fig. 1, the wage "required to enable the labourer to maintain a stationary population" in the above quotation, and in the second edition of the *Principles of Political Economy* Malthus saw this critical profit rate as perhaps around $6\frac{2}{3}$ per cent when he wrote, "Nor is it probable that profits would admit of a greater reduction than from $16\frac{2}{3}$ to $6\frac{2}{3}$ before accumulation would be nearly at a stand,"[7] Malthus made it very clear that his theory of population could be applied in a parallel manner to the growth of the capital stock:

> "The laws which regulate the rate of profits and the progress of capital, bear a very striking and singular resemblance to the laws which regulate the rate of wages and the progress of population."[8]

> ". . . a further proof of a singular resemblance in the laws that regulate the increase of capital and of population, is to be found in the rapidity with which the loss of capital is recovered during a war which does not interrupt commerce. The loans to government convert capital into revenue, and increase demand at the same time that they at first diminish the means of supply. The necessary consequence must be an increase of profits. This naturally increases both the power and the reward of accumulation; and if only the same habits of saving prevail among the capitalists as before, the recovery of the lost stock must be rapid, just for the same kind of reason that the recovery of population is so rapid when by some cause or other, it has been suddenly destroyed,"[9]

Figs. 1 and 2 are completed with the schedules N_1N_1 and N_2N_2 which show the ability of the economy to absorb increased population and capital respectively. To consider increased population first, in Fig. 1 a low wage will produce a slow rate of growth of *supply* of population and therefore labour (through schedule *PP*), but at the same time it will be associated with a high rate of profit and therefore rapid capital accumulation. N_1N_1 shows the rate of capital accumulation at each wage rate, and it shows faster accumulation *and therefore a faster growth of demand for population*, the lower the wage

---

[7] *Principles*, Second Edition, p. 205; no corresponding passage in First Edition.
[8] *Principles*, First Edition, p. 370; Second Edition, p. 327.
[9] *Principles*, First Edition, pp. 373–4; Second Edition (worded almost identically), pp. 327–8.

Where the wage is low, the increased *demand* for population as indicated by N_1N_1 exceeds *supply* as indicated by *PP*. Conversely, where the wage is high and the rate of profit is therefore low, the *supply* of population (from *PP*) increases faster than the *demand* for population (from N_1N_1). At a wage of *OW* the *supply* of population and the *demand* increase equally, and *OW* is therefore the equilibrium wage where labour and capital both grow at the same equilibrium rate of *OG*.

Similarly, in Fig. 2, N_2N_2 indicates the growth of population and the labour force entailed by different rates of profit. At a low rate of profit the *supply* of capital indicated by the schedule *KK* increases slowly, i.e. capital "breeds" slowly, but the wage will be high, and the increase in population supply—indicated on this diagram by N_2N_2 will exceed the rate of growth of capital. At a high rate of profit the supply of capital will increase rapidly, but the wage will be low and the increase in population indicated by N_2N_2 will be less than this fast rate of increase of the capital stock. At the equilibrium rate of profit of *OR*, capital and labour will grow at the equilibrium rate of *OG*.

Equations for the functions in the two diagrams can be set out very simply.

PP, the population supply function, can be written as:

$$n = B(w - w_s) \qquad (1)$$

where w is the wage measured in commodities, w_s is the wage where the labour force is constant, n is the rate of growth of the labour force, and B is a positive constant.

KK, the population supply function applied to capital can be written similarly as:

$$k = X(r - r_s) \qquad (2)$$

where r is the rate of profit, r_s is that rate of profit where the capital stock is constant, k is the rate of growth of the capital stock, and X is a positive constant.

N_1N_1 and N_2N_2 are derived with the help of the basic relationship:

$$Z \cdot \frac{Y}{L} = w(1 + r \cdot F) \qquad (3)$$

where $\frac{Y}{L}$ is average output per worker in the commodity producing sector of the economy, and $(1 - Z)$ is the ratio of rents in total output so that $Z \cdot \frac{Y}{L}$ is that part of output per worker which is available for wages and profits. If circulating capital to pay wages one period in advance of production were the sole form of capital, $Z \cdot \dfrac{Y}{L}$ would pay wages of w plus $w \cdot r$ to compensate capitalists for the need to advance wages, which would come to $w(1+r)$. If total capital per worker is F times the wage, the capitalists will need to receive $w \cdot F \cdot r$, so $Z \cdot \dfrac{Y}{L}$ will equal $w(1 + r \cdot F)$ as in equation (3).

Malthus himself made a similar assumption in response to the problem:

> "But it will be asked, how are we to compare the value of the produce with the labour required to obtain it, when the advances of the capitalist do not consist of labour alone."[10]

He assumed, neglecting the complications due to the influence of income distribution on the relative *value* of fixed and circulating capital:

> "In cases of this kind, the following very simple mode of proceeding presents itself. It will be allowed that the capitalist generally expects an equal profit upon all the parts of the capital which he advances. Let us suppose that a certain portion of the value of his advances, one-fourth for instance, consists of the wages of immediate labour..."[11]

Malthus then works through a series of examples where the financing of wages paid in advance requires one-quarter of total capital, however wages fluctuate, while fixed capital forms most of the remaining three-quarters. In these examples, he makes assumptions very close to those which lie behind the above formula with $F = 4$, so it does correspond to his own way of setting out the relationship between output per worker, the wage, and the rate of profit.

The schedule $N_1 N_1$ which is needed to provide a functional relationship between the wage and the rate of growth of capital for Fig. 1 can be derived from (2) and (3):

$$w = \frac{Z \cdot \dfrac{Y}{L}}{1 + F\left(r_s + \dfrac{k}{X}\right)} \tag{4}$$

(1) and (4) together now provide the two schedules of Fig. 1 which link the wage to the rate of growth. As (1) must slope upwards with n, and (4) must slope downwards with k, they can only intersect at one rate of growth where $n = k$. It is evident that the equilibrium wage at this rate of growth must lie between a lower limit set by the subsistence wage, w_s, (from schedule (1)), and an upper limit of $\dfrac{Z \cdot (Y/L)}{1 + F \cdot r_s}$ derived from (4). Hence wages will be higher

----

[10] *Principles*, Second Edition, p. 267: no corresponding passage in First Edition.
[11] *Principles*, Second Edition, pp. 267–8: no corresponding passage in First Edition.

cet. par.) the higher the wage that is needed to keep population constant. "Moral restraint" will therefore raise the standard of living of the working class as Malthus reiterated on innumerable occasions from 1798 onwards. The equilibrium wage will also vary with $\frac{Y}{L}$. Higher labour productivity, i.e. a higher $\frac{Y}{L}$ will permit higher profits and therefore faster capital accumulation which will raise the equilibrium wage. The precise equilibrium values of the wage, the rate of profit and the rate of growth will be derived in Part II of this paper, but a certain amount can be inferred from Fig. 1 alone together with equations (1) and (4).

Turning to Fig. 2 and the determination of the equilibrium rate of profit from the schedules KK and N_2N_2, the schedule N_2N_2 is derived from (1) and (3):

$$r = \frac{1}{F}\left(\frac{Z \cdot \frac{Y}{L}}{w_s + \frac{n}{B}} - 1\right) \tag{5}$$

and this must slope downwards with n, while KK slopes upwards with k, so again the two schedules can only intersect once where $k = n$. The rate of profit must lie between a lower limit of r_s (from (2)) and an upper limit of $\left(\frac{Z \cdot (Y/L)}{w_s} - 1\right)$ (from (5)), so higher output per worker will also influence this favourably.

Clearly in actual economies the wage and the rate of profit will fluctuate round the equilibrium wage and the equilibrium rate of profit derived from the schedules of Figs. 1 and 2—and this is indicated by the dotted "cobweb" lines. The "cobweb theorem" operates where there are significant lags between market signals which call for an increase in supply and actual increases. Malthus suggested that in the case of population the lag between the favourable standard of living which calls forth an increase in population and the subsequent addition of extra population to the labour force could be as long as sixteen to eighteen years, with in consequence very lengthy fluctuations in the rates of growth of employment and the capital stock in the two diagrams.[12] Where the wage is below equilibrium because labour is temporarily plentiful in relation to the capital stock with the result that the wage is below its equilibrium value, it could therefore take a very long time before the numbers available for employment started to grow more slowly than the capital stock. Once they did, the wage would rise above equilibrium, and the growth of population would, after a suitable time-lag, start to

[12] *Principles*, First Edition, p. 287 (1820 Edition), p. 307, p. 357.

overtake the now slower rate of growth of capital to pull the wage dow
again.

The period of adjustment will be long if adjustment falls largely on th
rate of population growth, and this is essentially the view that Malthus too
in the very clear account of fluctuations which corresponds closely to tha
provided by the two diagrams in the first *Essay on Population*:

> "We will suppose the means of subsistence in any country just equal t
> the easy support of its inhabitants. The constant effort towards populatio
> which is found to act even in the most vicious societies, increases th
> number of people before the means of subsistence are increased. The foo
> therefore which before supported seven millions, must now be divide
> among seven millions and a half or eight millions. The poor consequentl
> must live much worse, and many of them be reduced to severe distress
> The number of labourers also being above the proportion of the work i
> the market, the price of labour must tend toward a decrease; while th
> price of provisions would at the same time tend to rise. The laboure
> therefore must work harder to earn the same as he did before. During thi
> season of distress, the discouragements to marriage, and the difficulty c
> rearing a family are so great, that population is at a stand. In the mea
> time the cheapness of labour, the plenty of labourers, and the necessity c
> an increased industry amongst them, encourage cultivators to emplo
> more labour upon their land; to turn up fresh soil, and to manure an
> improve more completely what is already in tillage; till ultimately th
> means of subsistence become in the same proportion to the population a
> at the period from which we set out. The situation of the labourer bein
> then again tolerably comfortable, the restraints to population are in som
> degree loosened; and the same retrograde and progressive movement
> with respect to happiness are repeated,"[13]

One of Malthus's clearest accounts of fluctuations is the one he set ou
twenty-nine years later in 1827 in one of his last publications, the *Definition
of Political Economy*:

> "All the most common causes of an acceleration or retardation in th
> movements of the great machine of human society, involve variations, an
> often great variations, in the real wages of labour. Commodities i
> general, and corn most particularly, are continually rising or falling i
> money-price, from the state of the supply as compared with the deman
> while the money-price of labour remains much more nearly the same. I
> the case of a rise of corn and commodities, the real wages of commo
> day-labour are necessarily diminished: the labourer obtains a smalle
> portion of what he produces; profits necessarily rise; the capitalists have

---

[13] *An Essay on the Principle of Population*, First Edition, pp. 29–31.

greater power of commanding labour; more persons are called into full work, and the increased produce which follows, is the natural remedy for that state of the demand and supply, from whatever cause arising, which had occasioned the temporary rise in the money-price of commodities. On the other hand, if corn and other commodities fall in money-price, as compared with the money-price of labour, it is obvious that the day-labourer, who gets employment, will be able to buy more corn with the money which he receives; he obtains a larger proportion of what he produces; profits necessarily fall; the capitalists have a diminished power of commanding labour; fewer persons are fully employed, and the diminished production which follows, is the natural remedy for that state of the demand and supply, from whatever cause arising, which occasioned the temporary fall in the money-price of commodities. The operation of these remedial processes to prevent the continuance of excess or defect, is so much what one should naturally expect, and is so obviously confirmed by general experience, that it is inconceivable that a proposition should have obtained any currency which is founded on a supposed law of demand and supply diametrically opposed to these remedial processes.

It will be recollected, that the question of a glut is exclusively whether it may be general, as well as particular, and not whether it may be permanent as well as temporary. The causes above mentioned act powerfully to prevent the permanence either of glut or scarcity, and to regulate the supply of commodities so as to make them sell at their natural prices."[14]

Here the burden of adjustment falls mainly on the rate of capital accumulation, which can be expected to adjust more quickly to the rate of profit than population growth to the wage. The period of the fluctuations could therefore be less than the sixteen to eighteen year gap between generations which had the dominant influence in the 1798 version of the argument.

The two accounts are however essentially the same, and they describe the fluctuations inherent in Figs. 1 and 2. The schedules there together with some lagging will produce what Malthus describes: self-correcting fluctuations. It is to be noted that the labour market takes time to clear in both the 1798 and the 1827 accounts of the cycle. In 1798, "the number of labourers is above the proportion of work in the market" where the wage is high; while in 1827, when "profits necessarily fall," "the capitalists have a diminished power of commanding labour; fewer persons are fully employed...". Product markets in contrast clear instantly, but future investment is adversely affected if, as in "general guts," they clear at a price which yields a rate of profit which is insufficient to encourage future production.[15]

---

[14] *Definitions of Political Economy*, pp. 60–2.
[15] See Definitions 37, 38, and 55 in *Definitions of Political Economy*.

28   MALTHUS'S THEORY OF EFFECTIVE DEMAND AND GROWTH

Professor Sowell has seen Malthus's analysis of "general gluts" in terms of diagrams like these and the economic forces they represent.[16] That this is an important part of the story is evident from the quotation from *Definitions of Political Economy* which describes "general gluts" entirely in terms of a slump in a self-correcting cycle.

In so far as Malthus saw "general gluts" in these terms, it is natural that he should have wished to reduce the amplitude and severity of the cycle, especially as this had particularly adverse effects on the working class.

"...eight or ten years, recurring not unfrequently, are serious spaces in human life. They amount to a serious sum of happiness or misery, according as they are prosperous or adverse, and leave the country in a very different state at their termination. In prosperous times the mercantile classes often realize fortunes, which go far towards securing them against the future; but unfortunately the working classes, though they share in the general prosperity, do not share so largely as in the general adversity. They may suffer the greatest distress in a period of low wages, but cannot be adequately compensated by a period of high wages. To them fluctuations must always bring more evil than good; and, with a view to the happiness of the great mass of society, it should be our object, as far as possible, to maintain peace, and an equable expenditure."[17]

The severe fall in government expenditure in the transition from war to peace after 1815 produced a sharp fluctuation additional to those which were in any case occurring, and so added to the severity of the cycle for a considerable time. Writing in terms of short-period policy prescription—and Keynes insisted that he was the first Cambridge economist[18]—in the slump phase of the cycle in 1820, Malthus argued for extra unproductive consumption, i.e. for more government expenditure. Government was responsible for the *extra* severity of the post 1815 slump by increasing expenditure massively during the war and then cutting it back severely after 1815. If government could avoid such severe fluctuations in its own expenditure, the cycle would be less severe which would above all benefit the working class. Smoothing out the cycle in 1820, i.e. maintaining an "equable expenditure," meant raising unproductive government expenditure because, "An expenditure, which would have absolutely crushed the country in 1770, might be little more than what was necessary to call forth its prodigious powers of production in 1816."[19]

Here Malthus is almost speaking as an early fine-tuner, which was a role

[16] Thomas Sowell, 1963 and 1972.
[17] *Principles*, First Edition (1820), pp. 521–2: Second Edition, p. 437.
[18] J. M. Keynes, (1933).
[19] *Principles*, First Edition (1820), p. 502: Second Edition, pp. 422–3.

that Ricardo never sought, or given the self-correcting mechanisms, considered desirable. As Ricardo said in a letter to Malthus which has been much quoted:

> "It appears to me that one great cause of our difference in opinion, on the subjects which we have so often discussed, is that you have always in your mind the immediate and temporary effects of particular changes—whereas I put these immediate and temporary effects quite aside, and fix my whole attention on the permanent state of things which will result from them. Perhaps you estimate these temporary effects too highly, whilst I am too much disposed to undervalue them."[20]

Malthus was of course far more than the first Cambridge demand manager. In Part II of this paper which now follows, his analysis of the determination of the underlying rate of growth around which the economy fluctuates will be explained. Finally in Part III the theory of effective demand will be outlined. This provides the true underpinning of Malthus's analysis of unproductive expenditure—and explains how economies can stagnate indefinitely—and it certainly represents a crucial part of his thought.

II. The rate of economic development

Fortunate economies develop. There are statements by Malthus as early as 1798 on how agricultural techniques and agricultural output will steadily improve over the centuries:

> "Were a country never to be over-run by a people more advanced in arts, but left to its own natural progress in civilization; from the time that its produce might be considered as an unit, to the time that it might be considered as a million..."[21]

Five pages on he used the phrase, "till the whole earth had been cultivated like a garden." What determines the rate of improvement? It is clear that he believed that profits and demand play a vital role.

> "If a great and continued demand should arise among surrounding nations for the raw produce of a particularly country, the price of this produce would of course rise considerably; and the expenses of cultivation, rising only slowly and gradually to the same proportion, the price of produce might for a long time keep so much a head, as to give a prodigious stimulus to improvement, and encourage the employment of much capital

---

[20] Letter from Ricardo to Malthus of 24th January, 1817, David Ricardo, *Works and Correspondence*, Vol VII, p. 120.

[21] *Essay on the Principle of Population*, First Edition, p. 138.

in bringing fresh land under cultivation, and rendering the old much more productive."[22]

More directly, "Inventions to save labour seldom take place to any considerable extent, except when there is a decided demand for them."[23] Conversely, in the absence of demand, productivity can be expected to stagnate, or indeed fall:

"...the tenant...if there were no foreign vent for the raw produce, and the commodities which contribute to the conveniences and luxuries of life were but little known, would have but small incitement to call forth the resources of his [the landlord's] land, and give encouragement to a rapid increase of population. By employing ten families he might perhaps, owing to the richness of the soil, obtain food for fifty; but he would find no proportionate market for this additional food, and would be soon sensible that he had wasted his time and attention in superintending the labour of so many persons. He would be disposed therefore to employ a smaller number; or if, from motives of humanity, or any other reason, he was induced to keep more than were necessary for the supply of the market, upon the supposition of their being tolerably industrious, he would be quite indifferent to their industry, and his labourers would naturally acquire the most indolent habits. Such habits would naturally be generated both in the masters and servants by such circumstances, and when generated, a considerable time and considerable stimulants are necessary to get rid of them."[24]

Hence, where demand for produce is high, there is a "prodigious stimulus to improvement," while where it is lacking it is likely that labourers will be allowed to acquire "the most indolent habits," and these will be generated "both in the masters and servants." Malthus believed that people are not easily motivated to develop their economies, and the range of goods available is an important factor:

"The greatest of all difficulties in converting uncivilized and thinly peopled countries into civilized and populous ones, is to inspire them with the wants best calculated to excite their exertions in the production of wealth. One of the greatest benefits which foreign commerce confers, and the reason why it has always appeared an almost necessary ingredient in the progress of wealth, is, its tendency to inspire new wants, to form new tastes, and to furnish fresh motives for industry. Even civilized and

---

[22] *An Inquiry into the Nature and Progress of Rent* (1815), republished in *The Pamphlets of Thomas Robert Malthus,* pp. 195–6.

[23] *Principles,* First Edition (1820), pp. 401, Second Edition, p. 351.

[24] *Principles,* First Edition (1820), pp. 376–7, Second Edition, pp. 331–2.

improved countries cannot afford to lose any of these motives. It is not the most pleasant employment to spend eight hours a day in a counting-house. Nor will it be submitted to after the common necessaries and conveniences of life are attained, unless adequate motives are presented to the mind of the man of business. Among these motives is undoubtedly the desire of advancing his rank, and contending with the landlords in the enjoyment of leisure, as well as of foreign and domestic luxuries."[25]

It will already be evident that motivation is central to Malthus's account of economic development. A passage in an important letter to Ricardo underlines the significance of this:

"You constantly say that it is not a question about the motives to produce. Now I have certainly intended to make it almost entirely a question about motives. We see in almost every part of the world vast powers of production which are not put into action, and I explain this phenomenon by saying that from the want of a proper distribution of the actual produce adequate motives are not furnished to continued production."[26]

In other words, for lack of a market, for lack of "a proper distribution of the actual produce" underdevelopment continues.

An important point to grasp is that Malthus did not see the level of production as closely connected to quantities of physical inputs. One approach to growth is to ignore motivation and to make output solely a function of inputs. The production function:

$$Y = f(K, L, A, N) \qquad (6)$$

where Y is output, K the capital stock, L the labour force, A the state of knowledge, and N natural resources including land, is an example. Malthus would have argued that such a production function ignores what matters no less vitally than the rest—motivation. He could have brought this in by adding a term, E, for energy, or more narrowly entrepreneurship (though this would be to miss the motivation of workers which he also considered vital). Hence a Malthus production function could read:

$$Y = f(E, K, L, A, N) \qquad (7)$$

Ricardo never perceived the vital distinction, and many of today's economists are content to set out a production function in the mechanical form of the first equation.[27] But any attempt to encapsulate the factors to which

---

[25] *Principles*, First Edition, p. 470, Second Edition, p. 403. See also an equally striking statement to the same effect on pp. 405–6 (First Edition).

[26] Letter from Malthus to Ricardo of 7th July, 1821, David Ricardo, *Works and Correspondence*, Vol IX, p. 10.

[27] The work of Harvey Leibenstein (summarised in 1978) comes closest to recognising the modern significance of E, which he labels X-efficiency. The significance of motivation in Malthus's *Principles* is stressed in J. F. Wright (1965).

32   MALTHUS'S THEORY OF EFFECTIVE DEMAND AND GROWTH

Malthus attributed the motivation to develop an economy in algebraic form is likely to miss much that is significant. One may however capture some of his insight into the the vital element that motivation plays in the productive process by linking technical progress to profitability. That is certainly the burden of the first quotations. A technical progress function which serves that purpose is:

$$a = a_0 + a_1(r - r_s) \tag{8}$$

where a is the rate of technical progress, formulated below as an annual augmentation of a production function, while a_0 and a_1 are the parameters of this technical progress function. It produces the result that the rate of technical progress varies with the rate of profit, which in turn depends on the demand for aggregate output in relation to the supply—which was the key factor in motivation as Malthus reiterated. In view of the significance which Malthus also attached to the range of goods available, it should be recognised that a_0 will be higher, the greater the significance of industry and commerce in the total output of the economy.[28] It may suffice to write that:

$$a_0 = f\left(\frac{Y - Y_a + T}{Y}\right) \qquad f' > 0 \text{ (subject to the constraint that } Y_a \geq C_a)$$

$$\tag{9}$$

where Y is total physical output, Y_a is agricultural output and C_a the domestic consumption of food, while T represents international trade. Hence it is assumed, following Malthus's argument, that the rate of technical progress (or the rate of "improvement" as he would call it), will vary with the proportion of manufacturing output in total output, and with the extent of international trade. The constraint that agricultural output should at least equal domestic consumption is necessary because Malthus was convinced, and reiterated in a series of publications, that great dangers of several kinds were involved in any significant dependence on imported food.[29]

Growth does not depend solely on technical progress: it is also influenced by capital accumulation and the growth of the labour force. As capital-labour substitutability plays a subordinate role in Malthus's various explanations of economic development,[30] a production function which allowed this to have a significant effect on the rate of growth would be misleading. It is

[28] The important role that manufacturing and commerce plays in providing the incentives that lead to growth and development is emphasised in J. J. Spengler (1945), and also in J. F. Wright (1965).
[29] See in particular the pamphlet "The Grounds of an Opinion on the Policy of Restricting the Importation of Foreign Corn" (1815). *An Essay on the Principle of Population.* Fifth Edition (1817), Book iii, Chapters IX–XII, and *Principles*, First Edition, pp. 217–25.
[30] However, see *Principles*, First Edition, pp. 261–5 and 301–8, (Second Edition, pp. 236–40, 276–82) for two quite full and detailed statements of the scope for capital-labour substitutability, and its influence on income distribution.

more accurate to assume that the growth of Y depends on technical progress—the rate at which "improvements" are occurring—and on the rate of growth of the labour force, which is interdependent with the rate of growth of the capital stock in the manner set out in Part I of this article. There will, of course, be diminishing returns from the employment of extra labour in agriculture, which is one of Malthus's first and most fundamental propositions. The consequent production function can be written as:

$$Y = A \cdot e^{at} \cdot L^Z \qquad 1 > Z > 0 \tag{10}$$

where A is a constant, L is labour employed and Z is less than 1 to an extent which depends on the strength of diminishing returns in agriculture. Z would of course equal 1 with constant returns. With competitive factor pricing, which would reflect Malthus's thinking, $1 - Z$ will be the share of rents in total commodity output as in equation (3). Z will increase over time for two reasons. First Malthus believed that there was a historical tendency for the share of rents to fall in agriculture.[31] Second, the share of rents in total output will fall in so far as the share of agriculture falls. Hence, like a_0 from the technical progress function, Z rises through time if $\dfrac{Y - Y_a}{Y}$ rises.

From (10) it is possible to obtain a growth equation for each constant value of Z. If g is the rate of growth of commodity output:

$$g = a + Z \cdot n \tag{11}$$

and (8) can be used to substitute for a to obtain:

$$g = a_0 + a_1 \cdot (r - r_s) + Z \cdot n \tag{12}$$

Now, $(r - r_s)$ equals $\dfrac{k}{X}$ from the investment function (2), so that:

$$g = a_0 + a_1 \cdot \frac{k}{X} + Z \cdot n \tag{13}$$

and in equilibrium growth where output, capital and labour all grow at the same rate:

$$g = k = n = \frac{a_0}{1 - Z - a_1/X} \tag{14}$$

Thus the economy's equilibrium rate of growth will depend on the coefficients of the technical progress function, a_0 and a_1, and on the coefficient of the investment function, X. It will also depend on the strength of the diminishing returns factors in the productive process, represented by $1 - Z$—which equals the share of rents in total commodity production. If

[31] *Principles*, First Edition, pp. 176–7, and the slightly more qualified statement on pp. 171–3 of the Second Edition.

$(1 - Z)$ becomes lower as a result of industrialization, as well as because of the natural tendency for the share of rents in agricultural output to fall, the economy's equilibrium rate of growth will become faster according to equation (14). Industrialization will also raise the equilibrium rate of growth because there is a more favourable production function with a higher a_0 in industry, and here Malthus followed Smith. A vital factor is that through its effect on motivation, industrialization also leads to a faster rate of advance in agricultural productivity.

Provided that $(1 - Z - a_1/X)$ remains positive, there will be a steady growth path for each value of Z where output, capital and the labour force can grow in line with each other in the very long-run. It was entirely Malthus's view that the strength of diminishing returns in agriculture, and the significance of agriculture in the standard of living of the working class, would ensure that output and the capital stock would not grow faster than the labour force in the very long-run. The Malthusian population supply mechanism would always ensure that the growth of the labour force could be expected to catch-up with the growth of output if this moved temporarily ahead. There is no doubt therefore that in a Malthus growth model, Z is always sufficiently below 1 to keep $(1 - Z - a_1/X)$ positive.

With the advantages of hindsight we should now of course say that at some point in the eighteenth and nineteenth centuries output and the capital stock started to grow substantially faster than the labour force in some fortunate countries, with the result that these actual economies broke clear of this constraint. In the present model, output, capital and labour simply *cannot* grow in line with each other if $(1 - Z - a_1/X)$ once becomes negative, and output and the capital stock can then race ahead of the labour force to produce the strong rising trend in living standards which so many economies have experienced in the past century. Malthus never thought this possible. His own world, and his detailed study of the published evidence from other countries convinced him that capital and output would only grow substantially faster than the labour force in transitory periods while the economy was benefitting from some favourable institutional change. With given institutions and "habits" economies would settle down to growth rates where *living standards* rose slowly if at all—results entirely compatible with an equation like (14).

The equilibrium wage which results from this process is of course above subsistence. When equation (14) is substituted into the basic population supply and capital supply equations ((1) and (2)), to produce expressions for the equilibrium wage and the equilibrium rate of profit in Figures 1 and 2:

$$w = w_s + \frac{a_0/B}{1 - Z - a_1/X} \tag{15}$$

and

$$r = r_s + \frac{a_0/X}{1 - Z - a_1/X} \tag{16}$$

so both the equilibrium wage and the equilibrium rate of profit that the argument of part I produced will be influenced by the strength of the technical progress function. Moreover, if there is a historical tendency for Z and for a_0 to rise with industrialization, the appropriate steady growth wage and profit rates will rise as the parameters of the model become increasingly favourable.

The view of the world which has been presented so far, even within Malthus's constraints, has been a relatively favourable one. Self correcting cycles, and increasingly favourable parameters for the steady growth paths of industrializing countries present a relatively benign view of the world. It is obviously not Malthus's whole view. A major part of his analysis of growth was concerned with the role of effective demand in the determination of profits, and how a lack of this could make growth an impossibility. His belief that many countries realised none of their growth potential has already been demonstrated. There are no results of this kind in the argument so far. Cyclical slumps have been the worst that can happen to an economy. There must therefore be more to Malthus's theory of growth, and his theory of the determination of effective demand is what is missing up to this point. It must be presented with care. McCulloch, the *Edinburgh Review*'s principal political economy reviewer wrote to Ricardo in the year *before* the *Principles of Political Economy* appeared, "... I think that justice will not be shown either to the science or the country if it be not handled pretty roughly."[32] With the advantages of writing one hundred and sixty years after publication instead of a year before, what do we know that McCulloch did not?

III. Malthus's theory of effective demand

The key to Malthus's approach to demand is that a commodity is effectively demanded if it can be sold at a price which covers the necessary costs of production including "the usual profits upon advances of capital." A commodity will only be produced if entrepreneurs expect to be able to sell it at a sufficient price:

"If the nature of the object to be obtained requires advances in the shape of capital, as in the vast majority of instances, then by whomsoever this capital is furnished, whether by the labourers themselves or by others, the commodity will not be produced, unless the estimation in which it is held

[32] Letter from J. R. McCulloch to Ricardo of 5 December, 1819, David Ricardo, *Works and Correspondence*, Vol VIII, pp. 138–9.

36   MALTHUS'S THEORY OF EFFECTIVE DEMAND AND GROWTH

by the society or its intrinsic value in exchange be such, as not only to replace all the advances of labour and other articles which have been made for its attainment, but likewise to pay the usual profits upon those advances; or, in other words, to command an additional quantity of labour, equal to those profits."[33]

If profits are adequate in the present, a commodity will continue to be produced for future sale. If profits are insufficient, "the commodity will not be produced" in future. Profits are therefore crucial because they motivate future production:

"By inquiring into the immediate causes of the progress of wealth I clearly mean to inquire mainly into motives. I dont at all wish to deny that some persons or others are entitled to consume all that is produced; but the grand question is whether it is distributed in such a manner between the different parties concerned as to occasion the most effective demand for future produce:..."[34]

How must the produce be distributed to motivate future production? A demand for produce from workers alone will not suffice to motivate future production:

"And no productive labour will ever be in demand unless the produce when obtained is of greater value than the labour which obtained it. No fresh hands can be employed in any sort of industry merely in consequence of the demand for its produce occasioned by the persons employed. No farmer will take the trouble of superintending the labour of ten additional men merely because his whole produce will then sell in the market at an advanced price just equal to what he had paid his additional labourers. There must be something in the previous state of the demand and supply of the commodity in question, or in its price, antecedent to and independently of the demand occasioned by the new labourers, in order to warrant the employment of an additional number of people in its production."[35]

and

"It is indeed most important to observe that no power of consumption on the part of the labouring classes can ever, according to the commo

[33] *Principles*, Second Edition, p. 302: the corresponding passage in the First Edition (p. 34) omits, "...or, in other words, to command an additional quantity of labour, equal to thos profits."
[34] Letter from Malthus to Ricardo of 7 July 1821, David Ricardo, *Works and Correspon dence*, Vol. IX, p. 10.
[35] *Principles*, First Edition (1820), pp. 348–9: Second Edition, p. 312, has "And no produc tive labour can ever be in demand with a view to profit unless...."

motives which influence mankind, alone furnish an encouragement to the employment of capital. As I have before said, nobody will ever employ capital merely for the sake of the demand occasioned by those who work for him. Unless they produce an excess of value above what they consume, which he either wants himself in kind, or which he can advantageously exchange for something which he desires, either for present or future use, it is quite obvious that his capital will not be employed in maintaining them."[36]

From where therefore can adequate demand come to permit the continuing or better still expanding employment of labour? From the landlords is clearly one possibility:

"It may be thought perhaps that the landlords could not fail to supply any deficiency of demand and consumption among the producers, and that between them there would be little chance of any approach towards redundancy of capital. What might be the result of the most favourable distribution of landed property it is not easy to say from experience; but experience certainly tells us that, under the distribution of land which actually takes place in most of the countries in Europe, the demands of the landlords, added to those of the producers, have not always been found sufficient to prevent any difficulty in the employment of capital."[37]

As for the capitalists, they will be saving rather than consuming, out of a desire to accumulate wealth, so where is sufficient demand to come from?

"...if the master-producers, from the laudable desire they feel of bettering their condition, and providing for a family, do not consume sufficiently to give an adequate stimulus to the increase of wealth; if the working producers, by increasing their consumption, supposing them to have the means of so doing, would impede the growth of wealth more by diminishing the power of production, than they could encourage it by increasing the demand for produce; and if the expenditure of the landlords, in addition to the expenditure of the two preceding classes, be found insufficient to keep up and increase the value of that which is produced, where are we to look for the consumption required but among the unproductive labourers of Adam Smith?

Every society must have a body of unproductive labourers; as every society, besides the menial servants that are required, must have statesmen to govern it, soldiers to defend it, judges and lawyers to administer justice and protect the rights of individuals, physicians and surgeons to cure diseases and heal wounds, and a body of clergy to instruct the

---

[36] *Principles*, First Edition, pp. 471–2, Second Edition, p. 404.
[37] *Principles*, First Edition (1820), p. 475: Second Edition, p. 405.

ignorant, and administer the consolations of religion. No civilized state has ever been known to exist without a certain portion of all these classes of society in addition to those who are directly employed in production. To a certain extent therefore they appear to be absolutely necessary. But it is perhaps one of the most important practical questions that can possibly be brought under our view, whether, however necessary and desirable they may be, they must be considered as detracting so much from the material products of a country, and its power of supporting an extended population; or whether they furnish fresh motives to production, and tend to push the wealth of a country farther than it would go without them."[38]

Malthus appears to add the demand for produce by the various classes to see whether in sum there is a sufficient excess over costs of production to produce adequate profits to encourage future production:

"There must therefore be a considerable class of persons who have both the will and power to consume more material wealth than they produce, or the mercantile classes could not continue profitably to produce so much more than they consume. In this class the landlords no doubt stand pre-eminent; but if they were not assisted by the great mass of individuals engaged in personal services, whom they maintain, their own consumption would of itself be insufficient to keep up and increase the value of the produce, and enable the increase of its quantity more than to counterbalance the fall of its price. Nor could the capitalists in that case continue with effect the same habits of saving. The deficiency in the value of what they produced would necessarily make them either consume more, or produce less; and when the mere pleasure of present expenditure, without the accompaniments of an improved local situation and an advance in rank, is put in opposition to the continued labour of attending to business during the greatest part of the day, the probability is that a considerable body of them will be induced to prefer the latter alternative, and produce less. But if, in order to balance the demand and supply, a permanent diminution of production takes place, rather than an increase of effective consumption, the whole of the national wealth, which consists of what is produced and consumed, will be decidely diminished."[39]

---

[38] *Principles*, First Edition (1820), pp. 476–7: Second Edition, pp. 406–7, worded slightly differently in places. In particular, the Second Edition has "Every society must have a body of persons engaged in personal services of various kinds..." for "Every society must have a body of unproductive labourers..."
[39] *Principles*, Second Edition, pp. 400–1; the corresponding passage in the First Edition (p. 466) is a little less fully set out.

Malthus's proposition that insufficient effective demand will produce "a permanent dimunition of production" and a "decidedly diminished" national wealth appears to rest on a Kalecki-like relationship between a summation of the demand for commodities by the various classes, and the level of commodity production.[40] This relationship can be set out formally to produce Malthus's results:

The total gross incomes received in commodity production, i.e. in the "productive sector" as defined by Malthus, must equal the total *ex-post* purchases of domestically produced commodities. Hence:

Wages + Profits + Rents ≡ Commodities purchased by productive labour
+ Commodities purchased by unproductive labour in the private sector
+ Commodities purchased by government and with government financed incomes
+ Commodities purchased by capitalists and landlords for private consumption
+ The net increase of the capital stock of the productive sector
+ Exports less imports of commodities

This equation can be simplified:

(i) It can be assumed as is fully implicit in Malthus's work, and indeed in that of Smith and Ricardo, that workers spend their entire incomes on commodities. Hence they don't save and they purchase no services. With this "classical" assumption, "Wages" (in commodity production) will equal "Commodities purchased by productive labour," so these two terms can be cancelled from the equation.

(ii) The total consumption of capitalists and landlords will consist of the physical goods they buy—"Commodities purchased by capitalists and landlords for private consumption," plus the private services that they purchase. If the private service workers (who derive their entire incomes from this source) buy no services themselves, they will purchase physical commodities with all the money that capitalists and landlords spend on the consumption of private services. Hence the "private consumption (of goods and services) by capitalists and landlords" will equal the sum of, "Commodities purchased by capitalists and landlords for private consumption" and "Commodities purchased by unproductive labour in the private sector," and this can be substituted in the equation.

[40] Cf. M. Kalecki (1956), Chapter 3. R. G. Link (1959) has derived a similar interpretation from these passages.

40   MALTHUS'S THEORY OF EFFECTIVE DEMAND AND GROWTH

The equation can therefore be rewritten as:

Profits + Rents = Private consumption (of goods and services) by capitalists
    and landlords.

+ Commodities purchased by government and with government financed incomes.

+ Exports less imports of commodities

+ The net increase of the capital stock of the productive sector   (17)

It is clear from the Malthusian investment function (equation (2)), $k = X(r - r_s)$ that aggregate investment will depend on aggregate profits. If we now go over to period analysis, and, for later simplicity, make investment depend solely on r, the rate of profit, and no longer on the excess of this over r_s, a required minimum profit rate, we can write down the investment function as, $k_t = X \cdot r_{t-1}$, and since $k = \dfrac{\text{investment}}{\text{capital}}$ and $r = \dfrac{\text{profits}}{\text{capital}}$, we can write the investment function as:

$$(\text{Investment})_t = X \cdot (\text{Profits})_{t-1} \qquad 1 > X > 0 \qquad (18)^{41}$$

If this equation is used to substitute $X \cdot (\text{Profits})_{t-1}$ for (The net increase of the capital stock of the productive sector)$_t$ in equation (17):

$(\text{Profits})_t + (\text{Rents})_t - X \cdot (\text{Profits})_{t-1} =$ (Private consumption by
    capitalists and landlords)$_t$

+ (Commodities purchased by government and with government financed incomes)$_t$

+ (Exports less imports)$_t$ (19)

Hence profits depend vitally on the private consumption of capitalists and landlords, on government financed unproductive consumption and on the trade balance. Since rents will only rise after profits have already risen, the equation states very clearly that profits can only increase if one of the terms on the right hand side of the equation increases. There must therefore be an increase in private consumption by capitalists or landlords, an increase in government consumption or an improved trade balance if profits are to rise.

---

[41] In this equation, and in those that follow, profits need to be defined gross of tax, because they are gross of tax in the previous equation (17) based on the necessary identity between the income categories and expenditure flows. X, the coefficient of the investment function in equation (18) therefore relates investment to the *gross of tax* profits of the previous period. Hence X will depend on the rate at which profits are taxed as well as on the willingness of entrepreneurs to invest. It will be seen below that Malthus believed that taxation fell largely on rents, directly or indirectly, so X will be only slightly influenced by profits taxation. The predominant influence must be the entrepreneurial willingness to invest and reinvest.

Similarly as rents will only fall in the short-run after profits have already fallen, a reduction in consumption by landlords, capitalists or the government, or a trade deterioration, must cut profits. This cut in profits will be followed by a reduction in investment which will produce falling employment if it is sufficiently severe. It must be remembered that investment is quite substantially an advance of wage goods to workers so that they can produce in the following period. If profits are lower in one *year* (the agricultural period) than in the previous one, they will be inadequate in some activities where businessmen will then cease to repeat the production level of the previous year. Equation (19) which is arrived at very simply and directly therefore reproduces much of what Malthus said on effective demand. The influence on profits, effective demand and future employment of consumption by landlords, capitalists and the government has been very fully documented already. On exports, the following passage may be cited:

> "It is obvious then that a fall in the value of the precious metals, commencing with a rise in the price of corn, has a strong tendency, while it is going on, to encourage the cultivation of fresh land and the formation of increased rents."
> "A similar effect would be produced in a country which continued to feed its own people, by a great and increasing demand for its manufactures. These manufactures, if from such a demand the money value of their amount in foreign countries was greatly to increase, would bring back a great increase of money value in return, which increase could not fail to increase the money price of labour and raw produce. The demand for agricultural as well as manufactured produce would thus be augmented, ..."[42]

Perhaps the clearest indication that the relationship set out in equation (19) goes to the core of Malthus's argument is the structure of his argument on "The Progress of Wealth" in the *Principles of Political Economy*.[43] After a brief introduction, Section II is entitled, "Of the Increase of Population considered as a Stimulus to the continued Increase of Wealth," Section III, "Of Accumulation, or the Saving from Revenue to add to Capital, considered as a Stimulus to the Increase of Wealth," Section IV, "Of the Fertility of the Soil, considered as a Stimulus to the continued Increase of Wealth," and Section V, "Of Inventions to save Labour, considered as a Stimulus to

---

[42] *Principles*, Second Edition, P.166: the equivalent passage in the First Edition (p.170) has "value" in place of "money value," and "value of the raw produce" in place of "money price of labour and raw produce." There is a similar passage in *An Inquiry into the Nature and Progress of Rent.* p.196.

[43] In the First Edition this is Chapter VII entitled, "On the Immediate Causes of the Progress of Wealth," while in the Second Edition it is Book II with the single Chapter, "On the Progress of Wealth" divided into the same ten sections.

the continued Increase of Wealth." These Sections are all concerned with the supply-side factors which may contribute to growth, and Malthus concludes Section V with the paragraph:

> "The three great causes most favourable to production are, accumulation of capital, fertility of soil, and inventions to save labour. They all act in the same direction; and as they all tend to facilitate supply, without reference to demand, it is not probable that they should either separately or conjointly afford an adequate stimulus to the continued increase of wealth." [44]

These Sections can be likened to the left hand side of an arch. The top of the arch is Section VI, "Of the Necessity of a Union of the Powers of Production with the Means of Distribution, in order to ensure a continued Increase of Wealth." It opens:

> "We have seen that the powers of production, to whatever extent they may exist, are not alone sufficient to secure the creation of a proportionate degree of wealth. Something else seems to be necessary in order to call these powers fully into action. This is an effectual and unchecked demand for all that is produced." [45]

The right hand side of the arch consists of the demand-side factors which contribute to growth, Section VII, "Of the Distribution occasioned by the Division of landed Property considered as the Means of increasing the exchangeable Value of the whole Produce", Section VIII, "Of the Distribution occasioned by Commerce, internal and external, considered as the Means of increasing the exchangeable value of Produce," and Section IX, "Of the Distribution occasioned by unproductive Consumers, considered as the Means of increasing the exchangeable Value of the Whole Produce." These three demand-side headings come close to describing the terms on the right hand side of equation (19).

There profits are favourably affected by higher consumption by landlords and capitalists, which the break-up of the great estates favours:

> "It is physically possible indeed for a nation, with a comparatively small body of very rich proprietors, and a large body of very poor workmen to push both the produce of the land and manufactures to the greatest extent, that the resources and ingenuity of the country would admit . . . but, in order to call them forth, we must suppose a passion among the rich for the consumption of manufactures, and the results of productive labour, much more excessive than has ever been witnessed in

---

[44] *Principles*, Second Edition, p.360, First Edition, p.413.
[45] *Principles*, Second Edition, p.361: the First Edition (p.413) does not have the final sentence.

human society. And the consequence is, that no instance has ever been known of a country which has pushed its natural resources to a great extent, with a small proportionate body of persons of property, however rich and luxurious they might be. Practically it has always been found that the excessive wealth of the few is in no respect equivalent with regard to effective demand, to the more moderate wealth of the many. A large body of manufacturers and merchants can only find a market for their commodities among a numerous class of consumers above the rank of mere workmen and labourers." [46]

Therefore the "division of landed property," the subject of one of the three demand-side Sections of Malthus's argument will undoubtedly raise the consumption of landlords and capitalists which is one of the three determinants of the change of profits in equation (19). The correspondence between the other two, government financed expenditure and exports less imports, and the subjects of the further demand-side Sections of Malthus's argument, namely the influence of unproductive consumption and commerce both internal and external on demand does not require further explanation.

The argument of the present paper is close to Malthus's own up to this point, and it has only stepped beyond him in the use of some algebraic presentation to set out the necessary consequences of some of his premises. The argument has emphasised the factors to which he himself attributed increased or reduced profits, and therefore the motivation to produce a greater or a diminished future supply.

The argument will now move a stage further. Malthus believed that inadequate strength of the demand side factors could, "... produce only, after the lapse of many thousand years, the scanty riches and scanty population, which are at present scattered over the face of the globe." He believed that, "... without [an easy division of landed property], a country with great natural resources might slumber for ages with an uncultivated soil, and a scanty yet starving population." [47] A complete account of Malthus's theory of effective demand and growth therefore requires a model where growth will be *an impossibility* if the demand side factors are too weak.

An "impossibility of growth" equation can in fact be derived very simply and straightforwardly from equation (19). An assumption which can reasonably be grafted onto (19) is that of a balanced budget. Malthus did not advocate deficit financing. His argument was essentially the balanced-budget-multiplier one that demand can be raised by taxing those who would otherwise save a high fraction of their incomes and passing this money on to

[46] *Principles*, First Edition (1820), pp.430–1: Second Edition, pp.374–5 has "below the rank of the great proprietors of land" for "above the rank of mere workmen and labourers."
[47] *Principles*, First Edition, (1820) p.440; Second Edition, p.382.

44   MALTHUS'S THEORY OF EFFECTIVE DEMAND AND GROWTH

those who would definitely spend it. That unproductive consumers are supported by taxation and not by budget deficits is evident from the following passage:

> "The effect therefore on national wealth of those classes of unproductive labourers which are supported by taxation, must be very various in different countries, and must depend entirely upon the powers of production, and upon the manner in which the taxes are raised in each country. As great powers of production are neither likely to be called into action, or, when once in action, kept in activity without great consumption, I feel very little doubt that instances have practically occurred of national wealth being greatly stimulated by the consumption of those who have been supported by taxes." [48]

With the assumption of a balanced budget and the further assumption that all taxes fall on capitalists and landlords who alone produce a taxable surplus, "Taxes paid by capitalists and landlords" can be substituted for "Commodities purchased by government and with government financed incomes" in equation (19). If it is now assumed for simplicity that imports equal exports, equation (19) can be rewritten as:

$$\text{(Profits} - \text{consumption and taxes paid by capitalists)}_t$$
$$+ \text{(Rents} - \text{consumption and taxes paid by landlords)}_t$$
$$- X \cdot \text{(Profits)}_{t-1} \qquad\qquad = 0 \qquad (20)$$

If s_c is written for the fraction of their pre-tax incomes which capitalists save, and s_r for the fraction of pre-tax incomes that landlords save, while P *is written for total profits, and R* for total rents, this expression can be rewritten as:

$$\frac{X}{s_c} \cdot \frac{P_{t-1}}{P_t} = 1 + \frac{s_r \cdot R_t}{s_c \cdot P_t}$$

and since, $1 + \dfrac{s_r \cdot R_t}{s_c \cdot P_t}$ equals $\left(\dfrac{\text{Total saving}}{\text{Saving from profits}}\right)_t$:

$$\frac{P_t}{P_{t-1}} = \frac{X}{s_c} \cdot \left(\frac{\text{Saving from profits}}{\text{Total saving}}\right)_t \qquad (21)$$

Moreover, it is evident from equation (18) that:

$$I_t/I_{t-1} = P_{t-1}/P_{t-2},$$

[48] *Principles*, First Edition, pp.480–1, Second Edition, Worded slightly differently, p.410.

so that:

$$\frac{I_t}{I_{t-1}} = \frac{P_{t-1}}{P_{t-2}} = \frac{X}{s_c} \cdot \left(\frac{\text{Saving from profits}}{\text{Total saving}}\right)_{t-1} \tag{22}$$

The modern economic principle which lies behind this equation is the necessary relationship between saving and investment. To produce stationary demand conditions in a closed economy (and equation (22) is derived with that assumption) planned investment must equal planned saving, and this will come about if capitalists who are responsible for all investment decisions, plan to invest in excess of their saving, precisely the aggregate amount that landlords save. This will ensue if X/s_c, the ratio of capitalists' investment to capitalists' saving, is precisely equal to the ratio, $\frac{\text{Total saving}}{\text{Saving from profits}}$, and in this event the right hand side of equation (22) will come to unity which will then produce stationary levels of profits and investment. If X/s_c exceeds $\frac{\text{Total saving}}{\text{Saving from profits}}$, capitalists will plan to invest more than they save to an extent greater than that needed to absorb landlords' saving, and demand will in consequence expand. In equation (22) the right hand side will exceed unity where X/s_c exceeds $\frac{\text{Total saving}}{\text{saving from profits}}$ to produce a rising investment and profits trend. Demand will of course contract if X/s_c is less than $\frac{\text{Total saving}}{\text{Saving from profits}}$.

Hence a rising trend in investment, profits and of course effective demand is only a possibility at all if X/s_c, the ratio of the coefficient of capitalists' investment to profits to the coefficient of their saving to profits exceeds the ratio, $\frac{\text{Total saving}}{\text{Saving from profits}}$. With a very small capitalist class in relation to the landlords, or a greater tendency for capitalists to save than to invest, growth will be a sheer impossibility.

In his own early nineteenth century statements, Malthus did not of course set out the problem of generating sufficient effective demand in these twentieth century terms, but his proposed public policies are entirely appropriate to the difficulty as set out here. It was his belief that taxation fell largely on rents;

"Though it is by no means true, as stated by the Economists, that all taxes fall on the neat rents of the landlords, yet it is certainly true that they have little power of relieving themselves. It is also true that they possess a fund more disposable, and better adapted for taxation than any other. They are in consequence more frequently taxed, both directly and indirectly. And if they pay, as they certainly do, many of the taxes which fall on the capital of the farmer and the wages of the labourer, as well as those directly imposed on themselves, they must necessarily feel it in the diminution of that portion of the whole produce, which under other circumstances would have fallen to their share."[49]

If taxation falls predominantly on the landlords, and greatly reduces their saving without at the same time significantly reducing the real resources of the capitalist class, and Malthus actually indicates that landlords will pay "many" of such taxes as "fall on the capital of the farmer," an increase in taxation together with a corresponding increase in government expenditure will cut the ratio $\frac{\text{Total saving}}{\text{Saving from profits}}$, and reduce this to unity if saving by landlords can be totally eliminated, which must favour *the growth of demand.* Demand can therefore be raised through government action, and incidentally without any need for deficit financing, which Malthus never specifically favoured.

While he did not publish arguments which supported deficit financing he did in fact argue in 1811 that extra note issues by the Bank of England, then a private company, raised effective demand by transferring real purchasing power from landlords and rentiers to capitalists:

"... if such a distribution of the circulating medium were to take place, as to throw the command of the produce of the country chiefly into the hands of the productive classes, —that is, if considerable portions of the currency were taken from the idle, and those who live upon fixed incomes, and transferred to farmers, manufacturers and merchants,—the proportion between capital and revenue would be greatly altered to the advantage of capital; and in a short time, the produce of the country would be greatly augmented.

Whenever, in the actual state of things, a fresh issue of notes comes into the hands of those who mean to employ them in the prosecution and extension of a profitable buisness, a difference in the distribution of the circulating medium takes place, similar in kind to that which has been last supposed; ... all the industrious classes,—all those that sell as well as buy. are, during the progressive rise of prices, making unusual profits; and even when this progression stops, are left with the command of a greater portion of the annual produce than they possessed previous to the new issues." [50]

[49] *Principles*, First Edition, p.204: Second Edition, p.193.
[50] "Depreciation of Paper Money" (1811), reprinted in *Occasional Papers of T. R. Malthus* p. 96. R. G. Link (1959) has drawn attention to the same passage and its significance.

A further element in the range of policies which is relevant to encouraging the growth of capitalist incomes in relation to rentier incomes of all kinds is of course the break-up of the largest estates into smaller ones, which, as we have seen, Malthus favoured. He argued that the growth of industrial and commercial capital is encouraged by a proliferation of small landowners rather than a handful of great estates:

"The possessor of numerous estates, after he had furnished his mansion or castle splendidly, and provided himself with handsome clothes and handsome carriages, would not change them all every two months, merely because he had the power of doing it. Instead of indulging in such useless and troublesome changes, he would be more likely to keep a number of servants and idle dependants ... Thirty or forty proprietors, with incomes answering to between one thousand and five thousand a year, would create a much more effective demand for wheaten bread, good meat, and manufactured products, than a single proprietor possessing a hundred thousand a year..."

"And experience shews us that manufacturing wealth is at once the consequence of a better distribution of property, and the cause of further improvements in such distribution, by the increase in the proportion of the middle classes of society, which the growth of manufacturing and mercantile capital cannot fail to create." [51]

A high ratio of capitalist incomes in relation to rentier incomes is essential if stagnation is to be avoided in the modern restatment of Malthus's argument which was set out above. It will be evident from the above passages that Malthus himself attached very great importance to this. It was Malthus's view that in early nineteenth century Britain, saving actually did come predominantly from profits, and that is obviously a precondition for growth in the present restatement of his argument. That is because a significant excess of the capitalists' investment propensity (X) over their saving propensity (s_c) was scarcely to be expected in the early nineteenth century when capital markets were relatively underdeveloped. Capitalists could therefore reinvest their saving from their own profits, and some could invest more as a result of fixed interest loans of limited size, but capitalists as a whole could hardly be expected to invest that much more than they saved. It was therefore absolutely essential if a rising trend of profits and investment was to be achieved, that the bulk of rents were consumed, either by the landlords themselves, or indirectly through the government.

To realise a country's full growth potential, it is not of course sufficient that profits and investment achieve a rising trend. The trend must be strong enough to raise profits, investment and demand at a rate at least equal to

[51] *Principles*, First Edition (1820), p. 430, 431: Second Edition, p. 374, 375.

48   MALTHUS'S THEORY OF EFFECTIVE DEMAND AND GROWTH

the economy's long-term growth potential. It was found in Part II of this article that the maximum sustainable rate of growth of the economy is $\dfrac{a_0}{1-Z-a_1/X}$ (equation (14)), so there is a final equation for the maximum sustainable rate of growth, i.e. that:

$$\frac{X}{s_c} \cdot \left(\frac{\text{Saving from profits}}{\text{Total saving}} \right) - 1 \geqslant \frac{a_0}{1-Z-a_1/X} \tag{23}$$

The left hand side of this final equation shows the growth of profits and investment, and this will need to be at least as great as the growth of potential output shown on the right hand side. An economy will not be prevented from achieving its maximum potential growth rate in the long-term if the demand-side factors on the left hand side of the equation are stronger than the supply-side factors on the right. A cycle of the kind set out in Part I will hold down the rate of growth of demand during the slump phase of the cycle, so that, over the cycle as a whole, demand grows no more rapidly than supply potential.

Let us see however why *long-term* stagnation can ensue where the demand-side factors on the left hand side of equation (23) are weaker than the long-term potential growth rate on the right. Should not the self-correcting cycle, outlined in Part I of this article, lift the economy off the floor, and lift the growth of demand to at least temporary equality with the potential rate of growth of supply? Where *ex-ante* demand is below *ex-ante* supply at the existing price level, prices fall, and:

> "As long as this fall in the money price of produce continues to diminish the power of commanding domestic and foreign labour, a great discouragement to production must obviously continue; and if, after labour has adjusted itself to the new level of prices, the permanent distribution of the produce and the permanent tastes and habits of the people should not be favourable to an adequate degree of consumption, the clearest principles of political economy shew that the profits of stock might be lower for any length of time than the state of the land rendered necessary; and that the check to production might be as permanent as the faulty distribution of the produce and the unfavourable tastes and habits which had occasioned it." [52]

Ought not the higher real wage that should accompany falling commodity prices and a low rate of profit, encourage population growth, and so force the wage down and profits up again to produce the self-correcting cycle of Part I?

[52] *Principles*, First Edition, pp.446–7: Second Edition, Slightly reworded (In particular, the Second Edition has "effectual consumption" for "consumption"), p.387.

"There is another cause, besides a change in the habits of the people, which prevents the population of a country from keeping pace with the apparent command of the labourer over the means of subsistence. It sometimes happens that wages are for a time rather higher than they ought to be, in proportion to the demand for labour. This is the most likely to take place when the price of raw produce has fallen in value, so as to diminish the power of the cultivators to employ the same or an increasing number of labourers at the same price. If the fall be considerable, and not made up in value by increase of quantity, so many labourers will be thrown out of work that wages, after a period of great distress, will generally be lowered in proportion. But if the fall be gradual, and partly made up in exchangeable value by increase of quantity, the money wages of labour will not necessarily sink; and the result will be merely a slack demand for labour, not sufficient perhaps to throw the actual labourers our of work, but such as to prevent or diminish task-work, to check the employment of women and children, and to give but little encouragement to the rising generation of labourers. In this case the quantity of the necessaries of life actually earned by the labourer and his family, may be really less than when, owing to a rise of prices, the daily pay of the labourer will command a smaller quantity of corn. The command of the labouring classes over the necessaries of life, though apparently greater, is really less in the former than in the latter case, and upon all general principles, ought to produce less effect on the increase of population."[53]

"If a labourer commands a peck instead of $\frac{3}{4}$ of a peck of wheat a day in consequence of a rise of wages occasioned by a demand for labour, it is certain that all labourers may be employed who are willing and able to work, and probably also their wives and children; but if he is able to command this additional quantity of wheat on account of a fall in the price of corn which diminishes the capital of the farmer, the advantage may be more apparent than real, and though labour for some time may not nominally fall, yet as the demand for labour may be stationary, if not retrograde, its current price will not be a certain criterion of what might be earned by the united labours of a large family, or the increased exertions of the head of it in task work.

It is obvious, therefore, that the same current corn wages will, under different circumstances, have a different effect in the encouragement of population."[54]

In other words, where demand is slack, profits *and the earnings of a family* can be low at the same time, so there will be no encouragement to

---

[53] *Principles*, first edition, pp.257–8; second edition, pp.231–2 with extensive amendments.
[54] *Principles*, First Edition, pp. 289–90, Second Edition, pp.258–9 With extensive amendments.

50   MALTHUS'S THEORY OF EFFECTIVE DEMAND AND GROWTH

population. Low effective demand leads to both low profits *and low productivity*—per family—and this in turn leads to slack work through the various incentive effects, and a slower rate of "improvement," and indeed," ... the check to production might be as permanent as the faulty distribution of the produce and the unfavourable tastes and habits which had occasioned it." An economy can thus be trapped in a situation where effective demand, earnings, incentives, and profits are all low, and there is no way out of this trap apart from a change in the "faulty distribution of the produce."

That appears to be Malthus's theory of underdevelopment, and of how an advanced economy can relapse if it oversaves and underspends. There was no apparent recognition by Ricardo that effective demand will influence both *the level* and the rate of growth of productivity, and he insisted in much of his argument with Malthus that if profits were low, real wages must be high.[55] If, where effective demand is low, profits are low and the output of a family is also reduced, profits and real incomes per family—which is what determines population—can of course be low at the same time as Malthus insisted.

Equation (23) describes the conditions for this trap in the language of twentieth century economics. Can it be said to largely reflect Malthus's own argument? There is a reasonable case that the argument to equation (19) which makes profits and rents dependant on the consumption expenditures of capitalists, landlords and the government, and on the trade balance, follows his reasoning quite closely. It reflects accurately his own understanding and it is not far from the precise statements of his which have been quoted. The extension of the argument to equation (23)—which incidentally also describes some of the conditions which must be met if savings propensities are to be optimal[56] when the equation becomes an equality—is quite another matter. One can only say that the premises are Malthus's, the

---

[55] See, in particular, Ricardo's Notes on Chapter 7, Section 3, of the First Edition of Malthus's *Principles*, (Ricardo, Vol. 2, pp. 301–31).

[56] Malthus himself was convinced that there was an optimum savings ratio. "Adam Smith has stated, that capitals are increased by parsimony, that every frugal man is a public benefactor, and that the increase of wealth depends upon the balance of produce above consumption. That these propositions are true to a great extent is perfectly unquestionable ... but it is quite obvious that they are not true to an indefinite extent, and that the principle of saving, pushed to excess, would destroy the motive to production. If every person were satisfied with the simplest food, the poorest clothing, and the meanest houses, it is certain that no other sort of food, clothing and lodging would be in existence ... If consumption exceed production, the capital of the country must be diminished, and its wealth must be gradually destroyed from its want of power to produce; if production be in great excess above consumption, the motive to accumulate and produce must cease from the want of will to consume. The two extremes are obvious; and it follows that there must be some intermediate point, though the resources of political economy may not be able to ascertain it, where, taking into consideration both the power to produce and the will to consume, the encouragement to the increase of wealth is the greatest." *Principles*, First Edition, pp.8–9: Second Edition, pp.6–7, worded slightly differently. See also, First Edition, pp.489–90: Second Edition p.413 for a reference to optimum unproductive consumption. O. Lange (1938) discusses the optimum propensity to save in Malthus's work.

conclusions are his, and that he perceived intuitively that an impossibility of growth result *could* follow from his premises. He was in fact a little hesitant about the "impossibility of growth" argument, or at any rate its possible applicability to Britain. He asserted it in the places which have been quoted, but he could not establish it with entirely verbal reasoning and he may have developed doubts about its applicability to Britain.

In the 1820 edition of the *Principles of Political Economy*, he wrote, ". . . it is obvious that the adoption of parsimonious habits in too great a degree may be accompanied by the most distressing effects at first, and by a marked depression of wealth and population permanently." In the posthumously published edition of 1836 there is merely,". . . a marked depression of wealth and population afterwards." [57] The account of the self-correcting cycles in the *Definitions of Political Economy* of 1827 which has been quoted is not qualified with the reservation that recovery may not occur. On the contrary, he wrote, "The causes above mentioned act powerfully to prevent the permanence either of glut or scarcity . . .".[58] But the posthumous edition of the *Principles of Political Economy* leaves quite unaltered the statements about the large areas of the world which are undeveloped for lack of effective demand. It may well be that in 1820 Malthus held the view that an "impossibility of growth" argument was applicable to Britain. By 1827 he had perhaps become confident that Britain had safely reached the territory of self-correcting cycles, but there were still many countries far less fortunate which could not start to develop because of a "faulty distribution of their produce."

In conclusion, there are at least two features of this restatement of Malthus's argument which may surprise some of those who have studied the literature on his theory of effective demand. The first is the lack of any reference to the rate of interest. There has in fact been no reference to the rate of interest because Malthus himself made none when he was considering these vital matters. Malthus has been criticised for failing to recognise its significance.[59] An investment function which attributed investment to profits was the one on which Malthus and Ricardo focused attention in the early nineteenth century, precisely because this may well have been the appropriate assumption at a time when there were not financial markets in the private sector sufficiently sophisticated to allow *a high fraction* of investment to be financed by borrowing at a competitively determined interest rate. Until 1833 there were even usury laws, though easily evadable ones, which fixed the maximum legal rate of interest at 5 per cent.[60] It is anachronistic to expect Malthus to write as if sophisticated modern capital

[57] *Principles*, First Edition, p.369: Second Edition, p.326
[58] *Definitions of Political Economy*, p.62.
[59] See, for instance, B. A. Corry, (1959), p.722.
[60] See J. H. Clapham, pp.347-9.

markets with an equilibrating rate of interest to reconcile the needs of would be savers and investors were already in existence. There may indeed be economists today who consider Malthus's assumption of profit determined ex-ante investment more relevant to the determination of the rate of investment than the assumption of an investment function where the rate of interest is especially significant.

A second point of departure from the work of several scholars is the suggestion that Malthus had distinct saving and investment functions, in other words, that there are different functional relationships between investment and profits and saving and profits. It has been argued by several scholars that he assumed that saving and investment were identical.[61] The textual substantiation for this assumption is partly derived from the Section of *Principles of Political Economy* entitled "Of Accumulation, or the Saving from Revenue to Add to Capital, considered as a Stimulus to the increase of Wealth." In this Section he very carefully outlined what the effects would be of a willingness to reinvest substantial ex-ante savings, but that assumption is almost wholly confined to this Section where reinvestment is an expository assumption.

A further quotation on which weight has been placed in the secondary literature is the italicised passage below.[62] This is from the Section of the *Principles of Political Economy*, "On Productive and Unproductive Labour" from the Chapter, "On the Definitions of Wealth and Productive Labour."

"Almost all the lower classes of people of every society are employed in some way or other, and if there were no grounds of distinction in their employments, with reference to their effects on the national wealth, it is difficult to conceive what would be the use of saving from revenue to add to capital, as it would be merely employing one set of people in preference to another, when, according to the hypothesis, there is no essential difference between them. How then are we to explain the nature of saving, and the different effects of parsimony and extravagance upon the national capital? *No political economist of the present day can by saving mean mere hoarding*; and beyond this contracted and inefficient proceeding, no use of the term, in reference to national wealth, can well be imagined, but that which must arise from a different application of what is saved, founded upon a real distinction between the different kinds of labour which may be maintained by it.

If the labour of menial servants be as productive of wealth as the labour of manufacturers, why should not savings be employed in their maintenance, not only without being dissipated, but with a constant increase of value? But menial servants, lawyers, or physicians, who save from their

[61] See, for instance, Mark Blaug, (1958) pp. 86–8 and B. A. Corry, (1959), pp. 719–21.
[62] See, for instance, Mark Blaug, (1958), p.86; and Lionel Robins (1958). p. 248.

salaries, are fully aware that their savings would be immediately dissipated again if they were advanced to themselves instead of being employed in the maintenance of persons of a different description . . ." [63]

"I am hardly aware how the causes of the increasing riches and prosperity of Europe since the feudal times could be traced, if we were to consider personal services as equally productive of wealth with the labours of merchants and manufacturers." [64]

" . . . in every case of productive labour, as explained by Adam Smith, there is always a period, though in some cases it may be very short, when either the stock destined to replace a capital, or the stock reserved for immediate consumption is distinctly augmented by it; . . ." [65]

It will be evident that in this section, Malthus was primarily concerned with the correct borderline between the productive and unproductive sectors of the economy— and its significance—and the reference to hoarding comes in quite incidentally. Moreover, even in the context of this Section, the employment of productive labour increases the *stock* (not necessarily *capital*, see below) which may be used in the next period, either for consumption, or for accumulation. There is therefore not much weight in the sentence in question to substantiate the interpretation of the secondary literature that Malthus assumed that ex-ante savings and investment were always identical. As we shall see below, there is in fact very strong evidence that differences between them were central to his argument. This will now be outlined.

First, Malthus distinguishes carefully between the physical capital of a country which is used to earn profits and provide employment, and the physical wealth which is not so used:

"Stock is a general term, and may be defined to be all the material possessions of a country, or all its actual wealth, whatever may be its destination; while capital is that particular portion of these possessions, or of this accumulated wealth, which is destined to be employed with a view to profit. They are often, however, used indiscriminately; and perhaps no great error may arise from it; but it may be useful to recollect that all stock is not properly speaking capital, though all capital is stock." [66]

[63] *Principles*, First Edition, pp. 32–3; Second Edition. (worded slightly differently), pp. 38–9.

[64] *Principles*, First Edition (1820), p.35. Not in Second Edition. See however, *Definitions of Political Economy*, p. 97," . . . I will venture to affirm, that if we once break down the distinction between the labour which is so directly productive of wealth as to be estimated in the value of the object produced, and the labour or exertion, which is so indirectly a cause of wealth, that its effect is incapable of definite estimation, we must necessarily introduce the greatest confusion into the science of political economy, and render the causes of the wealth of nations inexplicable."

[65] *Principles*, First Edition (1820), p.45: Second Edition, P.46.

[66] *Principles*, First Edition, p.293: Second Edition, p.262, has " . . . employed with a view to profit in the production and distribution of future wealth."

54   MALTHUS'S THEORY OF EFFECTIVE DEMAND AND GROWTH

All *realised* or *ex-post* saving must add to stock, but it will not necessari
add to capital. *Ex-post* saving and *ex-post* capital accumulation are ther
fore distinct, both practically and theoretically.

Capital accumulation can occur at home or overseas:

> " . . . the saving from revenue to add to capital, instead of affording t
> remedy required, would only aggravate the distresses of the capitalis
> and fill the stream of capital which was flowing out of the country." [67]

Hence even that part of *ex-post* saving which results in capital accumulatic
does not necessarily add to the capital of the saving country. Saving
Britain and investment in Britain—or in any other country— will differ in
far as investment crosses national frontiers, and it can clearly flood out of
country where there is a lack of effective demand and therefore a low rate
profit.[68]

Still more important and fundamental, Malthus very clearly distinguish
ex-ante intentions from *ex-post* results. The role of motivation in Malthu:
thought has already been discussed. When he says," . . . from the want of
proper distribution of the actual produce adequate motives are not furnishe
to continued production. . . I don't at all wish to deny that some persons
others are entitled to consume all that is produced; but the grand question
whether it is distributed in such a manner between the different parti
concerned   as   to   occasion   the   most   effective   demand   for   futu
produce: . . ." [69] he is distinguishing *ex-post* saving from *ex-ante* investmer
The accumulation of property rights over existing produce does not guara
tee its reproduction, let alone its expansion. This depends on new *ex-an*
decisions to invest which will only be made if profits are sufficiently high.

> "Unless the estimation in which an object is held, or the value which a
> individual, or the society places on it when obtained, adequately compe
> sates the sacrifice which has been made to obtain it, such wealth w
> not be produced in future.
>
> In individual cases, the power of producing particular commodities
> called into action, in proportion to the intensity of effectual demand f
> them; and the greatest stimulus to their increase, independent of ir
> proved facilities of production, is a high market price, or an increase

---

[67] *Principles*, First Edition, p.492: Second Edition, p.415.

[68] See also the reference to an international flight of capital due to low profits in "Six lette
from Malthus to Pierre Prevost." (G. W. Zinke (1942)). Samuel Hollander (1969) argues th
Malthus's saving and investment functions are distinct, and cites the letters to Prevost and oth
evidence to point to the significance of overseas investment in a situation where domes
investment is unprofitable.

[69] Letter from Malthus to Ricardo of 7 July 1821, David Ricardo *Works and Corresponden*
Vol IX, p.10.

their exchangeable value, before a greater value of capital has been employed upon them.

In the same manner, the greatest stimulus to the continued production of commodities, taken altogether, is an increase in the exchangeable value of the whole mass, before a greater value of capital has been employed upon them." [70]

There is thus an *ex-ante* investment function for the manufacture of each commodity, and for the manufacture of commodities as a whole. Finally:

"... the labouring classes of society may be thrown out of work in the midst of an abundance of necessaries, if these necessaries are not in the hands of those who are at the same time both able and willing to employ an adequate quantity of labour." [71]

A redistribution of incomes from profits to rents has no kind of adverse effect on *ex-post* saving—there will still be "an abundance of necessaries"— but there will be a very clear effect on the *ex-ante* investment of the next period, because only capitalists are "able and willing to employ an adequate quantity of labour."

It is of course the essence of the story that saving and investment are distinct, *ex-ante*, and this is something which Malthus fully appreciated and repeatedly said. Like modern Keynesians, Malthus sometimes correctly equates saving to investment, *ex-post*.

Malthus's theory of effective demand is only a part of his total contribution. Like Marx he was concerned with the laws of motion of societies. This article has sought to show that a logically coherent theory of growth and development can be derived from his *Principles of Political Economy*.

Exeter College, Oxford

REFERENCES

BLACK, R. D. C. "Parson Malthus, the General and the Captain," *Economic Journal*, Vol. 77, March 1967.
BLAUG, M., *Ricardian Economics: A Historical Study*, Yale University Press, 1958.
CLAPHAM, J. H., *An Economic History of Modern Britain: The Early Railway Age* 1820–50, Cambridge University Press, 1926.
CORRY, B. A., "Malthus and Keynes—A Reconsideration," *Economic Journal*, Vol. 69, December 1959.
CORRY, B. A. *Money, Saving and Investment in English Economics*, Macmillan 1962.
EAGLY, R. V., *The structure of Classical Economic Theory*, Oxford University Press, 1974.
ELTIS, W. A., *Growth and Distribution*, Macmillan, 1973.

[70] *Principles*, Second Edition, p.361: the First Edition, pp. 413–4, does not have the first paragraph of the quotation, and the second paragraph has several significant differences in wording.

[71] *Principles*, First Edition, p. 446: Second Edition, p. 387.

56   MALTHUS'S THEORY OF EFFECTIVE DEMAND AND GROWTH

GORDON B. J. and JILEK T. S., "Malthus, Keynes et l'Apport de Lauderdale," *Revue d'Economie Politique*, Vol. 75, January 1965.

HOLLANDER S., "Malthus and Keynes: A Note," *Economic Journal*, Vol. 72, June 1962.

HOLLANDER, S., "Malthus and the Post-Napoleonic Depression," *History of Political Economy*, Vol. 1, Fall 1969.

KEYNES, J. M. "Thomas Robert Malthus: the First of the Cambridge Economists," *Essays in Biography* (1933), reprinted in *The Collected Writings of John Maynard Keynes*, Macmillan, 1972, Vol. IX, Chapter 12.

LAMBERT, P., "The Law of Markets Prior to J. B. Say, and the Say-Malthus Debate," *International Economic Papers*, No. 6, 1956.

LAMBERT P., "Lauderdale, Malthus and Keynes," *Annals of Public and Cooperative Economy*, Vol. 37, January 1966.

LANGE O., "The Rate of Interest and the Optimum Propensity to Consume," *Economica*, February 1938.

LEIBENSTEIN, H., *General X-Efficiency Theory and Economic Development*, Oxford University Press, 1978.

LEVY, D., "Ricardo and the iron law: a correction of the record," *History of Political Economy*, Vol. 8, Summer 1976.

LINK, R. G. *English Theories of Economic Fluctuations* 1815–48, Chapter 2, "Thomas Robert Malthus." Columbia, N. Y., 1959.

KALECKI, M. Theory of Economic Dynamics, Allen and Unwin, 1954.

MALTHUS, T. R. *An Essay on the Principle of Population*, First Edition, 1798, Third Edition, 1806, Fifth Edition, 1817.

MALTHUS, T. R., "Depreciation of Paper Money," *Edinburgh Review*, February 1811, reprinted in Occasional Papers of T. R. Malthus, edited Bernard Semmel, New York, 1963.

MALTHUS, T. R., *The Grounds of an Opinion on the Policy of Restricting the Importation of Foreign Corn*, 1815.

MALTHUS, T. R., *An Inquiry into the Nature and Progress of Rent*, 1815. (This pamphlet and "The Grounds of an Opinion..." are reprinted in *The Pamphlets of Thomas Robert Malthus*, Kelley, 1970.)

MALTHUS, T. R., *Principles of Political Economy: Considered with a View to their Practical Application*, First Edition, 1820, Second Edition, 1836 (reprinted Kelley, 1951).

MALTHUS, T. R., *Definitions of Political Economy*, 1827.

O'BRIEN, D. P., *The Classical Economists*, Oxford University Press, 1975.

O'LEARY, J. J., "Malthus and Keynes," *Journal of Political Economy*, Vol. 50, December 1942.

O'LEARY, J. J., "Malthus' General Theory of Employment and the Post-Napoleonic Depression," *Journal of Economic History*, November 1943.

RICARDO, D., *Works and Correspondence*, Edited P. Sraffa, Cambridge University Press, 1951 onwards.

ROBBINS, L., *Robert Torrens and the Evolution of Classical Economics*, Macmillan, 1958.

SKINNER, A. S. "Of Malthus, Lauderdale and Say's Law," *Scottish Journal of Political Economy*, Vol. 16, June 1969.

SOWELL, T., "The General Glut Controversy Reconsidered," *Oxford Economic Papers*, Vol. 15, November 1963.

SOWELL, T., *Say's Law*, Princeton University Press, 1972.

SPENGLER, J. J. "Malthus's Total Population Theory: a Restatement and Reappraisal," *Canadian Journal of Economics and Political Science*, Vol. 11, February and May 1945.

VATTER. H. G. "The Malthusian Model of Income Determination and its Contemporary Relevance," *Canadian Journal of Economics and Political Science*, Vol. 25, February 1959.

WRIGHT, J. F. "British Economic Growth, 1688–1959," *Economic History Review*, Vol. XVIII No. 2, 1965.

ZINKE, G. W. "Six Letters from Malthus to Pierre Prévost," *Journal of Economic History* November 1942.

8

11

Ricardo on Machinery and Technological Unemployment

WALTER ELTIS

he statements that Ricardo made in the last two years of his life concerning
ie tendency of machinery to reduce the demand for labour and to cause
echnological unemployment are very strong indeed. On 30 May 1823 it is
ecorded that, in the House of Commons,

> Mr Ricardo said, his proposition was, not that the use of machinery was
> prejudicial to persons employed in one particular manufacture, but to
> the working classes generally. It was the means of throwing additional
> labour into the market, and thus the demand for labour, generally, was
> diminished. (Ricardo, *Works*, vol. V, p. 303)

In the chapter 'On Machinery', which he added to the third edition of
Principles of Political Economy and Taxation in 1821, he wrote:

> the same cause [investment in machinery] which may increase the net
> revenue of the country, may at the same time render the population
> redundant, and deteriorate the condition of the labourer. (vol. I, p. 388)

While in a letter to McCulloch on 30 June 1821 he wrote:

> If machinery could do all the work that labour now does, there would
> be no demand for labour. Nobody would be entitled to consume any
> thing who was not a capitalist, and who could not buy or hire a
> machine. (vol. VIII, pp. 399–400)

These statements about the possible effects of mechanization on the demand for labour are no less strong than Marx's, although, as will become
evident, Ricardo's reasons for arriving at them are different.

The author is a Fellow of Exeter College, Oxford. He is grateful to Alberto Chilosi and to Samuel
Hollander for helpful comments on an earlier draft of this paper.

The statements that Ricardo made from 1821 onwards about the influence of machinery contrast very sharply with those that he had made earlier. For instance, in his *Essay on the Influence of a Low Price of Corn on the Profits of Stock* (1815),

> The effects [of a lower price of corn] on the interests of ... [the labouring] class would be nearly the same as the effects of improved machinery, which, it is now no longer questioned, has a decided tendency to raise the real wages of labour. (vol. IV, p. 35)

And in a letter to McCulloch of 29 March 1820:

> The employment of machinery I think never diminishes the demand for labour—it is never a cause of a fall in the price of labour ... (vol. VIII, p. 171)

This was a comment on an 1820 *Edinburgh Review* article on Barton's *Observations on the Conditions of the Labouring Classes*, where McCulloch had written:

> The fixed capital invested in a machine, must always displace a considerably greater quantity of circulating capital,—for otherwise there could be no motive for its erection; and hence its first effect is to sink, rather than increase, the rate of wages. (McCulloch, 1820, p. 171)

McCulloch then went over to what he believed to be Ricardo's position in an article he published in the *Edinburgh Review* in 1821, just 15 months after his previous article:

> It appears, therefore, however much it may be at variance with the common opinions on the subject, that an improvement in machinery is always more advantageous to the labourer than the capitalist. In particular cases, it may reduce the profits of the latter, and destroy a portion of his capital; but it cannot, in any case, diminish the wages of the labourer, while it must raise their value relatively to commodities, and improve his condition. (McCulloch, 1821, p. 116)

The third edition of Ricardo's *Principles* was published in the same month as McCulloch's new article, and McCulloch read with consternation in the new chapter:

> Ever since I first turned my attention to questions of political economy, I have been of opinion, that such an application of machinery to any

branch of production, as should have the effect of saving labour was a general good, accompanied only with that portion of inconvenience which in most cases attends the removal of capital and labour from one employment to another. It appeared to me, that provided the landlords had the same money rents, they would be benefited by the reduction in the prices of some of the commodities on which those rents were expended, and which reduction of price could not fail to be the consequence of the employment of machinery. The capitalist, I thought, was eventually benefited precisely in the same manner. He, indeed, who made the discovery of the machine, or who first usefully applied it, would enjoy an additional advantage, by making great profits for a time; but, in proportion as the machine came into general use, the price of the commodity produced, would, from the effects of competition, sink to its cost of production, when the capitalist would get the same money profits as before, and he would only participate in the general advantage, as a consumer, by being enabled, with the same money revenue, to command an additional quantity of comforts and enjoyments. The class of labourers also, I thought, was equally benefited by the use of machinery, as they would have the means of buying more commodities with the same money wages, and I thought that no reduction of wages would take place, because the capitalist would have the power of demanding and employing the same quantity of labour as before, although he might be under the necessity of employing it in the production of a new, or at any rate of a different commodity .... .

These were my opinions, and they continue unaltered, as far as regards the landlord and the capitalist; but I am convinced, that the substitution of machinery for human labour, is often very injurious to the interests of the class of labourers.

My mistake arose from the supposition, that whenever the net income of a society increased, its gross income would also increase; I now, however, see reason to be satisfied that the one fund, from which landlords and capitalists derive their revenue, may increase, while the other, that upon which the labouring class mainly depend, may diminish .... . (*Works*, vol. I, pp. 386–8)

McCulloch's reaction was to tell Ricardo how appalled he was 'to see an Economist of the highest reputation strenuously defending one set of opinions one day, and unconditionally surrendering them the next' (*Works*, vol. VIII, p. 382).

Ricardo and his contemporaries undoubtedly believed that he had changed his opinion on a major issue of great practical importance. It has been shown that much of the underlying argument that led to Ricardo's new thinking on the influence of machinery on the demand for labour was in fact implicit in the previous editions of the *Principles*.[1] It is at the same time entirely clear that Ricardo began to perceive the full implications of this aspect of his argument only in 1821.

There are also important new elements in the machinery chapter. The most striking of these is Ricardo's arithmetical example, which shows how the construction of machinery may reduce the subsequent demand for labour. This bears a considerable resemblance to the arithmetical example that Barton published in 1817. Sismondi and Malthus published examples of the same kind in 1819 and 1820[2] and John Stuart Mill went on to reproduce the essentials of Ricardo's example in his *Principles of Political Economy* (1848) and to draw conclusions very similar to Ricardo's (Mill, *Works*, vol. II, pp. 93–9).

Barton's book is one of the very few that Ricardo cited and quoted from, and as it includes the first of the four arithmetical examples to be published, he undoubtedly deserves credit for originating an important element of the argument that Ricardo went on to develop. His example to show how the construction of machinery can reduce the demand for labour therefore merits quotation in full:

It does not seem that every accession of capital necessarily sets in motion an additional quantity of labour. Let us suppose a case.— A manufacturer possesses a capital of £1,000, which he employs in maintaining twenty weavers, paying them £50 per annum each. His capital is suddenly increased to £2,000. With double means he does however hire double the number of workmen, but lays out £1,500 in erecting machinery, by the help of which five men are enabled to perform the same quantity of work as twenty did before. Are there not then fifteen men discharged in consequence of the manufacturer having increased his capital?

But does not the construction and repair of machinery employ a number of hands?—Undoubtedly—As in this case a sum of £1,500 was expended, it may be supposed to have given employment to thirty men for a year, at £50 each. If calculated to last fifteen years, (and machinery seldom wears out sooner) then thirty workmen might always supply fifteen manufacturers, with these machines;—therefore each manufacturer may be said constantly to employ two.—Imagine also that one man is always employed in the necessary repairs. We have then five weavers, and three machine-makers, where there were before twenty weavers.

But the increased revenue of the manufacturer will enable him to

[1] See, for instance, Hollander (1971, 1979).
[2] Sismondi (1819, vol. II, pp. 324–6); and Malthus (1820, pp. 261–2; reprinted in Ricardo, *Works*, vol. II, pp. 235–6).

maintain more domestic servants.—Let us see then how many.—His yearly revenue, being supposed equal to ten per cent on his capital, was before £100—now £200. Supposing then that his servants are paid at the same rate as his workmen, he is able to hire just two more. We have then, with a capital of £2,000, and a revenue of £200 per annum,

5 weavers,

3 machine-makers,

2 domestic servants,

10 Persons in all, employed.

With half the capital, and half the revenue, just double the number of hands were set in motion.

The demand for labour depends then on the increase of circulating, and not of fixed, capital. Were it true that the proportion between these two sorts of capital is the same at all times, and in all countries, then indeed it follows that the number of labourers employed is in proportion to the wealth of the state. But such a proposition has not the semblance of probability. As arts are cultivated, and civilization is extended, fixed capital bears a larger and larger proportion to circulating capital. The amount of fixed capital employed in the production of a piece of British muslin is at least a hundred, probably a thousand times greater than that employed in the production of a similar piece of Indian muslin.— And the proportion of circulating capital employed is a hundred or a thousand times less. It is easy to conceive that under certain circumstances, the whole of the annual savings of an industrious people might be added to fixed capital, in which case they would have no effect in increasing the demand for labour. (Barton, 1817, pp. 15–17)

Ricardo quoted the last of these four paragraphs in the third edition of his *Principles* and constructed a far sharper example than Barton's to show how the construction of machinery can reduce the demand for labour by cutting the total amount of circulating capital. Wage goods have to be made available to workers in advance of production in all classical models, so a reduction in the stock of consumable commodities, which forms a high fraction of circulating capital, must reduce a classical economy's ability to pay wages and therefore to support labour.[3] Ricardo's example is not cluttered with the presence of maintenance workers and of servants who become newly employed as a result of an increase in profits. Still more important, it does not involve a doubling of the capital stock. Ricardo's analysis of the problem (which naturally ran deeper than Barton's) showed him, for reasons which will become clear, that extra capital will always raise employment. It is only the conversion of part of the existing capital stock

[3] See Hicks (1969, p. 151), for an account of the underlying foundations of this line of argument.

from circulating capital to machinery that can reduce employment. His example therefore required an unchanged total capital, and within that total, a change in the composition of capital.

In Ricardo's example, a capitalist has a total capital valued at £20,000, which is initially £13,000 circulating and £7,000 fixed. The profit to the capitalist is £2,000, which is entirely consumed, so his total capital is constant. In a particular year he converts £7,500 of his circulating capital into fixed capital by making use of Barton's assumption that some of the workers are employed to construct a machine instead of to produce provisions. In consequence, in the following year his total capital will still be £20,000, but his fixed capital will be up from £7,000 to £14,500 as a result of the construction of the machine, while his circulating capital will be down from £13,000 to £5,500. Ricardo concludes that in this case, where there is no net accumulation of capital, the capitalist's 'means of employing labour, would be reduced in the proportion of £13,000 to £5,500, and, consequently, all the labour which was before employed by £7,500, would become redundant' (*Works*, vol. I, pp. 388–9). At first sight surprisingly, as he appears to have made use of vital elements in Barton's argument, Ricardo supplements his quotation from him with the qualification:

> It is not easy, I think, to conceive that under any circumstances, an increase of capital should not be followed by an increased demand for labour; the most that can be said is, that the demand will be in a diminishing ratio. (*Works*, vol. I, p. 396)

It will become evident that this qualification can be derived straightforwardly from some of the fundamental propositions of Ricardo's *Principles*, and this has been widely shown.[4]

For an argument concerned primarily with the interrelationship between capital accumulation and employment, when the ratio of fixed to circulating capital is changing, the most convenient unit to work with is clearly a physical commodity unit. Until recently this would have had to be corn, but Hicks (1972) has reminded us that a consumption basket consisting of a variety of goods can be brought into the analysis as a single composite commodity, provided that the individual items in the consumption basket are consumed in relative proportions which remain unaltered. There are many passages where Ricardo explicitly or implicitly assumes that workers consume the food and manufactures which make up their necessary consumption in fixed proportions (see e.g. vol. I. pp. 102–4), so it will not misrepresent him if the unit in which output is measured is the basket of commodities that makes up the natural wage. As Hicks has pointed out, some of the items in the

---

[4] See, for instance, Blaug (1958, 1978), Hollander (1971, 1979), O'Brien (1975) and Berg (1980).

basket will be produced with diminishing returns and others with constant or increasing returns. However, in a Ricardian model the diminishing returns items in the basket have more effect on the behaviour of costs as output expands, so costs rise as the output of necessities is increased and extra units of the composite good are produced. With Hicks's reformulation, many of the results of the 'corn' model can be extended to a world where, as in the *Principles*, workers consume both food and manufactures.

In the present brief statement of how the model can be used to analyse the influence of the adoption of machinery, k_c will be written for circulating capital per worker, and k_f for fixed capital per worker. If the wage is at the natural level, and if wage goods provided in advance of production are the sole element in circulating capital, k_c will equal 1, since the wage goods that provide the natural wage are the unit of output. k_c will then exceed 1 to the extent that the wage exceeds the natural wage and to the extent that there are further elements in circulating capital. k_f may rise relative to k_c for two reasons. First k_f will rise if there is no change in the physical capital goods with which a labourer works, but the relative prices of these goods rise in relation to the price of the consumption basket. It will also rise, of course, if relative prices are unchanged but there is an increase in the quantity of fixed capital per worker.

If N is written for total employment and K for the total capital stock, then

$$K = (k_c + k_f)N. \tag{1}$$

If F is written for $(k_c + k_f)/k_c$, the ratio of total capital per worker to circulating capital per worker, (1) can be rewritten as:

$$K = k_c FN \tag{2}$$

and from (2) it is evident that

elasticity of N with respect to K

$$\tag{3}$$

$$= \frac{1}{1 + \left(\begin{array}{c}\text{elasticity of } k_c \\ \text{with respect to } N\end{array}\right) + \left(\begin{array}{c}\text{elasticity of } F \\ \text{with respect to } N\end{array}\right)}.$$

With the assumptions that are often made in restatements of Ricardo's argument that the wage does not persistently depart from the natural level, and that wage goods form the whole of circulating capital, the elasticity of k_c with respect to N will be zero. If it is also assumed that the ratio of total capital to circulating capital is constant, F will be constant, and in that event the elasticity of F with respect to N will also be zero. In equation (3) the elasticity of N with respect to K will then be unity: employment will grow in proportion to the capital stock. That is what Ricardo usually says, so he generally discusses the relationship between employment and the capital stock *as if* there is no persistent tendency for the wage to depart from the natural level, and no clear tendency for total capital per worker to grow faster than circulating capital per worker.

There was, however, a line of argument that was actually present in the first two editions of the *Principles* in embrionic form, which could have made Ricardo aware that, in a rigorous version of his model with the assumptions as stated, employment would grow more slowly than the capital stock. In the first chapter of the *Principles* Ricardo explains the determination of the relative prices of machinery and necessities, and measures these in money that is produced by a gold mining industry. In the third edition he assumes that machinery necessities and gold are produced by workers who use the same constant and circulating capital per head, so the marginal output of a year's labour in each industry will be sold for the same sum of money, which will go only to wages and profits since marginal production yields no rent. If a worker in gold mining produces G pieces of money a year, while a worker in necessity output produces Q units of necessities, these Q units must sell for G pieces of gold, so the price of a unit of necessities will be G/Q pieces of gold. As the natural wage is one unit of necessities, this will also be G/Q pieces of gold. As capital accumulation and consequent population growth force the economy on to inferior land, Q, the output of necessities per worker, will fall, with the result that G/Q, the money wage and the money price of a unit of necessities, will rise correspondingly.[5] In contrast, the productivity of the workers who produce machinery will not fall.

Ricardo always writes about the production of machinery and its cost in terms of gold, as if it is produced at constant cost. The constant amount of machinery a worker produces in a year will therefore sell for the G pieces of money that a gold miner produces in the same period. As the capital stock and employment grow, therefore, the price of the machinery a worker produces in a year will stay constant at G pieces of gold, while the wage and the price of necessities, which is G/Q pieces of gold, will rise continuously.

In the first two editions of the *Principles*, Ricardo arrived at the result that a rise in wages would not raise the cost of machinery, and of course made it very clear (after chapter 1) that the real cost of producing necessities, and therefore of employing labour, would tend to rise as capital and population grew. He did not however bring the two lines of argument together and state explicitly that the incentive to employ machinery would increase as the

---

[5] This exposition follows Pasinetti (1960) in the explanation of the prices of 'corn' and 'gold' and their divergence in his mathematical restatement of Ricardo's system.

economy developed. There is merely a general remark in the second edition (but not the first) referring to 'the early stages of society, before much machinery or durable fixed capital is used' (*Works*, vol. I, p. 62), but there is no explanation of the introduction of machinery as a direct consequence of a relative change in the price of machinery and the wage. It is no wonder, since there is no evidence that Ricardo actually inferred that machinery would be increasingly resorted to as labour productivity in necessity production fell, that he did not go on to perceive that, as a consequence of increasing mechanization, employment would grow more slowly than the capital stock.

Ricardo's failure to draw that inference at that stage could have been because, in the early editions of the *Principles*, gold mining did not in fact involve the same capital intensities as machinery and necessity production. Gold was produced without fixed capital, with the result that a rise in wages reduced the prices of both necessities and machinery measured in gold. What happened to the relative prices of machinery and necessities, and to the wage as the economy developed, therefore came out very much less clearly than with the assumptions made in the third edition, on which the argument stated above was based. With the assumption made there that there are equal capital intensities in machinery production, necessity production and gold mining, it becomes crystal clear that, as a population presses on to inferior land, money wages rise while the price of machinery does not, and this may well have led Ricardo to understand the full implications of his argument. It is only with the third edition that he added the footnote to chapter 1:

We here see why it is that old countries are constantly impelled to employ machinery, and new countries to employ labour. With every difficulty of providing for the maintenance of men, labour necessarily rises, and with every rise in the price of labour, new temptations are offered to the use of machinery. This difficulty of providing for the maintenance of men is in constant operation in old countries, in new ones a very great increase in the population may take place without the least rise in the wages of labour. (*Works*, vol. I, p. 41)

A parallel passage in the new machinery chapter reads:

In America and many other countries, where the food of man is easily provided, there is not nearly such great temptation to employ machinery as in England, where food is high, and costs much labour for its production. The same cause that raises labour, does not raise the value of machines, and, therefore, with every augmentation of capital, a greater proportion of it is employed on machinery. (vol. I, p. 395)

With these two new passages Ricardo was home, and he fully perceived the implications of what is nowadays called 'the Ricardo effect'. As wages rise as a result of the increasing marginal cost of necessities (relative to gold and machinery produced with unchanging productivity), the ratio of total capital per worker to circulating capital per worker, F in equation (3), rises. The elasticity of F with respect to L is therefore positive, with the result that the elasticity of L with respect to K is less than 1. If, for instance, a 1 per cent increase in employment raised the wage by $\frac{1}{2}$ per cent, and this raised the ratio of total capital relative to circulating capital by $\frac{1}{2}$ per cent, the elasticity of F with respect to L would be $\frac{1}{2}$. Equation (3) shows that, if circulating capital per worker is constant (as Ricardo implicitly assumes where he analyses the influence of mechanization on employment), the elasticity of L with respect to K will then be $\frac{2}{3}$; in other words, employment will grow at a rate of just 2 per cent when the capital stock grows at 3 per cent. It would be quite wrong to graft on to Ricardo the assumption of a constant elasticity of the wage with respect to employment, or a constant tendency to mechanize as the wage rises. Where he gives numerical examples of the relationship between employment and the real cost of food, this rises at a faster proportional rate than employment.[6] The Ricardo effect therefore may be weak at first (as the first of the two above quotations implies) as population expands relative to territory, and then may become very much stronger. The elasticity of employment in relation to the total capital stock may therefore be little less than 1 for a considerable time and then become sharply less than 1.

It is of course only if employment, and therefore the demand for food (and other necessities produced with diminishing returns), rises that the effects set out in equation (3) are triggered off. Without a rise in the demand for necessities, there will be no rise in their real cost and therefore no rise in the wage relative to the cost of machinery. There will therefore be no temptation to substitute machinery for labour. That is why Ricardo believed that Barton had gone too far when he said that capital could grow and employment fall at the same time. It is only if employment is actually growing that the relative cost of labour will be pulled up to produce a lasting incentive to mechanize. If mechanization actually cut employment, the demand for food would fall back, and so reduce the wage again relative to the cost of machinery, with the result that those who had mechanized would discover that they had been mistaken. Mechanization must be associated with rising employment in this strand of Ricardo's argument, and that is why he says, in the paragraph where he goes on to quote Barton and to explain why there will be an increasing use of machinery as wages rise. 'The demand for labour will continue to increase

---

[6] The examples are in Ricardo's *Works* (vol. IV, p. 17, and vol. I, p. 81), where successive increases in capital produce increasing *proportional* reductions in marginal corn output, i.e., increasing proportional rises in the real cost of corn.

with an increase of capital, but not in proportion to its increase; the ratio will necessarily be a diminishing ratio' (vol. I, p. 395). That is precisely the relationship set out in equation (3).[7]

There is an additional aspect to the manner in which a higher wage leads to increased mechanization in Ricardo's argument, and this is seen most clearly in terms of Hicks's new analysis in *Capital and Time* (1973, pp. 97–9). Hicks distinguishes there between construction labour and operating labour, and an invention with a 'forward bias' is one that raises the labour needed to construct capital equipment relative to the labour required to operate it. That is precisely Ricardo's machinery example, an increase in construction labour and a reduction in operating labour. Ricardo has several examples involving varying time-periods between incurring costs and bringing products to market, of which the construction of machinery is an example, and he states:

> On account then of the different degrees of durability of their capitals, or, which is the same thing, on account of the time which must elapse before one set of commodities can be brought to market, they will be valuable, not exactly in proportion to the quantity of labour bestowed on them ... but something more, to compensate for the greater length of time which must elapse before the most valuable can be brought to market. (*Works*, vol. I, p. 34)

And

> Every rise of wages, therefore, or, which is the same thing, every fall of profits, would lower the relative value of those commodities which were produced with a capital of a durable nature, and would proportionally elevate those which were produced with capital more perishable. (vol. I, pp. 39–40)

Thus while Ricardo does not quite state Hicks's argument, he all but states it. Durability of machinery is the same thing as a longer time that must elapse before commodities can be brought to market, and a rise in wages is favourable to those commodities that are produced with a capital of a more durable nature. It is a very small jump from this to the proposition that a higher wage leads to the substitution of construction labour for operating labour in the terms of Hicks's argument.

---

[7] Meacci's account of Ricardo's analysis of mechanization in this volume is quite close to that presented here at this point. He agrees that there cannot be an economy-wide trend towards mechanization in the absence of accumulation, and that in Ricardo's analysis this will also generally entail growth in the absolute amount of circulating capital and therefore in the demand for labour.

That relationship is simply another that influences the elasticity of F with respect to L in equation (3). If it makes this larger, the elasticity of L with respect to K will fall that much more below 1, and total employment will grow still more slowly in relation to the capital stock. As with the previous argument that Ricardo stated, however, there must be a rising trend in wages before these incentives towards mechanization are triggered off, and this requires an increasing pressure of population on territory, so these trends will persist only if the demand for labour is on balance advancing.

There are, however, as has been shown, passages in the new machinery chapter, and in speeches in Parliament and in his correspondence, in which Ricardo certainly spoke as if machinery could produce absolute falls in employment. This can occur in the particular conditions he assumed at the start of the chapter, namely:

> To elucidate the principle, I have been supposing, that improved machinery is *suddenly* discovered, and extensively used .... (*Works*, vol. I, p. 395)

He then went on to state the argument that in practice mechanization is a process that is endogenous to the rising wage that is central to his argument:

> the truth is, that these discoveries are gradual, and rather operate in determining the employment of the capital which is saved and accumulated, than in diverting capital from its actual employment.
>
> With every increase of capital and population, food will generally rise, on account of its being more difficult to produce. The consequence of a rise of food will be a rise of wages, and every rise of wages will have a tendency to determine the saved capital in a greater proportion than before to the employment of machinery. Machinery and labour are in constant competition, and the former can frequently not be employed until labour rises. (*Works*, vol. I, p. 395)

As Hollander (1971, 1979) has pointed out, therefore, Ricardo has two distinct arguments. There is first the argument in which increasing mechanization is endogenously associated with the rising wage which is a central element of Ricardo's account of what occurs as economies develop. That process can never produce a declining trend in employment. Second, there is the case where 'improved machinery is suddenly discovered'. These exogenous discoveries of machinery can obviously take any form and have any kind of effect on employment.

It is Ricardo's argument in his machinery chapter 'That if the improved means of production, in consequence of the use of machinery, should increase the net produce of a country in a degree so great as not to diminish the gross produce, (I mean always quantity of commodities and not value), then the situation of all classes will be improved' (vol. I, p. 392). In a letter to McCulloch written on 18 June 1821, Ricardo assumes a cloth manufacturer who can produce 10,000 yards of cloth, with a labour-intensive technique, spending £18,000 on labour and selling the cloth at £2 a yard for £20,000 to yield a profit of £2,000 on his circulating capital of £18,000. He goes on to say that, if he invested the same capital in machinery and still obtained an output of 10,000 yards of cloth, society could still employ the same quantity of labour because 'you would have the same quantity of food, cloth, and all other commodities annually' (vol. VIII, p. 389). The conversion of £18,000 of circulating capital into fixed capital would involve no aggregate loss of circulating capital because the 10,000 yards of cloth the machine produced would at once make good the circulating capital used up in the year of its construction. The 10,000 yards of cloth and the proceeds from marketing it would belong to the capitalist and the income of the previously employed workmen in cloth production would cease, but the capitalist would be able to employ more menial servants, and the society's circulating capital as a whole would be in no way reduced. Therefore it is only if the *sudden* discovery of machinery involves a fall in output that there is a loss of circulating capital and therefore a fall in the demand for labour.

Here there is a temptation to suggest that Ricardo had not thought the problem through completely (as he had not thought through the case of endogenous invention prior to the third edition). He asserts in his letter of 18 June 1821 to McCulloch that the substitution of machinery for an equal circulating capital quite categorically 'will diminish the quantity of gross produce'. 'Diminish the quantity of exchangeable articles, and you diminish the demand for commodities;—you diminish the means of enjoyment of some one, or more, of the classes of the community' (vol. VIII, p. 388). He goes on to say that if, using circulating capital alone, a capitalist produces 10,000 yards of cloth, obtains 1,000 yards as profit and sells this at £2 a yard, he will be less well off than if, by using machinery but not increasing his total capital, he produces 3,000 yards of cloth, obtains 1,500 yards of this as profit and sells it for just £1.10s a yard. With a profit of 1,000 yards of cloth out of 10,000 and a price of cloth of £2 a yard, he makes £2,000 profit. With a profit of 1,500 yards out of 3,000 and a price of cloth of £1.10s a yard, he makes £2,250 profit. Mechanization is therefore profitable even if the gross output of cloth falls by 70 per cent.

But it in no way follows from this example and the argument behind it that, if inventions involving the use of machinery are *suddenly* and *spontaneously* made, employment will fall. It has been shown that spontaneous inventions are the only ones that can be associated with a falling demand for labour in the economy as a whole: but if an invention is an exogenous event there is no reason why because it would be profitable to exploit it, even if it involved 70 per cent less output from the same capital, output should actually fall 70 per cent. The output of cloth could equally rise 70 per cent, and that quite probably is what happened during much of the industrial revolution, namely a simultaneous substitution of fixed for equal circulating capitals, and very great increases in the output of physical commodities (measured in yards) from that capital. If inventions are spontaneous, there is no reason why this should not occur, and it surely often did. Ricardo himself admitted that the effects of machinery could be extremely favourable to labour if the inventions resembled a gift from nature.

> To obtain an indestructible steam engine now, we are obliged annually to bestow a quantity of labour upon it, and therefore it is of great value. I have not said that if Almighty power would give us steam engines ready made, and capable of doing work for us without the assistance of human labour, that such a present would be injurious to any class—it would be far otherwise ... . (*Works*, vol. VIII, pp. 389–90)

Newly invented machinery that simultaneously reduced the labour needed to operate it, and raised the physical output produced with an unchanged total capital cost, would resemble the addition of these steam engines to the capital stock. Such inventions occurred, and according to Ricardo's analysis they in no way reduced the demand for labour.

All of Ricardo's actual examples are in fact of inventions and machinery that reduce the *physical* gross output obtainable from a given total capital. The case for adopting these inventions becomes greater the higher the wage. It is not worth adopting them at all at an extremely low wage, and there is always a critical wage where they become more profitable than the previous labour-intensive method of production. They are therefore all examples of the kind of mechanization that is to be expected as a result of endogenous invention. Spontaneous invention may take this form, but it may equally take the 'gift of nature' form of more physical output and lower labour requirements with a given capital investment. Ricardo's logic is therefore tight only where he speaks of endogenous technical change associated with the rising wage (in relation to the cost of machinery) that is central to his whole argument. It is the influence of this on his total argument that therefore merits attention, and given the textual evidence and his statement that he assumed the *sudden* discovery of machinery only for expositional reasons—'to elucidate the principle'—it is very probably endogenous invention associated with a rising wage that he principally had in mind when he analysed the causes and effects of mechanization.

How will continuing endogenous invention influence the growth of the Ricardian economy? This has been analysed far more closely than before by Hicks and Hollander and by Casarosa in their very similar restatements of

Ricardo's theory of economic growth.[8] Their models describe disequilibrium growth, in which the wage tends to be above the natural wage and the rate of profit tends to be higher than the minimum to which the rate of profit is reduced in the eventual stationary state. Both Hicks–Hollander and Casarosa assume that the labour force and the capital stock will tend to grow at similar rates in the long progression of an early nineteenth-century economy towards the eventual stationary state. In Casarosa's model,

$$\frac{1}{N}\frac{dN}{dt} = \psi\left(\frac{w-w_s}{w_s}\right) \quad 0 < \psi < 1 \tag{4}$$

where N is the population, w_s is the natural wage where population is constant and w is the market wage, both expressed in corn or, it could easily be said, necessities. That is simply the Malthusian population supply function which Ricardo adopted. The supply of capital is given by the equation

$$\frac{1}{K}\frac{dK}{dt} = \lambda\left(\frac{f'(N)-w}{w}\right) \tag{5}$$

where $f'(N)$ is the marginal product of labour in the production of corn—or preferably 'necessities'. The term $f'(N)-w$ is the surplus of output per worker at the margin over the wage, and Casarosa assumes that a fixed fraction of this surplus is invested. Casarosa then assumes that

$$\frac{1}{N}\frac{dN}{dt} = \frac{1}{K}\frac{dK}{dt}. \tag{6}$$

It was shown above that more generally:

$$\frac{1}{N}\frac{dN}{dt} = \frac{1}{K}\frac{dK}{dt} \frac{1}{1+\left(\begin{array}{c}\text{elasticity of } k_c \\ \text{with respect to } N\end{array}\right)+\left(\begin{array}{c}\text{elasticity of } F \\ \text{with respect to } N\end{array}\right)} \tag{7}$$

Casarosa assumes a tendency for circulating capital per worker, k_c, to fall as the economy moves towards its eventual stationary state. He therefore has a negative elasticity of k_c with respect to N which would allow employment and population (their rates of growth are not distinguished) to grow a little faster than the capital stock. He does not take this effect (which may well be slight) into account. He also, of course, ignores the tendency of total capital to grow

[8] Hicks and Hollander (1977) and Casarosa (1978). Their argument is developed in Eltis (1984, ch. 6).

faster than circulating capital, which makes the elasticity of F with respect to N positive. Which effect is stronger, that of the negative elasticity of k_c with respect to N, or the positive elasticity of F with respect to N?

Ricardo himself explains, in the fifth chapter of the *Principles* 'On Wages', that 'in the natural advance of society' wages will tend to fall 'as far as they are regulated by supply and demand', because the rate of growth of capital will fall which will tend to reduce the excess of the wage over the natural wage. At the same time, wages will tend to rise as a result of the continuing rise in the price of necessities. When these two effects are combined, Ricardo says, the worker would 'receive an addition in his money wages, though with that addition he would be unable to furnish himself with the same quantity of corn and other commodities, which he had before consumed in his family' (vol. I, pp. 101–2). When all the effects shown in equation (7) are allowed for by Ricardo, therefore, there is still, on balance, a rise in the cost of labour in relation to the cost of machinery which has a constant gold price, because, like gold, it is produced with unchanging technology. There is therefore a continuing tendency to substitute machinery for labour with the result that the effect of the positive elasticity of F with respect to N is decisive. The wage does rise all the time relative to the cost of machinery; machinery is substituted for labour; the ratio of total capital to circulating capital per worker rises, and employment therefore has a continuing tendency to grow less than the capital stock.

If the sole effect of a continuing tendency towards mechanization was that employment had to grow less than the capital stock, the effect on Casarosa's model would be to lower the market wage at all points of time, since the slower growth of population needed could be provided by a smaller excess of the wage over the natural wage. That is not however the sole effect of mechanization. A more extensive use of machinery could be expected to make $f'(N)$, the marginal product of labour in the production of necessities, greater than it otherwise would be at each point of time. Through equation (5) this then raises the excess of the marginal product of labour over the wage, which increases the rate of growth of capital. If continuing mechanization raises the marginal product of labour and so the rate of growth of capital because it raises the investible surplus, and at the same time increases the rate of growth of the total capital stock that is needed to provide the extra capital to equip more workers, it is not clear whether employment will, on balance, grow more or less quickly. Blaug was surely right when he wrote in 1978:

> Ricardo seems to have realized by this time [when he wrote the machinery chapter] that the rise in money wages and the fall in the rate of profit implied by his model must lead to a constantly rising ratio of machinery to labour. This contradicts his usual assumption that capital and labour grow at equal rates and creates new complications. No

wonder that this chapter seems glued on to the rest of the book as an afterthought. (Blaug, 1978, p. 138)

In Casarosa's model, which, with Hicks and Hollander's, arguably provides the clearest analysis of the long-term behaviour of the Ricardian economy, a process of continuing mechanization raises both the economy's investible surplus at the margin and the amount of surplus that is needed to provide the capital for a given increase in employment. How this influences the long-term demand for labour is therefore unclear.

Ricardo himself recognized the favourable element due to machinery in the very long run:

> I have before observed, too, that the increase of net incomes, estimated in commodities, which is always the consequence of improved machinery, will lead to new savings and accumulations. These savings, it must be remembered are annual, and must soon create a fund, much greater than the gross revenue, originally lost by the discovery of the machine, when the demand for labour will be as great as before, and the situation of the people will be still further improved by the increased savings which the increased net revenue will still enable them to make. (*Works*, vol. I, p. 396)

That recognizes the favourable effect of higher net output on the rate of capital accumulation, which must permanently raise the rate of growth of demand for labour. In the above quotation mechanization has a once-for-all negative effect on the demand for labour, which the permanent favourable effect must in due course outweigh. But what if, as the logic of Ricardo's argument demands, there is further mechanization as the wage continues to rise, and this produces a series of further once-for-all negative effects on the demand for labour, and also further permanent positive effects? There must then be uncertainty about what will happen to the demand for labour in the long run.

Ricardo himself offered his readers the immediate unfavourable effect by setting out an example where mechanization occurs haphazardly at a particular point of time. If that example were truly haphazard, it could as plausibly have raised gross physical output as reduced it, so its adverse influence on employment was no more than a fluke. Ricardo's many amendments and additional references to machinery in the third edition of the *Principles* do however make it very clear that the mechanization he had in mind in 1821 did not occur haphazardly, but was a direct consequence of rising wages. There are therefore two trends that go on continuously: (1) mechanization all the time raises the investible surplus; (2) at the same time, it raises the amount of new capital that is needed to create a job.

Ricardo nowhere resolved the question of which influence is the stronger. He resolved it favourably to employment in the above passage only by making the investment cost of extra mechanization occur just once, while the benefits of a larger investible surplus continued indefinitely. In other passages he mentioned only the unfavourable effect. He had to leave the resolution of the problem to his great successors John Stuart Mill and Karl Marx.

Mill took up the challenge, in his *Principles of Political Economy*, by repeating Ricardo's machinery example virtually without amendment; and, as was not uncommon at the time, without acknowledgement to Ricardo:

Suppose that a person farms his own land, with a capital of two thousand quarters of corn, employed in maintaining labourers during one year (for simplicity we omit the consideration of seed and tools), whose labour produces him annually two thousand four hundred quarters, being a profit of twenty per cent. This profit we shall suppose that he annually consumes, carrying on his operations from year to year on the original capital of two thousand quarters. Let us now suppose that by the expenditure of half his capital he effects a permanent improvement of his land, which is executed by half his labourers, and occupies them for a year, after which he will only require, for the effectual cultivation of his land, half as many labourers as before. The remainder of his capital he employs as usual. In the first year there is no difference in the condition of the labourers, except that part of them have received the same pay for an operation on the land, which they previously obtained for ploughing, sowing, and reaping. At the end of the year, however, the improver has not, as before, a capital of two thousand quarters of corn. Only one thousand quarters of his capital have been reproduced in the usual way: he has now only those thousand quarters and his improvement. He will employ, in the next and in each following year, only half the number of labourers, and will divide among them only half the former quantity of subsistence. The loss will soon be made up to them if the improved land, with the diminished quantity of labour, produces two thousand four hundred quarters as before, because so enormous an accession of gain will probably induce the improver to save a part, add it to his capital, and become a larger employer of labour. But it is conceivable that this may not be the case; for (supposing, as we may do, that the improvement will last indefinitely, without any outlay worth mentioning to keep it up) the improver will have gained largely by his improvement if the land now yields, not two thousand four hundred, but one thousand five hundred quarters; since this will replace the one thousand quarters forming his present circulating capital, with a profit of twenty-five per cent (instead of twenty as before) on the whole capital, fixed and circulating together. The improvement, therefore, may be a very profitable one to him, and yet very injurious to the labourers. (Mill, *Works*, vol. II, p. 94)

Mill's example is of an agricultural improvement while Ricardo's was of a machine, but Mill had already pointed out that

all increases of fixed capital, when taking place at the expense of circulating, must be, at least temporarily, prejudicial to the interests of the labourers. This is true, not of machinery alone, but of all improvements by which capital is sunk; that is, rendered permanently incapable of being applied to the maintenance and remuneration of labour. (Mill, *Works*, vol. II, pp. 93–4)

Mill goes on to repeat the two effects of the conversion of circulating into fixed capital on the demand for labour. As for the unfavourable effect,

All attempts to make out that the labouring classes as a collective body *cannot* suffer temporarily by the introduction of machinery, or by the sinking of capital in permanent improvements, are, I conceive, necessarily fallacious. (Mill, *Works*, vol. II, p. 96)

As for the long-term favourable effect,

even if improvements did for a time decrease the aggregate produce and the circulating capital of the community, they would not the less tend in the long run to augment both. They increase the return to capital; and of this increase the benefit must necessarily accrue either to the capitalist in greater profits, or to the customer in diminished prices; affording, in either case, an augmented fund from which accumulation may be made, while enlarged profits also hold out an increased inducement to accumulation. In the case we before selected, in which the immediate result of the improvement was to diminish the gross produce from two thousand four hundred quarters to one thousand five hundred, yet the profit of the capitalist being now five hundred quarters instead of four hundred, the extra one hundred quarters, if regularly saved, would in a few years replace the one thousand quarters subtracted from his circulating capital. (*Mill, Works*, vol. II, p. 98)

Mill has followed Ricardo up to this point with an exactitude that is a compliment to the depth of Ricardo's logic, for Mill took on board for his Victorian readers only what he firmly believed to be correct. With this foundation, Mill could at last introduce his own insights. Ricardo believed that the eventual stationary state was distant and that there was still immense potential for future investment and growth. The fourth and fifth chapters of Mill's book IV, 'Of the Tendency of Profits to a Minimum' and 'Consequences of the Tendency of Profits to a Minimum', suggest that societies can easily and rapidly approach a state of development where they have exploited all their present investment opportunities. Given this, the extra opportunities arising from newly invented methods of mechanization can only help all classes by pushing ahead the frontiers of the stationary state and permitting further growth which could otherwise not occur:

> This tendency of improvements in production to cause increased accumulation, and thereby ultimately to increase the gross produce, even if temporarily diminishing it, will assume a still more decided character if it should appear that there are assignable limits both to the accumulation of capital, and to the increase of production from the land, which limits once attained, all further increase of produce must stop; but that improvements in production, whatever may be their other effects, tend to throw one or both of these limits farther off. Now, these are truths which will appear in the clearest light in a subsequent stage of our investigation. It will be seen, that the quantity of capital which will, or even which can, be accumulated in any country, and the amount of gross produce which will, or even which can, be raised, bear a proportion to the state of the arts of production there existing; and that every improvement, even if for the time it diminish the circulating capital and the gross produce, ultimately makes room for a larger amount of both, than could possibly have existed otherwise. It is this which is the conclusive answer to the objections against machinery; and the proof thence arising of the ultimate benefit to labourers of mechanical inventions even in the existing state of society, will hereafter be seen to be conclusive. But this does not discharge governments from the obligation of alleviating, and if possible preventing, the evils of which this source of ultimate benefit is or may be productive to an existing generation. (Mill, *Works*, vol. II, pp. 98–9)

A vivid instance of the 'evil . . . to an existing generation' which the substitution of fixed for circulating capital may impose is provided when he gives an instance of agricultural improvements in practice:

> The remarkable decrease which has lately attracted notice in the gross produce of Irish agriculture, is, to all appearance, partly attributable to the diversion of land from maintaining human labourers to feeding cattle; and it could not have taken place without the removal of a large part of the Irish population by emigration or death. We have thus . . .

recent instances, in which what was regarded as an agricultural improvement, has diminished the power of the country to support its population. (Mill, *Works*, vol. II, p. 95)

Ricardo's argument does indeed apply to Ireland and the Irish famine, as Mill perceived. The failure of the potato crop raised the wage that capitalists had to pay for labour in Ireland. At the former wage the workers could be expected to live largely off potatoes; after the failure of the potato, they had to be able to afford dearer food. That rise in wages persuaded capitalists to prefer a more capital-intensive agriculture, which required more farm animals (which Ricardo also regarded as a part of fixed capital—see vol. I, pp. 394–5) and fewer workers. Hence the evictions and the starvation, which continued long after the potato crop failed. Mill satisfied himself that the long-term effects of inventions and continuing mechanization must be beneficial to all classes, with his new argument that capital was at most times close to its limits, which technical progress extended; but he and Ricardo also rightly emphasized the dark side of this progress. Before the welfare state, machinery often killed, and Mill remembered and reminds us that, in the nineteenth century as in the sixteenth, sheep and indeed cattle were the 'devourers of men' (More, 1516). In England in 1581, as in Ireland three centuries later, 'wheare XL persons had theire lyvinges, nowe one man and his shepard hathe all' (Lamond, 1929, p. 15). Ricardo explained why.

In Marx's argument, written between 20 and 40 years after Mill's, this darker side to mechanization became dominant. Marx praises Ricardo and Barton,[9] and develops their argument in two important ways. First, he assumes continuing mechanization, where Ricardo restricted his examples to a single substitution of fixed for circulating capital. With Ricardo, as has been shown, the demand for labour therefore falls just once, and the benefits from the extra accumulation that results from the higher profits arising from mechanization continue indefinitely. In Marx, both the displacement of labour and the increase in profits occur all the time.

Marx's wage goods are variable capital, while machinery and raw materials or means of production are constant capital; and

With the progress of accumulation, therefore, the proportion of constant to variable capital changes. If it was originally say 1 : 1, it now becomes successively 2 : 1, 3 : 1, 4 : 1, 5 : 1, 7 : 1, etc., so that as the capital grows, instead of $\frac{1}{2}$ its total value, only $\frac{1}{3}, \frac{1}{4}, \frac{1}{5}, \frac{1}{6}, \frac{1}{8}$, etc., is turned into labour-power, and, on the other hand, $\frac{2}{3}, \frac{3}{4}, \frac{4}{5}, \frac{5}{6}, \frac{7}{8}$, into means of production. Since the demand for labour is determined not by the extent of the total

---

[9] Marx (1969–71, vol. II, pp. 555–85; and 1867–83, vol. I, pp. 591–2) (Moscow edition for Lawrence and Wishart: missing from Penguin edition).

capital but by its variable constituent alone, that demand falls progressively with the growth of the total capital .... With the growth of the total capital, its variable constituent, the labour incorporated in it, does admittedly increase, but in a constantly diminishing proportion .... This accelerated relative diminution of the variable component, which accompanies the accelerated increase of the total capital and moves more rapidly than this increase, takes the inverse form, at the other pole, of an apparently absolute increase in the working population, an increase which always moves more rapidly than that of the variable capital or the means of employment. But in fact it is capitalist accumulation itself that constantly produces, and produces indeed in direct relation with its own energy and extent, a relatively redundant working population, i.e. a population which is superfluous to capital's average requirements .... (Marx, 1867–83, vol. I, pp. 781–2)

In addition to assuming that means of production are increased all the time in relation to wage goods, and not merely once, as Ricardo assumes, Marx also differs in the assumptions he makes about the influence of relative factor prices on the substitution of capital for labour. In Ricardo's argument mechanization occurs predominantly because of the continuing rise in the wage relative to the cost of machinery. In Marx there are no references to the substitution of capital for labour as a result of changes in relative costs, and mechanization occurs because advances in productivity are achievable only if capitalists continuously increase the means of production they use relative to the labour they employ in the manner set out in the above passage. This continual increase in the ratio of means of production to labour can make possible vast increases in productivity, as the following up-dating of Adam Smith's pin factory makes clear:

According to Adam Smith, ten men in his time, using the system of the division of labour, made 48,000 sewing-needles every day. A single needle-making machine, however, makes 145,000 needles in a working day of 11 hours. One woman or one girl superintends four such machines, and so produces nearly 600,000 needles in a day, and over 3,000,000 in a week. (Marx, 1867–83, vol. I, pp. 588–9)

Hence in Marx's Victorian England, one woman or one girl produced four times as many needles in a day as ten men in Smith's time. This advance in productivity is attributed by Marx to the immense extensions of the division of labour and the extra mechanization that had occurred since the last half of the eighteenth century. According to Marx, the productivity benefits from the further division of labour are obtainable only if capitalists mechanize to the extent required. They must also keep expanding their firms in order to take advantage of the scale economies which permit the increases in efficiency that they need to achieve in the competitive struggle with other firms:

> The battle of competition is fought by the cheapening of commodities. The cheapness of commodities depends, all other circumstances remaining the same, on the productivity of labour, and this depends in turn on the scale of production. Therefore the larger capitals beat the smaller. It will further be remembered that, with the development of the capitalist mode of production, there is an increase in the minimum amount of individual capital necessary to carry on a business under its normal conditions. (Marx, 1867–83, vol. I, p. 777)

It is as if output expands using the sequence of techniques linked by the dotted line in figure 1. These are drawn with little scope for substitutability between capital and labour to reflect the lack of weight that Marx places on the influence of relative factor prices on the technique of production. The achievement of the successive equilibria involves far faster increases in means of production than in labour to reflect Marx's assumption that this is one of the inevitable characteristics of technical progress. Finally, the distance between the isoquants narrows to represent the underlying assumption of increasing returns which permeates chapter after chapter in the first volume of *Capital*.[10] With these technological developments, capital has to increase more and more to provide a given rate of growth of employment. If capital fails to expand in this way, the growth of employment will fall continuously.

It is also simple to show algebraically how lethal for employment a combination of an ever-rising capital–output ratio and increasing returns is liable to be.[11]

Marx's assumptions about technology can be described with the help of two equations. Suppose, first, in order to reflect Marx's assumption that means of production have to be increased consistently faster than wage goods and employment, which will almost always entail an ever-rising capital–output ratio that:

$$\frac{1}{K}\frac{dK}{dt} = H\frac{1}{Y}\frac{dY}{dt} \quad H > 1. \tag{8}$$

Suppose, second, in order to make the simplest possible assumption, that there is a linear relationship between labour requirements and the growth of capital and output; i.e.,

[10] Marx's *Capital* (vol. I, pp. 439–639) is quite largely concerned with the influence of co-operation and the division of labour and increasing mechanization on industrial organization and efficiency.

[11] The restatement of Marx's argument which is outlined below is presented at greater length and developed more fully in Eltis (1984, ch. 8).

$$A\frac{1}{N}\frac{dN}{dt} = \frac{1}{Y}\frac{dY}{dt} - B\frac{1}{K}\frac{dK}{dt} \qquad (9)$$

where A and B are constants. It is easy to show that, if there are increasing returns as Marx believed (in contrast to Ricardo's assumption of diminishing returns in the production of necessities), B will have to equal $(Z - A)$ in this equation, with $Z > 1$ and $A < 1$. Rewriting equation (9) with that substitution,

$$A\frac{1}{N}\frac{dN}{dt} = \frac{1}{Y}\frac{dY}{dt} - (Z - A)\frac{1}{K}\frac{dK}{dt} \quad \begin{cases} Z > 1 \\ A < 1 \end{cases}. \qquad (10)$$

It is evident that increasing returns lies behind this labour requirements equation, because if both labour and capital increase at a rate of x per cent, output grows at a rate of $Z \cdot x$ per cent, and Z exceeds 1. Output therefore grows Z times as fast as labour and capital where these grow at the same rate, and, since Z exceeds 1, total factor productivity will grow at a rate of $(Z-1)$ per cent for each 1 per cent increase in labour and capital. Total factor productivity will not grow at all in the absence of growth in labour and capital, so there is no productivity growth in the absence of investment, which reflects Marx's many statements about the interconnection between productivity growth and capital accumulation.

Equation (10) describes the many possible ways in which an economy can achieve higher productivity. There is however only one way in which an economy will in practice raise productivity, if Marx is right to believe that the ratio of constant to variable capital and the capital–output ratio must rise continually if the particular techniques of production which permit continuous productivity growth are to be achieved. The attainment of the series of optimum techniques that Marx had in mind, like those shown in figure 1, entails the continual increase in the capital–output ratio shown by equation (8) as well as the 'increasing returns' labour requirements function shown by equation (10). When equations (8) and (10) are both satisfied,

$$\frac{1}{N}\frac{dN}{dt} = \left\{1 - \frac{Z - (1/H)}{A}\right\}\frac{1}{K}\frac{dK}{dt}. \qquad (11)$$

This equation shows that, when the influence of a rising capital–output ratio (i.e. an H greater than 1) and increasing returns (a Z greater than 1) are taken into account, employment always grows more slowly than the capital stock. If $Z = 1$ and $H = 1$, as on a neoclassical steady-growth path, which always entails a constant capital–output ratio and constant returns,

$$\frac{1}{N}\frac{dN}{dt} = \frac{1}{K}\frac{dK}{dt}$$

so employment grows at the same rate as the capital stock. If, in contrast, it is assumed that $Z = 1.2$, so that a 1 per cent increase in capital and labour would raise output 1.2 per cent, and $H = 1\frac{1}{3}$, so that capital grows $1\frac{1}{3}$ times as fast as output, and $A = \frac{3}{4}$, which means, from equation (10), that in the absence of capital accumulation a 1 per cent increase in employment would permit a 0.75 per cent increase in output, then

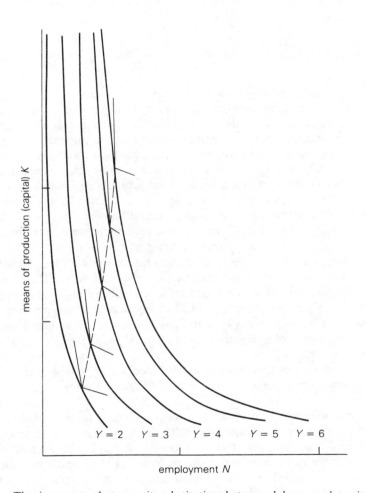

means of production (capital) K

$Y = 2$ $Y = 3$ $Y = 4$ $Y = 5$ $Y = 6$

employment N

FIGURE 1 The isoquants that permit substitution between labour and capital are drawn from equation (10) with the assumption that $A = 0.75$ and $Z = 1.20$. The fixed coefficient techniques which are linked by the dotted line also satisfy the condition set out in equation (8) with $H = 1.33$, so they describe the sequence of tecnniques of production a Marx economy would follow in these conditions.

$$\frac{1}{N}\frac{dN}{dt} = \frac{2}{5}\frac{1}{K}\frac{dK}{dt}.$$

Hence, with this quite modest degree of increasing returns, and this relatively moderate tendency towards a rising capital–output ratio, employment would grow just two-fifths as fast as the capital stock. Figure 1 illustrates this example. Employment could quite easily decline as the capital stock grows. It follows from equation (11) that

$$\frac{dN}{dK} \begin{array}{c}> \\ <\end{array} 0 \text{ depending on whether } A \begin{array}{c}> \\ <\end{array} Z - \frac{1}{H}. \qquad (12)$$

With neoclassical steady-growth assumptions where $Z = 1$ and $H = 1$, dN/dK will always be positive, but it can easily be negative if Z and H exceed 1 as Marx believed. If, for instance $A = \frac{3}{4}$, which is the kind of coefficient for the increase in output owing to extra employment alone that is generally assumed, positive accumulation will be associated with a decline in employment if $Z > 1.75$ and $H = 1$, i.e. if the capital–output ratio is constant and a 1 per cent increase in capital and labour would raise output more than 1.75 per cent. Proponents of increasing returns do not believe they are as strong as this. Alternatively, positive accumulation would be associated with declining employment if $Z = 1$ and $H > 4$, i.e. if there were constant returns and capital increased more than four times as fast as output. Most would regard that as an implausibly rapid increase in the capital–output ratio. It is however by no means implausible that $Z > 1.25$ where $H = 2$, or that $Z > 1.35$ where $H = 1\frac{2}{3}$, which would suffice to reduce employment as capital accumulates. Fairly strong but not implausibly strong increasing returns plus quite a sharp rate of increase in the capital–output ratio could therefore produce the result of a negative association between capital accumulation and employment.

Marx suggested that, as capitalism developed, a stage might conceivably be reached where the demand for labour would begin to decline:

> A development in the productive forces that would reduce the absolute number of workers, and actually enable the whole nation to accomplish its entire production in a shorter period of time, would produce a revolution, since it would put the majority of the population out of action .... The barrier to capitalist production is the surplus time of the workers. The absolute spare time that the society gains is immaterial to capitalist production. (Marx, 1867–83, vol. III, pp. 372–3)

More often, as in the passage quoted on p. 278 above, Marx stated that employment 'does admittedly increase. but in a constantly diminishing

Ricardo on Machinery and Unemployment   283

proportion' as capital accumulates. The kind of development illustrated in figure 1 may therefore come closest to giving an impression of the inter-relationship between accumulation and employment as he saw it. He believed, in other words, that the demand for labour would grow in an economy that invested massively, but still too little to keep pace with even a minimal rate of population growth.

Marx and Mill therefore provided very different answers to the fundamental questions that Ricardo's analysis of the machinery question raised. Is either answer satisfactory? The difficulty with Marx's approach to the problem has proved to be his assumption that the capital–output ratio has an inevitable upward trend. The best evidence available indicates that the capital–output ratio has been relatively stable in the century since the publication of *Capital*.[12] That would make H equal to 1 in the above equations, which removes much of the pessimism from Marx's analysis by bringing the growth of employment far closer to the growth of capital. The demand for labour has indeed risen in most of the past century, which has helped to pull up wages in a way Marx never thought possible. Marx's analysis is still, however, a valid warning of what could occur in some future period, if the capital–output ratio resumes the upward progression that he predicted.

Mill's answer to Ricardo's problem has worn better. Keynes (1936, pp. 220–1) echoed his belief that in developed economies capital accumulation would rather quickly and easily exploit available investment opportunities. When real interest rates are close to their practical floor, as they sometimes have been in recent decades, the output of efficient economies has been close to practical limits. Extra invention leading to further mechanization, which will always raise labour productivity, must extend those limits and raise a society's potential output, which modern fiscal policy can in principle redistribute so that all can benefit. That answer to Ricardo's problem has been dominant since he wrote. Marx's wholly different answer is a frightening indication of what can happen if technological progress has the capital-using bias that it may well have had in Ricardo's lifetime.

REFERENCES

Barton, John (1817). *Observations on the Circumstances which Influence the Condition of the Labouring Classes of Society*. London.

[2] The work of Matthews, Feinstein and Odling-Smee (1982) on the measurement of the growth of capital and output in Britain from 1856 to 1973 is the most professional to date, and they find that the ratio of the domestic British capital stock to the gross domestic product, measured at constant prices, averaged 4.0 in 1856–73, 4.1 in 1873–1913, 4.8 in 1924–37 (when the level of output was depressed as a result of generally weak effective demand) and 4.1 in 1951–73 (p. 133). See Klein and Kosobud (1961) for evidence on the United States capital–output ratio.

Berg, Maxine (1980). *The Machinery Question and the Making of Political Economy, 1815–1848*. Cambridge: CUP.

Blaug, Mark (1958). *Ricardian Economics: A Historical Study*. New Haven: Yale University Press.

Blaug, Mark (1978). *Economic Theory in Retrospect* (3rd edn). Cambridge: CUP.

Casarosa, Carlo (1978). 'A New Formulation of the Ricardian System'. *Oxford Economic Papers*, 30, 38–63.

Eltis, Walter (1984). *The Classical Theory of Economic Growth*. London: Macmillan.

Hicks, J. R. (1969). *A Theory of Economic History*. Oxford: OUP.

Hicks, J. R. (1972). 'Ricardo's Theory of Distribution'. In Bernard Corry and Maurice Peston (eds), *Essays in Honour of Lord Robbins*. London: Weidenfeld & Nicolson.

Hicks, J. R. (1973). *Capital and Time*. Oxford: OUP.

Hicks, J. R. and Hollander, Samuel (1977). 'Mr Ricardo and the Moderns'. *Quarterly Journal of Economics*, 91, 351–69.

Hollander, Samuel (1971). 'The Development of Ricardo's Position on Machinery'. *History of Political Economy*, 3, 105–35.

Hollander, Samuel (1979). *The Economics of David Ricardo*. Toronto: Toronto University Press.

Keynes, John Maynard (1936). *The General Theory of Employment Interest and Money. Vol. VII of the Collected Writings of John Maynard Keynes*. London: Macmillan.

Klein, L. R. and Kosobud, R. F. (1961). 'Some Econometrics of Growth: Great Ratios of Economics'. *Quarterly Journal of Economics*, 75, 173–98.

Lamond, E. (ed.) (1929). *A Discourse of the Common Weal of this Realm of England* (1581). Cambridge: CUP.

Malthus, Thomas R. (1820). *Principles of Political Economy*. Partly reprinted in Ricardo *Works* (1951–73), vol. II. Cambridge: CUP.

Marx, Karl (1867–83). *Capital* (3 vols). Harmondsworth: Penguin, 1976–81 edn.

Marx, Karl (1969–71). *Theories of Surplus Value* (3 vols). Moscow: Progress Publishers for Lawrence & Wishart.

Matthews, R. C. O., Feinstein, C. H and Odling-Smee, J. C. (1982). *British Economic Growth, 1856–1973*. Oxford: OUP.

McCulloch, J. R. (1820). 'Taxation and the Corn Laws'. *Edinburgh Review*, 33, 155–87.

McCulloch, J. R. (1821). 'The Opinions of Messrs Say, Sismondi and Malthus, on the Effects of Machinery and Accumulation Stated and Examined'. *Edinburgh Review*, 35, 102–23.

Mill, John Stuart (1963ff.). *The Collected Works of John Stuart Mill* (17 vols to date). Toronto: Toronto University Press.

More, Thomas (1516). *Utopia*.

O'Brien, D. P. (1975). *The Classical Economists*. Oxford: OUP.

Pasinetti, Luigi L. (1960). 'A Mathematical Formulation of the Ricardian System'. *Review of Economic Studies*, 27, 78–98.

Ricardo, David (1951–73). *The Works and Correspondence of David Ricardo* (11 vols), ed. P. Sraffa. Cambridge: CUP.

Sismondi, J. C. L. Sismonde, de (1819). *Nouveaux Principes d'Economie Politique* (2 vols). Paris.

9

3 Sir James Steuart's Corporate State

WALTER ELTIS

It is well known that Smith and Hume have had great influence on conservative economic policy in the twentieth century. Hume argued that the balance of payments was self-correcting so that governments could ignore the international implications of their policies, and that money was neutral in the long run so that monetary expansion offered no long-term benefits. Smith showed that the demand for labour depended on the capital stock and its effectiveness which would be maximised if capital was always allowed to earn the highest possible return. This required that the allocation of capital be in no way interfered with by government regulation and control, and that all investment decisions be taken by those who actually stood to benefit. It followed that workers' living standards would be maximised if capitalists were left entirely free to invest in whatever they regarded as the most profitable ways, while the role of government was restricted to the creation of an environment where capitalist property rights were guaranteed. Government investments would reduce living standards because they would yield less than private investments since those who took the decisions would have no inducement to get them right. All interference with trade would make workers poorer because the effectiveness of the capital stock would be reduced. Government consumption would be still more damaging because it would actually reduce the capital stock and not merely its effectiveness. The connection between these propositions and twentieth-century conservative economic policy is patent.

Eighteenth-century economics left a wholly different legacy which is less well known. An eighteenth-century Scottish aristocrat, Sir James Steuart, went into exile in 1745 (as a prospective Minister if the Stuarts had triumphed)[1] where he absorbed a good deal of the interventionism which prevailed in Europe, and published a 1200 page treatise, *An Inquiry into the Principles of Political Oeconomy*, in 1767 after his return from the continent.[2] This offered his countrymen heavy taxation, an unlimited public debt, monetary expansion to reduce interest rates to 2 per cent, import controls, export subsidies, government-managed corporations, and the Agricultural Policy which the EEC went on to adopt 200 years later. Still more astonishingly he described as, 'the most perfect plan of political oeconomy . . . anywhere to be met with' (218), one where there was no private property, no imports, no foreign travel, and no private consumption beyond the barest necessities. The potential effectiveness of such a society where the entire non-agricultural population was available for war was such that if any European nation adopted it, 'every other nation' would be obliged 'to adopt, as far as possible, a similar conduct, from a principle of self-preservation'. (227)

In the period of Keynesian ascendancy, Steuart's economics was preferred to Smith's by admirers of his cheap money and full employment policies,[3] and a distinguished Indian planner welcomed his collectivism and justification for unlimited intervention,[4] but soviet economists have yet to follow up the admiration for Steuart which Marx repeatedly expressed.[5]

An Inquiry into the Principles of Political Oeconomy was referred to by Smith in 1772 in a well-known letter to William Pulteney: 'Without once mentioning it [Steuart's book], I flatter myself, that every false principle in it, will meet with a clear and distinct confutation in mine'.[6] Smith succeeded so well that Steuart remarked shortly before his death that a book of equal length about his dog would have excited as much interest as the treatise on political economy which occupied 18 years of his life.[7]

As with most economists who merit attention, Steuart's conclusions, including his twentieth-century policy proposals, follow straightforwardly from his premises. The present restatement will start with an account of Steuart's assumptions and how these led him to conclude that a nation would suffer a variety of economic maladjustments leading to inevitable economic decline, in the absence of very detailed interventions by an enlightened *statesman*. The actual policies Steuart put forward to enable a nation to develop fully its physical and human resources and so prevent the economic decline which would otherwise be inevitable, will be the subject of the second part of the paper. Finally something will be said about Smith's reasons for regarding these policies as utterly misconceived. It will become evident that the sharply different policy implications of these two major eighteenth-century economic treatises have echoes, and indeed, considerably more than echoes, in the economic debates of the 1980s.

SIR JAMES STEUART'S ASSUMPTIONS AND HOW THEY LED HIM TO CONCLUDE THAT ONLY AN ENLIGHTENED STATESMAN COULD PREVENT SEVERE ECONOMIC MALADJUSTMENT AND DECLINE

Steuart divided the people of a country into two classes, 'The first is that of the farmers who produce the subsistence, and who are necessarily employed in this branch of business; the other I shall call *free hands*; because their occupation being to procure themselves subsistence out of the superfluity of the farmers, and by a labour adapted to the wants of the society, may vary according to these wants, and these again according to the spirit of the times'.(43)

Steuart anticipated Malthus in linking population closely to the growth of agricultural output. The non-agricultural population which depends on the surplus that farmers produce for the consumption of 'free hands' will rely on powers of coercion in a society where slavery prevails, but most of Steuart's book is concerned with market economies, and here the amount that farmers produce in excess of their own needs will depend on the range of manufactured goods which can be offered in exchange for their surplus food, and since these will be more extensively available in a monetised than a barter economy, agricultural productivity and therefore the size of the agricultural surplus will also vary with the degree of monetisation:

When once this imaginary wealth (money) becomes well introduced into a country, luxury will very naturally follow; and when money becomes the object of our wants, mankind become industrious, in turning their labour towards every object which may engage the rich to part with it; and thus the inhabitants of any country may increase in numbers, until the ground refuses farther nourishment. (45)

Steuart was convinced like Malthus that the level of agricultural productivity and output would vary sharply with the effective demand of other classes for food. If the demand for food falls for any reason:

The laziest part of the farmers, disgusted with a labour which produces a plenty superfluous to themselves, which they cannot dispose of for any equivalent, will give over working, and return to their ancient simplicity. The more laborious will not furnish the food to the necessitous for nothing . . . Thus by the diminution of labour, a part of the country, proportional to the quantity of food which the farmers formerly found superfluous, will again become uncultivated.

Here then will be found a country, the population of which must stop for want of food; and which, by the supposition, is abundantly able to produce more. Experience every where shews the possible existence of such a case, since no country in Europe is cultivated to the utmost: and that there are many still, where cultivation, and consequently multiplication, is at a stop. (41–2)

Agriculture and industry therefore have to grow together. Industrial growth provides the incentives for farmers to produce the surpluses which industry's free hands require for their subsistence.[8] 'agriculture, when encouraged for the sake of multiplying inhabitants, must keep pace with the progress of industry; or else an outlet must be provided for all superfluity'. (41)

The free hands whom the agricultural surplus supports (who amounted to approximately half the population in the Britain of 1767 according to Steuart (54–5)) may produce manufactures for home consumption or for export, provide personal services for the wealthy, or be employed by the state in the armed forces, or else to produce public works or services, The 'wants of society' and the 'spirit of the times' will determine which of these predominate.

Steuart believed a historical sequence which is often found is that the development of agriculture is first associated with a reciprocal growth in manufacturing. As industry develops, costs are low initially because surplus labour can be drawn cheaply from the land ('The desertion of the hands employed in a trifling agriculture' (183)) while industrialists have not yet become accustomed to high personal incomes which will in due course be 'consolidated' into manufacturing prices. Industry will then be internationally competitive, and there will be a fruitful period in which the free hands are predominantly employed in industry to produce luxuries for home consumption and for export. This will produce a comfortable period in which there is parallel growth in industry and agriculture, but industrial expansion contains the seeds of subsequent decline.

First, the relative price of food will rise and raise wages in a Ricardian manner:[9]

> Now the augmentation of food is relative to the soil, and as long as this can be brought to produce, at an expence proportioned to the value of the returns, agriculture without any doubt, will go forward in every country of industry. But as soon as the progress of agriculture demands an additional expence, which the natural return, at the stated prices of subsistence, will not defray, agriculture comes to a stop, and so would numbers, did not the consequences of industry push them forward, in spite of small difficulties. The industrious then, I say, continue to multiply, and the consequence is, that food becomes scarce, and that the inhabitants enter into competition for it.
>
> This is no contingent consequence, it is an infallible one; because food is an article of the first necessity, and here the provision is supposed to fall short of demand. This raises the profits of those who have food ready to sell; and as the balance upon this article must remain overturned for some time . . . these profits will be consolidated with the price, and give encouragement to a more expensive improvement of the soil . . .
>
> This augmentation on the value of subsistence must necessarily raise the price of all work . . . (197)

The consequent rise in wages and the prices of manufactures will weaken industrial competitiveness, reduce exports of manufactures and increase imports.

At the same time as industry advances, any high profits and wages which are earned over any considerable period will tend to be consolidated into the income levels that producers come to expect, and a subsequent weakening of demand will not reduce their incomes to the former level. Moreover, as industry advances, all kinds of barriers to competition will develop, and manufacturers will acquire peculiar privileges which enable them to sustain prices at high levels. According to Steuart, monopoly and monopsony are widespread, and departures from perfect competition will be greater, the more mature a country's industry, so in time any successful country will become increasingly vulnerable to international competition.

Finally export markets will inevitably weaken and competition from imports increase as foreign industry develops as it must.

when the inhabitants themselves foolishly enter into competition
with strangers for their own commodities; and when a statesman
looks coolly on, with his arms across, or takes it into his head, that it
is not his business to interpose, the prices of the dexterous workman
will rise above the amount of the mismanagement, loss, and
reasonable profits, of the new beginners; and when this comes to be
the case, trade will decay where it flourished most, and take root in a
new soil. (205)

As soon as foreign manufacturers begin to outcompete domestic
producers, a country will find it increasingly difficult to employ its free
hands in industry.

Trade having subsisted long in the nation we are now to keep in our
eye, I shall suppose that, through length of time, her neighbours
have learned to supply one article of their own and other people's
wants cheaper than she can do. What is to be done? Nobody will buy
from her, when they can be supplied from another quarter at a less
price. I say, what is to be done? For if there be no check put upon
trade, and if the statesman do not interpose with the greatest care, it
is certain, that merchants will import the produce, and even the
manufactures of rival nations; the inhabitants will buy them
preferably to their own; the wealth of the nation will be exported;
and her industrious manufacturers will be brought to starve. (284)

The lost jobs due to increasing import penetration present considerable problems for a society in Steuart's analysis because the economy's
'free hands', approximately half the labour force, will necessarily have
to find work outside agriculture, but he does not believe that there is a
satisfactory mechanism to clear the labour market at an acceptable
wage. He believes that attention should be continually focused on the
relationship between *demand* and *work* in an economy:

when we say that the balance between work and demand is to be
sustained in equilibrio, as far as possible, we mean that the quantity
supplied should be in proportion to the quantity *demanded*, that is,
wanted. While the balance stands justly poised, prices are found in
the adequate proportion of the real expence of making the goods,
with a small addition for profit to the manufacturer and merchant.
(189)

If demand falls while work (or potential supply) remains unchanged, 'reasonable profits will be diminished', and perhaps workmen will be obliged to sell 'below prime cost' with the result that 'workmen fall into distress, and that industry suffers a discouragement'. If on the contrary demand exceeds work, 'the manufacturers are enriched for a little time, by a rise of profits', 'but as soon as these profits become *consolidated* with the intrinsic value, they will cease to have the advantage of profits, and, becoming in a manner necessary to the existence of the goods, will cease to be considered as advantageous'. The continual tendency for import penetration to rise will reduce demand in relation to work with the result that manufacturers will be 'forced to starve' (192–4).

A further result of increased imports is that any consequent balance of payments deficit will lead to a continual drain of the precious metals, and therefore a loss of part of the money supply:

> if . . . a nation . . . be found to consume not only the whole work of the inhabitants, but part of that of other countries, it must have a balance of trade against it, equivalent to the amount of foreign consumption; and this must be paid for in specie, or in an annual interest, to the diminution of the former capital. Let this trade continue long enough, they will not only come at the end of their metals, but they may render themselves virtually tributary to other nations, by paying to them annually a part of the income of their lands, as the interest due upon the accumulated balances of many years' unfavourable trade. (359)

Steuart rejects Hume's argument that a loss of specie will produce self-correcting adjustments in relative prices.

A loss of specie will continue indefinitely in a country which is spending more than its national income so that it not only suffers adverse trade but also a continual need to sell real assets to foreigners and to borrow internationally:

> [Mr Hume] is led from his principles to believe, that there is no such thing as a wrong balance of trade against a nation, but on the contrary thinks that the nature of money resembles that of a fluid, which tends every where to a level . . . [N]othing is so easy, or more common than a right or a wrong balance of trade; and I observe, that what we mean by a balance, is not the bringing the fluid to a level, but either the accumulating or raising it in some countries, by the

means of national industry and frugality, which is a right balance; or the depressing it in others, by national luxury and dissipation which is a wrong one. Thus the general doctrine of the *level* can only take place, on the supposition that all countries are equally frugal and industrious . . . (1767 i.515–16)

Steuart also objects to Hume's assumption that prices will rise smoothly in countries which gain specie and fall in those which lose gold and silver, because an increased supply of the precious metals may stagnate in countries with surpluses, where, because of all the imperfections in competition, 'prices remain regulated as before, by the complicated operations of demand and competition'. (363)[10] If a gold inflow does not raise prices:

What then will become of the additional quantity of coin, or paper-money? . . . if upon the increase of riches it be found that the state of demand remains without any variation, then *the additional coin* will probably be locked up, or converted into plate; because they who have it, not being inspired with a desire of increasing their consumption, and far less with the generous sentiment of giving their money away, their riches will remain without producing more effect than if they had remained in the mine . . . Let the specie of a country, therefore, be augmented or diminished, in ever so great a proportion, commodities will still rise and fall according to the principles of demand and competition . . . Let the quantity of coin be ever so much increased, it is the desire of spending it alone which will raise prices. (344–5)

A drain of money in countries with deficits is liable to produce irreversible adverse effects if there is an accompanying decline in the degree of monetisation, which is so important to the creation of incentives to produce. If a country with a trade deficit is also borrowing internationally, or selling assets to foreigners, because its aggregate expenditure exceeds its domestic production, which can all too easily occur in a country with declining real incomes, then, as in the case of Ireland (where the improvidence of heirs is supposedly shifting property rights to England):

so soon as . . . demand . . . comes to fail, for want of money, or industry, in Ireland, to purchase it, what remains on hand will be sent over to England in kind; or, by the way of trade, be made to circulate with other nations (in beef, butter, tallow, &c.) who will give silver and gold for it, to the proprietors of the Irish lands. By such a diminution of demand in the country, for the fruits of the earth, the depopulation of Ireland is implied; because they who consumed them formerly, consume them no more; that is to say, they are dead, or have left the country. (371)

Thus adverse specie flows as a result of lack of demand for domestic produce, may lead to demonetisation and depopulation.

Steuart was deeply concerned that a country which threw its frontiers open to international competition, could easily arrive at a situation where its manufactures were overpriced, with the result that it had a chronic tendency to raise its imports and to export less. At the same time the monopolistic and restrictive practices which emerged while its industry was internationally viable would prevent prices from falling to a competitive level, for in so many states, 'domestic luxury, taxes, and the high price of living, have put out of a capacity to support a competition with strangers' (1767 i.505). If foreigners are neverthe-less permitted to sell manufactures freely to an increasingly fickle population which often prefers foreign goods merely because they are foreign, domestic industry will provide employment for diminishing numbers of 'free hands'. There will then be an inevitable excess of 'work' or potential output over 'demand' resulting in inevitable unemployment and starvation for industrial workers. The failure of domestic manufacturing will moreover reduce demand for surplus food from the farmers, for there will be insufficient demand from 'free hands' to buy up the agricultural surplus. The continuing loss of the domestic money supply which accompanies these adverse trends will compound the decline in both industry and agriculture, which, Steuart believed, had often occurred in the past as once prosperous states fell:

If . . . there be found too many hands for the demand, work will fall too low for workmen to be able to live; or, if there be too few, work will rise, and manufactures will not be exported.

For want of this just balance, no trading state has ever been of long duration, after arriving at a certain height of prosperity. We perceive in history the rise, progress, grandeur, and decline of Sydon, Tyre, Carthage, Alexandria, and Venice, not to come nearer home. (195)

But this decline in great manufacturing nations is avoidable because:

> When a nation, which has long dealt and enriched herself by a reciprocal commerce in manufactures with other nations, finds the balance of trade turn against her, it is her interest to put a total stop to it, and to remain as she is, rather than to persist habitually in a practice, which, by a change of circumstances, must have effects very opposite to those advantages which it produced formerly. Such a stop may be brought about by the means of duties and prohibitions, which a statesman can lay on importations, so soon as he perceives that they begin to preponderate with respect to the *exportations* of his own country. (1767 i.504)

The further stages of historical development of a nation therefore depend on the decisions of statesmen, and the second part of this paper will be concerned with Steuart's detailed theory of state intervention.

SIR JAMES STEUART'S THEORY OF ECONOMIC POLICY

Steuart was very optimistic about the motivation of statesmen and their desire to further economic welfare. Like Smith, he believed that self-interest is the ruling principle which governs humanity, and 'From this principle, men are engaged to act in a thousand different ways, and every action draws after it certain necessary consequences'; but self-interest will not similarly influence the conduct of a statesman,[11] 'Self-interest, when considered with regard to him, is public spirit; and it can only be called self-interest, when it is applied to those who are to be governed by it.' (142) Steuart's statesman desires nothing less than to plan the functioning of the whole economy in order to advance the good of all:

> When the statesman knows the extent and quality of the territory of his country, so as to be able to estimate what numbers it may feed; he may lay down his plan of political oeconomy, and chalk out a distribution of inhabitants, as if the number were already compleat. It will depend upon his judgement alone, and upon the combination of circumstances, foreign and domestic, to distribute, and to employ the classes, at every period during this execution, in the best manner . . . (384)

Steuart's statesman requires vast knowledge in order to plan the economy successfully:

There is no governing a state in perfection, and consequently no executing the plan for a right distribution of the inhabitants, without exactly knowing their situation as to numbers, their employment, the gains upon every species of industry, the numbers produced from each class. (70)

The more perfect and more extended any statesman's knowledge is of the circumstances and situation of every individual in the state he governs, the more he has it in his power to do them good or harm. I always suppose his inclinations to be virtuous and benevolent. (333)

Steuart's statesman becomes indispensable as soon as a country's industry begins to become less competitive in relation to foreign producers, because that is the point from which employment, output and population will continually fall if the statesman 'looks coolly on, with his arms across, or takes it into his head, that it is not his business to interpose'. What should the statesman then do to preserve industry at its peak? His desire above all is to sustain the nation's capital at this maximum level.

The first object of the care of a statesman, who governs a nation, which is upon the point of losing her foreign trade, without any prospect or probability of recovering it, is to preserve the wealth she has already acquired. No motive ought to engage him to sacrifice this wealth, the safety alone of the whole society excepted, when suddenly threatened by foreign enemies. The gratification of particular people's habitual desires, although the wealth they possess may enable them, without the smallest hurt to their private fortunes, to consume the productions of other nations; the motive of preventing hoards; that of promoting a brisk circulation within the country; the advantages to be made by merchants, who may enrich themselves by carrying on a trade disadvantageous to the nation; to say all in one word, even the supporting of the same number of inhabitants, ought not to engage his consent to the diminution of national wealth. (293)

Since it is a loss of trade competitiveness that is threatening the wealth of the nation, the statesman's immediate desire will be to restrict imports and encourage exports so as to attempt to overcome the increasing competitive advantages of other nations. The statesman will need to have extremely detailed knowledge if he is to restrict imports to the best effect:

> He must first examine minutely every use to which the merchandize imported is put: if a part is re-exported with profit, this profit must be deducted from the balance of loss incurred by the consumption of the remainder. If it be consumed upon the account of other branches of industry, which are thereby advanced, the balance of loss may still be more than compensated. If it be a mean of supporting a correspondence with a neighbouring nation, otherwise advantageous, the loss resulting from it may be submitted to, in a certain degree. But if upon examining the whole chain of consequences, he find the nation's wealth not at all increased, nor her trade encouraged, in proportion to the damage at first incurred by the importation; I believe he may decide such a branch of trade to be hurtful; and therefore that it ought to be cut off, in the most prudent manner . . . (293)

The declining competitiveness of exports can be counteracted in a variety of ways. Most directly, exports can be subsidised. '[P]ublic money must be made to operate upon the price of *the surplus* of industry only so as to make it exportable, even in cases where the national prices upon home consumption have got up beyond the proper standard'. (235) An example of a proposal to subsidise exports is:

> Let me suppose a nation which is accustomed to export to the value of a million of sterling of fish every year, to be undersold in this article by another which has found a fishery on its own coasts, so abundant as to enable it to undersell the first by 20 *per cent*. In this case, let the statesman buy up all the fish of his subjects, and undersell his competitors at every foreign market, at the loss to himself of perhaps £250,000. What is the consequence? That the million he paid for the fish remains at home, and that £750,000 comes in from abroad for the prices of them. How is the £250,000 to be made up? By a general imposition upon all the inhabitants. This returns into the public coffers, and all stands as it was. If this expedient be not followed, what will be the consequence? That those employed in the fishery will starve; that the fish taken will either remain upon hand, or be sold by the proprietors at a great

loss; they will be undone, and the nation for the future will lose the acquisition of £750,000 a year. (256–7)

If the decline in exports is the result of an inevitable Ricardian rise in food and raw material prices as the country develops, then the statesman may use public money to counteract the adverse effects on competitiveness of these fundamental developments:

When the progress of industry has augmented numbers, and made subsistence scarce, he must estimate to what height it is expedient that the price of subsistence should rise. If he finds, that, in order to encourage the breaking up of new lands, the price of it must rise too high and stand high too long, to preserve the intrinsic value of goods at the same standard as formerly; then he must assist agriculture with his purse, in order that exportation may not be discouraged. This will have the effect of increasing subsistence, according to the true proportion of the augmentation required, without raising the price of it too high. (200)

If it is a consolidation of previous inflated incomes that has made export prices unduly high, new export producers can be set up in green field sites uncontaminated with consolidation:

All methods . . . should be fallen upon to supply manufacturers with new hands; and lest the contagion of example should get the better of all precautions, the seat of manufacturers might be changed; especially when they are found in great and populous cities, where living is dear: in this case, others should be erected in the provinces where living is cheap. The state must encourage these new undertakings; numbers of children must be taken in, in order to be bred early to industry and frugality . . . (251)

Steuart also supports a state role in the day-to-day management of industrial companies:

in the infancy of such undertakings . . . the want of experience frequently occasions considerable losses; and while this continues to be the case, no complaints are heard against such associations. Few pretend to rival their undertaking, and it becomes at first more commonly the object of raillery than of jealousy. During this period, the statesman should lay the foundation of his authority; he ought to spare no pains nor encouragement to support the undertaking; he ought to inquire into the capacity of those at the head of it; order their projects to be laid before him; and when he finds them reasonable, and well planned, he ought to take unforeseen losses upon himself: he is working for the public, not for the company; and the more care and expence he is at in setting the undertaking on foot, the more he has a right to direct the prosecution of it towards the general good. This kind of assistance given, entitles him to the inspection of their books; and from this, more than any thing, he will come to an exact knowledge of every circumstance relating to their trade. (391)

It will already be evident that Steuart's interventionism is not confined to industry, because fisheries are also receiving support, and the statesman's purse has been opened to agricultural improvement. In 1759, before his return from exile, he wrote a paper which was only published in 1805 in which he proposed 'a Policy of Grain' in 'the Common Markets of England'. In this he proposed that the government should be prepared to buy up all the grain that farmers were prepared to produce at 'the minimum price expedient for the farmers', sell all that could be sold at 'the maximum price expedient for the wage-earners', and store any excess in state granaries. This proposal for the Common Markets of England in grain which he wrote for his countrymen from Tübingen has, of course, become the extremely controversial policy of grain of the European Common Market.

The detailed interventions in industry and agriculture which have been set out, were avoidable while industrial and agricultural growth were compatible with international competitiveness, but they become increasingly necessary as soon as foreign industry threatens to undermine the employment of the country's 'free hands'. Actual intervention in industry would of course be unnecessary if there was blanket protection against all imports. But a consequence of this would be that domestic monopoly incomes would grow and the home production of an extensive range of luxury consumer goods for the landlords and the recipients of consolidated monopoly incomes would occupy the free hands who formerly produced for international markets. But a shift into luxury production where domestic producers have no need to fear foreign competition has several disadvantages:

The consequences of *excessive luxury, moral and physical*, as well as the dissipation of private fortunes, may render both the statesman, and those whom he employs, negligent in their duty, unfit to discharge it, rapacious and corrupt. (267)

The growth of domestic luxury production will tend to encourage the formation of large private fortunes. The need to compete internationally acted as a constraint in the former period, but there is now no limit to the extent to which prices can be raised. This will lead to great personal inequalities; and the growth of private fortunes which will tend to dominate money markets also threatens the power and prestige of the state. Here there are remedies:

> The statesman looks about with amazement; he, who was wont to consider himself the first man in the society in every respect, perceives himself eclipsed by the lustre of private wealth, which avoids his grasp when he attempts to seize it. This makes his government more complex and more difficult to be carried on; he must now avail himself of art and address as well as of power and authority. By the help of cajoling and intrigues, he gets a little into debt; this lays a foundation for public credit, which, growing by degrees, and in its progress assuming many new forms, becomes from the most tender beginnings, a most formidable monster, striking terror into those who cherished it in its infancy. Upon this, as upon a triumphant war-horse, the statesman gets a-stride, he then appears formidable anew; his head turns giddy; he is cloaked with the dust he has raised; and at the moment he is ready to fall, he finds, to his utter astonishment and surprise, a strong monied interest, of his own creating, which, instead of swallowing him up as he apprehended, flies to his support. Through this he gets the better of all opposition . . . (181–2)

Steuart saw great potential advantages from the establishment of state controlled banks and issues of government bonds to create paper assets, and he believed that these would simultaneously raise the money supply and reduce interest rates. He argued that John Law's Mississippi scheme could have been successful in France with only a few minor modifications in the manner in which it was set up and administered; and that this would have established a long-term rate of interest of 2 per cent in France (557–63).

As well as asserting his authority via the market for public debt, a statesman also has the power to tax, which offers to governments the most powerful means to influence the economy and society:

By taxes a statesman is enriched, and by means of his wealth, he is enabled to keep his subjects in awe, and to preserve his dignity and consideration.

By the distribution of taxes, and maner of levying them, the power is thrown into such hands as the spirit of the constitution requires it should be found in. (304)

[T]he intention of taxes as I understand them, is to advance only the public good, by throwing a part of the wealth of the rich into the hands of the industrious poor . . . (334)

In addition to furthering income redistribution and social improvement, large sums of public money are needed to finance Steuart's policies to sustain the competitiveness of industry, so tax revenues will become increasingly necessary as foreign industry advances:

[T]axes become necessary; in order, with the amount of them, to correct the bad effects of luxury, by giving larger premiums to support exportation. And in proportion as a statesman's endeavours to support by these means the trade of his country becomes ineffectual, from the growing taste of dissipation in his subjects, the utility of an opulent exchequer will be more and more discovered; as he will be thereby enabled both to support his own authority against the influence of a great load of riches thrown into domestic circulation, and to defend his luxurious and wealthy subjects from the effects of the jealousy of those nations which enriched them. (336–7)

Another use of taxes, after the extinction of foreign trade, is to assist circulation, by performing, as it were, the function of the heart of a child, when at its birth that of the mother can be of no farther use to it. The public treasure, by receiving from the amount of taxes, a continual flux of money, may throw it out into the most proper channels, and thereby keep that industry alive, which formerly flourished, and depended upon the prosperity of foreign commerce only.

In proportion, therefore, as a statesman perceives the rivers of wealth . . ., which were in brisk circulation with all the world, begin to flow abroad more slowly, and to form stagnations, which break out into domestic circulation, he ought to set a plan of taxation on foot, as a fund for premiums to indemnify exportation for the loss i must sustain from the rise of prices, occasioned by luxury; and also for securing the state itself, against the influence of domestic riches, as well as for recompensing those who are employed in its service. (337–8)

The need for high taxation in order to finance Steuart's industrial policies is underlined by the need to pay high salaries to administer them. As the role of government increases, it needs to attract a proportion of those with high ability to execute the vast array of tasks which Steuart has in mind, and top people (which meant aristocrats to Steuart who had lived more in France than in Smith's Edinburgh and Glasgow) need to be well paid:

> Is it not very natural, that he who is employed by the state should receive an equivalent proportioned to the value of his services? Is it to be supposed, that a person born in a high rank, who, from this circumstance alone, acquires an advantage in most nations, hardly to be made up by any acquired abilities, will dedicate his time and his attendance for the remuneration which might satisfy an inferior? The talents of great men deserve reward as much as those of the lowest among the industrious; and the state is with reason made to pay for every service she receives. (337)

Steuart also needed high taxation in order to finance his full employment policies, and these have attracted much favourable twentieth-century attention:[12]

> The nation's wealth must be kept entire, and made to circulate, so as to provide subsistence and employment for every body. (1767 i.506)
>
> The more money becomes necessary for carrying on consumption, the more it is easy to levy taxes; the use of which is to advance the public good, by drawing from the rich, a fund sufficient to employ both the *deserving*, and the *poor*, in the service of the state . . . (1767 i.512–3)

If there is insufficient demand for labour:

> When home-demand does not fill up the void, of which we have spoken, a vicious competition takes place among those that work for a physical-necessary; the price of their labour falls below the general standard of subsistence . . .

A statesman therefore, at the head of a luxurious people, must endeavour to keep his balance [between 'work' and 'demand'] even; and if a subversion is necessary, it is far better it should happen by the preponderancy of the scale of demand. Here is my reason for preferring this alternative.

All subversions are bad, and are attended with bad consequences. If the scale of work preponderates, the industrious will starve, their subsistence will be exported; the nation gains by the balance, but appears in a manner to sell her inhabitants. If the scale of demand preponderates, luxury must increase, but the poor are fed at the expence of the rich, and the national stock of wealth stands as it was. (1767 i.506–7)

The poor should be employed above all on public works to carry through major investments in the social infrastructure:

If a thousand pounds are bestowed upon making a fire-work, a number of people are thereby employed, and gain a temporary livelihood. If the same sum is bestowed for making a canal for watering the fields of a province, a like number of people may reap the same benefit, and hitherto accounts stand even; but the fire-work played off, what remains, but the smoke and stink of the powder? Whereas the consequence of the canal is a perpetual fertility to a formerly barren soil. (1767 i.519)

I say that whoever can transform the most consumable commodities of a country into the most durable and most beneficial works, makes a high improvement. If therefore meat and drink, which are of all things the most consumable, can be turned into harbours, high roads, canals, and public buildings, is not the improvement inexpressible? This is the power of every statesman to accomplish, who has subsistence at his disposal; and beyond the power of all those who have it not. (383)

As policies which require public expenditure are pushed further, rates of taxation and borrowing will have a continual tendency to increase, and Steuart believed that taxation should rise continually as competitiveness declines and the government has to create a demand for labour to fill the gap left by declining foreign sales. He was convinced that higher taxation would have a clear tendency to raise effective demand, since the state definitely spends what might only be partly spent if left in private hands:

[T]axes promote industry; not in consequence of their being raised upon individuals, but in consequence of their being expended by the state; that is, by increasing demand and circulation . . .

Every application of public money implies a want in the state; and every want supplied, implies an encouragement given to industry. In proportion, therefore, as taxes draw money into circulation, which otherwise would not have entered into it at that time, they encourage industry; not by taking the money from individuals, but by throwing it into the hands of the state, which spends it; and which thereby throws it directly into the hands of the industrious, or of the luxurious who employ them.

It is no objection to this representation of the matter, that the persons from whom the money is taken, would have spent it as well as the state. The answer is, that it might be so, or not; whereas when the state gets it, it will be spent undoubtedly. (725–6)

If the demand-side effects of higher taxation are favourable as Steuart and present-day Keynesians insist for precisely these reasons, what of the supply-side effects which are now so often believed to be unfavourable? Steuart differed from almost all his successors in that he believed that higher taxation would actually have *favourable effects upon supply*.

When in any country the work of manufacturers, who live luxuriously, and who can afford to be idle some days of the week, finds a ready market; this circumstance alone proves beyond all dispute, that subsistence in that country is not too dear, at least in proportion to the market prices of goods at home; and if taxes on consumption have, in fact raised the prices of necessaries, beyond the former standard, this rise, cannot, in fact, discourage industry: it may discourage idleness; and idleness will not be totally rooted out, until people be forced, in one way or other, to give up both superfluity and days of recreation. (691)

When the hands employed are not diligent, the best expedient is to raise the price of their subsistence, by taxing it. By this you never will raise their wages, until the market can afford to give a better price for their work. (695)

Since higher taxation will thus have favourable effects upon both *demand* and *supply*,[13] there really are no problems in raising it whenever this is necessary for the financing of social, or industrial, or full employment policies. Steuart's attitude to private incomes has twentieth-century echoes:

> [M]y original plan, . . . was to keep constantly in view those virtuous statesmen who think of nothing but the good of their subjects. Taxes and impositions in their hands, are the wealth of the father of the family; who therewith feeds, clothes, provides for, and defends every one within his house. (703)
>
> If the money raised be more beneficially employed by the state, than it would have been by those who have contributed it, then I say the public has gained, in consequence of the burden laid upon individuals; consequently the statesman has done his duty, both in imposing the taxes, and in rightly expending them. (709)

With economic activity increasingly concentrated in public hands where normal market incentives do not apply. there are clear risks of abuse which Steuart recognised, and he recommended penalties for economic sabotage which have been widely applied in the twentieth century; though not quite his insistence that the appropriate method of execution for the abuse of public money was drawing and quartering (the eighteenth-century penalty for high treason) and not mere hanging (the penalty for highway robbery):

> [I]f there be a crime called high treason, which is punished with greater severity than highway robbery, and assassination, I should be apt (where I a statesman) to put at the head of this bloody list, every attempt to defeat the application of public money, for the purposes here mentioned . . . If severe punishment can . . . put a stop to frauds, I believe it will be thought very well applied. (257)

Steuart was of course far ahead of his time in his eulogies of high taxation, and in the emphasis he placed on the public sector. He recognised this, but because he was confident that his argument was logically correct, he believed a time would surely come when his propositions would also be politically acceptable:

> In treating of taxes, I frequently look no farther than my pen, when I raise my head and look about, I find the politics of my closet very different from those of the century in which I live. I agree that the

difference is striking; but still reason is reason, and there is no impossibility in the supposition of its becoming practice. (1767 i.514)

Steuart's attitude to public debt is equally modern, but here it is Latin America that has gone furthest in the directions he advocated. He reasoned that there is no limit to the heights that domestically held public debt can reach. He first posed the question:

> If the interest paid upon the national debt of England, for example, be found constantly to increase upon every new war, the consequence will be, that more money must be raised on the subject for the payment of it. The question then comes to be. First, How far may debts extend? Secondly, How far may taxes be carried? And Thirdly, What will be the consequence, supposing the one and the other carried to the greatest height possible? (645)

Steuart's answer is that, 'debts may be increased to the full proportion of all that can be raised for the payment of the interest', and the land-tax, for instance:

> may be carried to the full value of all the real estate of England. The notion of actually imposing 20 shillings in the pound upon the real value of all the land-rents of England, appears to us perfectly ridiculous. I admit it to be so; and could I have discovered any argument by which I could have limited the rising of the land-tax to any precise number of shillings under twenty, I should have stated this as the maximum rather than the other. (646)

But the upper limit to government debt is not even the level where the interest upon it equals the revenue of a 100 per cent land-tax plus all the other taxes which can be levied. '[T]he state will then be in possession of all that can be raised on the land, on the consumption, industry and trade of the country; in short, of all that can be called income, which it will administer for the public creditors.' (646) In effect, the property rights of all former property owners will then have been transferred to the state, since their wealth no longer yields a net of tax income, but there will then be a new set of property owners, the holders of public debt, or gilt-edged stock. The government can go on to finance still further borrowing by taxing their income at 100 per cent, and so an, *ad infinitum*:

64   *Sir James Steuart's Corporate State*

> If no check be put to the augmentation of public debts, if they be
> allowed constantly to accumulate, and if the spirit of a nation can
> patiently submit to the natural consequences of such a plan, it must
> end in this, that all property, that is income, will be swallowed up by
> taxes; and these will be transferred to the creditors, the state
> retaining the administration of the revenue.
>
> The state, in that case, will always consider those who enjoy the
> national income as the body of proprietors. This income will
> continue the same, and the real proprietors will pay the taxes
> imposed; which may be mortgaged again to a new set of men, who
> will retain the denomination of creditors; until by swallowing up the
> former, they slip into their places, and become the body of
> proprietors in their turn, and thus perpetuate the circle. (1767
> ii.633–4)

Such reasoning appeared strange to Steuart's contemporaries, but the
analytical device he is using which is extremely familiar today is the
limiting case. He says, 'Do not be put off from raising taxes when this
appears correct in the short term, for there is no theory which says that
a land-tax, for instance, cannot be raised to 100 per cent; and Britain
(levying just four shillings in the pound) is far short of that. Do not be
put off from borrowing for fear of the size of the public debt, because
immeasurably greater debt is conceivable'. Finally, to explain his
praise for a wholly collectivist and egalitarian society which has been
remarked on,[14] do not fear to restrict freedom of choice in consumption by restricting imports and taxing the better off heavily in order to
reduce their luxury consumption, because a society which pushed such
trends immeasurably further would still be agreeable to live in, and
militarily formidable to boot. In each of these examples, Steuart is
careful to point out that they are chimerical. Thus, the scheme of
taxing property owners at 100 per cent in order to finance massive
government borrowing, and then going on to tax the holders of gilt-
edged shares in order to provide the interest to finance still more
borrowing is 'destitute of all probability; because of the infinite variety
of circumstances which may frustrate such a scheme'. (647) As for the
egalitarian collectivist society where none consume imports or luxuries, this has been, 'introduced purposely to serve as an illustration of
general principles, and as a relaxation to the mind, like a farce between
the acts of a serious opera'. (227) Steuart's solid and substantial
argument is the detailed case he consistently develops for the

establishment of what is nowadays called 'a corporate state', where the interests of both capitalists and workers as producers are paramount. His fundamental approach to economy and society is summarised in the passage below:

> Cities and corporations may be considered as nations, where luxury and taxes have rendered living so expensive, that goods cannot be furnished but at a high rate. If labour, therefore, of all kinds, were permitted to be brought from the provinces, or from the country, to supply the demand of the capital and smaller corporations, what would become of tradesmen and manufacturers who have their residence there? If these, on the other hand, were to remove beyond the liberties of such corporations, what would become of the public revenue, collected in these little states, as I call them?
>
> By the establishment of corporations, a statesman is enabled to raise high impositions upon all sorts of consumption; and notwithstanding these have the necessary consequence of increasing the price of labour, yet by other regulations . . . the bad consequences thereby resulting to foreign trade may be avoided, and every article of exportation be prevented from rising above the proper standard for making it vendible, in spite of all foreign competition . . .
>
> Cities having obtained the privilege of incorporation, began, in consequence of the powers vested in their magistrates, to levy taxes: and finding the inconveniences resulting from external competition (foreign trade), they erected the different classes of their industrious into confraternities, or corporations of a lower denomination, with power to prevent the importation of work from their fellow tradesmen not of the society . . . Nobody ever advanced, that the industry carried on in *towns*, where living is dear, ought to suffer a competition with that of the *country*, where living is cheap . . . (286–7)

Steuart himself underlines the importance of this example of a social contract between rulers who tax, and unionised citizens whose livelihood they then protect from competition, when he summarise this chapter:

> I shew how [incorporated cities] may be considered as so many states, which domestic luxury, taxes, and the high price of living,

have put out of a capacity to support a competition with strangers (that is with the open country) which here represents the rest of the world. I show the reasonableness of such exclusive privileges, in favour of those who share the burthens peculiar to the community, in so far only as regards the supply of their own consumption; and I point out, by what methods any discouragements to industry may be prevented, as often as that industry has for its object the supplying the wants of those who are not included in the corporation.

From the long and constant practice of raising *taxes* within incorporated cities, I conclude, that *taxes* are a very natural consequence of luxury, and of the loss of foreign trade; and as Princes have taken the hint from the cities, to extend them universally, it is no wonder to see foreign trade put an end to, in consequence of such injudicious extensions. (1767 i.504–5)

Steuart thus perceived a parallel between a country which is no longer competitive in trade and therefore incapable of providing employment for its 'free hands', and a mature city state, and he proposed that the remedies for the problems of the mature nation were precisely those that successful city states had discovered in their efforts to sustain an adequate standard of living for all within their corporations. The full range of Steuart's policy proposals is explicable in this context,[15] and also the extensive support for very similar policies in the twentieth century by those who see the problems of their countries in similar terms.

It is thus central to the analysis of the Cambridge Economic Policy Group that British industry ceased to be internationally competitive in the 1970s, for reasons which echo several of Steuart's, and the consequent damage to employment to which they attach the same overriding importance can only be averted by import controls and positive job-creating industrial policies which resemble those that Steuart specifically outlined. At the same time, like Steuart, they foresee little damage from higher taxation, heavier government borrowing and a narrower range of availability of 'luxury' consumer goods.[16] Similar analyses have naturally emerged elsewhere.

Smith considered this analysis entirely mistaken in 1776. This paper will conclude with a summary of why he objected so strongly to Steuart's interventionist policies. The reasons for his opposition to Steuart's corporatist approach naturally have much in common with the arguments used today by those who oppose moves towards a corporate state in the Britain of the 1980s.

∕HY ADAM SMITH BELIEVED THAT SIR JAMES TEUART'S POLITICAL OECONOMY WAS MISTAKEN

here are several obvious reasons why Smith believed strongly that ɩeuart's analysis was misconceived. First and most fundamentally, his ɩew of the knowledge, skill and motivation of statesmen was entirely ɩfferent. The contrast between Steuart's omniscient and benevolently ɩtentioned statesmen, and those to be found in *The Wealth of Nations* ɩlow[17] could hardly be greater:

> The stateman, who should attempt to direct private people in what manner they ought to employ their capitals, would not only load himself with a most unnecessary attention, but assume an authority which could safely be trusted, not only to no single person, but to no council or senate whatever, and which would nowhere be so dangerous as in the hands of a man who had folly and presumption enough to fancy himself fit to exercise it. (456)

> What is the species of domestick industry which his capital can employ, and of which the produce is likely to be of the greatest value, every individual, it is evident, can, in his local situation, judge much better than any statesman or lawgiver can do for him. (456)

ᴧs well as lacking the knowledge of entrepreneurs, Smith also ɛlieved that statesmen were by nature extravagant, and prone to ɩaladministration:

> The uniform, constant, and uninterrupted effort of every man to better his condition, the principle from which publick and national, as well as private opulence is originally derived, is frequently powerful enough to maintin the natural progress of things towards improvement, in spite both of the extravagance of government, and of the greatest errors of administration. (343)

`he eighteenth-century readers of Smith and Steuart who actually ɛtermined which would be taken seriously, recognised Smith's ːatesmen, but not Steuart's Utopian supermen (who re-emerged only ɩ the detailed blueprints for 'the economics of control' which followed ɩe Keynesian revolution').[18] There is one point where some of the ːatesmen whom Steuart must actually have encountered surface, ˊhen he writes,

In my inquiries. I have constantly in my eye, how man *may* be governed, and never how *he is* governed. How a righteous and intelligent statesman may restrain the liberty of individuals, in order to promote the common good; never how an ignorant and unrighteous statesman may destroy public liberty, for the sake of individuals. (708)

It is precisely because Smith described how man *is* governed, while Steuart merely sought to show how he *may be* governed that his analysis carried extra conviction to his contemporaries. And today there is an equal difference between those who believe governments have sufficient information to execute complex interventionist policies in order to maximise social welfare functions over immense (and sometimes infinite) time horizons, and those who believe that in practice politicians will often be concerned with little more than the parochial interests of their own party over a period little longer than the memory of an electorate. These 'realists' are as unready as Smith to expect benefits from government control over the minutiae of economic life.

An equally far-reaching objection to Steuart stemmed for Smith's belief that economies were sufficiently self-correcting in the short term to avoid many of the ills that Steuart predicted. In particular, in *The Wealth of Nations* the demand for labour always depends on the capital stock, and this will be used most effectively if it is allowed to earn as much profit as possible for those who own it. The prosperity of workers which Smith and Steuart both desired depended on continual growth in the stock of capital, and Smith analysed the conditions which can be expected to contribute to accumulation with great care. It has been widely pointed out that potential supply in Steuart's economy, 'work' as he calls it, is merely the available labour force.[19] Smith's perception that 'stock' influences the demand for labour is lacking. Even if many of Steuart's full employment policies actually raised demand in the short term, they would undoubtedly reduce the rate of capital accumulation afterwards, and therefore reduce the demand for labour in the medium term. Smith did not refer to the possibility of unused capital even in the short term, but even if the short run is conceded to Steuart, the lack of a concept of 'stock' means that he fails to provide an analysis of the progression of the demand for labour, and of how the growth of government expenditure may inhibit this, and of how private saving will generally increase it. Today there is equal disagreement between those like Steuart who focus on the correction of immediate demand deficiencies at whatever cost, and those like Smith who believe that the trend demand for labour must react favourably if the appropriate conditions for long-term private sector capital accumulation can be established.

Finally, because he believed that private capitalists would always be able to find profitable openings for the physical capital at their disposal, Smith had no need for the paraphernalia of the corporate state:

> The general industry of the society never can exceed what the capital of the society can employ. As the number of workmen that can be kept in employment by any particular person must bear a certain proportion to his capital, so the number of those that can be continually employed by all the members of a great society, must bear a certain proportion to the whole capital of that society, and never can exceed that proportion. No regulation of commerce can increase the quantity of industry in any society beyond what its capital can maintain. It can only divert a part of it into a direction into which it might not otherwise have gone . . . (453)

If foreign competitors provided some goods more cheaply than home producers, Smith's industrialists can be expected to switch their capital to the production of alternative products. An eighteenth-century capital stock consisted largely of food and raw materials which could be used to produce a variety of final products. If one of these became uncompetitive, production could switch to others at a trivial cost in comparison with the twentieth-century penalty for having to switch capital out of textiles, a car, or an aircraft industry, because these are losing out to foreigners. Smith believed that competition would always steer the capital stock into the directions which would maximise returns. Steuart believed that the extent of domestic competition was extremely limited, and that the superior knowledge of the statesman would generally enable him to out-think the market, and that the powers of government to limit competition would in any case ensure that whatever the statesman produced was sold. Smith believed that such departures from the competitive process would misdirect investment, and reduce the aggregate returns a nation derived from its physical capital. Today there are equally those who wish to set up a corporate state behind tariff walls, and others who believe that maximum competition will ensure that the best use is made of a country's productive resources.

70   *Sir James Steuart's Corporate State*

A vital difficulty which economies encounter today that never occurred to Smith is that a country's general price or cost level may be stuck above those of competitors. Smith readily accepted Hume's argument that gold losses by such a country would reduce its domestic costs and prices to a level where domestic markets cleared. Today's market economists are perfectly ready to echo Smith and Hume, but Steuart's rejection of Hume's argument because many domestic costs and prices are fixed independently of the money supply, and because a country can lose gold cumulatively like Ireland and never find equilibrium, also finds eloquent and persuasive support. It is difficult to believe that eighteenth-century economies had sufficient wage and price rigidities to defeat Hume's argument, but in the Britain of 1985 Steuart's belief that a country's wage or price structure can get so far out of line that its industries cannot remain sufficiently competitive to sustain full employment is accepted by many ranging from the Cambridge Economic Policy Group to the Chancellor of the Exchequer.

NOTES

1. The best accounts of Sir James Steuart's life are to be found in Skinner (1966) and Chamley (1965).
2. References and quotations will, wherever possible, be to the Scottish Economic Society's 1966 edition, edited by Andrew Skinner, and page references will be to this edition, unless a passage is only to be found in the original edition in which case a page reference will be preceded by 1767 The publishers of the 1966 edition unfortunately insisted on the omission of approximately one-quarter of Steuart's text.
3. See, in particular, Sen (1957), Stettner (1945), and Vickers (1959) and (1970).
4. See Sen (1957), 'Steuart's historical and evolutionist approach, his views on the economic structure, his conception of labour as a social category his theory of perpetual crisis facing the exchange economy, his analysis of inner contradictions as transforming one economic stage into another, his treatment of Spartan communism and general anti-individualist bias had undoubtedly a profound influence on Marx' (pp. 187–8).
5. There are, for instance, 13 references to Steuart in the first volume of *Capital*, 'Sir James Steuart, a writer altogether remarkable for his quick eye for the characteristic social distinctions between different modes of production' (p. 314); and 'Sir James Steuart is the economist who has handled this subject [population] best. How little his book, which appeared ten years before *The Wealth of Nations*, is known, even at the present time, may be judged from the fact that admires of Malthus do not even know that the first edition of the latter's work on population

contains, except in the purely declamatory part, very little but extracts from Steuart, and in a less degree, from Wallace and Townsend' (p. 333).
6. See, Smith, *Correspondence*, p. 164. Skinner (1981) in his magisterial article written to commemorate the bicentenary of Steuart's death, discounts the evident contempt for Steuart's economics that this letter conveys: 'it will be noted that remarks such as these are not overtly hostile or even hypercritical, and that Smith's reply to Pulteney cannot be fully assessed until the latter's opinion is known' (p. 39).
7. See Skinner (1966), p. lv, and Steuart (1767) vol. 2, p. 646
8. See Eagly (1961) for an account of the importance of incentives and aspirations in Steuart.
9. Hollander (1973) has drawn attention to the presence of agricultural diminishing returns in Steuart.
10. The relationship between Steuart's monetary theory and the quantity theory is discussed in detail in Skinner (1967), and Skinner also explains (1981) the importance for Steuart's interventionist approach to economic policy of his rejection of Hume's self-correcting specie flow propositions.
11. Skinner (1962) provides a valuable account of the relationship of Steuart's politics to his economics.
12. See especially, Vickers (1959) and (1970), Meek (1967), Schumpeter (1954), Hutchison (1978) and Stettner (1945).
13. It is not easy to reconcile Steuart's argument here that higher taxation may have *favourable* effects on the supply produced by, for instance, farmers, with the propositions referred to above (pp. 45–6) that the availability of a greater variety of manufactures in exchange for food will often persuade them to produce more. Brian Loasby drew my attention to this contradiction, which may be a by-product of Steuart's evident desire to set out a strong case for high taxation.
14. Anderson and Tollison (1984) suggest that Steuart seriously desired the establishment of an egalitarian collectivist society of this kind, without referring to the context in which he outlines his account of this society. Their doubts about the uncritical praise for Steuart's interventionism in the secondary literature are similar to those in the present article.
15. Skinner (1966) has suggested that Steuart 'appeared too often in the guise of a "political matron"' (p. lxxxii). This is certainly a plausible interpretation of his attitude to policy, but it is also possible that he was systematically setting out the case for the establishment of 'a corporate state' rather than outlining a series of piecemeal remedies for every difficulty.
16. See the successive issues of the *Cambridge Economic Policy Review* which this group published from 1975 to 1981, after which they apparently lost hope of influencing policy in Britain, for the publication of the Review ceased.
17. Page references are to the Glasgow Edition of *The Wealth of Nations*, edited by R. H. Campbell and A. S. Skinner.
18. Sen (1957) has suggested that, 'It would not be any great exaggeration to say that A. P. Lerner's chapter on functional finance seems almost a paraphrase of Steuart' (p. 122).
19. See, for instance, Meek (1967) and Akhtar (1978 and 1979). In 1979

72   *Sir James Steuart's Corporate State*

Akhtar wrote 'The most serious flaw in his treatment is that it completely neglected the subject of capital accumulation, and the role of capital in the production process' (p. 301). Perelman (1983) has shown that there are valuable accounts of primitive accumulation in Steuart.

REFERENCES

Akhtar, M. A. 'Steuart on Growth', *Scottish Journal of Political Economy*, 25 (1978) pp. 57–74.

Akhtar, M. A. 'An Analytical Outline of Sir James Steuart's Macroeconomic Model', *Oxford Economic Papers*, 31 (1979) pp. 283–302.

Anderson, G. M. and R. B. Tollison 'Sir James Steuart as the Apotheosis of Mercantilism and His Relation to Adam Smith', *Southern Economic Journal*, 51 (1984) pp. 456–68.

Cambridge Economic Policy Group *Cambridge Economic Policy Review* (Farnborough: Gower, 1975–81).

Chamley, P. *Documents Relatifs à Sir James Steuart* (Paris: Dalloz, 1965).

Eagly, R. V. 'Sir James Steuart and the Aspiration Effect', *Economica*, 28 (1961) pp. 53–81.

Hollander, S. *The Economics of Adam Smith* (Toronto: Toronto University Press, 1973).

Hume, D. *Political Discourses* (Edinburgh: 1752).

Hutchison, T. W. *On Revolutions and Progress in Economic Knowledge* (Cambridge: Cambridge University Press, 1978).

Lerner, A. P. *The Economics of Control* (New York: Macmillan, 1944).

Malthus, T. R. *An Essay on the Principle of Population as it Affects the Future Improvement of Society* (London: 1798).

Marx, K. (1867) *Capital* (Moscow: Progress Publishers for Lawrence & Wishart, 1974, reprint).

Meek, R. L. *Economics and Ideology and Other Essays* (London: Chapman and Hall, 1967).

Perelman, M. 'Classical Political Economy and Primitive Accumulation: The Case of Smith and Steuart', *History of Political Economy*, 15 (1983) pp. 451–94.

Ricardo, D. *On the Principles of Political Economy and Taxation* (London: 1817).

Schumpeter, J. A. *History of Economic Analysis* (New York: Oxford University Press, 1954).

Sen, S. R. *The Economics of Sir James Steuart* (London: Bell, 1957).

Skinner, A. S 'Sir James Steuart: Economics and Politics', *Scottish Journal of Political Economy*, 9 (1962) pp. 275–90.

Skinner, A. S. 'Biographical Sketch', and 'Analytical Introduction', in the Scottish Economic Society's edition of Sir James Steuart, *Principles of Political Oeconomy* (Edinburgh: Oliver & Boyd, 1966).

Skinner, A. S. 'Money and Prices: A Critique of the Quantity Theory', *Scottish Journal of Political Economy*, 14 (1967) pp. 275–90.

Skinner, A. S. 'Sir James Steuart: Author of a System', *Scottish Journal of Political Economy*, 28 (1981) pp. 20–42.

Smith, A. (1776) *An Inquiry into the Nature and Causes of the Wealth of Nations*. Republished as R. H. Campbell and A. S. Skinner (eds) *The Glasgow Edition of the Works and Correspondence of Adam Smith*, II (Oxford: Oxford University Press, 1976).

Smith, A. *The Correspondence of Adam Smith*, E. C. Mossner and I. S. Ross (eds) *The Glasgow Edition of the Works and Correspondence of Adam Smith*, VI (Oxford: Oxford University Press, 1977).

Stettner, W. F. 'Sir James Steuart on the Public Debt', *Quarterly Journal of Economics*, 59 (1945) pp. 451–76.

Steuart, Sir James (1759) *A Dissertation on the Policy of Grain, with a view to a Plan for preventing scarcity or exorbitant prices in the Common Markets of England* in Sir James Steuart (ed.) *Works, Political, Metaphysical and Chronological* (1805).

Steuart, Sir James *An Inquiry into the Principles of Political Oeconomy: being an Essay on the Science of Domestic Policy in Free Nations*, 2 vols (London: 1767). Reprinted (abbreviated) for the Scottish Economic Society in 2 vols, A. Skinner (ed.) (Edinburgh: Oliver & Boyd, 1966).

Steuart, Sir James (ed.) *Works, Political, Metaphysical and Chronological*, 6 vols (London: 1805).

Vickers, D. *Studies in the Theory of Money 1690–1776* (Philadelphia: Chilton, 1959).

Vickers, D. 'The Works, Political, Philosophical and Metaphysical of Sir James Steuart: A Review Article', *Journal of Economic Literature*, 7 (1970) pp. 1190–5.

PART III

PRACTICAL MACROECONOMICS: HOW GROWING PUBLIC EXPENDITURE DESTABILIZES

1 Where Britain Went Wrong

Those who seek to manage economies or advise on their management are either tinkerers or structuralists. Tinkerers believe that a country's economic ills can be cured by adjusting demand, the exchange rate or the money supply, and by persuading workers to accept periods of wage restraint. Structuralists are concerned with the underlying structure of economies, and believe that tinkering about will not suffice where this is out of line. Treasury civil servants are generally tinkerers, and they usually seek to put things right by adjusting what they actually control. Many politicians are also tinkerers, and indeed in many economies minor adjustments to this and that are all that is needed to produce highly satisfactory results. In these economies — West Germany, Japan and recently France are examples — the underlying structure has been such in the past fifteen years that government control of effective demand, the money supply and the exchange rate were really all that was needed to produce an economic environment where businessmen and workers could co-operate to increase wealth and real incomes at very rapid rates.

There are other economies with an inappropriate under-lying structure where tinkering is not enough, and it is becoming increasingly recognised that Britain — like many underdeveloped countries — has an economy with serious structural problems. This is now recognised by a growing number of economists, and politicians ranging from Mr Tony Benn on the left of British politics to Sir Keith Joseph on the right. Mr Benn has drawn attention to the problems raised by Britain's declining industrial base, while Sir Keith Joseph has been concerned about the continuing fall in the proportion of the economy that is allowed to respond to

1

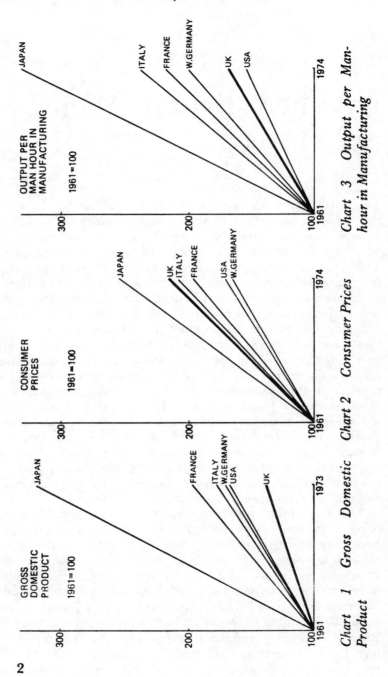

Chart 1   Gross   Domestic   Chart 2   Consumer Prices   Chart 3   Output per Man-
Product   *hour in Manufacturing*

2

market forces, and to produce outputs that consumers are actually prepared to pay for. The account of the deterioration in the structure of the British economy which will be given in this book will support those who believe that Britain's industrial base should be strengthened and also those who think that Britain's problems would be easier to solve if a higher fraction of output was marketable. The tinkerers, in contrast, can provide no viable solution. All their remedies, tax reductions, tax increases, devaluations, incomes policies of various kinds, have been tried again and again, and they have failed to arrest the underlying deterioration of the economy that has occurred.

That there has been serious deterioration is only too obvious. Crisis has followed crisis; government packages have become increasingly drastic, and each failure has reduced the reputation of Britain's leading politicians with the people. Charts 1—5 show the well-known evidence that Britain's growth rate has been one of the slowest of any major Western economy since 1961, that Britain's share of investment has been one of the two lowest, that Britain's share of world trade has been falling while others have had rising shares, and that Britain's rate of inflation has been one of the fastest in the Western world.* Some of these trends have a very long history. Britain's share of exports in world markets has been falling fairly continuously since about 1870, and Britain's growth rate has also been low compared to those of the United States and Germany for about a century. That the British economy has performed comparatively poorly for a very long time is well known.

What is less well known is that Britain's economic performance, as measured by the usual statistical yardsticks, has become incredibly worse in the last decade than it was (even by British standards). Industrial production increased 35 per cent in the decade 1955—65, and it increased less than half as much, 17 per cent in 1965—75. This is partly, but only partly, the result of the world recession.[1] As all

* The statistical sources on which the various charts in this book are based, and their derivation, are set out in detail at the end of the book in the order in which the charts appear in the text. The derivation of Charts 1—5 is explained on pp. 160—2.

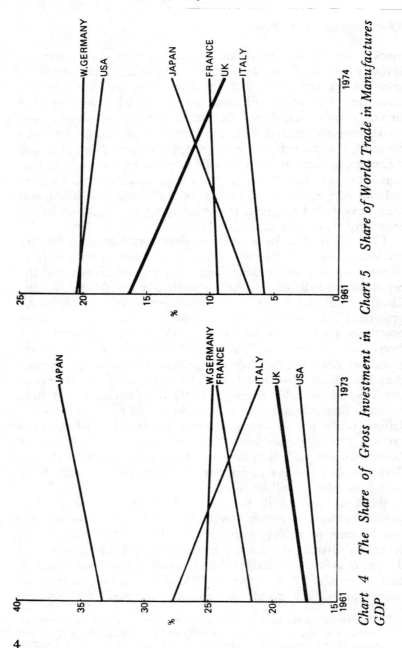

Chart 4   The Share of Gross Investment in   Chart 5   Share of World Trade in Manufactures
GDP

manufactured exports, all building of houses and factories, indeed investment of all kinds in the public and private sectors, and all consumption of consumer durables like cars, not to mention clothing and even nowadays quite a lot of packaged food, must come from industry (or foreign industry), the slower growth of industrial production says much about the underlying causes of Britain's problems. Apart from growth, the economic targets are usually considered to be price stability, full employment and balance of payments equilibrium. There was substantial deterioration in each case in 1965—75. Britain's inflation rate averaged 3.1 per cent in 1955—65, and it doubled to over 7 per cent in 1965—74, and it has accelerated fairly steadily in that dreadful decade to 26 per cent in 1974—75. Unemployment was much higher in the second decade than the first. It averaged 1.9 per cent in 1955—65 and 2.7 per cent in 1965—75, and in 1975 it reached 5 per cent. In 1955—65 the pound kept its international value and its exchange rate actually rose as an average of those of France, Italy, West Germany, the USA and Japan. In 1965—75 the pound fell 38 per cent compared to these other currencies. That industrial disputes became increasingly virulent with 2.1 times as many days lost through strikes in 1965—74 as in 1955—65 scarcely needs to be said. Some of this accelerated deterioration in 1965—75 can be put down to the quadrupling in the price of oil at the end of the decade. However, the whole Western World suffered from this and Britain's difficulties have been far more acute, so something other than oil has contributed to Britain's crisis. Indeed no other major economy suffered an equal failure to achieve every economic objective. In 1965 at the beginning of the decade that was to prove so disastrous for Britain, the examination question 'Can economies have simultaneously, zero growth, rapid inflation, substantial unemployment and a balance of payments deficit?' was set in Oxford. Undergraduates answered that this combination of failures was only possible in an underdeveloped country. It has now been achieved in Britain.

It must be emphasised that this has happened, in spite of the fact that every gimmick suggested by the tinkerers has been adopted by successive governments. The great nostrum

6   *Britain's Economic Problem*

of the 1960s was devaluation, and successive British governments allowed the exchange rate of sterling to fall more often and more sharply in 1965—75 than ever before. Incomes policies, a second important and improved method of tinkering, were repeatedly used in tougher and tougher forms, and after each attempt the rate of inflation became faster than before. The tax tinkerers persuaded British governments to introduce five radically new taxes, and virtually every new tax that any economist of repute advocated in 1965—75 was actually introduced (if only to be withdrawn and replaced by another). Finally, the tools of demand management were used repeatedly, and in both directions. It must be universally agreed that the tinkerers had an innings in which they enjoyed overwhelming support from successive governments, and that results have never been more disappointing. The case for looking for a structural explanation of the deterioration of the British economy is therefore overwhelming.

The underlying factors that are most commonly blamed for the deplorable situation that has been outlined are either militancy and obstruction to progress by the trade unions, or inadequate industrial productivity. It is a little implausible that trade unions have the power and desire to destroy the British economy when they do nothing of the kind in the successful capitalist economies where communism is actually strong. Those who believe that the trade unions are responsible for Britain's troubles must therefore argue that they are able and willing to disrupt an economy in a society which has, by objective tests, less support for extremists than most others.

What has in fact happened, and this is shown in Chart 6, is that deductions from paypackets grew so much from 1963 to 1974 that the average living standard in terms of what can actually be bought in shops rose only 1.6 per cent per annum — and since 1973 it has actually fallen. The same has been broadly true for workers and salary-earners on average earnings, one-and-one-third times average earnings, and two-thirds of average earnings. Compared to 1963, between 10 per cent and 12 per cent more of the paypackets of all three groups is now deducted for income tax and social security

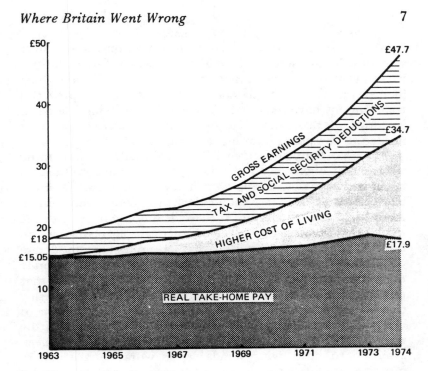

Chart 6   Gross and Net Earnings for the Average Male Worker

contributions to pay for the higher 'social wage'. Without this increase in 'deductions' what the average workers' wages could buy would have risen 39 per cent in eleven years instead of the 19 per cent they actually rose.[2] Workers and salary earners with just average earnings now suffer deductions of nearly 30 per cent from their paypackets, which is more than bank managers and university professors had to pay in tax and National Insurance contributions in 1963.

It is often argued that workers and salary earners do not notice higher taxation in their wage negotiations, and that they welcome the higher 'social wage' that greater public spending represents. The 'social wage' does not, however, enter into the money wage bargains that trade unions negotiate, and the period 1963 to 1974 when deductions from paypackets increased so sharply was one when there was growing pressure for higher money wages. Some workers have been better organised than others to achieve high increases in money earnings, and these workers with powerful trade unions have managed to increase their living standards in terms of take-home pay by much of the extra amount needed to compensate for higher taxation.

What has happened since 1963 is that all too often those who sought higher living standards, or the mere continuation of car and home ownership (which have risen in cost far more than prices in general) found that they could only obtain these by making full use of their trade union power, with the result that ordinary workers turned to aggressive union leaders to produce results. That a politically moderate population has chosen to be represented by immoderate trade unions is plausibly explained once it is appreciated that this was in many cases a response to a situation where a rising cost of living and rising taxation made the preservation of living standards increasingly difficult. With a halving of the rate of growth of industrial production, less has been available to raise living standards; so workers have had to progress at the expense of other groups rather than by accepting a roughly constant share of a rapidly growing national product. It is consequently possible to argue that the failure to achieve reasonable growth in living standards in recent years has led to the militant and obstructive trade union activity from which Britain has suffered. Hence this has been a consequence of Britain's great economic failures. It has not caused them, and things started to go wrong long before unions became militant. The underlying cause of Britain's troubles must therefore lie elsewhere.

Britain's lamentable productivity record is often seen as the root of the trouble. Certainly Britain's industrial productivity is low by international standards, and it is still falling in relation to productivity elsewhere. However, the evidence that has been outlined shows that Britain's general economic performance deteriorated sharply when the period 1965—75 is compared with the previous decade. What is not often appreciated is that in contrast industrial productivity increased very much more quickly in the second decade.

Output per man hour in manufacturing industry increased at an annual rate of only 3.0 per cent from 1955—65, but it increased 4.0 per annum from 1965 to 1974. Thus, if productivity is what matters most as many suppose, things should have gone very much better after 1965 than in the previous decade. Efficiency increased more quickly, which should have meant that all Britain's problems were easier to solve. Certainly Britain's growth rate of industrial productivity was still low by international standards after 1965, but it was not all that low. West Germany, France and Italy achieved growth at an average rate of 6.0 per cent against Britain's 4.0 per cent, but Britain's growth rate was still exceedingly high by historical standards, and it could have led to the 'economic miracle' that so many have expected for so long. That productivity rose faster is compatible with the view that many of the industrial policies of successive governments were beginning to produce results. There may have been contributions here from the tougher approach to restrictive practices from the end of the 1950s onwards, which meant that there were fewer price agreements which sheltered the inefficient. There may also have been contributions from the 'little Neddies' set up in the early 1960s which examined the particular productivity problems of a wide range of industries. There was also a great takeover movement in the early 1960s which was often assisted by the government and led to the absorption of a number of small and sometimes inefficient firms by larger and more favoured ones. There were also great increases in the numbers receiving education in virtually all the relevant age groups. Finally, successive governments gave substantial tax assistance to investment, and this must have led to the replacement of much obsolete plant. Our machine tool survey showed that by 1971 the service life and average age of British machine tools were almost exactly the same as in the USA over a very wide range of machine tool categories and user industries.[3] These helpful developments which almost certainly resulted from sensible and beneficial government industrial policies could have set the foundation for an acceleration in Britain's growth rate. This would then have provided the extra resources to satisfy the aspirations of workers for higher

10   *Britain's Economic Problem*

material living standards, and at the same time increased the capital stock in both the public and the private sectors, provided a sufficient supply of goods for overseas markets to pay for the country's import requirements, and produced in due course the kind of growth in welfare services that successful economies have achieved. In practice, the great improvement in the rate of growth of industrial productivity for which so many worked intensively in government and industry did none of these things. In the event, and only partly because of the world recession, industrial production increased less than half as fast as productivity, with the result that more than half the benefits from extra productivity resulted, not in the production of more goods but in the employment of fewer men for shorter hours. Higher productivity meant sackings, and a decline in the availability of overtime. This was not true over all industries, but it was true in the great majority.

A 40 per cent increase in productivity in ten years could have allowed the same number of men to produce 40 per cent more in the same number of hours. In the event more than half the potential increase in output was lost because the number of men employed in industry fell 14 per cent and hours of work also fell substantially. It is from this basic fact that the disastrous course the British economy followed in 1965–75 stems, and this was one result of the real structural maladjustment of the British economy that has occurred in these ten years and is still occurring. If Britain manages to cut overmanning in industry, which many regard as the economy's greatest weakness, productivity will advance still more rapidly than in the recent past, and the reduction in overmanning will produce still faster falls in industrial employment and in hours of work.* It must then be

---

* It is essential to distinguish *overmanning*, the use of too many men to produce a *given level of output* in a particular factory from *underproduction*. With the latter, a given number of men working in a particular factory produce *less output* than they could. The correction of *overmanning* leads to redundancies and the need to absorb surplus workers elsewhere. The correction of *underproduction* increases output and raises the rate of return on capital without any redundancies. It is therefore exactly what the British economy (or indeed any economy) always needs and unlike a reduction of overmanning, it would create no further problems.

Where Britain Went Wrong   11

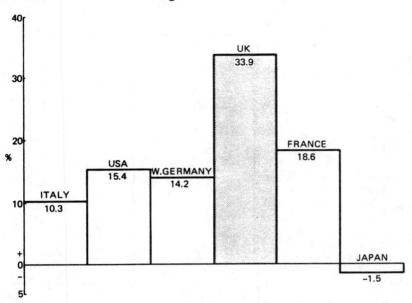

*Chart 7   Ratio of Non-industrial to Industrial Employment:
Percentage Change, 1961—74*

emphasised that it is not the rate of growth of productivity
that has let Britain down. What has let Britain down is that
this has been allowed to produce growing numbers of
redundancies instead of the increase in employment, and
growth in the availability of real resources that should have
resulted. It is this basic fact, and the reasons for it, which
needs to be explained, and one of the purposes of this book
is to show just what went wrong and why.

It is beginning to be appreciated that a very great
structural shift in employment has occurred in the British
economy since about 1961, and this can be looked at in
several ways. Perhaps the most significant is that employment
outside industry increased by over one-third relative to
employment in industry from 1961 to 1974 and that this
increase was most rapid into the public sector. The facts,
which are of crucial importance, are set out in Charts 7 and
8. These also show that the shift in employment from
industry to services, and public services in particular, had no

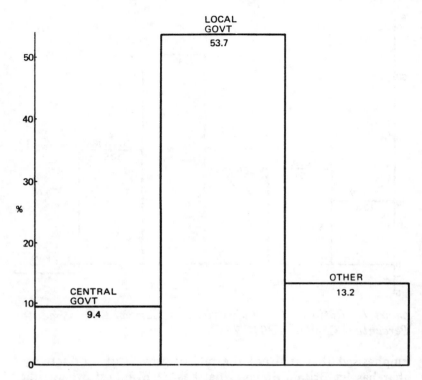

Chart 8   Percentage Change in Employment by Category in Great Britain, 1961—74

parallel in any other large Western developed economy. Virtually all modern economies gradually shift workers out of industry and into services as industrial efficiency rises, and aspirations grow for better education and welfare services, as well as for the many services provided in the private sector. They do not, however, have 34 per cent shifts in just thirteen years, and cannot without great strain.

In Britain's case the actual strain may not have been quite as great as the crude figures indicate. The employment of women (including many who work only part-time) increased 55 per cent faster in services than in industry, while the employment of men increased only 23 per cent faster. Hence, in so far as men are more important to industry (and women

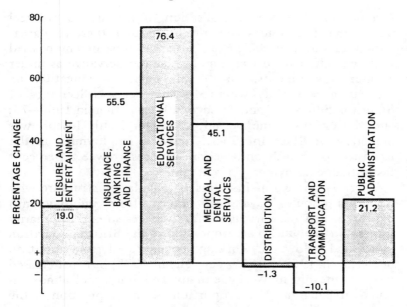

Chart 9 Percentage Increase in Service Sector Employment by Category in Great Britain, 1961—74

have become a vital part of the labour force in many firms) the strain caused by the structural shift in the labour force was less than the 34 per cent figure would indicate. But even a 23 per cent shift is greater than any other major economy's.

The details of the shift which occurred in Britain are set out in Charts 8 and 9 which show where the extra workers in British service occupations went. It will be seen that employment by local authorities rose 54 per cent, and that central government employment rose 9 per cent. By contrast, in the remaining services like retail distribution, banking, finance, insurance, entertainment, and so on, employment expanded only 13 per cent on average, so the shift from industry has been most rapid into public-employment. The Oxfordshire County Council now employs more workers in Oxfordshire than British Leyland. Within the public sector, employment in education at all levels has risen, and employment in the provision of health and welfare services has risen. All would agree that these are vital to any civilised

14   *Britain's Economic Problem*

community, and it is a realisation of this by all political parties that has done so much to bring about these very great structural shifts in the labour force. It must be emphasised that the shift has been as rapid under Conservative as under Labour governments, and employment in education increased more rapidly when Mrs Thatcher was Secretary of State for Education and Science (1970–4) than in 1964–70; and during the same period, when Sir Keith Joseph was Secretary of State for Social Services, employment in the provision of health and welfare services grew 8.2 per cent faster than employment in general.

There is no reason in terms of population structure why resources should have been moved from industry into education and the various welfare services so extraordinarily quickly in Britain.[4] The proportion of the British population above and below the working age increased from about 35 per cent in 1962 to 37½ per cent in 1973, but it increased more than this in West Germany and Italy, and almost as much in Belgium. The proportion of the population in the age groups that need education was very similar in Britain and the major EEC economies in both 1962 and 1973, but only West Germany increased its number of teachers as rapidly as Britain. The proportion at schools or universities rose from 17 per cent to 20 per cent in Britain between 1964 and 1973, but it rose from 13 per cent to 17 per cent in West Germany in the same period, and from 15 per cent to 18 per cent in Italy. Staff to pupil ratios in primary and secondary education improved 10 per cent in Britain from 1961 to 1971, but they also improved in Italy, West Germany and Japan. This suggests that increases in employment in education need not have differed markedly from those in other countries. Turning to the health services, doctors per head of population rose 20 per cent in Britain from 1961 to 1971, but they rose 27 per cent in West Germany and 29 per cent in France; and only Italy, with a 9 per cent increase, improved this aspect of health services more slowly than Britain. The availability of hospital beds per head of the population actually fell 11 per cent in Britain from 1961 to 1971, and it increased 10 per cent in West Germany and 15 per cent in Italy, falling slightly in France. These figures only describe a small part of the vast range of social indicators, but what they suggest is interesting. There was not apparently a greater improvement in the proportion of the population that was receiving education, or in the availability of doctors or hospital beds than other economies were providing. There may therefore have been a much larger shift of labour into the public sector service occupations taken as a whole to achieve rather similar results. Britain may then have achieved a far slower increase in the real 'outputs' of public services than in the expenditures needed to produce those outputs. This might help to explain why workers apparently failed to take the increase in the 'social wage' much into account in their wage bargaining. Perhaps the social wage did not rise very significantly, measured as an increase in the *output* of social services. It rose enormously, of course, as an increase in *expenditure* on social services, which is how the great spending departments like to measure it.

The increase in employment to provide more public services continued through boom and recession, and until 1975, each increase was permanent; so the workers taken on in recession were not available to industry in subsequent booms. There was, therefore, a kind of ratchet effect, with employment in health and education rising and never falling. One reason why public sector employment could be expanded particularly rapidly was that extra jobs could be provided without an immediate need for extra capital investment. More workers can be fitted into existing offices (though new and expensive town halls and expanded office space follow an increase in civil service numbers after a few years). In industry in contrast a lot of extra workers will be taken on only if there is additional machinery with which they can work, as the high costs of present-day labour can normally be covered (and industry must cover the costs of taking on extra men through extra sales) only if workers have a considerable amount of machinery with which they can operate. The extra workers were therefore drawn into the public sector because all wanted improved social services, and because to increase public sector employment appeared a cheap and socially desirable way of achieving full employment in times of recession. The Departments of Health,

Education and the Environment therefore found it easier to persuade the Treasury to approve their expansion plans at such times. The workers, often unskilled ancillary workers who were taken on by the public sector in this way, were inexpensive to employ when decisions were first taken to authorise higher public-sector employment. However, subsequent wage settlements were particularly high in the public sector; Houghton gave very large increases to teachers, administrative grade civil servants have had increases of almost 100 per cent in three years while at the other end of the scale some of the worst paid National Health Service workers have had increases of up to 70 per cent in just one year. There have been other increases which have turned what was originally cheap labour into a major element in the costs of local authorities and the central government, and this has had much to do with subsequent explosive rate and tax increases.

Much research is needed to discover whether the great increase in public-sector service employment that occurred in Britain in 1961–74 produced substantial improvements in public services of a kind that other economies which increased public-sector employment less quickly failed to achieve, or whether the improvements to services were peripheral in comparison to the extra costs involved. Whether the social benefits were minor or substantial, the shift had very great consequences for the rest of the economy, and a strong case can be made out that this very great structural change played a significant role in the deterioration in Britain's economic performance that has been recorded.

The deterioration occurred in the following way. Industrial production must supply the entire investment needs of the nation, and a very high fraction of its consumption; for durable consumer goods like cars, television sets and so on, clothing, and even quite a high proportion of what workers nowadays spend on food, have to be provided by British or foreign industry. In addition to this, a country like Britain that needs to import a high fraction of its food and raw material requirements must export more industrial products than it imports. The various private-sector service industries make a valuable contribution to the balance of payments, but

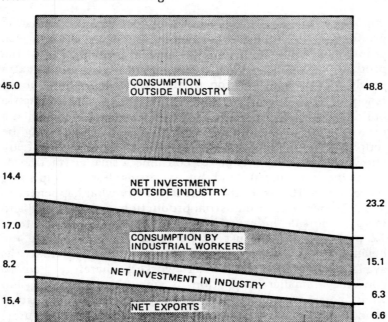

Chart 10   Where Industrial Production Went

this has never been sufficient, and it is never likely to be to finance the food and raw materials that Britain must buy from overseas, so a large export surplus of industrial production is always likely to be needed.

Now if non-industrial employment grows by one-third in relation to industrial employment, as happened in Britain after 1961, there will be added pressures on industrial production. With more workers employed outside industry, more industrial production will be required for the consumption of those who have played no direct part in producing it. Similarly, more investment outside industry will be needed, and the capital goods will all have to be taken from the output of the industrial sector itself. It must follow that less industrial production will be available for investment and consumption by those who actually produce it or that all the extra goods the non-industrialists require will have to be imported. All these needs can, of course, be met if industrial production can be increased rapidly, but it has already been pointed out that in Britain the rate of growth of industrial production was exceedingly slow. Hence most of the extra goods for the consumption of the vastly larger numbers of teachers, social workers and civil servants, and the extra buildings to house them (which were particularly needed as a result of local government reorganisation), could only be supplied by building fewer factories in industry itself, by allowing industrial workers to consume a smaller fraction of what they produced, and by exporting less or importing more. Chart 10 shows that this is exactly what happened. In 1961 59 per cent of industrial production was consumed and invested outside industry itself. By 1974 non-industry took 72 per cent, leaving just 28 per cent for industry and the balance of payments in place of the 41 per cent that was available in 1961. Industrial workers therefore had to consume a smaller proportion of what they produced, and what matters crucially is that the proportion of industrial production that was exported (less imports of manufactures) fell from 15½ per cent to 6½ per cent; and the proportion that was invested in industry itself, net of capital consumption, fell by one-quarter from 8 per cent to 6 per cent of sales of industrial production. The great increase in non-industrial employment and the accompanying increase in non-industrial investment therefore took resources away from the balance of payments and industrial investment, and this is precisely what Britain could not afford to cut if the country was ever to escape from the trap of an industrial sector too small to provide all that was required of it. It is also obvious that the reduction in the fraction of industrial output that industrial workers were themselves allowed to consume was only achieved at a cost of the increase in industrial conflict that has been remarked upon as group after group of workers attempted to ensure that it was not they who suffered reductions in living standards to pay for the increased employment in the public services. Chart 6 showed how tax increases greatly slowed down the growth of real living standards of all but those who got sufficient increases in money wages to compensate for higher taxation.

But the wage increases that the more militant obtained squeezed profits and industrial workers paid only 2 per cent of the 13 per cent extra that had to go outside industry. Hence most of the non-industrial sector's extra consumption and investment has grown at the expense of net exports and of investment in industry itself, which the government has squeezed by making deflationary periods predominate to an increasing extent in the stop-go cycle.

The squeeze on industrial investment is perhaps the most serious effect of all, because it influences the whole future development of the economy. Net industrial investment fell, as a fraction of final sales of industrial production, to 3 per cent in 1972, 3½ per cent in 1973 and 6.3 per cent in 1974 (about half the increase from 1973 to 1974 was investment for North Sea oil) from levels of 8 per cent to 9 per cent in the mid-1960s. This has had two devastating consequences for the economy. First, a halving of the share of investment has greatly reduced the rate of growth of industrial capacity. Thus, while Britain was investing enough to raise industrial production 3 per cent per annum or 35 per cent in a decade until the mid-1960s the rate of growth of industrial capacity is probably only about two-thirds of this today.[5] This means that when demand is expanded as the economy recovers from depressions as in 1972–3, the plant is just not there to meet the country's requirements for goods. Hence articles which are normally produced in Britain have to be imported and the goods are just not available to exploit export opportunities. With a lower share of net investment this has become true over an increasing range of industrial products. In consequence attempts by governments to move towards full employment produce vast balance of payments deficits, which make continued expansion impossible. A share of net investment of only 3 per cent to 6 per cent in industry will gradually reduce the rate of growth, with the result that the Treasury's expansion plans which used to be based on growth rates of 2.5 per cent to 3.5 per cent will need to be revised downwards extremely drastically.[6] In addition, the deep problem that declining industrial investment is producing is unemployment which is becoming increasingly structural — the unemployment due to insufficient factories from which underdeveloped countries suffer — and this will undermine the whole fabric of society if the trend is allowed to continue. It has been pointed out that output per man-hour has been rising about 4 per cent per annum in manufacturing industry since 1965. If this continues — and it is likely to — and there is only sufficient capacity to raise industrial production 2 per cent per annum, the number of men that firms employ must fall 2 per cent every year or hours of work must fall 2 per cent each year. In practice these have both been falling sharply in recent years.

The fall in industrial employment in relation to non-industrial employment is what has caused Britain's difficulties, and this trend will continue, making the situation worse each year unless investment recovers to its pre-1965 levels. Indeed, it will need to rise above them if industrial employment is to be maintained. This is because productivity now rises more quickly than it did. Economic progress is a complicated process in which technology advances, new factories are built, and more is produced. Now the faster technology advances, the greater the number of new factories that need to be built. Advances in technology mean that the same goods can be produced by fewer men or that better goods can be produced which make others out-of-date. These advances cause a great many redundancies. The factories which adopt more efficient processes need fewer men to produce old levels of output while the better products (which will come in from abroad if Britain does not manufacture them) cause whole factories to be closed down as their products become obsolete or obsolescent. In a successful economy all the workers who are made redundant by productivity growth and technical advance get jobs producing the new and better goods or jobs that result from expanded production of old goods, but the creation of all these new jobs requires capital investment; and net investment in industry has fallen by one-quarter in Britain since 1965. *Hence, Britain has suffered from technical progress instead of gaining from it.* The faster technical progress has produced redundancies on a growing scale but new investment has not absorbed the redundant workers. Hence, Britain has not expanded production as fast as this could have been

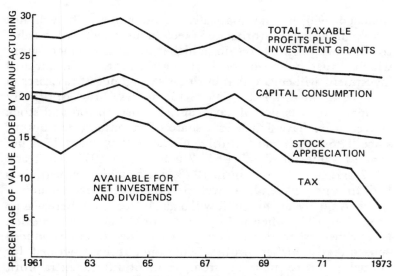

Chart 11   Profits of Manufacturing Companies

done, and increasing numbers of workers are finding that there is just not enough work. Given this, it is hardly surprising that trade unions obstruct technical progress in so many cases. What is tragic is that all the good work that is being done to raise efficiency in factories and workshops, by the little Neddies and by the Restrictive Practices Court, work which has raised Britain's rate of productivity growth to two-thirds of the West European rate, has reduced job opportunities instead of increasing the rate of growth of output.

How this has come about is obviously one of the most important elements in the collapse of Britain's economic performance. It is something that ought not to happen according to the theories either of Britain's Cambridge economists or of orthodox United States economists; yet it has happened. Cambridge economists, if they accept Lord Kaldor's theory of income distribution, believe that if industrialists raise investment, they will, at the same time, raise the share of profits in the National Income so that the profits from which this higher level of investment can be financed will be automatically forthcoming.[7] It will not matter how much profits are taxed. Industrialists will be able to pass any profits taxes on in higher prices and a mechanism which must raise national saving in line with national investment will ensure that business saving, net of tax, rises in line with investment. Chart 11 shows how drastically company profits net of tax, capital consumption and stock appreciation have fallen as a share of manufacturing output since 1964. In manufacturing industry they were 17.5 per cent of value-added in 1964, 7 per cent in 1970, 1971 and 1972 and only 3 per cent in 1973, out of which industrialists had to find dividends as well as finance for capital investment. A glance at this chart will make it clear that there was no year after 1969 when industrialists could have set in motion a sequence where substantially higher investment produced subsequently higher profits. They might have wished for enough profit to finance more investment but this extra profit could not be obtained for two reasons. First, governments (and here Mr Heath's government is particularly to blame) have not allowed companies to obtain the kind of profit margins that were needed to finance more investment. Since 1972 prices and incomes policies have forced companies to cut profit margins when they wished to increase them. Second, foreign competition sets an upper limit to profit margins in an economy where imports compete with home production over almost the entire range of output. Devaluations give domestic firms a temporary competitive edge but if devaluations are followed, as they have been, by increased wage inflation this competitive edge is soon lost; so that companies cannot maintain the higher profit margins that devaluation first makes possible. This means in practice that profit margins in Britain have been determined much more by government prices and incomes policies, trade unions and foreign competition than by the saving-investment mechanism that is crucial to the Cambridge theory. Hence, businessmen have not been able to pass higher company taxation on to the consumer through wider profit margins — the opposite has happened. This has meant that companies have just not been able to afford to invest the amount that the country has needed. In addition, the high taxes which have followed higher public spending have made trade unions more militant so that they have not been prepared to see a higher share of the National Income going to profits. Their activity forced the prices and incomes policies like Mr Heath's that so damaged profits, and they prevented companies from benefiting substantially from potentially profitable developments like devaluations and bursts of technical progress.

Orthodox United States economists would not expect companies to be able to get whatever profits they needed to finance investment, but they would expect that any level of investment would be sufficient to provide equipment for all the men who wanted work. With their approach a large reduction of investment should cause capital to be spread more thinly so that new factories were built according to designs which provided more jobs at lower cost. Any number of men could always be fitted into industry if factory designs were wholly flexible and there was equal flexibility with old plant.[8] The difficulty with this approach is that new factories which use much labour and little capital will only be built if labour is cheap and capital is very expensive. In theory structural unemployment should make labour cheap, but this has just not happened in Britain. Employment taxes have risen very steeply; the unions have succeeded in doing still more to raise the cost of labour, so companies have had no inducements at all to build new factories which use more workers than the factories they replace.[9] In consequence the 'impossible' has happened and a major developed economy is suffering from growing structural unemployment that is the result of too little modern industrial plant to provide work for more than a sharply falling fraction of the labour force. Only more industrial investment can arrest this process but the very process itself squeezes industrial profits and investment so that the economy moves into even deeper trouble.

As the unemployment figures rise, extra jobs can only be provided outside industry and only the government can provide jobs where there is no prospect of profits. Hence, governments are tempted to create still more jobs in the public services, and as they raise taxation to pay for them, in due course company profits and workers' living standards are further squeezed with the result that there is still more pressure against company profits in industry. In consequence industry invests still less, more industrial workers become redundant and still more workers need to be fitted into the public sector. This ever-accelerating spiral leads nowhere except to total economic collapse and it is so deep-rooted in structural maladjustment that it is in no way amenable to tinkering.

There is therefore a basic explanation of a structural kind of the underlying deterioration in Britain's economic performance and the succession of crises that have become increasingly severe until they threaten to undermine the repute of orthodox political parties and all that can follow from this. The explanation is that successive governments have allowed large numbers of workers to move out of industry and into various service occupations, where they still consume and invest industrial products and produce none themselves; their needs have, therefore, been met at the expense of the balance of payments, the export surplus of manufactures, and investment in industry itself, so the deterioration in the balance of payments and in Britain's rate of growth can be explained. Once the effect of taking away an increasing proportion of what workers produce is recognised, the great acceleration of wage inflation also becomes readily explicable, and the need for tougher and tougher incomes policies (which other major developed economies have not needed) to attempt to contain inflation. In monetarist terms, the unemployment rate that is compatible with stable prices (produced by a money supply that grows at the same rate as production) has risen drastically — in other words, there has been a great increase in what Professor Milton Friedman calls the *natural* rate of unemployment.[10] An economy that will not accept this exceedingly high *natural* rate of unemployment will have extraordinary inflation or draconian incomes policies instead, like Britain. Hence the whole range of economic options deteriorates sharply and societies in this terrible position must choose between very high unemployment or extra-rapid inflation, which is now undoubtedly the case in Britain, as it is in much of Latin America.

However, this explanation for Britain's decline needs to be refined. In 1776 Adam Smith said:

> The labour of some of the most respectable orders in the society is . . . unproductive of any value, and does not fix or realise itself in any permanent subject, or vendible commodity. . . . The sovereign, for example, with all the officers both of justice and war who serve under him, the whole army and navy, are unproductive labourers. They are the servants of the public and are maintained by a part of the annual produce of the industry of other people. Their service, how honourable, how useful, or how necessary soever, produces nothing for which an equal quantity of service can afterwards be procured.

He was right thus far, but he included in the same class 'men of letters of all kinds . . . opera singers, opera dancers, etc . . .'[11] and it is a mistake to assume that only physical goods represent tradable wealth. It is not only industry that exports. A British opera singer who stars at the New York Metropolitan Opera and brings home dollars is an exporter. So, more substantially, are the bankers, insurers, shippers and other specialists for whom Britain is famous. Unlike most industrial production, Britain does these things better than a great many competitors. Britain's invisible exports, that is, exports of services, have risen massively since 1967 and there is scope for them to rise much further. The economy's private service industries also sell increasing amounts to workers, for more is spent on leisure activities as incomes grow. Moreover, all industrial production must pass through shops to reach consumers, and it must be transported, and this represents a high fraction of the total cost of turning raw materials into finished goods in the homes of those who want them. It would therefore be a great oversimplification to suppose that industry necessarily makes the predominant contribution to consumption and the balance of payments.

There are, of course, service activities that make virtually no contribution but the same is true of some industrial work. Concorde, for instance, has taken far more resources out of the economy in the form of consumer goods for the workers who make it, and plant and machinery specifically needed for it, than will ever be recovered when it starts to be sold. Other successful firms, and even some in the City of London, have therefore had to give up some of the results of their fruitful activities to make it possible for the workers who make Concorde to continue to produce something that will hardly sell enough to recover more than a small fraction of its costs. The fact that it is industrial does not mean that it relieves pressures on the remainder of the economy; it has created them instead.

This means that an argument like Mr Tony Benn's, based solely on the need to have adequate resources in industry, is incomplete; it leaves open the possibility that a government could apparently correct the imbalances of the economy by curtailing services that are essential to its functioning and substitute industrial products that people will only buy if there is no alternative. With sufficient errors by the government and the civil service, a crude pro-industry policy which increased the output of the wrong products at the expense of services that sold heavily overseas could make the balance of payments still worse (for it is British and not foreign airlines that will lose money with Concorde), curtail investment still further, and leave yet greater shortages of the goods that workers actually want. It is unlikely that an interventionist government working to expand industry on Bennish lines would do as much damage as this, but it could conceivably do so (particularly when the appalling record of mismanagement of civil service interventions in the aircraft industry is examined). This means that a crude pro-industry and anti-service approach to the deterioration of Britain's economic structure is not enough.

There is, fortunately, an alternative approach which gets round these difficulties and this has been outlined in a most interesting article on inflation by Professor J. Johnston of the University of Manchester.[12] Instead of dividing economic activities into those that are *industrial* and those that are *non-industrial* they can be divided instead between those that produce *marketed* outputs and those which do not. Almost everything that industry produces is *marketed*, that is, it is sold to someone. The private-sector services are sold, so they are *marketed*. Defence, on the other hand, is not marketed;

no one now pays for the use of a regiment or frigate. What the National Health Service provides, and most schools, is also not marketed, and the services provided by policemen and civil servants are not marketed; so they must spend their incomes on the marketed products of the rest of the community.

These cases are clear-cut but others are less so; thus, the Post Office only markets a fraction of its output because it makes substantial losses. If sales revenue covered only half its total costs one could say that half its output was marketed, like that of an industrial company, while the other half would correspond to the non-marketed output of a civil service department. Concorde will cost Britain over £1000 millions but it will probably produce marketed outputs of only £100 millions, so its effect on the economy will resemble those that would be produced by a second University of Bristol located at Filton (with more money to spend than ten ordinary universities). In short, industrial production is only marketed in so far as it is sold, so all subsidies to any firm whatsoever must be subtracted from industrial production to show what industry's marketed output is. At the same time all the services that are sold contribute to the economy's total of marketed output, which is a total that matters a great deal.

All exports are marketed, so the economy's entire exports of goods and services must be drawn from the economy's total pool of marketed output. All investment is marketed so this must also come from the economy's total marketed output. Finally, all the money that workers, salary earners and pensioners spend must necessarily go to buy marketed output. *Hence the marketed output of industry and services taken together must supply the total private consumption, investment and export needs of the whole nation.*

A difficulty Britain has suffered from since 1961 is that the proportion of the nation's labour force that has been producing marketed output has been falling year by year; at the same time those who have had to rely on others to produce marketed output for them, civil servants, social workers and most teachers and medical workers, have become increasingly numerous, and they have had to satisfy

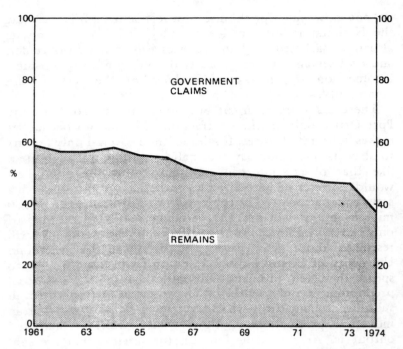

Chart 12   Pre-tax Government Claims on Marketed Output

their requirements by consuming goods and services that diminishing numbers of market-sector workers are producing. In addition, loss-making firms in the public and private sectors have been taking more out of the economy's pool of marketed output than they have been putting into it. Finally, pensioners and all those who receive money from the government are entitled to consume marketed output and produce none. Chart 12 shows that in 1961 the entitlement to buy marketed output by those who did not produce it directly was 41½ per cent (before tax). By 1974 the entitlement of those who did not produce marketed output had risen to 60½ per cent, so 19 per cent less remained for those who actually produced the economy's entire marketed output. Their own consumption needs and the export requirements of the whole economy and resources for investment in the market-sector of the economy had to come almost entirely from what was left after the non-market sector had taken nearly 19 per cent more. Put in these terms the argument is absolutely clear-cut.

If the entitlement to consume marketed output by people who do not produce it directly rises, and it rose from 41½ per cent to 60½ per cent (before tax) in thirteen years in Britain, those who produce it may agree and think it right that they should consume less of what they produce. If taxes are raised heavily to pay for more civil servants, teachers and social workers in these circumstances, and everyone acqui- eseces in the higher taxation that is needed, workers will simply get a higher 'social wage' and less to spend in the shops; and all will be well. If, however, they do not acquiesce in what is happening they will try to make up for the marketed output they are losing as a result of higher taxation with higher wage demands, and these can lead to explosive wage inflation.[13] If militant workers preserve their living standards in terms of marketed output in this way the government will only be able to get its extra marketed output at the expense of investment or the balance of payments, for there is nowhere else it can come from. In Britain the growth of non-market expenditure as a ratio of marketed output from 41 per cent to 60½ per cent (before tax) has had all these effects, explosive wage inflation, a squeeze on invest- ment in the market sector and balance of payments deterior- ation. This is the same argument as before but it can now be presented without qualifications of any kind. *All* exports and everything on which money is spent must be produced by an economy's market sector. With the industry/services dis- tinction, in contrast, industry provided *most* consumption needs and *most* exports, but not all of them; so a crude pro-industry and anti-services policy could conceivably go wrong.

It must be emphasised that the distinction between the market and non-market sectors of the economy is not the same as the distinction between the public and private sectors. A profit-making nationalised industry is in the public sector but its entire output is marketed. Council houses, if they are let at rents which cover all costs, also provide

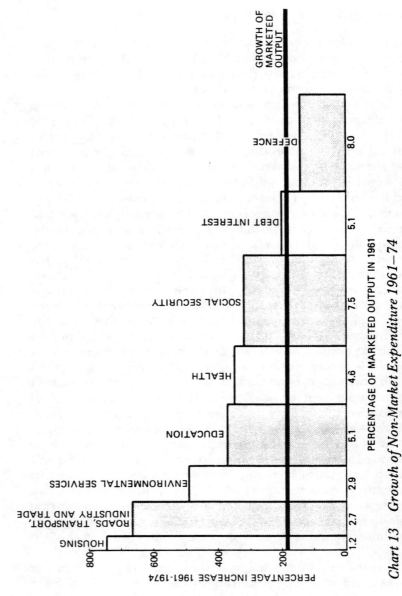

Chart 13   Growth of Non-Market Expenditure 1961–74

Defence, the biggest spender in 1961 with 8 per cent of marketed output grew least. Roads, etc., and Housing grew most.

30

much-desired marketed output. It is only in so far as nationalised industries make losses and houses are let at rents which fail to cover costs that they are part of the non-market sector which has to draw on the market sector for its consumption and investment requirements. In reality much of nationalised industry makes a loss, and council house rents cover only a fraction of costs, so perhaps half the amount spent on them is non-market expenditure. Chart 13 shows exactly where the great increase in non-market expenditure in Britain has gone, and it shows that education, health, subsidies to industry, both private and nationalised, subsidies to housing and entitlements to buy marketed output by the old, the sick and the unemployed, have all grown sharply. These are all immensely desirable activities which most support, but they can still have adverse effects if a society will not acquiesce in a diversion of private consumption in these socially beneficial directions.

It must be emphasised that almost all the civilised activities of a modern society are wholly or largely non-marketed. Both Covent Garden and Glyndebourne cover only a fraction of their costs by selling tickets, and universities, schools, art galleries, libraries and hospitals produce outputs which are almost entirely non-marketed. Defence is also non-marketed so, in times of war, countries perforce vastly increase the non-market sector of their economies. It can almost be said that a country with a larger non-market sector than another similar country will be either militarily stronger or more civilised, but it must be able to afford to maintain its large non-market sector. If its people are prepared to give up marketed output to the government on the necessary scale it will manage this, and in all economies that manage successful transitions from peacetime to wartime conditions, people pay the taxes the government requires without causing hyperinflation or diverting goods from investment, military production and the balance of payments; but if it is peacetime and people are not prepared to part with as much of their marketed output as the government wants the three great difficulties from which Britain suffers must occur in some combination or other. Wages and prices will be pushed up sharply; investment in the market sector will be curtailed; or the balance of payments will deteriorate.

There are two clear ways out of this difficulty and these will be the subject of Chapter 3. First, the market sector of the economy can be made larger compared to the non-market sector by cutting public spending and nationalised industry losses and subsidies. That is the solution that some members of the Labour party and government started to favour in 1975, and it is also the solution of the new leadership of the British Conservative party. As Mrs Thatcher said on 15 September 1975:

> The private sector creates the goods and services we need both to export to pay for our imports and the revenue to finance public services. So one must not overload it. Every man switched away from industry and into government will reduce the productive sector and increase the burden on it at the same time.

Alternatively, all the powers of government can be used to achieve a viable industry-based economy with a large non-market sector by financing this at the expense of private services and the better off. That is inherently the solution of the British Left, and in a still more extreme form it is the solution of the Peoples' Democracies of Eastern Europe. A Left solution along these lines is however perfectly compatible with social democracy. None of the large Western economies which are usually compared with Britain has had a shift into public services as great as Britain's, but the shift in three Scandinavian economies Sweden, Norway and Denmark, has been even faster, and these countries have not suffered from Britain's difficulties. There are therefore examples of a viable social democratic solution involving high public expenditure which Britain has not yet found and others have. There is therefore more than one viable democratic solution, and more will be said about these in Chapter 3. Before this something must be said about Britain's past, for to understand fully where one is one must first see how one got there. Britain's experience in the various attempts that were made to put things right by Mr Maudling, Mr George Brown, Mr Jenkins and Mr Barber will be set out in the next chapter. Much can be learned from their interesting and important initiatives.

NOTES

1. See n.5 below where it is argued that the rate of growth of *productive capacity* in industry fell from 3.3 per cent per annum in 1955—65 to about 2.5 per cent in 1965—73 and perhaps 2.0 per cent since then.
2. Income tax and social security contributions are actually deducted from most workers' paypackets by their employers, and Chart 6 shows the effects of this for the average worker. Many workers also pay local authority rates, and Table 6.1 (row (8)) on pp. 164—5 shows what remains after they too are deducted.
3. Bacon and Eltis, *The Age of US and UK Machinery*.
4. The evidence cited in this paragraph is derived from official EEC statistics. It is to be found in, for instance, various issues of *Basic Statistics of the Community*.
5. The rate of growth of productive capacity can be estimated by calculating the rate of growth of output between similar points in the cycle. Thus, industrial production increased 35 per cent between the cyclical peaks of 1955 (fourth quarter) and 1965 (first quarter) or at 3.3 per cent per annum. Capacity also grew at this rate if both booms peaked when there were similar margins of slack in the economy. Industrial production increased 22 per cent from 1965 (first quarter) to the cyclical peak of 1973 (first quarter), or at only 2.5 per cent per annum; and investment has been so much less since 1973 than in 1965 to 73 as a whole that the rate of growth of productive capacity is now almost certainly less than 2.5 per cent per annum, — probably as little as 2.0 per cent.
6. See David Smith, 'Public Consumption and Economic Performance', *National Westminster Bank Quarterly Review*, November 1975.
7. See N. Kaldor, 'Alternative theories of distribution', *Review of Economic Studies*, vol. XXIII (1955—6).
8. The first detailed exposition of the modern neo-classical theory of growth, where structural unemployment cannot occur, is by R. M. Solow, of MIT ('A contribution to the theory of economic growth', *Quarterly Journal of Economics*, vol. LXX, February 1956).
9. There is indeed evidence that the capital-output ratio has been rising in Britain. It certainly cost more capital investment to achieve each one per cent of growth in 1965—75 than in 1955—65 (i.e. the Incremental Capital Output Ratio or ICOR was higher in 1965—75). Britain's ICOR has also been the highest of any major developed economy. Those who regard a high ICOR as a low rate of return on investment see this as the result of British managerial weaknesses. It is also compatible with a bias towards labour-saving investment, due to high wages and employment taxes and low profitability.

10. See M. Friedman, 'The role of monetary policy', *American Economic Review*, vol. LVIII, March 1968.
11. Adam Smith, *An Inquiry into the Nature and Causes of the Wealth of Nations* (1776) II 3.
12. J. Johnston, 'A macro-model of inflation', *Economic Journal*, vol. 85, June 1975.
13. This propostion has been tested by J. Johnston and M. Timbrell ('Empirical tests of a bargaining theory of wage rate determination', *The Manchester School of Economics and Social Studies*, 41 June 1973). Cf. also, Dudley Jackson, H. A. Turner and Frank Wilkinson, *Do Trade Unions Cause Inflation?*, Cambridge University Press, 1972, Chapter 3.

[11]

THE IMPLICATIONS FOR INFLATION, EMPLOYMENT AND GROWTH OF A FALL IN THE SHARE OF OUTPUT THAT IS MARKETED

By R. W. BACON AND W. A. ELTIS

In 1974–75 there was an increasing realization that the United Kingdom was experiencing a very substantial structural shift in employment from industry to various public sector service occupations. The present authors,[1] economists in the Cambridge University Department of Applied Economics,[2] and Mr. Benn and those associated with him,[3] have all drawn attention to the great shift that has occurred and is occurring, and set out some of its implications. In addition, Professor J. Johnston has set out some of the implications for inflation of a shift of this kind in a most interesting model.[4]

In the present paper, after an introductory section which says something about the argument in general terms, the theoretical implications of a shift in employment to the public sector with an accompanying fall in the proportion of the economy's output that is marketed, will be set out in two stages. First two economies in steady growth with different ratios of marketed output will be compared, so as to identify some of the long-term implications of very different ratios of marketed output in total output. After this the problems involved in moving from a low to a high share of non-marketed output will be set out, including the possibility that there may be no viable growth path the economy can move to, with the result that inflationary pressures grow and the productive base of the economy runs down at an accelerating rate from year to year.

I. INTRODUCTION

The model which will be used to analyse the effects of a lower ratio of marketed output is an elaboration of the growth model with which the classical economists argued that the rate of growth depended on the proportion of an economy's economic activities that were 'productive' and the rate of surplus earned in the 'productive' sector.[5] In a simple classical model it can be assumed that the output

---

[1] R. W. Bacon and W. A. Eltis, 'A Budget Message for Mr. Healey: Get More People into Factories', *The Sunday Times*, 10 November 1974; and 'Stop-Go and De-industrialization', *National Westminster Bank Review*, November 1975, and articles in *The Sunday Times*, 2, 9 and 16 November 1975; and Walter Eltis, 'How Public Sector Growth Causes Balance of Payments Deficits', *International Currency Review*, Vol. 7, No. 1, January–February 1975.

[2]. See Vivian Woodward, 'The Need to Avoid Higher Government Employment', *The Times*, 7 July 1975, and (an article based on research by R. J. Tarling, C. J. Allsopp, V. Woodward, J. Morley and D. A. C. Heigham) 'A View of Industrial Employment in 1981', *Department of Employment Gazette*, May 1975.

[3] See 'Tony Benn Writes About Industrial Policy', *Trade and Industry*, 4 April 1975.

[4] J. Johnston, 'A macro-model of inflation', *Economic Journal*, Vol. 85, June 1975.

[5] The basic account of the classical theory of economic growth is set out in Book 2 of Adam Smith's *The Nature and Causes of the Wealth of Nations* (1776). See J. R. Hicks, *Capital and Growth* (Oxford University Press, 1965), Chapter IV; and W. A. Eltis, 'Adam Smith's Theory of Economic Growth' (in *Essays on Adam Smith* edited A. Skinner and T. Wilson, Oxford University Press, 1975) for modern restatements of the theory.

of the productive sector where all growth producing activities originate is O_p of which C_p is consumed by productive workers, C_u is consumed unproductively (by workers who do not work in the productive sector and by non-workers), while the remaining output of the productive sector, I_p, is invested. Then the surplus of the productive sector, i.e. its output less the consumption of its own workers, is $O_p - C_p$, and this must equal C_u plus I_p. Hence:

$$\frac{O_p - C_p}{O_p} \equiv \frac{C_u}{O_p} + \frac{I_p}{O_p}$$

Now $(O_p - C_p)/O_p$ is the surplus earned in the productive sector as a fraction of its own output, and e_p can be written for this, while c_u can be written for C_u/O_p, the proportion of the output of the productive sector that is consumed unproductively. If i_p is written for I_p/O_p, the proportion of productive sector output that is invested, then

$$i_p \equiv e_p - c_u \tag{1}$$

It can be assumed that the output of the productive sector will be constant in the absence of investment (and both output and investment must be defined net of capital consumption to produce this result), while it will grow if there is accumulation and decline if there is decumulation. Equation (1) shows that a classical economy will grow if e_p exceeds c_u, while output will decline if c_u, the proportion of output consumed unproductively, exceeds e_p, the rate of surplus in the productive sector. A stationary state will be achieved if e_p equals c_u, for instance if a 'corn' economy produces a surplus of 50 per cent of output in the 'corn' sector, while one-half of each harvest is diverted to the civilized and/or wasteful activities of the unproductive sector. If the rate of surplus was only 25 per cent, just one-quarter of each year's output could be diverted to the unproductive sector, while a rate of surplus of 75 per cent would allow three-quarters of output to be used in unproductive activities. Growth requires that the unproductive sector be smaller so that part of the surplus of the productive sector can be invested.

The classical economists differed about the correct practical dividing line between the productive and unproductive sectors. There must clearly be something arbitrary in where the borderline is drawn, but there is also an important element of sense in the classical proposition that the economy's ability to support non-surplus-producing activities depends on the ratio of outputs to inputs in the sector of the economy where surpluses are produced. Typical positions taken up by the classical economists were Malthus's that only the activities that produced physical and therefore investable outputs were productive, and Smith's that all profit-making activities were productive with the result that the productive sector included all marketed services.[6] These differences are echoed in recent analyses of de-industrialization where the economy has been divided between an industrial and a non-industrial sector: a sector producing tradable goods and services and

[6] The case for the various possible dividing lines between 'productive' and 'unproductive' and who used them is set out very comprehensively by Malthus in *Principles of Political Economy* (2nd Edition, 1836) Chapter 1, 'Of the Definitions of Wealth and of Productive Labour'.

sector producing non-tradables: and a sector producing marketed goods and services and one producing non-marketed outputs.[7]

There are obvious weaknesses in the industry and non-industry dividing line. Transport, communications, and distribution which are all services are part of any process by which inputs are transformed into final outputs in the hands of domestic or foreign producers and consumers, and a line drawn between the manufacturing and distribution stages of this process must be an arbitrary one.

Some of these disadvantages remain with the tradable/non-tradable dividing line. Thus retail distribution is largely untradable, and so are domestic transport and most building and construction activity, and these are indispensable parts of the processes by which raw materials are transformed into finished goods in the hands of producers and consumers and foreign purchasers.

The present authors therefore believe that the best division is between activities which produce marketed outputs and those which do not. The economy's market sector then produces all the output that is marketed at home and overseas, and this automatically includes all exports, all investment, and all the goods and services that workers buy. It is to be noted that the market sector will include the nationalized industries in so far as these cover their costs through sales of output, as well as the private sectors of modern economies. It will exclude public services which are provided free of charge.

Where the economy is divided into a market and a non-market sector, marketed output net of capital consumption is O_m and C_m of this is consumed by the market sector workers who produce it so the market sector's surplus of marketed output is $(O_m - C_m)$. Of this, C_u will be consumed by non-market sector workers and by non-workers such as pensioners, I_u will be used up outside the market sector in the form of investment and material purchases, I_m will be net investment in the market sector, and B_m will be the trade surplus of marketed output. With consistent definitions, this is the identity:

$$\frac{O_m - C_m}{O_m} \equiv \frac{C_u}{O_m} + \frac{I_u}{O_m} + \frac{I_m}{O_m} + \frac{B_m}{O_m}$$

Now e_m can be written for $(O_m - C_m)/O_m$ as in the basic classical formula (here e_m is the proportion of marketed output that is surplus to the consumption of market-sector workers), while c_u, i_u, i_m and b_m can be written for C_u/O_m, I_u/O_m, I_m/O_m and B_m/O_m. Hence:

$$i_m + b_m \equiv e_m - c_u - i_u \tag{2}$$

This equation is clearly very similar to the classical equation (1). Here the proportion of marketed output that can be reinvested in the market sector (net of capital consumption), plus the proportion that can be exported net is identically equal to the rate of surplus of marketed output achieved in the market sector, less the fractions of marketed output that are personally consumed and used up as raw materials and investment outside the market sector.

[7] The distinction between industrial and non-industrial activities is the one favoured by Mr. Benn and the present authors in some of their previous publications. Walter Eltis, 1975 (*op. cit.*) however used the tradable/non-tradable distinction and J. Johnston (*op. cit.*) the one between marketables and non-marketables.

There was a large shift from industry to public sector service employment in the United Kingdom in 1961–74 and this increased both the ratio of non-marketed to marketed output and the entitlement to consume marketed output by those who did not produce it directly.   The latter also increased because there was a large increase in pensions and social security benefits which entitled non-producers to buy an increasing proportion of marketed output.   Table 1 shows that the pre-tax entitlement to buy United Kingdom marketed output by those who did not produce it directly increased from 41.4 per cent of marketed output in 1961 to 60.3 per cent in 1974.   This increased c_u and i_u substantially and because e_m did not rise commensurately, b_m and i_m necessarily fell.   As all traded goods and services are marketed, b_m is the current account of the balance of payments (expressed as a fraction of marketed output).   Similarly as all investment is marketed, i_m is simply total market sector net investment (expressed as a fraction of marketed output).   We have argued that a squeeze on b_m and i_m resulted from the increase in the pre-tax entitlement to consume market sector output by non-market sector producers from 41.4 per cent to 60.3 per cent and that this put pressure on the current account of the balance of payments and market sector investment.

TABLE 1

Ratio of Pre-Tax Non-Market Sector Claims to
Marketed Output in the United Kingdom

1961	0.414	1968	0.504
1962	0.427	1969	0.505
1963	0.429	1970	0.515
1964	0.422	1971	0.516
1965	0.440	1972	0.529
1966	0.448	1973	0.534
1967	0.487	1974	0.603

NOTES:
(a) Non-market sector claims are total public expenditure less local authority housing less GDFC of public corporations (all from Table 58 of *National Income and Expenditure*) less debt interest paid by public corporations (Table 57 of *NIE*).
(b) Marketed output is GDP at factor cost less public administration and defence less public health and educational services (Table 11 of *NIE*) less income from private non-profit making bodies (Table 13 of *NIE*).

It is universally agreed that many of the most indispensable and civilized activities of a modern society produce unmarketable outputs.   The argument is not that increasing unmarketable activities in relation to total output is in any way wrong, but that this must have effects compatible with equation (2) which must always hold as it is an identity.   Hence the consumption and investment involved in the provision of unmarketed activities can only be increased without damage to investment and the balance of payments if e_m, the rate of surplus in the market sector, rises commensurately.   This happens in any society that achieves a successful transition from a peacetime to a wartime economy (for war involves a great increase in the ratio of output that is unmarketable) and in war-time conditions societies often accept very high rates of taxation without explosive wage inflation.   If resources are transferred to the provision of unmarketables on a similar scale in peacetime, and people still wish to buy growing quantities of goods in the shops, one of two things must happen. Either e_m will stay unchanged (i.e. governments fail to apply wartime rates of taxation or the share of wages and salaries fails to fall drastically) and in this case an increase in c_u and i_u must squeeze i_m and/or b_m. Alternatively taxation will be raised enough to prevent this, but ex-ante wage demands may still be based on the marketed goods and services workers expect to be able to buy, and when these ex-ante demands are frustrated ex-post because of higher taxation etc., wage demands in the next period are likely to be that much higher, producing a continuing acceleration of inflation (at given rates of unemployment) so long as the economy fails to meet workers' ex-ante wage demands in terms of marketed output.[8] A substantial shift from marketed to non-marketed output of the kind that has taken place in Britain since 1961 may therefore have far-reaching effects on the functioning of the economy. This much is apparent from the simple equations so far presented.

It is now time to develop the argument more fully, and to show first how basic economic interrelationships such as money flows and factor shares will differ in economies in steady growth with different ratios of marketed output. Following this, the precise form of the problems of transition from a low to a high share of unmarketed output will be outlined.

II. A Steady Growth Comparison Between Two Economies with Different Ratios of Marketed Output

An economy with two sectors is assumed. One, the market sector, has companies which produce outputs that they sell. The other, the public sector, produces non-marketed outputs.[9] The argument will be set out in two stages. First, a number of basic relationships which must always hold—whether there is steady growth or not—will be set out. After this, the further relationships which must hold in steady growth will be added, to produce a complete account of the long-term effects on economies of different ratios of marketed to non-marketed output.

(i) *Relationships which Must Always Hold*

The market sector produces output which sells for O_m (which is defined net of the depreciation of the market sector's own capital stock), and the corresponding pre-tax incomes are profits of $\Pi \cdot O_m$, and wages of $(1-\Pi) \cdot O_m$, where Π is the share of profits in the market sector. The government taxes all incomes at the same proportional rate of T. Fractions s_Π of net tax profits and s_w of net of tax wages are saved, and saving from profits is wholly in the form of company saving. All market sector investment, $i_m \cdot O_m$, is done through companies, and i_m, the fraction of marketed output invested, is defined net of capital consumption. The basic relationships of the market sector can be very easily derived from these assumptions, and they are written down in Tables 2, 3 and 4.

The public sector spends $G_o \cdot O_m$ directly on marketed output, and in addition,

[8] This possibility is clearly and fully set out in J. Johnston (*op. cit.*).
[9] Public sectors produce some marketed outputs, but it will obviously simplify the argument to have a complete dichotomy between a private sector that markets its output and a public sector that does not.

TABLE 2
Companies

Profits	$\Pi \cdot O_m$
Taxes paid	$T \cdot \Pi \cdot O_m$
Profits net of tax	$(1-T) \cdot \Pi \cdot O_m$
of which: saved	$s_\Pi (1-T \cdot \Pi \cdot O_m$
consumed	$(1-s_\Pi)(1-T)\Pi \cdot O_m$
Investment	$i_m \cdot O_m$
Financial Surplus (Saving—Investment)	$[s_\Pi(1-T)\Pi - i_m]O_m$

TABLE 3
Workers in Market Sector

Wages	$(1-\Pi) \cdot O_m$
Taxes paid	$T(1-\Pi) \cdot O_m$
Wages net of tax	$(1-T)(1-\Pi) \cdot O_m$
of which: saved	$s_w(1-T)(1-\Pi) \cdot O_m$
consumed	$(1-s_w)(1-T)(1-\Pi) \cdot O_m$
Financial Surplus (Saving—Investment)	$s_w(1-T)(1-\Pi) \cdot O_m$

TABLE 4
Total Market Sector—Workers and Companies

Output	O_m
Taxes paid	$T \cdot O_m$
Incomes net of tax	$(1-T) \cdot O_m$
of which: saved	$[s_\Pi \cdot \Pi + s_w(1-\Pi)](1-T) \cdot O_m$
consumed	$[1-s_\Pi \cdot \Pi - s_w(1-\Pi)] \cdot (1-T) \cdot O_m$
Investment	$i_m \cdot O_m$
Financial Surplus	$[s_\Pi \cdot \Pi + s_w(1-\Pi)(1-T) - i_m] \cdot O_m$
Marketed Output Balance (Market Sector Output available to Other Sectors)	$[1 - i_m - \{1 - s_\Pi \cdot \Pi - s_w(1-\Pi)\}(1-T)]O_m$

it pays $G_p \cdot O_m$ to persons for services, or simply as transfers. Hence total public expenditure is $(G_o + G_p)O_m$. The $G_p \cdot O_m$ that is paid to persons is taxable at the uniform rate of T, and the recipients save a fraction, s_w, of the net of tax incomes they receive from the government.[10] $G_o \cdot O_m$, total direct public expenditure on marketed output, includes public sector investment and all purchases of currently used materials, and these have identical effects on the equations.[11]   The basic public sector equations are set out in Tables 5 and 6.

TABLE 5
Recipients of Public Sector Incomes

Incomes received	$G_p \cdot O_m$
Taxes paid	$T \cdot G_p \cdot O_m$
Incomes net of tax	$(1-T) \cdot G_p \cdot O_m$
of which: saved	$s_w(1-T) \cdot G_p \cdot O_m$
consumed	$(1-s_w)(1-T) \cdot G_p \cdot O_m$
Financial Surplus	$s_w(1-T) \cdot G_p \cdot O_m$
Marketed Output Balance (Market Sector output produced less that consumed)	$-(1-s_w)(1-T) \cdot G_p \cdot O_m$

[10] The proportion of marketed output that is consumed *by persons* outside the market sector is $G_p(1-T)(1-s_w)$, and this equals c_u in equation (2).
[11] G_o is equivalent to i_u in equation (2).

TABLE 6
Government

Taxes received	$T \cdot O_m + T \cdot G_p \cdot O_m$
Expenditure	$(G_o + G_p) \cdot O_m$
Financial Surplus	$[T(1 + G_p) - (G_o + G_p)] \cdot O_m$
Marketed Output Balance	$-G_o \cdot O_m$

There are two basic equations which state the size of $b_m \cdot O_m$, the current account surplus of the balance of payments, in terms of the economy's other relationships. First, in terms of Marketed Output Balances:

Current account surplus =
Sum of Marketed Output Balances of the economy's various sectors,

i.e. the current account surplus must equal the market sector output that is surplus to that sector's investment and consumption, less the marketed output that is purchased by the government and the recipients of public sector incomes.

Second, as the New Cambridge school has reiterated:[12]

Current account surplus =
Sum of financial balances of the economy's various sectors.

The Marketed Output Balance equation is in fact the same as the Cambridge financial balance equation. Using the Tables, both equations can be written as:

$$b_m = T[1 + G_p - \Pi s_\Pi - s_w(1 - \Pi + G_p)] - i_m - G_o - G_p + \Pi s_\Pi + s_w(1 - \Pi + G_p) \quad (3)$$

It is to be noted that b_m is the *ratio* of the current account surplus to marketed output.

(ii) *A Steady Growth Comparison*

Two economies in steady growth will be compared where one has a substantially higher $(G_o + G_p)$ than the other, i.e. one uses up a substantially higher fraction of marketed output in the public sector. To focus attention on this difference and its consequences, it will be assumed initially that both economies have the same rate of Harrod neutral technical progress, a, in their market sectors. This assumption will be relaxed later, as it is plausible that the size of the public sector will influence the rate of technical progress, for instance because education and defence spending may have some favourable long-term effects on this, but so long as it holds, both economies will be assumed to have the same rate of growth of productivity in their market sectors. With constant rates of taxation, and unchanging income distribution, wages net of tax will increase at the same rate as productivity. Then wages will increase at rate a in both economies in terms of marketed real output, and this rate of increase of private consumable income will apply to the workers of both sectors, and it will be assumed that these always receive the same wage. It will also be assumed that the labour force grows at rate n in both economies. Then with constant shares of employment in the market and public sectors, employment will grow at rate n in both sectors of both economies. As output per

[12] See *National Institute Economic Review*, No. 64, May 1973, pp. 20–24 for an account of some of the propositions of the New Cambridge school.

worker grows at rate a, total market sector output will grow at rate (a+n) in both economies. Public expenditure will also grow at rate (a+n), and this will allow the government to increase the *goods* that it buys for investment, etc., at rate (a+n), but in steady growth it will only increase its direct employment at rate n, the rate at which the labour force grows, and the cost of this rises at an annual rate of (a+n) because wages (in terms of marketed output) rise at rate a

Up to this point, the growth paths of the two economies appear extremely similar. Both have the same rates of growth of public and private sector output and employment, and the same rate of growth of living standards in terms of both marketed and non-marketed outputs. The sole difference is that in the case of one economy a higher fraction of what is provided (and this grows at the same rate in both economies) is not marketed. It is now time to turn to the differences.

First the two economies will have very different rates of taxation. These can be calculated very easily as the natural first assumption to make in a steady state growth comparison is that the budgets of both economies balance.[13] As exports can be assumed continually equal to imports in steady growth, there will be no financial surplus or deficit in transactions with foreigners.

With the budgets of both economies balanced, governments which spend $(G_0+G_p)O_m$ and receive $T(1+G_p)O_m$ will need to set the rate of taxation at:

$$T=\frac{G_0+G_p}{1+G_p} \tag{4}$$

In the UK, according to Table 1, it can be said that (G_0+G_p) increased from 45 per cent in 1961 to 60 per cent in 1974. In both years approximately five ninths of non-market expenditure was in the G_p category (payments to persons) and four-ninths in the G_0 category (investment and material purchases).[14] The uniform rate of tax needed to balance the budget would then have been of the order of 36 per cent in 1961 and 45 per cent in 1974, so a 9 per cent increase in taxation on all incomes would have sufficed to allow an extra 15 per cent of marketed output to be used by the government. Substantially less extra taxation than 15 per cent is needed because with the present assumptions the government gets tax back at the uniform rate of T on all its payments to persons. Indeed it follows from (4) that if G_0 and G_p always increase in the same proportion:

$$\frac{dT}{d(G_0+G_p)}=\left(\frac{1}{1+G_p}\right)^2 \tag{5}$$

This was about 0.64 in the United Kingdom in 1961 when G_p was about 0.25 and 0.56 in 1974 when G_p was about 0.33, so an increase in non-market expenditure of 10 per cent of marketed output may now require an increase in overall taxation of less than 6 per cent, because civil servants' salaries, like those of others, are taxed

[13] If the budgets were not balanced and trade was balanced, the private sectors of the two economies would have persistent financial surpluses or deficits which would have monetary implications that are best avoided in the initial statement of the argument.

[14] In 1962 58.7 per cent of non-market expenditure went to persons: Wages and salaries 27.1 per cent, debt interest 12.8 per cent, and grants to the personal sector 18.8 per cent. In 1974 these totalled 56.5 per cent (wages and salaries 27.0 per cent, debt interest 9.5 per cent and grants 20.0 per cent). *National Income and Expenditure.*

It might be thought that the above equations would suffice to show how workers' living standards in terms of marketed output would be affected by various different ratios of public expenditure to marketed output. Thus it might be believed that if one economy required a T of 45 per cent while another required a T of only 36 per cent, then workers and profit receivers in the first economy would keep 55 per cent of the marketed output they produced, while those in the second economy would keep 64 per cent, with the result that in any given year both workers and profit receivers would be 9/64, or about 14 per cent, worse off in terms of marketed output in the economy with a T of 45 per cent. This calculation only holds if the share of profits is the same in both economies. If a larger public sector is associated with a higher or lower share of profits this will obviously have crucial effects on how living standards, etc., differ between the two economies.

A first approach to how income distribution will be affected is to follow through the effects of the condition that the private sectors of both economies have balanced financial transactions, which follows from the assumptions that foreign trade is balanced and that the governments' budgets are balanced. With no private sector financial surpluses or deficits, it can be inferred from Tables 4, 5 and 6 that:

$$\Pi = \left(\frac{1}{1-T}\right)\left[\frac{i_m}{s_\Pi - s_w} - (1 - G_o)\frac{s_w}{s_\Pi - s_w}\right] \tag{6}$$

This is close to $1/(1-T)$ times the share of profits in Lord Kaldor's celebrated equation for the share of profits,[15] and the equation shows that with the present assumptions the share of profits is of the order of $1/(1-T)$ times what it would be in the absence of public expenditure and taxation. As companies then pay a rate of tax of T on these profits, they keep about $(1-T)$ times $1/(1-T)$ of the profits they would have obtained in the absence of public expenditure and taxation, so their net of tax profits will be only slightly influenced by the rate of public expenditure. This means that the entire cost of the public sector is borne by labour. A simple example illustrated in Fig. 1 on p. 279 shows how this comes about.

The share of profits in marketed output is 25 per cent (net of capital consumption) in the left-hand block, approximately the British percentage in 1961, and the uniform rate of tax is the hypothetical 36 per cent needed to balance the British budget in that year. Thus 16 per cent of the 25 per cent profit is left after tax, and for simplicity it is assumed that this is half invested and half consumed. It is also assumed that all saving comes from profits and s_p is one-half so profit receivers always consume half of profits net of tax. With all saving coming from profits, workers consume the entire net of tax incomes that they receive, and these amount to the share of wages and salaries (75 per cent) less taxation at 36 per cent, or 48 per cent of marketed output.

In the right-hand block the rate of taxation is 45 per cent, the hypothetical rate needed for a 60 per cent share of non-market expenditure in 1974. Companies pass this on, so the entire 9 per cent cost of the larger public sector is financed at

[15] N. Kaldor, 'Alternative theories of distribution', *Review of Economic Studies*, Vol. XXIII, 1955–56. Equation (6) would give precisely $1/(1-T)$ times Professor Kaldor's share of profits if G_o was zero, or s_w was zero.

the expense of workers' consumption—partly through the higher taxation of wages (at 45 per cent instead of 36 per cent), and partly through the lower share of wages (71 per cent instead of 75 per cent) that results from the passing on of profits taxation.

A crucial assumption in the above analysis is the one that the proportion of marketed output invested in the market sector is unaffected by the rate and share of profits. In steady growth this will equal $V(a+n)$, where V is the capital–output ratio in the market sector. It has been assumed that $(a+n)$, the 'natural' rate of growth, will be the same with all rates of public expenditure, but it is far from clear that V, the capital–output ratio, will be unaffected by this. Pasinetti has suggested that since factor prices have such uncertain effects on V, it is best to assume (where something must be assumed) that V depends mainly on technical factors, and that it is independent of relative factor prices.[16] This result would be arrived at with neoclassical analysis where ϕ, the elasticity of substitution between labour and capital, is zero. With this assumption, V will be the same whatever the rate of public expenditure, and as $(a+n)$ is also independent of this, i_m will be the same in two economies in steady growth, whatever the rate of taxation and the relative size of their public sectors. Then the above calculation will be correct, and *in steady growth* the entire cost of the public sector will be financed by labour. Suppose however that *faute de mieux* the capital-output ratio depends in an old-fashioned way on the relative cost of labour and capital. If use is made of Pasinetti's steady growth equation that the rate of profit net of tax must equal $(a+n)/s_c$, where $(a+n)$ is the natural rate of growth and s_c is the net of tax propensity to save of those who have no earned incomes, it is evident that the rate of profit net of tax must be the same in all economies with the same s_c and $(a+n)$, whatever their rates of taxation. Then the pre-tax rate of profit will always be $1/(1-T)$ times Pasinetti's net of tax rate of return of $(a+n)/s_c$. Companies will choose the technique of production which is expected to maximize the rate of profit before tax and if the production function is CES, each 1 per cent by which the rate of profit is higher will be associated with a capital-output ratio that is ϕ per cent lower. This has implications for the share of investment and the share of profits. A number of relationships can be set down formally. First, making use of Pasinetti's proposition which points to the complete passing on of a tax on profits, so far as the rate of profit is concerned:

$$\text{Elasticity of the rate of profit with respect to public expenditure} = \frac{G_o + G_p}{(1 - G_o)(1 + G_p)} \qquad (7)$$

The denominator of this expression is likely to be close to unity, so (7) states that the rate of profit will vary in a similar proportion to $G_o + G_p$, total public expenditure as a fraction of marketed output. Making use of the proposition that a 1 per cent higher rate of profit will be associated with a ϕ per cent lower capital-output ratio:

$$\text{Elasticity of the capital-output ratio with respect to public expenditure} = -\phi\left[\frac{G_o + G_p}{(1 - G_o)(1 + G_p)}\right] \qquad (8)$$

[16] L. L. Pasinetti, *Growth and Income Distribution*, Cambridge University Press, 1974, pp. 133–34.

Thus if ϕ is 0.7, 10 per cent higher public expenditure will be associated with a capital-output ratio which is something like 7 per cent lower. Now i_m, the share of investment in marketed output, is $V(a+n)$, so with $(a+n)$ given, i_m is proportional to V. Hence:

$$\text{Elasticity of } i_m \text{ with respect to public expenditure} = -\phi\left[\frac{G_o+G_p}{(1-G_o)(1+G_p)}\right] \tag{9}$$

Thus, apart from the fixed coefficients case, higher public expenditure will be associated with a lower share of investment in marketed output. Finally, the share of profits is identically equal to the capital-output ratio times the rate of profit, so the elasticity of the share of profits with respect to public expenditure will be the elasticity of the rate of profit *plus* the elasticity of the capital-output ratio with respect to this. Thus:

$$\text{Elasticity of the share of profits with respect to public expenditure} = (1-\phi)\left[\frac{G_o+G_p}{(1-G_o)(1+G_p)}\right] \tag{10}$$

This states that in the fixed coefficients case where $\phi=0$, there will be complete passing on of any profits taxation, and this was the case in the examples set out above where the whole cost of the public sector was borne by labour. However, if $\phi=1$, a Cobb–Douglas case, the above elasticity is zero, and the share of profits is independent of the rate of taxation. Then the cost of the public sector will be shared between workers and profit receivers, and these will give up equal proportions of income shares that are unaffected by taxation. If ϕ has some intermediate value, for instance 0.7, there will be partial passing on, and a public sector that

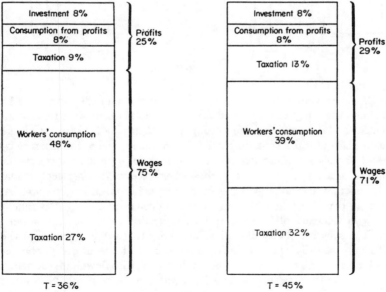

Fig. 1

took 10 per cent more of marketed output would be associated with a share of profits that was about 3 per cent higher. In the full passing on example that was outlined in Fig. 1, 75 per cent of net marketed output went to wages and 25 per cent to profits where the required tax rate was 36 per cent, and 29 per cent went to profits when it was 45 per cent, with the result that the ratio of workers' consumption to marketed output was a full 9 per cent lower at 39 per cent of marketed output in place of 48 per cent.

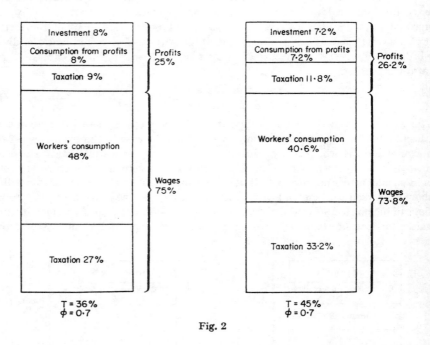

Fig. 2

Fig. 2 shows what will happen instead if ϕ is 0.7, and the right-hand block of Fig. 2 shows the effect of a required tax rate of 45 per cent with this assumption. Investment and consumption from profits each then take 7.2 per cent of marketed output in place of 8 per cent (in the left-hand block), where the tax rate is 45 per cent.[17]   26.2 per cent of marketed output has to go to profits to provide for these and profits taxation at 45 per cent, so workers receive 73.8 per cent of marketed output, and they consume 40.6 per cent after taxation at 45 per cent. As they consume 48 per cent where the tax rate is 36 per cent, they pay as much as 7.4 of the extra taxation of 9 per cent that is needed to finance the larger public sector. The substitutability of capital for labour that is now allowed for therefore disturbs only slightly the previous proposition that the larger public sector is financed from workers' consumption. Moreover with lower investment and a lower capital-output ratio, marketed output per worker will be lower in the

---

[17] This can be inferred from equation (9).

right-hand block on Fig. 2 than on Fig. 1 where there was no substitutability between capital and labour, so workers may be no better off than in the fixed coefficients case. There workers' consumption fell to 39 per cent of marketed output, and output per worker was unaffected . In Fig. 2 workers' consumption falls to 40.6 per cent of marketed output, but the capital-output ratio is about one-tenth lower.

It will be evident that the assumption that the budget is balanced, with the result that the private sector has neither a financial surplus nor deficit, makes it virtually certain that workers will have to finance (in one way or another) almost the whole cost of the public sector. This is because something very like Kaldor's income distribution equation must hold with this assumption, and profits taxes are then largely passed on. They are wholly passed on where V is independent of relative factor prices, and partly passed on where there is some substitutability of capital and labour (with $\phi < 1$)—when workers lose additionally because output per worker is lower. It follows that workers' living standards must always be lower to a rather greater extent than that indicated by the tax rate. At the same time, profit receivers are largely protected from the high taxation that must result from a large public sector. With Kaldor's equation, their ability to finance investment is independent of the rate of tax, because profits always generate a rate of saving from companies and workers that is sufficient to finance the steady growth share of investment. With these assumptions therefore, net of tax profits are never squeezed relatively to investment, with the result that companies face no financing problems when the non-market sector is large that they do not face equally when it is small. The sole pressure is on labour.

It is perhaps unrealistic to set up a model where workers are certain to give way to this pressure, as has been assumed so far. It is true that the analysis of this section is based on the assumptions of steady growth where the workers of different economies consume (and have always consumed) different fractions of the marketed output they produce. There is therefore never pressure on workers to move down to a growth path where private consumption per head is lower— pressure which trade unions might be expected to resist. Nevertheless it may be worthwhile to set out the implications of an alternative set of assumptions where the shares of wages and profits in marketed output depend on the relative market power of labour and capital. It could for instance be assumed that the degree of monopoly in Kalecki's sense is independent of the rate of taxation and the relative size of the non-market sector. Then the ratio of prices to direct costs of production will always be the same, with the result that Π, the share of profits in marketed output, will be a constant and not a variable.[18]

With this assumption, the cost of the public sector will be shared by workers and profit receivers. The latter will receive Π times marketed output before tax, where Π is a constant, depending on the degree of monopoly, and workers will receive $(1 - \Pi)$ times marketed output before tax. After tax they will receive $(1 - T)\Pi$ and $(1 - T)(1 - \Pi)$ times marketed output respectively. As the share of

[18] M. Kalecki, 'The determinants of distribution of the national income', *Econometrica*, Vol. VI, April 1938.

profits and pre-tax relative factor prices will then be the same in different economies with different rates of taxation etc., the capital-output ratio and therefore the share of investment will also be the same at all rates of taxation. Then different economies with different sized non-market sectors but the same degree of monopoly will all have the same share of profits before tax, the same rate of profit, the same capital-output ratio, and the same share of investment. The principal difference between economies with large and small public sectors will simply be that the former will have higher rates of taxation, with the result that their workers and profit receivers will be entitled to consume and invest (with internal finance) smaller fractions of marketed output. As the steady growth share of investment in the market sector will be the same in low and high tax economies, while high tax economies will have less net of tax company saving, the latter will have to use more outside finance to invest the fraction $V(a+n)$ of marketed output that all must invest in steady growth. With the previous assumptions, Π was adjusted to tax rates and investment requirements, with the result that the ratio of investment to internal finance was the same at all rates of taxation. A low Π (due to a low degree of monopoly) might however now create the problem that companies could only invest $V(a+n)$ if they were prepared to use a very high ratio of external finance—and it will be evident after the next stage of the argument that this might have to come from the government.

This emerges when the second principal effect of the assumption that Π depends on the degree of monopoly is analysed. It is a consequence of this that the budget will no longer be balanced (apart from a fluke). With Π given independently of investment requirements and saving propensities, the market sector of the economy may have a financial deficit or surplus so the assumption of a balanced budget which has been made hitherto cannot be retained. However, the assumption of balanced trade on a steady growth path can be retained, and this produces the condition that the market sector and the government taken together must have neither a surplus nor a deficit. This condition will be fulfilled where the tax rate is (from equation (3)):

$$T=\frac{G_o+G_p+i_m-\Pi(s_\Pi-s_w)-(1+G_p)s_w}{1+G_p-\Pi(s_\Pi-s_w)-(1+G_p)s_w} \tag{11}$$

Now when this tax rate is compared with $(G_o+G_p)/(1+G_p)$, the balanced budget tax rate, it emerges that:

T is lower than the balanced budget tax rate, producing a consequent budget deficit, where:

$$\Pi>\left(\frac{1+G_p}{1-G_o}\right)\left[\frac{i_m}{s_\Pi-s_w}-(1-G_o)\frac{s_w}{s_\Pi-s_w}\right] \tag{12}$$

and, conversely, T is higher and the budget is in surplus where Π is less than this.

It will be evident when (12) is compared with (6) that, not unexpectedly, the crucial point is whether the degree of monopoly share of profits exceeds or falls short of Kaldor's Π, which is what the right-hand side of (12) is equivalent to. If the degree of monopoly share of profits is greater, the market sector of the economy will generate excessive saving with the result that a budget deficit is needed to balance trade at full employment. Conversely, if the degree of monopoly factors produce a lower share of profits than Kaldor's equation (in the modified form appropriate to the present model), the government must run a budget surplus to generate the savings that are not coming from profits. Companies must then continuously borrow this surplus from the government to finance the fraction of the steady growth investment of $V(a+n)$ that company saving and workers' saving will not finance. Thus, where the degree of monopoly produces a 'low' share of profits, companies must be prepared to borrow from the government to finance investment, and where it produces a 'high' share of profits, the private sector must be prepared to invest a fraction of its saving in government bonds.

Where two economies with different rates of non-market expenditure and similar saving propensities, etc., are compared, the one with a higher ratio of non-market expenditure, i.e. a higher (G_o+G_p), will have a higher Kaldor share of profits, i.e. a higher share of profits from equation (6). If both economies have the same degree of monopoly share of profits, which is what their shares of profits will have to be with Kalecki-like assumptions, the one with a high (G_o+G_p) could well be in the situation where a budget surplus is needed, and the one with low public expenditure could need continuous deficits. Then the economy with high public expenditure could well require institutions to channel government tax revenues to the finance of company investment, while the economy with low public expenditure would require continuous budget deficits with private sector subscriptions to public debt. Certainly with the degree of monopoly Π given, higher public expenditure must be associated with a lower required budget deficit or a higher required surplus, so at a certain point it is bound to place an economy in the budget surplus situation where companies must borrow from the government to finance the steady-growth share of investment.

It is now time to summarize some of the basic implications of the argument. Where the share of profits is determined independently of the degree of monopoly, steady growth with a high rate of public expenditure requires that workers give up consumption to finance almost the entire cost of the public sector, while the size of this has no adverse effects on the availability of private sector finance. The economy simply generates whatever profits are needed net of tax to produce sufficient private sector saving to finance investment. On the other hand, where the share of profits depends on the degree of monopoly, workers' consumption is reduced by the uniform rate of tax needed to finance the public sector, and it is reduced no more than this. Savings are however squeezed net of tax in relation to the required steady growth investment ratio in the market sector, and this means that companies may need to invest much more than their savings, and to borrow from the government as well as from workers to do so. There are therefore two kinds of obstacle which may set an upper limit to the ratio of public expenditure which is compatible with steady growth: a certain minimal *share* or else *quantity* of marketed output may be required for workers' private consumption, and companies may be unwilling to increase their borrowing beyond a certain point. These potential constraints will be considered in turn, and the possibility that there might be a lower limit to workers' consumption will be considered first.

All would agree that there must be a Malthusian lower limit to workers' consumption of marketed output, i.e. workers will need a minimum wage in terms of marketed output if the labour force is not to decline. It is usually assumed that this classical minimum wage is fixed as an absolute quantity of goods and not a proportion of marketed output per head, so an economy could always overcome this constraint if its output per worker was sufficiently high. Thus if the classical minimum wage was w_s, and a society's desired rate of public expenditure left workers only 25 per cent of what they produced per head in the form of marketed output, there would be a feasible steady growth path once output per worker reached $4w_s$. Until then the workers in the market sector would need to consume more than 25 per cent of market sector output. Clearly in this case a steady growth path can exist provided that

$$(1 - \Pi)(1 - T) \geqslant w_s \qquad (13)$$

where w_s is the classical subsistence wage expressed as a fraction of output per worker in the market sector.[19] In poor societies (or rich societies with extraordinary rates of public expenditure) this condition will set an upper limit to T and therefore to public expenditure as a fraction of marketed output.

In rich societies there is a modern version of the classical subsistence minimum and this has been most clearly described by Joan Robinson:

> There is a limit to the level to which real-wage rates can fall without setting up a pressure to raise money wage-rates. But a rise in money wage-rate increases money expenditure, so that the vicious spiral of money wage chasing prices sets in. . . . Either the system explodes in a hyper-inflation, o some check operates to curtail investment.[20]

She argues that workers, through trade union pressure, have the power to set a 'inflation barrier' of this kind which sets a lower limit to wages in terms of markete output. An 'inflation barrier' at a wage of w_i expressed as a fraction of outpu per worker in the market sector would impose the condition that:

$$(1 - \Pi)(1 - T) \geqslant w_i \qquad (1$$

which would set an upper limit to T, and therefore to $(G_o + G_p)$ in exactly the sam way as the classical subsistence wage. Again, the 'inflation barrier' minimu wage might need to be sufficient to purchase a particular quantity of output an not a fraction of marketed output per worker, so that an economy with high outp per worker could get past this barrier and have a large public sector.[21] In contras an economy with lower output per worker would have minimum private consum tion demands (including perhaps sufficient post-tax income to finance car owne ship, etc.) which could set the 'inflation barrier' so high in relation to output p worker that T had to be relatively low. An economy in this situation would ha

---

[19] Expressed as a *quantity* of output, (13) would be: $(1 - \Pi)(1 - T)(O_m/L_m) \geqslant w_s$ whe O_m/L_m is output per worker in the market sector.
[20] Joan Robinson, *The Accumulation of Capital*, Macmillan, 1956, p. 48.
[21] Expressed as a *quantity* of output (14) would read $(1 - \Pi)(1 - T)(O_m/L_m) \geqslant w_i$.

o wait until output per worker was high enough to provide both for workers' rivate consumption at rate w_1 and desired non-market activities before public xpenditure could be raised to the desired fraction of marketed output. From his point onwards, steady growth with the desired public expenditure ratio would e practicable.

While all would accept the validity of the classical constraint that $(1-\Pi)(1-T) \geqslant w_s$, it would not be as universally agreed that $(1-\Pi)(1-T) \geqslant w_1$ vill also set a constraint in a modern developed economy. It would be argued y some that balanced budgets and money supply growth at a rate of $(a+n)$ vould ensure stable prices, whatever the aspirations of workers. With this view f the problem, workers would have to accept any real wage in excess of w_s, and his would set the only effective constraint (and advanced economies would hardly eed to concern themselves with it, so for them virtually any tax rate would be ompatible with steady growth at stable prices). A difficulty with this line of rgument is that it is universally admitted that trade unions, influenced by the act that private consumption per worker is less than the inflation barrier mini- num, can *temporarily* raise money wages rather rapidly. Monetarists would ssume however that the unemployment this caused (when the money supply vas increased only at rate $(a+n)$) would arrest such inflation, and make it im- ossible that it should persist in the long term. If this is accepted, it could still e supposed that there will always be substantial upward wage pressure *at full mployment* whenever workers cannot buy w_1 of marketed output. Then steady rowth *at full employment* requires that workers are able to purchase w_1 with their vages, and $(1-\Pi)(1-T) \geqslant w_1$ is a constraint that must be satisfied on any steady rowth path. Monetarists might prefer to allow that private consumption per mployed worker of less than w_1 will produce a 'natural' rate of unemployment hat exceeds the merely frictional rate. Thus steady growth will be incompatible vith just frictional unemployment where $(1-\Pi)(1-T) < w_1$.

The second obstacle that may set an upper limit to the ratio of non-market xpenditure in steady growth is that companies may require a minimum ratio of et of tax profits to marketed output, if they are to invest the fraction $V(a+n)$ hat they must invest in steady growth. Where outside finance is borrowed on ixed interest terms, companies may go bankrupt while they are still achieving an perating surplus, for this must be sufficient to pay interest on all debt. A com- any which has no fixed interest debt is less likely to face bankruptcy where things o wrong than a company which has much debt and therefore a high gearing ratio: nd the higher the gearing ratio (i.e. the higher the ratio of debt to equity) the reater will be the danger that outsiders will obtain control of the company. his means that risk is always involved in borrowing on fixed interest terms, and ompanies are therefore likely to set upper limits to the ratio of fixed interest ebt to equity that they are prepared to make use of. The risks involved in ccepting government finance are likely to be particularly great unless there are nancial institutions which make this available to companies without the risk of ncreasing government managerial interventions. Obviously none of these ifficulties will arise with nationalized companies, which do not face risks of take-

over if they borrow too heavily and then make inadequate surpluses to service
the loans.   However non-nationalized companies will face increasing risk as they
increase their ratio of debt to equity,[22] and this means that it may be right to
assume that there will be an upper limit to the investment they will undertake in
relation to their own undistributed profits net of tax.   There are, of course, no
risks to companies in general on a steady growth path, but it can still be assumed
sensibly, that companies will refuse to borrow more than a particular fraction of
the capital they use.   Company profits net of tax are $(1-T)\Pi$, and companies
save a fraction, s_Π, of these, so the internal finance available to them will be the
fraction $s_\Pi(1-T)\Pi$ of total market sector output.   If it is assumed for simplicity
that only fixed interest finance can be obtained externally (and it forms most outside finance) and that the maximum external debt companies as a whole are prepared to incur each year is D times the increase in their equity, i.e. D times the
profit they can themselves reinvest then the maximum investment that companies can finance is the fraction $s_\Pi(1+D)(1-T)\Pi$ of marketed output.   Hence
the achievement of steady growth is subject to the constraint that:

$$s_\Pi(1+D)(1-T)\Pi \geqslant V(a+n) \tag{15}$$

If profits taxes are passed on as is the case with Kaldor's equation, this constraint
will be equally easy to meet at all levels of T, because $(1-T)$ times Π will not vary
inversely with T—but if instead Π is determined by 'degree of monopoly' factors
there may be trouble.   A higher T (as a result of higher public expenditure as a
ratio of marketed output) will then reduce the left-hand side of equation (15)
and increase the likelihood that companies will be unable to invest the fraction
$V(a+n)$ of marketed output because to do so would involve excessive fixed interest
borrowing.   Too low a share of profits, or too high a rate of taxation, may then
prevent the achievement of steady growth because companies fail to undertake
the investment in the market sector necessary for this.

The argument has suggested that two obstacles may stand in the way of steady
growth (in addition to all the usual ones that stand in the way of steady growth in
any model).   First, workers may set off inflation if consumption per head in terms
of marketed output is less than a certain minimum.   Second, companies may have
inadequate internal finance for the steady growth share of investment if their
profits net of tax do not reach a certain minimum proportion of this.   Either of
these constraints, or both together, may set upper limits to the ratio of public
expenditure to marketed output that is compatible with steady growth.   If
neither constraint operates, economies with very different ratios of non-market
expenditure will be able to grow at rate $(a+n)$ with the effects set out above.

It has been assumed so far that the economy's long-term rate of growth will
be the same, $(a+n)$, whatever its ratio of public expenditure to marketed output.
It has thus been assumed that the long-term rate of growth of productivity is
independent of the size of the public sector and the rate of taxation.   In fact the
size of the public sector can be expected to have two general effects, one favourable

[22] See M. Kalecki, 'The principle of increasing risk', *Essays in the Theory of Economic
Fluctuations*, London, 1939.

nd one unfavourable, on the long-term rate of growth of productivity. First, many public sector activities which do not result in marketed outputs are likely o have favourable effects on the rate of growth of productivity. Of these, education, government financed research and defence spending can all be expected to ave favourable though sometimes severely lagged effects on technical progress hat are not easily quantifiable.[23] On the other hand, the larger the ratio of employment in the public sector, the smaller will be the aggregate amount of market ector output in any given year, and this means that market sector investment which is a *fraction* of market sector output) will be less. Growth models have een put forward by Arrow and others which make technical progress a function f the amount of investment,[24] and if there is less market sector investment, esearch and development departments may be smaller with the result that they iscover less per annum. On this line of argument, productivity will rise faster vhere the market sector is larger in relation to the non-market sector. Kaldor has uggested that returns to scale will be more favourable in industry than in services, nd industry is likely to form a high though historically diminishing fraction of he market sector, and it might be thought that this would be a further factor eading to a strong association between the size of the market sector and productivity growth.[25]

However, where economies of scale and Verdoorn effects have been formulated that they can play a part in growth models, it has been shown that they apply multiplier to growth from other sources. This means that two economies with qual rates of labour growth, n, and equal rates of technical progress, a, in their ndustrial sectors will both have growth rates of $(a+n) \cdot \psi$ where ψ is the economies scale multiplier, even if the size of their industrial sectors is very different.[26] hus an economy with a larger market sector will not have a faster *steady growth te* of output than another with the same $(a+n) \cdot \psi$ which has a larger non-market ector. It will obviously have a higher *level* of output, but it will only enjoy ster growth if it has a higher a or n (Kaldor himself has attached particular nportance to the industrial n, but this must be the same as the economy's n in eady growth comparisons). The crucial advantage of a large market sector is ien that this will be associated with high industrial investment which will have vourable effects on research and development. The crucial advantage of a rge non-market sector is that this will include education, much research, defence, nd so on. It is not possible to say at present which of these can be expected to provide the greater stimulus to the long-term rate of growth of productivity, so the ssumption that has been made throughout this section that $(a+n)$ will be the

[23] The positive feedback from public expenditure to the rate of growth of labour productivity the market sector is an important element in Professor J. Johnston's model (*op. cit.*).
[24] K. J. Arrow, 'The economic implications of learning by doing', *Review of Economic udies*, Vol. XXIX, June 1962. See W. A. Eltis, *Growth and Distribution*, Macmillan, 1973, hapter 6, for an account of further arguments which lead to this result.
[25] N. Kaldor, *Causes of the Slow Rate of Growth of the United Kingdom* (inaugural lecture), ambridge University Press, 1966.
[26] See F. H. Hahn and R. C. O. Matthews, 'The theory of economic growth: a survey', conomic Journal, Vol. LXXIV, December 1964, p. 833, and W. A. Eltis, *Growth and Distribu- m*, Ch. 11.

same in economies with different rates of public expenditure that are being com
pared may well be the best working assumption to make for the time being.

This means that the basic results that have been arrived at can be carrie
forward to the next section without further modification.   Thus, it is not clear tha
a larger non-market sector will be associated with faster or slower growth in th
long term, but it will certainly be associated with higher taxation—and it is likel
to be associated with a higher share of profits also (provided that $\phi < 1$) if this i
not determined exclusively by degree of monopoly factors.   Finally a minimun
wage in terms of market sector outputs, and minimum required profits net o
tax, may both set upper limits to the proportion of marketed output that ca
be diverted to the public sector in the very long run.

III. The Problems Involved in Increasing the Size of the Non-Market Sector

It has been shown in the previous section that it may or may not be possib
to increase the relative size of the non-market sector of the economy in the ver
long run.   It will be possible to do this in principle in a growing economy if th
new and larger non-market sector is compatible with steady state growth
and it will be impossible if it is not.   The case where steady growth can be achieve
with the new and larger non-market sector will be considered first.   After thi
the case where the larger public sector is incompatible with steady growth will b
outlined, and just how the economy breaks down as attempts are made to main
tain an 'impossible' ratio of non-market expenditure will be explained.

If steady growth can be achieved with the new and larger non-market secto
neither of the constraints outlined in the last section operate.   Hence the worker
in the market sector are prepared to consume a lower fraction of marketed outpu
and companies are if necessary prepared to finance a larger fraction of investmen
through borrowing.   The simplest case which will be considered first is the on
with fixed coefficients, where companies pass on their share of the larger cost c
the public sector through an increase in the share of profits with the result tha
workers bear the entire cost of this.   Then if, as a result of a larger non-marke
sector, T (which equals $(G_o + G_p)/(1 + G_p)$) has to be increased from T_1 to T_2, th
fraction of marketed output that the workers in the market sector will be able t
receive net of tax will need to fall by $(T_2 - T_1)$.   As they originally receive th
fraction $(1 - \Pi_1)(1 - T_1)$, where Π_1 is the original share of profits, they will have t
forgo the fraction

$$\left(\frac{T_2 - T_1}{(1 - \Pi_1)(1 - T_1)} \right)$$

of their net of tax incomes.   These grow at an annual rate of a on any stead
growth path, but workers must lose the above fraction to move from one stead
growth path to another where there is less private consumption.   If this transitio
takes z years, private consumption per worker will increase at less than rate a i
this period when its growth rate, g_c, will be (on the assumption of a constant pr

pensity to save from wages so that workers' consumption rises at the same rate as their net of tax incomes)

$$g_c = a - \frac{1}{z}\left[\frac{T_2 - T_1}{(1-\Pi_1)(1-T_1)}\right] \tag{16}$$

In the United Kingdom in 1961–74 when expenditures by the non-market sector increased by something like 15 per cent of marketed output, the hypothetical budget-balancing tax rate had to rise from about 36 per cent to 45 per cent, so $(T_2 - T_1)$ was 0.09, while $(1-\Pi_1)$ was about 0.75 and $(1-T_1)$ was 0.64. With these hypothetical figures, and a thirteen year transition period from 1961 to 1974, equation (16) would be:

$$g_c = a - 1.44 \text{ per cent}$$

The United Kingdom's growth in output per worker in the market sector (i.e. a) was about 3.0 per cent per annum in 1961–74 so the growth of private consumption per worker would have had to be limited to about 1.56 per cent per annum if the entire cost of the public sector had been financed at the expense of workers' consumption as in equation (16).

This example is illustrated in Fig. 3. The line C_1C_1 shows what consumption per worker would be if the hypothetical uniform 1961 tax rate of 36 per cent was maintained continuously, and this line rises at an annual rate of 3.0 per cent which

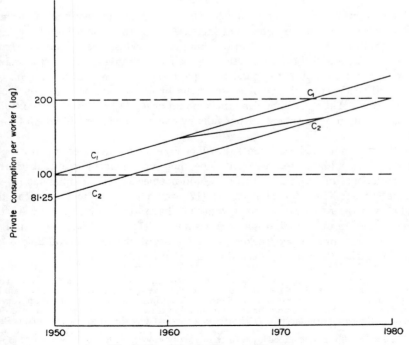

Fig. 3. Transition to larger public sector

is the assumed increase in marketed output per worker from 1961 to 1974. Th
line C_2C_2 shows what consumption per worker would be if the hypothetical 197
tax rate of 45 per cent was maintained continuously and the whole extra cost o
the higher tax rate was met from workers' private consumption as is being assumed
C_2C_2 is drawn 18.75 per cent below C_1C_1 because that is the extent to which a
higher tax rate of 9 per cent reduces workers' private consumption in the con
ditions assumed.   From 1961 to 1974 workers move from C_1C_1 to C_2C_2 so in thi
thirteen-year transition period their private consumption only advances somethin,
like half as quickly as on C_1C_1 and C_2C_2.   Once the costs of transition have bee
paid (in 1974), the growth rate of private consumption per worker can return t
3.0 per cent per annum and it can follow the growth path C_2C_2 which advance
at this annual rate.   Clearly the more rapid the transition period required to attai
the new ratio of non-market expenditure the larger the fall in the ratio of consump
tion relative to that in steady state growth.[27]

With the complete passing on of profits taxation that is being assumed, com
panies in the market sector invest the fraction $V(a+n)$ of marketed output o
both the original and the new steady growth paths without any increase in gearing
i.e. any increase in fixed interest borrowing as a ratio of their own net of ta
profits.

In terms of the basic equation (2) with $V(a+n)$ substituted for i_m,

$$V(a+n)+b_m = e_m - c_u - i_u \tag{17}$$

An increase in (c_u+i_u), the proportion of marketed output required in the non
market sector, calls for an equivalent increase in e_m, the proportion of markete
output that is surplus to consumption in the market sector.   That is what i
required if there is to be no reduction in the share of investment in the marke
sector, or deterioration in the balance of payments.   In the full passing on cas
with fixed coefficients, the whole cost of the higher (c_u+i_u) is borne by labou
with the result that e_m rises by the same amount as (c_u+i_u) and workers' consump
tion as a fraction of marketed output falls by exactly the extent to which (c_u+i_u)
rises.

If there are not fixed coefficients, V will be lower on the new steady growth path
where (c_u+i_u) is higher to an extent depending on the elasticity of substitutio
between labour and capital.   Then e_m would not need to rise as much as (c_u+i_u)
because the left-hand side of equation (17) would be lower to the extent tha
$V(a+n)$ was lower.   Hence workers would not have to give up as great a fractio
of marketed output as has so far been assumed.   This would not mean that th
growth of consumption per worker would necessarily be more favourable in th
transition period than that indicated in equation (16).[28]

---

[27] This example serves to show what will happen to consumption during a transition perio
of given length which attains a new ratio of non-market expenditure.   It is possible to analys
the optimal path to a new ratio and the choice of an optimal ratio itself given an appropriat
utility function for society, using the methods developed by Kenneth J. Arrow and Mordeca
Kurz in *Public Investment the Rate of Return, and Optimal Fiscal Policy*, Johns Hopkins Press
1970.

[28] The lower capital-output ratio on the new steady growth path would be associated wit
less output per worker in the market sector.   Workers would be able to consume a highe

The assumption that profits taxes are passed on (which follows from the balanced-budget assumption on which this case like the last is based) ensures that companies will face no liquidity problems at high rates of taxation that they do not face equally at low rates. Hence the effect the larger public sector has on workers' consumption is what primarily needs to be considered.

This is not the case where the share of profits is determined by 'degree of monopoly' factors which are unaffected by the size of the public sector. In this situation workers and companies must both give up the extra fraction $(T_2 - T_1)$ of their incomes to the government, while the distribution of incomes between wages and profits is unchanged. As workers receive $(1 - \Pi)(1 - T_1)$ times marketed output before the increase in the size of the non-market sector, and $(1 - \Pi)(1 - T_2)$ after the transition is completed, private consumption per worker falls by the proportion $(T_2 - T_1)/(1 - T_1)$ in the z year transition period. Hence over the transition period, consumption per worker grows at the rate given by

$$g_c = a - \frac{1}{z}\left(\frac{T_2 - T_1}{1 - T_1}\right) \tag{18}$$

It will be observed that consumption now increases less slowly in the transition period. Taking the approximation to the British 1961–74 case as an example where $a = 3.0$ per cent per annum, T_1 is 0.36 and T_2 0.45; g_c is 1.92 per cent per annum in the transition period with equation (18) in place of the 1.56 per cent rate suggested by equation (16).

The growth of net of tax profits, g_Π, is $(a+n)$ on any steady growth path, but like wages it will fall short of this by $(T_2 - T_1)/(1 - T_1)$ during a z year transition period in which the rate of taxation rises from T_1 to T_2 and the distribution of income is unchanged. Thus:

$$g_\Pi = a + n - \frac{1}{z}\left(\frac{T_2 - T_1}{1 - T_1}\right) \tag{19}$$

Consumption from profits will grow at this rate, but the case of investment is more complex. Once steady growth is resumed with a higher ratio of public expenditure, investment will need to be the fraction $V(a+n)$ of marketed output that it must be on all steady growth paths, and V will be unchanged with constant income distribution, but company saving will have fallen from the fraction $(1 - T_1)s_\Pi$ to $\Pi(1 - T_2)s_\Pi$ of marketed output. Companies will need to borrow an extra $\Pi(T_2 - T_1)s_\Pi$ of marketed output on the steady growth path where public expenditure is higher. If they are prepared to increase their gearing to the required extent, the economy can achieve a new steady growth path with the same share of investment in marketed output, $V(a+n)$, and lower ratios of private consumption from wages and profits than on the old path. Once the new path is achieved, marketed output will grow at rate $(a+n)$, consumption per worker at rate a, and so on.

It can be noted that as the greater cost of the public sector is likely to be

action of this lower output because e_m would not need to rise as much, but it is not clear on *priori* grounds whether they would gain or lose from the lower share of investment. They might gain because less marketed output was needed for investment, and they might lose because marketed output per worker was lower, see pp. 280–1 above.

financed with different rates of taxation on profits and wages, the costs of tran
tion to a larger non-market sector could be borne more by capital or by labo
than the previous analysis would indicate.   If taxes were increased mainly
profits, the gearing ratio would need to rise more than has so far been indicat
while if taxes were increased mainly on wages and salaries, the costs of transit
would fall predominantly on labour.   The result of this would approximate
that shown by equation (16) which described the effects of complete passing
There it made no difference where higher taxation was actually levied, si
workers paid it all in any case.

It has been assumed so far that the constraint that prevents workers' priv
consumption from falling below a certain fraction of marketed output, and
constraint that sets an upper limit to company borrowing, do not operate.
either constraint operates, the economy will not be able to achieve steady grow
with a higher ratio of non-market expenditure, and it will be interesting to
what form this failure will take if the government raises public expenditure to
desired extent.

If company taxes are completely passed on, only the wage constraint can op
ate.   If it does, money wages will start to rise rapidly at full employment as so
as $(1 - \Pi)(1 - T)$ becomes less than w_1.   It will be immaterial whether the hig
taxes that follow too large a public sector are levied predominantly on wages or
profits, for higher profits taxes will simply be passed on and so raise Π, and the
fore reduce $(1 - \Pi)(1 - T)$ below w_1.   This inflation could presumably be elimina
by a sufficient rate of unemployment which would mean that economies with a lar
public sector either had more inflation or more unemployment than econom
with a smaller public sector, once the w_1 constraint began to operate.   It is to
noted that an economy with a larger public sector and therefore more unempl
ment (if this is preferred to extra and perhaps accelerating inflation)[28] would
this reason have a still higher ratio of public expenditure since the market sec
could be expected to have to produce whatever unemployment was needed
stabilize prices.   Thus if the market sector produced 100 at full employment
which the public sector took 60 and this was sufficient to set off a rapid wage-pr
spiral because the 'inflation barrier' was breached, and the authorities reacted
creating market sector unemployment while leaving public expenditure unc
market sector output might fall to for instance 96, with the result that the ra
of public expenditure to this became 60/96 or 62.5 per cent in place of 60 per ce
This would accentuate the effect of the high ratio of public expenditure with
result that still higher unemployment would be needed, both to compensate for
original failure to give the workers w_1 at full employment, and for the fact that s
less could be given as a result of the inability of the economy to allow the mar
sector to use the share of resources available to it at full employment. With
passing on of any profits taxes, investment would be adequate in the long term
produce growth in marketed output at a rate of $(a + n)$.

[28] The rate of inflation will accelerate if Professor Friedman's theory of the effect of
employment below the 'natural' rate is correct. See 'The role of monetary policy', *Ameri
Economic Review*, Vol. LVIII, March 1968.

It is to be expected that the policy options of rapid and perhaps accelerating
flation or high unemployment which followed failure to meet the w_1 constraint
ight lead governments in societies in this situation (which did not wish to reduce
e size of their public sectors) to attempt to introduce prices and incomes policies
 contain the inflation that resulted from a net of tax wage of less than w_1 in
rms of marketed output. Such policies often seek to control profits as well as
ages, with the result that the assumption of complete passing on of profits taxes
uld hardly be made in these circumstances. This means that the constraint of
limit to investment set by undistributed profits net of tax plus the fixed interest
rrowing firms are prepared to undertake could begin to operate. It could operate
 any case, even if the real wage constraint did not, in the case where the share of
ofits is determined by 'degree of monopoly' factors, so it will be important to see
w a failure of investment in the market sector to reach the fraction $V(a+n)$
ll affect the economy.

The most direct approach to this problem is the following. If the fraction
(a+n) of marketed output must be invested in the market sector to increase
ployment in that sector at rate n, less investment than this while new plant
s an unchanged capital-output ratio will create fewer employment opportunities.
ith zero net investment, it could be assumed that the output capacity of the
arket sector would be constant, and that productivity growth at rate a would
ake a fraction a of the labour force redundant. This redundant labour, and the
tra labour, n, can be employed with new plant if $V(a+n)$ is spent on this, but if,
r instance, only $V \cdot a$ is spent, then new plant will be adequate to reabsorb those
ade redundant by technical progress, but it will be inadequate to provide for
owth in employment in addition. It follows from this approach to the problem
at the number of workers who can be employed in the market sector will only
ow if more than the fraction $V \cdot a$ of marketed output can be invested in that
ctor. It will only grow at the steady growth rate n if $V(a+n)$ is invested, and
will actually decline if less than $V \cdot a$ is invested

The rationale for this approach—and it has crucially important implications—
as follows. With substitutability between capital and labour with old plant,
y number of men can be fitted into any given capital stock if the wage is low
ough. However if, as is being assumed here, there are factors which prevent the
are of wages in the market sector from falling, extra men cannot be found jobs
 that sector without new investment. It can be assumed that companies will
t employ extra men if this reduces aggregate profits, and as the cost of employ-
g workers in terms of marketed output rises at rate a (with a constant share of
ofits) fewer men and not more must be employed in the absence of investment.
V, the capital-output ratio with new plant, were flexible, a halved share of invest-
ent would still allow new plant to provide employment for the fraction (a+n)
 the labour force if V was also halved. But in terms of neoclassical theory com-
nies will only choose to invest in new plant with a lower V if the cost of capital
es in relation to the cost of labour (and non-neo-classics would perhaps prefer to
eat V as fixed in any case by the available technology). If competitive conditions
 the labour and product markets prevent the share of profits from rising, while

the government taxes employment as much as investment, companies will hav
no incentives of any kind to invest in new plant with a lower V. If employment i
taxed more heavily (as in Britain) or the share of profits falls, companies wi
indeed choose new plant with a higher V. Any shortfall in the share of investmen
from the steady growth share will then undoubtedly have the consequence tha
insufficient employment opportunities will be created in the market sector t
permit steady growth.

This will not necessarily do harm in a transition period from a steady growt
path with a small public sector to another with a larger one. A smaller fractio
of the labour force will need to work in the market sector on the second growt
path, so it will be right that investment should be less than $V(a+n)$ in the trans
tion period when the public sector is growing relative to the market sector. How
ever, the share of investment in the market sector must be restored to $V(a+n)$ a
soon as it is desired that this process of structural change in favour of the publi
sector should cease. If it is not, employment opportunities in the market secto
will decline indefinitely, and this means that the full employment ratio of publi
expenditure to market sector output will rise each year. This will require eve
rising tax rates if trade is to be balanced, and this will continuously reduce th
proportion of marketed output that workers can consume, and put increasin
pressure on company liquidity. In consequence what workers receive in terms o
marketed output can be expected to fall short of w_1 to an increasing extent if thi
constraint operates, while at the same time, with rising taxation of profits, com
panies with constraints on the amount of their borrowing can be expected t
invest a diminishing fraction of marketed output since they will receive a fallin
fraction of this net of tax. Then fewer jobs will be created or more lost in th
market sector in each successive year, with the result that the necessary annua
increase in taxation will accelerate, as will inflation if workers' private consumptio
is at all close to w_1. Correspondingly more unemployment or, alternatively
tougher incomes controls will therefore be needed in each successive year to arres
the inflation.

It will be evident that an economy must drift deeper and deeper into thi
territory in the conditions assumed, namely workers who bargain for private con
sumption per head of at least w_1, income distribution that does not automaticall
keep the share of profits net of tax in line with the investment that must be unde
taken to maintain market sector employment, and companies that will not borro
to finance investment to an unlimited extent. Once companies fail to borrow
sufficient amount, the share of investment must become less than $V(a+n)$, an
the proportion of the labour force that can be provided with jobs in the marke
sector of the economy must fall at an accelerating rate if the share of investmen
in the market sector remains less than $V(a+n)$, and falls with profits net of ta
Moreover prices will also rise at an accelerating rate after a time if Friedman'
analysis is correct.

Two points should be noted about this impasse. First an increase in pro
ductivity growth (i.e. an increase in a) will do nothing to relieve the situation
this faster technical progress is Harrod neutral. This is because faster productivit

rowth would *increase* the required share of investment, for being Harrod neutral, would leave V unchanged at the existing income distribution and so increase (a+n). Only technical progress or productivity growth with a capital-saving ias would be helpful, and faster neutral or capital-using technical progress would ctually increase the rate at which the market sector had to shed labour. It •llows that a continuing and accelerating decline of employment in the market ector in relation to the non-market sector with almost inevitably associated iflation could only be arrested through an end to the conditions that led to this ate of affairs. Thus the share of investment in the market sector would need > be raised to V(a+n) to prevent further relative decline, and an increase in the roportion of employment provided in the market sector would require a share of ivestment of more than V(a+n). Either of these would require a lower rate of >mpany taxation, and/or higher share of profits, and/or an increase in the willing-ess of companies to finance investment through borrowing. Real resources for 1ese would only become available given the equation:

$$i_m + b_m \equiv e_m - c_u - i_u$$

a country ran a balance of payments deficit during any transition period in hich the capital stock of the market sector was restored, or reduced private >nsumption in the market sector as a ratio of marketed output, or reduced the roportion of market sector output that was needed in the public sector.

It must be emphasized that the case of extreme and accelerating instability 1at has been outlined will only arise as a result of an increase in the proportion : marketed output required by the public sector if conditions in the economy are ich that the share of profits in marketed output cannot rise correspondingly, and >mpanies will not increase their ratio of investment to net of tax profits. These :e unfortunately conditions that are rather commonly found, and if nothing is >ne to maintain market sector investment in face of them, a proportionately .rger public sector will produce accelerating inflation and a rising unemployment end as efforts are made to correct this, together with an accelerating decline in nployment opportunities. These are what will be produced if market sector ivestment is allowed to fall in the long run, instead of the benefits which it was >ped a larger public sector would provide.

incoln College, Oxford
xeter College, Oxford

[12]

7

HOW RAPID PUBLIC SECTOR GROWTH CAN UNDERMINE THE GROWTH OF THE NATIONAL PRODUCT

by Walter Eltis*

Exeter College, Oxford

All economies have a sector which produces a surplus off which the rest of the economy lives. This is one of the oldest propositions in economics. It has always been understood that if the surplus is large, the economy will be able to support strong but unproductive armed forces and an extensive state establishment which meet their material needs from the extra output of agriculture, industry and commerce. If the surplus is small, the country cannot afford to employ many non-producers and if it attempts to finance them, it will push taxation to the point where agriculture, industry and commerce fail to function as they should. Their output will fall and tax revenues with it and governments will then find it increasingly difficult to finance their spending. If they push up rates of taxation as their surplus producing sectors decline, they will put these under increasing pressure and force cuts in output and employment until the conflict between the demands of government and the needs of the sector of the economy which must finance it becomes intolerable. An economic crisis then results characterised by rapid and accelerating inflation, growing unemployment, and a cessation of growth.

The surplus creating sector of economies is the market sector. This is because marketed output—output which is sold—must supply a nation's entire export needs since all exports are marketed. In addition, capital equipment is always sold to firms so all physical investment goods must come from the market sector. Finally all the consumer goods and services which are bought privately are marketed. Hence the marketed output of industry, agriculture and services taken together must supply the total private consumption, export and investment needs of all nations.

Much marketed output is required by those who produce none. The

*The author is grateful to Robert Bacon for extensive comments and help with the statistical work.

armed forces, the civil service, government employed teachers, doctors, nurses, policemen, dustmen and pensioners all produce no marketed output. They eat and require clothing and housing and most drive cars and work in buildings which have to be constructed and maintained: These are all marketed goods and they must be provided by the workers of the market sector, or obtained through international trade from the market sectors of other economies. Thus the market sector must produce marketed output in excess of its own needs to provide for all the requirements of those in the non-market sector. The market sector must therefore provide a surplus and the non-market sector lives off that surplus.

The transfer of resources from the market to the non-market sector is most efficiently achieved through the tax system. The market sector pays taxes and the non-market sector lives off the revenues obtained.[1] Market sector employment is therefore self-financing and the ultimate source of all tax revenues, while non-market employment is tax-financed. If the budget is balanced, the aggregate taxes paid in the market sector will equal the *net* taxes required to finance the non-market sector.

The market sector includes government controlled companies which market their output as well as privately owned corporations, and government companies can finance social services from the taxes derived from their surpluses (provided they earn them) in basically the same way as privately owned companies. The vital borderline is therefore not the traditional one between the public and private sectors. Instead the vital distinction is between the self-financing companies in the *public* and *private* sectors which market their output, and the tax-financed non-market sector which the market sector finances through the taxes that companies and their employees pay.

Where governments finance their spending through deficits instead of taxation, the position is basically similiar. Here part of the non-market sector may be financed through the voluntary savings of the market sector workers who buy government secutities which allow the state to spend. Alternatively, the state finances some of the spending of the

---

[1]Some do not perceive this basic fact because non-market sector workers also pay taxes, so everyone appears to be a taxpayer. A civil servant with an income of £20,000 must rely on others for his entire marketed output needs because he produces none, but he is not entitled to buy £20,000 worth of marketed output because he pays perhaps £7,000 of total taxes out of this. Hence the net cost to the market sector of employing him is at most £13,000 and not £20,000 and the basic fact is that the market sector must give up £13,000 of marketed output if he is to be employed at a salary of £20,000. Once the taxes paid by non-market sector workers and pensions are deducted from their gross pay, it is clear that where the budget and international trade are balanced, the total net taxes paid by the market sector must equal the total net of tax incomes received in the non-market sector plus purchases of capital goods and materials by the non-market sector.

non-market sector through the printing press. The latter has the same effect as a *tax* on all cash holdings. If printing money raises prices 10 per cent, market sector workers with cash of £100 will find they can only buy real goods and services which used to be worth £90. The other £10 their cash can no longer buy can then go to soldiers, pensioners and civil servants. Ultimately therefore, the great bulk of the non-market sector is tax-financed, whether the budget is balanced or not, but the tax will be an inflation tax on cash balances rather than a more obvious method of taxation where governments have to resort to the printing press because regular taxes will not suffice to finance non-market spending.[2]

1. How Smooth Growth to a Larger Non-Market Sector can be Achieved

The fact that the market sector ultimately finances the non-market sector does not mean that it is more important to the wellbeing of a society. Welfare and civilization depend on the efficiency of agriculture, industry and commerce, and equally on the effectiveness of education, health services, welfare systems, crime prevention and much more that is not bought and sold. In 1759 François Quesnay also listed "the beautification of the Kingdom" among the objectives of an economy:[3] he was right, and such eighteenth century objectives which cannot be measured in monetary units are often ignored by today's economists.

The expenditure patterns of the wealthy show that on average they spend more than the poor as a fraction of income on education, health, personal security and the arts. Therefore, it is reasonable to assume that as economic resources per head increase, the average citizen will expect a higher fraction of a nation's income to be spent on the improved education of his children, better medical treatment, greater security for his family and his property, and more opportunities to enjoy the theatre, music and opera which the wealthy value. It is consequently to be expected that a society will spend an increasing fraction of its resources in these directions as real incomes grow. If education and health are not marketed, and to a great extent they are not in modern societies, then non-market expenditures can be expected to grow, decade by decade, in relation to marketed output. If they did not, societies would be failing to raise consumption in the ways that consumers prefer when, like the wealthy, they are free to choose.

In addition, increasing numbers in many countries have come to

[2] The argument that excessive printing of money acts as an inflation tax on cash balances was set out by Keynes in his account of the German hyperinflation in *A Tract on Monetary Reform* (London, 1924) ch. II, 'Inflation as a Method of Taxation'.
[3] *Quesnay's Tableau Economique*, M. Kuczynski and R. L. Meek (eds.) (London, 1972), 3rd ed. (1759), p. 20.

consider that the co-existence of extremes of poverty and wealth in the same society are unacceptable. Hence there has been growing pressure to raise standards of support for non-producers such as pensioners and the unemployed, in relation to the average earnings of employed workers. This has necessarily raised the ratio of transfer payments to the National Income.

The fact that a growing share of resources to the non-market sector makes economic and social sense does not mean that the rule that the non-market sector must be financed from the surplus of the market sector can be broken. This rule must always be followed by any society which seeks to avoid economic breakdown. A failure to finance the non-market sector from the surplus of the market sector can only result in balance of payments collapse as efforts are made to use the resources of foreigners to provide what a population is unwilling to pay for, or physical shortages of capital as a society consumes its seed-corn in the form of extra social services, and so fails to maintain the employment creating capacity of its capital stock.

There are various ways in which economies can be destroyed by a failure to finance the non-market sector from the surplus of the market sector, but before these are explained in detail, the model of an ideal development of the non-market and market economies through time will be set out.

Suppose that for the reasons which have been explained, as a society becomes richer its population wishes to raise its spending on the resources the non-market sector provides one-and-a-half times as fast as on private consumption. Then whenever output per worker rises say 10 per cent, non-market spending per worker will rise, for instance, 12 per cent, while spending on the products of the market sector will then increase 8 per cent. Therefore, as the society progresses, each 10 per cent rise in average output per worker will allow social spending per family to rise 4 per cent more rapidly than private spending.

Over a longer period in which output per worker doubles, a rise in the non-market sector's share of marketed output of about 5 per cent from say 35 to 40 per cent will suffice to raise the resources available to the non-market sector about one-and-a-half times as fast as those which go to the average market sector worker, and this is illustrated in Table 7.1. The overall tax rate would need to rise by about 5 per cent in the market sector in the twenty to fifty year period over which output per worker doubles in this table, because the market sector is able to purchase 70 per cent of its own output at the beginning of the period and only 65 per cent at the end.

This example shows the effect of assumptions which are extremely favourable to the non-market sector, namely that a community wishes to increase unmarketed public services and pensions one-and-a-half times

TABLE 7.1.
The Non-Market Sector Grows
One-and-a-Half Times as Fast as the Market Sector

			Increase
Net Output per Worker	100	200	100%
Purchased by the Market Sector per Worker Employed	65 (65%)	120 (60%)	84.6%
Purchased by the Non-Market Sector per Worker Employed	35 (35%)	80 (40%)	128.6%

Non-Market Purchases rise 1.52 times as Fast as Market Sector Purchases

as fast per worker as the marketed output that is consumed privately by those who produce it. If the preference for unmarketed public services is weaker than this, taxation will need to rise less quickly than in the table. It will not need to rise at all if there is no desire that public services should grow faster than private consumption, and this will presumably be the case at some very high income level, because no population is likely to wish to increase taxation indefinitely, when its social services are already extensive.

The principal condition which must be fulfilled if a continuous transfer of resources from the market to the non-market sector of the kind illustrated is to be achieved is that the increase in taxation should be realized without damage to the underlying structure of production in the economy. What this requires is that extra taxation should be paid without damaging those economic activities which finance necessary imports and the capital investment which is indispensable to growth and long-term job creation. Taxation must therefore be paid from the surplus of the market sector and not with the economy's seed corn. If extra taxation leads to the substitution of public for private *consumption*, there can be no damage to the underlying structure of production. Workers produce for the non-market sector what they would otherwise produce for the market sector, and the government allocates what would otherwise be distributed by market forces. As private consumption foregone pays for extra public consumption, there is no damage to the balance of payments or to investment in job creation and growth. The economy can, therefore, grow as fast, provide as many jobs, and pay for the same imports, but services are given away which would otherwise be paid for, including pension rights which would otherwise require private insurance policies.

For this transfer from private consumption to the 'social wage' to be achieved, workers must either acquiesce in the continuous increase in

Public Sector Growth and Growth of the National Product 123

rates of taxation that is needed or alternatively governments must have adequate powers to ensure that workers will not pass the extra taxes on so that they fall on capital investment or the balance of payments.

It is, of course, vital if such acquiescence is to be achieved that the output of social services should rise as rapidly as expenditures upon them. If there is a preference for extra education, and taxation is raised continuously to finance it, while each generation of children is worse educated than the one before, either because the extra money is spent on administration instead of teaching, or because teachers fail to teach the technical skills which later life will require, taxpayers may not regard the extra 'social wage' as adequate compensation for private consumption foregone. In the ideal conditions assumed, it is therefore necessary that the non-market sector be as efficient as the market sector. A society will then be substituting unmarketed public services which are as efficiently produced as private goods and services for the extra private consumption it would otherwise obtain. Workers then obtain a combination of private and public goods and services which they can sensibly prefer to alternative combinations where there are fewer public goods and services. If the non-market sector is consistently less efficient, it is unlikely that combinations which take increasing fractions from this inefficient sector will be rationally preferred.

Finally, it is not enough that a continuous relative shift of resources into the non-market sector be acceptable to the average worker. Workers with above average incomes may regard the increasing 'social wage' they obtain (which will generally be no greater than the increase in the average worker's 'social wage') inadequate compensation for the above average taxes they will be expected to pay with progressive taxation. Ideally the increasing equality involved in an ever growing non-market share will need to be acceptable to a whole community and not merely to a majority, or to workers with average or below average incomes. Dissatisfied minorities of the better off can disrupt and interrupt a smooth progression to an ever growing non-market sector.

Difficulties have arisen in a number of countries since 1960 because the growth of the non-market sector at the expense of the market sector has not taken this ideal form. The difficulties that can arise are best illustrated by considering three general cases where economies or regions within economies have been destablized because extra rapid non-market sector growth prevented the market sector from growing as it should. These cases are first the British one where the non-market sector grew far more rapidly than in the example which has been illustrated, with the result that it grew largely at the expense of capital investment and not consumption. The second case is that of New York City where extra rapid growth of the non-market sector produced a destabilizing movement of market sector employment out of the city and of welfare receipients into it to produce all but insoluble social and financial problems. Finally, something will be said about the abortive revolutions in Chile and Portugal where attempts to superimpose a vastly greater non-market sector on a market sector which was simultaneously reducing output led to financial collapse and a loss of power by those who sought to produce a new society.

If the world's market sectors grow more slowly in the 1980s and 1990s than in the 1950s and 1960s as is now widely expected, other countries will be destabilized in similiar ways if they fail to reduce the growth of their non-market sectors to the new and slower rates which their market sectors can finance.

2. The Destabilization of Britain

The British case with which this examination of modern error will begin is illustrated in Table 7.2.[4]

TABLE 7.2.
*The Shift from the Market
to the Non-Market Sector in Britain: 1964–73*

	1964	1973	Increase
Net Output per Worker	100	126.6	26.6%
Purchased by the Market Sector per Worker Employed	66.0 (66.0%)	76.2 (60.2%)	15.5%
Purchased by the Non-Market Sector per Worker Employed	34.0 (34.0%)	50.4 (39.8%)	48.2%

Non-Market Purchases rise 3.1 times as fast as Market Sector Purchases

This shows that the average rate of taxation on market sector output rose considerably faster than in the previous example in Britain from 1964 to 1973, the last full year before the start of the world recession. The non-market share rose a great deal more from 1973 to 1976 but this was partly due to lack of growth of market sector output because of exceptionally unfavourable trading conditions during the recession. The period 1964-73 shown in the table was uninfluenced by such adverse factors and 1964 and 1973 are both expansion years which can safely be compared—and this period shows disproportionate non-market sector

[4]The statistical methods used to arrive at the split between market and non-market sector purchases in Britain were set out in general terms in R. Bacon and W. Eltis, *Britain's Economic Problem: Too Few Producers*, 2nd ed. (London, 1978), pp.243-7, and refined in their 'The Measurement of the Growth of the Non-market sector: and its influence' *Economic Journal*, Vol. 89, June 1979.

growth. In the previous example, non-market purchases of goods and services increased one-and-a-half times as quickly as market sector purchases per worker. But in Britain from 1964 to 1973 they actually increased over three times as fast. Personal preferences may give priority to public services over private consumption, but it is not plausible that many will wish the public services to grow over three times as fast. The increase in taxation involved in what occurred averaged about 6 per cent in the nine years in which output per worker rose 26.6 per cent in contrast to the previous example where a smaller increase in taxation was needed in a period over which output per worker doubled (about twenty-seven years at the British rate of growth) and the non-market sector grew one-and-a-half times as quickly as the market sector. Britain therefore compressed over twenty-seven years of increased taxation into a nine year period. The average worker with ordinary earnings was expected to pay the increased taxes like the rest of the community, and deductions from the average worker's paypacket increased by 6.7 pence in the pound from 1964 to 1973,[5] slightly more than the 5.8 per cent increase in average taxation indicated in the table.

It is reasonable to suppose that what occurred went much further than actual preferences in the community for higher public consumption. British workers wanted extra private consumption also. Many were unable to afford car ownership: many ate far less meat than they wished even before Britain joined the European Economic Community; many aspired to house ownership (55 per cent of British families live in houses they own) and house ownership was becoming increasingly expensive. Certainly more public services were desired, but it was desired that private consumption should rise rapidly also. It is probable that politicians of all British political parties appreciated this, but they made two major errors of analysis which led to the position illustrated in the table.

The first error was due to the Keynesism that dominated British economic thought and analysis across the whole political spectrum from 1964 to 1973.[6] There were thought to be unemployed resources in most years from 1964 to 1973, so few British politicians or civil servants or academic economists believed that extra growth of the non-market sector cost anything. On the contrary, all had been taught or themselves taught that each extra pound sterling spent by the non-market sector increased total incomes by between two and three pounds

---

[5] The statistical basis for this calculation is set out in Bacon and Eltis, op. cit. pp. 210–3.
[6] The line of argument set out here is developed more fully in Walter Eltis, 'The Failure of the Keynesian Conventional Wisdom', *Lloyds Bank Review* (Oct. 1976). See also Lord Kahn's reply 'Mr. Eltis and the Keynesians' (Apr. 1977), And my Rejoinder (July 1977).

126   *Slow Growth in Britain*

(to follow Keynes's own estimate of Lord Kahn's multiplier—the concept which taught two generations of English speaking economists that you can expand your cake and eat it faster at the same time), so the British happily allowed the non-market sector to increase at rapid rates in relation to the growth of the remainder of the economy whenever they wished to expand demand and production. It rarely occurred to those in power or their advisers that extra social spending would eventually need to be paid for. Therefore at election time, all political parties promised more expenditure on the social services and more private consumption also without ever indicating that taxation would need to rise to pay for the enlarged non-market sector. Voters never actually chose the growth imbalance which occurred. Instead they voted for more of everything many times.

The second error Britain made was that where governments actually made· long-term expenditure plans, the rate of growth on which the plans were based was overestimated. The long-term rate of growth of British expenditure on the social services was consistently based on the assumption that Britain would achieve a rate of growth of final out-put of around 4 per cent.[7] In reality, production grew by only 2.8 per cent a year from 1964 to 1973. An economy growing at 4 per cent could have financed the increases in social expenditures which occurred with much smaller increases in taxation, and far more growth of private consumption than was actually achieved. It will be seen that the rapid non-market sector growth itself contributed to the slow growth of the economy which undermined the financial foundations of the social services.

Britain's third error was to fail to ensure that the non-market sector would be managed as efficiently as the market sector. In the hospital service, for instance, there was a 51 per cent increase in the number of hospital administrators from 1965 to 1973 and an 11 per cent fall in the number of beds they were administering.[8] It took longer for the sick to get into hospital as waiting lists grew from year to year, but the real cost of administering each bed grew over 60 per cent. In British state education, employment grew 54 per cent from 1964 to 1974, but only 51 per cent of those employed actually taught anyone. The other 49 per cent administered, cleaned, served meals, but did not directly educate.[9] Vast sums also went on prestige projects, for instance, Concorde, instead of on goods and services which would have genuinely raised

[7]See *Growth of the United Kingdom Economy to 1966* (H.M.S.O., 1963); and *The National Plan* cmnd. 2764 (H.M.S.O., 1965).
[8]See Dr. Max Gammon, *Manpower and Number of Beds Occupied Daily 1965–73, UK N.H.S. Hospital Service*, St. Michael's Organisation (London, 1975).
[9]*Department of Employment Gazette* (1974), p. 1141.

the 'social wage'. These are just examples of what occurred. There was a widespread belief that much of the non-market sector was not giving full value for the taxes deducted to finance it.

Whether for this reason, or because it was allowed to grow far faster than workers' preferences for public goods, there was a clear departure from the ideal conditions for non-market sector growth which have been outlined. Workers did not acquiesce in the increased taxation that was needed to finance the extra-rapid growth of the non-market sector, and they therefore made every effort to increase their private consumption at rates almost as fast as public consumption was growing. Private real market sector incomes grew about 1.6 per cent per annum for each worker employed from 1964 to 1973 which was a far slower rate of increase than workers had obtained in the previous decade, and continued to expect. Each individual group of workers could only increase their private consumable income at more than 1.6 per cent per annum by gaining wage increases which were larger than those that other groups of workers were obtaining or by raising wages exceptionally at the expense of profits. Union leaders who were particularly likely to push for exceptional wage increases without inhibitions about the methods used to obtain them were therefore increasingly elected to positions of power in the labour movement, and these were often on the extreme left politically. Individual trade unions then went on to exploit each particular advantage they possessed regardless of the damage they were causing to the economy and the rest of the community. The coalminers demonstrated that the country could not function without electricity and obtained very large wage increases after long and significant strikes which set a lead for other settlements. The dockers also demonstrated their power and extracted for their members (partly in the form of high redundancy payments) a high fraction of the potential surplus value resulting from the technical advance of containerization. Most of the unions with the opportunity to obtain exceptional wage increases by disrupting the productive process did so with the result that money wages started to rise far faster than before. There is some rate of unemployment which would have checked this inflation—monetarists call this the 'natural' rate of unemployment—but the greater militancy of the trade unions raised this critical unemployment rate. Hence successive British governments were faced with the choice of either far more inflation than before if they maintained traditional unemployment rates, or else a much higher unemployment rate to check inflation. They found both of these alternatives unacceptable and introduced a series of official 'incomes policies' in their attempts to avoid having to choose between intolerable inflation and intolerable unemployment. In these the trade unions agreed to wage restraint for two years at a time, but only in exchange for a series of concessions which included price controls that

128   *Slow Growth in Britain*

severely reduced profits.

The unions managed to raise the share of wages in two additional ways. More militant union leadership at the local level meant that much of the surplus value resulting from technical advance which previously went to profits now went to wages instead, for workers only agreed to work new plant if much higher wages were paid or they were compensated in some other way. In addition, the more militant trade union leadership that resulted from workers' frustration increased the political power of the working class in the Marxist sense with the result that a considerable amount of legislation was passed which reduced companies' property rights. Companies therefore found it more difficult to choose the employment level of a factory (since they were often obliged to continue to employ workers whom they would have preferred to declare redundant), and they could not easily obtain possession of a factory or goods in it against the wishes of the unions in their area. This meant that companies earned lower profits from a given capital stock than before. As they also earned lower profits from the introduction of new technology, and less profit as a result of the government price controls which were frequently introduced, the share of wages rose markedly at the expense of the share of profits. In fact from 1964 to 1973 the share of profits fell by almost precisely the 5.8 per cent of output by which the non-market share rose, while the share of wages and salaries in the National Income increased.[10] Workers were therefore able to compensate for some of the 6.7 pence in the pound increase in taxation which fell on them by squeezing the share of profits, and raising the share of wages and salaries in the National Income. Their private consumption could therefore rise almost as fast as output, while the cost of financing the rapid growth of the non-market sector fell largely on profits. The non-market sector was therefore financed, not at the expense of consumption, but to an increasing extent at the expense of investment and the balance of payments, because the profits squeeze soon led to an investment squeeze. This was especially the case in industry where union pressures were strongest and profits were squeezed most,[11] and net industrial investment actually fell 46.2 per cent in 1964–73. In Industry the link

[10]In 1964 British Industrial and Commercial companies earned trading profits domestically of £3530m net of stock appreciation of £238m and capital consumption of £1072m, while the net national income was £26981m. In 1973 profits were £4268m net of these, while the national income was £57451m so that the share of net profits on this basis fell from 13.1 per cent of the national income in 1964 to 7.4 per cent in 1973. (*National Income and Expenditure* (H.M.S.O., 1964–74), Tables 1, 34 and 35.)

[11]See Bacon and Eltis, op. cit. (1978), pp. 231–8 for a comparison between profits in manufacturing companies and in British companies as a whole. The results are illustrated in Charts 11.1 and 11.2, pp. 21–2.

between investment and job creation is especially strong. It sometimes pays to put up buildings which provide little extra employment,
but new factories always need to be manned. It will be seen that the
fall in industrial investment had extremely serious consequences for the
economy.

It is to be noted that if the non-market sector's share in marketed
output rises as it did in Britain, while the consumption share of market
sector workers does not fall correspondingly, then the share of investment
and net exports (that is, exports less imports) must necessarily fall—as it
did in Britain. What actually happens is partly that the accompanying
profits squeeze may immediately incline companies to spend less on
investment, on research and development and on product promotion in
home and overseas markets—and this happened in Britain to a certain
extent. If, however, companies persist in expanding investment, despite
the profits squeeze, simple arithmetic decrees that the current account
of the balance of payments must then move sharply into deficit, for the
share of government and workers' consumption cannot rise without a
corresponding fall in the share of *net exports plus investment*. What
happens here in practice is that when output is near to its capacity limits,
investment *plus* net exports are crushed between the irreducible shares
of government and workers' consumption. If investment does not give
way of its own accord because profits are being squeezed, there is
absolutely certain to be a large import surplus corresponding to the
increased share of government and workers' consumption. If the import
surplus cannot be sustained, and this has been persistently the case in
Britain, governments necessarily respond by deflating the economy
which pulls job-creating investment down. Hence when the non-market
share of output rises, job creating investment falls, either because profits
are squeezed, or because of the effects of balance of payments deficits
on government policies and the adverse effects these will then have on
investment. In the simplest possible terms, investment and net exports
together must give way at full capacity working if the government and
workers together insist on taking a larger share of marketed output. If
the current account of the balance of payments must be balanced over
a period of years—and this was certainly the case in Britain—then the
cost of an increase in the government share must fall in one way or
another on investment. There is no other possibility.

Hence, Britain's non-market sector grew, not at the expense of the
economy's consumable surplus which any society can afford, but instead
at the expense of investment in job creation, the economy's seed-corn.
The effect of what happened was that employment in British industry
fell at a rate of 155,000 a year from 1966 until 1973, the final year
before the world recession. Therefore even before the beginning of the
recession, British industry had already lost 1,087,000 jobs. It lost these

130   Slow Growth in Britain

partly because of the fall in investment that resulted from the profits squeeze and the deflationary policies which followed balance of payments weaknesses, and partly because the union pressures which have been outlined made labour extremely expensive to companies so that they had strong incentives to substitute capital for labour. Hence such investments as firms managed to make created fewer jobs than before because each new job cost far more in real terms, and the new jobs were therefore insufficient to make good all the jobs any economy must lose each year because of the obsolescence of plant, wear and tear and technical change and improved designs in the rest of the world. An American study has estimated that 57 per cent of industrial jobs are lost each decade throughout the USA for these reasons, and these have to be made good through the creation of new jobs which will often involve new designs and new technologies.[12] The position in Britain is almost certainly comparable, and there was simply too little investment to create enough new jobs to make good those that were lost. Hence the industrial part of the market sector employed fewer and fewer people. Fortunately the private services raised their employment slightly so that overall market sector employment fell less than industrial employment—in fact by 625,000 from 1966 to 1973, but in the same period non-market employment rose by 810,000 so that in a mere seven years—and seven years of world expansion at that — self-financing employment fell over half a million, and tax dependent employment rose almost a million. Table 7.3 shows what would happen in Britain if that trend continues, and the total British labour force grows at the rate which is now expected.[13]

TABLE 7.3.

British Employment if the Trends of 1966-73 Continue

	1966	1973	1976	1980	1987
Total Labour Force	25,066,000	25,545,000	26,136,000	26,466,000	27,388,000
Self Financing Employment	20,707,000	20,082,000	19,467,000	19,457,000	18,832,000
Tax Dependent Employment	4,078,000	4,888,000	5,337,000	5,698,000	6,508,000
Unemployment	281,000	575,000	1,332,000	1,311,000	2,048,000
Number of Market-Sector Workers Available to Finance each Non-Market Worker	4.75	3.68	2.92	2.78	2.20

[12] See G. Breckenfeld, 'Business Loves the Sun Belt (and Vice Versa)' *Fortune*, June 1977.
[13] This Table is derived from data in the *Department of Employment Gazette*, the *Annual Abstract of Statistics, Economic Trends* and *National Income and Expenditure*. Table 1.11. It is assumed that the labour force will grow 0.5 per cent per annum from 1973 to 1987.

Public Sector Growth and Growth of the National Product 131

The continuation of past trends clearly produces an intolerable outcome, both because unemployment can be expected to rise to over three millions by 1987, and because the number of market sector workers who will be available to finance each non-producer of marketed output will fall from 4.75 in 1966 to 2.20 in 1987. From 1966 to 1973 British taxation had to rise sharply because the number of market sector producers available to finance each non-producer of marketed output fell from 4.75 to 3.68. If the same trends continue, only 2.78 producers will be available to finance each non-producer of marketed output in 1980 and only 2.20 in 1987. It is to be noted that the previous trend continued unchecked until 1976 when only 2.92 producers were available to finance each non-producer of marketed output. In 1966 there were 4.75. If this trend continues further, taxation will need to rise drastically for another decade, which would certainly mean that British governments would turn increasingly to the printing press with its consequent inflation 'tax' of cash balances to finance their expenditure. There were already tendencies in this direction in 1972–6 a period in which the non-market sector's share increased very rapidly. Conventional taxation just could not be increased to the extent needed if rapid non-market sector growth continues at the rate indicated in the table. If workers again succeeded in passing extra taxation on to companies as in 1966–73, profits would virtually disappear—they had become extremely low by 1974—and market sector employment would fall by more than the 89,000 per annum indicated, so unemployment would rise still faster than in the table. Soaring unemployment with a total collapse of company profitability and massive money printing by the government would certainly produce a crisis for British capitalism at some point in the 1980s.

This was well understood in Britain by 1976—at least in official circles. Early in that year the authorities decided that further growth in non-market employment would cease for a time. A glance at the table will show that this by no means suffices to correct Britain's growing structural imbalance. If tax-dependent non-market employment ceases to grow while market sector employment continues to decline by 89,000 a year, unemployment will grow all the faster.

In 1976 the British economy was in a trap. Employment in the market sector had been declining for ten years, but it is precisely the market sector which must ultimately finance the non-market sector and the consumption of the unemployed. Britain's Labour government of 1976 therefore had to attempt to reverse the decline of the market sector. To continue to expand the non-market sector, a Keynesian solution, through government inspired and financed job creation schemes, or further expansion of the public services, would have been no solution because it would have involved still higher taxation and worker frustration, or ever growing deficits involving an increasing use of the printing press to finance them.

The decline of market sector employment from 1966 to 1973 was largely due to the profits squeeze which reduced the real rate of return on British capital to as little as 3 or 4 per cent by 1973. Since 1973, the market sector has continued to cut employment, partly because of the world recession which began in 1974, and partly because it just could not afford to finance enough jobs to compensate for those lost as a result of technical progress and international competition. The government therefore had the urgent task of raising profitability in the market sector. It did this by deferring company taxation on profits that are the counterpart of inflation in the value of inventories, and by presiding over incomes policies in 1975-7 which cut the real wage by about 10 per cent so that profitability could be restored. British workers accepted the real wage cut because a collapse of the currency which few wanted was the obvious alternative. If these policies to raise company profitability are reinforced rather than reversed in 1978-80 and an internationally competitive currency is maintained so that British industrialists can earn adequate profits in export markets, British market sector employment could start to grow again after 1978 and the structural balance of the economy can start to be restored after this. Once it is, every four new market sector jobs created will provide the finance for one extra public service job at unchanged rates of taxation, so the creation of extra market sector jobs will have a multiplier effect on employment. It has already been pointed out that the belief that extra non-market jobs had a sustainable multiplier effect on employment contributed to Britain's policy errors and those of other English speaking countries.

The attempt to cure Britain's structural imbalance in 1976-7 was painful. In 1976-7 non-market employment fell 2 per cent as a result of the government's necessary economies, and market sector employment has continued to fall because government policies to help the market sector can only act slowly. Unemployment therefore increased to over 1,400,000 and the country has seen the government destroying public sector jobs at the very time that industry and commerce were also employing fewer people. That was a clear result of the imbalances of 1964-73. In that decade non-market sector growth was financed at the cost of investment instead of personal consumption. In consequence the market sector was unable to provide a sound financial foundation for growing non-market employment and jobs were destroyed in every sector of the economy in 1976 and 1977 because of this error. Once the market sector starts to expand again, employment in the non-market sector can begin to be restored, for the key point which Britain forgot and is painfully relearning is that it is a growing market sector which finances social welfare.

3. The Destabilization of New York

The imbalances created by rapid non-market sector growth in Britain have an extremely close parallel in North America, for New York's problems have been fundamentally the same. Non-market spending has increased still more rapidly in the United States than in Britain in recent decades.[14] There is, however, an important difference. In Britain the vast growth of non-market spending was predominantly financed by increases in national taxation because only a little over 10 per cent of total British taxation is local. In the United States over two-thirds of the increase in public spending and taxation from 1964-1974 was local—by states, cities, counties and townships. Federal taxation increased hardly at all as a share of output.[15] The difference would be immaterial if local taxation increased uniformly throughout the United States, but this is not at all what occurred. Taxation and public expenditure increased a great deal in some areas and hardly at all in others. In particular taxation and spending increased far more in the North and especially the North East than in the sun belt states. According to official United States statistics, a family of four paid about 10 cents in the dollar more in taxation in the four high tax cities, Boston, Buffalo, Milwaukee and New York, than in Houston, Jacksonville, Memphis and Nashville.[16] This difference is made up of higher state income taxes, higher property taxes, and higher local sales and corporation taxes. Companies to some extent compensate their workers for living in high tax areas like New York, so they earn less profit there, both because they are taxed more heavily themselves and because they have to pay higher salaries. Capital therefore tends to move out of the high tax neighbourhoods, so these acquire a diminishing ratio of market sector jobs. The expensive local non-market sector therefore has a diminishing productive base to support it as in Great Britain.

New York is a high tax city and real take home pay *fell* 3.5 per cent after all taxes in 1966-76[17] so workers paid for some of the rapid growth of its non-market sector, and companies have been expected to pay for the remainder. But their response has been to move more and more jobs out of New York, and market sector employment in the city fell from 3,130,000 in 1960 to 2,664,000 in 1976, a reduction of 15 per cent. The city's taxable surplus out of which its social services are

---

[14]See the statistical comparisons set out in Bacon and Eltis, op. cit. (1978), Ch. 6.
[15]See the *Statistical Abstract of the United States*, US Department of Commerce, Tables 418 and 425 of the 1976 edition, and equivalent tables in earlier editions.
[16]See the *Statistical Abstract of the United States*, US Department of Commerce, Table 450 of the 1976 edition.
[17]See the account of a New York State Labour Department study in the *New York Times* on May 15th, 1977.

financed has been moving South. In the same period non-market employment in New York City increased over 30 per cent. From 1960 to 1974 non-market employment actually increased 42 per cent. Then came the financial crisis and in the next two years public sector jobs had to be cut back by 50,000 at the very time that market sector jobs were also declining—by over 200,000.[18] The extra rapid initial expansion of non-market jobs with consequent local tax increases therefore contributed to a situation where market sector jobs were lost as firms moved out and contracted employment—until in the end both sectors were forced to cut employment at the same time exactly as in Great Britain.

There is a further important effect. United States evidence suggests that the better paid salaried workers move out of the high tax areas towards low tax ones.[19] At the same time, the poor move into the high tax and high public benefit areas. A former mayor of Houston put it colourfully. "Houston is a good place to be if you want to work. If you don't want to work you might get a better deal in New York."[20] As the rich and potential high earners move out of the high tax areas and the poor move in a vast unstable movement begins. The potential high tax payers congregate in areas where there is a wealth of skill in the population, and few poor people to support. In other areas, the unskilled and the deprived congregate, and there are a diminishing number of skilled workers to pay the taxes to support them, and to provide a magnet to market sector industry and commerce. These trends are slow but they are socially devastating. In New York City which has suffered from both a loss of market sector jobs and an influx of would-be beneficiaries from New York's fuller social services, unemployment increased from 4.8 per cent in 1970 to 10.6 per cent in 1976. In addition, employment in the 16-19 age group fell from 30 per cent in 1970 to a disastrous 22 per cent in 1976.[21] Among the ethnic minority groups, employment fell to a mere 14 per cent in this age group so the young had extremely few lawful opportunities to achieve living standards above the welfare minimum.

By contrast, in low tax Houston, aggregate employment grew rapidly in both the market and the non-market sector and employment in the 16 to 19 age group rose from 41 to 47 per cent from 1970 to 1976.

The destabilization of New York illustrates a general problem. In an

---

[18]See the *Thirteenth Interim Report* of the Temporary Commission on City Finances, New York City (May 1977), p. 15.
[19]See, for instance, J. R. Aronson and E. Schwarz, 'Financing Public Goods and the Distribution of Population in a System of Local Governments', *National Tax Journal* (June 1963).
[20]See Breckenfeld, op. cit.
[21]See the accounts of a United States Federal Government study in the *New York Times* on August 2nd and 7th, 1977.

economic area like the United States where capital and people can move freely, any region which offers non-market standards which are more expensive than companies and the better off wish to pay for is liable to suffer the gradual erosion of its productive base. Capital will leave a region where net of tax returns are below average. Some of the better off will leave an area where the benefits from the non-market sector social services are less than tax costs at their income level. The conditions for a smooth transition to a larger non-market sector which were outlined earlier are breached where the better off do not accept the redistributive element in higher taxation and have the power to react against it. Once capital and the better off start to depart, the high tax and high benefit areas must either cut public sector employment because they are losing the tax revenues which finance it, or they must raise rates of taxation still more. The latter will drive yet more taxpayers out and bring the final financial crisis nearer.

It is to be noted that if a combination of high non-market expenditure and high-taxation was attractive to the skilled and highly paid, they would move into the high tax areas and not away from them. The studies quoted suggest that what deters them from doing so is the redistributive element in the taxation that they are asked to pay. They can finance their own social services and have something left over in a low tax area. A further point is that, as in Britain, high taxation and high public expenditure often involves a proliferation of administrative expenditures and not the output of more public goods.

New York is the obvious example where instability due to these effects has gone furthest, but there are other cities and provinces which face similar difficulties. The Californian electorate has sought to avert them, well in advance, by passing the now celebrated proposition 13 to limit local spending in California. In Canada, Quebec has income tax rates which exceed those in the remainder of Canada by 6 cents in the dollar or more at the higher income levels, regulations which seek to enforce a higher minimum wage and further restrictions (obligations on Quebec based companies to do business in French) which are unattractive to many employers. Capital is therefore leaving Quebec which already has an unemployment rate one-and-a-half times the Canadian average.

Quebec like New York needs growing market sector employment so both are under overwhelming pressure to reverse the policies which have persuaded companies to locate elsewhere, and if the pressure is not obvious now in Quebec's case, it soon will be. If the European Economic Community continues to move towards truly free labour and capital mobility, Europe too will have its New Yorks and Quebecs. The problem is fundamentally that no city or province or country within a large economic union where labour and capital is free to move can afford to be relatively unattractive to the companies which create market sector

136   Slow Growth in Britain

jobs. These jobs will leave at a rate of 1 or 2 per cent a year and this will suffice over two decades to remove the foundations on which the financing of the non-market-sector rests.

4. The Destabilization of Chile

A final example of how rapid non-market sector growth can destabilize an economy is the case of a mismanaged revolution. Chile provides an example where statistics are beginning to emerge, and it is likely that Portugese figures will tell a similar story once they become available for the revolutionary period.

After Allende was elected President of Chile in September 1970, the rate of growth of government final consumption (which increased more slowly than government expenditure as a whole) rose from 2.2 per cent per annum for each worker employed to 7.0 per cent per annum. This would have involved increased taxation in itself but not necessarily an unacceptable rate of increase in taxation, at least in the short term, given the fact that many had voted for significant change—and that tax revenues would grow 2.2 per cent per annum for each worker with unchanged tax rates if the previous rate of growth of productivity of 2.2 per cent per annum was maintained.[22] What would have happened in 1970-3 would then have been something like the outcome set out in Table 7.4.[23] With this pattern of growth, the non-market sector would have grown about fifteen times as fast as the market sector.

What actually happened was far more serious for the market sector. For various reasons the previous rate of growth of productivity of 2.2 per cent per annum was not maintained after 1970. Indeed, according to ILO data, productivity fell 4 per cent in 1970-3. It fell for a number

---

[22] See the United Nations *Statistical Yearbook* for 1975, Tables 189-90, and the ILO *Year Book of Labour Statistics* for 1971 and 1976. Table 17 in the ILO Yearbook indicates that Chile's overall rate of growth of labour productivity was 2.2 per cent per annum in 1961-70 and −1.3 per cent per annum in 1970-3. It is inferred from this series and the United Nations' Table 189 that employment rose at a rate of 2.5 per cent per annum in both 1961-70 and 1970-3, and this information is needed to infer the rate of growth of government consumption *per worker* from the data in Table 189. It is assumed that the increase in government consumption in 1970-4 occurred entirely in the Allende years of 1970-3 for which a separate figure is not available.

[23] The basis for the assumptions about productivity growth and the growth of government spending in this table is set out in note 22 above, and the growth of government spending is if anything understated by using the growth of government consumption as a basis (see Table 201 of the UN *Statistical Yearbook* for 1975). The ratio of non-market purchases to market output is set at 25 per cent in 1970 because the ratio of total government spending to the National Income was 25.8 per cent in that year (Tables 201 and 185) and there is insufficiently detailed data to permit a breakdown between market and non-market purchases in the case of Chile.

Public Sector Growth and Growth of the National Product *137*

TABLE 7.4.
What Could Have Happened in Chile in 1970-3 with Unchanged Productivity Growth

	1970	1973	Increase
Output per Worker	100	106	+ 6.7%
Purchased by the Market Sector per Worker Employed	75 (75%)	76.1 (71.3%)	+ 1.5%
Purchased by the Non-Market Sector per Worker employed	25 (25%)	30.6 (28.7%)	+ 22.4%

Non-Market Purchases rise 14.9 times as fast as Market-Sector Purchases

of reasons including in particular a cessation of capital accumulation in some factories and farms, with indeed failures to renew capital in many cases. In addition, the function of managing many of Chile's farms and factories was taken over by the working class and its elected government before the necessary skills to manage the nation's capital equipment successfully had been acquired. The ILO's statisticians do not suggest that this destroyed the market sector—merely that productivity fell about 4 per cent on average instead of rising by 6.7 per cent. Table 7.5 shows that this was quite enough to destabilize the economy in three years, given the 22.4 per cent increase in non-market spending which was now more than a declining economy could sustain.

TABLE 7.5
What Happened in Chile in 1970-3

	1970	1973	Increase
Output per Worker	100	96	− 4%
Purchased by the Market Sector per Worker Employed	75 (75%)	65.4 (68.1%)	− 12.8%
Purchased by the Non-Market Sector per Worker Employed	25 (25%)	30.6 (31.9%)	+ 22.4%

The market sector which produces all investment all exports and all private consumer goods and services had 12.8 per cent less per worker in 1973 than in 1970. In consequence exports, private consumption and investment all fell. Investment per worker fell 16 per cent, while exports fell 8 per cent.[24] The fall in exports played its part in Chile's

[24]These figures are derived from Table 189 of the United Nations *Statistical Yearbook*, the growth of employment being inferred as in note 22, p.136. It is inferred that the reductions in exports and investment in 1970-4 were concentrated in the three years, 1970-3.

138   Slow Growth in Britain

balance of payments crises and the rapid destruction of the international value of the currency, but this was also due to the government's increasing resort to the printing press to finance its expenditures for conventional taxes could not be increased by 6.9 per cent of the National product in a mere three years. The fraction of expenditure financed by conventional taxes in fact fell from 87 per cent in 1970 to 65 per cent in 1973,[25] so up to one-third of the government's soaring expenditures were being financed by the printing press and consequent inflation taxes of cash balances by 1973. Conventional taxes might have financed an adequate proportion of expenditures if productivity had risen 6.7 per cent instead of falling 4 per cent in 1970-3, so this was a vital factor.

It is evident from the fact that exports per worker fell 8 per cent and investment 16 per cent that Chile failed to finance its increased social spending from the market sector's surplus. By presiding over policies which simultaneously reduced productivity and raised the real wage (where this includes the 'social wage'). the government destroyed most of the economy's surplus so that there was too little left for investment and the balance of payments. The Soviet Union was careful to precede its successful five year plans with the New Economic Policy which involved some use of capitalist managements in the early 1920s. Chile's and Portugal's Marxists in contrast preferred immediate reforms which sacrificed productivity and therefore most of their economies's potential surpluses of marketed output. If Marxists are to make more successful use of any future opportunities which European electorates may give them in the next decades, they will need to ensure that there are sufficient market sector surpluses in the period of transition to their preferred society for job creating investment and the provision of enough exportables to pay for necessary imports. If this is again forgotten, the New Left with its enthusiasm for immediate worker control, even at a cost of surplus destruction, will find that it has an infallible recipe for economic failure, and this is likely to be followed by political failure also, as in Chile and Portugal.

5. Conclusion

The world's viable economies are those which have an adequate market sector surplus to finance both the needs of the non-market sector and the job creation the economy requires. The examples of Britain, New York and Chile illustrate the slow or rapid destabilization which results if investment in job creation is neglected, or the surplus is destroyed.

The world's rate of growth of output has been much slower since 1973 than in the three previous decades. This may merely be the result of a recession which might conceivably prove temporary. Alternatively, the

[25]See the United Nations *Statistical Yearbook* for 1975, Table 201.

world may now have to face two or three decades of far slower growth. If the world's non-market sectors continue to grow at the rapid rates to which they became accustomed in the prosperous decades which followed the second world war, many countries will follow Britain, New York and Chile along the road to destabilization. A typical "successful" economy had a rate of growth of marketed output of 4 or 5 per cent per annum in 1950–73, and a rate of growth of real non-market expenditure of 6 or 7 per cent in this period. Hence non-market spending increased as fast as in Britain, but the economy's productive base typically increased about two-thirds as fast as rapidly growing non-market spending so taxation increased at an acceptable rate, given the rapid rate of growth of the National Product. Moreover, with 4 or 5 per cent real growth per annum, the market sector as well as the non-market sector obtained a rapid increase in real resources. If the rate of growth of marketed output now falls to 2 or 2.5 per cent in the typical "successful" economy, and real non-market spending continues to be expanded at 6 or 7 per cent each year, then a British style imbalance will begin to emerge in economies which have hitherto achieved balanced growth. 6 per cent non-market growth will cream off the entire growth of the economy if marketed output is only growing 2.5 per cent per annum, and this will leave no scope for increased private consumption in the market sector. If workers begin to pass on the consequent tax increases as in Britain, investment and the balance of payments will be undermined after a few years.

Therefore, if the 1980s and the 1990s prove to be decades of slow growth, the world's governments will have to become accustomed to far slower expansion in their own expenditures than in the prosperous 1950s and 1960s. If they continue to increase spending at the former rates—and this is bound to appear socially desirable to many—instead of the new and slower rates which market sector taxation will finance at tax rates workers are prepared to pay, destabilization will follow as surely as in Great Britain and New York. Other countries are certain to follow Great Britain's and New York's unwillingness to face the extra taxation needed to finance a sharp increase in the non-market sector's share. Like Britain and New York, they will therefore be drawn towards deficit financing, massive borrowing, and then the printing-press—which New York never had access to. Destabilization will certainly spread if it is not appreciated that when world growth decelerates, public expenditure must advance more slowly also.

PART IV

PRACTICAL MACROECONOMICS: HOW BORROWING AND INFLATION DESTABILIZE

The Failure of the Keynesian Conventional Wisdom

by Walter Eltis

It would be universally agreed today that Keynes's *General Theory of Employment, Interest and Money* is, together with Smith's *Wealth of Nations* and Marx's *Das Kapital* one of the three truly great books that political economists have written. It would also be widely agreed that it made a significant contribution to human welfare in the quarter-century after its publication. Those governments which, like Britain's, applied the tools that Keynes invented achieved full employment and, in addition, declining inflation rates for most of the 1950s.

But the 1960s and 1970s have been quite different. Inflation has accelerated throughout the world, and it must be particularly disturbing to Keynesian policy-makers that the countries where their influence was greatest are those which have suffered most. These countries, and Britain and Italy can be singled out, have suffered from faster inflation, slower growth, larger budget deficits and severer international currency collapses than their principal competitors where out-of-date pre-Keynesian methods of thought are still influential. So how is it, a sensible Keynesian might ask, that the countries where those in power and influence have the most correct understanding of how economies work manage to achieve the worst results and to be among the world's perpetual candidates for international financial support? Ironically, most of this has to come from countries which are managed in non-Keynesian ways.

One possibility is that Keynesian economists have been let down by the workers and managers of the countries they advise. This is a well-known explanation of

The author is a Fellow of Exeter College, Oxford, and currently Visiting Professor of Economics in the University of Toronto. In November 1975 he was co-author with Robert Bacon of the Declining Britain' articles in *The Sunday Times*, since republished in extended book form as *Britain's Economic Problem: Too Few Producers*, Macmillan, 1976. He is grateful to Robert Bacon and Nicholas Dimsdale for helpful comments on an earlier draft of this article.

1

Britain's failures, much favoured by Keynesians in British universities and in Whitehall, but the reverse is also possible. The time has surely now come to consider the possibility that the Keynesian conventional wisdom, so uncritically used as a guide for policy in *all* situations, has flaws which have had a devastating adverse effect on those countries where Keynesian economists have been influential. A strong case can indeed be made out that, in the hands of lesser men and women, certain Keynesian propositions are a recipe for international poverty and economic breakdown, rather than for growing wealth and prosperity, for they depend on assumptions which made sense in the Britain of the 1930s, but make none today.

All economic theories necessarily rest on unreal assumptions, and it is therefore vital that the simplifications made are those which can most safely be made. Keynesian theory rests on unreal assumptions no more and no less than others. The particular Keynesian simplifications which will be critically examined below are the following. First, that where there are unemployed resources, extra public investment, ie public works, raises the national income and employment until planned saving has risen by a corresponding amount. Second, that the only price which an increase in the money supply influences is the price of bonds. Third, that the rate of interest is determined by the quantity of money and liquidity preference and, finally, that the major influence on the level of output and employment in an economy is effective demand, so that hard work and the efficiency of resource allocation in the public and private sectors has a less significant effect on the wealth of nations than correct demand management policies Sophisticated Keynesians are of course aware that these crucial propositions rest on particular assumptions which may or may not be the most appropriate ones. But most Keynesians, like indeed most neo-classicals and most monetarists, are less sophisticated than that. Many Keynesian economists, not to mention those of their former pupils who are now senior civil servants, trade union leaders, journalists, broadcasters and politicians, still accept these propositions without serious qualification.

Public Expenditure and Employment

The proposition that extra government investment raises output and employment until planned saving has risen as much as planned investment is taught to British economics students at school or university as one of their first lessons in economics. More generally, it is explained at an equally early stage that extra government expenditure *of any kind* raises incomes and employment.

2

The Failure of the Keynesian Conventional Wisdom

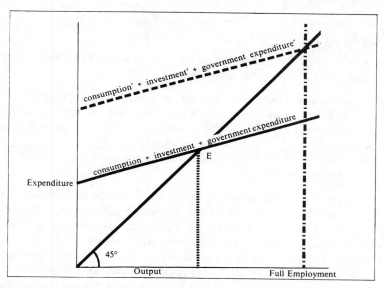

The Basic Equations

One of the basic diagrams which is used to explain this is illustrated here. The *consumption+investment+government expenditure* line shows the economy's aggregate expenditure, and the economy's equilibrium output must be where aggregate expenditure equals output, so it is at E where the expenditure line cuts the 45° line (where expenditure and output are equal). It intersects this below full employment and, therefore, the higher dashed expenditure line, *consumption' +investment'+government expenditure'* is needed if full employment is to be achieved. Therefore, to achieve full employment, governments must raise private consumption and investment and their own expenditures. As policy tools to raise private investment are notoriously inadequate, governments in practice raise *consumption+investment+government expenditure* by raising government expenditure and by raising private consumption through tax cuts. These are the traditional Keynesian recipes for full employment.

But the weakness in the argument is that it ignores international trade. In other words, it is true for the world as a whole, for all countries acting together, or for a great power acting on its own, but it does not work for a small country in international trade as Britain now is, and this can easily be shown.

With international trade included, the complete version of one of the celebrated Keynesian national income identities is as follows:

$$\text{government expenditure} + \text{private investment} + \text{exports} \equiv \text{taxation} + \text{private saving} + \text{imports}$$

and this equation can be rearranged as:

3

$$\left(\begin{array}{l}\text{government}\\\text{expenditure}\end{array} - \text{taxation}\right) \equiv \left(\begin{array}{l}\text{private}\\\text{saving}\end{array} - \begin{array}{l}\text{private}\\\text{investment}\end{array}\right) + (\text{imports} - \text{exports})$$

In other words, the budget deficit equals the balance-of-payments deficit *plus* the excess of private saving over investment.

Keynesian governments, faced by the situation illustrated in the diagram, consider it orthodox to raise *government expenditure* and cut *taxation* for the reasons that have been mentioned. These policies can be described as follows:

$$\underbrace{\left(\begin{array}{l}\text{government}\\\text{expenditure}\end{array}}_{+3\,000} - \underbrace{\text{taxation}}_{-3\,000}\right) \equiv \left(\begin{array}{l}\text{private}\\\text{saving}\end{array} - \begin{array}{l}\text{private}\\\text{investment}\end{array}\right) + (\text{imports} - \text{exports})$$

There is +3 000 under *government expenditure* and −3 000 under *taxation* to indicate that taxes have been cut by 3 000 and public expenditure increased by 3 000, policies like those which British and Italian governments have followed repeatedly in periods of unemployment. Now, these policies which have added 6 000 net to the left hand side of the identity must also add to the right hand side, and there is no doubt where the reader of an elementary Keynesian textbook would expect them to go. As in the diagram, a higher *consumption + investment + government expenditure* line will raise the national income and therefore *private saving*, and the national income will increase until private saving has risen sufficiently to finance the increase in the government's deficit. It does not need to rise by 6 000 because, at a higher national income, tax revenue will also be higher, and it will be supposed in the examples here that private saving and aggregate tax revenues rise equally as the national income rises, so these will both rise by 3 000. With 3 000 added to *private saving* and to *taxation* (which makes good the previous tax cuts), the Keynesian identity becomes:

$$\underbrace{\left(\begin{array}{l}\text{government}\\\text{expenditure}\end{array}}_{+3\,000} - \text{taxation}\right) \equiv \underbrace{\left(\begin{array}{l}\text{private}\\\text{saving}\end{array}}_{+3\,000} - \begin{array}{l}\text{private}\\\text{investment}\end{array}\right) + (\text{imports} - \text{exports})$$

Here extra *private saving* finances the increase in *government expenditure*. But that is not the end of the story. Expansion in the *national income* raises *private investment* as well as saving, albeit one year to eighteen months later, and in British booms since the second world war it has raised it about as much.[1] Theoretical accounts which fail to take this into account omit the initial

---

[1] For instance, from 1962 to 1965, private saving rose by £1 756 millions in Britain, while private investment (including investment in stocks) rose by £1 452 millions. From 1971 to 1974, private saving rose by £8 962 millions, while private investment (again including investment in stocks) rose by £9 038 millions. (*National Income and Expenditure*, 1973, Table 70, and 1964–74, Table 80.)

The Failure of the Keynesian Conventional Wisdom

celerator' or capital stock adjustment type effects of a change in the national ome on investment. Given that aggregate private savings and investment have en about equally in British booms, if we are to put +3 000 under *private ing*, we must also put +3 000 under *private investment*. And this leaves 3 000) much on the left hand side of the equation, unless we also add 3 000 to *ports—exports)*, the balance-of-payments deficit, which is what we must do to lance the identity. Hence, what truly happens is this:

$$\left(\begin{array}{c}\text{government} \\ \text{expenditure}\end{array} - \text{taxation}\right) \equiv \left(\begin{array}{c}\text{private} \\ \text{saving}\end{array} - \begin{array}{c}\text{private} \\ \text{investment}\end{array}\right) + (\text{imports} - \text{exports})$$

$$+3\ 000 \qquad\qquad +3\ 000 \quad +3\ 000 \qquad +4\ 500 \quad +1\ 500$$

vate investment rises just as much as *saving* in the course of expansion, and *orts* rise far faster than *exports*. Expansion favours exports slightly, but to lance the equation imports rise three times as fast. Hence, the ultimate effect the Keynesian deficit-financed expansion is to destroy the balance of payments. e Keynesian expansion to full employment through increased government ending contains a time-bomb in the form of an inevitable built-in collapse of : balance of payments. This then brings these Keynesian booms to an end as on as their balance-of-payments consequences become intolerable. This has ppened many times in Britain. Moreover, after the collapse of the boom, itish governments have had to maintain output at lower levels than it would ierwise need to be because of the balance of payments—so it is not clear that ise Keynesian deficit-financed booms raise output and employment at all in : long term.

ith further superficial thinking, orthodox Keynesian policies can be made to oduce results which differ still more from what Keynesians expect to achieve. ie problem with the expansion policies which have been outlined is that there is ly *one* policy lever, demand expansion by unbalancing the budget, while ire are *two* objectives, full employment and balance-of-payments equilibrium. , given the rule that there must be at least one policy lever for each objective, extra policy lever is needed. To meet this difficulty, it is widely supposed that, the government increases its expenditure *and devalues its currency at the same ie*, it will have the extra policy lever which will prevent the 3 000 under *ernment expenditure* from going to (*imports—exports*) to destroy the balance payments.

we have that historical low point of British economic management, the .rber boom of 1971–3 with vast government expenditure increases and tax ts and an 18 per cent devaluation in addition, the recipe for what may lay iims to be the most mismanaged boom since the publication of *The General*

5

Lloyds Bank Review

Theory. Of course *private investment* again rose about as much as *private saving* so that the balance of payments again deteriorated as much as the budget, in spite of devaluation. And all that the extra ingredient of devaluation achieved was a 4 per cent addition to Britain's rate of inflation, with food and commodity prices rising faster in Britain than in other major economies. The British Keynesians maintain that the rise in commodity prices in 1971–4 had nothing to do with their domestic policies, but it was these that produced a situation where commodity prices rose 40 per cent more in sterling than in Deutschemarks, which goes a long way to explain the greater inflationary strains that Britain experienced.

Three Ways to Increase Employment

Some of Cambridge's most senior economists were among the first to see through the argument that budget deficits and devaluation should be combined to take the economy to full employment and balanced trade.[1] They saw that *in expansion*, if the balance of payments is not to be destroyed, *government expenditure* and *taxation* must rise together since *private saving* and *private investment* rise together. And there are just three ways in which Keynesians can seek to raise employment if they accept this.

First, employment can be raised through beggar-my-neighbour measures against foreigners. With the budget held stable, employment can be raised through a return to the competitive devaluations and tariff wars of the 1930s, which raise employment by raising exports or cutting imports. But in a world recession the policies will be as self-frustrating as in the 1930s if several countries attempt to follow them at the same time. The Cambridge economists who favour this approach must therefore be persuasive enough to convert the British government without being so persuasive that they also convert foreigners, a delicate task in which they are at present succeeding.

A second way in which employment can be raised is by raising *government expenditure* and *taxation* equally and at the same time, for effective demand and employment will be higher in an economy with more public expenditure and taxation than in one with a smaller balanced budget (as a result of the 'balanced budget multiplier'). But this policy to achieve full employment through a large balanced budget entails more taxation at higher levels of public expenditure and employment. As taxes and public expenditure rise, a higher

[1]See, for instance, N Kaldor, 'Conflicts in national economic objectives', *The Economic Journal* Vol 81, March 1971; and R R Nield's articles in *The Times* on 19 and 20 July, 1973.

The Failure of the Keynesian Conventional Wisdom

d possibly growing) fraction of the labour force becomes dependent for its
ployment on the taxes paid by those workers who are not in tax-dependent
lic sector jobs. And if workers resist the payment of rising rates of taxation
keep others in employment, the result will be accelerating inflation and a
fits squeeze increasing still further the need for extra tax-dependent jobs.
is can lead all too easily into a spiral where extra tax-dependent job creation
ults in the creation of fewer self-financing jobs in the private sector, with the
ult that still more tax-dependent jobs are needed, which raises required tax
es still further, and cuts job creation in industry and commerce where the
-financing jobs are yet again. This spiral can all too easily result in soaring
es of taxation, accelerating inflation as everyone tries to pass on extra taxes,
d a growing fraction of the labour force which has to be found
-dependent government jobs if full employment is to be maintained.[1] If
vernments are to avoid these dangers, then, as soon as they judge that
ation has reached acceptable limits, they must stop creating extra
-dependent jobs in the public sector unless the private sector (and those
ionalized industries which cover their costs) are still creating profitable jobs.
th extra private sector jobs, more government jobs can of course be financed
constant rates of taxation. The British government judged that the limit to
eptable rates of taxation was reached by February 1976, and it is now
pared to increase public sector employment only after employment in industry
d commerce has risen.[2] So Keynesian job creation through a larger budget is
ed out, because taxes are too high to finance this without accelerating inflation
ding to a possible hyper-inflation.

ere remains a third possible solution to the problem of unemployment which
ynesians could adopt, and this is precisely the one to which Keynes devoted
last years of his life. It is relevant to the problem of a world recession where
employment is widespread. For the world as a whole there is no (*imports —
orts*) term in the equations that were set out earlier, so if *all countries*
ether raise *government expenditure* and cut *taxation*, they will achieve
ansion without collective balance-of-payments deterioration. World incomes
l rise until, with more wages and profits everywhere, *taxation* rises as much as
initial rise in *government expenditure*. Hence, budgets will be restored at
her levels of world income, and *private saving* and *private investment* can rise
ually in the course of expansion without destroying the balance of payments

---

is line of argument is set out in detail in Robert Bacon and Walter Eltis, *Britain's Economic
blem: Too Few Producers*, Chapter 1.
is is made extremely clear in *Public Expenditure to 1979–80*, Command 6393, HMSO, London,
ruary 1976.

7

Lloyds Bank Review

of the expanding countries, for the world as a whole cannot have a payments deficit.[1]

The argument suggests that the principal economic tools a small country seeking to achieve full employment by Keynesian means in a world recession has at its disposal are diplomatic ones if it is to avoid the beggar-my-neighbour policies which did so little good in the 1930s. It cannot fine-tune its way to full employment. Instead, it must persuade countries with economic power to act together if it is to achieve results. So it is the great and the powerful that must follow Keynesian deficit-financing policies. It is they whom Keynes addressed in 1936 (when he addressed the powerful by addressing his own countrymen). So, while for the great powers acting together Keynesian policies are indeed a way of achieving full employment, they can all too easily lead to the economic conditions of a banana republic if the economically insignificant use them on their own. Such countries may either destroy their currencies through repeated deficit-financed booms which destroy the exchange rate, or produce rubbish behind the protection of tariff walls and import quotas which is unmarketable against the competitive products of others. But the weaknesses in these policies have not been understood, so small countries like Britain in the 1960s and the 1970s, advised by Keynesian fine-tuners, have accelerated domestic inflation and destroyed the international values of their currencies, either deliberately or accidentally, under the mistaken belief that they were pursuing full employment. And they may at any time move still nearer to true banana republic conditions by setting up the import quota machinery which will destroy quality control in the manufacturing sector.

The Money Supply and Inflation

A second confusion of all but the more sophisticated Keynesians has stemmed from their failure to understand the role of the money supply in *The General Theory*. In that book, Keynes as a simplifying device assumed that portfolio holders—banks, insurance companies, pension funds, colleges and rich

---

[1]In terms of the Keynesian identity, a modest initial increase in *government expenditure* and reduction in *taxation* can be set out for the world as a whole as:

$$\left(\begin{array}{c}\text{government} \\ \text{expenditure}\end{array} - \text{taxation}\right) \equiv \left(\begin{array}{c}\text{private} \\ \text{saving}\end{array} - \begin{array}{c}\text{private} \\ \text{investment}\end{array}\right)$$
$$+1\,500 \qquad -1\,500$$

and after world incomes have risen—with *taxation* and *private saving* rising equally—and *private investment* rising as much as *private saving*:

$$\left(\begin{array}{c}\text{government} \\ \text{expenditure}\end{array} - \text{taxation}\right) \equiv \left(\begin{array}{c}\text{private} \\ \text{saving}\end{array} - \begin{array}{c}\text{private} \\ \text{investment}\end{array}\right)$$
$$+1\cdot500 \qquad +1\,500 \qquad +3\,000 \qquad +3\,000$$

so a country with a representative balance of payments would enjoy higher incomes without deterioration in either its balance of payments or its budget.

The Failure of the Keynesian Conventional Wisdom

individuals—could hold their wealth in the form of only two kinds of asset, money and bonds. Extra money went in the first instance to portfolio holders (who held it in the form of what Keynes called larger 'speculative balances') and this meant that, with an increase in the money supply, portfolios became unbalanced. Portfolio holders, if they were formerly in balance, now had too much cash in relation to their bond holdings. They therefore attempted to switch from cash to bonds (which collectively they could not do) but in the process they bid up the prices of bonds until portfolio balance was achieved at new and higher bond prices, where interest rates were of course lower. The assumptions that all extra money went in the first instance to portfolio holders, and that these could react only by bidding up the prices of fixed-interest shares gave money a severely limited role, but the role is still considerable to anyone who understands that it is only an economist's simplifying assumption that bonds are the sole alternative to cash. Keynes's real assumption is that extra money goes in the first instance to portfolio holders, and bonds are merely a typical portfolio asset. With as many portfolio assets as in the real world, more money in the hands of portfolio holders must lead them to bid up the prices of assets in general, and not merely the bonds in their portfolios. So, when the money supply rises, bond prices will indeed be influenced, but so will the prices of equity shares, urban real property, houses, farms, land, pictures, and even commodities. (And we all know that commodities often formed a considerable fraction of the portfolio of King's College, Cambridge, while Keynes was Bursar[1]). Therefore, in the true Keynes model that underlies *The General Theory*, an increase in the money supply will raise the prices of bonds, equity shares, houses, land and commodities, as Leijonhofvud and others have suggested.[2] It will not raise their prices equally, and as we shall see some may even fall, but it will tend to raise their weighted average. As soon as it is recognized that all these prices will be influenced, analysis becomes far more complex than in *The General Theory* because a far more complicated theory of portfolio choice is needed if all these prices are to be included. But many Keynesians have failed to notice that bonds should be regarded merely as one portfolio asset out of many, wherever the theory is applied to the real world. They have therefore jumped far too quickly from the simplified presentation of the argument in *The General Theory* to the real world, and assumed that there, too, according to Keynes, money influences the price of bonds and nothing else. As evidence soon began to emerge that the price of bonds (or rather its inverse, the rate of interest) had a relatively

---

There is the famous story of Keynes walking past King's College Chapel, and saying—'Too mall, too small, far too small to hold all the wheat I have just bought for the college, if we have to take delivery'.
Axel Leijonhofvud *On Keynesian Economics and the Economics of Keynes*, Oxford University Press, 1968.

insignificant effect on investment and consumption,[1] it was assumed by these so-called Keynesians that the money supply had an equally insignificant effect on investment and consumption, Therefore, even though the great Keynesian book is called *The General Theory of Employment, Interest and Money* (which would suggest today to anyone uninitiated that Keynes was a monetarist) the idea began to emerge that true Keynesians believed that the money supply influenced nothing of importance.

They should of course have traced the story back and appreciated that Keynes's insight was that extra money becomes a portfolio asset, and that an increase in the money supply therefore influences the prices of *all* other portfolio assets. Once this is understood, it immediately becomes clear that money is important, for no one can possibly imagine that government action which doubles the prices of housing and building land and puts pressure on commodity prices measured in domestic currency has negligible effects on the inflation rate. Apart from their immediate impact, these will have effects on other prices and the wages of building workers which will affect other wages. Moreover, an increase in portfolio prices in general will have far greater effects on investment (equity finance cheaper, house-building more profitable, companies wealthier) than the mere increase in the bond price that follows from the superficial interpretation of Keynes with which so many have been content. And this wider interpretation allows basic Keynesian stories to be told which the no-money Keynesians cannot tell. Thus, it is part of Keynes's vision of the world that, even if there is no fall in the expected profitability of investment or in the propensity to consume an increased psychological preference by the City of London for liquidity will produce falling share and property prices which can then move the economy towards a slump. This is straight Keynes: bankers can cause slumps.[2] But the no-money Keynesians could not possibly believe this. To them, bankers can influence only the bond price, and this has no influence on anything at all. These people therefore lost much of their Keynes. And, in the process, those they advised, including until recently the British Treasury, believed that the money supply influenced nothing at all that was worth including in their equations. Hence, the British Treasury was until recently one of the most cavalier in the world about the influence of money on economies, and this damaged British economic management in all sorts of obvious ways, of which the sad events of

---

[1]*Oxford Studies in the Price Mechanism*, ed T Wilson and P W S Andrews, Oxford University Press, 1951, and the Radcliffe Report (*Committee on the Working of the Monetary System*, Cmnd 827, HMSO, 1959) were influential in suggesting that interest rates were unimportant.
[2]It is interesting in this context that, when Keynes became a member of the London Political Economy Club, the first question he put (in 1913) was, 'How far are bankers responsible for the alternations of boom and depression?' (*Political Economy Club Centenary Volume*, 1921).

10

The Failure of the Keynesian Conventional Wisdom

1971–3 are among the clearest. It cannot be emphasized too much that Keynes always considered money important.

Inflation and the Rate of Interest

Keynes's simplification that money and bonds are the only portfolio assets has been even more damaging than has so far been suggested. because it has left Keynesians with an extremely unrealistic theory of the rate of interest. They insist and teach that an increase in the money supply will reduce the rate of interest. Now, from 1971 to 1974. when the money supply (M3) about doubled in Britain, the prices of irredeemable government bonds fell by almost one-half, and the long-term rate of interest the government had to pay rose from 9 to 17 per cent. Therefore, orthodox Keynesian teachers were teaching the professors and economic advisers of the future the precise opposite of what was going on in the world around them. If they had explained that it was the prices of portfolio assets in general that would rise as a result of a doubling of the money supply, their students could have seen that any consequent increase in the expected rate of inflation would have adverse effects on the prices of bonds (which have mere money yields), in comparison with houses and land (which have yields that can keep pace with inflation). Because an increase in the expected rate of inflation will depress bond prices in relation to other asset prices, the money rate of interest will be higher the higher the expected rate of inflation. This point is obvious as soon as it is appreciated that the money supply influences the prices of all portfolio assets, and by now many Keynesian economists have grasped this, but that was not the case even ten years ago. Then my co-examiners in economics in the Final Honours School of Politics, Philosophy and Economics in Oxford wished to write in our examiners' report that '. . . some candidates were so confused that they supposed that an increase in the rate of inflation would raise the rate of interest'. I dissuaded my two colleagues from this public confession of our own confusions. It will be evident below that even those very great and distinguished Keynesians, Sir Roy Harrod and Lord Kahn, told the Radcliffe Committee in 1958 that a large increase in the money supply must lower interest rates.

A further and connected confusion in the Keynesian theory of the rate of interest is that, as in so much of Keynes, it relates to an economy that is cut off from the rest of the world. In an open economy the rate of interest will be influenced by the balance of payments and, in particular, countries with falling exchange rates will have to pay higher short-term interest rates on internationally mobile holdings than countries with exchange rates that are expected to rise. In so far as expected falls in the exchange rate are associated with expectations

11

about rates of inflation, countries with rapid inflation will have high forward discounts on their currencies, and will therefore have to pay far higher short-term rates of interest than countries with slower inflation, so once again inflation influences interest rates. Joan Robinson, to her great credit, perceived as early as 1936 that the rate of interest of an individual country would be influenced by its balance of payments, and wrote something about this in her *Essays in the Theory of Employment* and sent the galley proofs to Keynes before publication. Keynes wrote to her, appalled, on 9 November 1936:

> I beg you not to publish. For your argument as it stands is most certainly nonsense . . You do not seem to realize that if you are right the whole theory of liquidity preference has to be thrown overboard. The rate of interest on English money no longer depends on the quantity of English money and the liquidity preference of the holders of it . . .

Four days later Joan Robinson wrote to Keynes, presumably to his great relief, 'I finally decided to cut all the controversial matter out of my exchange essay . . .'[1] The leading Keynesians therefore preserved a united front to the world in defence of what was to become complete nonsense. But their great prestige kept it in British textbooks for a further forty years.

Keynes's assumptions that the British interest rate is independent of foreign interest rates and that government bonds are a typical portfolio asset are comprehensible in the context of the Britain of the 1930s. London was then a great financial centre, so if he believed that world interest rates were determined in London, with sterling the *numéraire* against which other currencies were at a premium or discount, this would not have been absurd. And, with expectations of approximate price stability in London, bonds and equities and houses and land would not necessarily move in persistently divergent ways, so that in 1936 it might have been reasonable to regard bonds as a typical portfolio asset, for in 1936 commodity prices had risen relatively little in the previous century and a half. How much difference this makes is shown when Keynes's experience of centuries of relative price stability in his country is contrasted with that of Jean-Baptiste Say, the originator of Say's law. Say, writing in France after the Napoleonic wars, considered the possibility that a seller of commodities would hold on to the money he received and rejected it:

> When the producer has put the finishing hand to his product, he is most anxious to sell it immediately, lest its value should vanish in his hands. Nor is he less anxious to dispose of the money he may get for it; for the value of money is also perishable.

---

[1] *The Collected Writings of John Maynard Keynes*, Vol XIV, 'The General Theory and After', Macmillan, 1973, pp 146–7.

The Failure of the Keynesian Conventional Wisdom

But the only way of getting rid of money is in the purchase of some product or other. Thus, the mere circumstance of the creation of one product immediately opens a vent for other products.[1]

So this Frenchman who lived through the currency collapse of the revolution, which had followed a series of currency devaluations under the Bourbons, believed that the value of money was *perishable*. Therefore, said Say, as soon as someone gets money from selling commodities, he buys other commodities. Money is therefore no more than a medium for transactions. Not so, said Maynard Keynes, an Englishman living in a country where for most of his life the gold value of sterling was exactly where Sir Isaac Newton had fixed it early in the eighteenth century. This Englishman saw money as the most secure store of value available to portfolio holders, and his prestige is such that many of his countrymen still believe and teach this, even while the commodity value of money halves every five to ten years.

Those who have been taught these theories of money and interest which are contradicted by many of the observed facts of actual price and interest rate behaviour of the past twenty years include those British civil servants who have learned some formal economics, many of the politicians in the Labour and Conservative parties who have held cabinet rank (Britain now has, for the first time since 1964, both a Prime Minister and a Chancellor without a British economics degree) and, in addition, senior trade union leaders, for two of the three most recent General Secretaries of the Trades Union Congress had Oxford Politics, Philosophy and Economics degrees. So it is no wonder that, with general assent, successive British governments fine-tuned their way to balance-of-payments crisis after crisis and increased the money supply under the mistaken impression that this would reduce the rate of interest at which British governments borrowed, which would ease the cost of Keynesian deficit financing. In practice, of course, the monetary expansion made inflation faster than it would otherwise have been, weakened sterling and therefore raised the rate of interest in London to the bewilderment of the British authorities, who were reduced to pleading with foreigners for lower world interest rates so that British interest rates could also be reduced. They would have been reduced, of course, if British inflation rates had been less, and most would now agree that a necessary (though not sufficient) condition for this would have been a slower rate of increase in Britain's money supply. But this would have contradicted everything our policy-makers were taught while they were students.

---

[1] Jean-Baptiste Say, *Traité d'Economie Politique*, 4th Edition. English translation by C R Prinsep, London, 1821, Vol 1, p 167. The statement about the *perishable* value of money which prevents the circular flow of commodities from being blocked by 'hoarding' is not to be found in the early editions of Say's *Treatise*, so it has not been widely appreciated that a falling value of money is one of the presumptions on which Say's analysis is based.

13

Lloyds Bank Review

Investment, Company Profitability and Growth

A final weakness in the Keynesian conventional wisdom which has dominated British economic management since the second world war is a total lack of understanding of how growth and rising living standards are achieved. A vital point to note about *The General Theory* is that it was published three years before Sir Roy Harrod published his first essay on economic growth.[1] The model of production that underlies *The General Theory* is not far from a neo-classical stationary state. In this, full employment can be maintained continuously without perpetual investment in job creation, and the idea that economies must invest each year, possibly at a high rate, to provide enough new jobs to replace those which are destroyed by technical change seems never to have occurred to Keynes. He was always contemptuous of Marx. In *The General Theory*, largely following John Stuart Mill,[2] he said that[3]:

> . . . a properly run community equipped with modern technical resources, of which the population is not increasing rapidly, ought to be able to bring down the marginal efficiency of capital in equilibrium approximately to zero within a single generation; so that we should attain the conditions of *a quasi-stationary community* where change and progress would result only from changes in technique, taste, population and institutions . . .

> If I am right in supposing it to be comparatively easy to make capital-goods so abundant that the marginal efficiency of capital is zero, this may be the most sensible way of gradually getting rid of many of the objectionable features of capitalism. For a little reflection will show what enormous social changes would result from a gradual disappearance of a rate of return on accumulated wealth.

To see an economy in long-term equilibrium as a quasi-stationary one requiring no profits to finance job creation was indubitably a serious error, and Marx's belief that a collapse of the rate of profit would destroy capitalism shows much more understanding of a market economy's long-term needs. In 1939 Sir Roy Harrod converted Keynes's model from a static to a dynamic one (though Keynes and his Cambridge colleagues found Harrod's work puzzling at first) but the damage was done.

The Keynesian conventional wisdom saw no need for continuing investment *in job creation* at a high level as a necessary condition for full employment. It was therefore not widely perceived in Britain that economies with a high potential for growth needed high investment, and therefore high profits to finance this. There was no *technical* need for profits because Keynes saw no objection to their

---

[1]'An essay in dynamic theory', *The Economic Journal*, Vol XLIX, March 1939.
[2]John Stuart Mill, *Principles of Political Economy*, 1848, Book IV, Chapter 4, 'Of the tendency of profits to a minimum'.
[3]pp 220–1, my italics.

The Failure of the Keynesian Conventional Wisdom

being zero in the very long run, in spite of limited changes in population and technique. Also, as is evident from the quotation, profits were seen, not as a source of investment finance, but primarily as a source of social inequality. To Keynes, profits at any level at all were part of the unacceptable face of capitalism, for many of the objectionable features of capitalism would disappear if profits were zero. And the minimal investment necessary to maintain the economy on its long term *General Theory* quasi-stationary state would presumably be induced by the mere expectation of profits. The 30 per cent investment share of Japan and the 25 per cent share of West Germany could not of course have been financed from expectations alone, while workers and the government took nearly 90 per cent of the national income, as in Britain.

So the quasi-stationary state economics of 1936 was unable to provide what was needed for Britain's growth opportunities of the 1950s, 1960s and 1970s. Here the Keynesian failure was not as great or total as it was in the field of monetary economics and fine-tuning, for several distinguished Keynesian economists did produce models where fast growing economies had higher shares of profits and investment than those with slow growth rates, but the valuable models of Lord Kaldor, Joan Robinson and Luigi Passinetti[1] have been considered advanced and difficult by most students, the politicians and civil servants of the future, so they have not been widely absorbed into the ordinary thinking of men of affairs. But these did imbibe the quasi-stationary state world of *The General Theory*, so when they achieved power they destroyed the profitability of British industry (and this was true of both Labour and Conservative governments from 1964 to 1975) and then tried to boost investment by telling British industrialists that they could *expect* unprecedented growth.

This misconception of what is needed for growth should not have occurred for, with Roy Harrod's pioneering contribution, British economists should have become the first to understand the needs of a growing economy. But unfortunately Roy Harrod and many after him overlooked a vital point. He invented the 'natural' rate of growth, which was the growth rate that technical progress and population growth allowed, and the 'warranted' rate, which was the rate the country's saving (less government investment) was able to finance. He concluded that if the 'warranted' rate was greater, countries would have excessive saving at full employment so that, '. . . we must expect the economy to be prevailingly depressed'. This is generally agreed. He described the situation where the 'natural' rate was higher, ie where saving was insufficient to finance

---

[1] N Kaldor, 'A model of economic growth', *The Economic Journal*, Vol LXVII, December 1957; Joan Robinson, *Essays in the Theory of Economic Growth*, Macmillan, 1962, Chapter 2; and L L Pasinetti, 'Rate of profit and income distribution in relation to the rate of economic growth', *Review of Economic Studies*, Vol XXIX, October 1962.

the country's growth opportunities, as one with '. . . plenty of booms and a frequent tendency to approach full employment, the high employment will be of an inflationary and therefore unhealthy character'.[1]

But that is not the end of the matter. If saving is insufficient, the investment the country needs at full employment may well be crowded out by other expenditures, so the country simply will not realize its growth opportunities. And this will not merely slow down growth. It will also mean that there is insufficient new investment to create enough new jobs for school-leavers and those made redundant by technical change, so inadequate saving (net of government investment) can lead to diminishing private sector employment opportunities as well as to inflation. Roy Harrod was therefore over-optimistic when he thought that there will be 'a frequent tendency to approach full employment'. He and most of the British growth theorists who followed him failed to include this line of argument in the conventional wisdom, so inadequate saving was seen merely as a cause of inflation, and not of structural unemployment in addition. A fall in private sector jobs can of course be made good if a growing number of public sector jobs is created, and this has happened to a great extent in Britain, but, as has already been pointed out, these extra public sector jobs are 'tax-dependent', so this process involves ever-rising taxation, or else budgets which become increasingly unbalanced. So Keynesians never had a theory of long-term job creation. They simply assumed that enough jobs would always be there if governments created sufficient demand.

Equally seriously, to most Keynesians the rewards from higher effective demand almost always exceeded those from greater efficiency and such old fashioned virtues as thrift with resources and hard work. Keynes ridiculed de Mandeville's thrifty bees and the Gladstonian virtues.[2] In the great slump of the 1930s output could indeed be raised massively by increasing effective demand (provided the balance-of-payments consequences could be managed or negotiated) but since the second world war it is the economies with well-organized bee-hives, thrifty bees and a low ratio of drones in the hive that have prospered. Keynes's writings of the 1930s inadvertently set the economically literate in Britain on a course where hard work, efficient industrial organization and the employment of a high fraction of the labour force on productive and profitable work were considered to be of only secondary importance in relation to correct demand management. And, because of their confused understanding of the functioning of economies at the macro-level, the British Keynesians were even unsuccessful managers of effective demand, so that average excess capacity rose as the rate of

[1]*Towards a Dynamic Economics*, Macmillan, 1948, p 88.
[2]*The General Theory*, pp 359–62.

16

growth of output fell, thus doubly increasing the waste of resources that resulted from their demand management policies.

The Misuse of Keynes in Britain

This has been an increasingly depressing account of the misinterpretation of the work of a very great economist, but it has an interesting historical parallel. In 1815 the Duke of Wellington was the world's most successful general. Because of his overwhelming prestige, those who were at Waterloo with him ran the British army for the next forty years and insisted that everything must remain as it was under Wellington. The price for this conservatism was paid in the Crimean war. Since the second world war British economic policy has been dominated by a desire to maintain the momentum of Keynes's very great successes, and the automatic transference of his theories of the 1930s to a wholly different world in an attempt to do this was responsible for many of the disastrous policies of the 1960s and the 1970s.

To illustrate this, one need only quote from the memoranda that three of the greatest Keynesians who knew Keynes submitted to the Radcliffe Committee in 1958. This will allow us to see how Keynes's most distinguished successors were thinking at the start of the vital period in which the British economy was to decline so sharply in relation to its principal competitors.

First, Sir Roy Harrod, the author of some of the most notable and original contributions to economics after Keynes, wrote in a section of his memorandum entitled *Normal Long Term Interest Rate in Britain should be 3%*:

> The long term rate of interest is governed by the relation between the quantity of money and the money value of the national income. . . . If the quantity of money available were restored to a more normal relation to the money value of the national income, the long term rate of interest would come down to 3% quite naturally, without any fuss or bother.[1]

Here Roy Harrod's thinking was clearly still locked into the simple two-asset Keynes model of 1936, where extra money cannot raise the rate of interest. In the real world, Lord Barber raised the money supply vastly faster than the national income, and the rate of interest did not fall to 3 per cent. It rose towards 17 per cent, and the increase in the money supply was partly responsible for this.

---

[1] *Committee on the Working of the Monetary System, Principal Memoranda of Evidence*, HMSO, 1960, Vol 3, p 114.

Lloyds Bank Review

And Lord Kaldor, the great Keynesian who has had more influence over policy than any other since 1958, submitted a memorandum with a long section headed, *The Dangers of a Regime of Stable Prices.* He was concerned that the British economy would stagnate if the inflation rate was too low.[1] This illustrates how the belief emerged that to Keynesians the objectives of full employment and growth must always have priority over the objective of price stability. But it did not then occur to Lord Kaldor that rapid inflation could have adverse effects on employment and growth.

And, finally, there is Lord Kahn, the Keynesian with the highest reputation for intellectual rigour. In 1958 he wrote in his memorandum that:

> Either interest rates are dangerously low, in which case they should be raised, or they are not dangerously low, in which case there is no harm in the increase in the quantity of money which is called for to keep them down.[2]

We now know that raising the money supply may raise the rate of interest, so 'the increase in the quantity of money which is called for to keep [interest rates] down' is a meaningless concept—while raising the money supply in an attempt to achieve the unachievable has other adverse effects of which Lord Kahn is presumably now aware, but, like Roy Harrod, his thinking was clearly locked into the simplest version of Keynes's model of 1936 when he drafted this significant passage. Perhaps the statement in Lord Kahn's memorandum that most strongly foreshadowed what was to come is:

> To my mind the [government's] 'overall' deficit is of no significance.[3]

Because Keynes was prepared to tolerate budget deficits in slumps, his great successors apparently felt it necessary to show how Keynesian they were by accepting budget deficits of any size. Presumably Lord Kahn would now consider Britain's deficit of 11 per cent of the national product and Italy's of over 15 per cent significant.

The key point to note is that eighteen years ago three of the greatest Keynesians offered their countrymen monetary expansion, indifference to inflation and the irrelevance of deficits. Their advice was accepted, but its disastrous effects have underlined an important lesson. In a changing world a particular economic model has only a limited life-span before its simplifications become dangerously wrong, and the evidence is overwhelming that the precise simplifications of Keynes's model of 1936 are now obsolete.

[1]Ibid, pp 148–9.
[2]Ibid p 145.
[3]Ibid p 145.

18

14

13

Some Implications of Deficit-financed Tax Cuts: These Will Always Increase Demand, but Will They Reduce Supply?

WALTER ELTIS

I INTRODUCTION

It was widely argued in the 1970s and the 1980s that macro-economic policies would function more effectively in a country which was enjoying the benefits of falling taxation, than in one where taxes were rising.[1] It is uncontroversial that tax cuts with parallel reductions in public expenditure to produce a neutral overall effect on the budget should have some favourable effects on supply. But some supporters of supply side economics have gone further and argued that taxes can be cut as an element in macro-economic policy, even in the absence of parallel reductions in public expenditure.[2] They believe that tax cuts which produce an initial deterioration in the budget may involve no widening of the deficit in the medium term if their eventual favourable effects on supply are sufficient.

There is the additional and distinct possibility that tax cuts might be an ideal element in policies to expand an underemployed economy towards its equilibrium employment rate without the accelerating inflation that Keynesian policies might otherwise involve, because the inflationary impact of their tendency to raise effective demand may be counterbalanced by their favourable impact on the rates at which wages and prices increase,[3] for if tax rates are cut, wages and prices will be able to rise less and still provide workers and companies with the growth of net of tax incomes that they have come to expect.

The key question which must be answered before the viability of such short-term tax cutting policies to reduce unemployment can be assessed is the nature of any beneficial long-term effects on supply. If these are sufficient, then tax cuts which expand an economy rapidly in the short term might not produce unsustainable deficits in the medium term. The next section of this chapter will therefore be concerned with the long-term effects of tax cuts on supply. After that the question of whether deficit-financed tax cuts can be used to provide an expeditious cure for unemployment without adverse long-term real and financial effects will be considered. The United States cut taxes sharply after 1980, and then raised employment rapidly and reduced inflation at the same time, but a variety of adverse pressures are now emanating from the consequent structural deficit. The chapter will conclude with a few words about the possible relevance of the argument to the American case.

II THE LONG-TERM BENEFITS FROM LOWER TAXATION

As this section is concerned with the *long-term* influence of lower taxation, an economy with the labour market continually in equilibrium and unemployment therefore always at the natural rate will be assumed. Initially it will also be supposed that the budget is balanced so that the favourable supply-side effects of lower taxation are not being partly offset by unfavourable crowding-out effects from the higher interest rates that might accompany extra government borrowing.

Lower rates of taxation will have a variety of possible effects on supply in a fully employed economy with a balanced budget, and there is an enormous range of literature which bears on this subject.[4] Lower taxation will influence the supply of labour and capital and of other factors of production. It will influence the efficiency of resource allocation, and attitudes to risk. Out of these, attention will be focused here on the influence of lower rates of taxation on the supply of labour and capital, and through these on the level of capacity output and therefore the long-term tax base. Other influences, on the efficiency of resource allocation, on risk taking, and on the supply and quality of entrepreneurship may matter more in the longest of long runs, but they are exceedingly difficult to model. The effects of taxation on the supplies of labour and capital are in contrast mainstream problems which have received a great deal of attention.

It will be assumed that there is a uniform rate of tax of T on all incomes,[5] a uniform elasticity of labour supply of N_s and a uniform elasticity of demand for labour of N_d if employment is always at its equilibrium rate, and the (growing) capital stock is given at each point of time. N_d will be close to but not equal to the elasticity of substitution between labour and capital. With these assumptions, the formula for $E_{L/T}$, the elasticity of equilibrium employment with respect to percentage point changes in the rate of taxation is[6]

$$E_{L/T} = -\frac{1}{1-T}\ \frac{1}{1/N_s - 1/N_d} \tag{13.1}$$

This may be positive or negative depending on whether the elasticity of labour supply is positive or negative; that is, lower taxation may be associated with a higher or lower equilibrium level of employment. N_d, the elasticity of demand for labour, will always be negative, and $E_{L/T}$, the elasticity of equilibrium employment with respect to the rate of taxation, is certain to be negative (that is, lower taxation will be associated with higher employment) if N_s, the elasticity of supply of labour, is positive. Recent United States evidence appears to indicate that the elasticity of supply of male workers may be close to zero while the supply of female workers reacts positively to net of tax real wages with the result that the overall elasticity of supply of labour, N_s, may perhaps be of the order of $+0.15$.[7] If the elasticity of demand for labour is -0.75 (values of the elasticity of substitution between labour and capital of between 0.5 and 1.0 have been widely found,[8] then $E_{L/T}$, the elasticity of employment with respect to the rate of taxation will be $-0.125[1/(1 - T)]$, so that a 1 percentage point tax cut will raise the equilibrium level of market sector employment by only 0.14 percentage points where the rate of tax is 10 per cent, and by just 0.21 percentage points where it is 40 per cent, in which case a 5 percentage point tax cut would raise the supply of labour a mere 1 per cent. Thus the rate of tax will generally have little influence on the economy via increases in the equilibrium supply of labour at full employment – unless N_s is far larger than recent empirical work suggests.

There is one qualification to this negative result which may sometimes be important. At very high rates of taxation, for instance 90 per cent, even modest elasticities of labour supply, of the kind so far assumed, will have quite considerable effects. Thus at 90 per cent taxation, a 1 percentage point tax cut will raise the supply of labour by as much as 1.25 per cent, even if the elasticity of supply of labour is only $+0.15$. Average tax rates are rarely as high as 90 per cent, but marginal tax rates may often be as high as this in a complex tax and social security system, so there may indeed be instances where reductions in such extremely high rates have significant supply side effects. With the present arithmetic, a 5 percentage point tax cut from 90 to 85 per cent would raise equilibrium employment by over 6 per cent which is by no means an insignificant effect. But, in general, the supply-side benefits from lower taxation will be modest so far as the supply of labour is concerned. What of the supply of capital? Are larger benefits to be expected there?

The most straightforward assumptions to make about aggregate saving are that all net saving is private, and that this depends on permanent private incomes and upon the real rate of interest that savers receive. It can be assumed for simplicity that permanent incomes will be reduced, *pari passu*, by proportional taxation at rate T which is expected to be levied indefinitely, and that where the budget is balanced the level of T will not influence the net of tax rate of interest that savers receive.[9] Then total saving as a ratio of the national income, s, will always equal $(1 - T)s_p$, where s_p is the propensity to save permanent incomes.[10] If an economy has an exogenously given long-term or 'natural' rate of growth of g_n, its capital to output ratio will always tend towards s/g_n which equals $(1 - T)s_p/g_n$.[11] As the capital to output ratio will therefore be proportional to $(1 - T)$, any tax cuts which reduce T will raise the equilibrium capital to output ratio correspondingly.

With the customary neoclassical assumptions, if the elasticity of output with respect to the real capital stock is α (that is, if a 1 per cent increase in the capital stock raises output α per cent), then a 1 per cent increase in the capital stock will raise the capital to output ratio $(1 - \alpha)$ per cent. Thus a rise in the capital to output ratio of 1 per cent, that is, a rise in $(1 - T)s_p/g_n$ by 1 per cent, will be associated with a rise in the capital stock of $1/(1 - \alpha)$ per cent. It follows from this that the formula for $E_{K/T}$, the elasticity of the capital stock with respect to percentage point changes in the rate of tax is

$$E_{K/T} = -\frac{1}{1-T}\frac{1}{1-\alpha} \tag{13.2}$$

If α is 0.33, then the elasticity of the capital stock with respect to the rate of taxation will be $-1\frac{1}{2}[1/(1 - T)]$, so that a 1 percentage point cut in the rate of tax will raise the capital stock 1.67 per cent where the rate of taxation is 10 per cent, by $2\frac{1}{2}$ per cent where it is 40 per cent, and by 15 per cent where it is 90 per cent. The assumption that the elasticity of output with respect to the capital stock is 0.33 is in no way ambitious or controversial, and it will be evident that this suggests an elasticity of the capital stock with respect to the rate of tax which is quite considerable. Thus, at 40 per cent taxation, it appeared that a 1 percentage point tax cut might raise the supply of labour by only around 0.2 per cent, but it might well raise the capital stock in due course by as much as $2\frac{1}{2}$ per cent.

Equation 13.1 showed the elasticity of employment with respect to the rate of tax, and equation 13.2 the elasticity of the capital stock with respect to this. But what is of most interest is the elasticity of the equilibrium level of *output* with respect to the rate of tax, because this will show the full supply-side effects from the increase in both the labour force and the capital stock which are consequent on lower rates of taxation. The elasticity of real output with respect to percentage point changes in the rate of tax, $E_{Y/T}$, as a consequence of the tendency of tax cuts to raise both the capital stock and the labour force, will be α, the elasticity of output with respect to the capital stock times the increase in this, plus β, the elasticity of output with respect to the labour force times the increase in this. Thus, using equations 13.1 and 13.2

$$E_{Y/T} = -\frac{1}{1-T}\left[\frac{\alpha}{1-\alpha} + \frac{\beta}{1/N_s - 1/N_d}\right] \tag{13.3}$$

With a constant returns production function β will be 0.67, that is, a 1 per cent increase in the labour force will raise output 0.67 per cent, if α is 0.33; and if N_s is +0.15 and N_d is −0.75, the elasticity of output with respect to the rate of tax will become $-0.5825[1/(1 - T)]$. It is to be noted that with these assumed values which are intended to be plausible, the contribution of extra labour to output as a result of the supply-side effects of lower taxation is $0.0825[1/1 - T)]$, while the contribution of extra capital is six times as great at $0.50[1/(1 - T)]$, the combined effect of both together being to raise output by $0.5825[1/(1 - T)]$ per cent for each percentage point cut in the uniform rate of tax. The assumptions about the elasticities which produce these results are of course arbitrary, but few would wish to assume the far greater elasticity of labour supply which would be needed to disturb the result that the supply-side benefits from lower taxation as a result of the larger capital stock this should induce will be of an altogether greater order of magnitude than those from a larger labour force.

The implications of the proposition that lower taxation should be associated with higher equilibrium output, mainly because there will be a larger capital stock, but also because there will be an increased labour force, are important. This is because all increases in output raise the economy's tax base, for taxation can be levied on the extra wages and profits that result from additions to output. A percentage point tax cut may raise output by something like $0.5825[1/(1 - T)]$ per cent if the values of the various elasticities are close to those suggested, and the supply-side benefits of tax cuts can indeed produce more extra revenue in due course than the tax cuts themselves cost initially. In the present example, if the rate of tax is cut from 75 to 74 per cent, output will grow by 2.33 per cent from say 100 to 102.33, and 0.74 times 102.33 = 75.72 which exceeds 0.75 times 100, so once the supply-side effects of cutting taxation from 75 to 74 per cent are taken into account, it emerges that the government will actually obtain more revenue with 74 per cent taxation than with 75 per cent.

It can be said in general that if there are any supply-side effects at all, a 1 percentage point tax cut will always reduce the real resources available to governments by less than 1 per cent of the national income, while a 1 percentage point tax increase will always bring in less extra revenue than 1 per cent of the national income at the time the tax increase was imposed. The general relationship between tax rates and total tax revenues can be derived very straightforwardly from $E_{Y/T}$, the elasticity of the real national income with respect to the rate of taxation. Thus

$$Y = Y_0(1 - T)^{-(1-T)E_{Y/T}} \tag{13.4}$$

where Y_0 is the real national income with employment at the natural rate and zero taxation. Total tax revenue, R, will be T times Y, so that

$$R = TY_0(1 - T)^{-(1-T)E_{Y/T}} \tag{13.5}$$

These equations allow the real national income and total tax revenues to be estimated at different rates of tax for any given value of $E_{Y/T}$.

In table 13.1 these are set out for an elasticity of real output with respect to the rate of tax of $-0.5825[1/(1 - T)]$, the value of this that results when the values of the elasticities are those previously assumed.

Table 13.1   *The rate of tax, real national income, total tax revenue and the national income net of taxation where* $\alpha = 0.33$, $\beta = 0.67$, $N_s = +0.15$ *and* $N_d = -0.75$

Rate of tax %	National income $(\times Y_0)$	Tax revenue $(\times Y_0)$	Income net of tax $(\times Y_0)$
0	1.0000	0	1.0000
10	0.9404	0.0940	0.8464
20	0.8779	0.1756	0.7023
30	0.8122	0.2436	0.5686
40	0.7423	0.2969	0.4454
50	0.6674	0.3337	0.3337
60	0.5860	0.3516	0.2344
62.5	0.5643	0.35269	0.2116
63.16	0.5585	0.35275	0.2058
64	0.5510	0.35266	0.1983
70	0.4954	0.3460	0.1486
80	0.3911	0.3129	0.0782
90	0.2610	0.2349	0.0261
95	0.1742	0.1655	0.0087
99	0.0681	0.0674	0.0007

It will be seen that with these assumed values, total tax revenue rises at first as the rate of tax is increased, and reaches a maximum when the rate of tax is 63.16 per cent, after which it begins to fall.

The relationship which the table describes, where increases in rates of tax first increase and then reduce total tax revenue, and where all actual revenues apart from maximum revenue can be obtained with two alternative rates of tax (for instance, a revenue of 25 per cent of Y_0 can be obtained with either a tax rate of approximately 30 per cent, or one of around 88 per cent) is of course the Laffer curve.[12]

There will be a Laffer relationship of the kind illustrated in the table with all possible values of the elasticities (provided that the elasticity of labour supply is positive and not negative), and it follows from equations 13.3 and 13.5 that the formula for the revenue maximizing rate of tax is

$$\frac{\delta R}{\delta T} = 0 \quad \text{where } T = 1 \bigg/ \left(1 + \frac{\alpha}{1 - \alpha} + \frac{\beta}{1/N_s - 1/N_d} \right) \qquad (13.6)$$

This will always be less than 1 provided that N_s is positive and N_d negative, and with the present assumed values of α, β, N_s and N_d, the formula produces a revenue maximizing tax rate of 63.16 per cent. If the only supply-side benefits from lower taxation were those that follow from the favourable effects of lower taxation on the supply of labour, and N_s was indeed as low as +0.15, then the revenue maximizing rate of tax would be as high as 92.31 per cent (found by making α zero in the formula). If attention is focused instead on the far more important tendency for lower taxation to raise the savings ratio and thus to increase capital per worker and the capital to output ratio, while the effect of lower taxation on the supply of labour is ignored then the revenue maximizing rate (found by making β zero) will be 66.67 per cent. The two supply-side effects in combination produce a revenue maximizing tax rate of 63.16 per cent.

Two aspects of these conclusions must be emphasized. The first is that these results have rested on the assumption of the continuous achievement of equilibrium output with unemployment always at the natural rate, and in addition balanced budgets. Nothing has been said about the time required to obtain the full supply-side benefits from lower taxation. It may in fact take many generations before the capital to output ratio settles at the s/g_n which has been assumed, for this is the capital to output ratio in a steady state, and full adjustment of the capital to output ratio to the savings ratio will be a slow process.[13] The labour supply should adjust quite rapidly to higher net of tax incomes, but the principal supply-side benefits from lower taxation arise via the capital to output ratio where adjustment may be gradual. Therefore all that can be said is that where comparisons between steady states are made, which is what the table illustrates, economies with higher rates of tax will not enjoy extra real government revenues in anything approaching the same proportion. Economies with higher tax rates may only enjoy slightly higher real revenues, while market financed spending will often be vastly lower. But this will only be the case in long-run comparisons.

The second important caveat is one which follows from the assumption of balanced budgets. Countries will not be able to obtain the full long-term benefits from lower taxation by merely cutting rates of tax. A country on the second stage of the Laffer curve, with a tax rate in excess of the revenue maximizing one, will actually obtain a 'free lunch' by cutting taxation. In this situation reductions in tax rates will raise total tax revenues, so the budget can actually be improved while real government spending is increased and net of tax real incomes are raised. But in general, and in most economies, taxation will be below the revenue maximizing rate. So if the balanced budget assumption is to be retained, a lower rate of tax will only be feasible if real government spending is reduced at the same time.

As will be shown in detail in the next section where the long-term implications of *deficit-financed* tax cuts will be analysed, any attempt to reduce taxation without corresponding expenditure cuts will only produce a fraction of the supply-side benefits which have been set out. This is because they will raise the supply of labour *but reduce the supply of capital*. If there is lower taxation at full employment and these lower tax rates are expected to continue indefinitely, permanent private incomes will be higher with the result that private consumption will expand, and if consumption rises while the capital stock is at first unchanged, aggregate saving must fall. More marketed output will be consumed, but with an unchanged capital stock (and only the slight increase in labour supply that the previous argument suggests) little extra marketed output will be produced, so less marketed output than before will be saved and invested. In consequence the savings ratio in the economy's market sector will fall with the result that capital per worker, output per worker and the capital to output ratio will all become lower than they would have been in the absence of deficit-financed supply-side tax cuts. As the strongest favourable supply-side effects of lower taxation appear to follow from its tendency to raise the savings ratio, it follows that tax cuts unaccompanied by expenditure reductions will generally reduce aggregate supply and therefore the long-term tax base.

This does not mean that deficit financed tax cuts have no role to play in supply-side policies. Tax cuts financed through budget deficits may be handicaps so far as long-term growth is concerned, but they may be important for the rapid achievement of full employment.

III THE USE OF SUPPLY-SIDE TAX CUTS TO ACCELERATE TRANSITIONS TO FULL EMPLOYMENT WITHOUT ADVERSE EFFECTS ON INFLATION

Supply-side reflationary policies seek to make use of tax cuts with two objects in mind. In so far as these reduce prices, full employment may be approachable without the acceleration of inflation that is otherwise to be expected. In addition, tax cuts should raise effective demand in the traditional Keynesian manner (though less so than equal increases in public expenditure). The combined influence of a moderation of inflation and a stimulus to real demand can obviously be extremely helpful to the pace and sustainability of economic recovery.

Because their advocates expect supply-side policies to reduce inflation, they believe there is no accompanying need to raise the rate of growth of the money supply, so they hope to avoid this vulnerable aspect of traditional Keynesian policies. These lines of argument will now be developed.

To focus particular attention on the supply-side effects of the tax ratio, it will be assumed that real public expenditure grows at the economy's natural growth rate, g_n, and that the budget will be balanced at full employment at a uniform rate of tax of T_n. Total public expenditure is therefore $T_n Y_n$, where Y_n is the national income with employment at the natural rate. It is assumed that there is initially unemployment in excess of the natural rate, and inflation in excess of p^*, the target inflation rate, but the tax ratio is assumed to be T_n, the ratio that would produce a full employment balanced budget. This means that if the initial national income (Y_0) is below Y_n, then there will be a budget deficit because taxation will amount only to $T_n Y_0$ which is bound to be less than public expenditure which is always $T_n Y_n$. However, there is no structural deficit because taxation would equal $T_n Y_n$ at the existing tax rate of T_n if employment was actually at the natural rate so that output was Y_n.

It can now be supposed that in order to implement supply-side policies to achieve full employment at the target inflation rate, the government reduces the uniform rate of tax by one percentage point in each successive year, and that it maintains an unchanged rate of growth of the money supply, namely the rate calculated to sustain the target inflation rate at full employment.

These successive reductions in the uniform rate of tax will have three main influences upon the economy. First they will reduce the inflation rate by up to 1 per cent in each successive year, in relation to what it would otherwise have been. Second, the expenditure effects of the tax cuts will raise real demand in each successive year. Third, each year in which the tax cutting policy persists will open up a full employment budget deficit of 1 per cent of the national income, so if it takes J years to reach full employment and the target inflation rate, the structural deficit at the end of that period will be J per cent of the national income.

The beneficial effect on the rate of inflation could amount to as much as a full 1 per cent per annum reduction in this with adaptive expectations wage and price equations.[14] If, for instance, there is a wage equation of the general form

$$w = {}_eP + {}_eq + \delta T_d + f_1(U_n - U) \quad f_1' > 0 \tag{13.7}$$

where w is the annual rate of wage increases, ${}_ep$ the expected rate of inflation, ${}_eq$ the expected rate of increase in *net of tax* living standards, and δT_d the annual increase in direct taxation (expressed as a ratio of the national income at factor cost), while U_n is the natural rate of unemployment and U actual unemployment, workers will bargain for increases in excess of expected inflation plus the rate of increase in real living standards to which they have become accustomed where unemployment is less than the natural rate, and they will accept less than this where unemployment exceeds the natural rate. A corresponding price equation can be set out as

$$p = w - a + \delta T_i + f_2(U_n - U) \quad f_2' > 0 \tag{13.8}$$

where, when unemployment equals the natural rate, p, the rate of price inflation, equal annual money wage increases, *less a*, the annual rate of productivity growth, *plus* δT_i, the change in indirect taxes (expressed as a ratio of the national income at factor cost). The simplest adaptive expectations assumption for the expected inflation rate is that this is the actual inflation rate of the previous period, so that ${}_ep = p_{-1}$; while for the expected growth of workers' real living standards, it can be supposed that they have previously been able to raise these in line with annual productivity growth, and that this is therefore the rate of increase they have come to expect, so that, ${}_eq = a$. With these substitutions

$$p - p_{-1} = \delta T_d + \delta T_i + f(U_n - U) \tag{13.9}$$

so that inflation will accelerate, either if unemployment is below the natural rate which is well known, or (which is less well known) if direct or indirect taxation increases (when previous rises in taxation have not already depressed $_eq$, the increase in real living standards which workers have come to expect, below a, the increase which productivity growth actually allows the economy to deliver).

With these equations, annual tax cuts *which are unexpected* will conversely produce deceleration in the rate of inflation. Thus if direct or indirect taxes are reduced by 1 per cent of the national income per annum, workers' real incomes will be able to advance 1 per cent faster than they have come to expect. As a result, money wages will be able to rise 1 per cent less in the next period, and this will mean that prices will rise 1 per cent less which will permit a further cut in the pace of wage increases.

Table 13.2 is an example of the sequence which could follow successive reductions in the uniform rate of tax of 1 per cent per annum. There will be some extra tendency for inflation to fall, because throughout the process set out in the table, unemployment is presumed to exceed the natural rate, and any such excess will have an additional tendency to reduce the annual rate of wage and price increases. Table 13.2 abstracts from this effect and merely outlines the tendency of a succession of supply-side tax cuts to reduce inflation by 1 per cent per annum above such reductions as excess unemployment is producing at the same time.

In table 13.2 it is assumed that productivity growth, a, is a steady 2 per cent per annum, and δT_i the annual change in indirect taxation is -1 in years 1, 2, 3, 4 and 5, the years in which indirect taxes are cut by 1 per cent of the national income, while rates of direct taxation are unchanged. The result is that p, the rate of inflation, falls from an initial 10 per cent in year 0 to 5 per cent in year 5. If direct taxes are

Table 13.2 *The influence of successive annual reductions of 1 per cent of the national income in the rate of indirect taxation*

	Annual percentage increases			
Year	Increase in wages $w = p_{-1} + {}_eq$	Increase in productivity a	Increase in taxation δT_i	Increase in prices $p = w - a + \delta T_i$
0	12	2	0	10
1	12	2	−1	9
2	11	2	−1	8
3	10	2	−1	7
4	9	2	−1	6
5	8	2	−1	5
6	7	2	0	5

reduced instead by 1 per cent of the national income in each of years 1, 2, 3, 4 and 5, while indirect taxation is unchanged, the deceleration of wage and price inflation will be as set out in table 13.3.

Many would consider the sequence of events set out in table 13.2, where it is indirect taxation that is reduced, considerably more plausible. There is widespread agreement that changes in indirect taxation will have a short-term impact on the price level, and that this will have some influence on the expected rate of inflation and therefore on subsequent wage negotiations. The one-for-one impact of indirect tax cuts on inflation set out in table 13.2 is of course no more than a limiting case, but there would be general agreement that there may be effects of this nature. There would be less assent for the view that direct tax cuts would immmediately reduce inflation in anything approaching the parallel extent set out in table 13.3. Analytically there should of course be an eventual symmetrical response to changes which affect workers' real incomes equally, so it is tempting to predict similar results from the two kinds of tax reduction, but tax cuts are likely to reduce inflation more immediately where it is indirect taxation that is being reduced, and that is what will be assumed from now on.

With inflation reduced by up to 1 per cent per annum, but an unchanged rate of growth of the nominal money supply, the growth of the real money supply will accelerate by up to 1 per cent per annum, which will help to produce an accelerating rate of growth of real effective demand. This will also be raised by the demand stimulating effects of the tax cuts themselves.

These will raise real disposable income by 1 per cent of the initial national income, Y_0, in the first year after taxes begin to be reduced,

Table 13.3 *The influence of successive annual reductions of 1 per cent of the national income in the rate of direct taxation*

		Annual percentage increases		
Year	Increase in direct taxes δT_d	Increase in wages $w = p_{-1} + {}_e q + \delta T_d$	Increase in productivity a	Increase in prices $p = w - a$
0	0	12	2	10
1	−1	11	2	9
2	−1	10	2	8
3	−1	9	2	7
4	−1	8	2	6
5	−1	7	2	5
6	0	7	2	5

and this increase will boost both consumption and investment. Consumption will depend partly on the propensity to consume permanent incomes and partly on the propensity to consume transient incomes, and some of the beneficiaries of tax cuts will regard these as permanent while others will consider them transitory. Those who regard the tax cuts as permanent will increase their consumption in so far as their net wealth and hence their permanent incomes are raised. Barro has suggested in his well-known equivalence theorem (which follows Ricardo) that deficit financed tax cuts may have a zero net effect on wealth because new obligations on taxpayers and their heirs to finance consequent increases in the national debt will reduce private net wealth to precisely the degree that tax cuts themselves increase it.[15] Many taxpayers will, however, base their consumption on their expected incomes over merely their own lifetimes or else some still briefer time span, and, as Tobin has pointed out, the net wealth and permanent incomes of these taxpayers will rise as taxes are reduced. Clearly the actual rise in consumption that accompanies tax cuts will depend quite considerably on the extent to which they are regarded as permanent, and the extent to which those who regard them as permanent actually believe that their net wealth has risen.[16]

As those who benefit from tax cuts raise consumption, real incomes will rise which will increase the desired capital stock, and this will incline companies to increase investment. They will also raise investment in so far as this is favourably influenced by any rise in net of tax profits that is consequent upon reductions in taxation. The result is that both real investment and real consumption will rise as rates of taxation are reduced.

There are a number of ways in which the effects of successive reductions in taxation upon consumption and investment could be set out, and the simple propositions that follow outline the nature of some of the possible interrelationships. It will be assumed that the overall marginal propensity to consume extra net of tax incomes is c, and that this takes into account that some beneficiaries of tax cuts regard these as permanent and wealth increasing, while others consider them transitory, or else wealth neutral. Consumption will then rise by c per cent of the previous 'year's' natural income in the first year in which taxes are reduced by 1 per cent of the national income, if it is assumed (for simplicity) that consumption decisions are not revised (upwards or downwards) in the course of the year.

It will be supposed for simplicity that gross investment at an unchanged rate of interest is always determined by an investment function of the general form $I_t = vY_{t-1} - dK_{t-1}$, where v and d are constants, so investment will only start to be favourably influenced by tax cuts in the 'year' after these begin. Thus in the year in which taxes are first reduced, there will be no addition to investment and their sole effect will be to raise consumption by c per cent of the national income, so in the first year δY, where this is regarded as the direct influence of the tax cuts upon investment and consumption via their influence on real disposable incomes, will merely be c.

In the second year, consumption will rise by c per cent of the previous year's national income as a result of the second 1 per cent cut in taxation but this will not be the sole increase in real demand. The rise in the national income by c in the previous year will produce extra induced investment of v times this, and the fact that incomes are c per cent higher as a result of the growth of the previous year will produce extra consumption of $c(1 - T)$ times these higher incomes of the previous year. The total rise in demand as a consequence of the growth of the previous year will therefore be $v + c(1 - T)$ times the growth of that year. This means that the total growth in demand in the second year will be $c[1 + v + c(1 - T)]$. The investment function, $I_t = vY_{t-1} - dK_{t-1}$, assumes that investment, as well as being favourably influenced by the growth of the previous year, is unfavourably influenced by the rise in the capital stock in that year. For simplicity the negative effect of the growing capital stock in this brief tax-cut-induced recovery is neglected, so that sole influence on investment of which account will be taken is the increase in the national income of the previous year. These simplifications suggest that demand will rise by c in the first year of the tax cutting programme, and by $c[1 + v + c(1 - T)]$ in the second year. In the third year the immediate effect of the tax cuts will again be to raise consumption by c, but the secondary effect, a rise in consumption and investment by $[v + c(1 - T)]$ times the growth of the previous year will now produce extra demand of $c[v + c(1 - T)]$ plus $c[v + c(1 - T)]^2$. Hence the total rise in demand in the third year of the tax cuts is

$$c\{1 + [v + c(1 - T)] + [v + c(1 - T)]^2\}$$

Similarly, the growth of real demand in the nth year will be

$$c\{1 + [v + c(1 - T)] + [v + c(1 - T)]^2 + \ldots + [v + c(1 - T)]^{n-1}\}$$

Thus the multiplier and accelerator effects of the tax cuts will produce an accelerating rate of growth of real demand if the rate of interest is unchanged. If, for instance, c is 0.5, T is 0.4, and v is 1.1, the growth of real demand will be 0.5 per cent in the first year, 1.2 per cent in the second, 2.18 per cent in the third, 3.55 per cent in the fourth, and so on. Other assumed values for c, v and T would produce different results but they would all produce a considerable acceleration in the rate of growth of real demand. The expansion of demand only accelerates with conventional multiplier–accelerator interactions if the value of v exceeds some critical value, but those results which Hicks (1950, ch. 6) has categorized depend on the assumption that expansion is triggered off by a single impluse; here expansion is more powerful because the government repeatedly injects extra demand into the economy in a succession of tax cutting budgets. That the growth of demand is bound to accelerate is extremely helpful because it was shown above that the tendency of successive tax cuts to reduce the rate of inflation by up to 1 per cent annum could raise the rate of growth of the *real* money supply by up to 1 per cent per annum so that this would rise by an extra 1 per cent in the first year, 2 per cent in the second, 3 per cent in the third, and so on. Thus the real money supply and the rate of growth of real demand will both have a tendency to accelerate in each year in which taxes are cut, so there will be an accelerating rightward movement in both the Hicksian LM and IS curves, though not of course at parallel rates. If the tendency of the real money supply to accelerate is greater than that of the multiplier–accelerator interaction, the LM curve will tend to move rightwards faster than the IS curve with the result that interest rates will tend to fall in so far as these are determined by the relationships discussed up to this point. Interest rates will of course tend to rise if the multiplier–accelerator interaction advances more powerfully than the real money supply. There will be a strong acceleration of growth in either case, and the excess of unemployment over the natural rate should gradually be eliminated, while inflation should at the same time fall towards the target rate.

It may be that employment will reach the natural rate before inflation falls to the target rate. In that event, the joint policies of control of the nominal money supply and continuous tax cuts could be differently balanced. Monetary growth could be tighter for instance, so that employment grew less, while inflation fell somewhat faster because it took employment longer to reach the natural rate. Conversely, if it appeared that the inflation target would be reached before the employment target, more emphasis could be placed on the tax cutting programme, and less on reductions in the rate of growth of the money supply.

If the joint policies succeed in achieving both targets after J years, growth can proceed from that point with employment at the natural rate and inflation at the target rate, but the budget will have a structural deficit of J per cent of the national income. This will have implications which will be the subject of the next section.

IV   THE LONG-TERM CONSEQUENCES OF THE STRUCTURAL BUDGET
DEFICIT THAT RESULTS FROM THE USE OF TAX CUTS TO EXPAND TO
FULL EMPLOYMENT

The first consequence of the structural deficit is that real interest rates will need to be higher than if employment had reached the natural rate with a balanced budget. With the present assumptions, the share of consumption in the national income will be higher by cJ per cent (at unchanged real interest rates) than if taxes had not been cut by 1 per cent of the national income in J successive years. Interest rates will therefore need to be sufficiently above the rate they would reach if the natural rate of employment was attained with a balanced budget to raise the share of private saving in the national income or else to crowd out investment by cJ per cent of the national income. If 1 per cent higher interest rates raise the share of saving by A per cent of the national income, and cut the share of investment by B per cent, real interest rates will need to be higher by $cJ(A + B)$ percentage points. At these higher real interest rates the share of investment in the national income will be lower by $[B/(A + B)]cJ$ per cent of the national income, so if private saving and investment were previously s per cent of the national income, the fraction,

$$\frac{B}{A + B}\frac{cJ}{s}$$

of private investment will now be crowded out. In the fullness of time the capital to output ratio will also be lower to this extent. If the elasticity of output with respect to capital is α, this means that equilibrium output will eventually be lower by the fraction

$$\frac{\alpha}{1 - \alpha}\frac{B}{A + B}\frac{cJ}{s}$$

than it would have been if growth with employment at the natural rate had been achieved with a balanced budget.

There is another adverse effect which many consider still more serious. If there is a budget deficit of J per cent of the national income when employment reaches the natural rate, then Domar has shown that if this deficit persists, the national debt will converge upon J/g_n per cent of the national income.[17] Financing the interest on this debt will require future taxation of iJ/g_n per cent of the national income where i is the real interest rate which the government will have to pay finance continuous annual borrowing of J per cent of the national income.

If borrowing is to be held indefinitely at J per cent of the national income, that is if the deficit that is required to expand up to the natural rate of employment is sustained indefinitely after this, then a simple proposition follows. The interest cost of the resulting deficit of J per cent of the national income will need to be financed through extra taxation and this will build up towards an eventual iJ/g_n per cent of the national income. Taxes can be reduced by J per cent of the national income along the initial expansion path to full employment, but after this they will gradually need to be raised by iJ/g_n per cent of the national income to finance the interest on the gradual accumulation of debt. If taxes are first cut by J and subsequently increased by iJ/g_n per cent of the national income, they will end up higher than their initial level if i exceeds g_n. Thus if the real rate of interest at which the government has to borrow exceeds the long term rate of growth, governments will end up levying higher rates of taxation than the initial level before the tax cutting policies were adopted. If, conversely, the real rate of interest on government debt is less than the long-term rate of growth, then the government will be able to levy lower taxation indefinitely, because debt interest will always require less extra taxation to finance it than the J percentage points by which tax rates were cut initially. The critical real interest rate at which supply-side tax cuts produce lower rates of taxation in the distant future as well as the immediate present is therefore the interest rate that equals the long-term rate of growth. If governments can borrow at interest rates below this in the very long run, then they can reduce taxation indefinitely and follow a quick road to full employment at the same time. If, on the contrary, they have to pay real interest rates (net of such taxes as they receive back on the interest they pay out) which exceed the rate of growth, then supply-side tax cutting policies will only allow tax rates to fall in the short term and they will eventually entail larger anti-supply-side tax increases.

There are a number of qualifications and amplifications to this relatively simple proposition. It has been assumed in what has been said so far that the government ceases to expand borrowing after the equilibrium level of employment is reached. It thus acquires a structural deficit of J per cent of the national income in order to reach full employment expeditiously, but expands borrowing no further after that. The result is that it has to raise the rate of taxation in order to pay debt interest which builds up towards iJ/g_n per cent of the national income. This debt interest could be financed through further increases in borrowing, which would raise real interest rates further, crowd out yet more investment, and continually reduce capital and output per worker. If debt interest was financed through further borrowing instead of taxation, there would be all these unfavourable effects, but there would be no accompanying need to raise taxation so this would remain *J* percentage points below its initial level. But as debt interest and extra borrowing to finance it built up, a point would eventually be reached where governments could not continue to expand their debt to national income ratios further. The price of postponed tax increases would then be an eventual financial crisis with unpredictable consequences.[18] It will be assumed here that governments will not embark on policies which involve *indefinite* increases in debt, so they will only finance a growing deficit through borrowing instead of taxation if specific short-term benefits are attainable, and the borrowing ratio needed to attain these is *limited*. That is the case with the use of supply-side tax cuts to reach full employment expeditiously, when the effect on the structural deficit should be containable, but it is not the case if there is further borrowing to pay consequent debt interest, because this would involve an indefinite increase in the debt to income ratio and an inevitable financial breakdown in the end.

The second qualification to the relatively simple result that borrowing will reduce eventual taxation where the rate of interest is less than the long-term rate of growth, and raise it if the rate of interest is higher than this, is the assumption which has been implicit so far that the economy has no previous debt. It has been assumed that there was formerly a balanced budget at full employment with the result that the structural deficit rises from zero to *J* per cent of the national income as a result of the adoption of new expansionary policies. If there is already debt amounting to the fraction, *D*, of the national income, the interest cost of financing this will gradually increase as interest rates rise. The additional borrowing of *J* per cent of the national income that is consequent upon the adoption of supply-side tax cutting policies will raise real interest rates by the time full employment is reached by $J/(A + B)$ per cent of the national income. This rise in interest rates will have to be applied to the previous debt of *D* as soon as the interest on this comes up for renegotiation, and extra interest costs of $[J/(A + B)]D$ per cent of the national income will then have to be incurred.[19] Tax rates will have to be raised by $[J/(A + B)]D$ per cent of the national income to pay this extra interest if an indefinite growth of debt is to be avoided, so a country which has already incurred debt will cut taxes in recession by *J* per cent of the national income in order to trigger off a supply-led recovery, but it will then have to raise them again by $[J/(A + B)]D$ per cent of the national income soon after full employment is reached. This subsequent increase in taxation will exceed taxation will exceed the initial tax cuts if $D/(A + B)$ exceeds unity, and it will in any case amount to a considerable fraction of the initial tax cuts if D is at all significant.

Many countries finance their borrowing through short-period debt instruments where interest rates have to be renegotiated with considerable frequency, and such countries could easily find that most of the hoped for benefits from new borrowing were largely absorbed into extra obligations to pay interest on existing debt. This would be entirely the case once a country's debt reached $1/(A + B)$ per cent of its national income. Thus is $(A + B)$ totals $1\frac{1}{2}$ for instance (which means that an increase in government borrowing of $1\frac{1}{2}$ per cent of the national income will raise real interest rates 1 per cent at full employment), and borrowing is actually raised by $1\frac{1}{2}$ per cent of the national income, then if existing debt totals $1\frac{1}{2}$ times the national income, 1 per cent extra interest on this will cost the budget $1\frac{1}{2}$ per cent of the national income, precisely the amount by which borrowing is being increased. This means that a country with existing debt which has reached $(A + B)$ per cent of its national income can gain no extra resources as a result of further increases in borrowing. Any further borrowing will merely raise interest costs sufficiently to absorb all or more than the increment that is borrowed. Obligations to pay interest will rise as fast or faster than increases in the national debt. Once a country has reached this point, it will be unable to make any rational use of extra borrowing for any purpose, including of course, borrowing to finance supply-side policies. Any tax cuts along the path to full employment will need to be reversed once this is attained, and the anticipation of these future tax increases (or else a future monetization of debt) may mean that there will not even be transitional benefits. The weaknesses and failures of Keynesian debt-financed expansions in the 1970s and the 1980s may have resulted in part because by then their previous successes had led some countries to push their existing debt to levels where further borrowing was significantly absorbed into extra obligations to pay interest.

If past debt is not so high that extra interest almost immediately absorbs all the extra funds a government obtains from additional borrowing, there will of course be opportunities to reduce rates of taxation immediately, even if they will eventually need to be increased. Domar's well-known result that taxation will have to rise in the end if the real rate of interest at which the government borrows exceeds the economy's long-term rate of growth is demonstrable for an *infinite* time horizon, but government do not commonly look so far ahead.

If, for instance, the government borrows in order to pursue supply-side tax cutting policies, and the real interest rate rises to $1\frac{1}{2}$ times the natural rate of growth *after* this, and if this is the first government borrowing the country in question has embarked on and g_n is 3 per cent per annum, then it can be shown that debt interest will build up so that it equals the borrowing ratio after 37 years. If, however, the country had previous government debt amounting to say $\frac{1}{2}(A + B)$ as a ratio of the national income, then interest payments will catch up with the government's further borrowing after just 23 years. In these cases therefore taxes will be lower for a few decades, but after this the interest on accumulated borrowing will push them up above their levels before the supply-side policies were adopted.

Proponents of supply-side tax cutting policies would argue that such calculations miss the main point of their strategy. They advocate supply-side policies precisely because they believe the economy will function more effectively with lower taxation – that is after all what the expression supply-side policies is intended to convey. They expect these policies to lead to a higher level of output and to a faster long-term rate of growth, with the result that future tax revenues will rise to produce benefits which the above calculations ignore. If the level of the national income is actually higher *when the economy reaches full employment* than it would have been in the absence of supply-side tax cuts, then that larger national income will produce more tax revenue than has so far been supposed. But will deficit-financed tax cuts actually raise the level of Y_n, the real national income with employment at the natural rate?

It was shown in the first section that lower rates of taxation will be associated with higher full employment output, because there are likely to be increased supplies of both labour and capital. But those results depended on the assumption of a balanced budget. In the present analysis of the use of tax cuts to take an economy rapidly to full employment, the budget is in continuous deficit, with the result that interest rates will be higher when the economy reaches full employment than they would have been with a balanced budget.

This will not affect the analysis of the influence of lower taxation upon the full employment supply of labour because that will depend only on rates of taxation, and not at all on the rate of interest. However, the analysis of how lower taxation will raise saving and therefore the capital stock will be seriously affected. Lower taxation with unchanged government spending is certain to raise the share of consumption in the full employment national income, so it is bound to reduce the full employment share of investment. Therefore far from raising investment and capital per worker, as tax cuts were bound to do at full employment with a balanced budget, deficit financed tax cuts will actually have the opposite effect: because they will inevitably raise the share of consumption, they are certain to have an unfavourable influence on the share of investment.

Worse still, it emerged that where budgets are balanced, tax cuts have a stronger impact on long-term supply potential via their tendency to raise capital per worker, than through their favourable impact on the size of the labour force. With plausible values for the various elasticities, it appears that the eventual favourable effects of tax cuts on potential supply resulting from a larger equilibrium capital stock might be about six times as great as those that could be expected from a larger labour force. It is therefore disturbing that deficit-financed tax cuts will actually reduce the capital stock. The worrying probability appears to be that they will be supply reducing and not supply increasing.

It is of course only in the longest of long runs that a country will suffer the full disadvantages of a lower savings ratio. According to Sato (1963), the full neoclassical transition to a lower capital ratio may take 90 years in an economy permanently at full employment, so it may take this long for the full adverse effects on the capital stock of higher consumption and a higher rate of interest to come through, while the benefits from lower taxation upon the supply of labour which were one-sixth as great in the first part of this chapter will be enjoyed immediately. It is therefore likely that as a policy of deficit financed tax cuts is embarked upon, the favourable effects on labour supply will be the greater influence at first, but the unfavourable effects via the influence of higher consumption and higher interest rates on the capital stock will gradually come to outweigh them, and the initial favourable effects will be extremely slight if the elasticity of labour supply is as modest as recent empirical work suggests.

The question that immediately arises after this disappointing analysis is whether an economy which uses supply-side policies to reach full employment and the target inflation rate can avoid the adverse long-term effects by correcting the deficit as soon as full employment is reached. Could this allow an economy to enjoy the benefits of a rapid transition to full employment without adverse long-term effects? In order to correct the structural deficit, taxes would have to be increased by the J per cent of the national income by which they were cut in the rapid transition to full employment. Suppose they are raised by 1 per cent of the national income in each of the J years after the natural rate is first reached. Will this undo all that was achieved in the favourable transition to this?

On the face of it, the previous favourable results should be precisely reversed. The gradual tax increases would then lead to an annual acceleration of inflation of 1 per cent per annum if the previous wage and price equation still applied, and this would reduce the rate of growth of the real money supply by 1 per cent per annum. At the same time the reduction in disposable incomes that followed the tax increases would reduce effective demand at an accelerating rate, so that the economy gradually drifted into recession, and quite possibly a stagflationary recession in which inflation accelerated as employment declined. Are there possible asymmetries which might allow this dismal conclusion to be avoided?

A possible assumption that would rescue the case for deficit financed tax cuts is that productivity growth might rise faster at full employment which would allow workers to continue to enjoy their accustomed rate of growth of real living standards, despite subsequent tax increases which gradually removed the deficit. There is a wide range of theories which suggest that if the long-term rate of productivity growth is not an exogenously given constant, then it will tend to vary with aggregate investment or else the rate of capital accumulation.[20] If there is force in these lines of argument, then there will actually be unfavourable long-term effects on productivity growth if an economy is run with a structural deficit, because this will always reduce the long-term share of investment in relation to what it would have been with a balanced budget.

The only case where these policies may actually raise the long-term rate of productivity growth will arise if an economy simply cannot otherwise attain the natural rate of employment. If the alternative is that full employment will never be reached, or else that the average level of employment will be significantly lower, then an economy which adopts supply-side policies may achieve a level of output that averages out closer to full employment output (Y_n). Suppose an economy with a structural deficit of J per cent of its national income thereby manages to achieve a level of output that averages 98 per cent of Y_n, then its share of investment will average $0.98\{s - Jc[B/(A + B)]\}Y_n$. Suppose another economy with a structurally balanced budget has a level of output which averages only $0.92Y_n$, but invests a full s per cent of this lower average national income because private saving is at no point diverted to finance government borrowing. Then the economy willing to pursue supply-side policies would invest more in the long term if $0.98\{s - Jc[B/(A + B)]\}Y_n$ exceeded $0.92sY_n$. That would require an extraordinary average output gain as a result of the pursuit of deficit financed full employment policies, because $\{s - Jc[B/(A + B)]\}$ will often fall short of s by one-quarter or one-fifth, but the average output gain from using tax cuts to get closer to full employment can hardly amount to more than between one-twentieth and one-tenth of the national income at the utmost. There should then be few cases where aggregate investment will actually be higher over the cycle as a whole in economies where deficit financed tax cutting policies are pursued, which means that there will be few countries where these policies actually lead to faster productivity growth. Slower productivity growth because investment is lower seems far more probable in most cases.

The sad conclusion is that deficit financed tax cuts should indeed take an economy rapidly to full employment, but there will almost invariably be a price to pay. The share of investment will be lower at full employment and productivity growth therefore slower, with the result that such economies will almost always have an inferior long-term tax base. Worse still, any attempts to reverse tax cuts and rebalance the budget as soon as full employment is reached seem likely to reverse the beneficial effects on employment and inflation that expanded the economy so rapidly in the first place. Hence this particular line of policy, like several others, can only be expected to produce short-term benefits at a considerable long-term cost.

Moreover, this new variant of Keynesian policies will be entirely impractical over a series of cycles. If the structural deficit is raised by J per cent of the national income in each recession, the cumulative deficit will rise, with the result that the diversion of saving to consumption will all the time increase to produce a growing loss of capital per worker. In addition, the ratio of debt to the national income will rise in each successive cycle, and higher interest rates will need to be paid to finance extra borrowing on each occasion. These higher rates will need to be paid on previously incurred debt, which will absorb growing fractions of the extra sums that governments attempt to borrow, with the result that the time will come when no part of an increase in borrowing will actually be available to finance tax cuts. Because of the cumulative tendency of extra borrowing to raise the rate of interest, it may well be that countries will only be able to take advantage of a tax-cut-induced recovery once or twice or at most on perhaps three occasions. After that the ratio of structural borrowing to the national income is likely to reach a point where further attempts to increase borrowing will simply be absorbed into extra interest on previously incurred debt.

There is, however, one case where costless tax-cut-induced recoveries may still be feasible, and this may be one of the practical policy options that Keynes himself envisaged. It has been assumed so far that borrowing in recession will always lead to a structural deficit when full employment is reached. But what if a country has rates of taxation in recession that would actually produce a budget surplus at full employment? The public expenditure ratio might be the fraction T_n of full employment output, but tax ratios in excess of T_n could produce deficits in recession. This means that rates of taxation could then *be cut to* T_n in order to expand the economy in all the ways which have been set out, and still produce a balanced budget when full employment is reached. There are no long-term difficulties with supply-side recoveries which do not involve *a structural deficit*, so a country with *a structural surplus* would have the opportunity to cut taxes in order to accelerate economic recovery without painful consequences afterwards. But that appears to be the only case where the rapid attainment of full employment via tax cuts would be costless.

V   CONCLUSION

There may well be parallels between the financial problems of the United States and the adverse effects of deficit financed tax cuts in the above argument. The United States apparently had a small budget surplus in 1979 on a cyclically adjusted basis. Unemployment was at the low rate of 5.8 per cent and the budget deficit (including on and off budget items) was about $1\frac{1}{2}$ per cent of the national income. However, inflation of around 10 per cent per annum was reducing the real value of government debt, then 30 per cent of the national income, by perhaps 3 per cent of the national income. As new borrowing was adding $1\frac{1}{2}$ per cent of the national income to government debt, and inflation was removing 3 per cent, this was falling on balance by $1\frac{1}{2}$ per cent of the national income. In 1985 with unemployment again low, the nominal deficit is perhaps $5\frac{1}{2}$ per cent of the national income, and the real deficit around 4 per cent: since 4 per cent inflation is cutting government debt of 35 per cent of the national income by $1\frac{1}{2}$ percentage points. This suggests that the real structural deficit has widened by $5\frac{1}{2}$ percentage points from $-1\frac{1}{2}$ per cent to $+4$ per cent, while the nominal deficit has widened 4 percentage points from $1\frac{1}{2}$ to $5\frac{1}{2}$ per cent.

In the earlier argument a $5\frac{1}{4}$ percentage point widening of the structural deficit was entirely associated with lower tax rates, but in the American case less than one-third appears to be due to supply-side tax cuts, while over two-thirds is the result of increased government spending. The higher expenditure and the tax cuts were concentrated into the period 1981–84, in which the economy achieved a rapid recovery from recession while inflation fell simultaneously in the manner supply siders predict.

But it is entirely plausible that the larger structural deficit is now producing adverse financial effects of the kind set out in this chapter. Part of the $5\frac{1}{2}$ per cent percentage point increase in borrowing is being financed internationally, so domestic saving has not had to be crowded in or investment crowded out to this full extent, but extra foreign borrowing has raised interest rates and real United States rates are now high by historical standards.

It would be interesting to know if the share of private investment in the national income and the rate of productivity growth are lower than when the economy previously achieved high employment: preliminary data suggest that higher real interest rates may already be producing adverse effects on productivity growth of the kind neoclassical analysis predicts.

United States net of tax real interest rates are considerably higher than the rate of growth, and the ratio of government debt to the national income is rising in the manner economic analysis suggests, from around 30 per cent in 1979 to a predicted 50 per cent in 1989 (see Congressional Budget Office, 1984, Pt. III, p. 4). It will converge on more than 100 per cent of the national income, according to Domar's formula, if the *real* deficit remains 4 per cent of the national income, and the long-term rate of growth approximates to the post Second World War average of $3\frac{1}{2}$ per cent.

Adverse long-term effects on interest rates and capital investment can only be prevented from becoming continually more severe as the debt to income ratio rises towards and beyond 100 per cent, if taxation is now increased or expenditure reduced by around 3 per cent of the national income. This would cut the structural deficit to the 1 per cent which is compatible with a stable public debt to national income ratio of 30 to 35 per cent, at which there should be no new adverse financial pressures. But the argument of this chapter would suggest that tax increases might reverse some of the favourable effects on inflation and employment which were achieved in 1981–84.

The United Kingdom was not tempted towards a tax-cut-induced recovery after the Conservative election victory in 1979, and it has been estimated that the British budget was then in structural balance on an inflation adjusted basis so there was no genuine opportunity for this. But Mrs Thatcher's government may have forgone a genuine opportunity to take advantage of a tax-cutting 'free lunch' a few years into her first term when the economy was in deep recession, for it has been estimated that there may have been a structural surplus of over 4 per cent of the national income in 1981.[21] It might therefore have been possible to cut taxes faster than they were actually reduced from 1982 onwards to produce a tax-cut-led recovery of the kind set out in the tables without adverse long-term effects of the kind the United States is experiencing. Whether this was a genuine opportunity obviously depends on the assumptions on which the estimates of the full employment structural surplus are based, and these have often been overoptimistic in the past.

A key conclusion appears to be that there is only a clear case for tax-cut-led recoveries from a starting point of structural surplus. The United States probably had a small structural surplus in 1981 so it could have cut taxes slightly in the absence of simultaneous expenditure increases. Britain may well have had a larger structural surplus by then, so a series of supply-side tax cutting budgets might have been feasible in the years after 1981 without significant adverse effects on the ratio of government debt to the national income.

NOTES

1 See, for instance, Canto et al. (1983), Evans (1980; 1983), Laffer (1979; 1981), Roberts (1978), and Bacon and Eltis (1976).
2 This has been argued especially by Laffer (1979; 1981), but see also Fullerton (1980), and Canto et al. (1983).
3 See especially, Perkins (1979), Corden (1981) and Bacon and Eltis (1976).
4 Musgrave and Musgrave (1976) provide a comprehensive analysis of the various and disparate influences of taxation.
5 A uniform rate of indirect taxation which takes the fraction T of all value-added will have a similar effect, because it will remove approximately the fraction T of the purchasing power of wages. An important difference is, however, that indirect taxes such as value-added tax leave saving untaxed, so they are associated with a greater incentive to save at equal real revenues. Potential savers would allow for the need to pay the uniform value-added tax as soon as they sought to consume their accumulative saving, but they would still gain because the (untaxed) real interest rate at which saving accumulated would be higher.
6 In the absence of taxation, a supply of labour schedule of uniform elasticity can be written as $S_L = L_0 W^{N_s}$, while a demand for labour schedule can be written as $D_L = D_0 W^{N_d}$, where W is the cost of labour. A: a uniform income tax at rate T reduces the net of tax wage on which labour supply is based by the multiple $(1 - T)$, this will modify the supply of labour schedule to $S_L = L_0[W(1 - T)]^{N_s}$. The labour market will be in equilibrium where $S_L = D_L$, that is, where $W^{(N_s - N_d)} = (D_0/L_0)(1 - T)^{-N_s}$. Hence, $(1/W)(\delta W/\delta T) = [1/(1 - T)][1/(1 - N_d/N_s)]$. The elasticity of equilibrium employment with respect to T which is shown in equation 13.1, will be this proportional rise in the cost of labour with respect to T times N_d, the elasticity of demand for labour with respect to the real cost of labour.
7 Some recent econometric evidence on the elasticity of labour supply is summarized by Fullerton (1980). See also Hausman (1981).
8 The evidence is summarized by Sato (1970).
9 A higher rate of tax will have two broad influences on the steady state net of tax rate of return that savers receive, and therefore on the rate of return that can be expected to influence their saving decisions. First, in so far as a higher rate of tax reduces the economy's savings ratio, it will reduce the

steady state capital to output ratio in the same proportion, and *raise* the marginal product of capital and therefore the rate of profit (with competitive assumptions) by $1/\sigma$ times the rise in the capital to output ratio (where σ is the elasticity of substitution between labour and capital). Second, a higher rate of tax will *reduce* the net of tax rate of return that is associated with any particular rate of profit before tax. The tendency of a higher rate of tax to raise the rate of return because it raises the marginal product of capital, and to reduce it because savers receive a lower fraction of this, will precisely cancel out if $\sigma = 1$ and the economy's savings ratio is $s_p(1 - T)$ at a constant rate of interest. (This is because the elasticity of the net of tax rate of return with respect to T is then $[1/\sigma - 1][1/(1 - T)]$, which is zero if $\sigma = 1$.) It will obviously much simplify the analysis if the possibly complex effects of the rate of taxation on the savings ratio via their influence on the rate of interest are neglected, as they safely can be where the two effects offset each other.

10 The effect of taxation on saving is analysed by Boskin (1978), and Ture (1980) offers a general neoclassical analysis of the supply-side effects of lower taxation. The interconnection between taxation and investment has been most thoroughly analysed by Feldstein, and an important example is Feldstein (1980).

11 The classical account of the neoclassical growth model where this result is derived is provided by Solow (1956).

12 Arthur Laffer reputedly first drew the curve on a napkin while he was explaining the case for tax cuts to an aide to President Ford in 1974 (Wanniski, 1978: chapter 6 is devoted to an exposition of the Laffer curve). Its derivation is set out rigorously by Canto et al. (1983).

13 The time period required for this neoclassical adjustment has been investigated by Sato (1963).

14 The use of wage and price equations like those set out below is justified by Eltis (1983). There are quite similar equations given by Grubb et al. (1982), but in their analysis accelerating inflation is due to disappointment with the rate of growth of real incomes as a result of slower productivity growth and not unexpectedly higher taxation.

15 See, in particular, Barro (1974) who is following Ricardo (1817, ch. 17).

16 The relevance of the equivalence theorem to the influence of deficit spending in actual twentieth century economies has been criticized along these lines by Tobin (1980, ch. 2).

17 This formula was first derived by Domar (1944).

18 See Sargent and Wallace (1981) for a well-known account of the consequences of indefinite increases in borrowing.

19 By the time this higher rate of interest has to be paid on previously incurred debt, its ratio, D, to the national income will have fallen, because growth in the *money* national income continuously reduces the ratio of past debt to this. Hence, D has a persistent tendency to fall in the absence of new borrowing.

20 See Arrow (1962), Conlisk (1969) and Kaldor (1957). These are restated and developed by Eltis (1971).

21 See, for instance, Miller (1985) who reports two studies which estimate that the United Kingdom's cyclically adjusted budget was in surplus by over 4 per cent of the national income in 1981.

REFERENCES

Arrow, K.J. 1962: The economic implications of learning by doing, *Review of Economic Studies*, 29, 155–73.

Bacon, R. and Eltis, W. 1976: *Britain's Economic Problem: Too Few Producers*, Macmillan, London.

Barro, R.J. 1974: Are government bonds net wealth?, *Journal of Political Economy*, 82, 1095–1117.

Boskin, M.J. 1978: Taxation, saving, and the rate of interest, *Journal of Political Economy*, 86, 3–27.

Canto, V.A., Jones, D.H. and Laffer, A.B. 1983: *Foundations of Supply-Side Economics: Theory and Evidence*, Academic Press, New York.

Congressional Budget Office 1984: *A Report to the Senate and House Committees on the Budget*, US Government Printing Office, Washington.

Conlisk, J. 1969: A neoclassical growth model wih endogenously positioned technical change frontier, *Economic Journal*, 79, 348–62.

Corden, W.M. 1981: Taxation, real wage rigidity and employment, *Economic Journal*, 91, 309–30.

Domar, E.D. 1944: The 'burden of debt' and the national income, *American Economic Review*, 34, 798–827.

Eltis, W. 1971: The determination of the rate of technical progress, *Economic Journal*, September, 502–24.

Eltis, W. 1983: The interconnection between public expenditure and inflation in Britain, *American Economic Review*, 73, 291–6.

Evans, M.K. 1980: The bankruptcy of Keynesian econometric models, *Challenge*, January–February.

Evans, M.K. 1983: *The Truth About Supply-Side Economics*, Basic Books, New York.

Feldstein, M. 1980: Fiscal policies, inflation and capital formation, *American Economic Review*, 70, 636–50.

Fullerton, D. 1980: Can tax revenue go up when tax rates go down? United States Department of the Treasury, Office of Tax Analysis, Paper 41 (Washington).

Grubb, D., Jackman, R. and Layard, R. 1982: Causes of the current stagflation, *Review of Economic Studies*, 49, Special Issue.

Hausman. J.A. 1981: Labor supply. In H.J. Aaron and J.A. Pechman (eds) *How Taxes Affect Economic Behaviour*, Brookings Institution, Washington, DC.

Hicks, J.R. 1950: *A Contribution to the Theory of the Trade Cycle*, Oxford University Press, Oxford.

Kaldor, N. 1957: A model of economic growth, *Economic Journal*, 67, December, 591–624.

Laffer, A.B. 1979: An equilibrium rational macroeconomic framework. In N.M. Kamrany and R.H. Day (eds) *Economic Issues of the Eighties*, Johns Hopkins. Baltimore.

Laffer, A.B. 1981: Government exactions and revenue deficiencies, *Cato Journal*, 1, Spring.

Miller, M. 1985: Measuring the stance of fiscal policy, *Oxford Review of Economic Policy*, 1, 44–57.

Musgrave. R.A. and Musgrave, P.B. 1976: *Public Finance in Theory and Practice*, 2nd edn. McGraw Hill, New York.

Perkins. J.O.N. 1979: *The Macroeconomic Mix to Stop Stagflation*, Macmillan, London.

Ricardo, D. 1817: *On the Principles of Political Economy and Taxation*, Reprinted Cambridge University Press, Cambridge (1951).

Roberts, P.C. 1978: The breakdown of the Keynesian model. *The Public Interest*, 52, Summer.

Sargent, T.J. and Wallace, N. 1981: Some unpleasant monetarist arithmetic, *Federal Reserve Bank of Minneappolis Quarterly Review*, Fall.

Sato, R. 1963: Fiscal policy in a neo-classical growth model: an analysis of time required for equilibrating adjustment, *Review of Economic Studies*, 30, 16–23.

Sato, R. 1970: The estimation of biased technical progress and the production function, *International Economic Review*, 11, 179–208.

Solow, R.M. 1956: A contribution to the theory of economic growth, *Quarterly Journal of Economics*, 70, February.

Tobin, James 1980: *Asset Accumulation and Economic Activity*, Blackwell, Oxford.

Ture, N.B. 1980: The economic effects of tax changes: a neoclassical analysis. In Congress of the United States Joint Economic Committee, *Special Study of Economic Change* (vol. 4: *Stagflation*), Government Printing Office, Washington, DC.

Wanniski, J. 1978: *The Way the World Works*, Basic Books, New York.

15

Walter Eltis
The Borrowing Fallacy

On the World Debt Crisis

MUCH OF Latin America's debt has become unfinanceable, and in addition the government debt of several Western developed countries has increased massively in the 1970s and the 1980s. Several of these are rapidly approaching a condition where drastic corrective action will be needed if they are to avoid financial destabilisation. This recent growth of government debt in Latin America, North America, and Europe can be explained in two broad ways.

First, government expenditure is often popular, and it helps governments to realise many of their promised social and political objectives. Taxation, in contrast, always weakens popularity and reduces political support. Politically weak governments are therefore tempted to buy short-term popularity by raising public expenditure through borrowing—it allows them to reward their supporters and fulfil their objectives more rapidly. This borrowing will involve significant costs in due course; but a different group of politicians will often have to face the unpopularity involved in paying the interest, often to foreign countries, on debt which financed originally popular expenditures. A disregard for the eventual cost of policies which are popular in the short term is a feature of the politics of many countries.[1]

But this has always been a feature of the politics of democracy, for electorates are widely believed to have very short memories so that there are overwhelming pressures on politicians to spend more and to tax less as elections approach. And authoritarian governments are also often under overwhelming pressure to boost their popularity, or at any rate to reward the supporters of the régime.

---

[1] This line of argument is developed in James M. Buchanan and Richard E. Wagner, *Democracy in Deficit* (Academic Press, New York, 1977).

So why is it that government debt has grown so over-whelmingly in the 1970s and the 1980s, when this pattern of causation has always been present?

An important explanation of why 19th- and early 20th-century governments often resisted the political pressure to borrow is that electorates then believed that this was incorrect economics, with the result that deficit financing was not the political asset it subsequently became. Britain ran enormous Budget deficits in the great wars of 1793-1815 and 1914-18, for the need to borrow heavily to finance international conflict has always been accepted. But the economics of Adam Smith took over immediately peace was declared, and public debt fell year after year in relation to the national income. Disraeli was castigated by Gladstone for the ex-pedients he resorted to to balance the British Budget of 1852, and his Budget proposals were defeated in the House of Commons. Ramsay MacDonald's Labour government ran a modest deficit of £120 million in the 1931 world slump (just over 3% of the national income), but the May Committee advised that the Budget be balanced via reductions in un-employment benefits and only half the Labour Cabinet was prepared to support this. King George V urged Ramsay MacDonald to form a National Government in order to balance the Budget, and those members of the Parliamentary Labour Party who believed in deficit financing won only 60 seats at the subsequent general election. So far from being an election asset, *peacetime* deficit financing was actually a recipe for electoral catastrophe less than 60 years ago.

Part of the explanation of the growing debt of many Western countries since the Second World War is that the Keynesian Revolution reversed orthodox economists' ana-lyses of the desirability of deficit financing. Electorates—which had previously regarded peacetime government borrowing as a politically disreputable expedient which only weak governments resorted to—were gradually educated to believe that deficit financing was *correct* economics whenever domestic demand was deficient.

KEYNES'S SOLUTION to the unemployment problem of the inter-War years involved the generation of sufficient effective demand to sustain full employment. He argued that if the private sector failed to spend enough, it then became incumbent on the state to spend what the private sector would not. He accepted that most of this additional government ex-penditure would need to be financed by borrowing.

Keynes did not envisage that government borrowing would be necessary all the time to sustain full employment; for he believed Budgets should be balanced over a period of years. This optimism is reflected in the celebrated *White Paper on*

Employment Policy after the Second World War which the British government published in 1944:

> ". . . to the extent that the policies proposed in this paper affect the balancing of the Budget in a particular year, they [12] certainly do not contemplate any departure from the principle that the Budget must be balanced over a longer period."

Others—including the distinguished US economist, Evsey Domar—were less optimistic, and posed the question: Can Keynesian policies be used to sustain *continuous full employment* if that would entail *indefinite government borrowing*?

> "The theory of the multiplier and our actual experience during this war have demonstrated, I believe, that money income can be raised to any desired level if the volume of public expenditure is sufficiently high. This view will be accepted also by the opponents of deficit financing. Their objections to such a policy are based on several grounds, the most important being the belief that continuous government borrowing results in an ever-rising public debt, the servicing of which will require higher and higher taxes; and that the latter will eventually destroy our economy, or cause an outright repudiation of debt."[2]

E VSEY DOMAR addressed himself to the question: if the United States runs a deficit for ever, what will happen? He arrived at the classic answer that the ratio *Debt/Gross National Product* converges on and will eventually equal the ratio *Deficit/GNP* divided by the economy's long-term rate of growth. Thus if a Budget deficit which is sustained over an indefinite period is divided by the rate of growth, the result is the eventual ratio of the national debt to the national income.

An example to illustrate the conclusion which Domar himself derived from this formula is set out in the accompanying table. This compares the long-term influence of deficits of 0%, 3%, 6%, and 9% of GNP. Domar believed that US growth had averaged 3% over quite long periods, so he took a 3% growth rate for granted. If borrowing ratios of 0%, 3%, 6%, and 9% are divided by a growth rate of 3%, the ratios of government debt to the national income of 0, 1, 2, and 3 shown in the table are arrived at. Domar also assumed

---

[2] Evsey Domar, "The 'Burden of the Debt' and the National Income", in *American Economic Review* (Vol. 34, December 1944).

that the *real* rate of interest (that is, the nominal rate less the rate of inflation) is merely 2%, with the result that *Interest/ GNP*, which equals *Debt/GNP* times the rate of interest is 2% where the deficit is 3%; 4% where the deficit is 6%; and 6% where the deficit is 9%.

With these assumptions, deficit financing involves no long-term cost.

If government spending is increased or taxes reduced by

Domar's Optimism about the Long-Term Cost of Public Debt

Deficit/ GNP	Rate of Growth	Debt/ GNP	Interest Rate	Interest/ GNP
0%	3%	0	2%	0
3%	3%	1	2%	2%
6%	3%	2	2%	4%
9%	3%	3	2%	6%

Table 1

9% of the national income in order to sustain full employment (or else to buy popularity), then after an indefinite number of years taxes have to be raised by 6% of the national income to pay the interest on this continuous government borrowing of 9%. So the government never has to raise taxes by as much as it cut them (or raised expenditure) in the first instance. Domar was able to conclude:

"It is hoped that this paper has shown that the problem of the debt burden is essentially a problem of achieving a growing national income. A rising income is of course desired on general grounds, but in addition to its many other advantages it also solves the most important aspects of the problem of debt."

Domar's analysis became part of the Keynesian conventional wisdom. For several decades the vast majority of Western economists believed that there were no significant long-term problems if sovereign governments achieved full employment through *permanent* deficit-financed expenditures: the taxes required to pay the interest would never catch up with the expenditures. This view pervaded the economics textbooks through which the economically literate were educated; and the economics profession itself devoted extremely little attention in the 1950s and '60s to the long-term "burden" of public debt. This was seen as a *non-problem* because, as the sophisticated were aware, Domar had elegantly disposed of it.

THE FLAW IN THE TABLE is the assumption that the real rate of interest is always 2%, and that it will remain the same, however much governments borrow. For it is this that prevents the interest cost of debt from exploding. But in 1974 Milton Friedman wrote:

> "We have interest rate data over very long periods of time, and these indicate that rates are very similar at distant times, if the times compared have similar price behaviour. More recently, the Federal Reserve Bank of St Louis has been estimating the 'real rate', and their estimates are remarkably stable despite very large changes in nominal rates."[3]

So it wasn't just Domar who assumed that the interest rate would remain the same, however much governments borrowed, which led to the happy conclusion that governments will never have to pay back as high a share of the national income as they borrow. This rests on the crucial assumption that the real rate of interest is less than the rate of growth. However, most Western governments now have to pay real interest rates of 4%, 5%, or even more, while their real rates-of-growth have been only 2 or 3%.

It is evident, therefore, that the assumptions set out in the table are absurdly optimistic. How will extra borrowing [13] actually influence the real rate of interest? If it raises it, then the results set out in the table will need to be modified.

THERE ARE A NUMBER OF countries in the world today with entirely free capital movements. The USA, West Germany, the United Kingdom, and Switzerland are obvious examples. Money can be borrowed in any one of these and spent in others, so they form an international capital market.

Any increase in the demand for finance from anywhere in the world will *raise* interest rates in this unified capital market, while any increase in the funds available will *lower* world interest rates. The total supply of finance in this world capital market is the total saving of all the countries—while the demand for finance is their total investment, plus the demand for finance from countries outside the group who seek to borrow in New York, Frankfurt, or London. So a rise in world saving relative to investment will increase the total funds available and so allow long-term interest rates to fall; a substantial increase in investment in the world as a whole will raise world interest rates.

Government borrowing also has to be financed in the world's financial markets, so this has to compete with private

---

[3] Milton Friedman et al., *Milton Friedman's Monetary Framework: A Debate with his Critics* (University of Chicago Press, 1974).

investment for the finance available. If the aggregate saving that finds its way to the world's capital markets and aggregate private-investment demand are unchanged, but governments seek to borrow more, then world interest rates will be bid upwards. Governments will only obtain the extra finance they need by paying sufficient interest to attract more saving to world capital markets; or else by "crowding out" private investment, because projects will be less capital-intensive the higher the rate of interest.[4]

KEYNESIANS OBJECT TO this approach to the influence of deficits upon world interest rates. They believe the extra world demand that extra government deficits generate will raise world output and therefore aggregate world saving. If the world's budget deficits rise by $100 billion and aggregate world saving also rises by $100 billion (because of the expansion these deficits induce), then the demand for finance and the supply in the world as a whole will rise equally; so there will be no need for world interest rates to rise. Keynesians, therefore, argue that deficits will only raise real interest rates if there is full employment in the world as a whole.

In reality, there will always be some sectors of the world economy which are close to capacity limits, so any extra demand that results from deficit financing will fail to raise supply in at least part of the world. Hence, while global deficit financing may often raise saving to some extent, it will also raise world interest rates because supply will not be sufficiently elastic to allow all the saving required to come forth at an unchanged rate of interest. So deficits will *always* raise real interest rates; and the larger are overall world deficits, the more interests rates will rise.

The diagram below shows how markedly the aggregate deficits of the largest eleven Western economies have risen in the 1970s and the 1980s—so it is no wonder that real interest rates have risen so sharply. The increasing borrowing by developing and Latin American and COMECON economies from the pool of saving of the Western developed economies has naturally added to the upward pressure on world interest rates. But the aggregate deficits of *the developed economies* themselves have been far greater than Third World borrowing, and this has been especially the case in 1983, 1984, and 1985 when the US deficit of over $200 billion has amounted to *between one-third and one-half of total world borrowing by governments*. In 1984, the total US government

---

[4] This line of argument is developed in, for instance, Martin Feldstein, "Fiscal Policies, Inflation and Capital Formation", *American Economic Review* (vol. 70, September 1980).

debt outstanding was approximately $1,400 billion—while Latin American governments owed around $330 billion, South-east Asian governments $130 billion, African and Middle Eastern governments $150 billion, and COMECON governments perhaps $70 billion. US government debt, therefore, amounted to about twice the total debt of all these governments.[5]

Latin America borrowed these huge sums ostensibly to finance "economic development". But that is not where a good deal of the money actually went.

In Argentina successive governments borrowed $50 billion, which could have enabled $50 billion of extra capital equipment and vital raw materials to be imported in order to expand industry and commerce. As soon as the facts are examined, however, it emerges that the current account of the Argentinian balance of payments has been in overall

Aggregate Budget Deficit
(estimate of 11 major countries)

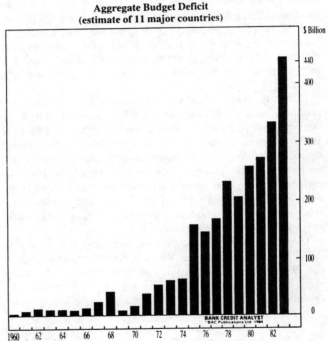

Includes Australia, Canada, France, Germany, Italy, Japan, Netherlands, Spain, Sweden, UK, US (including Federal Agency debt).

[16]

deficit by only $15 billion since 1970, so foreign borrowing financed extra imports of only $15 billion. The remaining $35 billion that Argentinian governments borrowed removed

[5] These statistics are derived from *The Bank Credit Analyst* (November 1984).

balance-of-payments constraints for a few years—and this enabled wealthy Argentinian families to get $35 billion of their personal assets out of the country.

The result today is that the Argentinian State has accumulated $50 billion of international debt (with a present value of perhaps $10 billion to the banks which misguidedly lent the money), while private Argentinian familes have acquired $35 billion of excellent foreign assets (in US and Swiss banks, and in share portfolios) which must be worth at least $50 billion today after the recent rises in the world's stock exchanges.

In other Latin American and Asian countries, a good deal of the money the State borrowed has also found its way to its political supporters and to the friends and relatives of those with the vast financial opportunities open to the families which can influence governments.

Some years ago Keith Griffin and John Enos showed that *there is no correlation between the extra finance that foreign aid makes available to developing countries and their subsequent investment and growth.*[6] On balance, they showed, the extra financial resources which the world made available to the governments of developing countries added little to total investment (though there was some substitution of projects which donors supported for the investments which would otherwise have been undertaken). In contrast, additional international finance very clearly raised consumption and (it can be conjectured) especially that of the political supporters of the fortunate governments which obtained it.

THERE HAVE, naturally, been governments which actually invested a good deal of the money they borrowed in the 1970s and the early 1980s (for instance, Mexico). The profitability of such investments has been drastically affected by the recent collapse in the oil price, and it is universally agreed that the financial return from what was borrowed from Western banks by Latin American and Asian governments will not even begin to service the interest on outstanding loans.

It must be remembered, however, that the bulk of the vast increase in government borrowing which has so raised world real interest rates has not gone to the world's poorer countries. Approximately half of total world government borrowing has recently been by the USA. Americans

[6] K. B. Griffin and J. L. Enos, "Foreign Assistance; Objectives and Consequences", *Economic Development and Cultural Change* (vol. 18, April 1970).

borrowed these vast sums because President Reagan was convinced of the overriding need to reverse the cuts in defence spending of previous administrations, and to reduce taxes in order to achieve the benefits that "supply-side economics" offered. In 1980-84, the US government raised real defence spending 37% and total Federal spending 19%; and it cut taxes substantially at the same time. Despite a remarkable growth performance (nearly in line with the predictions of Washington's "supply-siders"), these simultaneous boosts to expenditure and reductions in taxation have raised the Federal budget deficit to 5½% of the national income and the structural deficit to perhaps 4%. And today perhaps half of this structural deficit actually consists of debt interest, and a great deal of this is interest on the $1,000 billion that the Reagan Administration has itself borrowed. To quite a considerable extent therefore, it has been the rise in debt interest itself that has raised US and therefore world government borrowing to the present extraordinary levels.

THESE INTEREST COSTS rose so steeply because extra borrowing raises real interest rates throughout the world—which greatly surprised some of Washington's leading "supply-siders". Like Evsey Domar and Milton Friedman, they too had believed that real interest rates would not deviate significantly from the levels experienced over most of the 20th century. But the overall level of government borrowing in the early 1980s was unprecedented in peacetime; and it is widely understood today that if governments increase borrowing to this extent on a world scale, then real interest rates have to rise to equate the worldwide demand for saving to the total funds available.

Since the US government has been responsible for up to one-half of global government borrowing and outstanding world debt, it has also exercised the dominant influence on world interest rates. When the US government borrows more, all countries have to pay more for money. But so far world interest rates have been spoken of as if there is a single interest rate, when each country actually pays a different rate for the money its government borrows.

Countries with credit-worthiness as high as the USA's will pay what is in effect the US rate of interest, which is dominated by the level of world (and especially US) borrowing. Countries where there is judged to be a risk of default will have to pay higher dollar rates than the US, and higher interest rates in their own currencies to reflect the rate at which their exchange rate is expected to fall against the dollar.

Thus, the Brazilian, Mexican, and Argentinian governments pay dollar interest rates that exceed those the US government pays because there is a significant risk that they will default or, more probably, ask for a continual rescheduling of repayments which comes close to default. The British government now pays a sterling rate of interest that exceeds the dollar rate the US government pays by between 1% and 2% per annum because the pound is expected to fall against the dollar by between 1% and 2% per annum over the next ten to twenty years.

The Swiss and West German governments, conversely, pay about 2½% less than the US government because the Swiss franc and the Deutschmark are expected to rise against the dollar.

As an individual government raises its borrowings, it will, for two reasons, raise the rate of interest it has to pay. It will [17] raise it, first, because its borrowing adds to total world borrowing—and this raises the interest rates all countries have to pay. But this is only significant in the case of the United States, since other countries have an insignificant individual influence on aggregate world borrowing and saving.

Secondly, as each country raises its borrowing, it increases the risk that it will default or seek to reschedule its debts, or that its future inflation rate will rise—with the result that its exchange rate will fall in relation to the United States. These will all raise the interest rate its government has to pay in relation to US rates. It is a general proposition of "portfolio theory" that investors are less attracted to an asset the greater the relative amount of it that has to be disposed of; and extra government borrowing will always increase the relative quantity of an individual country's debt. Consequently, this will reduce its desirability as a portfolio asset, and therefore raise the interest rate the government has to pay.

THE GENERAL CONCLUSION—that governments have to pay a higher rate of interest, the more they borrow—devastates Domar's optimism. The table is recalculated below, on the assumption that each percentage point increase in a country's "Deficit/GNP" ratio raises the rate of interest its government has to pay by one third of 1%. That assumes a relatively modest linkage between extra government borrowing and the rate of interest; but it entirely alters Domar's conclusions.

Here raising the deficit by 3%—from, say, 3% to 6% of the national income—means that taxation eventually needs to be increased by 5%—from 3% to 8% of the national income—to pay additional debt-interest. Deficits, therefore, no longer offer a free lunch.

In this instance a 3% increase in the deficit allows the government to raise spending or to cut taxes by 3% of the national income. But it has to raise taxation or cut public expenditure by 5% of the national income at some point in the future to finance the 5% increase in debt interest.

Thus, if a government fulfils immediate political objectives by borrowing, a future government will have to impose larger sacrifices.

This conflict between present social and political benefits and future costs will arise wherever the real rate of interest exceeds the rate of growth.[7] If the rate of interest exceeds the rate of growth—as it does (in the second table) at all borrowing ratios in excess of 3% of the national income—then more has to be paid in the future (as a share of the

Additional Government Borrowing Raises Interest Rates

Deficit/ GNP	Growth Rate	Debt/ GNP	Interest Rate	Interest/ GNP
0%	3%	0	2%	0
1½%	3%	½	2½%	1¼%
3%	3%	1	3%	3%
4½%	3%	1½	3½%	5¼%
6%	3%	2	4%	8%
7½%	3%	2½	4½%	11¼%
9%	3%	3	5%	15%

Table 2

national income), in the form of additional debt interest, than the extra that is borrowed in the first instance.

It was because Evsey Domar assumed a rate of interest of only 2%—which was less than the 3% growth rate which he took for granted—that he got his comfortable result. The moment the real rate of interest the government has to pay *exceeds* the long-term rate of growth—as it has for almost all governments since 1981—a higher share of the national income will need to be sacrificed in the future for anything extra that is borrowed in the present.

IT HAS BEEN SUPPOSED so far that governments actually raise taxation, or cut expenditure, in order to pay growing debt interest. But recent experience has shown that they frequently fail to do this. Governments commonly

---

[7] Where a government borrows from and pays interest to its own citizens, it will levy tax on that interest, so the relevant interest rate in this calculation is the rate of interest it pays *less* the tax it claws back. Where it borrows from foreign governments or banks, it cannot recover tax in this way. So it is the *gross* rate of interest that will need to be compared with the future rate of growth.

seek to add debt interest to their borrowing. They aim to raise public expenditure or cut taxation in the first instance, and then to borrow this fraction of the national income *plus the accumulating interest on what they borrowed initially*. In 1981 it was shown by two distinguished American economists that wherever the rate of interest exceeds the rate of growth, the procedure of adding accumulating interest to what is borrowed initially must lead to an explosive and unlimited growth of debt, with the inevitable consequence of eventual repudiation, or else monetisation leading to hyperinflation.[8]

When a government reaches the limits of its power to borrow—as it inevitably will if it seeks to borrow accumulating debt interest when the interest rate exceeds the growth rate—it will be faced with the unattractive choice of repudiation or monetisation. If the debt is denominated in foreign currency, there is no choice—because the government cannot print foreign money. If it cannot finance debt denominated in foreign currency, it has no alternative but to seek to renegotiate, and in the last resort to repudiate, its debt.

The penalty for repudiation is that several generations may elapse before international finance again becomes available. Foreign governments and banks can be defrauded once; but after that decades may go by before they cease to regard promises from that country as worthless—so they will only make goods and capital available when these are paid for *in advance* and in hard currency. It is a considerable inconvenience for countries to be in a situation where commercial borrowing is impossible; and it is undignified for the people of a country to be governed by those whose signature is worthless. Countries and governments suffer these indignities and inconveniences from time to time, but the condition is unfortunate. Governments will not pursue [18] policies which inevitably involve default. They may, however, blunder into this situation rather easily if real interest rates exceed growth rates as they have in most of the world in the 1980s.

Governments that borrow in their own currency have the alternative option of printing money to pay the interest on previous borrowing. This will inevitably lead to hyperinflation if borrowing rises all the time because the real rate of interest exceeds the rate of growth. The sums which will need to be printed will rise exponentially. A consequence will be that the real value of monetary wealth, including all previous government debt, will be destroyed; and there will be subsequent unwillingness to hold money printed by that

---

[8] Thomas J. Sargent and Neil Wallace, "Some Unpleasant Monetarist Arithmetic", *Federal Reserve Bank of Minneapolis Quarterly Review* (Fall 1981).

government. It will take decades before such a government will be able to borrow significant sums again, in its own money or any other. Thus the procedure of adding accumulating interest to what is borrowed will again lead to financial disaster wherever the real rate of interest exceeds the growth rate. Governments will hardly embark on this if they foresee the consequences—but the debt of many Western economies *is* none the less growing at considerable rates.

One expert, John Bispham of the Bank of International Settlements, presented a comprehensive account of the borrowing trends of Western developed economies at a recent conference on public debt, and his most recent statistics include the data in Table 3.[9] This shows that Belgium, Italy, and Ireland already have ratios of government debt to the national income of over 100%, and their debt is continuing to grow rapidly.

Several other countries have more modest ratios, but these will rise towards 100% and beyond with present deficits, real interest rates, and growth rates. Thus The Netherlands, Canada and the USA have quite substantial deficits, and interest rates that are higher than their rates of growth. No corrective action to reduce the US deficit has as yet been taken (though some has been promised); and by 1986 United States public debt has risen considerably above the 29% of the national income ratio shown in the table. Debt to national income ratios are also continuing to rise rapidly in The Netherlands and Canada.

Nominal interest rates have fallen by several percentage points since 1985, but so have inflation rates; and real interest rates still exceed the rate of growth in most Western countries. Bispham has calculated that even if growth rises to 3% and real interest rates fall to 2%, the escalating cost of *existing* borrowing will raise the ratio of government debt to the national income to more than 100% in seven Western economies. Though growth may actually rise to 3% in many countries, there is, of course, virtually no possibility that real interest rates will fall to 2%.

Western economies will, therefore, find that the interest burden of growing public debt will raise increasingly difficult

---

[9] J. A. Bispham, "Rising Public Sector Indebtedness: Some More Unpleasant Arithmetic", in M. Boskin, J. S. Flemming and S. Gorini (eds), *Private Saving and Public Debt* (to be published in 1987 by Basil Blackwell). The data in the table are derived from his (less comprehensive) "Growing Public Sector Debt: A Growing Policy Dilemma" in *National Westminster Quarterly Bank Review* (May 1986). Bispham assumes that the net-of-tax cost of the interest that governments pay is always three-quarters the rate of interest on long-term government bonds (except for Italy where the interest paid on government bonds is free of tax).

Deficits and Debt in Several Western Countries in 1985

Country	Deficit/ GNP	Debt/ GNP	Interest Rate minus Growth Rate	Years before Debt/GNP reaches 100%
Belgium	9.8%	110.5%	1.3%	already 100%
W. Germany	1.1%	23.1%	0.3%	over 400
France	3.4%	17.4%	1.0%	30
UK	3.6%	49.9%	−0.7%	199
Italy	14.1%	104.2%	2.6%	already 100%
Netherlands	5.3%	67.4%	0.7%	45
Sweden	3.2%	17.7%	0.3%	32
Ireland	12.6%	107.5%	2.1%	already 100%
Denmark	2.7%	38.8%	0.9%	35
Japan	1.6%	27.5%	−1.4%	never
Canada	6.7%	36.9%	0.7%	14
USA	3.7%	29.1%	1.7%	25

Table 3

problems. Britain is a rare exception, as the British economy is one of the few where the debt to national income ratio has been stable in recent years, and the latest data show that the 1985-86 fiscal deficit has unexpectedly fallen to 1.6% of the national income (which is considerably below the 1985 ratio of 3.6% shown in the table). But, at almost 50%, Britain's ratio of public debt to national income is one of the higher ones, and the adoption of substantially looser fiscal policies could rapidly produce the same difficulties for Britain as others are experiencing.

IT GOES WITHOUT SAYING that there are many Latin American, Third World, and COMECON countries with public debt problems which are even more intractable than those of the hardest pressed Western economies. Their difficulties are, partly, a consequence of attempts to realise short-term political and economic gains via expenditure plans which have proved unfinanceable. There has also been the intellectual error stemming from the "Borrowing Fallacy" that growth rates always exceed interest rates.

The recent rise in real interest to rates far above economic growth in most of the world has exposed an intellectual error in the Keynesian analysis that dominated the 1950s and the 1960s. This made too strong a case for government borrowing by taking it for granted that growth rates would normally exceed real interest rates. That fallacy tempted many countries towards unsustainable deficits which are now producing unfinanceable public debt. For many countries the political costs now far exceed the benefits which governments derived when they spent so ambitiously a few years ago. Correcting these deficits is painful.

Examples abound of the dreadful social and political costs that are being paid today for the extravagant borrowing of governments in the 1960s and the 1970s. Latin America has had to cut imports by no less than 42% in the last four years. Mexico has reduced imports by 55%, Argentina by 43%, Venezuela by 40%, and Brazil by 24%. Real wages have fallen by 30% in Mexico and 23% in Brazil.[10] And this is merely paying the interest on what was borrowed. The debts remain. [19]

The Western banks which advanced vast sums to Latin America and Asia should have been using a proportion of their profits to write off some of the debt which they will never recover. The British banks certainly have, and it is to be hoped (but in some cases doubted) that the leading US banks have been equally prudent. The extra growth of the world economy which should in due course follow the collapse of the oil price will also ease these problems, at least for those banks which are not especially involved with the oil producers.

In the end, the principal sufferers from the intellectual errors that caused the debt explosion of the 1970s and '80s will be the populations of the countries with unfinanceable public debt.

---

[10] These statistics are derived from Christopher Allsopp and Vijay Joshi, "The International Debt Crisis", *Oxford Review of Economic Policy* (Vol. 2, Spring 1986). [20]

16

7. How Inflation Undermines Economic Performance

Walter Eltis*

INTRODUCTION

It is still widely believed, and especially by academic economists who follow the Keynesian tradition, that the control of inflation matters far less than output and employment. Their approach is at first sight compatible with the compensation test that is commonly applied to estimate whether an economic change is beneficial to welfare. Can the gainers compensate the losers and still remain better off after they have done so? Anything that raises an economy's aggregate output should pass that test, because if an economy produces more and the extra is correctly measured, those who benefit must by definition have enough extra GNP to compensate the losers and still gain themselves. The deflationary policies that are often needed to bring inflation down are liable to reduce GNP in the first instance, and many economists have been unwilling to recommend this temporary sacrifice of output, employment and growth, which must produce more losers than gainers until output recovers. For the same reason economists who follow the Keynesian tradition have been especially ready to recommend reflationary policies, even when these are likely to raise the inflation rate, because they believe that such increases in inflation will be of minor significance in comparison with the benefits from extra output, which are bound to produce more gainers than losers.

But if inflationary economies perform less well in the medium and long term, they will produce more losers than gainers if a long enough time horizon is considered and the future is not unduly discounted. It will be suggested in this chapter that there are several reasons why inflationary economies will eventually underperform those which achieve near-price stability and in that event the compensation test applied with a sufficiently long time horizon will not favour an acquiescence in inflation.

HISTORICAL ASPECTS

The high point of economists' growth-mindedness and indifference to inflation came in the period of high Keynesianism that followed the adoption of *The General Theory of Employment, Interest and Money* as the theoretical foundation for policy advice in all English-speaking countries in the decade after the Second World War. This is no accident. In the *General Theory* there is the statement (1936: 300), 'in general, supply price will increase as output from a given equipment is increased. Thus increasing output will be associated with rising prices, apart from any change in the wage unit.' So, disregarding any changes in wages, Keynes says that if output is raised from a given capital stock, prices will also tend to rise. If wages rise as well, the inflationary effect will be that much greater.

81

In the conditions of the 1930s when Keynes wrote, it was widely believed that it was a world-wide problem that prices had become too low in the slump and that it would be a beneficial consequence of reflationary policies if these restored 'adequate' prices. It is a central proposition in *The General Theory* that the application of Keynesian boosts to demand will raise, or rather restore, prices to more appropriate and higher levels. Some post-Keynesians have preferred to describe supply curves as horizontal and claim that modern industry will generally supply more at an unchanged selling price, but discount sales below list-prices are prevalent where demand is depressed, so *de facto* prices as against list-prices will certainly tend to be higher, the greater the level of demand in relation to productive capacity as Keynes himself insisted.

Keynesians initially welcomed the inflationary tendency of demand expansionary policies. The United Kingdom Treasury was gradually converted to a Keynesian approach during the Second World War, and in 1943 a Steering Group, contemplating postwar policy argued the advantages of moderate inflation:

> A rise in prices and incomes sufficiently slow to avoid a violent disturbance of the expectations of the recipients of fixed income, yet sufficiently perceptible gradually to unloose the dead hand of debt, has much to be said in its favour.   (Booth 1983: 113)

The Treasury evidently believed at this time that the inflation rate could be increased without a corresponding need to raise interest rates and without bond-holders noticing that the real value of their capital was diminishing. This belief had some plausibility until 1955 when Professor Sir Dennis Robertson remarked on hearing that the Church of England was switching from government bonds to equity shares, 'if you can't fool the Church of England, there is no one left you can fool any more'. After just 12 years the policy of running an inflationary economy in order gradually to eliminate government debt was played out.

But in the 1950s Keynesians discovered a new argument in favour of inflation, that it would have a favourable impact on long-term growth. Nicholas Kaldor (later Lord Kaldor), a senior adviser to United Kingdom Labour governments in 1964–70 and again from 1974–9 provided a foretaste of this approach in the advice (published in 1960) which he offered to the Radcliffe Committee on the Working of the Monetary System. His memorandum has a section headed 'The Dangers of a Regime of Stable Prices', and he goes on to say (Kaldor 1960: 149):

> it is dangerous for a weakly progressive economy to aim at a regime of stable prices . . . since when the rate of growth of production is low . . . stable prices are only consistent with low rate of profit which may be insufficient to maintain the inducement to invest. . . . in the United Kingdom the rate of growth of the 'real' gross national product in the period 1950–57 was three per cent a year. If inflation had been entirely avoided, the average rate of profit on new investment would have been . . . 6 per cent.

Kaldor regarded a 6 per cent nominal rate of return on capital as inadequate because with nominal interest rates in the plausible United Kingdom range of 4 to 7 per cent there would be too little incentive to invest. His calculations for the Radcliffe Committee were based on his recently discovered formula (Kaldor 1960: 148) for the determination of the rate of profit (r) that, 'as a first approximation' this can be taken 'as being equal to the rate of growth in the money value of the gross national product (g) divided by the proportion of profits saved (s_p)'. That is, $r = g/s_p$. He offers examples of 0.4 and 0.5 for s_p, the proportion of profits saved, and assumes for the quoted calculations he presents that half of profits are saved, so that $s_p = 0.5$ and $r = 2g$. This produces the remarkably simple result that industry's rate of return on capital can be expected to be twice the rate of growth of nominal GNP. So, if the inflation rate could be raised by 1 per cent which would raise g (the rate of growth of nominal GNP) 1 per cent, then r, the rate of profit on capital, would be raised by 2 percentage points. In the early Keynesian manner Kaldor made no reference to the possibility that nominal interest rates might rise as inflation increased. Hence each 1 per cent advance in inflation would raise the rate of profit 2 percentage points without any tendency to increase the rate of interest. It is no wonder that he went on to recommend that Britain's inflation rate which was no more than 1 per cent in 1959 should be raised to 4½ per cent because this together with the economy's underlying real growth of 3 per cent would produce a rate of growth of nominal GNP of 7½ per cent and a rate of return on capital of 15 per cent. United Kingdom inflation rose sharply after 1959 and it peaked at 27 per cent in 1975, a year in which company profitability virtually disappeared. Nobody today would wish to resurrect Kaldor's proposition that each 1 per cent addition to inflation raises the nominal rate of return on capital by 2 percentage points. Nor do economists believe any longer that the rate of interest can be held down when inflation rises.

During the 1960s and the 1970s there was a growing realization that if inflation raises the rate of profit it will also raise the rate of interest so inflation will not boost profit rates relative to interest rates and so stimulate the inducement to invest. The world's inflationary economies began to devalue regularly, and the United Kingdom with 7 per cent more inflation than West Germany in 1978 and 1979 had developed long- and short-term interest rates that were 6 per cent above Germany's. The market expectation was presumably that since the United Kingdom had 7 per cent more inflation than Germany it would have to devalue by something like 7 per cent per annum averaged over the years in relation to Germany's currency, and holders of sterling assets would need to be compensated for this regular tendency towards devaluation with extra interest of around 7 per cent per annum. The Keynesian policy of inflating to stimulate profits and growth was therefore played out by 1979 because the United Kingdom's extra inflation had raised the rate of interest as much as the rate of profit. In 1898 Knut Wicksell (1898: 3–4) had predicted that this would be the outcome of using inflation to generate an apparent increase in profitability:

It is . . . widely believed that what is most desirable of all is a state of affairs in which prices are rising slowly but steadily, . . . if a gradual rise in prices, in accordance with an approximately known schedule, could be reckoned on with certainty, it would be taken into account in all current business contracts; with the result that its supposed beneficial influence would necessarily be reduced to a minimum. Those people who prefer a continually upward moving to a stationary price level forcibly remind one of those who purposely keep their watches a little fast so as to be more certain of catching their trains. But to achieve their purpose they must not be conscious or remain conscious of the fact that their watches are fast; otherwise they become accustomed to take the extra few minutes into account and so after all, in spite of their artfulness, arrive too late. . . . (Wicksell 1898)

By 1979 the attempts to set the inflationary clocks of United Kingdom business ahead of the interest rate had failed and British industrialists were missing as many trains as in the 1920s and the 1930s when price stability had been the norm. This became increasingly understood in the late 1970s when there was also a growing concern whether, because of supply–side weaknesses and rigidities which were tending to produce near-vertical aggregate supply curves, United Kingdom industry would actually produce more in response to extra demand. Wage-setting behaviour appeared to be absorbing most injections of demand into higher pay with the result that the impact of higher demand was felt mainly in higher prices. In 1976 Mr James Callaghan, the Labour Prime Minister, launched a celebrated attack on the previous Keynesian orthodoxy which had recommended policies to raise employment whenever this was judged to be less than 'full', whatever the inflationary consequences:

> We used to think that you could spend your way out of a recession and increase employment by cutting taxes and boosting government spending. I tell you in all candour that the option no longer exists, and that in so far as it ever did exist, it only worked on each occasion since the war by injecting a bigger dose of inflation into the economy, followed by a higher level of unemployment as the next step. Higher inflation followed by higher unemployment. We have just escaped from the highest rate of inflation this country has known; we have not yet escaped from the consequences: high unemployment. That is the history of the last twenty years.

Mr Callaghan's government adopted monetary targets in 1976 and increased the priority attached to reducing inflation. The Conservative government, led by Mrs Margaret Thatcher which was elected in 1979, pushed the priority attached to reducing inflation still further and by 1981 her government's tight monetary and fiscal policies had more than doubled unemployment. At about this time economists developed the concept of 'hysteresis', which suggested that temporary sacrifices of employment and production could easily become long-term ones as unemployed workers lost skills and work-attitudes so that they became unemployable and formed part of a permanently larger pool of unemployment. The rise in unemployment from 1979 to 1981 and the growing belief that a good deal of this might become near-permanent caused great distress to the British economics profession, and many academic economists could not understand why it was right to sacrifice so much output and employment in order to reduce inflation.

POLITICAL CONSEQUENCES

In contrast, a number of politicians in several countries had become aware that there is considerable political mileage in reducing inflation. Two stylized political facts can be mentioned. In the United Kingdom since the Second World War no government which has significantly raised the rate of inflation has been re-elected, while four governments which reduced inflation, or stabilized it, have been re-elected. In the United States since the Second World War, no President where inflation rose significantly during his first term has been re-elected, while several Presidents who held or reduced inflation have been re-elected. Why is there this conflict between the apparent political appreciation of the damage that inflation causes and the belief of many economists that overriding priority should be attached to short-term output employment and growth? What is the damage to economies that politicians perceive which fails to enter into the calculus of many economists in English-speaking countries? Frank Hahn, who became a Professor of Economics in Cambridge University shortly before Lord Kaldor's retirement, is a notable recent example. In lectures he gave in Birmingham in 1981 he said (1982: 106), 'inflation as such is not an outstanding evil, nor do I believe it to be costly in the sense that economists use that term'. He also said, 'I am after all this left with the outstanding problem in inflation theory: why do people seem to hate it? Why does it drive politicians to destructive frenzy?' (101), and he cannot 'explain the election of governments whose top priority is the reduction of inflation whatever the consequence' (103).

So what is the economic damage that inflation causes which Hahn was unable to see ut which must be quite widely discernible in the political community at large? One vious cost of inflation is that if the general price level has a continual tendency to rise, rices in general will alter more frequently and by larger amounts. This will make it more fficult for producers and consumers to take efficient decisions because it will be harder r them to distinguish changes in relative prices which ought to elicit changes in resource location from changes in the general price level, which should, according to Hahn, be mpatible with neutral behaviour.

CONOMIC EFFECTS

ahn did not, of course, replicate Kaldor's error of supposing that inflation will be good r business because it raises the rate of profit without increasing the rate of interest. He lied instead on the proposition that two economies in steady growth with different rates f inflation are in essence the same real economy. Under steady growth with inflation erfectly anticipated, each percentage point addition to the rate of inflation will raise both e nominal rate of return on capital and the rate of interest 1 percentage point. If it is pposed that in a typical OECD economy in the late 1980s the real rate of return on apital was 10 per cent and the real rate of interest 5 per cent, then with zero inflation e nominal rate of return on capital would also be 10 per cent and the nominal interest te 5 per cent. With 10 per cent inflation, the nominal return on capital and the nominal terest rate would both become 10 percentage points higher, so the rate of profit would ecome 21 per cent instead of 10 per cent (allowing for compounding) while the nominal te of interest would be 15½ per cent instead of 5 per cent. At first sight the incentive invest should be the same in the inflationary economy with a nominal rate of profit of 1 per cent and an interest rate of 15½ per cent as it is in the economy enjoying the dvantages of price stability with a profit rate of 10 per cent and an interest rate of 5 per ent, for the profit rate is 5 percentage points above the interest rate in both economies. n real terms they appear to be the same economy.

If the government of the inflationary economy decided to reduce inflation to zero, the te of profit would gradually fall from 21 per cent to 10 per cent, and the interest rate om 15½ to 5 per cent, and it is not obvious at first sight what significant real advantages ould be attained, but a very high economic price in terms of transitional unemployment ould have to be incurred while inflationary expectations were squeezed out of the conomy. This price is liable to be especially great if, as appears to be the case in the Jnited Kingdom, prices and wages are 'sticky' downwards which will prolong the ecessionary conditions which prevail while the inflation rate is being brought down. Hahn nd others who use this line of argument insist that it is not worth this temporary sacrifice f real production and employment to move from 10 per cent to zero inflation when the eal benefits that price stability would confer are unclear.

But the proposition that economies with 10 per cent and zero inflation are essentially he same economy omits to bring out that the ratio of interest payments to profits is onsiderably higher in the inflationary economy. This is illustrated in Table 7.1, where ome of the detailed differences between these two hypothetical economies are brought ut. The share of profits will not in general be higher in the inflationary economy, because nflation does not normally allow companies to widen profit margins. Prices rise faster but o do wages and other costs. The aggregate interest bill will in contrast be a higher ratio

Table 7.1:   The general impact of inflation on companies in steady 3 per cent growth

	Company output	Capital stock	Company profits	Company debt	Interest payments	Profits net of interest
Zero inflation		K	P	D	$i \times D$	$P - i \times D$
5% interest rate						
Year 1	100.0	200.0	20.0	60.0	3.00	17.00
Year 2	103.0	206.0	20.6	61.8	3.09	17.51
10 per cent inflation						
15.5% interest rate						
Year 1	100.0	200.0	20.0	60.0	9.30	10.70
Year 2	113.3	226.6	22.66	67.98	10.54	12.12

It is assumed in this example that the real rate of growth is 3 per cent, and the real rate of interest 5 per cent. Where inflation is 10 per cent the growth of money output is therefore 13.3 per cent and the nominal rate of interest is 15.5 per cent. Physical company capital is assumed to be twice the value of output, and companies borrow amounts each year which maintain debt at three-tenths of the nominal value of their capital stock on which they pay 5 per cent when there is zero inflation and 15.5 per cent when there is 10 per cent inflation. Profits net of capital consumption are one-tenth of the value of physical capital. These are typical OECD ratios

of the national income in the inflationary economy. In the illustrations in Table 7.1, where the ratio of company debt to the capital stock is assumed to be 30 per cent whether inflation is zero or 10 per cent, net profits are 20 per cent of output in both economies, but interest is 3 per cent of output in the economy with price stability and 9 per cent of output in the economy with 10 per cent inflation. Hence interest costs absorb 3/20 of profits in the economy with price stability and 9/20 of profits where there is 10 per cent price inflation. It is therefore far from true that the two economies are essentially the same, because nominal interest payments are a far higher ratio of GNP in the inflationary economy, even in the steady-state conditions so far assumed where inflation is perfectly anticipated.

If interest costs are a higher ratio of output and profits in a steady state when inflation is faster, then as soon as there is a departure from steady-state conditions companies will be far more vulnerable to financial destabilization in the inflationary economy. Shock events that disturb the smooth growth of profitability will therefore leave companies less able to finance the payment of interest on debt.

Some would question whether it is realistic to suppose as in Table 7.1 that companies in inflationary economies carry as much debt as they have to bear where there is price stability. It is widely supposed, as the United Kingdom Treasury assumed in 1943, that inflation wipes out debt. Would it not be discovered in the inflationary economy that as inflation rises company debt gradually disappears? Sadly for the businessmen, in such economies this does not actually occur. Inflation does not improve companies' cash flow in relation to the costs they must incur. Wage and raw material costs generally rise at least as rapidly as final prices so, as in Table 7.1, net profit margins become no wider and companies' requirements for outside finance rise as fast as prices. In the United Kingdom recent inflationary episodes have greatly increased the need for companies to borrow. The assumption in Table 7.1 that companies borrow an amount each year which holds their ratio of debt to real capital stable is therefore a closer statement of their true financial

eeds in inflationary conditions, than the naïve belief that inflation assists them by wiping
ut their past debt.

If none the less companies preferred to respond to inflation by holding down their total
nterest payments to the proportion of profits that they regarded as appropriate in non-
flationary conditions, then in the example set out in Table 7.1, the ratio of debt to
apital would have to be reduced from 30 per cent to approximately 10 per cent. With a
hird as much debt companies could pay the three-times-higher interest rate that prevailed
ith 10 per cent inflation and still maintain the same ratio of interest payments to profits.
ompanies can therefore choose either to maintain their ratio of debt to capital, in which
ase they will have to pay far more interest as in Table 7.1, or to greatly reduce the level
f their debt if they wish to keep their interest outgoings down. This brings out starkly
ow the impact of inflation upon company finance cannot be neutral. Companies cannot
naintain the same level of debt to capital *and* the same ratio of nominal interest to profits
s equivalent companies in a non-inflationary economy. One or other of these must give.

able 7.2:   Impact of inflation on investment

		Present values					
		With zero inflation and 5% nominal interest rate			With 10% inflation and 15.5% nominal interest rate		
		Gross profits	Discount factor 5% PA	Net present values of future profits	Gross profits	Discount factor 15.5% PA	Net present values of future profits
ear	Cost						
0	100						
1		16.27	0.95	15.50	17.90	0.87	15.50
2		16.27	0.91	14.76	19.69	0.75	14.76
3		16.27	0.86	14.06	21.66	0.65	14.06
4		16.27	0.82	13.39	23.83	0.56	13.39
5		16.27	0.78	12.75	26.21	0.49	12.75
6		16.27	0.75	12.14	28.83	0.42	12.14
7		16.27	0.71	11.57	31.71	0.36	11.57
8		16.27	0.68	11.02	34.89	0.32	11.02
9		16.27	0.64	10.49	38.37	0.27	10.49
10		16.27	0.61	9.99	42.21	0.24	9.99
		Present value returns:		125.67	Present value returns:		125.67
			Cost:	100.00		Cost:	100.00
		Net present value:		25.67	Net present value:		25.67

he example shown in these tables compares projects with identical constant real rates of return of 10 per cent
nd neglects all tax questions). It shows the impact of an increase in inflation from zero (on the left-hand side)
• 10 per cent per annum (on the right-hand side) which leaves the real rate of interest unchanged at 5 per cent.
/hen inflation is 10 per cent the nominal interest rate rises from 5 per cent on the left to 15.5 per cent (allowing
•r compounding) on the right. The 10 per cent inflation which is assumed to influence wages and prices similarly
assumed to boost money profits (on the right) by a cumulative 10 per cent per annum. The discounted present
alue of aggregate future returns is exactly the same in the left- and right-hand tables. The extra inflation which
nises nominal interest rates equally has no effect on the discounted present value of expected future profits,
nd it has no impact on the net present value of the projects. This is 25.67 both where inflation is zero and
here it is 10 per cent.

The example set out in Table 7.1 is concerned with the way in which inflation put
pressure on the finances of companies in the aggregate. The precise way in which a
particular investment project may be influenced is set out in Table 7.2 which is drawn up
with assumptions parallel to those in Table 7.1. This shows in detail how an increase in
inflation from zero to 10 per cent reduces company liquidity and puts financial pressure
on to corporations. The same real capital investment project is compared in the two
hypothetical economies so far considered. On the left there is no inflation and nominal
interest rates are assumed to be 5 per cent, while on the right, there is 10 per cent inflation
and nominal interest rates are 15½ per cent, so as in Table 7.1 the real rate of interest
net of inflation is 5 per cent in both cases. The investments each have a real yield of 15
per cent and they are identical investments, so on a Net Present Value basis they provide
identical real returns and identical present value returns. But the effect of 10 per cent
inflation is that, on the right, every year's profits rise at a cumulative 10 per cent a year
because it is assumed that wages and prices rise at a cumulative 10 per cent a year.

What is the difference for companies between the positions on the left and on the right?
The main difference is that on the right where there is 10 per cent inflation they have to
pay 15½ interest on an investment of 100, so the first year's cash flow, the first year's
profit of 17.9, is almost entirely absorbed by interest. On the left, where there is no
inflation, they have much the same profit, 16.27, but interest of only 5 because the rate
of interest is only 5 per cent so profits are three-times interest. Where there is inflation
profits rise in the later years and come to much exceed interest, but at the beginning
having to pay 15½ per cent interest and receiving almost the same profits means that a
company is in a difficult cash-flow position.

Suppose the occurrence of one of the things that commonly happens to interrupt the
smooth working of an investment in the early years of its life. One possibility is that new
technology does not work as efficiently as expected, so there is difficulty in making
machinery work properly at the beginning of its life. A second possibility is that there is
a recession in the first two years which temporarily weakens markets, so that what a
machine can produce cannot all be sold. A third possibility is that there may be strikes
which disrupt the early cash flows. In these cases a company that is paying 15½ per cent
interest will find that its liquidity is severely damaged. A company that is paying only 5
per cent can far more readily survive such setbacks in the early years.

The result is that statistically (as Sushil Wadhwani (1985) has shown) there is a linkage
between inflation and bankruptcies. Wadhwani estimates that each 1 per cent on the
inflation rate adds 5.8 per cent to the number of bankruptcies. That is on the assumption
that each 1 per cent addition to inflation raises the rate of interest by a full 1 per cent (as
in Tables 7.1 and 7.2), so that the real rate of interest is unaffected. Wadhwani also
considers the case where, when the rate of inflation rises 1 per cent, the interest rate rises
by only one-half a percent. In that event, there is still a 3.4 per cent increase in the number
of bankruptcies. Now, because raising inflation adds to the number of bankruptcies it also
makes investments appear riskier, and because of this the Stock Exchange places them
in a higher-risk class. So there is the undoubted technical effect that, as soon as risk and
uncertainty are introduced into the economic argument to create the possibility that
investments may go badly in their early years, inflation creates a possible inhibition against
investment. This arises because when inflation increases, company profits rise far less than
the rate of interest, so interest costs increase enormously more than profits in the early
years of investments. Later, of course, companies get all this back, so there is no

ifference if perfect foresight or rational expectations are assumed, or if an investment an actually perform as expected right through its life.

Wadhwani also finds that because investments are in a higher-risk class, each 1 per cent ddition to inflation cuts Stock Exchange prices by 8 per cent. This has the effect (allowing or compounding) that where inflation is 7 percentage points faster, a company's equity hare price can be expected to be more than 40 per cent lower in relation to its earnings han in an economy with price stability (since $0.92^7 = 0.56$). It will also be that much ower in relation to the replacement cost of its physical assets. A foreign company that 'ishes to break into a market has the option of setting up its own plant or buying an xisting company. If a company's shares are half as expensive in relation to the :placement cost of its physical assets, takeovers will often become the cheaper option. .xtra inflation which damages the level of Stock Exchange prices will also therefore ender companies more vulnerable to domestic and international takeover, a phenomenon om which the United Kingdom has suffered in its inflationary periods.

One reason why production is riskier in an inflationary economy with adverse pressures n company cash flows and liquidity arises because the 10 per cent inflationary element f a 15½ per cent interest rate is in essence a capital repayment. With 10 per cent inflation, he real debt owed on money previously borrowed will be 10 per cent less after a year, nd what appears to be 10 per cent extra interest is actually compensation to creditors for ie reduction in the real value of their outstanding loans. The 10 per cent higher interest ite therefore has the same kind of impact as a compulsory 10 per cent capital repayment ould have in a stable price economy. A correctly anticipated 10 per cent inflation which aises the interest rate 10 percentage points has the effect of making such debt repayments ompulsory. With 10 per cent inflation, approximately half the real value of a loan will e eroded and have to be repaid via higher nominal interest payments within seven years, nd two-thirds in 10 years (since $0.90^7 = 0.48$ and $0.90^{10} = 0.35$). If a company wishes to orrow for 20 or 25 years, inflation renders this difficult, because the forced repayments imposes mean that loans have to be repaid rather fast. With 100 per cent inflation, half ie real value of a loan is eroded in one year, so the average period of a loan cannot xceed around two years.

In principle, companies can maintain the real value of their debt as in the assumed xample in Table 7.1 by taking out further loans each year. With 100 per cent inflation company which had an original debt of £1 million and wished to maintain its real value ould increase its debt to £2 million after one year, £4 million after two years and so on. . could thus maintain the real value of its debt and so continue to owe the same true mount if it borrowed a further £1 million after one year, and a further £2 million after vo years. It could ease its liquidity problems if it could continually add to its outstanding ominal debt with regular extra borrowing of this kind. By such means companies could effect borrow long-term and avoid the tendency for inflation to continually force them repay debt more quickly than ideal commercial considerations call for.

But there are two reasons why the effect of inflation on debt and interest cannot be so asily compensated through continual extra borrowing. It might not actually be practical borrow these extra sums each year. Lenders would have to judge all the time whether ie borrowing companies were still creditworthy. In addition the extra loans would involve ansaction costs – at a minimum in the form of extra time and trouble – so companies ould not be indifferent between borrowing £1 million in a stable price environment and orrowing an original £1 million and having to borrow further sums each year to maintain ie real period of debt in an inflationary environment.

THE IMPACT ON THE HOUSING MARKET

So far the argument has been concerned with the impact of inflation on companies, bu there are similar adverse effects when families borrow money to finance home ownership The market for housing has a pervasive influence in modern economies on both th economic condition of families and the efficiency with which the labour market function People commonly borrow to buy houses which cost between three and four times the annual salary, and aim to repay their loans over a period such as 20, 25 or 30 years. there is 10 per cent inflation and a worker has to pay 15½ per cent interest, then if h buys a house for between 300 and 400 when his salary is 100 he will have to pay betwee 46½ and 62 or 46½ and 62 per cent of his income as interest when he first buys the house With 10 per cent inflation, 30 or 40 of this 'interest' is in effect a capital repaymen inflation at 10 per cent is obliging the worker to repay the loan in little more than 1 years, when he would actually wish to pay for the house over 20, 25 or 30 years. But h cannot easily take out an extra loan each year. Transaction costs would stand in the wa of this, even if his creditworthiness remained adequate for a regular schedule of extr borrowing. So when there is inflation it is more difficult for the workers and the middl classes to buy houses. If, on the other hand, there is no inflation and interest rates ar only 5 per cent, then when the worker's salary is 100 and the house costs between 30 and 400, only 15 to 20 per cent of the worker's salary is needed to pay interest for th house, which he can finance without complications.

The greatest damage from inflation arises when workers buy houses when the intere rate is low, and then inflation increases and the interest rate rises and suddenly they hav to pay far more interest than they had expected, which puts enormous pressure on the and which therefore makes this aspect of higher inflation extremely unpopular wit workers and salary-earners. For those who are house buyers, if the interest rate they pa is adjusted upwards with inflation, they end up after a few years paying far more intere than they expected when they first bought their homes. The extra sums of money tha workers caught in this situation have to pay are potentially very high fractions of worker's income. If an employee still owes three times his income when inflation an interest rates rise by 5 percentage points, the extra interest he will have to pay will amour to approximately 15 per cent of his income, and this will very significantly reduce h standard of living. This is one of the aspects of an acceleration of inflation that may hel to explain why this is so unpopular with electorates. Those who receive 5 per cent extr interest on their deposits are merely being compensated for faster inflation, whil borrowers for home ownership see their family cash-flows devastated, although they wi subsequently find that the real value of their debt falls far faster.

There is a further impact of inflation on the housing market that is equally significan Local governments who build houses for poorer workers face the same inflatio arithmetic; namely, that when they borrow from central government at 15½ per cen they will have to pay interest of between 46½ and 62 per cent of the incomes of th workers who rent their new houses. As they can charge as rent no more than 25 per ce of a low-paid worker's income, building such houses will involve very large financi deficits. Faced by these, local governments mostly stop building houses for rent whe interest rates rise to 15 per cent or more with the result that government-funded housir becomes scarce. Like workers and companies, most local authorities are not prepared t undertake a programme of continual extra borrowing at nominal interest rates of 15 p cent or more in order to finance a housing programme. The result of a slow-down of loc uthority housing is then that the low-paid who cannot afford to buy houses become nmobile, because they are unable to obtain housing in a new district if they wish to move o take a job that happens to be available there, so they stay in their current houses where ney enjoy security of tenure. This then impedes the free movement of labour, with the esult that it becomes scarce in areas where there are growing employment opportunities, nd where there is at the same time insufficient housing for extra workers, which ccentuates inflation.

This difficulty does not arise in conditions of price stability because local governments hich build when interest rates are 5 per cent need charge no more than 15 to 20 per cent f a low-paid worker's wage to recover their interest, so they can build without incurring uge financial deficits when they let their houses at reasonable rents. The greater vailability of low-cost housing to rent goes on to improve the mobility of labour and it lso raises the welfare of low-income families which are less likely to suffer from nadequate housing in addition to their other difficulties.

OCIAL EFFECTS

1 addition to this damage to the housing market, inflation adds to the pressures that trade nions have to deal with, as Sir John Hicks explained in his account of *The Crisis in .eynesian Economics* (1974). If prices are stable, workers' standards of living remain ntact. Even if they do not get pay increases, what they are accustomed to buy can still e purchased, so they do not need tough bargaining with the underlying sanction of strike ction in order to protect living standards. But if there is 10 per cent inflation, then, if ney do not get pay increases, they will lose 10 per cent of their standard of living each ear, so they will need the protection of trade unions powerful enough to achieve results. any attempt is made to give workers less than 10 per cent or to delay the 10 per cent, ach group of workers will need effective trade unions to represent them in order to put ressure on the rest of the community for their annual 10 per cent. And some studies ave suggested that statistically there is a relationship in the United Kingdom which iggests that the faster the rate of inflation, the greater the amount of strike activity and idustrial action.

Strike activity by trade unions has, in the language of economics, a massive negative xternal effect. So far as the participants to a dispute are concerned, the position is iternalized. A union will call strike action if it judges that its members will gain more y a strike than they will lose. But, added to the effect on the welfare of the trade nionists, there is an impact on everyone else in the community that is negative, because iere will be disruption to many others whenever any group of workers strikes. If it is rguable that the faster the rate of inflation, the greater the degree of disruption due to rike action, it follows again that there is a possible explanation of why the people of a ountry who vote at elections appear to be hostile to inflation. They may be reacting as iuch to consequences such as a greater prevalence of strikes as to the faster price rises iemselves for which they may well be adequately compensated via faster rises in their ioney incomes. Voters are also bound to react adversely to the impression that a overnment does not appear to be in control if there are large numbers of strikes which iuse extensive personal inconvenience.

In addition to their effect on the lives of families, strikes seriously interrupt the smooth ow of production and the ability of companies to meet orders on time. Markets lost through delayed deliveries may go permanently to the producers of other countries Multinational companies are likely to respond by gradually shifting their manufacturing sites away from countries where production becomes unreliable.

An increased risk of interruptions to production also damages productivity by denying companies the use of 'just in time' ordering and stock-control systems which can produce very significant reductions in the cost of working capital and its integration into the production process. Inflation-prone economies will suffer industrially if they at the same time become strike-prone and it must be remembered that strikes in only a small fraction of companies can devastate production in a great many. Each manufacturing company typically buys components from several hundred others and the absence of any one of these can hold up the potential to produce and deliver.

The industrial relations costs of inflation are only partly captured by strike statistics There is a plethora of evidence to demonstrate that bargaining becomes a much more complex and time-consuming activity in inflationary periods, and concern about general inflation distorts consideration of the 'real' issues associated with the need to raise productivity in order to improve international competitiveness. This feeds through to worker attitudes and behaviour in many adverse ways. Strikes are only the tip of the iceberg.

There is a further way in which inflation damages a society and economy which is more difficult to clarify, and that is its influence upon the relative rewards of those who create value-added in industry and those who carry out financial transactions. If prices are stable and industrialists develop new products which create high value-added per worker they they will make money, but rarely more than 10 to 20 per cent of the costs they have to incur. If there is an inflationary situation with high interest rates and a good deal of uncertainty, it is possible for industrialists to create products with high value-added, and then to have to sell them in the wrong currency, to pay the wrong interest rates, to suffer all kinds of changes in money prices and wages which mean that the potential profit margins of 10 to 20 per cent that their high value-added production generates can very easily be eliminated. Because technically successful industrialists may be wiped out by the financial vicissitudes that accompany inflation, manufacturing companies will be placed in a higher-risk class than in economies where prices are stable, and as more capital investment has to be committed which is product-specific than in the financial sector the relative attraction of committing resources to production is diminished. There will be corresponding relative incentive for clever, intelligent and well-educated people to go into banking, insurance and finance and not into production, because the rewards from correct financial decisions and the purchase and sale of well-selected pieces of paper are raised relative to the rewards from the creation of value-added in the form of physical commodities. And so there is a tendency, with inflation, for a society's most talented and ambitious people to move away from industry and into the financial sector. This is one of the most insidious impacts of inflation.

THE IMPACT OF GOVERNMENT COUNTER-INFLATIONARY POLICY

Because of the extent of these various kinds of damage which politicians and electorate are becoming very much aware of, governments realize that inflation has to be stopped This adds to the uncertainty of business because it is not clear whether governments will

:ek to halt inflation mainly by cutting public exenditure or by raising taxation and in the
.tter case, which actual taxes are increased will matter a good deal to companies.
.lternatively, it may be that counter-inflation strategy will mainly take the form of higher
iterest rates and a consequent rise in the exchange rate. When inflation is unacceptably
igh the knowledge that one or more of these is in the offing will interfere with the long-
:rm planning of investment in capital equipment, research and development and
inovation which can take decades to bear fruit. Such business uncertainties lead to a
iort-termism which is absent in Germany, Japan and now France where, because
iflation is under control, companies have no reason to fear a major adverse shift in
overnment policy and its consequences.

Everyone in an inflationary economy is aware that at some point in the future deflation
ill follow, but because the Phillips curve is non-linear (since increases in demand have
far greater tendency to raise wages and prices than have reductions in demand to reduce
iem), the damage to the national income when the government tries to reduce inflation
ill be far greater than the gain when it acquiesces in an increase. So if there is a cycle
hich takes the form 'Keynes on, Keynes off, Keynes on, Keynes off' – expansion
illowed by contraction, expansion followed by contraction – its net effect will be very
amaging to production and efficiency, because the loss of GNP will be greater in the
ownside than the gains on the upside.

ONCLUSION

ine reason why inflation is damaging that has not been emphasized is the one that Milton
riedman has set out and which has become very familiar, namely, that the faster the rate
f inflation, the less use a society will make of money balances. because everybody
:onomizes in money balances when inflation destroys their real value. It is widely argued
iat this is statistically a modest effect at inflation rates of 10 per cent or less and the
dverse impacts to which most importance should be attached are those associated with
ie squeeze on company liquidity; the effect that workers acting defensively to protect
ieir standards of living disrupt the rest of the community; and the effect that the young
nd the educated find that there are greater rewards in the financial sector than in
roduction. These will all have a substantial adverse impact on the growth of output and
ving standards in the medium and the long term.

Some economists accept this but believe that the way to deal with any damage caused
y inflation is simply to index: that with indexing there is no need to worry about inflation,
ecause most of the difficulties referred to will disappear. If the companies illustrated in
'able 7.1 could sell indexed bonds, they could maintain their debt-to-capital ratio without
iising interest payments relative to profits. But if the experience of the countries which
ctually index is examined. they usually have indexes that are not entirely accurate: there
re often four or five indexes that matter, and people can exercise arbitrage advantages
y jumping from index to index. Indexing can also involve massive administrative costs,
nd even the best systems fail to avoid time-lags in adjustment. There is at present no
ountry where indexing deals satisfactorily with the difficulties that have been outlined.

Because in practice indexing has failed to protect the wealth and living standards of
iose who draw the short straws in inflationary periods, inflation inevitably redistributes
'ealth and it does so in an arbitrary manner. Those who are slow to react and adjust lose
'ealth, while others are rewarded because they are quick to see opportunities. There is

a consequent sense of injustice if it appears that it is the industrious and productive who are losing their wealth to those who are merely alert and manipulative. The perceptions of injustice that result from these arbitrary redistributions of wealth can have severe social effects as the losers feel that they have been let down by society. That may be inflation's most significant social effect, but there are also the several ways in which it damages economic and industrial efficiency. It is therefore worth considerable sacrifices to get it down towards the 3 per cent level which was achieved in 1990 by France, Germany, Belgium and Holland, the core economies in the European Exchange Rate Mechanism which the United Kingdom has now joined.

NOTE

* This article is developed with the benefit of comments and criticisms from Alex Bowen, Milton Friedman, Robin Matthews, Ken Mayhew, Martha Prevezer, Martin Ricketts and Howard White from the 1990 Bateman Memorial Lecture, 'How Inflation Undermines Industrial Success', a shortened version of which appeared in the *National Westminster Bank Quarterly Review* in February 1991.

PART V

PRACTICAL MACROECONOMICS: THE ACHIEVEMENT OF SOUND GROWTH

17

The Lessons for Britain from the Superior Economic Performance of Germany and Japan

Walter Eltis, Douglas Fraser and Martin Ricketts

A. The 'success' of Germany and Japan

In the last 30 years, Germany and Japan have achieved a superior economic performance to the United Kingdom in almost every respect. The following paragraphs briefly set out the record.

Productivity in the economy as a whole (Figure 1) indicates that Germany overtook the United Kingdom in the early 1970s while Japan is likely to do so in the early 1990s. In the manufacturing sector, Japan has made particularly large productivity gains since 1970 relative to both the United Kingdom and Germany.

Figure 1
Output per person
(1985 Sterling purchasing power parities)

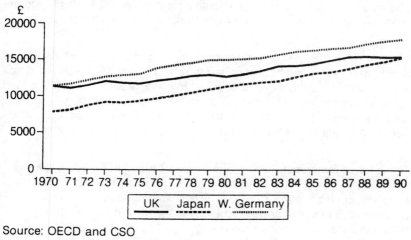

Source: OECD and CSO

Japan's capacity to resist unemployment has been remarkable (Figure 2).
Even in the 1980s the average level of unemployment was only 2.5 per cent
compared with 6.0 per cent in Germany and 10.0 per cent in the United
Kingdom.

Figure 2
Standardised unemployment rate
(as a percentage of total labour force)

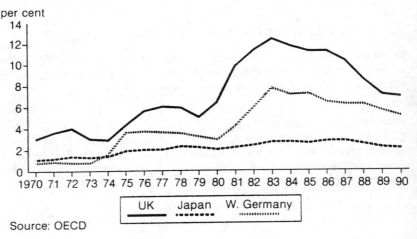

Source: OECD

In the sphere of international trade, Japan's share of total G10 (Group of
10 major countries) manufacturing exports has risen from around 12 per
cent in 1970 to 16 per cent in 1990 and the German share has remained
about 20 per cent throughout the same period, whilst the United Kingdom's
share has been in gentle decline from 10 per cent to around 8 per cent.

If Japan takes the prize for maintaining low unemployment and increasing
export share, Germany has managed to resist inflationary pressures most
effectively over the three decades from 1960 (Figure 3). In the 1960s and
early 1970s Japanese inflation was as high or higher than the United
Kingdom's, but it fell rapidly throughout the second half of the 1970s and
has been similar to the German rate in the 1980s.

These broad features of Japanese and German success are familiar and
inevitably lead to questions concerning the cause of Britain's lagging
performance. Productivity growth, which is what matters most in the
determination of both competitiveness and the growth of output, is
undoubtedly of key importance.

Figure 3
Inflation (3-year moving-average)
(percentage change in consumer price index)

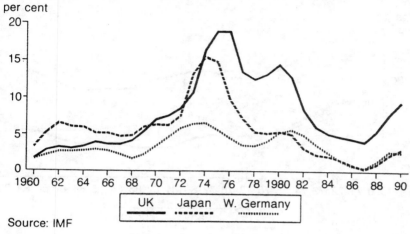

Source: IMF

B. Japan and Germany's faster growth of capital, technology and skills

The factors most often singled out to explain the United Kingdom's inferior productivity are the level, structure, composition and technical quality of investment in both physical and human capital. Gross Fixed Capital Formation as a proportion of GDP for the three countries (Figure 4) shows that the proportion of GDP invested has been consistently higher in Japan than in the United Kingdom, but Germany's investment has only slightly exceeded ours. A lower United Kingdom rate of return on capital appears to be a long standing phenomenon (Figure 5).

It is very widely recognised that the level of investment in human capital has been lower in the United Kingdom. Not only do a higher percentage of 16 to 18 year olds remain in full time education in Germany (47 per cent in 1987) and Japan (77 per cent in 1988) compared with the United Kingdom (35 per cent in 1988), but the availability of part-time education and of training in craft skills is greater. Germany has the famed 'Meister' system, which is described below, while Japan has a reputation for developing the potential of the less academically gifted.

Figure 4
Gross fixed capital formation
(percentage of GDP at current prices)

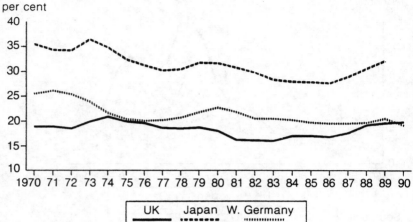

Source: OECD, Eurostat

Figure 5
Rates of return in manufacturing

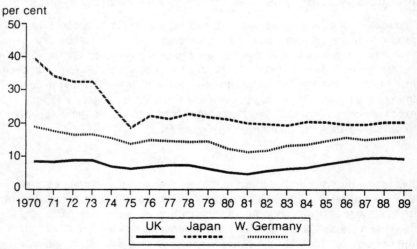

Source: OECD and NEDO estimates

nb. Definition of rate of return: Gross operating surplus
as a percentage of gross capital stock

In addition to deficiencies in the quantity and quality of capital and labour, attention has been drawn to the United Kingdom's poor record of innovation. The effort devoted to innovation can only be measured indirectly, but evidence based on research and development expenditure in the three countries and on trends in patent applications suggest that the United Kingdom is lagging behind both Japan and Germany.

The proportion of gross expenditure on research and development (R&D) to gross domestic product has not changed much over the last two decades in the United Kingdom (Table I). In Japan, the proportion has risen by about a full percentage point and is now close to the German level. The proportion of expenditure on R&D financed by government has been falling in all three countries but remains slightly higher in the United Kingdom than in Germany. Japan has an unusually low reliance on government finance. Government finance of R&D is considered significant because a high proportion (two thirds in the United Kingdom) is devoted to defence industries and aerospace, and this influences the sectoral distribution of research effort.

Table I

Gross expenditure on R&D as a percentage of GDP. In parenthesis: percentage of gross expenditure on R&D financed by government

	Germany	Japan	United Kingdom
1972	2.21	1.76	2.10
	(49.4)	(26.6)	(NA)
1975	2.24	1.81	2.17
	(47.4)	(27.5)	(55.0)
1981	2.42	2.14	2.41
	(40.7)	(24.9)	(49.0)
1985	2.71	2.62	2.31
	(36.7)	(19.1)	(43.4)
1988	2.83	2.72	2.20
	(33.9)	(18.1)	(36.5)

Source: OECD

In the United Kingdom, government R&D policy and funding of the science base has tended to be concentrated into 'glamour' products such as nuclear and astro physics. Such projects can impede the development and training of postgraduate science and engineering talent in other disciplines as well as weakening United Kingdom research efforts of potential commercial value in future high growth technology areas.

Information on patents is given in Table II which shows clearly the fast rate of growth of Japanese applications over time compared with the relatively static levels recorded for the United Kingdom and Germany.

Table II
Total patent applications (000s)

	1965	1970	1975	1980	1983	1988
Germany	38.1	32.8	30.2	30.6	32.1	32.6
Japan	60.8	100.5	135.1	175.7	227.7	308.8
United Kingdom	24.3	25.2	20.8	19.7	20.0	20.7

Source: OECD

Although comparisons of investment trends and innovative activity are suggestive, they do not in themselves provide immediate lessons for the United Kingdom. The perplexing questions relate to why, if there is still so much scope for 'catching up' with leading performers, greater investment does not appear profitable to British industry; or why if a highly skilled workforce is proving so valuable overseas it should appear so relatively unprofitable to individuals and companies in the United Kingdom. To understand why, it is necessary to focus on Japanese and German companies.

C. The superior performance of companies in Germany and Japan

Whilst most major nations can boast of some companies of international standing, there are certain highly traded sectors, electronics and automotives in the case of Japan, automotives and chemicals in the case of Germany, where virtually *all* companies are amongst the world's leaders. These companies moreover continue to be competitive despite relatively high domestic labour costs and an appreciating currency. Their robust underlying competitiveness is based upon the more effective use of people; the achievement of more consistent and superior quality; and constant innovation. These will be examined in turn.

C1. The superior use of people

In Japan, the high levels of labour performance can be ascribed to the effective working together of different skills and levels within teams, to a lack of rigid job definitions associated with a preparedness on the part of employees to attempt anything asked, and to a well educated and well trained workforce capable of undertaking a wide range of tasks. Furthermore, the workforce is actively engaged in looking for better means of undertaking the job in hand – for example: in 1990 the 17,000 employees of Toyota submitted 2 million suggestions, 87 per cent of which were implemented.

In Germany, much of the performance of the workforce can be ascribed to the superior level of vocational skills. In 1987, 20 per cent of school leavers entered university and 64 per cent concluded a vocational training contract. The dual system of vocational training typically involves two days a week over the ages 16 to 18 in a vocational school, where as much as 40 per cent of the time will be spent on continuing general education. The balance is spent in a company, but this on-the-job training is governed by federal laws and regulations. The system is very flexible, and is demand led by companies, although there is a common framework. Rooted in craft apprenticeships, the dual system has evolved to cover a wide range of industrial, commercial and administrative careers. One of the significant features of this system is the relatively low rates of pay of trainees. Employers thus have a positive incentive to take trainees and, indeed, many overtrain which gives them the opportunity of identifying and seeking to retain the best. Because vocational skills are so widely recognised throughout Germany, individuals have a positive incentive to train in order to gain access to interesting and well paid employment.

Japanese compulsory schooling produces disciplined pupils who achieve very high standards of educational performance, particularly in standardised mathematics and science tests. Compulsory schooling which ends at 15 is in mixed ability groups. After this point most young people (95 per cent) progress into different types of high schools, depending upon assessed ability. Over a quarter of young people pursue vocational courses at this point. Subsequently, around 30 per cent of the age group enter university or junior colleges, and over 20 per cent go into public and private training schools (senshu) where they undertake two-year vocational courses.

Recent research indicates that expenditure by Japanese firms on training is not high by international standards, if only training budgets are considered. However, Japanese firms are often 'learning organisations', using methods such as job rotation, quality circles and supervisors for informal training. Japanese workers also undertake considerable correspondence study in their own time with the encouragement and financial support of their employers, and the Ministry of Labour often contributes to the cost. Survey evidence suggests that individuals pursue this study primarily to improve their competence or because it is necessary for the performance of their jobs, rather than to improve their outside qualifications.

Positions in the hierarchy of Japanese companies are not associated with very specialised functions or jobs. On the contrary a person in a given rank will be expected to show great flexibility and gain experience of a wide variety of different functions. But co-operation and alertness are rewarded in the long run by promotion through the hierarchy. The structure encourages 'horizontal' communication, that is, knowledge sharing between team members. Because much of the knowledge and skill accumulated by an individual is not of immediate value to other firms and derives from production experience, 'poaching' is not a major problem. Where transferable skills or knowledge valuable to other firms have been developed by the workforce, mobility could be a bigger problem. However, Japanese firms do not make extensive use of outside markets in highly specialised types of skilled labour. The employment of an outsider may have disruptive effects on a firm's internal ranking hierarchy, effects which may outweigh any benefits that may accede from the use of the outsider's transferable skills.

As a result of these features of Japanese firms, employment tenure tends to be longer than in the United Kingdom or Germany. Long term 'obligational' relationships rather than short term 'arms length' relationships are therefore seen as a distinguishing feature of Japanese business structures. Lump sum separation payments related to length of tenure reinforce this by imposing a considerable penalty on leaving the firm for private reasons.

Close 'horizontal' links between marketing, production and development functions in Japanese firms have proved immensely beneficial. But they rely on the development of a climate of trust and require excellent industrial relations. Working days lost through industrial disputes in Japan have been well below those lost in the United Kingdom throughout the late 1970s and 1980s (Figure 6). The personnel function is of central importance in the Japanese firm. The 'enterprise union' is also important. Japanese managements place great significance on achieving agreement with the union on any change affecting employees and the union places equal significance on contributing to the success of the enterprise. Leadership within the union is often seen as a useful step in a young manager's career. Most wage negotiations are synchronised in the Spring when a great deal of economic data on the country and companies is made available. Payment differentials between levels in the hierarchy are low, there is single status in plants, and in many other ways all employees are made to feel respected and valued.

Figure 6
Working days lost through industrial disputes
(thousands)

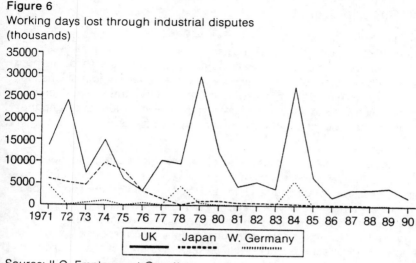

Source: ILO, Employment Gazette

Industrial relations in Germany are strongly influenced by the concept of social partners. The Works Council Constitution Act regulates the rights of employees at their place of work, where there is codetermination via a works council together with employee representation on a supervisory board. Firms with more than 100 employees must set up an economic committee which meets once a month and has access to extensive information on the situation of the firm. Trade unions, although having a strong and independent view of the changes needed to benefit their members, are also committed to low inflation and industrial success.

The higher skills of the German labour force also lead to a superior utilisation of machinery and the main reasons are to do with the training, treatment and attitudes of employees as touched on above. In Germany the role of the 'meister' – a well qualified supervisor with both technical and training functions – is critical. One German company with similar plants in both the United Kingdom and Germany reported that productivity in the United Kingdom plant was 40 per cent lower and ascribed the reasons to lower vocational skills levels and, especially, to the lack of a meister equivalent. The meister, dealing with all but major technical problems as they occur, maintains production and quality. In Japan it is customary for shop floor personnel to undertake first line maintenance. In the UK, the line too often grinds to a halt or starts to produce unacceptable products.

C2. Superior quality

Specific methods of quality management – statistical process control, quality circles, total quality management – were pioneered in the West, developed in Japan and are now being adopted worldwide. These methods can only be applied to their full effect where the underlying conditions are right. The most important of these conditions is a well trained workforce strongly motivated to find ways of improving its own performance and the quality of the product it produces, as already discussed.

A further requirement is the use of technical skills in depth throughout the organisation. The 'meister' system in Germany has been mentioned. In Japan it is usual for all engineers to start their careers on the shop floor. This means that the level of engineering capability on the shop floor is high and hence local problem solving capability is strong. More importantly, when those engineers subsequently gain responsibility for design, the resultant product reflects an understanding of the practicalities of production and can be produced economically and to specification. An 'engineering approach' pervades the whole of production in both Germany and Japan where meticulous attention is given to the systematic collection and analysis of data bearing on all aspects of product and production performance. There is a much greater emphasis than in the United Kingdom on process development. The dominance of world markets by the Japanese integrated circuit industry is almost wholly based upon superior process engineering together with high levels of capital investment.

The remaining critical factor in quality is dedication to customer satisfaction. Both Germany and Japan are highly competitive markets with demanding customers. In Japan in particular, industrial customers expect and receive a very high degree of technical support. The consequent involvement of engineers and other technical design staff feeds back into the design and production process which benefits from a full understanding of customer needs. Manufacturing companies are themselves demanding customers of their subcontractors and component suppliers, and work with them to achieve the highest quality. The effect is to integrate the production and quality management of customers and suppliers without an intermediate inspection stage. This is a necessary condition of 'just-in-time' manufacturing and pays off in reduced stocks, shortened production cycles and increased quality.

A further important element in the achievement of consistent high quality is the price and quality of subcontracted elements and components, which in engineering can account for 60 per cent of the final sales value. Germany has the benefit of a range of small and medium sized, usually family owned companies. This contains many highly competent engineering subcontractors and component suppliers with a strong craft and quality tradition.

Close relationships with suppliers including positive measures to develop their capability, are a particular characteristic of Japan. These relationships will often mean that the supplier firms are heavily dependent on a single customer. Suppliers are therefore under great pressure to meet quality standards, delivery times and requests for cost improvements. Such dependence is tolerable only because the buyer is under an obligation to continue the relationship, subject to satisfactory long term performance. A lower price quote from a competing supplier, for example, would not immediately result in the substitution of that supplier for an existing one. Information is exchanged on future plans; the buyer will often assist with technological improvements, staff training, and even with finance; and purchasing is conducted in such a way that the distinction between inside supply and outside contracting ceases to have much operational significance. Technological relationships with suppliers are particularly important. In many cases company investment in R&D is not just for application within the company, but on behalf of its whole supply chain. These relationships are frequently reinforced by cross shareholdings.

C3. Continuous innovation

The process described above, of close engineering liaison with customers and suppliers, intensive technical involvement throughout the organisation and constant small modifications to improve productivity and quality, also leads to continuing product improvement in respect of features of direct importance to the customer. The German and more especially the Japanese system of continuous product improvement is quite different from normal practice in the United Kingdom, where product innovation usually takes the form of major discrete steps arising from compartmentalised and highly specialised departments within organisations.

The principal driving force behind innovation in Germany and Japan appears to be competition in the market place. With several highly capable companies in each sector, the pressure is on companies to render their own products obsolete before their competitors do. This leads to an openness to new ideas and the Japanese in particular actively search outside the firm for new technologies and product ideas, and have no inhibitions about using them. Pressure to be the first to market has also led to 'simultaneous engineering' where the traditionally sequential processes of product development are allowed to overlap, permitting a halving of development timescales.

In the early part of the period under discussion, research outside the firm was of considerable importance in Japan. MITI (the Japanese Ministry of International Trade and Industry) organised a number of collaborative research programmes which had a major effect in developing strength in semiconductors and computers. Today, the main research and development activity takes place in companies; for example, Matsushita has 22,000 scientists and engineers working in 51 laboratories. There is still, however, a network of government laboratories working in a wide range of basic technologies; companies achieve technology transfer through seconding staff to joint projects organised through these laboratories. Many major companies report that 20 to 30 per cent of their research and development resources are deployed in this manner.

In Germany the principal source of technical development is within companies. However, institutes of higher and further education and independent research institutes are of greater importance than in Japan. The Hochschule at Aachen, for example, is recognised as one of the world's leading centres for manufacturing technology. It has a number of joint programmes with leading German companies to improve their manufacturing performance.

D. Continuity of purpose and the long term

The methods of achieving competitive success that have been outlined can only be fully effective in a situation of long term stability. For companies to invest in their employees, and the employees to work flexibly and creatively towards the success of the enterprise, both must have confidence in the long term security of their relationship. For companies to invest consistently in process and product innovation, investment funds must be available in bad times as well as good. It is in the long term commitment to their markets and the consistency of their actions that German and Japanese companies are most outstanding.

In the field of finance, the importance of long term stability in Japanese business practice is very apparent. Banks may hold stocks of non-financial companies up to a limit of 5 per cent, and the 'main bank' of a company will perform long term services both as a monitor of managerial performance and as the co-ordinator of a loans consortium with other banks. The role of the main bank as a monitor has particular significance because another source of managerial incentives much discussed in the

United Kingdom, the takeover threat, is virtually inoperative in Japan. In spite of an anti-monopoly law which restricts inter-corporate stockholding, financial corporate groupings have evolved which make takeover virtually impossible without the implicit consent of other members of the group.

Close relationships with banks have helped in the development of a further recognised characteristic of Japanese companies, a commitment to long term investment. For some investment purposes, for example the introduction of new equipment, the criteria used are purely financial and similar to those found in the United Kingdom. However, Japanese firms appear also to undertake investment of great importance to long term development where the purely financial implications are less important than strategic judgement. In this they are greatly assisted by the Japanese banks.

The system of universal banking in Germany has much in common with Japan. Banks may be represented on supervisory boards and their control of proxy voting rights from shares held in trust accounts makes them potentially very influential. Interconnecting shareholdings between companies and the role of the banks make hostile acquisitions much less common than in the United Kingdom.

Banks in Germany and Japan have provided consistent long term support for investment in companies. However, they themselves have been aided in doing this by a much more stable macroeconomic environment. The 'transactional banking' of Anglo-Saxon countries is a logical response to an unstable and unpredictable economy.

E. The superior macroeconomic environment for business in Germany and Japan

German and Japanese businesses have enjoyed important macroeconomic advantages; in particular inflation rates in these countries have been significantly lower over the last twenty years. A United Kingdom business knows that an acceleration of inflation of the kind that we have frequently suffered in the last 25 years will inevitably be followed by government deflationary policies within two to four years, which may take the form of far higher interest rates, increased taxation or public expenditure cuts which will include curtailments of government orders and contracts. The knowledge that one or more of these is inevitable within two to four years means that, once inflation rises, companies recognise that government inspired stop-go is inevitable. Throughout most of the last 25 years British companies were either producing in conditions of depression, as in 1991, or in conditions where prosperity was accompanied by the kind of acceleration of inflation that led to a general recognition that future government actions would not allow buoyant production to last.

In Germany and Japan in contrast where inflation was generally lower, business had no reason to expect that governments would have to act to remove the economic foundations of their markets. They could therefore plan ahead far more effectively. Because Germany and Japan had far less inflation, fluctuations of GNP were less, so there was less stop-go and consequently an absence of the expectations of stop-go that has made good long term decision taking and planning so difficult for British business.

It is notable that Japan and Germany have had far higher savings ratios and especially higher personal saving than Britain (Figure 7). The current account surplus of the balance of payments is identically equal to the excess of a country's saving over investment. Germany and Japan have built up a growing surplus of saving over investment (Figure 8). They have invested more than the UK, but their saving has been higher to a still greater degree. This has provided them with the macroeconomic foundations for their growing balance of payments surpluses and their businessmen had every reason to be confident that their governments would not interrupt growth to correct the balance of payments. British industrialists on the contrary have often known in the past twenty years as bad trade figures were announced, that some kind of government action that would disrupt their affairs was imminent and inevitable.

Figure 7
Personal savings ratio*

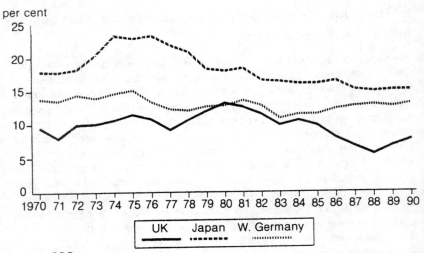

Source: CSO
*Household savings as a percentage of disposable income

Figure 8

Gross savings less gross fixed investment
as a proportion of GDP

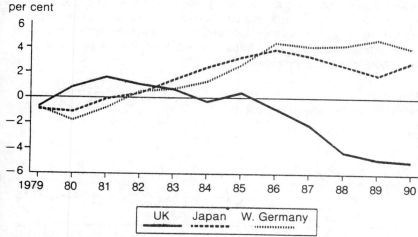

Source: OECD and NEDO estimates

An important advantage that lower inflation has conferred on German and
Japanese business is that it has gone on to produce a lower level of
nominal interest rates so that businesses were able to borrow more
cheaply. Figure 9 shows that real interest rates, the excess of nominal rates
over inflation, have been very similar in Britain, Germany and Japan. The
financially astute will invest heavily in any country offering the prospect of
a higher real rate of return and this process has tended to equalise real
rates of interest. As nominal interest rates are real rates plus inflation,
Britain, the high inflation country, has also been the country with
significantly higher nominal interest rates (Figure 10). High nominal interest
rates involve large negative cash flows in the early years after money is
borrowed, as became obvious to all who had to pay off home loans at 15
per cent in 1990 when inflation was 10 per cent. In Germany in 1990
inflation was 3 per cent and home loans cost 8 per cent so the real interest
rate was 5 per cent in both Germany and Britain, but British employees
had to find almost twice as much money to pay 15 per cent interest from
their current incomes, when German workers only had to find 8 per cent.
Where British workers ran into difficulty through temporary unemployment
or other misfortunes their homes were far more likely to be repossessed
because they had to find twice as much interest each month. Companies
are affected in exactly the same way by the need to pay higher nominal
interest because there is more inflation. If they borrow at 15 per cent to
finance investment and markets become temporarily weak or new

technology fails to perform as quickly and effectively as had been hoped, companies are as liable to be repossessed by their creditors as the houses of employees. For this reason it has been estimated that each 1 per cent of extra inflation adds almost 6 per cent to the number of bankruptcies. Because German and Japanese businesses have produced in less inflationary environments they were able to pay lower interest rates to their banks so they were less liable to become insolvent when events temporarily turned out less well than expected.

Figure 9
Nominal interest rates less inflation

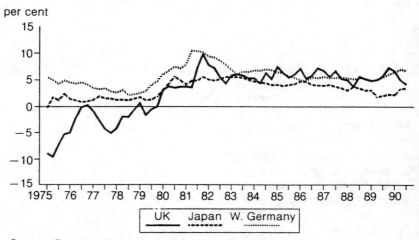

Source: Bank of England and NEDO estimates

The final and perhaps the greatest macroeconomic boon that German and Japanese business has enjoyed has been an average rate of return on capital of between two and three times the British level (Figure 5). With far higher profits and much lower nominal interest rates, German and Japanese companies have enjoyed far more breathing space between average profitability and interest. This has meant that companies could safely borrow to finance good projects without having to face a loss of ownership if something went wrong, and for the same reason banks could lend safely to companies without the equivalent fear that company insolvencies would deny them a full repayment. The far more favourable balance between profit rates and interest rates in Germany and Japan therefore goes a long way to explain the greater preoccupation with short term financial considerations in Britain than in Germany and Japan on the part of both lenders and borrowers.

Figure 10

Nominal short-term interest rates

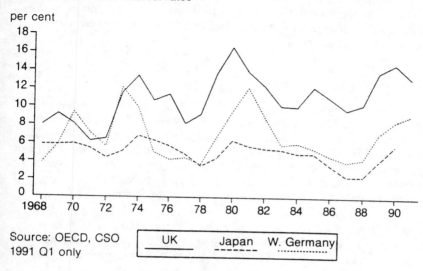

per cent

Source: OECD, CSO
1991 Q1 only

UK   Japan   W. Germany

One of the most significant impacts of Britain's less favourable financial environment has been on the proportion of time that senior managers have had to devote to financial questions while senior German and Japanese managers have been relatively free to focus most of their attention on the enhancement of technology and the management and development of the skills of the people for whom they are responsible. Given the sharp difference in macroeconomic environments it is not surprising that accountants and auditors so often reach the top in Britain, while engineers, technologists and scientists get so much further in Germany and Japan. Finance matters so much more in Britain because it can so easily go wrong with profits so much lower and interest rates so much higher.

That Germany and Japan achieved these lower inflation rates is no accident. Germany suffered catastrophically from inflation in the 1920s, which has provided a solid political basis for low inflation policies. In the 1960s Germany decided to detach the Deutschemark (DM) from the dollar to avoid the automatic importation of United States inflation into Germany and the DM soared above the dollar and the pound from then onwards. In 1967 the DM was worth 25 US cents and 9 British pence. Today it is worth 66 cents and 35 pence, a rise that reflects the lower inflation that Germany has achieved since the early 60s. German inflation has moved down towards the zero rate that most German policy makers regard as ideal. It is currently 4 per cent as the former East Germany is absorbed, but German policy will once again be aimed at a zero inflation target before very long and this will continue to give German businessmen the advantage of the lowest achievable nominal interest rates that they have enjoyed over so much of the last 25 years.

F. Transferable lessons

In the United Kingdom, successful attempts to learn from Japanese and German experience have been made in recent years. Obvious examples include the development of single union agreements on greenfield sites, greater attention to the supply chain and the introduction by some firms of 'preferred supplier policies', 'total quality management' and 'just-in-time production', recent efforts to improve the supply of vocational training, and the development of the concept of 'relationship banking'.

Many of these management practices have been introduced with varying degrees of success into British companies. More significantly, Japanese owned companies – Sony at Bridgend, Nissan and Sumitomo at Washington – have demonstrated that they can obtain quality and productivity in British plants comparable to that in Japan. Thus, those aspects of Japanese management concerned with the organisation of work and the management of people are directly transferable. However, Japanese owned companies often report difficulties in developing supplier relationships in the United Kingdom. As yet there is little product development conducted outside Japan. Here the ability of engineers with shop floor experience to design for low production cost and high quality is less transferable without a significant increase in the availability of engineers in the United Kingdom and changes in the way in which they are used. The remaining critical difference is that Japanese owned companies (and to some extent privately owned companies such as JCB) appear to be much more successful at implementing Japanese management practices than publicly owned British companies.

It is also clear that certain aspects of the German and Japanese systems are not transferable, nor is it necessarily desirable that they should be. Neither Japan nor Germany has a highly developed venture capital market. The Japanese system is much better at dealing with incremental than with radical change. Neither companies nor individuals in the United Kingdom have demonstrated that they would wish to experience the degree of dependence which is common in Japan. Indeed there are some signs that the Japanese themselves are changing in this respect. Mobility, both of capital and labour, acts as a force which allocates resources to those people who value them most highly and think they can make the most productive use of them. The stimulus to technical efficiency, not to mention civilised behaviour, which is induced by the ability of customers to leave suppliers, borrowers to change lenders, workers to quit unsatisfactory employers (and vice versa) is an essential element of the competitive process and should not be neglected.

The Japanese have shown, however, that the building of long term co-operation produces great advantages in some fields. These derive from ever closer knowledge, gradually acquired, of specific customer wants by suppliers, of supplier trustworthiness and competence by buyers, of employee skills by employers and so forth. The generation and use of this knowledge is something which it is difficult to accomplish with very short time horizons.

Both Germany and Japan share a good record of achieving macroeconomic stability. German inflation rates have been low by international standards and relatively stable. Japanese growth rates have been high and again subject to less variability than the United Kingdom's. At least some part of the lower cost of capital in Germany and Japan has been ascribed to this relative stability and the consequent reduction in risk to the lender.

The importance of vocational training is something which Germany shares with Japan. One lesson that might be drawn, therefore, is that a good system of vocational training may be more important than lifetime employment arrangements as a means of encouraging the accumulation of skills.

There is a high level of competition in both Germany and Japan in each of the sectors in which their industries excel. This is extremely important for there is a danger that, without competition, longer term associations could encourage restrictive agreements and the exclusion of newcomers.

G. The implications for Britain

The chairmen of the National Economic Development Council's (NEDC) Sector Groups and Working Parties, listed in the Appendix, considered that this account of the superior performance of Germany and Japan offered a number of lessons for the United Kingdom, which they presented to the NEDC in 1991. In particular they believed that there needed to be a national commitment to a target of near to nil inflation within 3 years. Once this was achieved British business would benefit by being able to borrow at the lowest sustainable level of nominal interest rates. They believed in particular that in the more stable macroeconomic environment that continuous low inflation would offer, industrialists would be able to devote far more energy to their products and customers.

They also believed that in Britain there had been conflict and controversy in the relationship between industry and finance where there should ideally be partnership. Changes for consideration in the view of some of the chairmen included those that would ease the conversion of some of the industrial debt held by the financial sector into equity and where this was achieved the City would to a greater extent be a partner to industry. In both Germany and Japan there are interlocking shareholdings between banks and some of their industrial clients which can increase the degree to which the financial sector has a direct interest in industry's success and a stronger motivation to participate in the quality of its decisions.

The NEDC chairmen also believed that companies must seek to involve employees more fully in all aspects of business, invest more strongly in their development and amend their reward systems to encourage the greater acquisition of skills and qualifications. They regarded a stronger research and development base and a competitive infrastructure as vital with higher investment by government in universities, polytechnics and the National Research Institutions to ensure that companies had access to world class centres of excellence in the key enabling technologies.

Trade unions along with institutional shareholders could play a major part in the management of change. The challenge to them was to look to their own organisations' structures and values to see how they needed to change in order to help their members to develop skills to contribute to the organisations they worked for. Unions could play an important and often crucial role in improving the quality of production and performance but only if they saw themselves and allowed others to see them as part of the team instead of as organisations that were sometimes resistant to improved industrial performance.

The chairmen believed that the successes of recent years in attracting high levels of inward investment from Japan, and the performance of some of the Japanese owned companies in this country which have matched their productivity levels in Japan, demonstrate that Japanese production management can be successfully transferred into the United Kingdom environment. But it is important not to allow the effectiveness of inward investment to be undermined by protectionist attitudes in Europe.

The Anglo-American economic and industrial tradition is based on short term maximising behaviour. Upwardly mobile workers and executives frequently change companies as their careers advance. Companies all the time search for cheaper suppliers and finance managers search between the world's finance houses for the cheapest loans. Britain needs to consider the alternative potential advantages of a culture where longer term relationships are encouraged between companies and their workers so that poaching between companies for labour is rarer; towards longer term relationships between companies and their suppliers so that relationships of trust concerning quality develop; and of course to longer term relationships between companies and their bankers. The critical similarity between Germany and Japan has been the commitment of all major institutions – companies, government, trade unions and banks to long term industrial success. The developments that have been set out could begin to have a similar impact in Britain.

Biographical Note
Walter Eltis is Director General, Douglas Fraser is Industrial Director, and Professor Martin Ricketts is Economic Director of the National Economic Development Office.

Appendix

The chairmen of the National Economic Development Council's Sector Groups and Working Parties

Dr John Ashworth DSc
Chairman, Traffic Management Systems Working Party

Professor George Bain
Chairman, Food Sector Group

David Barnes CBE
Chairman, Biotechnology Working Party

Alan A Benjamin OBE
Chairman, Electronic Applications Sector Group

Sir Ivor Cohen CBE
Chairman, Electronics Industry Sector Group

Angus Crichton-Miller
Chairman, Competitiveness Working Party on Tourism and Leisure

Sir John Cuckney
Chairman, European Public Purchasing Working Party

Sir Christopher Foster
Chairman, Construction Industry Sector Group

Ian Gibson CBE
Chairman, Engineering Skills Working Party

Sir Ronald Halstead
Chairman, Garment and Textile Sector Group

Eric Hammond OBE
Chairman, Electronic Components Sector Group

Bill Jordan CBE
Chairman, Engineering Industry Sector Group

Brian Street
Chairman, Specialised Organics Sector Group

Geoffrey A Truesdale
Chairman, Water & Effluent Treatment Technology Working Party

Sir Brian Wolfson
Chairman, Tourism & Leisure Industries Sector Group

Index

Economists of the Twentieth Century

Monetarism and Macroeconomic Policy
Thomas Mayer

Studies in Fiscal Federalism
Wallace E. Oates

The World Economy in Perspective
Essays in International Trade and European Integration
Herbert Giersch

Towards a New Economics
Critical Essays on Ecology, Distribution and Other Themes
Kenneth E. Boulding

Studies in Positive and Normative Economics
Martin J. Bailey

The Collected Essays of Richard E. Quandt (2 volumes)
Richard E. Quandt

International Trade Theory and Policy
Selected Essays of W. Max Corden
W. Max Corden

Organization and Technology in Capitalist Development
William Lazonick

Studies in Human Capital
The Collected Essays of Jacob Mincer, Volume 1
Jacob Mincer

Studies in Labor Supply
The Collected Essays of Jacob Mincer, Volume 2
Jacob Mincer

Macroeconomics and Economic Policy
The Selected Essays of Assar Lindbeck, Volume I
Assar Lindbeck

The Welfare State
The Selected Essays of Assar Lindbeck, Volume II
Assar Lindbeck

Classical Economics, Public Expenditure and Growth
Walter Eltis

Money, Interest Rates and Inflation
Frederic S. Mishkin

The Public Choice Approach to Politics
Dennis C. Mueller

The Liberal Economic Order
Volume I Essays on International Economics
Volume II Money, Cycles and Related Themes
Gottfried Haberler
Edited by Anthony Y.C. Koo

Economic Growth and Business Cycles
Prices and the Process of Cyclical Development
Paolo Sylos Labini